Society in Question

D1365551

Fifth Edition

Society in Question

Fifth Edition

Robert J. Brym
University of Toronto

Australia   Canada   Mexico   Singapore   Spain   United Kingdom   United States

THOMSON

NELSON

Society in Question, Fifth Edition

by Robert J. Brym

Associate Vice President, Editorial Director:
Evelyn Veitch

Editor-in-Chief, Higher Education:
Anne Williams

Executive Editor:
Cara Yarzab

Marketing Director:
Kelly Smyth

Senior Developmental Editor:
Lesley Mann

Permissions Coordinator:
Patricia Buckley

Content Production Manager:
Jaime Smith

Production Service:
Graphic World Publishing Services

Copy Editor:
Elizabeth Phinney

Proofreader:
Graphic World Inc.

Indexer:
Graphic World Inc.

Manufacturing Coordinator:
Loretta Lee

Design Director:
Ken Phipps

Interior Design:
Fernanda Pisani

Cover Design:
Johanna Liburd

Cover Image:
© J. A. Kraulis/Masterfile

Compositor:
Graphic World Inc.

Printer:
Thomson/West

Library and Archives Canada Cataloguing in Publication Data

Main entry under title:

Society in question / [edited by] Robert J. Brym. — 5th ed.

Includes bibliographical references and index.
ISBN 0-17-610281-7

1. Sociology—Textbooks.
2. Canada—Social conditions.

I. Brym, Robert J., 1951-

HM586.S654 2008 301
C2006-903303-X

In memory of Jim Curtis, 1942–2005

— RJB

Contents

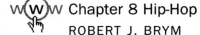

Preface

Society in Question is designed to supplement the main textbook in an introductory sociology course. I have therefore aimed for balanced coverage of major topics, approaches, and methods in current sociology. However, as the title suggests, this book also tries to convey more than just a sense of what sociologists do for a living. The readings, and my introductions to them, are intended to speak plainly and vividly to contemporary Canadians about how sociology can help them make sense of their lives in a rapidly changing and often confusing world. The book's title is thus a pun: as the nature of social life is called into question by vast and sometimes frightening forces over which we appear to have little control, sociological questioning offers the prospect of helping us understand those forces and make informed choices about how we can best deal with them.

This is a non-parochial collection of articles. I have not felt obliged to select only the works of authors who are Canadian citizens and hold Ph.D.s in sociology (although the large majority are and do). The sociological imagination has influenced other disciplines. I have chosen some works by non-sociologists because they are good examples of how cognate disciplines have repaid the favour by enriching sociological thought. Moreover, I strongly believe that, especially in this era of globalization, Canadian sociologists have as much to learn from non-Canadians as from non-sociologists. That is why several non-Canadians are among the authors represented here.

I consider some of the pieces reprinted here to be classics, but I have tried wherever possible to select items that speak to key issues of social life today. Three-quarters of the articles were written or extensively revised since 2000 and only a few were written more than ten years ago.

Finally, although I selected a few articles just because they cover important topics concisely and clearly, more rigorous criteria guided most of my choices. As I reviewed material for this collection, I tried to place myself in the shoes of a contemporary Canadian undergraduate who, entirely sensibly, takes the time to read only material that says something significant and non-obvious. Most of the articles in this book surprised me when I first read them and they continue to affect the way I see the world. Accordingly, the best indicator of the usefulness of this book will be the number of students who complete it and say that it helped ensure that they can no longer pick up a newspaper without thinking about the broader sociological significance of what they've read. That is just about the highest praise an introductory sociology instructor can receive.

ACKNOWLEDGMENTS

I am indebted to the Thomson Nelson team of Cara Yarzab (Executive Editor), Lesley Mann (Senior Developmental Editor), Kelly Smyth (Marketing Manager), Sandra de Ruiter (Developmental Editor), Jaime Smith and Anne Macdonald (Content Production Managers), Elizabeth Phinney (Copy Editor), and Graphic World Inc. (Proofreader) for their sage advice and tireless work in shaping this collection.

I would also like to thank the following colleagues, who critically reviewed preliminary material and helped to improve the quality of the book:

Roger Albert, North Island College
Anne Charles, Conestoga College
Thomas Groulx, St Clair College
Graham Knight, McMaster University
Malcolm MacKinnon, University of Toronto
Lois Stewart, Thompson Rivers University
Catherine Swanson, McMaster University
and others who prefer to remain anonymous

ROBERT J. BRYM
University of Toronto

NEW TO THIS EDITION

The fifth edition of *Society in Question* has been revised in the light of feedback provided by many instructors and students. Seven new articles were commissioned especially for this edition and cannot be found in any other volume. They are:

- Neil McLaughlin "The Sociological Imagination in Canada"
- Scott Davies and David Walters "The Value of a Sociology Degree"
- Sandy Welsh and Jayne Baker "Naming and Blaming: Gender Socialization and Women's Definitions of Sexual Harassment"
- Shyon Baumann "Movies and Society"
- Julie Ann McMullin and John Cairney "How Gender, Class, and Age Affect Self-Esteem"
- Jeffrey G. Reitz "Tapping Immigrants' Skills"
- Lawrence LeDuc "Political Volatility in Canada: Brokerage Parties and a Dealigned Electorate"

Other new articles include:

- Robert J. Brym "Sociology as a Life or Death Issue"
- Patricia A. Adler and Peter Adler "Peer Pressure and Adolescent Socialization"

Six articles that appeared in previous editions have been thoroughly updated:

- Robert J. Brym "Hip-Hop from Dissent to Commodity: A Note on Consumer Culture"
- Ann Duffy and Nancy Mandell "Poverty in Canada"
- Hugh Lautard and Neil Guppy "Multiculturalism or Vertical Mosaic? Occupational Stratification Among Canadian Ethnic Groups"
- Adie Nelson "What Is a Family? New Challenges in Defining an Everyday Term"
- Wallace Clement "Work and Society: Canada in Continental Context"
- Patricia Erickson "The Selective Control of Drugs"

We welcome new authors Neil McLaughlin, Scott Davies, David Walters, Jayne Baker, Shyon Baumann, Julie Ann McMullin, John Cairney, Jeffrey G. Reitz, Lawrence LeDuc, Patricia A. Adler, and Peter Adler to the *Sociology in Question* author team.

Finally, we are pleased to introduce a new feature in *Society in Question, Fifth Edition.* First-year students face the challenge of learning how to read sociological literature and use what they have read in their own writing and studying. Accordingly, Robert Brym prepared marginal annotations to guide students through the book's first reading, "Sociology as a Life or Death Issue." We hope these annotations will help students develop critical skills that will prove useful as they read the articles in *Society in Question* and other texts.

ANCILLARIES

This edition, like others before it, continues to support instructor teaching and student learning through a variety of additional resources.

FOR INSTRUCTORS

- **Computerized Test Bank in ExamView** (ISBN 0176105360). Create, deliver, and customize tests (both print and online) in minutes with this easy-to-use assessment and tutorial system. *ExamView* offers both a *Quick Test Wizard* and an *Online Test Wizard* that guide you step-by-step through the process of creating tests. The test appears on screen exactly as it will print or display online. Using *ExamView*'s complete word processing capabilities, you can enter an unlimited number of new questions or edit existing questions (over 270 multiple choice questions have been created for this edition of *Society in Question*). ExamView is offered in both PC and Mac platforms.

Companion Website

- **http://www.societyinquestion5e.nelson.com/instructors.** The Instructor's page of the companion website includes information about the book and a link to the Thomson Nelson Sociology Resource Centre.

 InfoTrac®

- **http://www.infotrac-college.com.** Ignite discussions or augment your lectures with the latest developments in sociology and societal change. Create your own course reader by selecting articles or by using the search keywords provided at the end of each chapter. *InfoTrac® College Edition* (available as a free option with this text) gives you and your students four months of free access to an easy-to-use online database of reliable, full-length articles (not abstracts) from hundreds of top academic journals and popular sources. Among the journals available twenty-four hours a day, seven days a week are the *Canadian Review of Sociology and Anthropology,* the *Canadian Journal of Sociology, Canadian Ethnic Studies, Public Policy,* the *American Journal of Sociology, Social Forces, Social Research,* and *Sociology.* Contact your Nelson representative for more information. *InfoTrac® College Edition* is available only to North American college and university students. Journals are subject to change.

FOR STUDENTS

  Companion Website

· **http://www.societyinquestion5e.nelson.com/.** Student Resources include online versions of two key readings on pop culture, Chapter 8, Hip-Hop from Dissent to Commodity: A Note on Consumer Culture; and Chapter 16, Love Online. In addition, the website includes online versions of the text's glossary and annotated bibliography, as well as information on Degrees and Careers, Study Resources, Search Engines, and the Online Dictionary of Sociology.

InfoTrac®

· **http://www.infotrac-college.com.** This website offers access to over 20 million articles from nearly 6,000 sources—a valuable resource when you do online research. See the description on the preceding page for more details.

There are many other Thomson Nelson Sociology products that will help instructors and students achieve their goals. For more information, please visit www.sociology.nelson.com or contact your local Thomson Nelson sales and editorial representative.

PART 1 | THE FIELD OF SOCIOLOGY

I have been writing my autobiography since I entered graduate school. As autobiographies go, it is pretty unconventional. It records no personal events or dates, nor does it sketch interesting characters. My friends, enemies, colleagues, parents, wife, and children are not mentioned in it. It is not written as a personal narrative. Yet, indirectly, it is the story of my life.

My life story is embedded in my sociological writings. The pressing issues that trouble me have somehow been transformed into a research agenda. But I alone can plainly see the connection between my life and my writings. To the degree that my writings have any value to others it lies in their contribution, however slight, to conversations and debates in which people who call themselves sociologists have engaged for more than a century. Those sociologists couldn't care less about whether I have found my research and writing useful in answering the political, ethnic, and economic issues that have weighed on me over the years.

Nor should they. Sociology is a science—a science that is not as precise as physics, which doesn't have to contend with human caprice, but a science nonetheless. That is, sociologists try to observe their chosen corner of reality in a systematic and controlled manner and to evaluate the validity of their ideas on the basis of whether their observations confirm or disconfirm them. The origins of those ideas are irrelevant, scientifically speaking. That is, I think, what the American writer Kurt Vonnegut meant when he wrote that the most beautiful marigold he ever saw was growing in a bucket of cat manure.

Here we have the great irony of much scholarship, sociology included. Scholars try to be dispassionate and objective, yet much scholarly activity is animated by real-life experiences and individual passions. Albert Einstein believed on philosophical grounds that the universe is a deterministic system operating according to iron laws and that it is the physicist's job to discover them. When he was confronted by evidence that certain subatomic processes can be described only in terms of probable rather than certain outcomes, he objected: "God does not play dice with the universe." In this case, the evidence did not sway Einstein; his personal bent of mind, even his religious outlook, affected his evaluation of the evidence.

In their laudable efforts to be objective, some scholars lose sight of the fact that personal experiences and individual passions help them define certain problems as urgent and certain solutions to those problems as preferable. But few thoughtful and honest scholars can fool themselves for long with pious statements about being purely objective in their research. The plain fact is that objectivity and subjectivity each have an important role to play in science, including sociology. Objectivity—the consensus viewpoint—is a reality check. Subjectivity—one's own viewpoint—leads us to define which aspect of reality is worth checking on in the first place.

In the book's first essay, I ask a question about the subjective, motivational side of sociology: Why study it? I reply that doing so is a matter of life and death. I do not make that claim for dramatic effect. I mean it literally. By helping us understand the social forces underlying the conditions of our death, sociology can help us figure out how to live better. That, I argue, is the promise and the urgency of higher education in general and sociological knowledge in particular.

Some students consider sociology's promise impractical. They may see in principle how sociology can help them to navigate in the world and contribute to improving it and themselves, but they wonder which jobs, if any, require or benefit from a sociology degree. Scott Davies and David Walters provide much useful up-to-date information on this subject in the book's second chapter. They demonstrate that sociology degrees lead to interesting and well-paying jobs in a variety of fields, and they give practical sociological advice to Canadian students on how to expand their job opportunities.

Finally, Neil McLaughlin offers a thumbnail sketch of sociology as it is practised in Canada—its strengths and challenges. Together with the authors of the other chapters in this section, McLaughlin provides the groundwork for all the chapters that follow.

CRITICAL THINKING QUESTIONS

1. What are the roles of subjectivity (one's own viewpoint) and objectivity (the consensus viewpoint) in sociological research?
2. What is the value of a sociology degree compared to degrees in other subjects?
3. What are the main features of Canadian sociology?

ANNOTATED BIBLIOGRAPHY

Brym, Robert J., John Lie, and Steven Rytina. *Sociology: Your Compass for a New World.* 2nd Canadian ed. Toronto: Nelson, 2007. Provides a comprehensive, introductory overview of the field of sociology from Canadian and global perspectives.

The Canadian Journal of Sociology 28, 3 (2003); 30, 1 (2005); 30, 4 (2005). These three issues of *The Canadian Journal of Sociology* feature a debate on the strengths, weaknesses, and challenges of sociology in Canada.

Stephens, W. Richard, Jr. *Careers in Sociology.* 2nd ed. On the World Wide Web at http://www.abacon. com/socsite/careers.html. Offers 18 informative case studies of what students did with their sociology degrees.

Chapter 1

Sociology as a Life or Death Issue[1]

Robert J. Brym

TO HELP STUDENTS LEARN HOW TO TAKE NOTES ON THEIR READINGS EFFECTIVELY, THIS ARTICLE IS ACCOMPANIED BY MARGINAL COMMENTS ON NOTE-TAKING.

DEATH

To inspire you, I will take the unusual course of talking about death. I apologize in advance if this makes you uncomfortable. I know it is customary when addressing first-year university students to remind them that they are young, have accomplished much, and are now in a position to make important decisions that will shape the rest of their lives. I will eventually get around to that. But to arrive at the optimistic and uplifting part, I feel I must take a detour through the valley of the shadow of death.

> The author doesn't tell the reader yet what the article is about, but uses a dramatic theme—death—and an unexpected tone—whimsy—to grab the reader's attention. This is a narrative or storytelling approach to beginning an academic article. An alternative and more common approach is to state plainly at the outset what the article is about and how the author intends to make his or her case. If the alternative approach is used, you should summarize the main argument and method of the article as stated in the opening paragraphs.

When I was seven years old, I lived across the street from a park where I engaged in all the usual childhood games with my friends. We played tag, hide-and-seek, baseball, and cops-and-robbers. We also invented a game that we awkwardly called "See Who Drops Dead the Best." We would line ourselves up on a park bench and choose one boy to shoot the rest of us in turn, using a tree branch as a machine gun. Once shot, we did our best to scream, fall to the ground, writhe, convulse, and expire. The shooter would choose the most convincing victim—the boy who dropped dead the best—to be the shooter in the next round. The game would occupy us for ten minutes or so, after which we'd pick ourselves up and move on to baseball. At the age of seven, death was entertaining.

I didn't live in a war zone and there were no deaths in my family during my youth, so I really didn't begin to take death personally until I was fifteen. Then, one Sunday evening, it quite suddenly dawned on me that someday I would *really* die, losing consciousness forever. The moment this realization hit, I ran to my parents in panic. I rudely switched off the TV and asked them to tell me immediately why we were living if we were going to die anyway. My parents looked at each other, stunned, and then smiled nervously, perhaps thinking their son had taken leave of his senses. They were not especially religious people, and they had only a few years of elementary schooling between them. They had no idea how to address questions about the meaning of life. Eventually my father confessed he didn't know the answer to my question, whereupon I ran to my bedroom, angrily shouting that my parents were fools to have lived half a century without even knowing why they were alive. From that moment and for the next three decades, death became a source of anxiety for me.

DENIAL

And so it is for most adolescents and adults. We all know that we might die at any moment. This knowledge makes most of us anxious. Typically, we react to our anxiety by denying death. To a degree, denying death helps us to calm ourselves.

The denial of death takes many forms. One is religious. Religion offers us immortality, the promise of better times to come, and the security of benevolent spirits who look over us. It provides meaning and purpose in a world that might otherwise seem cruel and senseless (James, 1976 [1902]: 123, 139).

In one of its extreme forms, religion becomes what philosophers call "determinism," the belief that everything happens the way it does because it was destined to happen in just that way. From the determinist's viewpoint, we can't really choose how to live because forces larger than we are control life. Even religions that say we can choose between good and evil are somewhat deterministic because they guarantee eternal life only if we choose to do good, and that requires submitting to the will of God as defined by some authority, not us. Many people worry less about death because they believe that the reward for submitting to the will of God is eternal life in heaven.

A second way in which we calm our anxiety about death involves trying to stay young. Consider the cosmetic surgery craze. Every week, millions of North Americans watch *Nip/Tuck*, *The Swan*, and *Extreme Makeover*—all popular TV series about cosmetic surgery. Every year, millions of North Americans undergo plastic surgery (including dermabrasion and Botox injections). In 2005 alone, 10.5 million plastic surgeries were performed in North America, up nearly 2 500 percent since 1992, when statistics were first collected (American Society of Plastic Surgeons, 2006). And that's not all we do to stay young. We diet. We exercise. We take vitamin supplements. We wear makeup. We dye our hair. We strive for stylishness in our dress. We celebrate youthfulness and vitality in movies, music, and advertising. We even devalue the elderly and keep them segregated in nursing homes and hospitals, in part so we won't be constantly reminded of our own mortality.

The search for eternal youth is a form of what philosophers call "voluntarism," the belief that we alone control our destiny. From the voluntarist's point of view, we can overcome forces larger than we are and thereby make whatever we want of our lives. Thus, many people worry less about death because they delude themselves into thinking they can cheat it.

A TRAP

Ladies and gentlemen, I have good news and bad news for you, and I'm going to deliver the bad news first. The bad news is that the denial of death is a trap. Denying death makes it more difficult to figure out how to live well and thus be happy.

The main themes of articles are often signified by subheadings, and they are typically stated at the beginning of each section. Here we have **the first main theme of the article:** knowing that they could die at any moment makes people anxious, and to cope with that anxiety, people typically deny death.

Typically, one or more examples are offered to illustrate a theme. Here we have an example of how people deny death: by turning to religion, which promises immortality, security, and meaning.

Definitions of important terms, usually indicated by italics, quotation marks, or boldface, should always be noted. Here, **determinism** is defined as the belief that everything happens the way it does because it is destined to happen just that way.

A second example of how people deny death: They try to maintain the *appearance* of being young.

First-year students frequently ask if they will be expected to know all the statistics in the material they read for tests. Different instructors answer that question differently, so you should check with yours, but most instructors say you should remember only the most important trends rather than the numbers themselves. For example, the important point to take from these highlighted sentences is that cosmetic surgery has become much more popular over the past decade.

Definition: **Voluntarism** is the belief that we control our destiny. Note that voluntarism is the opposite of determinism.

This is **the second major theme of the article**, again stated at the beginning of a new section: Denying death makes it harder to figure out how best to live.

Let's say, for example, that a religion promises you eternal life in exchange for obeying certain rules. One rule says you can marry people only of your own religion. Another says that once you marry you can't divorce. A third severely limits the steps you can take to limit the number of children you have. A fourth says you have to marry someone of the opposite sex. Many people respect these rules but they happen to make others miserable. That, however, is the price they must pay for the religion's promise of eternal life. In general, by denying people the opportunity to figure out and do what is best for them as individuals, the fatalistic denial of death can make some people deeply unhappy.

> An example of how the denial of death is a trap: religion can prevent some people from living well and being happy.

The voluntaristic denial of death can also make people unhappy. In the TV series *Nip/Tuck*, plastic surgeons Christian Troy and Sean McNamara begin each consultation with these words: "Tell me what you don't like about yourself." Notice that they don't ask prospective patients what they dislike about their bodies. They ask them what they dislike about their *selves*. They assume that your body faithfully represents your self—that your weight, proportions, colour, scars, and hairiness say something fundamentally important about your character, about who you are. If, however, you believe your happiness depends on your physical perfection and youthfulness, you are bound to be unhappy because nobody can be perfect and because you will inevitably grow old and die. And in the meantime, pursuing youthfulness in the belief that you are no more than your appearance distracts you from probing deeply and finding out who you really are and what you need from life to make you happy. I conclude that denying death for whatever reason prevents you from figuring out how to live in the way that is best for you.[2]

> A second example of how the denial of death is a trap: pursuing youthfulness distracts people from probing deeply and finding out who they really are and what they need from life to make them happy.

HIGHER EDUCATION

Finally, some good news: You don't have to deny death and thus become distracted from figuring out what you need to do to live a happy life. Instead, you can try to remain aware that you will die and that you could die at any moment. That awareness will inevitably cause you to focus on how best to achieve a meaningful life in your remaining time: the kind of career you need to pursue to make you happiest, the kind of person with whom you need to develop a long-term intimate relationship, the way you can best contribute to the welfare of others, the political principles you should follow, and so forth. As an old saying goes, the gallows in the morning focuses the mind wonderfully (cf. Frankl, 1959).

> **The article's third main theme,** again stated at the beginning of a new section: refusing to deny death focuses the mind on how best to live.

I have more good news. We have created an institution especially devoted to helping us discover what the good life is for each of us: the system of higher education.

I imagine your parents and teachers have told you to stay in school as long as you can because a degree is a ticket to a good job. They are right, at least in part. A stack of studies shows that each additional year of education will increase your annual income for the rest of your life. Moreover, the economic value of education increases year after year (Appleby, Fougère, and Rouleau, 2004). But the view that colleges and universities are places for job training is a half-truth. Above all, the system of higher education is devoted to the discovery, by rational means, of truth, beauty, and the good life. Said differently, if you treat higher education not just as job training but as a voyage of self-discovery, you will increase your chance of finding out what you value in life, what you can achieve, and how you can achieve it.

Colleges and universities are divided into different departments, centres, schools, and faculties, each with a different approach to improving the welfare of humanity.[3] The physician heals; the instructor in physical education teaches how to improve strength, stamina, and vigour; and the philosopher demonstrates the value of living an examined life. A good undergraduate education will expose you to many different approaches to improving your welfare and that of humanity as a whole and will give you a chance to discover which of them suits you.

What does the sociological approach offer?

SOCIOLOGY

The sociological approach to improving human welfare is based on the idea that the relations we have with other people create opportunities for us to think and act but also set limits on our thoughts and actions. Accordingly, we can better understand what we are and what we can become by studying the social relations that help shape us.

A classic illustration of the sociological approach to understanding the world and improving human welfare is Émile Durkheim's nineteenth-century study of suicide in France (Durkheim, 1951 [1897]). Most people think that suicide is the most non-social and antisocial action imaginable, a result of deep psychological distress, that is typically committed in private and involves a rejection of society and everything it stands for. Yet Durkheim showed that high rates of psychological distress often do not result in a high suicide rate while low rates of psychological distress sometimes do. He also argued that the rate and type of suicide that predominates in a society tells us something fundamentally important about the state of the society as a whole.[4]

According to Durkheim, the probability that your state of mind will lead you to suicide is influenced by the social relations in which you are embedded—in particular, the frequency with which you interact with others and the degree to which you share their beliefs, values, and moral standards. Durkheim referred to the frequency of interaction and the degree of sharing of beliefs, values, and morals in a group as its level of "social solidarity."

Simplifying for brevity's sake, Durkheim analyzed the effects of three levels of social solidarity on suicide rates:

- *Low solidarity:* According to Durkheim, groups and societies characterized by a low level of social solidarity typically have a high suicide rate. Interacting infrequently and sharing few beliefs, values, and moral standards, people in low solidarity settings lack emotional support and cultural guidelines for behaviour. They are therefore more prone to commit suicide if they experience distress. On a broader canvas, Durkheim viewed rising suicide rates as a symptom of the state of modern society. In general, social ties are weakening, he argued, and people share fewer beliefs, values, and moral standards than they used to.

The system of higher education can help people focus on how best to live because it is devoted to just that purpose; it is not merely for job training.

The various subjects taught in college and university represent different approaches to improving the welfare of humanity.

This rhetorical question anticipates **the article's fourth main theme:** what the sociological approach can offer to people engaged in a voyage of self-discovery.

Very important. This paragraph defines the **sociological approach** to improving human welfare: "The relations we have with other people create opportunities for us to think and act but also set limits on our thoughts and actions. Accordingly, we can better understand what we are and what we can become by studying the social relations that help shape us."

An example—Durkheim's study of suicide—illustrates one of the article's themes, namely, the sociological approach. While most people think that suicide is a non-social and antisocial act caused by deep psychological distress, Durkheim showed that this is not necessarily so. Instead, suicide is associated with how frequently people interact with others and share their beliefs, values, and morals. Thus, the likelihood of committing suicide is influenced by specifically *social* forces. Durkheim referred to the frequency of interaction and the degree of sharing of beliefs, values, and morals in a group as its level of **social solidarity.**

Low social solidarity is associated with a high suicide rate because people who lack emotional support and cultural guidelines have little to buffer them against adversity.

- *Intermediate solidarity:* It follows that if we want suicide rates to decline, we must figure out ways of increasing the strength of social ties and shared culture in modern society. For example, if Canadians created a system of universally accessible, high-quality daycare with national standards, then more children would be better supervised, enjoy more interaction with peers and adults, and be exposed to similar socializing influences. At the same time, more adults (particularly single mothers) would be able to work in the paid labour force and form new social ties with their workmates. By thus raising the level of social solidarity, we would expect the suicide rate to drop.

> An intermediate level of social solidarity is associated with a low suicide rate because people who enjoy emotional support and cultural guidelines are disinclined to commit suicide if adversity strikes.

- *High solidarity:* Despite a general decline in social solidarity, some groups are characterized by exceptionally high levels of social solidarity. When members of such a group perceive that the group is threatened, they are likely to be willing to sacrifice their lives to protect it. For instance, suicide bombers often see the existence of their group threatened by a foreign power occupying their homeland. They are willing to give up their lives to coerce the occupying power into leaving (Pape, 2005). The increased rate of suicide bombing in the world since the early 1980s is in part a symptom of increasing threats posed to high solidarity groups by foreign occupying forces. It follows that if we want fewer suicide bombings, one thing we can do is to figure out ways of ensuring that high solidarity groups feel less threatened.

> High social solidarity may be associated with a high suicide rate. If members of high solidarity groups perceive that the group is threatened, they are likely to be willing to sacrifice their lives to protect it.

Much of the best sociological research today follows Durkheim's example. Sociologists frequently strive to identify (1) a type of behaviour that for personal, political, or intellectual reasons they regard as interesting or important; (2) the specifically social forces that influence that behaviour; and (3) the larger institutional, political, or other changes that might effectively improve human welfare with respect to the behaviour of interest. By conducting research that identifies these three elements, sociologists help people to understand what they are and what they can become in particular social and historical contexts (Mills, 1959; Weber, 1964 [1949]).

> This paragraph summarizes the entire section. Such summary paragraphs often appear at the end of a section and are therefore worth highlighting.

LIFE

You have accomplished much and you are now in a position to make important decisions that will shape the rest of your life. At this threshold I challenge you not to be seduced by popular ways of denying death. I challenge you to remain aware that life is short and that by getting a higher education you will have he opportunity to figure out how to live in a way that will make you happiest. I personally hope you find sociology enlightening in this regard. But more importantly, you should know that higher education in general ought to encourage you to play the game of "See Who Lives Life the Best." You will be declared a winner if you play the game seriously. Socrates once said to his pupils: "What we're engaged in here isn't a chance conversation but a dialogue about the way we ought to live our lives." Accept nothing less from your professors.

> As soon as you complete an article you should summarize its main themes, examples, and definitions. Your summary will serve as a useful study guide before tests. It should be roughly 5–10 percent of the length of the article. There is no substitute for taking your own notes. Synthesizing and restating the material in your own words will help you remember it. Reading someone else's notes is far less effective.

- *Intermediate solidarity:* It follows that if we want suicide rates to decline, we must figure out ways of increasing the strength of social ties and shared culture in modern society. For example, if Canadians created a system of universally accessible, high-quality daycare with national standards, then more children would be better supervised, enjoy more interaction with peers and adults, and be exposed to similar socializing influences. At the same time, more adults (particularly single mothers) would be able to work in the paid labour force and form new social ties with their workmates. By thus raising the level of social solidarity, we would expect the suicide rate to drop.

  > Low social solidarity is associated with a high suicide rate because people who lack emotional support and cultural guidelines have little to buffer them against adversity.

- *High solidarity:* Despite a general decline in social solidarity, some groups are characterized by exceptionally high levels of social solidarity. When members of such a group perceive that the group is threatened, they are likely to be willing to sacrifice their lives to protect it. For instance, suicide bombers often see the existence of their group threatened by a foreign power occupying their homeland. They are willing to give up their lives to coerce the occupying power into leaving (Pape, 2005). The increased rate of suicide bombing in the world since the early 1980s is in part a symptom of increasing threats posed to high solidarity groups by foreign occupying forces. It follows that if we want fewer suicide bombings, one thing we can do is to figure out ways of ensuring that high solidarity groups feel less threatened.

  > Low social solidarity is associated with a high suicide rate because people who lack emotional support and cultural guidelines have little to buffer them against adversity.

Much of the best sociological research today follows Durkheim's example. Sociologists frequently strive to identify (1) a type of behaviour that for personal, political, or intellectual reasons they regard as interesting or important; (2) the specifically social forces that influence that behaviour; and (3) the larger institutional, political, or other changes that might effectively improve human welfare with respect to the behaviour of interest. By conducting research that identifies these three elements, sociologists help people to understand what they are and what they can become in particular social and historical contexts (Mills, 1959; Weber, 1964 [1949]).

> Low social solidarity is associated with a high suicide rate because people who lack emotional support and cultural guidelines have little to buffer them against adversity.

LIFE

You have accomplished much and you are now in a position to make important decisions that will shape the rest of your life. At this threshold I challenge you not to be seduced by popular ways of denying death. I challenge you to remain aware that life is short and that by getting a higher education you will have he opportunity to figure out how to live in a way that will make you happiest. I personally hope you find sociology enlightening in this regard. But more importantly, you should know that higher education in general ought to encourage you to play the game of "See Who Lives Life the Best." You will be declared a winner if you play the game seriously. Socrates once said to his pupils: "What we're engaged in here isn't a chance conversation but a dialogue about the way we ought to live our lives." Accept nothing less from your professors.

> As soon as you complete an article you should summarize its main themes, examples, and definitions. Your summary will serve as a useful study guide before tests. It should be roughly 5–10 percent of the length of the article. There is no substitute for taking your own notes. Synthesizing and restating the material in your own words will help you remember it. Reading someone else's notes is far less effective.

NOTES

1. This is an expanded version of a convocation address delivered in May 2005 to graduates of the "Steps to University" program, University of Toronto. Steps to University identifies promising senior high-school students who might otherwise not complete school or attend college or university because of their economic and social situation and offers them selected university courses to encourage them to pursue postsecondary education. I thank my colleagues, Malcolm Mackinnon and Jack Veugelers, for thoughtful criticisms of an early draft.

2. Some scientists believe we will conquer death before this century is over by developing the ability to upload our minds to robots (Kurzweil, 1999). If that happens I will have plenty of time to revise my argument accordingly.

3. Paradoxically, "hard" scientists such as physicists seem more likely than "soft" scientists such as sociologists to acknowledge that the purpose of their field is to contribute to human welfare. Many soft scientists think that their field lacks scientific status, and they believe that by denying the role of values in motivating their work they will appear more objective and therefore scientific. They fail to appreciate that (1) ideas become scientific not when they are motivated by a quest for "value freedom" (or anything else) but when they are systematically and publicly tested against evidence, and (2) human values are often a source of scientific creativity.

4. Dividing the number of times an event occurs (e.g., the number of suicides in a certain place and period) by the total number of people to whom the event could occur in principle (e.g., the number of people in that place and period) will give you the rate at which an event occurs. Rates let you compare groups of different size.

REFERENCES

American Society of Plastic Surgeons. (2006). On the World Wide Web at http://www.plasticsurgery.org/public_education/statistical-trends.cfm (14 September 2006).

Appleby, John, Maxime Fougère, and Manon Rouleau. (2004). "Is Post-Secondary Education in Canada a Cost-Effective Proposition?" Applied Research Branch, Strategic Policy, Human Resources Development Canada. On the World Wide Web at http://www11.hrsdc.gc.ca/en/cs/sp/hrsdc/arb/publications/research/2002-000150/page01.shtml (24 May 2005).

Durkheim, Émile. (1951 [1897]). *Suicide: A Study in Sociology,* ed. G. Simpson, trans. J. Spaulding and G. Simpson. New York: Free Press.

Frankl, Viktor E. (1959). *Man's Search for Meaning: An Introduction to Logotherapy,* trans. I. Lasch. Boston: Beacon Press.

James, William. (1976 [1902]). *The Varieties of Religious Experience: A Study in Human Nature.* New York: Collier Books.

Kurzweil, Ray. (1999). *The Age of Spiritual Machines: When Computers Exceed Human Intelligence.* New York: Viking Penguin.

Mills, C. Wright. (1959). *The Sociological Imagination.* New York: Oxford University Press.

Pape, Robert A. (2005). *Dying to Win: The Strategic Logic of Suicide Terrorism.* New York: Random House.

Weber, Max. (1964 [1949]). "'Objectivity' in Social Science and Social Policy." In Edward A. Shils and Henry A. Finch, trans. and eds., *The Methodology of the Social Sciences* (pp. 49–112). New York: Free Press of Glencoe.

Chapter 2

The Value of a Sociology Degree

SCOTT DAVIES AND DAVID WALTERS

FIELDS AND CAREERS

When university students search for a major, who can blame them for seeking career information on various fields? As individuals and families bear heavier debt loads from rising tuition fees, students are understandably curious about their job prospects. The average cost of a B.A. in Canada is still inexpensive relative to both elite American universities, where annual tuition fees can run up to US$30 000 and to deregulated professional programs (e.g., dentistry, medicine, M.B.A., law), the fees of which have recently soared from $8 000 to $20 000. Nonetheless, the expense of a B.A. is considerably higher than it was 20 years ago, and students are increasingly mindful of its economic potential.

This chapter presents a sociological analysis of the links between university and employment. It compares the job fortunes of Canadian sociology graduates to those from other liberal arts and sets its findings in the context of emerging labour market trends. For reasons of space we focus only on economic payoffs and point interested readers to a recent study of sociology's social, political, and intellectual benefits (Spalter-Roth et al., 2005). We urge students to select a field of study that is compatible with their interests and focus on the economic consequences to help guide their choices.

HIGHER EDUCATION TODAY

Today there is a lot of talk about how the emerging "knowledge economy" requires young people with higher-order cognitive skills acquired through postsecondary schooling. While some sociologists are skeptical about these claims (Livingstone, 1998; Wolf, 2002), Canadian governments are encouraging universities to expand their enrollments at all levels. From a historical vantage point, the sheer growth of university attendance is striking. Enrollments have never been higher and they are projected to grow despite substantial tuition fee hikes.

Faith in the economic value of university education is curious for two reasons. First, many students are choosing fields about which they have little knowledge. For instance, the social sciences attract many students. In fact, they have the highest enrollments in Canadian universities (Statistics Canada, 2005). Fields such as sociology, psychology, economics, business, political science, anthropology, and communications are popular in universities, yet they are not taught much (if at all) in secondary schools. These fields attract many students even though few high-school graduates have a firm sense of what they are about. This situation is quite unlike that of the traditional humanities and natural sciences, such as history, English, biology, and chemistry. Second, when we examine the links between university and job markets, they are remarkably loose. That is, few jobs are directly related to any of the major social sciences and humanities. Check your local newspaper and you won't find many positions for historians, geographers, psychologists, or sociologists. We conclude that the social sciences attract students with little prior knowledge of, and background in, the field and with few role models in the labour market.

The weak connection between the university and job markets is a result of the fact that most university disciplines emerged as research areas, not vehicles for vocational training. They were created to suit the interests of professors, governments, and students, not employers. Their content is shaped by the fascinations of researchers and instructors, not the requests of workplace managers. Their conventions may make sense to academics but not to employers. With the exception of a few professional programs, there are no institutional mechanisms by which economic authorities can influence what is taught in universities. While academic officials may occasionally call for more practical or vocational courses, established universities are governed by powerful norms of academic freedom that grant them considerable autonomy from politicians and employers. As a result, there are few procedures by which employers offer feedback to professors, and few professors are inclined to seek such feedback. To use the language of sociologists who study complex organizations, most university disciplines are "decoupled" from labour markets.

Why do so many students enter the social sciences and humanities given this decoupling? One answer is that a university degree pays off in the labour market. Sociological research shows that university graduates enjoy higher wages and fewer bouts of unemployment compared to graduates from high school, trade colleges, and community colleges (Walters, 2004). In fact, *all* studies of which we are aware reveal such advantages. The trick is to understand how these advantages emerge and persist despite the loose connections between most university fields and the vast majority of workplaces.

WHY SOCIOLOGY PAYS

Sociologists offer three broad explanations as to why social science fields such as sociology are valued in the labour market. The first explanation is that such fields nurture diffuse skills that are useful across a range of service-sector jobs even though they are directly relevant to only a few occupations. Thus, evidence suggests that liberal arts graduates have high levels of decision-making, interpersonal, and communication skills (Axelrod, Anisef, and Lin, 2001; Rush and Evers, 1985; Allen, 1998; Lowe and Krahn, 1995; Giles and Drewes, 2002; Krahn and Bowlby, 1999). They can think critically and explore new ideas with ease. They can think abstractly and theoretically, and quickly absorb different kinds of information. They can work well with others, manage conflict, and relate abstract ideas to real-life situations. They have a capacity to work effectively and assume authority in large organizations. Such skills allow on-the-job training to be quicker and easier. Many argue that today's labour market has a growing need for the abilities of social science graduates. In contrast, graduates from more applied disciplines, particularly those in trade and community colleges, often lack such breadth of knowledge. Graduates from social science fields such as sociology are thus said to enjoy a long-term advantage because their generic skills are portable across many different kinds of jobs. These skills may not be obvious or easily observed. Many students may be unaware that the abilities they develop in sociology courses are useful in any job where written, oral, and critical thinking skills are valued. Yet sociology undoubtedly develops these valued skills in students.

A second reason why general fields like sociology pay off is known as "credentialism" (Brown, 2001). In government and corporate bureaucracies, many applicants compete for few jobs. Employers therefore need legitimate and convenient criteria to whittle down the pool of qualified applicants. Educational credentials are often used as a convenient screening device.

Consider the changing value of the high-school diploma over the past half century. As high-school enrollments grew after World War II, most Canadian-born adults were able to obtain a diploma. Many employers began to demand diplomas as a minimum entry requirement. They did so not necessarily because they associated the diploma with any particular skill but because they associated it with dependability (Berg, 1970). Having a diploma signalled a capacity to follow instructions, complete tasks, and be punctual. However, as more young people with high-school diplomas flooded the job market, employers eventually altered their reasoning. As diploma holders became commonplace, employers interpreted the *lack* of a diploma as potentially problematic. They viewed dropping out of high school as an indicator of potential unreliability. Perhaps, they reasoned, dropouts are incapable of fitting in with people, heeding instructions, and completing tasks.

A similar style of thinking has now been applied to higher education. Before the 1970s, a young person with a bachelor's degree was a rarity in the labour market. Employers often assumed that people with B.A.s were especially able. Their assumption was rooted in the longstanding prestige that higher learning had enjoyed and its association with high status and a sense of social superiority. Employers would sometimes hire university graduates in the hope of bringing prestige to their firm. Before the 1980s, those who lacked university degrees were not stigmatized. High-school graduates could still vie for solid middle-class jobs since most job applicants lacked postsecondary credentials.

This situation appears to be changing. As more and more people graduate from university, degree holders become less rare; and with less rarity comes less prestige (Wolf, 2002). University diplomas no longer offer elite status, even when their holders possess exceptional ability. Such "credential inflation" is sparking a new trend: as long as employers continue to link degrees with some measure of ability, they will increasingly associate someone's lack of degree with mediocrity. Since so many people are earning degrees, employers might suspect that something is wrong with people who lack one. While a degree may no longer buy elite status, it appears to be becoming a general marker of trustworthiness and dependability.

Trust is increasingly important in higher education today, as many new suppliers of educational credentials emerge. These suppliers include online universities, for-profit universities, and private training colleges. Many of these new entrants, such as the online University of Phoenix, offer training only in "practical" fields such as business and information technology that are perceived as being in high demand. The entrance requirements of for-profit institutions are typically lower than those of traditional universities since they need to attract as many fee-paying students as possible to survive. Will their apparent job relevance allow them to take over the higher education marketplace? Will their graduates out-compete traditional liberal arts graduates in the job market? Almost certainly not—and for a stark reason: mainstream universities have the key advantage of being more difficult to enter. This difficulty will remain vitally important as long as employers continue to interpret a degree from a relatively selective university as a general marker of trustworthiness. Credentials from online universities, with their lower entry standards, are less likely to be recognized by employers. In a highly uncertain environment, employers are still inclined to trust a degree from a well-known and respected "brand name" university over a new competitor they may have never heard of and therefore suspect of having lower standards.

A third reason for the continuing popularity of fields of study such as sociology is that they offer a passport to valuable professional and graduate degrees. The highest financial payoffs in university accrue to graduates with advanced degrees in medicine, law, dentistry, and business, or graduates of Ph.D. programs. These programs usually require a previous degree, such as a B.A. or B.Sc. While sociology graduates rarely enter medicine or dentistry given their lack of natural science training (though some medical schools such as McMaster's accept humanities and social science graduates), they commonly enter law, M.B.A., Public Administration, and teaching, all of which offer solid career opportunities and wages (Walters, 2004). Thus, many social science and humanities disciplines continue to thrive by providing a "ticket" for an advanced degree (Collins, 2002). Research shows that humanities and social science graduates are more likely to pursue additional degrees than are other graduates (Statistics Canada, 2001: 27). This tendency seems to be increasingly important as more employers expect workers to return to university and upgrade their skills and credentials. In contrast, a community college diploma is largely a terminal credential and rarely offers eligibility for advanced degrees. Moreover, recent research shows that attending a community college after earning a university B.A. does not usually increase earnings or employability (Walters, 2003).

SOCIOLOGY GRADUATES COMPARED TO OTHERS

The career opportunities discussed previously are those that sociology shares with other liberal arts programs. We next address how sociology graduates compare to graduates from nearby fields. We use the best available evidence, Statistics Canada's *National Graduate Survey*, which for several decades has traced how Canadian university graduates from all fields perform in the work force. We report the latest available data on how individuals who graduated from university in 2000 were faring in the labour market in 2002.

Tables 2.1 and 2.2 compare graduates of several liberal arts fields, including sociology. We

TABLE 2.1 LIBERAL ARTS GRADUATES BY FIELD OF STUDY AND GENDER (IN PERCENT)

FIELD OF STUDY	PERCENT OF ALL LIBERAL ARTS GRADUATES	PERCENT OF ALL MALE LIBERAL ARTS GRADUATES	PERCENT OF ALL FEMALE LIBERAL ARTS GRADUATES	PERCENT MALE IN FIELD	PERCENT FEMALE IN FIELD	TOTAL
Sociology	8	7	9	29	71	100
English	8	7	9	28	72	100
Liberal Arts and Sciences	12	12	12	35	65	100
Fine Arts and Music	7	7	7	35	65	100
Film and Performing Arts	10	11	9	40	60	100
Media and Information Studies	7	6	8	29	71	100
Languages	7	4	9	20	80	100
Philosophy	4	6	3	57	43	100
Psychology	11	6	14	18	82	100
Economics	4	8	3	62	38	100
Political Science	6	6	6	36	64	100
History	7	11	5	52	48	100
Other (Hist/Anthro/ Religion/Geog)	8	9	8	38	62	100
Total	99*	100	102*			

*Does not equal 100 due to rounding.

Source: Adapted from Statistics Canada's 2000 National Graduates Survey (NGS), 2000.

TABLE 2.2 AVERAGE INCOME OF GRADUATES BY FIELD AND GENDER

FIELD OF STUDY	ALL GRADUATES	MEN	WOMEN
Sociology	31 574	33 367	31 137
English	29 437	28 062*	29 917
Liberal Arts and Sciences	31 423	31 668	31 263
Fine Arts and Music	27 477*	25 655*	28 413
Film and Performing Arts	25 046*	27 191*	23 544*
Media and Information Studies	33 740	33 658	33 777
Languages	27 730*	27 411	27 810*
Philosophy	28 811	28 593	29 025
Psychology	30 920	37 450	29 397
Economics	33 528	33 510	33 546
Political Science	32 171	31 007	32 980
History	30 589	31 561	29 803
Other (Hist/Anthro/Religion/Geography)	31 592	37 697	28 239*
All	**30 218**	**31 334**	**29 679**

*Indicates a 95 percent or greater chance that the sample figure is different from the actual figure for sociologists in the population.

Source: Adapted from Statistics Canada's 2000 National Graduates Survey (NGS), 2000.

combined history, anthropology, religion, and geography into an "Other" category because there were too few respondents in the sample from each of these fields to allow for reliable statistical comparisons. "Liberal Arts and Sciences" includes students in general studies, fields that are not classified, and those who did not declare a field. The first column in Table 2.1 shows that the largest group of employed graduates come from combined liberal arts and science programs (12 percent), while economics and philosophy have the smallest proportion of graduates (4 percent). The second and third columns display this information separately for males and females. Males are least likely to hold a degree in languages (4 percent), and most likely to have a combined liberal arts and science degree (12 percent). Females are most likely to hold a degree in psychology (14 percent) and are least likely to graduate in economics and philosophy (both 3 percent). The last two columns in Table 2.1 show that women outnumber men in every field of study except philosophy, history, and economics. The fields with the largest gender imbalance are psychology (82 percent female) and languages (80 percent female). Males are the majority in economics (62 percent). Sociology graduates make up 8 percent of the liberal arts, representing 7 percent of males and 8 percent of females.

Before going any further we must emphasize that all social surveys examine a part (the "sample") to make generalizations about a whole (the "population"). There is a certain danger in this practice, for a chance always exists that a sample will differ from the population from which it is drawn. To the degree the sample differs from the population, generalizations based on the sample will be inaccurate.

Thankfully, statisticians have developed ways of figuring out the chance of drawing faulty conclusions from different types of samples. In general, sociologists accept a 5 percent chance of being wrong (a 95 percent chance of being right) in the conclusions they draw from sample surveys. We follow that standard here.

In Table 2.2, for example, we report annual earnings in 2002 of graduates who obtained a bachelor's degree in 2000 and were no longer in school in 2002. We created Table 2.2 because we want to know which graduates earn more or less than sociology graduates. Given that each number in Table 2.2 has a certain margin of error, however, we are limited in the conclusions we can safely draw. Specifically, we can be 95 percent confident that the figures marked with an asterisk are actually below sociology graduates' annual income of $31 574. This means that graduates of programs in fine arts and music, film and performing arts, and languages almost certainly earn less than sociology graduates (see column 1; as columns 2 and 3 show, the below-average fields differ somewhat for men considered alone and women considered alone). We cannot, however, state with 95 percent certainty that annual income for graduates of other fields is either above or below that of sociologists in the population as a whole. Thus, economics graduates lead the pack with annual earnings of $33 528, but all we can safely say about them is that their annual earnings are not significantly more than the $31 754 earned by sociology graduates. In other words, in the Canadian population, sociology and economics graduates seem to enjoy roughly the same annual income two years after graduation.

Columns 2 and 3 reveal that, on the whole, men earn more than women. Two years after graduation, male liberal arts graduates earn $31 334, whereas females earn $29 679, about 95 percent of the male average. Most fields have rather small gender pay gaps. Only two fields exhibit big gender gaps in favour of men: males with psychology and "other" degrees earn, respectively, about $8 000 and $9 000 more than their female counterparts. But in seven of the thirteen fields listed in Table 2.2, women report higher annual earnings than men. This finding is consistent with other studies that have found shrinking gender pay gaps among university graduates in recent decades (Walters, 2005).

Overall, the data suggest that the income potential of sociology graduates is roughly the same as that of graduates in most other fields,

and perhaps above average. Graduates of a few fields in the humanities earn significantly less than sociology graduates do. Graduates from no field earn significantly more than sociology graduates do.

CAREERS FOR SOCIOLOGY GRADUATES

We have argued that sociology, like most other subjects in the social sciences and humanities, is both useful and decoupled from the labour market. Decoupling is evident from the fact that only a minority of sociology graduates in Canada and the United States report that their job is directly related to their schooling (Krahn and Bowlby, 1999; Spalter-Roth et al., 2005). Utility is evident in the fact that sociology graduates readily find good work in a variety of fields. We conclude that while employers place few job ads for sociologists, sociology is a flexible field that allows graduates to work in many occupations and organizations.

A study of McMaster University sociology graduates (Davies and Denton, 1997) from various degree levels found them in a great variety of jobs, including social work, teaching, journalism, business administration, health administration, criminal justice, policing, sales, public relations, private polling, government research, and so on. The National Graduate Survey provides data on the percentage of recent sociology B.A.s employed in various occupational categories (see Table 2.3). They illustrate that sociology graduates have opportunities across a broad range of sectors. The largest proportion (35 percent) is in occupations relating to business, finance, and administration. Jobs in the social sciences, education, and government services are the second-largest destination, employing 29 percent of recent graduates. Sales and service jobs are third, accounting for 18 percent of employed graduates; followed by management positions (nearly 7 percent); jobs in the primary industry (almost 5 percent); health (about 2 percent); and art, culture, and sport (about 2 percent).

TABLE 2.3 SOCIOLOGY GRADUATES BY OCCUPATIONAL CATEGORY (IN PERCENT)

OCCUPATION	PERCENT
Management Occupations	6.8
Business, Finance and Administrative Occupations	35.0
Natural and Applied Sciences and Related Occupations	1.2
Health Occupations	2.2
Occupations in Social Sciences, Education, Government Service	29.0
Occupations in Art, Culture, Recreation, and Sport	2.2
Sales and Service Occupations	18.0
Trades, Transport, Primary Industry, and Other	4.7

Source: Adapted from Statistics Canada's 2000 National Graduates Survey (NGS), 2000.

Amid this variety, there are some specific occupations for which sociology prepares its graduates. Most sociology programs have course requirements in research methods and statistics. Such applied research training can be extremely valuable. Many government agencies and companies, such as Statistics Canada, the Centre for Addiction and Mental Health, Proctor and Gamble, Angus Reid, and just about any corporation, federal or provincial ministry, or trade union involved in large-scale research, seek applicants with a strong aptitude for conducting surveys and analyzing data, and they regularly offer excellent employment opportunities to sociology graduates. In fact, every year Statistics Canada offers a national job competition for sociology graduates (information can be found at http://www.statcan.ca/english/employment/emplop.htm). Thus, there is a strong demand for graduates who are capable of administering and analyzing survey data.

In an analysis not reported in detail here, we also found that sociology graduates who specialized in an applied sub-area such as criminology, health, and population studies (demography) had substantially higher earnings than did other

sociology graduates. Although the small sample sizes for these subgroups do not permit accurate statistical comparisons with other fields, they suggest both the marketability of applied research areas within sociology and the range of opportunities sociology offers.

Beyond applied and quantitative subfields, many social agencies, hospitals, and market research companies employ graduates with a broad range of research skills that are taught in most sociology undergraduate programs. Many companies want employees with a strong background in qualitative techniques relating to interviewing, organizing, and administering focus groups, and who are capable of communicating research findings to audiences unfamiliar with technical terms. This is why the skills provided in research methods and statistics classes nicely compliment the communication and critical thinking and writing abilities acquired in theory courses.

ADVICE FOR STRATEGIZING IN NETWORKS AND INTERNAL LABOUR MARKETS

What then is the value of a sociology degree? Sociology resembles other social sciences and humanities: it pays off, but largely indirectly. While offering few unique paths to specific labour markets, sociology fosters generic skills, is a recognized credential in bureaucratic settings, and serves as a passport to graduate and professional school. Because it is loosely connected to job markets, sociology is linked to a variety of occupations.

Such wide-reaching links to job markets force graduates to use job search strategies creatively. For example, you have probably heard the old saying that to get a good job, who you know is as important as what you know. Sociological research suggests that there is much truth in that adage. Creating a wide range of social ties can lead to many job opportunities (Granovetter, 1995). For example, if you secure a middle management position after you graduate, your newly established contacts may lead to a permanent full-time position. Contacts are particularly useful for securing an interview. Often the people who are offered a job are not the most qualified. Instead, they may be the people with the most interview experience—they knew just what to say, when to say it, and who to say it to. Forming contacts allows you to gain such experience. After an unsuccessful interview—and for most of us there will be many—always follow up with the interviewer to find out how you can improve your performance.

Networking is important when applying to postgraduate programs, especially master's and doctoral programs. Not only do you need to know which programs suit your interests, but also which faculty members conduct research in your area. Having an undergraduate advisor to work with can often be as important as your grade point average for being accepted into a graduate program. The reputation of the professors writing your letters of reference can be extremely important in being admitted into graduate school and even securing a good job in your research area. Faculty members vary widely in their resourcefulness, their ability to fund graduate students as research assistants, and the quality of their connections in the labour market. Select your mentors wisely!

Diverse networks also allow you to obtain advice from multiple sources and thereby improve the breadth of your information. Whether applying to postgraduate studies or entering the labour market, use a variety of sources to research your options. Aside from personal contacts, seek guidance from career counsellors at your university, secretaries in your department, and of course, professors. Draw on as many resources as you can. For example, web sites (such as http://www.sociology.ca) offer information on research and employment opportunities for sociology graduates, as well as links to departments that offer master's degrees. Many departmental web pages provide Internet links to assist students in making academic or career decisions.

Note also that some entry-level jobs lead to better jobs than others. "Internal labour markets" exist when large organizations hire from within (Krahn and Lowe, 2002). Many government and corporate bureaucracies arrange their positions hierarchically, creating promotional paths that lead upward from entry-level jobs to management. This means that a relatively low-paying job can be worthwhile if its leads to something more, and also that seemingly lucrative summer jobs at shopping malls, bars, or factories may yield few long-term benefits. Students may find it difficult to resist such jobs if they pay well, but they are not selling features on a résumé and they offer little advancement potential. Unless you are absolutely confident of being admitted into a graduate or a professional program, you are much better off applying for summer positions at large organizations, even for clerical, volunteer, or unpaid positions, as long as they allow access to an internal labour market. Some initial grunt work may eventually lead to a position with more creative autonomy and authority. A university-educated, hardworking, ambitious employee who already has experience within a company is an ideal candidate for promotion to one of its well-paying full-time positions. If you eventually find fewer openings than you initially anticipated, use this experience to acquire a job elsewhere, and you may benefit from the additional interviewing know-how.

We conclude that although a sociology degree opens up a wide variety of employment opportunities, realizing that potential requires sociology graduates to use job search strategies creatively. Research suggests that social science graduates, including sociology graduates, initially fare less well than graduates with professional degrees, but they catch up somewhat over time (Finnie, 2001). This fact illustrates the importance of building networks and entering internal labour markets. Of course, luck helps in the job market, but you will significantly improve your chance of success by studying sociology and adopting sociological strategies for taking advantage of job market opportunities.

REFERENCES

Allen, Robert C. (1998). *The Employability of University Graduates in Humanities, Social Sciences and Education: Recent Statistical Evidence.* Available on the World Wide Web at http://www.econ.ubc.ca/dp9815.pdf.

Axelrod, Paul, Paul Anisef, and Zeng Lin. (2001). "Against All Odds? The Enduring Value of Liberal Education in Universities, Professions, and the Labour Market." *The Canadian Journal of Higher Education,* 31 (2): 47–78.

Berg, Ivar. (1970). *Education and Jobs: The Great Training Robbery.* New York: Praeger.

Brown, David K. (2001). "The Social Sources of Education Credentialism." *Sociology of Education,* (Extra Issue): 19–34.

Collins, Randall. (2002). "Credential Inflation and the Future of Universities." In Steven Brint, ed., *The Future of the City of Intellect: The Changing American University* (pp. 23–46). Stanford: Stanford University Press.

Davies, Scott, and Margaret Denton. (1997). "The Employment of Masters and Ph.D. Graduates from Eleven Sociology Departments." *Society/ Societe,* 21 (1): 9–14.

Finnie, Ross. (2001). "Fields of Plenty, Fields of Lean: The Early Labour Market Outcomes of Canadian University Graduates by Discipline." *Canadian Journal of Higher Education,* 31 (1): 141–76.

Giles, P., and T. Drewes. (2002). "Liberal Arts Degrees and the Labour Market." *Perspectives on Labour and Income,* 13 (3): 27–33.

Granovetter, Mark. (1995). *Getting a Job: A Study of Contacts and Careers,* 2nd ed. Chicago: University of Chicago Press.

Krahn, Harvey, and Jeffrey W. Bowlby. (1999). "Education-Job Skills Match: An Analysis of the 1990 and 1995 National Graduate Surveys." Applied Research Branch for Strategic Policy. Ottawa: Human Resources Development Canada.

Krahn, Harvey, and Graham S. Lowe. (2002). *Work, Industry, and Canadian Society,* 4th ed. Toronto: ITP Nelson.

Livingstone, David W. (1998). *The Education-Jobs Gap: Underemployment or Economic Democracy.* Toronto: Garamond Press.

Lowe, Graham S., and Harvey Krahn. (1995). "Job-Related Education and Training among Young Workers." *Canadian Public Policy,* 21 (3): 362–78.

Rush, J. C., and F. T. Evers. (1985). "Making the Match: Canada's University Graduates and Corporate Employers." *Business Quarterly,* 50 (Winter): 41–47.

Spalter-Roth, Roberta, William Erskine, Sylvia Polsiak, and Jamie Panzarella. (2005). *A National Survey of Seniors Majoring in Sociology.* American Sociological Association. Available at http://www.asanet.org/galleries/ default-file/B&B_first_report_final.pdf (12 December 2005).

Statistics Canada. (2001). "The School-to-Work Transitions of Post-Secondary Graduates in Canada: Research Findings Based on the National Graduates Surveys." *Applied Research Bulletin,* (Special Edition).

Statistics Canada. (2005). "University Enrollment." *The Daily,* Tuesday, 11 October. On the World Wide Web at http://www.statcan.ca/Daily/ English/051011/d051011b.htm (12 December 2005).

Walters, David. (2003). "Recycling: The Economic Implications of Obtaining Additional Post-secondary Credentials at Lower or Equivalent Levels." *Canadian Review of Sociology and Anthropology,* 40 (4): 463–80.

———. (2004). "A Comparison of the Labour Market Outcomes of Postsecondary Graduates of Various Levels and Fields over a Four-Cohort Period." *Canadian Journal of Sociology,* 29 (1): 1–27.

———. (2005). "Gender, Postsecondary Education and Field of Study." *Higher Education Policy.* In press.

Wolf, Alison. (2002). *Does Education Matter? Myths About Education and Economic Growth.* New York: Penguin.

Chapter 3

The Sociological Imagination in Canada

NEIL McLAUGHLIN

INTRODUCTION

Canada's first Department of Sociology was established at McGill University in 1925. Since then, sociology as a distinct academic discipline has found a home in universities throughout the country and is now a core element of Canadian liberal arts education and research-oriented social science. The discipline brings unique strengths to intellectual life and the social sciences. In this paper I outline the history of sociology in Canada and then discuss sociology's unique strengths, ending with an exploration of some of the challenges you might face as you engage with sociology in the classroom.

THE THREE ROOTS OF CANADIAN SOCIOLOGY

Sociology in Canada and the United States first emerged out of religious reform movements in the early twentieth century. Protestant ministers and social workers in English Canada and French-speaking Catholic intellectuals in Quebec wanted to use sociology to examine and eliminate social problems such as poverty and crime in cities populated by new immigrants. They believed it was a short step from preaching about religion, salvation, and moral values to studying society with an eye toward bringing about progressive social change. At the time, churches funded and ran Canadian universities. Baptists, Methodists, and Catholics were the most socially engaged churches, so sociology was first taught in Catholic Quebec at Laval University and at Baptist and Methodist institu-

tions including Acadia University in Wolfville, Nova Scotia, Wesley College in Winnipeg, McMaster University in Hamilton, and Mount Allison University in Sackville, New Brunswick (Brym, 1989; Helmes-Hayes, 2002; Hiller, 1982; Shore, 1987).

A second influence on early Canadian sociology was the British tradition of policy-oriented research on poverty, the social exclusion of new immigrants, and the welfare state. Important early Canadian sociologists—notably Leonard Marsh and John Porter—trained in Britain. From the 1940s to the 1960s they contributed enormously to legitimizing state spending on social welfare and the design of the Canadian welfare state (Helmes-Hayes, 2002; Marsh, 1940). Canadian government officials were more concerned with the practicality of policy proposals than theoretical arguments, so these early policy-oriented Canadian sociologists developed skill in gathering and presenting quantitative data. Numbers mattered in early Canadian sociology, and that emphasis continues today. The Canadian federal government sponsors much quantitative research on health care, poverty, immigration, racism, and other topics that form an important part of contemporary policy debates.

A third contributing factor to the emergence of sociology in Canada was the social turmoil and change of the 1960s. This was an era of protest around the world and government reform in Canada led by the "great society" policies of Prime Minister Pierre Trudeau. Canadian universities grew quickly in the 1960s. Tens of thousands of students entered higher education and transformed universities from elite-dominated religious institutions into organizations designed for popular and secular education and research. Sociology, as one of the newest additions to university education, was shaped by, and helped to create, the social movements of the 1960s. These movements helped Canadians to rethink their history and national identity, minimize racism and sexism, open up their culture to new ways of thinking about sexuality and the family, and democratize education.

In English Canada, sociologists played an important role in the Canadianization movement, an effort to ensure that Canadian universities hired Canadians and taught our history and culture rather than the history and culture of Britain and the United States (Cormier, 2004). In Quebec, sociologists were deeply engaged in the Quiet Revolution, an assertive and vibrant movement that sought to create a province no longer dominated by Anglo-Canadian culture, money, and political power. Canadians were not touched directly by the American civil rights movement. Protests against the war in Vietnam did not have the urgency they did in the United States (Breton, 1989; Brym and Saint-Pierre, 1997). But these movements nonetheless raised important questions for Canadians about the racism affecting our First Nations people and the immigrants we now call "visible minorities." They also encouraged Canadians to rethink their place in the world, raising the issue of our global responsibility as a rich nation in a world marked by enormous differences in living standards.

We see, then, that Canadian sociology began as a reformist intellectual movement, a policy-oriented research endeavour, and a product of the tumultuous social movements of the 1960s. These three roots have nurtured an academic tradition with unique strengths. Let us consider them in detail.

METHODOLOGICAL DIVERSITY

Sociologists employ three main research methods. First, they collect information using surveys and other techniques that allow them to turn people's attitudes and actions into numbers that can be analyzed statistically. Second, they collect information from historical materials (archival records, diaries, newspapers, secondary historical accounts, etc.), often comparing two or more places or periods to identify key sociological differences. Third, they observe people in natural social settings to gauge the meanings people attach to various aspects of social life. These three approaches are often called quantitative, historical–comparative, and interpretive, respectively (Alford, 1998).

Canadian sociology is marked by methodological diversity, by which I mean that Canadian sociologists tend to be open to using all three approaches to research (Guppy and Arai, 1994). The roots of this distinctive openness to different methods in Canadian sociology can be found in the early history of the discipline. Carleton University sociologist John Porter's classic *The Vertical Mosaic* (1965) pioneered quantitative research in Canada. The historical–comparative approach was introduced by University of Toronto's S.D. Clark in the late 1950s and 1960s (Clark, 1976). The famous University of Chicago/McGill ethnographer Everett Hughes wrote *French Canada in Transition* (1943), a work that helped establish a strong interpretive tradition in Canada. It is worth summarizing the major insights of these scholars before we focus on the work of some contemporary Canadian sociologists who have improved the methodological standards of the discipline beyond the contributions of its early practitioners.

Porter's *The Vertical Mosaic* (1965) is a study of nationality and ethnicity in the Canadian stratification system. It stimulated a rich tradition of quantitative research on elites, social stratification, and political sociology (Helmes-Hayes and Curtis, 1998; Clement and Myles, 1994). Porter challenged the widespread consensus that our nation is a cultural mosaic, which avoided the inequality and racial conflict of the American "melting pot." Canadian society, Porter showed, has its own problems of inequality and injustice. In the 1950s and 1960s, Canada's political and economic elites were dominated by English-speaking Protestant Canadians of British origin. New immigrants, francophones, Catholics, and Jews were located lower in a class system that was much more of a hierarchy than conventional wisdom suggested. Porter made his point with carefully gathered statistics on the social composition of elite groups.

Canada's historical sociology tradition originated with the work of S. D. Clark (Hiller, 1982). As the first Chair of the Department of Sociology at the University of Toronto, Clark stressed the need to understand the roots of contemporary Canadian society in its colonial past. He wrote about Canadians' early reliance on natural resources, fishing and fur trading, the complex relationships between the First Nations, the French in Quebec, and the British in Upper Canada, and Canada's ambivalent relationship with the United States. Clark also wrote about early social protest movements in Canada. He often focused on the Canadian hinterland, adding to our understanding of poverty in the Maritimes and western hostility to Ontario and central Canada.

Canadian sociology also has a rich ethnographic tradition. Everett Hughes wrote *French Canada in Transition* (1943) while teaching at McGill. Using the observational methods he had learned at the University of Chicago, Hughes studied changing ethnic relations in "Cantonville," Quebec, as it experienced rapid industrialization and urban development. His core argument was that the traditional rural stratification system of the parish and family farms was giving way to inequalities based on a division of labour between the managerial and working classes in the growing textile industry. Hughes observed that the industrial division of labour closely overlapped ethnic differences. The factories were all English-owned, while most of the workers were French. Somewhat controversially at the time, Hughes argued that the subordinate position of the French should be explained not primarily by cultural differences between English and French but by their economic position in relation to the ethnic division of labour and the colonial expansion of English Canada into Quebec. Hughes's book inspired generations of Canadian interpretive sociologists.

CONTEMPORARY OFFSHOOTS

Thanks to the foundational work briefly described above, Canada sociology became strong in quantitative, historical–comparative, and interpretive approaches. Contemporary Canadian sociology, however, is of an even higher scholarly quality. To demonstrate the discipline's progress and its multi-methods strengths, I now discuss important Canadian quantitative research on social stratification, historical–comparative writings on differences between the United States and Canada, and observational research on Newfoundland fisheries.

Quantitative research on elites in Canada, building on Porter, has contributed enormously to our understanding of Canadian society (Carroll, 1986; Clement, 1975, 2001; Fox and Ornstein, 1986). University of Victoria sociologist William Carroll, for example, recently produced a detailed "map" of the elite structure of Canadian society by examining the top 250 companies in the country (Carroll, 2004). He found continuity and change in the elite structure since Porter's research in the 1950s and 1960s. Carroll shows that, by 1996, 10 percent of the corporate elite in Canada were female. This is a significant if not enormous change from Porter's time, when women were entirely absent from the highest levels of economic power. In addition, Carroll found that the Canadian financial and political elites are not as dominated by British immigrants to Canada as they were in Porter's time. Carroll also documents a move away from the Toronto-centric corporate elite with the emergence of what he calls "prairie capitalism," promoted by an entrepreneurial Alberta government, the Calgary "oil patch," and large forestry and mining firms in British Columbia. At the same time, however, Carroll's data show that among the more than 1 000 000 businesses incorporated in Canada, the top 25 own fully 41 percent of the investment resources. And while French speakers make up about 30 percent of the Canadian population, they comprise only 6 percent of the corporate elite. Even in 1996, two-thirds of the corporate elite traced their family lineage to Great Britain. More women are in the top echelons of the Canadian economic elite, and there is some ethnic and linguistic diversity among the corporate class, but the dominance of this elite group of business people continues. Carroll's mapping also shows the increasingly global nature of corporate power in the modern world, raising important questions about how Canada differs from the United States and other countries.

Canadian historical–comparative sociologists have shown that many common perceptions of Canadian–American differences are wrong. For example, according to conventional wisdom, Canadians tend to be law-abiding while Americans tend to commit crimes, especially violent crimes. In their recent work, however, James Curtis and Edward Grabb show that such generalizations are far too simplistic (Curtis and Grabb, 2005). The Canadian rate of burglaries and car thefts is about the same as the American rate and is higher in some years. The view that Toronto is so crime free that people do not have to lock their doors is a gross exaggeration; this myth gained currency when American filmmaker Michael Moore reported it in *Bowling for Columbine*. Despite the recent increase in homicides in Toronto, however, the rate of murders in the United States remains three times higher than in Canada. So Canadians are hardly more law-abiding than Americans, even though they are less likely to shoot people.

Clearly, a more complex account of Canada–U.S. differences is required than is often presented in the mass media. Curtis and Grabb have contributed to such an account by demonstrating in their influential book that we can best think about North America as being made up of four distinct regions: French Quebec, English Canada, the Northern United States, and the American South (Curtis and Grabb, 2005). Instead of simplistic comparisons between two very large countries, the Curtis-Grabb historical–comparative perspective helps us to understand a number of interesting differences and similarities between these distinct regions. In addition, this angle on the topic allows us to see how remarkably similar English Canada is to the Northern United States. The American South and French Canada, in contrast, are really distinct societies, in a variety of ways. For example, when one looks at attitudes about family, sex, and traditional religious values, Quebec is the most liberal region in North America and the American South is the most conservative, but English Canada and the Northern United States are quite similar. In fact, when one breaks North America into regions in this way, the history and present culture of English Canada and the Northern United States look remarkably alike, challenging clichés about U.S.–Canadian differences.

Sociologists engaged in observational research have also contributed much to our understanding of Canadian society. Consider, for example, the exemplary ethnographic work on Newfoundland by Peter Sinclair and his colleagues (Sinclair, 1988). In the early 1990s, the Canadian government declared a moratorium on cod fishing in the Northwest Atlantic because cod stocks were depleted due to many years of overfishing. Twenty-five thousand rural Newfoundlanders suddenly found themselves out of work. To fashion policies that could help Newfoundlanders cope, it was necessary to observe and sympathetically understand their plight. That is precisely what Peter Sinclair and his team of researchers at Memorial University in St. John's did (Sinclair, 2003). Sinclair and his associates sent interviewers into the field to learn about the suffering, needs, and resourcefulness of Newfoundlanders as they attempted to cope with economic changes largely beyond their control.

In the Bonavista Peninsula, an area almost totally dependent on the fishery, they found that economic disaster was averted for several years by welfare and government programs aimed at encouraging people to learn new skills and leave the province for work elsewhere. But such programs failed to solve the problem of economic dislocation over the long term. Take the case of "Joe," who was 30 years old when the cod fishery closed down. His annual income dropped from $40 000 in 1993 to $15 000 in 1994. He took various government-sponsored training courses and moved to Saskatchewan to work on the railway but always found his way back to the Bonavista Peninsula.

Why did government policies designed to get Newfoundlanders to leave the economically devastated area not work well? Sinclair's interviews uncovered deep flaws in the economic models and political strategies developed in Ottawa— flaws that resulted from policy analysts failing to observe and talk to the people affected by the cod moratorium. Only by engaging in such observational research, Sinclair argued, is it possible to figure out people's options, the reasons they make certain choices, and their likely reaction to various policies. Thus, Joe strongly preferred to work rather than be on welfare, and he might have considered moving away permanently, but he owned a home in the Bonavista Peninsula that he was unable to rent or sell. Moreover, he and his wife benefited from help provided by family members in the area, especially child-care. Joe's elderly parents, who depended on Joe's family, were unwilling to move to Saskatchewan. While Joe supported aspects of the government training programs that were put into place after the closing of the cod fishery, he was angry that it took two years before anyone asked ordinary Newfoundlanders what should be done about the problem. As he put it, "Millions and millions, probably billions of dollars gone, and you're finally coming down asking the people that know what's wrong, what needs to be done and where it should go"

(quoted in Sinclair, 2003: 9). As Sinclair's work well demonstrates, the shortcomings of government policy were largely due to the failure of government officials to listen to people like Joe. One is compelled to conclude that, in general, observational research is essential for well-designed social policy.

CANADIAN PUBLIC SOCIOLOGY AND ITS CHALLENGE TO STUDENTS

An international debate is now taking place about how sociologists ought to use their professional research, policy skills, and often critical outlook on society to establish a dialogue with ordinary citizens outside the university. Sometimes this process of bridge building is referred to as the establishment of a "public sociology" (Burawoy, 2005). Canadian sociology is well placed to help construct such a bridge.

Canada's parliamentary system and its rough consensus around welfare state policies have created many opportunities for policy-oriented sociology. While American sociologists have often been excluded from the corridors of power, Canadian sociologists have enjoyed some measure of access to and influence in Ottawa— and even more in Quebec City. Co-optation by political authorities can weaken the scholarly contribution and autonomy of sociologists, as was the case in early twentieth-century Britain. Practical political demands can divert one's attention from the big picture. But there seems little danger of that in Canada, where sociologists enjoy plenty of opportunities to contribute to public policy debates on women's roles in society, gender and sexuality, families, visible minorities, criminal justice, health care, and other issues (Brym and Myles, 1989; Breton, 1989). Canada enjoys a particularly strong and vocal sociological tradition that is critical of mainstream and official points of view. That critical tradition further enlivens policy debates

(Curtis, 2001; Hiller, 2001; Hiller and Langlois, 2001; Eichler, 2001, 2002; Nock, 2001; Smith, 1975; Sydie, 1994).

The nature of Canadian sociology is such that students who major in the discipline typically learn a wide range of quantitative, qualitative, and historical research skills. The discipline's openness to critical perspectives enables students to examine the lives of people outside the mainstream of society—people who are marginalized by the colour of their skin, religion, class position, sexual orientation, region, or lifestyle. It is a discipline that often challenges students' moral and political assumptions and beliefs. The public policy relevance of Canadian sociology inevitably leads students into controversial yet pressing, practical questions about inequality, politics, and culture. The construction of a public sociology in Canada promises to be an exciting project. I invite you to join us.

REFERENCES

Alford, Robert. (1998). *The Craft of Inquiry: Methods, Theories and Evidence.* Oxford: Oxford University Press.

Breton, Raymond. (1989). "Quebec Sociology: Agendas from Society or from Sociologists?" *Canadian Review of Sociology and Anthropology,* 26: 557–70.

Brym, Robert, with Bonnie Fox. (1989). *From Culture to Power: The Sociology of English Canada.* Toronto: Oxford University Press.

Brym, Robert, and John Myles. (1989). "Social Science Intellectuals and Public Issues in English Canada." *University of Toronto Quarterly,* 58: 442–51.

Brym, Robert, and Céline Saint-Pierre. (1997). "Canadian Sociology." *Contemporary Sociology,* 26: 543–46.

Burawoy, Michael. (2005). "2004 Presidential Address: For Public Sociology." *American Sociological Review,* 70: 4–28.

Carroll, William K. (1986). *Corporate Power and Canadian Capitalism.* Vancouver: University of British Columbia Press.

———. (2004). *Corporate Power in a Globalizing World: A Study in Elite Social Organization.* Don Mills, ON: Oxford University Press.

Clark, S. D. (1976). *Canadian Society in Historical Perspective.* Toronto: McGraw-Hill Ryerson.

Clement, Wallace. (1975). *The Canadian Corporate Elite: An Analysis of Economic Power.* Toronto: McClelland and Stewart.

———. (2001). "Canadian Political Economy's Legacy for Sociology." *Canadian Journal of Sociology,* 26: 405–20.

Clement, Wallace, and John Myles. (1994). *Relations of Ruling: Class and Gender in Postindustrial Societies.* Montreal and Kingston: McGill-Queen's University Press.

Cormier, Jeffrey. (2004). *The Canadianization Movement: Emergence, Survival and Success.* Toronto: University of Toronto Press.

Curtis, Bruce. (2001). *The Politics of Population: State Formation, Statistics, and the Census of Canada, 1840–75.* Toronto: University of Toronto Press.

Curtis, James E, and Edward G. Grabb. (2005). *Regions Apart: The Four Societies of Canada and the United States.* Toronto: Oxford University Press.

Eichler, Margrit. (2001). "Women Pioneers in Canadian Sociology: The Effects of a Politics of Gender and a Politics of Knowledge." *Canadian Journal of Sociology,* 26: 375–403.

———. (2002). "Feminism and Canadian Sociology." *The American Sociologist,* 33: 27–41.

Fox, John, and Michael Ornstein. (1986). "The Canadian State and Corporate Elites in the Postwar Period. *Canadian Review of Sociology and Anthropology,* 23 (4): 481–506.

Guppy, Neil, and Bruce Arai. (1994). "Teaching Sociology—Comparing Undergraduate Curricula in the United States and English Canada." *Teaching Sociology,* 22: 217–30.

Helmes-Hayes, Richard. (2002). "John Porter: Canada's Most Famous Sociologist." *The American Sociologist,* 33: 79–104.

Helmes-Hayes, Richard, and James E. Curtis. (1998). *The Vertical Mosaic Revisited.* Toronto: University of Toronto Press.

Hiller, Harry. (1982). *Society and Change: S. D. Clark and the Development of Canadian Sociology.* Toronto: University of Toronto Press.

———. (2001). "Legacy for a New Millennium: Canadian Sociology in the Twentieth Century as Seen Through Its Publications." *Canadian Journal of Sociology,* 26: 257–63.

Hiller, Harry, and Simon Langlois. (2001). "The Most Important Books/Articles in Canadian Sociology in the Twentieth Century: A Report." *Canadian Journal of Sociology,* 26: 513–16.

Marsh, Leonard. (1940). *Canadians In and Out of Work: A Survey of Economic Classes and Their Relation to the Labour Market.* Toronto: Oxford University Press.

Nock, David. (2001). "Careers in Print: Canadian Sociological Books and Their Wider Impact, 1975–1992." *Canadian Journal of Sociology,* 26: 469–85.

Porter, John A. (1965). *The Vertical Mosaic: An Analysis of Social Class and Power in Canada.* Toronto: University of Toronto Press.

Shore, Marlene. (1987). *The Science of Social Redemption: McGill, the Chicago School, and the Origins of Social Research in Canada.* Toronto: University of Toronto Press.

Sinclair, Peter. (1988). *A Question of Survival: The Fisheries and Newfoundland Society.* St. John's, NF: Institute of Social and Economic Research, Memorial University of Newfoundland.

———. (2003). "A Very Delicate World: Fishers and Plant Workers Remake Their Lives on Newfoundland's Bonavista Peninsula after the Cod Moratorium." *Maritime Studies,* 2: 89–109.

Smith, D. E. 1975. "What It Might Mean to Do a Canadian Sociology—The Everyday World As Problematic." *Canadian Journal of Sociology,* 1: 363–76.

Sydie, R. A. 1994. "Sex and the Sociological Fathers." *Canadian Review of Sociology and Anthropology,* 31: 117–38.

PART 2 | FOUNDATIONS OF SOCIETY

Imagine standing at the end of a road 30 kilometres long. Allow each metre of the road to represent 100 000 years. The entire road will then signify the amount of time that has passed since life first appeared on the planet: about 3 billion years. From this long view, human beings are recent arrivals, first assuming their present form only about 100 000 years ago, or just a metre down the road.

Recorded human history spans a much shorter distance. The development of agriculture, undoubtedly the single most important event in human history, took place approximately 10 000 years ago (only 10 centimetres down the road). The beginning of modern industry, arguably the second most important event in human history, dates from just about 230 years ago (a mere 2.3 millimetres down the road).

The evolution of agriculture and modern industry hint at what makes humans different from other animals: our advanced ability to create complex symbols (**abstraction**), make and use tools that improve our ability to take what we want from nature (**production**), and develop a complex social life (**cooperation**). These are the characteristics that enabled humans to survive and multiply despite a harsh natural environment and relatively poor physical endowments.

The second section of this book focuses on the building blocks of social life, the basic social mechanisms and processes involved in human abstraction, production, and cooperation. You will explore how symbolic communication between people, or **social interaction,** enables us to engage in social learning, or **socialization.** By means of socialization people acquire the languages, laws, science, values, customs, and beliefs—in short, the **culture**—of the groups to which they belong. When social interaction assumes a regular or patterned form, the relations among people form a **social structure.** Social structures may be, for example, hierarchical or egalitarian, tightly integrated or loosely organized; and different social–structural forms influence human thoughts and actions in different ways. The patterned behaviour of people embedded in a social structure is called a **role.** For instance, in some types of hierarchy, some people perform the role of slave, others the role of master. You will see that social structures and cultures are paradoxical features of social life. On the one hand, they are constructed anew, and often modified, at least a little, by each person in society. On the other hand, because social structures and cultures exist before any particular individual does, they help define and limit what the individual can think and what he or she can do. Hence the answer of many sociologists to the philosophers' debate about whether people are free or determined: they are both.

GLOSSARY

Abstraction is the human ability to create symbols in order to classify experience and generalize from it.

Cooperation is the human ability to give and receive aid from other humans. Social structures are typically created to facilitate cooperation.

Culture consists of the symbols that people use to communicate and organize their social life.

Production is a distinctively human mode of interacting with nature. It involves inventing tools and using them to make and improve the means of survival.

Roles are the behaviour patterns of people embedded in a social structure.

Social interaction is symbolic communication between people.

Social structures are the patterns of social relations in which people are embedded and that provide opportunities for, and constrain, action.

Socialization is the social process by which culture is learned.

CRITICAL THINKING QUESTIONS

1. If we accept that social structures influence human thought and action, are people responsible for what they think and do? Should criminals, for example, be held responsible for their crimes? Should society be held responsible for producing criminals? Or is there a middle ground between these two extreme views?

ANNOTATED BIBLIOGRAPHY

Lenski, Gerhard, Patrick Nolan, and Jean Lenski. *Human Societies: An Introduction to Macrosociology.* 7th ed. New York: McGraw-Hill, 1995. Imaginatively traces the evolution of human societies, focusing on the relationship between technological innovation and social stratification.

PART 2A

SOCIAL INTERACTION AND SOCIALIZATION

Three main social–psychological models inform the socialization literature. The **developmental model** compares people to acorns that have growth potential and develop in stages set by their inherent characteristics. The **normative model** likens people to empty bowls into which society and culture pour a defined assortment of beliefs, symbols, values, and roles. The **interactive model** views people as the imaginative, two-legged creatures you and I deal with every day. From the interactive point of view, socialization is a creative process that takes place in groups. Inherent biological and psychological traits may set broad potentials and limits to what people can become. The broader society and culture may define the general outline of people's beliefs, symbols, values, and roles. But people become socialized in face-to-face settings where they interact with others. In those settings they imaginatively interpret, accept, and reject the opportunities and demands of socialization in ways that suit them.

Patricia and Peter Adler adopt the interactive model in this section's first chapter, which focuses on gender relations during preadolescent socialization (from preschool through grade 6). They closely observed preadolescents in schools and discovered a complex pattern of integration, separation, and reconnection between boys and girls over time. Developmental stages were evident and sociocultural pressures abounded, but the children were agents of the socialization process, adapting circumstances to their needs as much as they were compelled to adapt to their circumstances. They were socialized into masculine and feminine roles but in innovative and sometimes surprising ways. They were not born with gender, nor did they simply learn it; they had to "do" gender before it became theirs.

Playing gender roles can be a risky and costly business. Consider, for instance, that in 2003, women working full-time in Canada's paid labour force earned about 71 cents for every dollar earned by men. Although that was up from 64 cents in 1985, there were still nearly five times more men than women in high-paying jobs. In 2005, women held just 14.4 percent of corporate officer positions in Canada's 500 biggest companies. Nearly 40 percent of those companies had no women at all in their executive ranks. Meet the **glass ceiling,** a sociological barrier that makes it difficult for most women to rise to the top rungs of the job ladder.

What is the glass ceiling made of? Over 100 male chief executives and 400 female senior managers were asked in a Canadian survey to indicate the top three barriers to women's advancement to senior levels. The barrier most frequently mentioned by the women: male stereotyping and preconceptions of women's roles and abilities. The barrier most frequently mentioned by the men: lack of job experience. These responses are not necessarily contradictory. In corporations and the public bureaucracy, male managers may slot talented women into communications and human resource jobs because of their preconceptions of what women are good at. Because of this bias, women may fail to get the kind of operational experience in the field or on the production line that could lead them to top managerial positions. In any case, the men and women who participated in the survey certainly agreed on one thing. The second most frequently chosen response by both groups was "commitment to family responsibilities." Married women still do most of the housework, child-care, and senior care while governments and corporations provide little in the way of support. The resulting career disruption, absenteeism, use of the part-time job option, and sheer physical and emotional exhaustion impede the rise of women in the job hierarchy. Not surprisingly, therefore, among full-time workers in the paid labour force, *never-married* women earn about 90 percent as much as never-married men, but *married* women earned only about 65 percent as much as married men. Given current domestic, state, and corporate arrangements, women are penalized economically to the degree that their families are important to them.

In Chapter 5, Deborah Tannen explores another fascinating aspect of the glass ceiling: gender-specific conversational styles. Because the socialization of women usually differs from that of men, they typically communicate in different ways at work. These differences matter in terms of career advancement. According to Tannen, "women's and men's conversational styles affect who gets heard, who gets credit, and what gets done at work." In other words, much miscommunication between men and women takes place on the job. Due to the distribution of power in the workplace and the nature of this miscommunication, the important contributions made by women often go unnoticed or even get mistaken for incompetence by male managers. Tannen's revealing case studies drive home the point that women's careers will benefit if women become more assertive at work and if male managers improve their ability to understand everyday, gendered, face-to-face interaction. Indeed, by assessing the impact of typical male and female conversational styles, Tannen's research contributes to this role change.

Other costs of gender interaction and socialization include violence and harassment. Sociological surveys show that men have physically or sexually assaulted about half of Canadian women. It will perhaps surprise you to learn that rates of female violence against men are about the same as rates of male violence against women. It will undoubtedly be less startling to hear that men's violent acts against women are much more likely to result in medical treatment and police intervention than women's violent acts against men. Men, moreover, sexually harass women a lot more than the reverse. In this section's final chapter, Sandy Welsh and Jayne Baker show that male sexual harassment, like gendered action in the primary school classroom and the corporate office, is partly the result of learned stereotypical gender roles. Welsh and Baker thus demonstrate that women are unlikely to define unwanted acts as sexual harassment if they are situated in social locations where stereotypical gender roles are routinely stressed. But they also show that women are more likely to define unwanted acts as sexual harassment if workplaces are organized in certain ways. We are obliged to conclude that while gender socialization at school and at work is important, it is not a straightjacket. Social forces increase the probability that people will act in certain ways, but ultimately people are agents of their own destiny.

GLOSSARY

The **developmental model** of socialization likens people to acorns that have growth potential and develop in stages set by their inherent characteristics.

The **glass ceiling** is a sociological barrier that makes it difficult for most women to rise to the top rungs of the job ladder.

The **interactive model** regards socialization as a creative process that takes place in groups.

The **normative model** of socialization likens people to empty bowls into which society and culture pour a defined assortment of beliefs, symbols, values, and roles.

CRITICAL THINKING QUESTIONS

1. What are the strengths and limitations of the three main social–psychological theories of socialization? Exactly how does the interactive theory improve upon earlier developmental and normative theories?

2. What is meant by "the glass ceiling?" Do you agree with Deborah Tannen that conversational style differences between men and women play a significant role in establishing the glass ceiling? What are some conversational rituals common among women? What are some other examples of language differences in the workplace that make women's experience different from men's experience?
3. What social factors decrease the probability that women will define unwanted sexual advances as harassment? What circumstances increase that probability?

ANNOTATED BIBLIOGRAPHY

Goffman, Erving. *The Presentation of Self in Everyday Life.* Garden City, NY: Anchor, 1959. The classic sociological analysis of social interaction as theatrical performance.

Kanter, Rosabeth Moss. *Men and Women of the Corporation.* New York: Basic Books, 1977. Analyzes the ways in which social interaction and group formation reinforce gender inequality in a setting where no formal gender discrimination exists.

Chapter 4

Peer Pressure and Preadolescent Socialization

PATRICIA A. ADLER AND PETER ADLER

GENDER INTEGRATION: THE EARLY YEARS

Children began their early lives and their education with a much greater attitude of gender neutrality than they later developed. Although they experienced intensive gender socialization and labeling as infants, they remained fairly open to cross-gender friendships throughout the preschool and earliest of elementary school years (Oswald et al., 1987; Voss, 1997). When children were very young, the primary determinant of someone's suitability for friendship was propinquity: a nearby child was acceptable as a friend. Young children readily acquiesced to forming play groups and to spending time with relatives, neighbors, and family friends selected by their parents based on their availability.

FRIENDSHIP PATTERNING

When they entered into preschool and early elementary years, children brought with them a strong gender awareness. They were learning the role parameters of their gender and experimenting with gender-varied clothing, role modeling, and identification. For instance, when Stacey was four, she cast off her jeans and shirts, and wore nothing but dresses for the whole year. Five-year-old Mark carefully noted aloud each time he encountered an occupation that seemed to be male- or female-associated, fixing these patterns in his mind. Yet children at this stage, ranging in age from three to six and educationally located between prekindergarten and first grade, were socially open to gender in ways that they might not be later. They were somewhat more likely to socialize with members of their own gender, but there was little stigma attached to cross-gender companionship. When Katy was in kindergarten she mostly played with girls, but she also had two friends from school who were boys. She and her male friends would spend time together at school, but they would also make arrangements to play together at home, after school, or on the weekends.

Other girls leaned more heavily toward cross-gender friendships. Betsy, in third grade, described her current attitude toward boys, comparing it with the way she used to feel when she was younger. "Brett, he and I used to be best friends, but then he sat on my stomach at my friend's birthday party, was squeezing me, like he was trying to kill me. And now we're just not friends. But we still talk. Or like Matt, we used to be best friends. There was a period of time in kindergarten and preschool where I only liked boys, and I wouldn't go hang out with girls, and then now I can't stand boys except my dad." As Betsy noted, the openness toward cross-gender friendships that predominated in the early school years was temporally bounded. Children's ease of interactions and lack of self-consciousness about playing with members of the other gender did not last.

Paul, the third grader with few friends, offered his recollections about the age demarcations that changed boys' and girls' friendship relations:

Q: *So do you think it's kind of common for boys and girls to be friends, or it's not that common?*

Paul: Um, I don't think, it depends what grade you're talking about. Like this grade, it's not that common I don't think. Other grades . . .

Q: *Older grades or younger grades?*

Paul: Well, mostly really old grades. Really old grades and really young grades, 'cause young grades it's just like a bunch of kids who really, like the whole class, like, likes each other, they just look for friends to call and play with. Sometimes that's what it's like with very small kids, they have girlfriends, a lot of people think for friends. In the second grade I don't really think it's like that, but when you get really old I think you could have a girlfriend.

Preschool and early elementary school children's cross-gender friendships were thus most recently comfortable and unselfconscious, not rigidly marked by gender boundaries. Children played along mixed lines, unrestricted by cultural roles or norms prohibiting such interaction.

ROMANTIC ALTERNATIVES

Young preadolescents did not usually interact with each other in a romantic or sexualized way. This was something they associated with their parents or older siblings, but not with themselves. There was not a complete lack of interest, however, and every group contained modes of behavior for selected boys and girls to explore this area. Some boys and girls were more regularly interested in dabbling with romance or sexuality, while others became drawn into it from time to time or seasonally, when such pursuits

developed momentum. At times this romantic interest was held privately, without being shared among friends.

Nancy, the fifth-grade girl, recalled with embarrassment her early desire for a boyfriend and the way she simulated romantic attachment to one of her classmates:

Q: *Have you ever had any interest in boys, kind of a boyfriend type of thing?*

Nancy: Uh, yeah. In kindergarten I wanted to like somebody, and so I just picked somebody and said to myself, "Okay, I like you."

Q: *And so what kinds of things did you do with him?*

Nancy: Nothing. I didn't show it in any way, I didn't tell anybody about it. I just said, "Okay, I like him." And that was that. I have no idea why I did that. It's embarrassing now to think of that.

Marcia, when she was in kindergarten, decided she liked one of the boys in her class and told her friends about it. This was a boy with whom she was friends, and with whom she used to play frequently. She never spoke to him about these thoughts, though. She never allowed it to surface in their interaction, keeping it a secret.

Children rarely spoke openly of romantic feelings for age mates, generally acting toward their peers only as friends. The behavior that offered a generalized exception to this was the chasing and kissing games, which provided a way for children to more openly explore cross-gendered romantic expressions. In these games, groups of boys and girls ran after each other and chased groups or individuals of the other gender. Such games varied in nature, but the object was to chase or be chased. When individuals got close to getting caught, they often turned around and reversed the roles, chasing rather than being chased. When people actually got caught, they sometimes were kissed, but usually the chasers lost their nerve and just backed away or pushed them. Other games were more elaborate, involving locking up the apprehended individuals in makeshift jails. Delivering or receiving an actual kiss, however, was the most exciting outcome to an exhilarating chase.

John, a fifth-grade boy, looked back nostalgically on his first kiss. "Some boys like some girls right now, and I think it started about first grade, that boys started liking girls. That's when me and my friend got our first kiss."

Q: *How'd that happen?*
John: Um, Alex, a girl in our grade, she was one of the "kissing girls." She was always chasing the boys and trying to kiss them. Me and Travis thought this was fun. We would chase the girls too. But one day we wanted to see what would happen if we let her catch us. So we ran down behind the slides area, and we slowed down so she could catch us. No one else was around. So she caught us, and she gave us each kisses. Then we ran away.

Chasing and kissing games, then, were not practiced by all members of the grade, only the "kissing girls" and "kissing boys." This ensured that people who were not willing participants did not get molested. People signaled their interest in entering the game through previous participation, or by running away and looking back or shouting and jeering at members of the other gender.

Kevin, a fifth grader, spoke of his experiences with chasing and kissing, offering his estimate of the extent of the participation:

Q: *When do people start getting interested in the opposite sex?*
Kevin: It really depends. Like for me it started in the first grade. Some I'm sure haven't started until third grade. But I definitely started in the first grade.
Q: *And what were your early experiences?*
Kevin: Boys chase girls, girls chase boys. And like, "You know who I have a crush on?" and stuff.

Q: *At that age is everyone into the chasing stuff and the liking stuff, or is it just a certain portion of them?*
Kevin: Thirty percent or something, not very much.

Children in the preschool or early elementary school years generally interacted readily, then, both within and across gender groups for platonic friendship. More romantic interest and interactions were restricted by peer norms to games of chasing and kissing. Children participating in such games were generally the more precocious and popular individuals, those who had more friends and more visibility in the grade. Individuals did not feel free to express any other forms of romantic interest.

GENDER SEGREGATION: THE MIDDLE YEARS

Once they were firmly settled in elementary school, children moved into the stage of strict gender separation. This generally began in about first or second grade and lasted until fourth or fifth grade. Like Paul, who noted the difference between the way children interacted with members of the other gender at the "really young grades" and the "really old grades," most children were aware of this patterned movement into and out of contact with members of the other gender.

Kenny, the fifth grader, reflected back on the phases of gender relations through which he and his friends had passed:

Q: *Do you think that it is common that most boys of your age are not as good friends with girls?*
Kenny: Yes, we don't hang out with any girls. We are like a different race from them.
Q: *Thinking back when you were younger, when you were little, did you used to be friendly with girls?*
Kenny: Yes. I had a couple of friends who were girls.

Q: *When did you think that boys and girls separated out of the same race?*

Kenny: 'Bout second to fourth grade.

Kenny marked the main boundaries of the middle period, where boys and girls "separated out of the same race," noting that boys and girls were generally not friendly with each other during this time.

INTERESTS AND ACTIVITIES

One of the primary reasons boys and girls separated into different races and ceased to interact with each other on a friendly basis was that their interests sharply diverged. Boys and girls moved into highly gendered worlds where their concerns and recreational activities were different (see Thorne, 1986). Boys pursued sports; fantasy card games; sport card collecting; and rough-and-tumble play; while girls engaged in relationship building and intimacy work; dressing up; playing with dolls; and pursuing dance, art, and gymnastics. Paul, the third grader, supported the notion of different interests as the source of the chasm between boys and girls: "Well, in the middle grades boys have other friends, and they think that girls aren't that, they don't really like them all that much unless the boys like dolls or something." With few overlapping interests, boys and girls had little to do with each other, aside from school activities. They were engaged in developing gendered groups, and identities that left little room for transgression.

Craig, the third grader, indicated the rarity for boy-girl friendships:

Q: *Are there many boys and girls who are friendly?*

Craig: Not many. I have one girl that I'm friendly with, Adair.

Q: *What kinds of things might you and Adair do at school together?*

Craig: Well, I usually play with my friends that are boys, and she usually plays with her friends that are girls.

ATTITUDES TOWARD THE OTHER GENDER

During this phase of gender segregation, boys and girls tended to lose the positive feelings they had toward each other. At best, they regarded each other neutrally. At worst, they moved into the "cooties" stage, thinking of each other as contaminated (Thorne, 1993).

Kyra, the third grader, expressed the negative perspective that girls at this stage commonly held toward boys. This included a lack of interest in romantic attitudes as well as platonic ones:

Q: *Do girls of your age have any interest in boys?*

Kyra: Not really. We don't like boys.

Q: *Do you think any of the guys in your class are cute?*

Kyra: Um mum. They're more annoying.

Q: *If they're annoying, what kinds of annoying things do they do?*

Kyra: Well, Colin falls out of his chair purposely, they're always talking, so they could be called jitterboxes instead of boys, and they talk too much, and they're just annoying.

Like Kyra, most girls regarded boys as violent, uncouth, dirty, and mean-spirited. Boys were disgusting and had nothing that would interest girls in them.

Seth, a third grade boy from the popular crowd at another school, reinforced Kyra and Brett's sentiments, expressing disdain for members of the other gender:

Q: *Do you have any friends who are girls?*

Seth: I used to have one back in second grade, last year. But she just like started to say well, "I don't like you because I want to be with my friends," and I bet her friends just started saying, "Oh my god, you're playing with him?"

Q: *What would be wrong with being friends with you?*

Seth: People would say, "You're friends with the opposite sex!"

Q: *But you're not really friendly with girls?*

Seth: They're okay. Sometimes they can be nice. Sometimes they can be just sort of dorks.

Q: *And so just as far as just liking girls, do you have a little bit of interest, or no interest?*

Seth: None of my friends has any interest. No interest.

Seth's remarks indicate the presence of a second factor influencing the contours of boy-girl relations: the peer culture. During this period, boys and girls began to frown on cross-gender associations and delivered informal negative sanctions to each other for violating these boundaries. Such attitudes were more powerful among the popular boy crowds than in the less popular middle circles, and in the middle girl friendship circles than among the more precocious girls, but they set the tone for the entire grade.

ALTERNATIVES: FRIENDLY CONTACT

While the predominant mode of social life involved gender segregation, there were patterned exceptions. Cross-gender relationships inside school were harder to maintain due to peer pressure, leaving middle elementary school students with more cross-gender family and neighborhood friends than those from school. Some boys and girls who had been close friends during the younger years managed to retain their friendships, however. In addition, there were times when groups of girls or boys drifted together for occasional play. These group interactions were usually oriented around play rather than relationships and were short-lived. More lasting cross-gender friendships were usually pursued on an individual basis. Several people indicated that they were the type who had kept close friends of the other gender during the years of segregation. This was often the case with girls who enjoyed playing sports. Yet playing with boys did not necessarily mean establishing friendships.

ALTERNATIVES: CHASING AND TEASING

During the middle elementary school years the interactions between boys and girls were the most problematic. Beyond the large-scale gap were chasms of awkwardness and misunderstanding. Boys and girls were unsure of how to relate to each other, had uncertain spurts of interest in each other, and alternated these with strong negative feelings about each other. Part of membership in boys' and girls' gendered cultural worlds involved expressing and enacting hostility toward the opposing group. This happened between individuals and groups, involving teasing and deriding. The chasing and kissing games of the early years were replaced by a more mean-spirited gender play. Some of the excitement of the chase remained, but the outcome was more frequently tinged with hurt and injury.

Nancy, the fifth-grade girl, recalled that in first grade a group of boys tried to catch girls and make them eat grasshoppers. She viewed this behavior as cruel and degrading, with the boys taking advantage of the girls.

Betsy, the third grader, noted that teasing and negative interaction were not the exclusive domain of boys. Girls, too, acted mean to boys they did not like. She described one of her friends who teased boys a lot: "She'll just yell to them. Sometimes, even, to get on their nerves. Like when they're playing basketball, she likes getting on their nerves. And she does that very easily. She's very good at it, and sometimes, like, when I'm mad at somebody, like sometimes I get mad at Brett, and so I'll go up to him and I'll take his hat and throw it. And I do that a lot."

ALTERNATIVES: FLIRTING AND LIKING

Despite the prevailing feeling that boys and girls had no romantic interest in each other during the period of segregation, there were people who departed from this norm. In contrast to the clear patterns relating social status and types of behavior noted thus far, individuals who flirted with members of the other gender or who developed a crush on someone could come from any rank of the stratification hierarchy. Quiet and shy people who were not popular could like someone of another gender as readily as those who were outgoing and highly visible. Whether they had the courage to act on those feelings was another matter.

PEER REACTIONS

The power of negative peer reactions was enough to deter most people interested in romantic liaisons from acting on these interests. Children were concerned with fitting in and being accepted, fearful of ridicule. The elementary school years were characterized by acutely fierce ridicule, untempered by the gentility of politeness that comes to cloak most interactions later in life. When boys or girls latched onto an item that violated peer norms, their reactions usually followed a predictable pattern.

Kenny, the fifth grader, recalled an incident of ridicule that he experienced in third grade, after placing his only phone call to a girl:

> Q: *Was it a serious call or kind of a prank?*
> Kenny: Both. I asked her if she liked me, and she said not really.
> Q: *Sounds like a serious call.*
> Kenny: Then she told everybody that I called her.
> Q: *So what happened?*
> Kenny: Everybody knew that I had called her.
> Q: *Did they make fun of you?*
> Kenny: Really badly for a while. It was horrible. But then it died down.

During the period of ridicule, most people suffered severe anguish. Some tried to avoid problems by isolating themselves from people, waiting for the storm to blow over, while others were so engulfed by it that they never saw an end in sight. Their distress, and others' perceptions of it, was vivid, as Seth, a popular third-grade boy, described: "Most kids, if they're interested in a girl, they won't tell anyone. They'd just keep it a secret, because people now make fun of them. Like, 'Oh god, you like her!'"

> Q: *Has that ever happened to anyone in your grade?*
> Seth: Some people, yeah.
> Q: *What happens when people get made fun of?*
> Seth: Usually they just walk away and look like they feel bad. They try not to let it show, or people will just lay it on more, but they look bad. You can just tell.

Very few people were willing to submit themselves to the anguish and humiliation of public ridicule. They had seen it inflicted on others and understood what it was like. Paul, the third grader, explained how this unfolded: "If you'd really like to be friends with a girl, you know why you don't usually? 'Cause they say, 'You're friends with a girl?' And 'Blah, blah blah, blah blah blah.' And they make fun of you. And I realize that usually I don't tell people that I like them until I think it's the right timing."

LIKING IN SILENCE

Fear of the fallout from peer reaction led most people in the middle years to keep from approaching individuals they liked and revealing their feelings. People who did not realize what might happen if their secret got out to the wrong crowd quickly learned the hard way. Kenny, the fifth-grade boy who called a girl in third grade and told her he liked her, only to have his deed turned into fodder for class ridicule, spoke about the consequences of that event for him: he did not stop liking her, but rather "liked her in silence." Kenny thus moved into the great morass of secrecy in which most preadolescents held feelings or experiences that they thought would be mocked by the peer group.

THE LATER YEARS

After the years of segregation, cross-gender contact began to reemerge. Throughout this later period, comprising fourth through sixth grades, people initiated cross-gender relationships for two purposes: friendship and romance. The movement back toward members of the other gender was fraught with excitement, tension, and danger, however. Many less sophisticated individuals chose to remain within the relative safety of their own gender group, letting others forge this path. During these years, then, children engaged in the widest diversity of cross-gender contact patterns, with some firmly rooted in the separated mode of the middle years, others beginning tenuous platonic friendships, and others testing the romantic waters. We consider the range of feelings and behaviors along this continuum.

SEPARATION

A significant portion of the boys and girls, nearly one-quarter of those in this age range, showed little or no interest in bridging the gender divide. These people had spent so many years holding divergent interests that they found it difficult to socialize casually with each other. Their preoccupations did not overlap enough to support platonic relations, and they did not feel comfortable pursuing romantic attraction. Some individuals made attempts at reintegration, but these were often uneasy. Early forays into the cross-gendered world tended to be furtive; boys and girls made "gender jabs" at one another.

FRIENDLY INTERACTION

In contrast to the middle years, a sizable number (roughly one-half) of boys and girls developed friendly relations. Early boy-girl platonic contact continued, as it had during the gender segregation phase, to flourish primarily when girls played sports with boys.

Tucker, the fifth grader in a middle friendship circle, described the nature of the boy-girl friendships he observed:

> Q: *What about friends who are girls?*
> Tucker: My world is more filled up with boy friends. I mean, there are some girls that have been my friends since the first grade, ones that play sports and

stuff, but I don't hang out with them and talk to them.

> Q: *Do girls have to come into boys' sports worlds for boys to play with them? Do boys ever go into girls' activities to play with them?*
> Tucker: Yeah.
> Q: *Like what kinds of girls' activities do boys participate in?*
> Tucker: I don't know. Jump rope, hopscotch maybe, I haven't seen that, but um, that's what they could do.

Tucker struggled to think of ways that boys moved into the realm of girls' worlds because this crossover was decidedly more rare.

Girls' gender roles expanded during the 1980s and 1990s to a much greater extent than did boys'. Consequently, it was more likely that a girl who liked to play sports could count boys among her friends than a girl who did not, and there were not many boys who ventured into the activities described above.

Outside of sports, boys and girls found other bases for friendships. Some who had been friendly years before revived their shelved relationships. Others forged cross-gender friendships that grew out of shared school interests. The incidence of cross-gender neighborhood and after-school activities increased. But not everybody pursued platonic boy-girl relationships; some people preferred to keep their distance. Those who were willing to move beyond their segregated spheres had to take the risk of getting teased or feeling awkward.

ROMANTIC INTEREST

Slowly, and more tentatively than for platonic friendships, boys and girls began to put out romantic feelers. This began with very few individuals and increased in fits and starts. Everyone watched with riveting interest as the front-runners made their romantic forays. Some were quickly rebuffed, while others received more tentative response.

Individuals developed greater interest in members of the other gender and got up the courage to speak openly about these feelings. Kevin said the turnaround in boy-girl relations occurred in fourth grade: "We no longer had boys chase girls and stuff. It just wasn't that immature any longer. It became, like, cool." Chuck, the more popular fifth-grade boy, offered a more differentiated view of individuals' transitions out of the segregation stage into cross-gender rapprochement. He talked about the range of grades at which people began to make this passage: "Early starters, I guess you could call them, in around third or fourth grade. Late starters, not until fifth grade. By now it's big. There's four people going out. Four couples. Going on a date, serious."

A fifth grader, Mariah, described her first encounter with boy-girl activity as reflecting a simultaneous rise of boy-girl interest: "All of my friends all of a sudden just kind of had an interest in boys. All of the girls in my class." This rapidly changing dynamic might reflect either the tendency for groups to swing from one set of interest to another, or the sudden release of people's pent-up romantic interests when the constraining social norms loosened. Many preadolescents reported that they waited eagerly for other people to break the ice before they felt free to discuss or act on their interest in members of the other gender.

Laura, a popular fifth grader, saw her friends' increased interest in boys as a more gradual phenomenon: "Fourth grade is when we really first started. We'd be just like walking around and talking, but in fourth grade we didn't really do much. In fifth grade is when we just, kinda, started talking about like the dating crowd and stuff."

Multiple patterns—with people moving into romantic interest individually, by friendship group, or in a swing encompassing a whole crowd—were thus possible. While different groups of boys and girls began moving toward romantic integration at different times and at different speeds, by fifth grade enough people had become interested in the other gender that it attained a foothold of legitimacy in the peer cul-

ture. Many individuals still held no interest, but the more popular groups were definitely roused. Less popular people watched this behavior and commented about or ignored it, but they knew that it had begun. Roughly one-third of the people we observed had made romantic overtures by the end of this time period.

ATTRACTIVE CHARACTERISTICS

Before they began flirting, boys and girls had to decide whom they liked. They used different criteria to determine what they found attractive in members of the other gender. For boys, the preeminent determinant was appearance: they had crushes on girls they found cute. Girls, in contrast, followed a more complex and intangible set of criteria.

Mariah, a popular fifth grader, described what she looked for in a boyfriend:

Q: *So when did you first start developing a crush on a boy?*

Mariah: Like two moths into the year.

Q: *What kids of thing is it based on?*

Mariah: They have to be nice to you, or else forget it.

Q: *Is there anything else you look for in a guy?*

Mariah: How intelligent the person is. Because if the person's not very smart, then, I don't know, that can get kind of annoying. 'Cause they're always asking questions, and uhhhhhhh! You're supposed to know this stuff.

Joanna, another popular fifth grader, elaborated further on similar concerns:

Q: *What are girls or boys looking for in each other?*

Joanna: Usually it's because they're nice, and mature. Not like embarrassing like, "You have cooties." Like, Eric [was] always really embarrassed and stuff. And that was one of the reasons I decided it wouldn't be a very good idea to go to the movies and stuff with him. But Rob is ten times more mature. He doesn't get embarrassed. Sometimes he gets embarrassed, but it's like me. Sometimes I get embarrassed, but not usually.

These girls, then, were more concerned with boys' intelligence and maturity than their appearance. What they left unsaid is that social status represented the first-cut factor in their romantic selection. Popular boys and girls, who were the people primarily involved in cross-gender relations at this age, restricted their focus to other people of similar position. Being friendly with, flirting with, or going with people who were less popular than them would lead to a diminution in individuals' own status; making a connection with people in the popular crowd would increase their status.

It was not only popular people who were romantically attracted to members of the popular crowd; everyone was. Popular boys attracted the attention and interest of girls who were popular, unpopular, and socially isolated. The same was true for the popular girls. This was a common pattern, where a small segment of the population was sought after by the entire population of the other gender. It led to many people lingering, frustrated, around individuals who were chronically "over their heads." Attractive characteristics, then, were a relatively elite commodity.

Nancy, a fifth-grade girl, described a popular boy whose attention was desired by many girls. "We kind of expected him to ask Alice out. But then he just surprised everyone and asked Mariah out. Because, we knew he would ask somebody out."

> Q: *How'd you know what?*
> Nancy: Well, because all of the other girls like him. And some of my lower-down friends that are not as popular like him too.

> Q: *So there are a lot of girls who like this one guy?*
> Nancy: Yeah.

SEXUAL INTEREST

Boys and girls often had different goals in a preadolescent romantic relationship. While they were both spurred by the excitement, status, and aura of maturity inherent in a romantic liaison, their divergences were rooted in differences between male and female culture.

For boys, a status preoccupation centered on sex. Kevin was the first to introduce this topic:

> Q: *Do you think that boys get interested in girls first, or that girls get interested in boys first?*
> Kevin: Boys get interested in girls first.
> Q: *What makes you say that?*
> Kevin: I don't know. Uh. I think it might be sexual attraction at first. I know one thing, in some guys, if they see a nice girl, they kind of want a kiss from her. And then, a lot of boys, not myself, but a lot of boys, 'cause they've been sexually attracted to a girl, they wonder if the girl wants to have sex or whatever it is. And I used to wonder about that. It is kind of an interesting question. I think that's really interesting.

Not only were boys interested in sexual exploration for its own sake, but they sought it to enhance their social status. Boys derived peer prestige for "scoring" with girls and talking about it. It is at this age that the "baseball" analogy of sexual exploration (first base, second base) surfaced, leading boys to talk about sexual matters that they barely understood.

Girls, however, were socialized to derive their status from having boys pay attention to them, from having boys do things for or give things to them, and from resisting sexual pressure. When Joanna was asked whether she thought girls were interested in boys "for sexual attraction," her reply was typical of the prevailing attitude in the girls' culture: "No. They kind of want a boyfriend, but just to hang out with, you know, watch good movies. Usually it's a boyfriend thing."

APPROACHING THE OPPOSITE GENDER

Even more frightening than liking someone or participating in sex games at a party was openly committing oneself to tell such people of one's interest or asking them for a date. Although this was risky and scary, some individuals eventually approached each other more directly. These mavericks were the trailblazers, who faced the most uncertainty and censure while having the least social support and established groundwork on which to build. Those who waited until dating became a more established practice found it somewhat less traumatizing to approach the people they liked. Preadolescents were especially concerned, here, with gender-appropriate norms. While girls have traditionally had to wait for boys to make the first move, these patterns have become somewhat moderated, so that girls were occasionally the first to approach boys. Girls' assertiveness in romance was accepted in the peer culture. Yet, at the same time, the norm remained that boys were ultimately responsible for the assertive role. Other girls cleaved tightly toward the demure demeanor and would not think of being the one to make the first approach. With positively sanctioned exceptions, then, boys generally found themselves in the role of approaching girls whom they liked.

INDIRECT APPROACHES

Beyond considerations of gender, people approached individuals they liked in both direct and indirect manners. The safer way to do this indirectly (see Eder and Sanford, 1986), inquiring through intermediaries if one's approach would be positively received. If the answer was no, the would-be approachers avoided the pain of direct rejection, enabling them to save both feelings and face. People usually used their closest friends

as intermediaries. It helped if the intermediaries were friends with the intended contacts, but this was not a requirement. If intermediaries were friendly with the desired targets, they might feel those persons out more discretely, avoiding having to admit that their friend liked the person. When the envoy had no particularly close relationship with the target, a more unsubtle approach was necessary.

DIRECT APPROACHES

The indirect approach required less courage on the part of the approacher, because the responsibility for talking to the target was passed on to a friend. Yet there were advantages associated with the direct approach as well. Kenny described how the direct approach could generate peer status:

Q: *Do you know of boys who actually got up enough nerve to tell girls that they liked them?*

Kenny: Yes, it happened in the fifth grade.

Q: *How did he do that?*

Kenny: I was standing real close to him, and he asked her.

Q: *He asked her directly straight out?*

Kenny: Yes, and everybody, after he asked her, everybody was patting him on the back.

Q.   *What happened! What did he say?*

Kenny: I don't know. That he liked her, he thought she was cute, that he wanted to go out with her, stuff like that.

Q: *And why were they congratulating him?*

Kenny: Because she didn't outright reject him, so that's a victory.

The boy in this case gained the respect of his peers because he had the courage to make a direct approach and because his tender was not immediately rejected. Other reasons people chose to make a direct approach included their ability to present themselves in their best light and their ability to safeguard their privacy. If the girls rejected them, there was less chance of other people knowing or talking about it.

GETTING REJECTED

Not everyone who made a direct or indirect approach received a positive response. People tried to manage others' reactions to them, increasing their chances of success by limiting their approaches to targets they thought would receive them positively. This was risky business, however, and people's feelings and status were fragile. Rejections stung more intensely than acceptances felt good. The safest way to manage an approach, in the event of a possible rejection, was to employ both indirection and discretion.

Jake spoke about a rejection he received that was managed so well by the intermediary that the target never even knew she was rejecting him:

Q: *Do people ever keep it a secret if they like someone or are going with someone?*

Jake: A lot. I'd say 70 percent. That's the thing, I like this girl now, and I have Laura for a friend, so I had Laura talk to her about me. So you get somebody to pull a plan or something.

Q: *So what happened when she pulled this plan?*

Jake: It didn't work very well. The girl I like, she likes this boy named Ian, and Ian doesn't like her, and she knows that.

Q: *So she said she liked somebody else?*

Jake: Well, not really. Laura asked her what if somebody else liked her, was there somebody else she would like back if they liked her? Nobody was on that list. The only person that no matter what, was going to be on the list, was Ian. So then she came back and told me. She was very cool about it because she did it in a safe way that didn't embarrass me by not mentioning my name.

DATING

For people who successfully approached a member of the other gender and got them to agree to "go" with them, the next issue was dating. Not all "going together" couples went out on dates, but it often happened. Preadolescents were very excited about the possibility of dating. Dating was one of the first things people talked with each other about, after they confirmed a mutual romantic interest. Early daters attracted greater attention due to the unusual nature of their activity. As time passed, this ceased to be as unusual, and they were joined by other courageous souls. By fifth grade, significant numbers of people in the popular circles were dating and "going with" others (see Merten, 1996), and this behavior was accepted as less shocking.

Uncertainty about dating behavior made individuals nervous, even though they saw their prospective dates every day at school. Cultural lore was passed around about what to do on a date. Jake discussed what boys and girls might do together when they were involved in a "going with" relationship. "Mostly go shopping or go to movies. A lot of times if you have an activity, you will get the other person to go to that activity and watch."

Boys and girls also went on more formal dates, where they made plans to go out together without their parents or teammates. These might be alone or in the company of other dating couples. Kevin gave some examples of good "date activities" for preadolescents: "You go to the movies, the movie thing is like really strong. Or like you might, maybe, go to like the Rock Creek Festival or something."

Q: *How about the mall?*

Kevin: The mall you don't want to go to because you don't want to just go shopping. The reason you don't go to a mall is because people don't want to think that they have to entertain the other person. Just go to a movie, which is very easy.

Q: *Because there's other awkwardness of what are you going to do together?*

Kevin: Yeah. And what are you going to talk about and stuff. I mean, if you go to a movie, you get to talk in the car, too. It's just perfect timing. When you're running out of talk, the car stops.

By carefully planning their time on dates, boys and girls managed the interaction to maximize the excitement and minimize the anxiety. Conversation was somewhat strained, for boys and girls felt uncomfortable talking about the things they normally discussed in school. Unable to rely on topics of conversation revolving around their routine activities, they gossiped about other people, discussed their plans, and talked about what to do. Avoided at all costs was emotions or relationship talk.

PEER REACTIONS

When the first "daters" embarked upon their activities, they often faced gossip and social stigma. Ben described the kinds of rumors that led to embarrassment among early romantically linked couples: "they start calling them names like loverboy. Make fun. Start a rumor and everybody would find out." Although curiosity still abounded, social embarrassment diminished as romantic relationships became less novel and people got used to them. Individuals could still face humiliation for some kinds of romantically linked situations, but these no longer encompassed all romantic encounters.

This lessening of embarrassment, then, was related to the development of romantic and dating peer norms. As such norms arose or were learned and accepted from older friends and siblings, preadolescents had firmer ground on which to base their activities. Peer norms were structured and serious. Departures could bring on the tyranny and shame of social censure. One universal norm was romantic monogamy. The peer culture had no concept of individuals "playing the field." It was absolutely forbidden, from elementary through high school, to be engaged in romantic relations with more than one person at a time. Any person who conceived of himself or herself as not completely attached and free to romantically experiment on a multiple basis encountered fierce negative sanctioning.

CONCLUSION

The popular people set the normative tone for the entire social spectrum throughout their preadolescent careers. While they held cross-gender friendships, these remained socially accepted. When they moved away from cross-gender interaction, it became stigmatized. When they reforged platonic cross-gender relationships, and later became interested in romance, these became not only accepted but status generating. They were the ones to break these grounds first, and although they suffered initially for it, they benefited socially over the long run. Individuals who lagged in the cross-gender game were eventually labeled nerds and faggots.

The peer culture opened the pathway for platonic and romantic cross-gender relations slowly and grudgingly, define the forms that these could take, retroactively accorded participants elevated status, defined the outer limits of romantic behavior, and ultimately diminished the social status of those who did not participate. This culture normatively traced a single acceptable route through the progression of boy-girl relationships and negatively sanctioned, through censure and ridicule, those who deviated from it. There were boys and girls, form the popular crowd down through the pariahs, who desired to stray from the normative path and cultivate romantic relations out of the approved sequence. Most of them were inhibited by their knowledge of the censure they would encounter if they breached these informal constraints.

The character and progression of relationships between preadolescent girls and boys, as shown here, are not as simple as most have described. The pattern dominating both the cultural wisdom and the scholarly literature, of preadolescent boys and girls living in discrete, gendered cultures and worlds, was not exclusive. Throughout these several stages of cross-gendered relations, there were always people who desired to violate the normative behaviors. Although a few had the courage to breach these norms, the majority did not. Most individuals were held in check by the sanctions embodied in the peer culture and the consequences individuals faced when they departed from the normative track. Freed from this constraining model, preadolescent boys and girls might have more freely intermixed platonic and romantic interactions throughout the elementary school years, adopting a range of behaviors that blended the traditional gender roles to a greater extent. They were discouraged from doing so by the powerful grip of their peer culture, which intermediated between them and the greater society at large, incorporating into its own formulation those features of society at large that it desired and rejecting others for which it was not yet ready.

REFERENCES

Eder, Donna, and Stephanie Sanford. (1986). "The Development and Maintenance of Interactional Norms among Early Adolescents." In P. A. and P. Adler, ed., *Sociological Studies of Child Development* (vol. 1, pp. 283–300). Greenwich, CT: JAI.

Merten, Don E. (1996). "Going-With: The Role of a Social Form in Early Romance." *Journal of Contemporary Ethnography,* 24: 462–84.

Oswald, Hans, Lothar Krappmann, Irene Chowdhuri, and Maria von Salisch. (1987). "Gaps and Bridges: Interactions between Girls and Boys in Elementary School." In P. A. and P. Adler, ed., *Sociological Studies of Child Development* (vol. 2, pp. 205–33). Greenwich, CT: JAI.

Thorne, Barrie. (1986). "Girls and Boys Together, but Mostly Apart: Gender Arrangements in Elementary Schools." In W. Wartup and Z. Rubin, ed., *Relationships and Development* (pp. 167–84). Hillsdale, NJ: Lawrence Erlbaum.

———. (1993). *Gender Play.* New Brunswick, NJ: Rutgers University Press.

Voss, Laurie Scarborough. (1997). "Teasing, Disputing, and Playing: Cross-Gender Interactions and Space Utilization among First and Third Graders." *Gender and Society,* 11: 238–56.

Chapter 5

The Glass Ceiling

DEBORAH TANNEN

A man who heads up a large division of a multi-national corporation was presiding at a meeting devoted to assessing performance and deciding who would be promoted into the ranks of management. One after another, each senior manager got up, went down the list of individuals in his group and evaluated them, explaining whether or not they were promotable, and why. Though there were significant numbers of women in every group, not a single person singled out for advancement was female. One after another, every senior manager pronounced every woman in his group not ready for promotion because she lacked the necessary confidence. The division head began to doubt his ears. How could it be that all the talented women in the division suffered from a lack of confidence?

The situation described by this manager seemed to me to hold a clue to one described by a top executive at another multinational corporation who contacted me for help: "We started full of hope but we've reached an impasse. We are very successful at recruiting top women—they're creative, motivated, with fabulous credentials. They look just as good as the men when we hire them, if not better. But they don't get promoted. Years into our affirmative-action program, we still don't have any women in top management." The women who had been hired either were stuck at the level of middle management or had left the company or the field. He was describing what is sometimes referred to as the glass ceiling: an invisible barrier that seems to keep women from rising to the top. The problem is considered so widespread and serious that a Glass Ceiling Commission was created as part of the U.S. Civil Rights Act of 1991, chaired by the secretary of labor.

Many earnest executives sincerely believe that there is no glass ceiling but only a pipeline problem: When women have been in the pipeline long enough to work their way up, some will reach positions at the top. But the longer this situation prevails, the less tenable the pipeline theory becomes. According to a 1991 report by the United States Department of Labor, progress has been extremely slow. During the ten-year period from 1979 to 1989, the representation of women and minorities in the top executive positions of the one thousand largest American corporations rose from 3 percent to 5 percent. Another 1991 survey based on 94 randomly selected Fortune 1 000–sized companies found women comprised 37 percent of employees, 17 percent of managers, but only 6½ percent of executive-level managers.

The temptation is to see the cause of the glass ceiling as "sexism," and surely there is truth in this characterization. But "sexism" tells us where we are without telling us how we got there, and without providing help in getting out. I do not doubt there are men (as well as women) who do not wish to see women advance. It may be that the presence of women in their work lives is a complication that they did not bargain for when they chose their life's work. They may see every

---

woman who fills a job in their field as taking that job from a man (rather than seeing half the men in their field as taking jobs that should have gone to qualified women). They may even feel that women do not belong in positions of authority, certainly not in authority over them. But not all men fit this description. There are many men who sincerely want to see women advance and are trying to do something about it.

In all the companies I visited, I observed what happened at lunchtime. I saw women who ate lunch in their offices and women who skipped lunch to run or exercise in the gym and women who ate in groups with other women or with men. I observed men who ate alone or with colleagues and a few who went home to have lunch with their wives. I observed young men who made a point of having lunch with their bosses, and men at high levels of management who ate lunch with the big boss. I rarely noticed women who sought out the highest-level person they could eat lunch with.

Early on, I became aware of an irony. On one hand, it was from men that I heard that if women weren't promoted, they simply weren't up to snuff, whereas women everywhere agreed that something outside themselves prevents women from advancing. But on the other hand, it was women, more often than men, who seemed to feel that all that was necessary for success was to do a great job, that superior performance would be recognized and rewarded. Yet looking around, I could see that much more seemed to go into getting recognized and rewarded, and I saw men more often than women behaving in these ways.

In addition to doing excellent work, you must make sure that your work is recognized. This may consist of making a point to tell your boss, or your boss's boss, what you have done—either orally, or by sending reports or copies of pertinent correspondence. If a group meets, the person who is the first to report the group's results may get the most credit for them, whether or not that person was the source of the ideas in the first place. When lunchtime comes, the one who eats lunch with the boss may be doing more to get ahead than the one who stays in the office, eating a sandwich and working. Doing brilliantly at a project that no one knows about will do little good in terms of personal advancement; doing well in a high-profile project, or one that puts you into contact with someone in power who will thereby gain firsthand knowledge of your skill, may make the big difference when that person speaks up in a meeting at which promotions are decided. All of these dynamics could be derisively dismissed as "office politics," but they are simply a matter of human nature. How are the bosses to know who's done what? It is understandable (though not necessarily admirable) if they notice what happens before them and fail to notice what they would have to rout around to see. Put another way, influence flows along lines of affiliation and contact.

Here is a brief explanation of how conversational-style differences play a role in installing a glass ceiling. When decisions are made about promotion to management positions, the qualities sought are a high level of competence, decisiveness, and ability to lead. If it is men, or mostly men, who are making the decisions about promotions—as it usually is—they are likely to misinterpret women's ways of talking as showing indecisiveness, inability to assume authority, and even incompetence. A woman who feels it is crucial to preserve the appearance of consensus when making decisions because she feels anything else would appear bossy and arrogant begins by asking those around her for their opinions. This can be interpreted by her bosses as evidence that she doesn't know what she thinks should be done, that she is trying to get others to make decisions for her.

Again and again, I heard from women who knew they were doing a superior job and knew that their immediate co-workers knew it but the higher-ups did not. Either these women did not seem to be doing what was necessary to get recognition outside their immediate circle, or their superiors were not doing what was necessary to discern their achievements and communicate these upward. The kinds of things they were doing, like quietly coming up with the ideas that influence their groups and helping those around them to do their best, were not easily observed in the way that giving an impressive presentation is evident to all.

Even so small a linguistic strategy as the choice of pronouns can have the effect of making one's contributions more or less salient. It is not uncommon for many men to say "I" in situations where many women would say "we." One man told me, "I'm hiring a new manager; I'm going to put him in charge of my marketing division," as if he owned the corporation he worked for and was going to pay the manager's salary himself. Another talked about the work produced by all the members of his group in the same way: "This is what I've come up with on the Lakehill deal." In stark contrast, I heard a woman talking about what "we" had done, but on questioning discovered that it was really she alone who had done the work. By talking in ways that seemed to her appropriate to avoid sounding arrogant, she was inadvertently camouflaging her achievements and lessening the chances they would be recognized.

Sociolinguist Shari Kendall spent two days shadowing the technical director for a news/talk show at a local radio station. The woman, Carol, was responsible for making sure all the technical aspects of the show went smoothly, and she did her job very well. The following incident, presented and analyzed by Kendall, reveals both why Carol was so good at her job and why her excellence was likely to go unrecognized.

Carol knew she had a challenge on her hands: the "board op," the technician who sits at the soundboard (the radio show's control tower), was out sick, and Harold, the man filling in, was very, very nervous. He had to get all the right prerecorded bits of music and talk onto the air at the right time, make sure that callers got on just when the host wanted to talk to them, and generally throw switches in the right direction at the right moment—switches chosen from a dizzying

array that made up the soundboard. Though Harold had a thorough technical knowledge of the equipment, he was unfamiliar with the routines of the show and inexperienced in this role. He was so nervous, he was shaking. For her part, Carol knew that if Harold fouled up, she would be blamed. She also knew that it is hard to throw a switch in the right direction with split-second timing when your hands are shaking. So, in addition to making sure he knew all the routines, she had to help Harold relax, which meant she had to make him feel competent and up to the job.

First Carol made sure that she gave Harold the information he needed to run the show and cautioned him about potential errors, all in a way that did not make him feel incompetent. Kendall points out that Carol gave Harold information phrased so as to imply it was not general technical knowledge (which he should have) but information particular to this show (which he could not be expected to have). For example, instead of saying, "Don't forget that tapes have a one-second lead-in," she said, "On this show everything has that one-second dead roll." Rather than saying, "Don't mix up the tapes; make sure you get them on in the right order," she said, "The only thing that people usually have trouble with is that they end up playing the promos and cassette tags and stuff in the wrong order." She avoided giving direct orders by saying, for example, "Probably we will want to re-cue the switch" when obviously it was he who had to re-cue the switch. In other words, Carol managed to apprise Harold of what he had to do without giving the impression she thought he was in danger of getting it wrong, and without framing him as potentially incompetent.

When she had done all she could to ensure that Harold knew what he had to do, Carol did not consider her job finished. She still wanted to make sure he felt calm and in control. She could have done this directly, by assuring him: "Now, look, you're a techie—you know a lot about this equipment; you'll do just fine," but when you think about it, that sounds condescending. Reassuring him would position her as superior and him as a novice needing reassurance. So she built up his confidence indirectly by framing him as an expert in an area in which he knew he was competent. She picked up his copy of *Mac Weekly* and engaged him in conversation about computers. He took this opportunity to give her information about purchasing used Macs. Kendall, who was in the room observing, noticed that Harold sat back, put his feet up, and visibly relaxed during this conversation. Right before her eyes, he was transformed from the nervous novice to the self-assured teacher. As I pictured this scene in my mind, it was as if someone had inserted a tube in his foot and blown him back up. Carol remained with Harold throughout the show, and when it proceeded without requiring anything of him, she again asked him questions about computers. She later told Kendall that she sometimes keeps technicians talking during periods when they're not working the soundboard to reduce tension and prevent errors.

Carol's efforts paid off. The self-confidence she inspired in Harold carried him through the show, which went without a hitch—a success that no one would know was due in part to Carol. Quite the contrary, imagine the impression their supervisor might have gotten had he come into the studio shortly before airtime and found Harold with his feet up, answering Carol's questions about computers. It is likely he would have thought, even if he didn't think it through, that Harold was very much in command of the situation, and Carol was a rather underqualified technical supervisor who needs technical advice from her pinch-hitting board op. How different this impression would have been had she been less competent—say, if she had rushed into the studio at the last moment, rather than early, and had been busily giving direct orders to the board op right up to airtime. Now that would have created an image of firm control, even as it would have rattled Harold and caused him to make errors.

In two other conversations Kendall analyzed, Carol was working with a colleague named Ron, the manager of another control room. It was Carol's job to see that all went smoothly with the technical aspects of her show; it was Ron's to see that everything went well with all shows. In this instance, Carol foresaw a potential problem with the telephone hookup to be used when her show went on the road the following week. Ron, however, had not foreseen any problem. Carol managed to call the potential problem to Ron's attention and to enlist his aid in heading it off. This show too went off without a hitch.

The proof of the pudding is in the eating. Carol had a low rate of technical errors on her watch. But the proof of her competence was invisible: the *absence* of errors. How do you get your bosses to see something that did not happen? Carol herself expressed concern that her excellent work and job skills might not be recognized when new appointments were made.

This example is hauntingly similar to one described by journalist Sharon Barnes, who tells of an office that had to switch from manual to computer operations. Barnes contrasts the way two managers, a man and a woman, handled the switch. The woman foresaw the need for computerization and gradually hired secretaries with computer experience, so the transfer to computerization took place without a ripple. The man did not prepare, so when the time came to switch to computers, his staff was in revolt. He mollified them by catering a lunch at which a consultant taught them what they needed to know. His troubleshooting was rewarded with a letter of commendation and a bonus. Barnes calls this "the white knight method"—letting problems happen and then ostentatiously solving them. This attracts attention, whereas making sure the problems don't arise in the first place is likely to go unnoticed—and unrewarded. According to Barnes, the white knight method is more common among men, the problem-preventing method more common among women.

Here is another example of a woman getting others to do their best at the risk of her own credibility. It comes from the curator of a private art collection. The young men who were responsible for constructing the art installations were generally competent with tools, but they were artists, not construction workers, so they did not always know how to execute what she wanted. Her job was complicated by the fact that they would not tell her when they didn't know how to do something. She noticed that one of the three had more knowledge and skill than the other two. He often set about doing a job while the others stood by—not asking, but not working either. She figured out that if *she* asked for an explanation, the other two, hearing the explanation they needed, would start working. In her own words, she got the information out by taking the stance "I'm just a girl who doesn't understand." Like Carol, she framed herself as ignorant in order to get the job done. In this situation, the curator was the boss. There was no one over her to observe the interaction, miss her intent, and conclude that she was underqualified. The knowledgeable man *did* once explode, "Every time we do something, you ask the same stupid questions!" She simply walked away and explained later—in private— what she was doing and why; he immediately understood and apologized.

This corrective was simple enough, but not likely to happen with a boss who might well say nothing but form his opinion and keep his counsel. Once again, there is no harm in assuming the ritual appearance of incompetence so long as everyone knows that it is ritual. When it is taken literally, and when only one person in an interaction is using that style, the strategic use of an appearance of incompetence can be mistaken for the real thing.

In these examples, women adjusted their ways of speaking to make sure the job got done. In a study I conducted, together with a colleague, of doctor–patient communication, I observed a pediatrician who spoke in a seemingly unsure way in order to buffer the emotional impact of what she was saying. Because her work involved not only examining her young patients and consulting with their parents but also reporting to other clinical staff, we had an unusual opportunity to hear her talking about the same information under different circumstances, where she made a very different impression.

My colleague Cynthia Wallat and I analyzed the videotapes of the pediatrician talking in several different contexts about a child with cerebral palsy who had recently been diagnosed as having an arteriovenous malformation in her brain. In one of the videotapes, the doctor was examining the child in the presence of the mother. She pointed out that hemangiomas, visible as red marks on the child's face, were basically the same type of malady as the arteriovenous malformation in the brain. This gave the mother an opportunity to express a concern, and the doctor responded to the indirect question by providing an explanation:

Mother: I've often wondered about how dangerous they—they are to her right now.

Doctor: Well, um, the only danger would be from bleeding. *From* them. If there was any rupture, or anything like that. Which *can* happen. . . . um, That would be the danger. *For* that. But they're . . . mm . . . *not* going to be something that will get worse as time goes on.

Mother: Oh, I see.

Doctor: But they're just *there*. Okay?

The doctor seemed rather insecure in this excerpt. Her talk was full of hesitations ("Well," "um," pauses). She uttered extra verbiage that didn't add meaning ("or anything like that," "which *can* happen"). She added phrases after her sentences were done ("the only danger would be from bleeding. *From* them." "That would be the danger. *For* that.") Emphasis seemed to fall in odd places.

But the doctor's hesitance and circumlocution in this setting contrasts sharply with her fluency and assurance when she talked about the same condition in a meeting with her peers. There she articulated part of the reason for her lack of fluency in speaking to the mother: She did not know how much information the parents already possessed about the danger of the child's condition, and she was not hesitant about the information she was imparting but about the effect it might have on the mother:

> uh, I'm not sure how much counselling has been *done, with* these parents, around the issue . . . of the a-v malformation. Mother asked me questions, about the operability, inoperability of it, um, which I was not able to answer. She was told it was inoperable, and I had to say, "Well, yes, some of them are and some of them aren't." And I think that this is a—a—an important point. Because I don't know whether the possibility of sudden death, intracranial hemorrhage, if any of this has ever been *discussed* with these parents.

The physician, who showed so much hesitation and repetition in explaining the danger of the a-v malformation in the child's brain to the mother, expressed the same information in the staff meeting strongly and directly: There is a possibility of "sudden death, intracranial hemorrhage." When my colleague and I talked to the doctor, we were not surprised to learn that in speaking to the mother, she had been considering the emotional impact of telling a mother that her child might die suddenly because the a-v malformations could cause a hemorrhage in the brain at any time. When the mother asked this question, the doctor was in the midst of examining the child, so she could not take a half hour to discuss the danger and deal with the mother's reaction. Furthermore, the child was not her regular patient; she was examining her in connection with an educational placement. So she wanted to make sure that anything she said was coordinated with what the parents had been told by their own doctors.

The doctor's seeming lack of articulateness stemmed from her sensitivity to the potential impact of her diagnosis on the mother. And the mother appreciated this. She told us that of all the doctors she had taken her daughter to (and there had been many), she found this one to be the most considerate. In contrast, she said, she had been given devastating diagnoses and prognoses by doctors with no regard to how the information might make her feel. For example, early in the child's life one doctor had told her in a matter-of-fact way, "Your child will be a vegetable," and then moved on to other topics.

Considering how the doctor spoke to the mother in comparison with how she spoke in a meeting with other medical staff makes it clear that her hesitance and other disfluencies did not reflect her level of competence but her awareness of the impact of what she was saying on the person she was talking to. But how often do we have a tape recording of the same person talking about the same topic in another setting? And how often, when women talk in tentative, even seemingly confused, ways in order to soften the impact of what they are saying, are they seen as lacking in competence or confidence?

We judge others not only by how they speak, but also by how they are spoken to. If we hear people asking lots of questions and being lectured to, an impression takes root that they don't know much and that those lecturing to them know a lot. This is why girls used to be told to make boys feel good on dates by asking them about subjects they're expert on and listening attentively to their answers. It is also what Japanese subordinates are supposed to do to make the boss feel important when they spend an evening with him, according to Japanese anthropologist Harumi Befu. Ellen Ryan and her colleagues have found that when a health care provider behaves in a patronizing way toward elderly patients, observers evaluate the patient as less competent.

If people are being spoken to as if they know nothing, we assume they know nothing. If people are addressed as if they are pretty smart, we assume they're pretty smart. This probably has some basis in most of the conversations we hear around us; it is a reasonable way to approach the world, trusting it to give us clues. But if women routinely take the position of novice or listener to make others feel smart, it is highly likely that those others, as well as observers, will underestimate their abilities.

Even worse, how a woman is addressed by others may have little to do with how she spoke in the first place. A consultant who worked fairly regularly with a small company commented to me that the new manager, a woman, was challenged and questioned by her subordinates more than her predecessor had been. He hadn't noticed any direct evidence that would lead him to question her competence, but he didn't really know the area they were working in. He added, "Maybe they know something about her abilities that I don't know." This seemed to me a double whammy. A woman who assumes a role that has previously been held by men will likely begin work with an aura of suspicion about whether she is up to the job, and this may well lead at least some of her co-workers to press her to justify her decisions. This very questioning then becomes evidence that she lacks competence—regardless of her real abilities.

Women may get more flak not only because their competence is in question but also because they are perceived as more vulnerable. A man who sails competitively commented that in a race, if he's looking for a hole, he picks a boat skippered by a woman or an older man; if you yell at them, he said, they are more likely to get out of the way. In the same spirit, Nancy Woodhull, a media and workplace consultant, points out that when corporate leadership changes and people jockey for position, they are especially likely to try to move in on turf held by women.

This insight helped me understand an experience that had puzzled and troubled me. I took part in a joint presentation together with a man whose style was different from mine. When I speak alone, as I generally do, I rarely get hostile comments from audience members because I always make sure to show the positive side of every style I mention and show the logic of *both* speakers when I give an example of a misunderstanding. I'm always careful not to make anyone look bad. My co-speaker, however, was more provocative. Many of his anecdotes made either women or men look foolish.

When the question period came, this different tone had sparked a different response from the audience: some of the questions were hostile—especially from women. But most of the hostile questions were directed at me—including those that took issue with statements he alone had made. At the time, I was hurt and baffled, but in retrospect I could see what probably had happened. These women, riled by his tone and possibly put off by how he talked about women in some of his examples, looked at the stage and saw a large, gray-haired man with a caustic tone who did not hesitate to ruffle feathers, and a younger woman who was always conciliatory and eager not to offend. I was an easier target. My "open" manner left me open to attack.

Conversational rituals common among women involve each saving face for the other. One speaker is freed to take the one-down position (ritually, of course) because she can trust the other to, ritually again, bring her back up. Neither has to worry too much about casting herself in the best possible light because everyone is working together to save face for everyone else. I save your face, and you save mine.

Put another way, many of the conversational rituals common among women are designed to make others feel comfortable, and this often involves the speaker taking a one-down role herself, though as we have seen, this is usually a ritual the other person is expected to match. At the same time women who observe these rituals are not investing a lot of energy in making sure they themselves do not appear one-down, which means that's just where they may end up.

A couple of years ago, I arrived at a class I was teaching and found a newspaper journalist waiting outside the door. She told me she had been trying to get me on the phone, but because she had not succeeded in reaching me at my office, she had come ahead to the class because she wanted to sit in and write a short piece about me. Now the number of people who want to sit in on my classes, for various reasons, is considerable, so I have long had a firm policy that I do not permit auditors or visitors for any reason. Since I always conduct classes not as lectures but as discussions among students sitting in a circle, a stranger in our midst is a significant intrusion. There was no question in my mind that had the journalist gotten me on the phone beforehand, I would have told her this. But here I was faced with a poor woman who had made the trek all the way to my class, had waited for a long time, and was now looking at me directly and plaintively. I felt culpable for not having been in my office when she was trying to reach me, and I have a strong impulse to help everyone and inconvenience no one. I had to make a snap decision; I let her in.

At the end of the class, I collected assignments, and a few students had not followed my instructions. To save face for them, I said something like, "I'm sorry if my instructions weren't clear." I suspect some readers will be able to foresee what happened: Lo and behold, in the article she wrote, the journalist took this ritual apology as a literal admission of fault and used it to make me look bad: Imagine, she wrote, here's this expert on communication, and she can't even give comprehensible assignment instructions to her students.

I am sure that some people will think, "It serves her right. She opened herself up to this." And they are correct. The impulses that drove me to make others feel comfortable were driving me in a direction opposite from self-protection, which would have led me to deny the journalist entrance to my class (it was her problem, not mine, if she made the trip without getting permission to sit in), or, once she was there, would have led me to monitor my behaviour so as not to say anything that might appear as weakness—the kind of self-monitoring that leads others (including many men) not to apologize, take blame, admit ignorance, and so on.

It is interesting to consider, however, how well my impulse to accommodate the journalist worked for her. She risked rejection by showing up at the door of my class unannounced. In a way, she was counting on me to observe interactional rituals common among women, and in this case her hunch paid off.

All these examples dramatize how ways in which women are likely to talk may mask their true competence in the view of those who are required to judge their performance. When forced to evaluate people they do not work with day-to-day, executive and high-level managers will necessarily be influenced by what little exposure they have had to the people they are judging. In addition to the fleeting impressions of chance encounters, for many top executives this may mean the few times they have observed lower managers directly—when they are making presentations. And this is yet another situation in which knowing a lot doesn't automatically transfer into showing what you know. If most women's conversational rituals have prepared them for private speaking, the importance of formal presentations is yet another aspect of moving through "the pipeline" that puts many women at a disadvantage.

Public speaking is frightening for almost everyone. But standing up in front of a large group of people, commanding attention, and talking authoritatively are extensions of the socialization most boys have been forced to endure, as boys in groups tend to vie for centre stage, challenge the boys who get it, and deflect the challenges of others. Many of the ways women have learned to be likable and feminine are liabilities when it comes to public presentations. Most girls' groups penalize a girl who stands out or calls attention to herself in an obvious way.

A woman who works as a trainer for business people coming to the United States realized that a disproportionate amount of the criticism she and her colleagues delivered to the trainees was directed at women, especially in the nebulous category of "professional presence." They found themselves telling women, more often than men, that they did not speak loudly enough, did not project their voices, should stop cocking their heads to one side, should try to lower the pitch of their voices. A few women were told that their way of dressing was too sexy, their manner too flirtatious, if they wanted to be taken seriously in the American business environment. In a sense, they were appearing too "feminine." But there were also women who were told that they were too challenging and abrasive. They launched into questions without a lead-in or hedges; they asked too many insistent questions; they did not tilt their heads at all or seemed to be tilting them in challenging ways. Although the trainers did not think of it in these terms, you could say that these women were not "feminine" enough.

In at least one case, a particular trainee had to be told that she was coming across as both too flirtatious and too confrontational. In wondering why such a large percentage of women in her program (a small one to start with) had the basic skills down cold, yet seemed to be undermining their own effectiveness by their nonverbal behaviour, the trainer concluded that they had a very fine line to walk: The range of behaviours considered acceptable for them was extremely narrow. And, perhaps most important, the American professional business culture in which they were learning to fit was not only American but also American male.

All of the factors mentioned by the trainer indicate that making presentations is a prime example of an activity in which behaviour expected of women is at odds with what is expected of an effective professional. In fact, the very act of standing up in front of a group talking about ideas is something that was unthinkable for women not so long ago. The nineteenth-century abolitionist Abby Kelley was reviled as a "Jezebel" and "fornicator" because of her public speaking. Because she was physically attractive, men saw her as a dangerous seductress.

Once a woman (or man) does make public presentations, she (or he) is open to challenge or even attack. Many women have been told they cave in too quickly rather than stand their ground. Being able to deal effectively with public challenges is not something that comes easily to many women (or men). And there are regional and cultural differences in styles as well. One man, a sociologist from a small town, was invited to give a lecture at a major East Coast university where he was being considered for a faculty posi-

tion. The questions from the floor were so authoritative that he became convinced he was talking to people who had obviously done research in his area, research that he had somehow missed in his review of the literature. After the talk, which he was sure he had bombed, he went to the library and scoured the sources for references to these men's work—references that did not exist. To his amazement (he had taken literally the tone of contempt in their questioning), he got the job. So he had occasion to discover that they had done no work in the field at all; they were simply challenging him to see how well he could defend his claims—and were satisfied and pleased with his rebuttals. Although he had successfully defended himself against this ritual assault, he had gotten the impression that they had more basis for their challenges than they actually had.

There are many women who are very successful public speakers. I once noted the different public-speaking styles of two presenters at a meeting—a man and a woman. Both were excellent speakers, but he filled the room with his expansive presence, whereas she brought the room in close. He told stories as if he were in church preaching to a crowd; she told them as if she were sitting in her living room with friends. (An audience member commented on how "natural" she sounded.) She did not tell jokes, as he did, but she was humorous. Whereas he remained straight-faced after saying something funny, she laughed along with her audience. The woman's public speaking was successful in a private-speaking sort of way, whereas his was successful in a more public-speaking, oratorical way.

This is not to say that there is only one way for a woman or a man to give successful presentations. Both women and men must learn to handle this special situation well in order to get recognition for the work they do, but women's socialization is usually more at odds with the requirements of presenting to a group.

If one of the reasons women are not promoted is that they are spending more time doing their jobs and less time promoting themselves, can the solution be for women to begin promoting themselves more? Veronica had an observant boss who noticed that many of the ideas coming out of the group were hers, but it was often someone else in the group who trumpeted the ideas around the office and got credit for them. The boss told Veronica she should take more credit for her ideas. But Veronica wasn't comfortable doing that. She tried and found she simply didn't enjoy work if she had to approach it as a grabbing game. She liked the atmosphere of shared goals and was comfortable in the knowledge that she was part of a group effort. Striving to get credit for herself felt like a lonely and not very admirable endeavour. Trying to follow her boss's advice made coming to work a lot less fun.

In a related pattern, I spoke to many women who claimed they simply were not comfortable standing out. And I spoke to men who had noticed women who seemed to feel that way. For example, a man who headed an educational film company called a woman into his office and told her the good news that one of the clients with whom she had dealt in the past had decided to make a large purchase for a new film library. Rather than saying, "Great! I'll give them a call right away," the woman said, "Maybe someone else should follow up this time, since I've already got the highest sales in the group for the month." Even though the sales staff did not work on commission, the manager was incredulous. "They *asked* for you," he said. "They liked working with you before, and you're the one they want. What kind of a company would I be running if I didn't give my clients the person they ask for?" This convinced her, and she accepted the assignment. But she had to think of it in terms of what was good for the company rather than what was good for her—or at least be *assigned* the job rather than appear to be *taking* it.

I saw this same force at work in a talented graduate student who had been working for me as a research assistant in addition to participating in a seminar I taught. One day I told her, in pri-

vate, that I owed her two apologies. The first was because she had handed me a bill for her services as research assistant as we were leaving class, and I had misplaced it. The second was that I feared I had embarrassed her in class when I unthinkingly corrected a minor grammatical error she had made while speaking. She told me that, since I was bringing it up, there was something that had bothered her, but it wasn't either of the two things I mentioned. It was something else entirely. The students had gathered around me after the last class meeting of the term, discussing who would take the next course. She had expressed frustration that she could not afford to take the course, and everyone knew my policy against allowing auditors. But I had said, "Maybe I can make an exception for you." She had not been bothered by my publicly correcting her grammar or by my neglecting to pay her on time. What bothered her was my singling her out for special treatment.

Favouritism can wreak havoc in any group. But whereas anyone can see that those not in favour would resent those who are, it seems that many women are uncomfortable not only being out, but also being too obviously in. This has resounding implications for promotability. Unobtrusively doing excellent work does not threaten group belonging. But getting special recognition does. It may well spark resentment from co-workers. Resentment, in fact, can result from almost any action that ensures getting credit, especially from those above. In a large organization, everyone is really the servant of many masters. Whereas you are taking direction, or even orders, from an immediate supervisor, that supervisor is answerable to someone above, who is answerable to someone above that. And somewhere in the upper layers are those who determine your fate when it comes to ranking and promotion. Much depends, therefore, on your ability to make contact with the people above your boss. But if you do, you may well incur the rancour of your immediate boss and your peers. And this may be a burden that more women than men are hesitant to risk.

Besides the danger of provoking peer resentment (or related to it) is the different ways women and men are inclined to view self-aggrandizing talk. Letting others know about what you have done is almost always labelled boasting by women, and boasting is something most women have learned early on to avoid. In contrast, many men assume they have to let others know what they've done in order to get the recognition they deserve. Bragging about his exploits got Othello the hand of Desdemona; Kate had to learn to keep her mouth shut to marry Petruchio—the "shrew" who spoke up had to be "tamed."

The example of a professional couple illustrates the attitudes many women and men have toward displaying or downplaying their own accomplishments. Bridget and Sean were both successful real estate agents, but they had different habits of self-presentation. Sean made sure to let new acquaintances know what he had done; Bridget played down what she had done and assumed people would eventually learn of it from others and like her all the more for her modesty when they did. Bridget thought Sean was boastful; he thought she was foolishly and inappropriately self-deprecating. Neither thought of the other's way of talking as related to gender; they thought they were dealing with issues of personal character.

A widely publicized incident involving political consultant Ed Rollins is evidence that talking about one's accomplishments is a ritual common among men. Rollins managed the campaign of Republican candidate Christine Todd Whitman in her 1993 bid for the governorship of New Jersey. At a breakfast for journalists shortly after Whitman's victory, Rollins boasted that he had won the election for his candidate by his successful efforts to keep blacks from voting—for example, by making donations to African American churches in exchange for the ministers' agreement not to preach get-out-the-vote sermons. When this boast hit the headlines, there was talk of knocking the candidate out of office and sending Rollins to jail. So he quickly explained that his boasts had been groundless, designed to embarrass his opponent James Carville, who was campaign manager for the Democratic candidate Jim Florio.

It is not clear whether Rollins was telling the truth when he first made the boast or when he later claimed it had been baseless. Whichever it was—and this may never be known—the case is a revealing example of the ritualized role of boasting. Rollins saw his role of campaign manager as a head-to-head fight with another man, Carville, and wanted to take ostentatious credit for his victory, so he boasted in a group about what he had done—or felt he could get away with claiming to have done. Another famous (or infamous) instance of boasting occurred when police located one of the men who allegedly had arranged an attack on figure-skater Nancy Kerrigan in part because he—rival skater Tonya Harding's "bodyguard"—had boasted openly to fellow students about what he had accomplished.

This incident, and the story of Ed Rollins's boasting, brought to mind an intriguing statement by Rupert Allason, a British member of Parliament who is an authority on the British intelligence services. He was explaining why he thinks women make better spies than men. On the occasion of the appointment of Stella Rimington as the first female director-general of the British Internal Security Service, Allason commented, "Women have always been good security operatives. While men tend to gossip about their job to impress friends, women gossip about trivia and keep their real secrets."

Linguist Penelope Eckert made similar observations of high school girls' and boys' secret-keeping habits. The high school girls Eckert studied told her that boys were better at keeping secrets than girls. Eckert hypothesized that this is not because boys are morally superior to girls but because, given the sex-separate social structure of the high schools, girls have something to gain by revealing other girls' secrets, whereas boys do not. Girls gain status by their social network—whom they are friends with. So showing that you know a girl's secrets is a good way to prove to others that you are friends with her.

Boys, on the other hand, gain status by their own accomplishments. They gain nothing by demonstrating that they are close friends with girls, so they have no incentive to repeat their secrets. Instead, the boys are tempted to talk about what they've done or can claim to have done. This explains why, in the situation of a spy or a campaign manager, males' and females' abilities to hold their tongues are not-so-mysteriously reversed.

Whatever the motivation, women are less likely than men to have learned to blow their own horns—which means they may well not get credit for the work they have done, or, as Ed Rollins at least claimed, try to get credit for what they have not done. More women than men seem to have a sense that if they do this, they will not be liked. And the spectre of working in an environment where they are not liked may be more than they are willing to risk. The congeniality of the work environment is important to everyone, but the requirement that everyone like each other may be more central to women's notion of congeniality, whereas men may value other types of congeniality, such as easy banter. One man who heads a large division of a corporation commented that in recruiting for diversity, they usually get the minority men they want by offering them the most generous package of remuneration. In recruiting women, however, they are most successful by sending women to recruit other women. If the recruiter can convince a prospective woman that the company provides a positive work environment, it is successful in recruiting her even if she has competing offers that are more lucrative. In addition to providing evidence that a congenial work environment is very important to many women, this may also say something about why women are chronically paid less than men in comparable positions.

The most eloquent and amusing description I know of why someone fails to get credit for her work and how she changes her behaviour to rectify the situation is in a short story by the Irish writer Maeve Binchy entitled "King's Cross." As the story opens, Sara Gray, an overworked and underappreciated assistant manager in a travel office, is interviewing a prospective secretary named Eve, who turns out to be a mixture of the Lone Ranger and Mary Poppins. Eve swoops into Sara Gray's life and transforms it by showing her how to get recognition—and promotion.

The first thing Eve does is insist on addressing her boss as "Miss Gray," even though Sara protests that it sounds "snooty." Eve points out that the male managers and assistant managers all call Sara by her first name, though she addresses many of them as "Mr." When speaking of Miss Gray to others, she adopts a tone of respect bordering on awe that gradually creeps into the attitudes of others in the office. Eve tells Sara that "it is absolutely intolerable the way that people think they can come barging in here, taking advantage of your good nature and picking your brains, interrupting us and disturbing you from whatever you are doing." To put a stop to this, Eve sets herself up at the door to Sara's office and insists that anyone who wants to see Miss Gray must make an appointment.

Eve discovers that Sara has not been taking advantage of available perks such as an account at a taxi firm, a clothing allowance, and a small fund for redecorating her office. With the latter, Eve acquires a conference table and suggests how Sara might use it. She points out that when Sara last developed a wildly successful marketing idea, no one but her boss, Garry Edwards, knew that it had been hers, so he got the credit and the reward, since it came out of his division. Eve counsels:

> Next time, I suggest you invite Mr. Edwards and his boss and the marketing director and one or two others to drop in quite casually,—don't dream of saying you are calling a meeting, just suggest that they might all like to come to your office one afternoon. And then, at a nice table where there is plenty of room and plenty of style, put forward your plans. That way they'll remember you.

When Sara prepares work for Garry Edwards, Eve sends copies to others, so everyone knows it's her work. She encourages Sara to get an assistant who can cover her desk, so indispensability will not be an excuse for failing to send her to conferences or, eventually, promote her. She makes sure that Sara's name is on the list of guests to social events attended by executives. When Garry Edwards tries to undo Sara by blaming her for his own mistake, Eve's filing system yields a document proving that Sara had recommended the correct course of action. Garry Edwards is out, and Sara Gray gets his job, which she had, after all, been doing, without remuneration, all along.

This is, sadly for us all, just a fantasy, a work of fiction, though a delightful one to read. How nice it would be if Eve swept into each of our lives and ensured we got the credit we deserve. But the story, oversimplified (and entertaining) as it is, captures some of what individuals can do (and often fail to do) to achieve that felicitous result on their own.

I do not wish to imply that all inequities in recognition and promotion result from the behaviour—linguistic or otherwise—of individuals. Some forces are out of our hands, or at least extremely difficult to influence. A phenomenon having little to do with conversational style that may handicap women is mentoring.

An academic position was advertised at a major university. Everyone was welcome to apply. But one candidate was a favourite of someone on the faculty. The faculty member saw to it that his candidate was the last one scheduled for a presentation, and he let him know when the other candidates were giving their presentations. This enabled his candidate to attend the others' presentations and gauge the reaction of the audience—what went over well, what fell flat, what concerns were reflected in the questions asked. He took this information into account in planning his own talk, and he wowed the department enough to get the job. At least one woman who had applied for the job felt that she had been locked out by an "old-boy network."

Similar patterns can obtain in promotion, where one candidate has established a relationship with someone involved in the search. He may be informed of the opening earlier, told what is best to emphasize in his application or interview, and given an advantageous position in the queue. Is this illegal preferential treatment or just "mentoring," a system by which a younger person has a supporter and ally higher up who "brings him along"? If such supporter relationships are likely to spring up between someone established in the organization and someone new to it, it is likely that the older person will be male (since he probably entered the organization when there were few or no women in it) and also likely that the established person will be drawn to someone who reminds him of himself at that stage—who is therefore probably male too. It is not intentional "sexism," yet it is a pattern that favours men over women—not all men, of course, but it is a structure women are less likely to fit into.

At the same time that we seek to understand how ways of talking can work against women, we also must bear in mind that it may be harder for women to get promoted regardless of how they speak. Marjorie and Lawrence Nadler list a number of studies that show that stereotypes work against women. They cite, for example, Lea Stewart, who found that women are often given different task assignments than men with similar positions and qualifications, and the ones they are given are not those that lead to advancement. They also cite Cynthia Fink, who shows that there is a widespread belief that men are simply more suited to management. Finally, Garda Bowman, Beatrice Worthy, and Stephen Grayser show that managers believe women just don't have the decision-making skills or aggressiveness needed to succeed in managerial positions.

Not every woman, or every man, wants to be promoted, though the argument that women don't really want high-pressure jobs has been used to avoid giving them the chance. There are women and men who choose downward mobility, but I do not think there are many people who would choose not to have their work recognized. People whose contributions are appreciated become motivated to continue and increase their efforts, whereas those whose contributions are overlooked are more likely to leave, perhaps citing other reasons for their decision. So failing to recognize the achievements of those with styles that do not call attention to themselves is a loss not only to the individuals but also to the companies.

Talking, like walking, is something we do without stopping to question how we are doing it. Just as we cheerfully take a walk without thinking about which foot to move forward (unless a puddle blocks our path), we simply open our mouths and say what seems self-evidently appropriate, given the situation and person we are talking to. In other words, ordinary conversation has a ritual character, and the conversational rituals typical of women and men, though they obviously have a lot in common—otherwise we couldn't talk to each other—can also be different. And even subtle differences can lead to gross misinterpretation. In a situation in which one person is judging another and holds the key to a gate the other wants to pass through, the consequences of style differences can be dire indeed.

If more and more people understand the workings of conversational style, they will be able to adjust their own ways of talking and stand a better chance of understanding how others mean what they say. But at the same time, the more people gain an understanding of conversational style, the less necessary it will be for others to adjust their style. If supervisors learn to perceive outstanding performance regardless of the performer's style, it will be less necessary for individuals to learn to display their talents. On that happy day, the glass ceiling will become a looking glass through which a fair percentage of Alices will be able to step.

Chapter 6

Naming and Blaming:

GENDER SOCIALIZATION AND WOMEN'S DEFINITIONS OF SEXUAL HARASSMENT[1]

SANDY WELSH AND JAYNE BAKER

WHEN IS IT SEXUAL HARASSMENT?

Surveys show that between a quarter and a half of Canadian women in the paid labour force experience unwanted sexual attention at work (Welsh and Nierobisz, 1997; Gruber, 1997). Yet not all women define unwanted sexual attention—including sexual touching, jokes, and comments—as sexual harassment (Dellinger and Williams, 2002, Giuffre and Williams, 1994, Welsh et al., 2006). Why is this so? In this chapter we focus on gender socialization as a possible explanation.

To be sure, other factors also play a role. For example, some workplace cultures are less tolerant of sexual harassment than others, and less tolerance may encourage more women to define unwanted sexual attention as harassment (Dellinger and Williams, 2002). In contrast, women from some ethnic and racial groups and women who lack citizenship may be less inclined to define unwanted sexual attention as harassment because of their background and status (Welsh et al., 2006). Women who immigrate to Canada may be initially unaware of what constitutes "sexual harassment" in Canada. They may also be unwilling to label unwanted sexual attention as harassment if it means putting their potential Canadian citizenship status at risk. In our judgment, however, gender socialization plays a primary role in the way women define their experiences and is therefore chiefly responsible for the way women label unwanted sexual attention in the workplace.

Using data from a study of women in Ontario, we demonstrate how gender socialization leads some women to blame themselves for unwanted sexual attention and to dismiss their experiences as unimportant. We begin by defining sexual harassment. We next outline how gender socialization influences women's ability (or inability) to label their experiences as sexual harassment. We then analyze our data, which show how women in Ontario often blame themselves for sexual harassment while others have trouble defining sexual harassment as such. Finally, we demonstrate that gender socialization is not destiny. With the proper social support, some women are able to re-evaluate their experience of sexual harassment as unacceptable behaviour and take action to have it corrected.

SEXUAL HARASSMENT

Sexual harassment involves two forms of behaviour: quid pro quo harassment and hostile environment harassment. Quid pro quo harassment involves sexual threats or bribery linked to getting a job, keeping a job, or receiving a promotion or training opportunity. Hostile environment sexual harassment includes sexual jokes, comments, and touching that may create a sexualized environment or one that degrades women. By law, it is up to the person committing the behaviour to know the difference between welcome and unwelcome sexual behaviours (CHRC, 2004). At its core, sexual harassment lets women know they are not welcome in certain workplaces and that they are not respected members of the work group (Reskin and Padavic, 1994).

GENDER SOCIALIZATION

Gender socialization focuses on how we learn to become male or female according to the cultural standards of the social collectivities to which we belong. While recognizing the existence of biological differences between boys and girls, gender socialization researchers study how children learn the attitudes, behaviours, and expectations associated with masculine and feminine roles by interacting with teachers, parents, and role models, including the role models portrayed in the mass media. Such interactions reinforce behaviours that fit culturally acceptable forms of femininity and masculinity—and punish behaviours that don't. For example, young girls are often given dolls to play with and encouraged to display affection toward them. Such behaviour conforms to cultural expectations about femininity and nurturance. Yet people typically discourage young boys from playing with dolls, reinforcing expectations about a widely accepted form of masculinity that sees men as less nurturing and affectionate than women.

The aspect of gender roles that is most relevant to sexual harassment concerns the way men learn to become relatively dominant, powerful, and competitive while women learn to become relatively nurturing, concerned with the quality of social relations, and passive. As a result of this differential learning, most men learn to treat women as sexual objects or "conquests," while most women learn to believe that being treated as such is normal. For example, women generally learn to be non-confrontational when they are sexually harassed by men; they are inclined not to report such behaviour to the proper authorities. Meanwhile, men come to believe that women want and expect them to flirt, even in the workplace.

Focusing on how people learn gender roles carries with it the danger of emphasizing the existence of only one form of masculinity and one form of femininity—what are often called traditional "gender stereotypes" (Connell, 2002). Said differently, some analysts make it seem as if gender socialization happens to unwitting individuals who lack the capacity to influence, let alone resist, what they are taught. Such analysts downplay the extent to which people enjoy agency and choice. Below, we argue that their determinism is misplaced; people influence and resist traditional gender roles all the time.

GENDER SOCIALIZATION AND SEXUAL HARASSMENT

Early research emphasized how traditional gender role socialization teaches women to tolerate unwanted sexual attention from men and avoid confronting them about it (Gwartney-Gibbs and Lach, 1992; Lach and Gwartney-Gibbs, 1993). From this point of view, by teaching women to avoid conflict and doubt their perceptions, gender socialization makes it more likely that women will not label their experiences as sexual harassment and will not report it (Fitzgerald, Swann, and Magley, 1997; Hotelling and Zuber, 1997).

Researchers then noted that organizational culture contributes to employees' ability and willingness to label certain behaviours as sexual harassment (Folgero and Fjeldstad, 1995). In some masculine work cultures, women may not define their experiences as sexual harassment in order to ensure that they will be seen as competent team players (Collinson and Collinson, 1996). For example, new female coal miners may consider sexualized hazing rituals part of their initiation into work groups (Yount, 1991). In other workplaces, sexual behaviours commonly understood as sexual harassment may be requirements of the job (Williams, 1997: 4). For instance, restaurants may encourage customers to "talk dirty" to waitresses by promoting drinks with sexually loaded names such as "Screaming Orgasm" (Williams, 1997: 22; Giuffre and Williams, 1994: 387) or by requiring waitresses to wear short tight skirts and revealing tops (Loe, 1996). In these sexually charged or permissive work cultures, degrading sexual behaviours become an expected component of work that may not be considered sexual harassment by employees, be they men or women (Williams, 1997). Yet, even in these organizational contexts, gender socialization plays a role since it is part of what leads to the acceptability of sexually harassing behaviours in the first place.

In the remainder of this chapter, we discuss the role that gender socialization plays in how women make sense of the sexual behaviours they experience at work. We show that women's gender socialization affects how women interpret their experience and make decisions about how to respond to it.

METHODS

Our analysis is based on a project designed to evaluate how women define harassment and harassment reporting mechanisms in Ontario. For our study we selected women with a wide variety of social characteristics so we could learn how race, citizenship, class, language, age, disability, and sexuality help to shape their experiences. In the summer and fall of 2000, we conducted six focus groups, following this up with six additional focus groups and seventeen in-depth interviews in the spring of 2002. Data for our analysis comes from these interviews and focus groups, which included a total of 67 women (for details, see Welsh et al., 2006).

RESULTS

NOT NAMING: NORMALIZING UNWANTED SEXUAL ATTENTION

Several women in our study initially viewed their experiences of sexual harassment as "normal" flirting in the workplace or as sexual attention that they simply had to endure. Consider the experience of one francophone woman who worked in a government office. She experienced touching, suggestive talk, and comments from coworkers suggesting she was a sexual "con-

quest." She mentioned that she wasn't even aware at first that she was being harassed. Instead she viewed the behaviour as simply flirtatious:

> I welcomed, contributed to, and responded to the flirting. . . . It wasn't possible to say anything, to do anything because I was so naive, unaware that it was possible to do something, that it was harassment. It didn't happen! I was appealing to the guys. Afterward I told myself that the guys were mean, rather than believing that it was harassment. I minimized the situation, though I warned a new employee to be aware of the two men, so I had some kind of awareness. After the physical confrontation, I experienced a great deal of stress and understood that the situation was serious.

The "physical confrontation" that led her to realize that the men's actions were in fact not "normal" involved their trapping her in a room. She concluded:

> I minimized, I talked about it to my girlfriends, but as if it was flirtation, and that allowed me to vent. [This was] my way of rationalizing and of minimizing, because if I'd seen the situation clearly, I wouldn't have been able to go in to work.

This woman's experience demonstrates how traditional gender socialization can complicate the ability to identify and label behaviour as sexual harassment. What turned out to be sexual harassment was seen as "normal" flirting between men and women, at least initially.

Some women also had initial difficulty naming the sexual harassment due to their race and/or ethnicity or citizenship status. One example of this comes from the group of Filipina domestic workers in our sample. They came to Canada through the Live-In-Caregiver program, which gives them a limited work visa requiring that they hold a domestic worker job for 24 months of a 36-month period in order to apply for Canadian citizenship. One Filipina who cared and cleaned for an elderly man discussed the conflict between her background and Canadian definitions of sexual harassment:

> I remember my first year, he is always telling me why don't you come with me in bed and make me warm? . . . So I just, I don't know the way to take it in Canada, because in the Philippines if somebody say that to you and they don't touch you, nothing happens, it's just a word, but here in Canada, it's something.

These women also talked about how they were unwilling to file a complaint because it might put their employment and future Canadian citizenship in jeopardy. They were afraid that they would be fired from their job and that they would be unable to find a replacement job that would give them the necessary 24 months of work experience. As one Filipina domestic worker stated: "Even if you don't like your situation, you just wait for the time [when you have more permanent citizenship status] to leave."

BLAMING ONESELF

As a result of traditional gender socialization, women often take on a passive role when confronting uncomfortable and unpleasant situations. In the case of sexual harassment, this tendency initially leads most women to blame themselves for unwanted sexual behaviour. This is just what we found in our study. In the words of one white respondent: "I used to blame myself for the harassment and ask myself constantly what I was doing to make them want to treat me this way."

Women did not enjoy sexual advances from male colleagues, yet they believed they were the ones to blame for the men's behaviour (Fitzgerald et al., 1997). Other researchers have shown how blaming oneself for harassment reinforces the way in which women are socialized to respond to issues in a non-confrontational manner. If women blame themselves for the unwanted sexual attention, they will not speak up and attempt to end the harassment.

Like women who experience rape and other forms of sexual violence, the women in our study often blamed their youthfulness or their clothes for inciting men to harass them. Here is what two white women in our study had to say on the subject, the first, anglophone, the second, francophone:

> I did blame myself sometimes for the harassment, asking what it was that made them do this, and also I would think that it was because I was young and the clothes that I wore caused this. I also tried to dress differently so that I wouldn't be attractive at work.

> I asked myself whether the clothes I was wearing were too sexy, even though every day I wore a smock over my clothes since I worked in a hospital setting.

The Native women in our study also struggled to define their experiences as harassment, especially when the perpetrator was in a position of authority, such as a respected elder in the Native community:

> I felt uncomfortable. I don't like doubting myself, I was questioning: maybe that's just the way he is as an elder but it didn't feel right. Sometimes it's just knowing that something doesn't feel right.

This woman experienced sexual comments, touching, and invasion of personal space. Her case illustrates that the authority of the harasser is an important determinant of the victim's ability to identify her experience as harassment: the greater the authority of the harasser, the more difficult such identification becomes (Carr et al., 2004).

NAMING AND NOT BLAMING: BEYOND GENDER SOCIALIZATION

Some women in our study moved beyond blaming themselves. They re-defined their experiences as sexual harassment by talking with someone knowledgeable about the issue.

Women began to understand that what they were experiencing should not be tolerated as normal behaviour between men and women. As one white woman said:

> I worked at a bar and I always kept my looks up, you know, that's where your tips come from. I always thought it was because maybe I was wearing the wrong kind of clothes. I was never trashy looking or anything—but I thought maybe that was what it was. Or I thought maybe I was flirting a little bit with him like when I was being nice to him when he first came in, but then I kept thinking to myself, there's no way. I know I wasn't. And especially I got to see [the support worker] from the sexual assault centre—she really helped me. I realized it was about that.

This case demonstrates how some women resist their early gender socialization. The woman in question decided to re-evaluate behaviour that at first seemed normal to her and, through the assistance of a support worker, was able to reject her initial beliefs and stop blaming herself.

A Black woman who worked in a temporary position demonstrates the same process. She had the following conversation with the interviewer:

> *Respondent:* How did I cope with it? I started going to talk to [the support worker] a lot. But I, you know how you question yourself. I started thinking it was something that I wore or I had too much makeup on or what was it? You know, I don't know why he started off that way. And I said to her, "You know I had my hair down." Sometimes I wore my hair in a bandanna. I wore a scarf. I wore a T-shirt to cover my body like, you know what I mean, and I didn't wear short, short shorts. And I was like "Why was he doing that to me?"

> *Interviewer:* So, did you get an answer to that question?
> *Respondent:* Well she [the support worker] told me that it was nothing that I was wearing or anything. That it didn't have anything to do with that, that it was the person himself.
> *Interviewer:* Do you believe that? Do you believe that it had nothing to do with you?
> *Respondent:* Not at the moment because you know, you question yourself. I guess I questioned myself for a while.
> *Interviewer:* Now how do you look at it?
> *Respondent:* Now how do I look at it? That he was just an ignorant pervert. Stuff like that—he's got some issues he needs to deal with. He's got some problems.

Our interviews show, then, that gender socialization is not the only variable affecting women's ability to define their experience. The nature of workplace culture, the authority of the harasser, the lack of Canadian citizenship, and the intervention of trained support personnel are among the factors that affect the capacity of women to define sexual harassment as such. The fact that some of the women we interviewed first blamed themselves for the harassment they experienced but were later able to re-evaluate their experience and report it to the relevant authorities shows that, while gender socialization constrains self-perceptions, it is by no means a lifetime straight-jacket (Morgan, 1999). For example, by placing support personnel in the workplace—officials who can discuss incidents of harassment with workers, educate them about what constitutes appropriate and inappropriate behaviour, inform them about their rights and mechanisms for seeking a resolution of grievances—organizations can do much to help women who experience sexual harassment. They can help them to recognize it for what it is and do something about it.

NOTES

1. Research for this project was funded by Status of Women Canada. We thank Jacquie Carr, Barbara MacQuarrie, and Audrey Huntley for collaboration on this project. Michael Schreiner and Robert Brym provided helpful comments on this paper. Finally, we are grateful to the women in our study for sharing their experiences with us.

REFERENCES

Canadian Human Rights Commission. (2004). "Discrimination and Harassment." On the World Wide Web at http://www.chrc-ccdp.ca/discrimination/what_is_it-en.asp (31 January 2006).

Carr, Jacquie, Audrey Huntley, Barbara MacQuarrie, and Sandy Welsh. (2004). Workplace Harassment and Violence. Centre for Violence Against Women and Children. University of Western Ontario. On the World Wide Web at http://www.crvawc.ca/research_crvawcpubs.htm (31 January 2006).

Collinson, M., and D. Collinson. (1996). "It's only Dick: The Sexual Harassment of Women Managers in Insurance Sales." *Work, Employment and Society,* 10: 29–56.

Connell, R.W. (2002). *Gender.* Oxford: Polity Press.

Dellinger, Kirsten, and Christine Williams. (2002). "The Locker Room and the Dorm Room: The Cultural Context of Sexual Harassment in Two Magazine Publishing Organizations." *Social Problems,* 49: 242–57.

Fitzgerald, L.F., S. Swann, and V.J. Magley. (1997). "But was it Really Harassment? Legal, Behavioral and Psychological Definitions of the Workplace Victimization of Women." In W. O'Donohue, ed., *Sexual Harassment: Theory, Research, and Treatment* (pp. 5–28). Boston: Allyn and Bacon.

Folgero, I.S., and I.H. Fjeldstad. (1995). "On Duty—Off Guard: Cultural Norms and Sexual Harassment in Service Organizations." *Organization Studies,* 16: 299–313.

Giuffre, Patti, and Christine Williams. (1994). "Boundary Lines: Labeling Sexual Harassment in Restaurants." *Gender and Society,* 8: 378–401.

Gruber, J.E. (1997). "An Epidemiology of Sexual Harassment: Evidence from North America and Europe." In W. O'Donohue, ed., *Sexual Harassment: Theory, Research, and Treatment* (pp. 84–98). Boston: Allyn and Bacon.

Gwartney-Gibbs, Patricia A., and Denise H. Lach. (1992). "Sociological Explanations for Failure to Seek Sexual Harassment Remedies." *Mediation Quarterly,* 9 (4): 363–73.

Hotelling, Kathy, and Barbara A. Zuber. (1997). "Feminist Issues in Sexual Harassment." In W. O'Donohue, ed., *Sexual Harassment: Theory, Research, and Treatment* (pp. 99–112). Boston: Allyn and Bacon.

Lach, Denise H., and Patricia A. Gwartney-Gibbs. (1993). "Sociological Perspectives on Sexual Harassment and Workplace Dispute Resolution." *Journal of Vocational Behavior,* 42 (1): 102–15.

Loe, M. (1996). "Working for Men at the Intersection of Power, Gender, and Sexuality." *Sociological Inquiry,* 66 (4): 399–421.

Morgan, Phoebe. (1999). "Risking Relationships: Understanding the Litigation Choices of Sexually Harassed Women." *Law and Society Review,* 33 (1): 67–92.

Reskin, Barbara, and Irene Padavic. (1994). *Women and Men at Work.* Thousand Oaks: Pine Forge Press.

Welsh, Sandy, Jacquie Carr, Barbara MacQuarrie, and Audrey Huntley. (2006). "I'm Not Thinking of It As Sexual Harassment: Understanding Harassment across Race and Citizenship." *Gender and Society,* 20: 87–107.

Welsh, Sandy, and Nierobisz, Annette. (1997). "How Prevalent Is Sexual Harassment? A Research Note on Measuring Sexual Harassment in Canada." *Canadian Journal of Sociology,* 22: 505–22.

Williams, Christine L. (1997). "Sexual harassment in organizations: A critique of current research and policy." *Sexuality and Culture* 1: 19-43.

Yount, K.R. (1991). "Ladies, Flirts, and Tomboys: Strategies for Managing Sexual Harassment in an Underground Coal Mine." *Journal of Contemporary Ethnography,* 19 (4): 396–422.

PART 2B

CULTURE

Earlier I defined culture as the languages, laws, science, values, customs, and beliefs of the groups to which people belong. This broad definition includes the elements of popular culture that are the focus of this section and that we all know well: movies and music.

In Chapter 7, Shyon Baumann outlines the ways in which society influences movies, and the ways in which movies influence society. He finds good reason to believe that economic and cultural forces shape both the content of movies and the way movies are produced. Baumann notes the difficulty of demonstrating that movies exert society-wide influences but finds convincing evidence that movies influence some individuals' patterns of behaviour. For example, some children and adolescents who watch violent films tend to become more physically and verbally aggressive, at least in the short term and possibly in the long term.

Chapter 8 discusses a specific aspect of contemporary culture: consumerism. **Consumerism** is the practice of defining oneself in terms of the commodities one buys. The use of jewelry and clothing to establish rank is as old as human society. Therefore, it is not exactly news that most people buy particular styles of clothes, cars, and other commodities partly to project an image of power, sexiness, coolness, athleticism, or sophistication. Nor will it shock anyone to learn that advertising seeks to sell image more than substance. In the immortal words of one advertising executive in the 1940s, "It's not the steak we sell, it's the sizzle." Less obvious, however, is the way consumer culture markets *dissent* to mass audiences and thereby tames it; that is, consumer culture often turns expressions of radical protest into harmless commodities. In Chapter 9, I illustrate this process by examining the evolution of hip-hop music.

GLOSSARY

Consumerism is the practice of defining oneself in terms of the commodities one buys.

CRITICAL THINKING QUESTIONS

1. How, specifically, does society shape the movies? How, specifically, do movies shape society? Apply insights from Baumann's analysis of movies to another element of popular culture, such as music.
2. On the Web, read the Angus Reid Group's "Why Is It Important to Track Pop Culture?" at http://www.angusreid.com/pdf/publicat/pop.pdf. Do you think the kind of research described in this article is valuable? Why or why not?
3. Can you think of elements of contemporary culture other than hip-hop that began as forms of radical protest and then developed mass appeal? Was the main force underlying the transformation commercial, or did other forces also come into play?

ANNOTATED BIBLIOGRAPHY

Gleick, James. *Faster: The Acceleration of Just About Everything.* New York: Vintage, 2000. A breathless tour of one of the most pervasive features of Western culture.

Gruneau, Richard, and David Whitson. *Hockey Night in Canada: Sport, Identities and Cultural Politics.* Toronto: Garamond, 1993. Canada's national sport is placed under the microscope in this engaging account, which shows how the global marketplace for commercial spectacle has altered the game and, along with it, Canadians' sense of themselves.

Spillman, Lyn, ed. *Cultural Sociology.* Oxford, UK: Blackwell, 2002. A compendium of leading articles in the field.

Chapter 7

Movies and Society

SHYON BAUMANN

THE SOCIOLOGY OF FILM

Quick—name a movie star. Is there anyone who cannot name one, or twenty? Is there anyone who does not know where Hollywood is, or who has not seen an image of the Hollywood sign, spelling out the place name in giant white letters on a hillside? The movies occupy a central place in our popular culture, just as they do in many other cultures around the world. Millions of Canadians see movies in theatres every year, and millions more see movies aired on television or recorded on DVD.

As an integral part of our popular culture, movies merit close sociological examination. The primary question of interest for sociologists of film is, "What is the relationship between movies and society?" There are two secondary questions built into the primary question. First, how do social factors influence the kinds of movies that are made? In other words, how do the social and organizational conditions in which movies are made affect their content? The second question reverses the causal arrow. How do movies influence society, particularly the attitudes and behaviours of audience members? As we will see, there is good evidence for arguing that, just as society influences movies, movies influence society.

TWO PERSPECTIVES ON HOW SOCIETY INFLUENCES FILM

ORGANIZATIONAL ANALYSIS

Do films represent the creative thoughts and actions of filmmakers? Of course they do. For example, the six *Star Wars* films bear the mark of the primary creative force behind them, writer and producer George Lucas. The distinctive characters and plot lines are his inventions. But a sociological perspective can show how movies reflect more than individual creativity. A review of the film industry's organizational history demonstrates that the way in which filmmaking was organized played a role in shaping the kinds of films that were made (Peterson, 1994). The organizational foundations of filmmaking were, in turn, influenced by wider social factors.

Depending on which sources you consult, the invention of a camera that could take moving pictures was either a French or an American invention, though inventors in both countries probably contributed equally to the final product. Regardless of who receives the credit, moving pictures were invented in the final decade of the nineteenth century without any awareness that they would form the basis of a major cultural industry and art form. In fact, moving pictures were first used to document everyday events for scientific and informational purposes. Not long after they were invented, however, cultural entrepreneurs realized their entertainment potential.

To capitalize on audience interest, many owners of shops and lunch counters converted their stores and restaurants into makeshift cinemas. Initially, movies were just a few minutes long, but the new technology so dazzled audiences they would pay just to see footage of a train approaching or a horse galloping. By the second decade of the twentieth century, however, movies had already begun to develop in length and content and to adopt the narrative style with which we are familiar today. As movies evolved, so did the industrial organization of film production and distribution. Movie theatres seating hundreds and even thousands of people were built. A small group of companies emerged as forerunners in film production. Their production facilities were located in Los Angeles to take advantage of the consistently favourable weather for filming.

Before long, this small group of companies was responsible for the vast majority of films being made in the United States, which also meant that they were responsible for the vast majority of films being *seen* in the United States, as well as in many other countries, including Canada. Before television became widespread in the late 1940s and early 1950s, movies were the primary form of mass entertainment. A large proportion of the population attended a movie theatre weekly, and it was not uncommon for people to go to the movies several times a week (Brown, 1995). Movies were big business, and they continue to be big business today even though people see fewer movies than they used to.

Despite the economic success of the film industry, movies were heavily criticized at the time for being formulaic; that is, critics found movies to be bland, predictable, and altogether too similar (White, 1936). Part of their criticism of the movies was directed at the way movies were made.

Because they were the default entertainment option for many people, films were virtually guaranteed a minimum audience size. The incentive for the film companies, then, was to produce a large number of films to meet the high demand. This supply and demand dynamic encouraged a production process for films that resembled that of most other mass-produced goods. For the sake of efficiency, film companies made films in assembly-line fashion. Moreover, the centralization of production by a handful of companies meant that there were relatively few opportunities to create diversity in the kinds of films that were being made. Adding to uniformity was the system of "block booking" that studios forced on theatre owners (Hanssen, 2000). Theatre owners leased movies from studios, but rather than being allowed to choose which movies they leased, they were required to lease whole "blocks" of films, ranging from three or four to about twenty at a time. Of these blocks of films, only one or two would be "A" movies, and the rest would be cheaply made "B" movies. To book "A" movies, theatre owners had to book the more numerous "B" movies as well. For the most part, this method "encouraged the production and consumption of as vast an avalanche of triviality as has ever been inflicted on a public." The workers involved in producing "B" movies "seemed to consider the assignment a chore below their personal dignity, to be performed perfunctorily, carelessly and ineptly" (Mayer, 1948).

As a whole, the films produced in Hollywood during the era of the "studio system" bear the stamp of the method through which they were created. A "Fordist" assembly-line production model fashioned films that were largely standardized. Unlike cars, however, there were some standout films that exhibited the artistic impulses of particular directors, producers, and screenwriters. Orson Welles, the director of films such as *Citizen Kane* and *The Magnificent Ambersons*, fought hard for his artistic independence from studio executives and was able to make lasting works of art as a result. Walt Disney founded his own studio to pursue the art of animation and was able to create *Snow White and the Seven Dwarfs* and *Fantasia* among many other treasured films. Although these great films are still appreciated today, they are exceptions to the general character of films produced by the studio system.

The studio system came to an end in the 1950s. For a variety of reasons, including the introduction of television, suburbanization, and a rising birth rate, film audiences fell dramatically. In the absence of guaranteed audiences, the assembly-line production method of the studio system was no longer effective. Over the next few decades, new modes of production emerged to suit the changing economic circumstances of the film industry.

The current model for film production is the "blockbuster" model. Production companies make a smaller number of films, and within that smaller pool they select a few to receive most of the funding for production and promotion. In effect, they put most of their eggs in a few baskets. This production logic has, again, an economic foundation. Great uncertainty surrounds every film; producers do not know if an audience will turn up at the theatres. By investing large sums in the production and promotion of certain films, studios increase the likelihood that audiences will flock to them. A recent example is *Batman Begins*, which was made for about $135 million and grossed over $370 million worldwide. Despite these efforts, big budget films often fail. A recent failure was *Catwoman*, starring Halle Berry. It cost approximately $85 million to produce but failed to gross anywhere near that amount. For this reason, the studios hedge their bets and produce smaller budget films on the off chance that they will strike a chord with audiences. While many of these films also lose money, others are surprisingly successful. The original *Texas Chainsaw Massacre*, for example, was made for around $140 000 and grossed over $30 million in 1974. In 2003, the remake of that movie was produced for about $9 million and grossed over $80 million in the United States and tens of millions of dollars more in overseas markets (http://www.imdb.com). The blockbuster production model is profitable for studios because the popular films generate more than enough profit to cover the losses incurred by unpopular films.

As with the studio system, the blockbuster system involves a correspondence between the production model and the nature of the films that are made. The blockbuster system encourages the making of narrative and visual spectacles designed to generate fascination, mass interest, and big profits. Films such as *Titanic*, *Spiderman*, and *The Lord of the Rings* trilogy rely on stunning visual effects and archetypal story lines of good versus evil to appeal to as wide an audience as possible, not just domestically but around the globe. Such films require enormous capital investment, so film studios want to franchise them. After all, spinoff toys, video games, and sequels can add much to the bottom line. Films that can be franchised are more likely to be produced and to be given large budgets.

Films that do not receive as much funding for production and promotion tend to experiment more with narrative elements and lesser known actors. Sometimes these lower budget productions pay off hugely and become hits, as in the case of *My Big Fat Greek Wedding*.

In sum, an organizational perspective offers an important corrective to the conventional view that cultural productions such as movies represent only the work of individual creators. Individual creators surely have an influence on the final product, but if we wish to understand the character of movies it is crucial to take into account the organizational conditions under which they are made.

CULTURAL REFLECTION

A second perspective for understanding how social factors influence the content of films points to the elements of culture reflected in them. In this view, films mirror society for two main reasons. First, filmmaking occurs within a social context and is constrained by that context. Second, films are designed to be popular with audiences and so are made to reflect the interests and concerns of audience members.

As with other artistic media, movies are preoccupied with universal themes such as love and intimacy, family life, growing up, and examining what constitutes true happiness. Because these issues are an integral part of our culture, they enjoy a central place in movies.

Films also mirror society at the level of everyday life. Thus, movies today differ in many ways from the movies of, say, the 1920s. That is partly because the technology of filmmaking has evolved. Today, sound, editing, lighting, camera work, and special effects create movies that look entirely different from the films of the past. Today's movies also look different from movies made in the past because (with the exception of movies set in the future or in the past) they must realistically depict the lives of characters in contemporary social settings, and these settings, including the objects people encounter in everyday life, change over time.

Just as the facts of our everyday existence evolve over time, so do important social problems, concerns, and interests. Consider the villains that populate movies. During the cold war (1947–91), many people in North America felt threatened by Communism, particularly Communist infiltration of Western democracies and nuclear annihilation at the hands of Communists. Films from that period often featured Communists, especially Soviets, as archetypal bad guys. Since the fall of Communism in the Soviet Union and Eastern Europe, these threats no longer loom large in the public consciousness. Communist villains are neither plausible nor interesting to today's audiences. As a result, they generally no longer appear in films. The public is now preoccupied with the threat of terrorism, and that is reflected in an increase in the depiction of terrorist villains in recent films such as *The Sum of All Fears*, *Spy Game*, *The Siege*, and *Collateral Damage*, among many others.

The cold war is just one of many evolving social concerns and interests that are reflected in the movies. Following the rise of feminism in the 1960s, people became more interested in exploring the roles of women in society, and films reflected that interest. The same can be said of such issues as environmental protection, corporate crime, government corruption, genetic engineering, and HIV/AIDS.

Film scholars argue that social concerns also influence films at a deeper, metaphorical level. Accordingly, even films not explicitly dealing with the cold war can be interpreted as expressions of the anxiety associated with it. Science fiction films in which aliens seek to expand their dominion by colonizing Earth were especially popular in the 1950s when cold war anxieties were at their peak. The aliens embodied many of the qualities that were attributed to Communists; they were godless, emotionless invaders intent on destroying Western democracy, traditions, and prosperity (Hendershot, 1999). Similarly, horror films often depict creatures that afflict humans through implantation or infection. They often end up inside people or they take the form of people. One interpretation of this recurring theme is that it reflects our anxiety over health and illness, particularly illness caused by viruses, bacteria, and cancers that invade and destroy their human hosts (Guerrero, 1990). *Alien* and its three sequels, for example, involve a vicious monster that reproduces itself by inhabiting a human host who is killed when the creature is eventually "born." At a certain level, a film in which people are saved from the dangers of bodily invasion and destruction reassures the audience that it can be saved from the dangers of real-world illness.

HOW FILMS SHAPE SOCIETY

Having considered two ways in which society influences the movies, let us now examine how movies influence society. For almost as long as movies have been made, people have feared that they may corrupt us. Initially, concern arose from the fact that moving images proved to be a captivating and fascinating innovation. Observers predicted disastrous consequences, including the thoughtless imitation of dangerous activities, the learning of criminal techniques, and the rapid deterioration of moral standards.

By the late 1920s, such concern initiated the Payne Fund Studies, which attempted to assess whether going to the movies influenced children negatively. The studies have been thoroughly criticized for their flawed methods and suspect findings. Nevertheless, they indicate the high level of early concern over the possibility—and, in some people's minds, the certainty—that movies were corrupting youth.

Eighty years later, that fear has not abated. New articles about the dangers of movies appear in the popular press without any pretence of social scientific rigour. We often read that movies are responsible for promiscuity, materialism, violence, depression, loss of religion, sexism, agism, racism, and much else. These are serious allegations, but before we conclude that movies actually have these effects, we need strong evidence.

Movies may influence people on both the societal and the individual level. *Societal-level* influences include those that change the nature of our culture, particularly our norms and values. Consider materialism—the view that wealth buys happiness. Some people note that movies typically depict wealthy lifestyles as a source of happiness. The lavish and hedonistic lives of movie stars reinforce the message. How many North Americans envied Jennifer Lopez when Ben Affleck proposed to her with a pink diamond engagement ring worth more than $1 million? People are more inclined to accept the notion that wealth buys happiness when they are surrounded by such images and exposed to such events.

The problem with arguments about societal-level influences is that they are difficult to support or refute with data. There are two reasons for this. First, our culture is affected by many social forces of which the movies are only one. We have no way of separating the effect of movies from all other effects. In the case of materialism, for example, we cannot know if changing values result from changing levels of wealth, changing levels of wealth inequality, messages contained in mass media other than movies, or many other factors. Movies may play a large role, a small role, or no role at all. Given what we know about the complexity of cultural change in general, however, it seems highly unlikely that the movies play a large role in shaping society's values. It is more likely that they reflect existing values.

The second reason for doubting arguments about the societal-level influence of films is that such arguments assume films are understood by members of society in the same way and affect them similarly. We know, however, that some people never or infrequently see films and that different people take away different messages from the same film. For example, do people become more tolerant of promiscuity when they see it portrayed in movies, or more repulsed? Without knowing what messages audience members are receiving from films, it is impossible to form an argument about how films influence society.

Arguments about certain kinds of *individual-level* effects stand on firmer empirical ground. These arguments hold that movies shape the attitudes and behaviours of individuals in specific ways. For example, one vein of research on the effects of movies investigates whether exposure to movies in which the characters smoke increases the likelihood that young people will take up smoking. The most recent study on this topic asked a large number of adolescents about the movies they had seen in recent years, as well as whether they had ever tried smoking (Sargent et al., 2005). It found that increased exposure to movies in which characters smoked was correlated with the likelihood that an adolescent would try smoking, even after taking into account many other factors usually associated with starting smoking. Thus, while movies are by no means the only relevant factor, they seem to have an influence on smoking initiation among some adolescents. Research done in this fashion, however, only gains general acceptance by scholars as reliable after many replications. Time will tell if these initial results hold up.

A much larger body of research conducted over the last 40 years has been done on the topic of violence, again focusing on the potential effects on children. This research attempts to understand whether and in what ways individuals are affected by on-screen violence. Studies take the form of laboratory experiments (in which some children are shown violent content and compared to a control group of children who are shown non-violent content); field experiments (in which the same kinds of comparisons are made in natural social settings); cross-sectional studies (in which surveys allow researchers to examine correlations between exposure to on-screen violence and real-world violence in different segments of the population); and longitudinal studies (in which researchers track samples of people for months or years and look for correlations between exposure to on-screen violence and violent behaviour).

Several recent reviews of the research literature find strong evidence that in the short term, children and adolescents who watch violent films become physically and verbally aggressive. The evidence for long-term effects is significant but requires further research before firm conclusions can be drawn (Anderson and Bushman, 2002; Browne and Hamilton-Giachritis, 2005; Office of the Surgeon General, 2001).

Research shows that violent movies increase the likelihood that *some* audience members will behave more aggressively. Significantly, however, not all individuals are affected in the same way or to the same extent by violent movies. Moreover, violent behaviour has many causes, of which media violence is only one and by no means the most important. It is also important to note that critics have expressed much concern about the graphic nature of violence, as in horror movies where people are butchered. However, on-screen violence tends to have more of an effect on audience members if it is presented without a reasonable moral context. Violence is sometimes presented as a legitimate way to resolve conflict, as an action that goes unpunished, and without a depiction of the devastating emotional consequences that it has on people's lives. It is more the lack of contextualization of violence than its graphic quality that makes on-screen violence problematic (Potter, 1999).

Frequently lost in the conversation about how movies influence society is consideration of their positive effects. Yet movies benefit us by entertaining us and by addressing important issues that deserve public awareness and understanding. *On the Beach* (1959) sparked debate about the nuclear arms race, *Guess Who's Coming to Dinner* (1967) provoked dialogue about interracial relationships, *Philadelphia* (1993) generated widespread discussion about discrimination

against people with AIDS, *The Insider* (1999) raised awareness of the influence of the tobacco industry on the mass media, and *Syriana* (2005) raised questions about the oil industry's manipulation of politicians in the United States and the Middle East. As these examples suggest, the influence of movies on society is often informative and progressive.

REFERENCES

Anderson, Craig A., and Brad J. Bushman. (2002). "The Effects of Media Violence on Society." *Science*, (29 March): 2377–78.

Brown, Gene. (1995). *Movie Time: A Chronology of Hollywood and the Movie Industry from Its Beginnings to the Present.* New York: Macmillan.

Browne, Kevin D., and Katherine Hamilton-Giachritis. (2005). "The Influence of Violent Media on Children and Adolescents: A Public-Health Approach." *The Lancet*, (19 February): 702–10.

Guerrero, Edward. (1990). "AIDS as Monster in Science Fiction and Horror Cinema." *Journal of Popular Film and Television*, 18 (3): 86–93.

Hanssen, Andrew F. (2000). "The Block Booking of Films Reexamined." *Journal of Law and Economics*, 43 (2): 395–426.

Hendershot, Cyndy. (1999). *Paranoia, the Bomb, and 1950s Science-Fiction Films.* Bowling Green, OH: Bowling Green State University Press.

Mayer, Arthur L. (1948). "An Exhibitor Begs for 'B's.'" *Hollywood Quarterly*, 3 (2): 172–77.

Office of the Surgeon General. (2001). *Youth Violence: A Report of the Surgeon General.* Washington, DC: Dept. of Health and Human Services, U.S. Public Health Service.

Peterson, Richard. (1994). "Cultural Studies Through the Production Perspective: Progress and Prospects." In Diana Crane, ed., *The Sociology of Culture: Emerging Theoretical Perspectives* (pp. 163–89). Cambridge, MA: Blackwell Publishers.

Potter, James W. (1999). *On Media Violence.* Thousand Oaks, CA: Sage Publications.

Sargent, James D., Michael L. Beach, Anna M. Adachi-Mejia, Jennifer J. Gibson, Linda T. Titus-Ernstoff, Charles P. Carusi, Susan D. Swain, Todd F. Heatherton, and Madeleine A. Dalton. (2005). "Exposure to Movie Smoking: Its Relation to Smoking Initiation among US Adolescents." *Pediatrics,* 116 (5): 1183–91.

White, William Allen. (1936). "Chewing-Gum Relaxation." In William J. Perlman, ed., *The Movies on Trial* (pp. 3–12). New York: The Macmillan Company.

Chapter 8

Hip-Hop from Dissent to Commodity:

A NOTE ON CONSUMER CULTURE

ROBERT J. BRYM

MUSIC AS DISSENT AND CONSENT

Music can sometimes act as a kind of social cement. Reflecting the traditions, frustrations, and ambitions of the communities that create it, music can help otherwise isolated voices sing in unison. It can help individuals shape a collective identity. Sometimes, music can even inspire people to engage in concerted political action (Mattern, 1998).

Under some circumstances, however, music can have the opposite effect. It can individualize feelings of collective unrest and thereby moderate dissent. This occurs, for example, when music that originated as an act of rebellion is turned into a mass-marketed commodity. Music that develops in opposition to the mainstream typically gets tamed and declawed when it is transformed into something that can be bought and sold on a wide scale. By commodifying dissent and broadening its appeal to a large and socially heterogeneous audience, consumer culture renders it mainstream. The way it accomplishes this remarkable feat is well illustrated by the musical genre called hip-hop.[1]

THE SOCIAL ORIGINS OF HIP-HOP

Hip-hop originated in the appalling social conditions facing African-American inner-city youth in the 1970s and 1980s. During those decades, man-

ufacturing industries left the cities for suburban or foreign locales, where land values were lower and labour was less expensive. Unemployment among African-American youth rose to more than 40 percent. Middle-class Blacks left the inner city for the suburbs. The migration robbed the remaining young people of successful role models they could emulate. It also eroded the taxing capacity of municipal governments, leading to a decline in public services. Meanwhile, the American public elected conservative governments at the state and federal levels. They cut school and welfare budgets, thus deepening the destitution of ghetto life (Wilson, 1987).

Understandably, young African-Americans grew angrier as the conditions of their existence worsened. With few legitimate prospects for advancement, they turned increasingly to crime and, in particular, to the drug trade.

In the late 1970s, cocaine was expensive and demand for the drug was flat. So, in the early 1980s, Colombia's Medellin drug cartel introduced a less expensive form of cocaine called rock or crack. Crack was not only inexpensive. It offered a quick and intense high, and it was highly addictive. Crack cocaine offered many people a temporary escape from hopelessness and soon became wildly popular in the inner city. Turf wars spread as gangs tried to outgun each other for control of the local traffic. The sale and use of crack became so widespread it corroded much of what was left of the inner-city African-American community (Davis, 1990).

The shocking conditions described above gave rise to a shocking musical form: hip-hop. Stridently at odds with the values and tastes of both whites and middle-class African-Americans, hip-hop described and glorified the mean streets of the inner city while holding the police, the mass media, and other pillars of society in utter contempt. Furthermore, hip-hop tried to offend middle-class sensibilities, Black and white, by using highly offensive language. In 1988, more than a decade after its first stirrings, hip-hop reached its political high point with the release of the CD *It Takes a Nation to Hold Us Back* by Chuck D and Public Enemy. In "Don't Believe the Hype," Chuck D accuses the mass media of maliciously distributing lies. In "Black Steel in the Hour of Chaos," he charges the FBI and the CIA with assassinating the two great leaders of the African-American community in the 1960s, Martin Luther King and Malcolm X. In "Party for Your Right to Fight," he blames the federal government for organizing the fall of the Black Panthers, the radical Black nationalist party of the 1960s. Here, it seemed, was an angry expression of subcultural revolt that could not be mollified.

HIP-HOP TRANSFORMED

However, there were elements in hip-hop that soon transformed it (Bayles, 1994: 341–62; Neal, 1999: 144–48). In the first place, early radical hip-hop was not written as dance music. It therefore cut itself off from a large audience. Moreover, hip-hop entered a self-destructive phase with the emergence of Gangsta rap, which extolled criminal lifestyles, denigrated women, and replaced politics with drugs, guns, and machismo. The release of Ice T's "Cop Killer" in 1992 provoked strong political opposition from Republicans and Democrats, white church groups, and Black middle-class associations. "Cop Killer" was not hip-hop, but it fuelled a reaction against all anti-establishment music. Time/Warner was forced to withdraw the song from circulation. The sense that hip-hop had reached a dead end, or at least a turning point, grew in 1996, when rapper Tupac

Shakur was murdered in the culmination of a feud between two hip-hop record labels, Death Row in Los Angeles and Bad Boy in New York (Springhall, 1998: 149–51).

If these events made it seem that hip-hop was self-destructing, the police and insurance industries helped to speed up its demise. In 1988, a group called Niggas with Attitude released "Fuck the Police," a critique of police violence against Black youth. Law enforcement officials in several cities dared the group to perform the song in public, threatening to detain the performers or shut down their shows. Increasingly, thereafter, ticket holders at rap concerts were searched for drugs and weapons, and security was tightened. Insurance companies, afraid of violence, substantially raised insurance rates for hip-hop concerts, making them a financial risk. Soon, the number of venues willing to sponsor hip-hop concerts dwindled.

While the developments noted above did much to mute the political force of hip-hop, the seduction of big money did more. As early as 1982, with the release of Grandmaster Flash and the Furious Five's "The Message," hip-hop began to win acclaim from mainstream rock music critics. With the success of Public Enemy in the late 1980s, it became clear there was a big audience for hip-hop. Significantly, much of that audience was composed of white youths. As one music critic wrote, they "relished . . . the subversive 'otherness' that the music and its purveyors represented" (Neal, 1999: 144). Sensing the opportunity for profit, major media corporations, such as Time/Warner, Sony, CBS/Columbia, and BMG Entertainment, signed distribution deals with the small independent recording labels that had formerly been the exclusive distributors of hip-hop CDs. In 1988, *Yo! MTV Raps* debuted. The program brought hip-hop to middle America.

Most hip-hop recording artists proved they were eager to forego politics for commerce. For instance, the rap group WU-Tang Clan started a line of clothing called WU Wear, and, with the help of major hip-hop recording artists, companies as diverse as Tommy Hilfiger, Timberland,

Starter, and Versace began to market clothing influenced by ghetto styles. By the early 1990s, hip-hop was no longer just a musical form but a commodity with spinoffs. Rebellion had been turned into mass consumption.

DIDDY

No rapper has done a better job of turning rebellion into a commodity than Sean Combs, better known as Puff Daddy, later as P. Diddy, and most recently as Diddy. Diddy seems to promote rebellion. For example, the liner notes for his 1999 hit CD, *Forever*, advertise his magazine, *Notorious*, as follows:

> There is a revolution out there. Anyone can do anything. There are no rules. There are no restrictions. Notorious magazine presents provocative profiles of rebels, rulebreakers and mavericks—Notorious people who are changing the world with their unique brand of individuality.
>
> Our goal is to inform and inspire, to educate and elevate the infinite range of individual possibility. . . . In essence, Notorious is for everyone who wants to live a sexy, daring life—a life that makes a difference. After all, you can't change the world without being a little . . . Notorious. (Combs, 1999)

Although he says he's committed to changing the world, Diddy encourages only individual acts of rebellion, not collective political solutions. Diddy's brand of dissent thus appeals to a broad audience, much of it white and middle class. As his video director, Martin Weitz, observed in an interview for *Elle* magazine, Diddy's market is not the ghetto: "No ghetto kid from Harlem is going to buy Puffy. They think he sold out. It's more like the 16-year-old white girls in the Hamptons, baby!" (quoted in Everett-Green, 1999).

It is also important to note that Diddy encourages individual acts of rebellion only to the degree they enrich him and the media conglomerate he works with.[2] And rich he has become. Diddy lives in a multimillion dollar mansion on Park Avenue in Manhattan and a multimillion dollar house in the Hamptons. In 2005, *Forbes* magazine ranked him the 20th most important celebrity in the United States and the third biggest money earner among musicians, with an annual income of US$36 million ("The Celebrity 100," 2005). Diddy is entirely forthright about his apolitical, self-enriching aims. In his 1997 song "I Got the Power," Diddy refers to himself as "that nigga with the getting-money game plan" (Combs and the Lox, 1997). And in *Forever*, he reminds us: "Nigga get money, that's simply the plan." From this point of view, Diddy has more in common with Martha Stewart than with Chuck D and Public Enemy (Everett-Green, 1999).

One indicator of the importance of the "getting-money game plan" among hip-hop artists is the near-worship of luxury commodities in their music. Consider Table 8.1, based on the top 20 songs of 2005 on the Billboard charts, almost all of which were in the hip-hop genre. The left half of Table 8.1 shows how many times the ten most frequently mentioned brands were referred to in the top 20 songs. The right half lists the eight recording artists who made it into the top 5 by referring to brands most frequently. The numbers tell a fascinating story. Each of the top 20 songs of 2005 mentioned brands 25.5 times on average. Assuming the average song is two and a half minutes long, that works out to 1 brand mentioned every 6 seconds. From this point of view, popular music is a lot like a commercial. The good life in the world of hip-hop—especially the music of 50 Cent—is strongly associated with driving a Mercedes, wearing Nikes, drinking Hennessy cognac, and packing an AK-47 assault rifle.

STREET CRED

One of the great difficulties deriving from the financial success of Diddy and other hip-hop artists is that earning millions of dollars a year robs them of what they call "street cred." One's

TABLE 8.1 BRAND NAMES IN POPULAR MUSIC, 2005

Brands Mentioned in Top 20 Songs

BRAND	NUMBER OF MENTIONS
1. Mercedes-Benz automobile	100
2. Nike sports shoes	63
3. Cadillac automobile	62
4. Bentley automobile	51
5. Rolls-Royce automobile	46
6. Hennessy cognac	44
7. Chevrolet automobile	40
8. Louis Vuitton luggage	35
8. Cristal champagne	35
9. AK-47 assault rifle	33
Total	509
Mentions/song	25.5

Top 5 Brand-Dropping Artists

SINGER	NUMBER OF MENTIONS
1. 50 Cent	20 brands in 7 songs
2. Ludacris	13 brands in 6 songs
2. The Game	13 brands in 2 songs
4. Ciara	10 brands in 4 songs
5. Jamie Foxx	6 brands in 1 song
5. Kanye West	6 brands in 1 song
5. Lil' Jon	6 brands in 2 songs
5. Trick Daddy	6 brands in 2 songs
Total	80 brands in 25 songs
Brands/song	3.2

Source: Agenda Inc. (2006). "American Bandstand 2005," 4–7. On the World Wide Web at http://www.agendainc.com/brandstand05.pdf (27 March 2006). Reprinted with permission of Agenda, Inc. (www.agendainc.com).

claim to be a gangster, a pimp, and a cop killer loses credibility when one shops at Salvatore Ferragamo on Fifth Avenue. One way of maintaining street cred is by staging fake gun battles. For example, in March 2005, a sidewalk gunfight broke out near hip-hop radio station WQHT in New York City between the entourages of rap star, the Game, and his former mentor, 50 Cent. The Game had hinted that he might record with one of 50 Cent's rivals, so 50 Cent expelled the Game from his inner circle. The gunfight followed. Four years earlier, on the same street corner, a similar incident occurred between followers of Lil' Kim and rival rap star, Capone, after Capone's group had referred to Lil' Kim as "lame" in a recording. In both gunfights, the rap stars' followers discharged many rounds of ammunition at close range but damage was minor. Total casualties: one man was shot in the leg in 2005. It seems reasonable to conclude that the gunfights were really for show. They help to reinforce the violent image and the street cred of the rap stars involved. Rap stars are multimillionaire members of the music elite but the gunfights confer "the illusion of their authenticity as desperate outlaws" (Hajdu, 2005). The shootouts are properly seen as low-risk investments by savvy businesspeople.

POP CULTURE AND THE COMMODIFICATION OF DISSENT

Hip-hop emerged among poor African-American inner-city youth as a counsel of despair with strong political overtones. Although there are still radical currents in contemporary hip-hop, it has largely become an apolitical commodity that increasingly appeals to a white, middle-class audience. Hip-hop is thus testimony to the capacity of consumer culture to constrain expressions of freedom and dissent (Frank and Weiland, 1997).

Interestingly, some sociologists play a big role in the containment process. In Canada, for example, most of the big public opinion firms (Angus Reid, Goldfarb, and Environics) are owned and run by sociologists. One of the tasks they have set themselves is to understand better the popular culture of North American youth. By conducting surveys and regularly organizing focus groups with young consumers in major North American cities, they identify new tastes and trends that marketers can then use to sell products. Angus Reid sells its reports on pop culture for $20 000 a copy (Angus Reid Group, 1999). By producing such reports, public opinion firms help to routinize the commodification of dissent.

Vladimir Lenin, leader of the Russian Revolution of 1917, once said that capitalists are so eager to earn profits they will sell the rope from which they themselves will hang. However, Lenin underestimated his opponents. Savvy entrepreneurs today employ sociologists and other social scientists to help them discover emerging forms of cultural rebellion. They take the edge off these dissenting cultural forms, thereby making them more appealing to a mass market. They then sell them on a wide scale, earning big profits. Young consumers are fooled into thinking they are buying rope to hang owners of big business, political authorities, and cultural conservatives. Really, they're just buying rope to constrain themselves.

NOTES

1. Scholars and music buffs disagree about the exact difference and degree of overlap between hip-hop and rap. They seem to agree, however, that rap refers to a particular tradition of Black rhythmic lyrics while hip-hop refers to a particular Black beat (often jerky and offbeat) mixed with samples of earlier recordings and LP scratches (now largely passé). See Mink-Cee (2000). In this chapter, I use the terms interchangeably.
2. *Forever* is marketed, manufactured, and distributed by a unit of BMG Entertainment, the multibillion dollar entertainment division of Germany's Bertelsmann AG, the third-largest media company in the world.

REFERENCES

Agenda Inc. (2005). "American Bandstand 2005." On the World Wide Web at http://www.agendainc.com/brandstand05.pdf (27 March 2006).

Angus Reid Group. (1999). "Why Is It Important to Track Pop Culture?" On the World Wide Web at http://www.angusreid.com/pdf/publicat/pop.pdf (22 March 2000).

Bayles, Martha. (1994). *Hole in Our Soul: The Loss of Beauty and Meaning in American Popular Music.* Chicago: University of Chicago Press.

"The Celebrity 100." (2005). *Forbes.com,* 15 June. On the World Wide Web at http://www.forbes.com/celebrity100 (27 March 2006).

Combs, Sean "Puffy." (1999). *Forever.* Liner notes. New York: Bad Boy Entertainment (CD).

Combs, Sean "Puffy," and the Lox. (1997). "I Got the Power." On the World Wide Web at http://www.ewsonline.com/badboy/lyrpow.html (22 March 2000).

Davis, Mike. (1990). *City of Quartz: Excavating the Future in Los Angeles.* New York: Verso.

Everett-Green, Robert. (1999). "Puff Daddy: The Martha Stewart of Hip-Hop." *The Globe and Mail,* 4 September, C7.

Frank, Thomas, and Matt Weiland, eds. (1997). *Commodify Your Dissent: Salvos from the Baffler.* New York: W.W. Norton.

Hajdu, David. (2005). "Guns and Poses." *New York Times,* 11 March. On the World Wide Web at www.nytimes.com (11 March 2005).

Mattern, Mark. (1998). *Acting in Concert: Music, Community, and Political Action.* New Brunswick, NJ: Rutgers University Press.

Mink-Cee. (2000). "Rap vs. Hip-Hop." On the World Wide Web at http://www.geocities.com/BourbonStreet/9459/rapvshiphop.htm (23 March 2000).

Neal, Mark Anthony. (1999). *What the Music Said: Black Popular Music* and Black Public Culture. New York: Routledge.

Springhall, John. (1998). *Youth, Popular Culture and Moral Panics: Penny Gaffs to Gangsta-Rap, 1830–1996.* New York: Routledge.

Wilson, William Julius. (1987). *The Truly Disadvantaged: The Inner City, the Underclass, and Public Policy.* Chicago: University of Chicago Press.

PART 2C

SOCIAL STRUCTURE

Social structures are the patterns of social relations that bind people together and give shape to their lives. Consider hierarchy, one feature of social structure. Hierarchy refers to the degree to which power is unequally distributed in a social group. The more unequal the distribution of power, the greater the degree of hierarchy. In a family, for instance, the degree of hierarchy and the position of a child in the hierarchy profoundly influence the quality of his or her life. In a highly hierarchical family the child may grow up to resent authority or cringe before it—or both. In a family without hierarchy, the child may be spoiled and remain selfish. As these examples illustrate, who you are is partly the result of the social structures through which you pass.

Despite its importance in shaping who we are, we seldom notice social structure in our everyday lives. In fact, we often deny its significance. That is because our culture places such strong emphasis on individual freedom and responsibility. Accordingly, we learn three rules about human behaviour from an early age:

- People are perfectly free to act as they wish.
- People can therefore choose right over wrong.
- If people choose wrong, we should judge them as moral inferiors.

Such thinking may be good for our egos, but it has little in common with sociology and is one of prejudice's most stubborn roots.

Chapter 9 offers a chilling illustration of the power of social structures. It reports an experiment in which middle-class American and Canadian university students were assigned the role of prisoner or guard in an artificial jail constructed by the experimenter. Almost immediately, the subjects were unable to distinguish between their roles and their former selves. Even though none of the subjects was instructed in how to behave, the "guards" quickly learned to take pleasure in causing pain while the "prisoners" were wracked with hatred as they planned their escape. A lifetime of learning was suspended. The experiment had to be abandoned within a few days. Social structure had revealed its influence.

Émile Durkheim's *Suicide* is a forceful, classical exposition of the way one aspect of social structure—**social solidarity**—helps to shape us. A group's level of social solidarity is higher to the degree its members share the same values and interact frequently and intimately. In the section reprinted here as Chapter 10, Durkheim argues that social solidarity anchors people to the social world. It follows, he argues, that the lower the level of social solidarity in a group, the more a group member will be inclined to take his or her own life if he or she is in deep distress. Durkheim tests his argument by examining the level of social solidarity that characterizes the major religious groups in Europe. He demonstrates that the propensity of group members to take their own lives does indeed vary inversely with social solidarity. On the strength of Durkheim's argument one is obliged to conclude that social structure powerfully affects even an uncommon antisocial action that is usually committed in private.

GLOSSARY

Social solidarity is higher in a group to the degree its members share the same values and interact frequently and intimately.

CRITICAL THINKING QUESTIONS

1. Are there parallels between the Zimbardo experiment and the treatment of Iraqi prisoners by American forces at Abu Ghraib prison in Iraq? For a simulation of the Zimbardo experiment on the Web and links to the parallels with Abu Ghraib, visit http://www.prisonexp.org/.
2. "Suicide varies inversely with the degree of integration of the social groups of which the individual forms a part." Explain this statement and give examples to support your answer.
3. How might the degree of integration of social groups affect actions other than suicide?

ANNOTATED BIBLIOGRAPHY

Brym, Robert J. "Regional Social Structure and Agrarian Radicalism in Canada: Alberta, Saskatchewan and New Brunswick." *Canadian Review of Sociology and Anthropology* 15 (3) (1978): 339–51. Analyzes how the different social structures of Canadian regions shaped political protest before World War II.

Hochschild, Arlie Russell. "Emotion Work, Feeling Rules, and Social Structure." *American Journal of Sociology* 85 (1979): 551–75. Shows how social structures shape the emotional life of people in different work settings.

Merton, Robert K. "Social Structure and Anomie." *American Sociological Review* 3 (1938): 672–82. One of the most frequently cited articles in sociology. Merton argues that different types of social structure give rise to different criminal activities and other coping mechanisms.

Chapter 9

Pathology of Imprisonment

PHILIP E. ZIMBARDO

In an attempt to understand just what it means psychologically to be a prisoner or prison guard, Craig Haney, Curt Banks, Dave Jaffe, and I created our own prison. We carefully screened over 70 volunteers who answered an ad in a Palo Alto city newspaper and ended up with about two dozen young men who were selected to be part of this study. They were mature, emotionally stable, normal, intelligent college students from middle-class homes throughout the United States and Canada. They appeared to represent the cream of the crop of this generation. None had any criminal record, and initially all were relatively homogeneous on many dimensions.

Half were arbitrarily designated as prisoners by a flip of a coin, the others as guards. These were the roles they were to play in our simulated prison. The guards were made aware of the potential seriousness and danger of the situation and their own vulnerability. They made up their own formal rules for maintaining law, order, and respect, and were generally free to improvise new ones during their eight-hour, three-man shifts. The prisoners were unexpectedly picked up at their homes by a city policeman in a squad car, searched, handcuffed, fingerprinted, booked at the Palo Alto station house, and taken blindfolded to our jail. There they were stripped, deloused, put into a uniform, given a number, and put into a cell with two other prisoners, where they expected to live for the next two weeks. The pay was good . . . and their motivation was to make money.

We observed and recorded on videotape the events that occurred in the prison, and we interviewed and tested the prisoners and guards at various points throughout the study. Some of the videotapes of the actual encounters between the prisoners and guards were seen on the NBC News feature "Chronolog" on November 26, 1971.

At the end of only six days, we had to close down our mock prison because what we saw was frightening. It was no longer apparent to most of the subjects (or to us) where reality ended and their roles began. The majority had indeed become prisoners or guards, no longer able to clearly differentiate between role playing and self. There were dramatic changes in virtually every aspect of their behaviour, thinking, and feeling. In less than a week, the experience of imprisonment undid (temporarily) a lifetime of learning; human values were suspended, self-concepts were challenged, and the ugliest, most base, pathological side of human nature surfaced. We were horrified because we saw some boys (guards) treat others as if they were despicable animals, taking pleasure in cruelty, while other boys (prisoners) became servile, dehumanized robots who thought only of escape, of their own individual survival, and of their mounting hatred for the guards.

We had to release three prisoners in the first four days because they had such acute situational traumatic reactions as hysterical crying, confusion in thinking, and severe depression. Others begged to be paroled, and all but three were willing to forfeit all the money they had earned if they could be paroled. By then (the fifth day), they had been so programmed to think of themselves as prisoners that when their request for parole was denied, they returned docilely to their cells. Now, had they been thinking as college students acting in an oppressive experiment, they would have quit once they no longer wanted the [money] we used as our only incentive. However, the reality was not quitting an experiment but "being paroled by the parole board from the Stanford County Jail." By the last days, the earlier solidarity among the prisoners (systematically broken by the guards) dissolved into "each man for himself." Finally, when one of their fellows was put in solitary confinement (a small closet) for refusing to eat, the prisoners were given a choice by one of the guards: give up their blankets and the incorrigible prisoner would be let out, or keep their blankets and he would be kept in all night. They voted to keep their blankets and to abandon their brother.

About a third of the guards became tyrannical in their arbitrary use of power, in enjoying their control over other people. They were corrupted by the power of their roles and became quite inventive in their techniques of breaking the spirit of the prisoners and making them feel they were worthless. Some of the guards merely did their jobs as tough but fair correctional officers, and several were good guards from the prisoners' point of view because they did them small favours and were friendly. However, no good guard ever interfered with a command by any of the bad guards; they never intervened on the side of the prisoners, they never told the others to ease off because it was only an experiment, and they never even came to me as prison superintendent or experimenter in charge to complain. In part, they were good because the others were bad; they needed the others to help establish their own egos in a positive light. In a sense, the good guards perpetuated the prison more than the other guards because their own need to

be liked prevented them from disobeying or violating the implicit guards' code. At the same time, the act of befriending the prisoners created a social reality that made the prisoners less likely to rebel.

By the end of the week, the experiment had become a reality. . . . The consultant for our prison, Carlo Prescot, an ex-convict with sixteen years of imprisonment in California's jails, would get so depressed and furious each time he visited our prison, because of its psychological similarity to his experiences, that he would have to leave. A Catholic priest, who was a former prison chaplain in Washington, DC, talked to our prisoners after four days and said they were just like the other first-timers he had seen.

But in the end, I called off the experiment, not because of the horror I saw out there in the prison yard, but because of the horror of realizing that I could have easily traded places with the most brutal guard or become the weakest prisoner full of hatred at being so powerless that I could not eat, sleep, or go to the toilet without permission of the authorities. . . .

Individual behaviour is largely under the control of social forces and environmental contingencies rather than personality traits, character, will power, or other empirically unvalidated constructs. Thus we create an illusion of freedom by attributing more internal control to ourselves, to the individual, than actually exists. We thus underestimate the power and pervasiveness of situational controls over behaviour because (a) they are often non-obvious and subtle, (b) we can often avoid entering situations in which we might be so controlled, and (c) we label as "weak" or "deviant" people in those situations who do behave differently from how we believe we would.

Each of us carries around in our heads a favourable self-image in which we are essentially just, fair, humane, and understanding. For example, we could not imagine inflicting pain on others without much provocation or hurting people who had done nothing to us, who in fact were even liked by us. However, there is a growing body of social psychological research that underscores the conclusion derived from this prison study. Many people, perhaps the majority, can be made to do almost anything when put into psychologically compelling situations—regardless of their morals, ethics, values, attitudes, beliefs, or personal convictions. My colleague, Stanley Milgram, has shown that more than 60 percent of the population will deliver what they think is a series of painful electric shocks to another person even after the victim cries for mercy, begs them to stop, and then apparently passes out. The subjects complained that they did not want to inflict more pain but blindly obeyed the command of the authority figure (the experimenter) who said that they must go on. In my own research on violence, I have seen mild-mannered coeds repeatedly give shocks (which they thought were causing pain) to another girl, a stranger whom they had rated very favourably, simply by being made to feel anonymous and put in a situation in which they were expected to engage in this activity.

Observers of these and similar experimental situations never predict their outcomes and esti-mate that it is unlikely that they themselves would behave similarly. They can be so confident only when they are outside the situation. However, because the majority of people in these studies do act in non-rational, non-obvious ways, it follows that the majority of observers would also succumb to the social psychological forces in the situation.

With regard to prisons, we can state that the mere act of assigning labels to people and putting them into a situation in which those labels acquire validity and meaning is sufficient to elicit pathological behaviour. This pathology is not predictable from any available diagnostic indicators we have in the social sciences, and it is extreme enough to modify in very significant ways fundamental attitudes and behaviour. The prison situation, as presently arranged, is guaranteed to generate severe enough pathological reactions in both guards and prisoners as to debase their humanity, lower their feelings of self-worth, and make it difficult for them to be part of a society outside their prison.

Chapter 10

Egoistic Suicide

ÉMILE DURKHEIM

If one casts a glance at the map of European suicide, it is at once clear that in purely Catholic countries like Spain, Portugal, Italy, suicide is very little developed, while it is at its maximum in Protestant countries, in Prussia, Saxony, Denmark. The averages in Table 10.1 compiled by Morselli confirm this first conclusion.

The only essential difference between Catholicism and Protestantism is that the second permits free inquiry to a far greater degree than the first. The Catholic accepts his faith ready made, without scrutiny. He may not even submit it to historical examination since the original texts that serve as its basis are proscribed. A whole hierarchical system of authority is devised, with marvelous ingenuity, to render tradition invariable. All *variation* is abhorrent to Catholic thought. The Protestant is far more the author of his faith. The Bible is put in his hands and no interpretation is imposed upon him. The very structure of the reformed cult stresses this state of religious individualism. Nowhere but in England is the Protestant clergy a hierarchy; like the worshippers, the priest has no other source but himself and his conscience. He is a more instructed guide than the run of worshippers but with no special authority for fixing dogma. But what best proves that this freedom of inquiry proclaimed by the founders of the Reformation has not remained a Platonic affirmation is the increased multiplicity of all sorts of sects so strikingly in contrast with the indivisible unity of the Catholic Church.

We thus reach our first conclusion, that the proclivity of Protestantism for suicide must relate to the spirit of free inquiry that animates this religion. . . . And if Protestantism concedes a greater freedom to individual thought than does Catholicism, it is because it has fewer common beliefs and practices. Now, a religious society cannot exist without a collective *credo*, and the more extensive the *credo* the more unified and strong is the society. For it does not unite men by an exchange and reciprocity of services, a temporal bond of union that permits and even presupposes differences, but that a religious society cannot form. It socializes men only by attaching them completely to an identical body of doctrine and socializes them in proportion as this body of doctrine is extensive and firm. The more numerous the manners of action and thought of a religious character are, which are accordingly removed from free inquiry, the more

TABLE 10.1 SUICIDE RATE BY RELIGIOUS COMPOSITION OF COUNTRY

RELIGIOUS COMPOSITION OF COUNTRY	SUICIDES PER MILLION INHABITANTS
Protestant	190
Mixed (Protestant and Catholic)	96
Catholic	58
Greek Catholic	40

the idea of God presents itself in all details of existence, and makes individual wills converge to one identical goal. Inversely, the greater concessions a confessional group makes to individual judgement, the less it dominates lives, the less its cohesion and vitality. We thus reach the conclusion that the superiority of Protestantism with respect to suicide results from its being a less strongly integrated church than the Catholic Church.

This also explains the situation of Judaism. Indeed, the reproach to which the Jews have for so long been exposed by Christianity has created feelings of unusual solidarity among them. Their need of resisting a general hostility, the very impossibility of free communication with the rest of the population, has forced them to strict union among themselves. Consequently, each community became a small, compact and coherent society with a strong feeling of self-consciousness and unity. Everyone thought and lived alike; individual divergences were made almost impossible by the community of existence and the close and constant surveillance of all over each. The Jewish church has thus been more strongly united than any other, from its dependence on itself because of being the object of intolerance. By analogy with what has just been observed apropos of Protestantism, the same cause must therefore be assumed for the slight tendency of the Jews to suicide in spite of all sorts of circumstances that might on the contrary incline them to it. Doubtless they owe this immunity in a sense to the hostility surrounding them. But if this is its influence, it is not because it imposes a higher morality but because it obliges them to live in greater union. They are immune to this degree because their religious society is of such solidarity. Besides, the ostracism to which they are subject is only one of the causes producing this result; the very nature of Jewish beliefs must contribute largely to it. Judaism, in fact, like all early religions, consists basically of a body of practices minutely governing all the details of life and leaving little free room to individual judgement.

The beneficent influence of religion is therefore not due to the special nature of religious conceptions. If religion protects man against the desire for self-destruction, it is not that it preaches the respect for his own person to him with arguments *sui generis;* but because it is a society. What constitutes this society is the existence of a certain number of beliefs and practices common to all the faithful, traditional and thus obligatory. The more numerous and strong these collective states of mind are, the stronger the integration of the religious community, and also the greater its preservative value. The details of dogmas and rites are secondary. The essential thing is that they be capable of supporting a sufficiently intense collective life.

So we reach the general conclusion: suicide varies inversely with the degree of integration of the social groups of which the individual forms a part.

PART 3

SOCIAL INEQUALITY

Social inequality is a core—some would say the central—sociological problem. It has provoked and confounded analysts since the founding of the discipline. For example, the simplification of the capitalist class system forecast by Marx never took place. Instead of polarizing around a large class of impoverished workers and a tiny class of wealthy capitalists, the stratification system became more complex. Small business owners did not disappear. In recent years they have actually become more numerous as a proportion of the economically active population. What C. Wright Mills called an "occupational salad" of "white-collar" personnel—professionals, educated office holders, clerks, and so forth— became the largest component of the stratification system. Manual or "blue-collar" workers experienced a rising standard of living (at least until the early 1970s) while their numbers as a proportion of the total labour force shrunk. The revolution that Marx expected never happened.

Poverty persists nonetheless. According to the government-funded National Council of Welfare, about one out of nine Canadians was in the low-income category in 2004. Moreover, poverty has been feminized: a substantial majority of poor adults are women. True, most adult women now work for a wage in the paid labour force, a development unforeseen by Marx, Weber, Durkheim, and other classical sociological writers. On the other hand, women tend to be segregated in "pink-collar" jobs—occupations that pay relatively low wages and are analogous to women's traditional family roles as servers, teachers, and nurturers. Even today, it is uncommon for women to have authority over men in the workplace, and even intimate relations between women and men are strongly influenced by the distribution of authority between the sexes.

Another unanticipated development in the realm of social stratification concerns the tenacity of ethnic and racial inequality, which the founders of sociology expected to disappear under capitalism. They believed that large factories and bureaucracies would, in effect, homogenize people, forcing them to work together, treating them all the same, and making cultural differences between them less pronounced. In the event, although ethnic and racial stratification has declined in Canada and many other places, different ethnic and racial groups still tend to occupy definite niches in the social hierarchy.

These are some of the key problems in stratification research and some of the chief issues examined in the chapters that follow.

PART 3A

CLASS AND GENDER INEQUALITY

The results of the first survey of ultra-affluent Canadians were released in 2006. With a net worth of $10 million or more, the ultra-affluent can easily afford more than two luxury cars each on average. Mercedes, BMWs, and Porsches are their top choices. They typically collect art (90 percent), antiques (72 percent), and fine wines (69 percent). The ultra-affluent are apparently pragmatic. Thus, while they contribute generously to philanthropic causes, their main reason for doing so is that it provides strategic personal tax and estate benefits. Their second reason for giving to charities is that it makes good sense in terms of providing opportunities for developing business relationships. Just like you and me, the ultra-affluent worry. After all, the rate of inflation for luxury items, including high-end German automobiles, art, antiques, and fine wines, is two or three times higher than the inflation rate for the goods and services consumed by the general population. And they are deeply concerned that their children will develop "affluenza," a rare disease whose symptoms include a lack of ambition brought on by a life of extraordinary privilege. (Okay, so maybe they don't worry just like you and me.)

Meanwhile, since the early 1970s, the average real income (or "purchasing power") of Canadians has risen little, substantially modifying the post–World War II trend to higher real incomes. Also since the early 1970s, income inequality has increased. The richest 20 percent of Canadians earn a larger share of total national income than they did 30 years ago, the middle 60 percent earn less, and the poorest 20 percent earn about the same. In 2004, the share of total after-tax national income earned by the richest 20 percent of Canadian families was 40 percent. The middle 60 percent of Canadians earned about 53 percent of after-tax national income. The share of after-tax national income earned by the bottom 20 percent of Canadian families was just 7 percent.

Poverty remains a serious and persistent problem in Canada, as Ann Duffy and Nancy Mandell show in Chapter 11. Statistics Canada sets **Low Income Cut-offs (LICOs).** These are the income levels below which people are considered to live in "straitened circumstances." Below the LICOs, people must spend more than 54.7 percent of their gross income on bare essentials (food, clothing, and shelter). Using that standard, the percentage of Canadians below the LICOs fell between the end of World War II and the early 1970s, remained fairly steady at about one-eighth of the population up to the early 1990s, and rose to about one-sixth of the population by the end of the 1990s. In 2004, 11.2 percent of Canadians—about 3.5 million people—earned a low income. Most low-income people work for a living, but lone women and their small children comprise a higher proportion than formerly. As Duffy and Mandell document, the social and personal costs of poverty remain staggering.

Although fundamentally important, it would be naive to reduce social inequality to the economic dimension. As Max Weber emphasized a century ago, inequalities in power and prestige also stratify society, and they do not precisely parallel economic inequalities. A poor priest may be held in high esteem, just as a rich criminal may be vilified.

Nor do inequalities exist simply as objective facts in the world outside our minds. We internalize inequalities, bringing them into our consciousness and our self-image. High self-regard is by no means the least important privilege that accompanies money, power, and honour, and low self-esteem can crush one's spirit every bit as effectively as hunger.

In a rare type of study, Julie Ann McMullin and John Cairney use survey data to trace the effects of gender, class, and age on Canadians' self-esteem. They find that self-esteem declines with age, is lower for women than men, and declines with income only when people reach middle age. For reasons that McMullin and Cairney examine in fascinating detail in Chapter 12, gender and age wear away inexorably at one's self-esteem, but, as in so many other areas of social life, class softens their effects remarkably effectively.

GLOSSARY

The **Low Income Cut-off** is the income level below which people are considered to live in "straitened circumstances." Below the LICO, people must spend more than 54.7 percent of their gross income on bare essentials (food, clothing, and shelter).

CRITICAL THINKING QUESTIONS

1. Why are Canadian women and children at greater risk of being poor than men? What social factors are responsible for this?
2. How do gender, class, and age influence Canadians' self-esteem? Describe their independent and combined effects; that is, how each factor influences self-esteem on its own and how the factors operate together.

ANNOTATED BIBLIOGRAPHY

Armstrong, Pat, and Hugh Armstrong. *The Double Ghetto: Canadian Women and Their Segregated Work.* 3rd ed. Toronto: Oxford University Press, 2001. A classic account of gender inequality in Canada.

Breen, Richard, and David B. Rottman. *Class Stratification: A Comparative Perspective.* New York: Harvester Wheatsheaf, 1995. A concise and incisive overview of class stratification theories.

Curtis, James, Edward Grabb, and Neil Guppy, eds. *Social Inequality in Canada: Patterns, Problems, Policies.* 4th ed. Scarborough, ON: Prentice-Hall Canada, 2003. A definitive collection of up-to-date research on social stratification in Canada.

Chapter 11

Poverty in Canada

ANN DUFFY AND NANCY MANDELL

POVERTY IN CANADA TODAY

Poverty is one of the great unresolved and often ignored social issues facing Canadians. Although Canada numbers among the wealthiest countries in the world, many of its citizens, especially children, the disabled, and single mothers, are unable to escape the debilitating effects of poverty. In some respects, the public record reveals not only failure but growing failure as the poverty profile of Canada has worsened in some segments of the population, notably among recent immigrants.

Evidence of the problem is everywhere. In virtually every small town and city, the persistent appeals from food banks speak to the hunger in our midst. By 2005, 823 856 Canadians had used a food bank at some time. Since 1989, food bank use has increased 118 percent. There are now 650 food banks across the country. Despite the 16-year-old promise to end child poverty, 41 percent of food bank clients are children. Most food bank users depend on social assistance, suggesting that current welfare payments are inadequate to meet families' basic needs for food (Canadian Association of Food Banks, 2005). Equally grim reminders of poverty can be found during any walk through the inner core of one of our major cities. There, huddled on hot air gratings or squatting in bus shelters, it is easy to find some of the estimated 33 000 homeless Canadians (Covenant House Toronto, 2006). About one-third of homeless Canadians are under the age of 25. Often driven out of their homes by years of abuse, they seek refuge in shelters or squats, and rely on panhandling, prostitution, or other crime to survive the violence and exploitation that pervade the street. These are the most visible symptoms of Canada's poverty. But behind closed doors are hundreds of thousands more poor Canadians—some relying on social assistance or disability income, some depending on minimum wage employment, and all struggling to keep going in a society that ignores their plight.

Despite solid evidence, it is difficult for some people to appreciate the extent of poverty in Canada. It is easy to see that hordes of homeless, starving children in nineteenth-century Montreal (or modern Somalia) were poor; it is more difficult to identify contemporary Canadians who have too little to get by, who need to choose between paying the rent or feeding the kids, and who are unable to participate in any meaningful fashion in the social, political, educational, and spiritual life of the nation. While these individuals are not necessarily starving or homeless, they are deeply deprived.

For years, government agencies, social researchers, and advocacy groups have struggled to arrive at meaningful standards of impoverishment—level of family income, cost of housing, food, clothing, fuel, and so on. To date, Canada has not arrived at an "official" definition of poverty. In recent years the definitional debate has persisted since almost any definition of poverty draws a somewhat arbitrary line below

Source: This is a revised and updated version of Ann Duffy and Nancy Mandell, "Poverty in Canada," in Dan Glenday and Ann Duffy, eds., *Canadian Society: Meeting the Challenges of the Twenty-First Century.* Don Mills, ON: Oxford University Press, 2001, pp. 86–101. Copyright © Oxford University Press Canada 2001. Reprinted by permission of Oxford University Press Canada.

which the "poor" live (Broadbent, 2005; National Council of Welfare, 1999; *Toronto Star*, 1999; Burman, 1996: 19–23; Sarlo, 1992). The resultant definitions of poverty are always vulnerable to political pressures and agendas. Employing a stricter or more lenient definition to count the poor may, at the stroke of a pen, dramatically reduce or increase the number of poor. For governments who are seeking to respond painlessly and inexpensively to pressures for social reform, "reduction by redefinition" is a tempting alternative.

Keeping in mind these ongoing definitional debates, the best known and most widely used poverty measure in Canada is the Statistics Canada definition (adopted in 1973; reset in 1992). It establishes income cut-offs below which people are considered to live in "straitened circumstances." The cut-offs are based on the notion that poor families must spend more than 54.7 percent of their gross income on food, clothing, and shelter, leaving few or no funds for transportation, health, personal care, education, household operation, recreation, or insurance. These income cut-offs vary by household size and the size of one's area or residence, resulting in 35 low income cut-offs. For example, a single person living in Toronto in 2004 on less than $20 337 was considered "poor" by the Statistics Canada definition (1992 base), while a two-person family living on less than $17 429 in a rural area was deemed poor (National Council of Welfare, 2005: 94).

While the Statistics Canada parameters provide us with a revealing picture of poverty in Canada, it has serious limitations. Specifically:

- It leaves out Aboriginal reserves; institutional inmates (homes for the aged, prisons); residents of the Yukon, the Northwest Territories, and Nunavut; and the homeless. It tells us nothing about the duration of poverty; that is, how long any one individual is poor (Canada and the World Backgrounder, 2005a).

- Considerable debate exists about adjustments by location. According to Statistics Canada, it is 31 percent less expensive to live in rural areas. But while research suggests that shelter costs are lower in rural areas than in the city, transportation costs are higher. Furthermore, access to subsidized public services such as child-care, health services, and education, as well as to competitively priced goods, are less accessible in many rural areas. The Canadian Council on Social Development calculates that rural costs are probably about 88 percent of those in large urban centres, but also points out that there are considerable differences between cities. In short, adjustments by location are likely inaccurate.

- Some analysts argue that, given the large tax bite, income cut-offs should be based on after-tax income.

- Statistics Canada measures ignore differences in the actual level of need in the household. For example, caring for a child with a severe disability while lacking access to subsidized services may significantly increase household economic needs (Canada and the World Backgrounder 2005a; Ross, 2000).

- Finally, the Statistics Canada measure of poverty reinforces the notion that there are two kinds of people: the poor and the non-poor. This is a split that is too easily translated into "us" and "them" and sustains stereotypes of the poor as somehow different and, possibly, defective. In fact, poverty is a fluid category. In the course of a year or two, low-income Canadians may drift in and out of officially defined poverty. Research examining low-income patterns between 1982 and 1993 found that most people had only one spell of low income within this time, lasting on average two years. The chance of a period of low income ending after one year was better than 50 percent; for 60 percent of the poor, a period of low income was a temporary setback, not a persistent problem (Laroche, 1998). Unemployment, illness, accident, marital breakup, or disability may, even in the course of a month, tip the balance. Similarly, in the course of a lifetime, a variety of factors (gender, age, marital status, and number of children) may trigger a slide into poverty. Given these patterns, the problem of poverty needs to be understood as encompassing a broad continuum of individuals and families both below and above the designated poverty line and influenced by powerful social forces.

The poor are far from a homogeneous group. In the first place, they do not consist solely of people on welfare. Many poor Canadians are employed, but their wages are so low that they do not exceed Statistics Canada's Low Income Cut-off (LICO) levels. However, without exception across Canada, if you are among the 1.7 million Canadian children, women, and men living on welfare income, you are living in poverty, that is, below the LICO (National Council of Welfare, 2005: IX). For example, in 2004, basic welfare assistance plus various benefits and credits resulted in a total annual income of $12 684 for a single Nova Scotian parent with one child. The same family would receive a total income from the same sources of $13 778 in British Columbia. If we examine the LICOs for 2004 we see that regardless of whether this family was living in a big city, a small town, or a rural area, they would be living significantly below the LICO. Welfare income levels range from a high of $25 319 for a two-person family living in a big city to a low of $14 000 for the same family living in a rural area (National Council of Welfare, 2005: 17, 20, 94). Indeed, the best possible welfare outcome is for a single parent with one child living in Newfoundland, who would be earning $15,228; in other words, 70 percent of the low-income level set by Statistics Canada. The worst off are single employable people living in New Brunswick, who receive $3 388—a scant 19 percent of the LICO. Most Canadians who rely on welfare payments must get by with about 50 percent of the low-income levels (National Council

of Welfare, 2005: 29). Note also that over the course of the past two decades, the dollar value of welfare benefits has steadily eroded because of cuts in welfare benefits as well as the lack of annual cost-of-living adjustments. The net result is that welfare benefits for a single parent with one child living in Quebec dropped by 29.1 percent from 1994 to 2004 and in Ontario by 71.2 percent (National Council of Welfare, 2005: 44–46). These patterns help explain why so many food bank clients are welfare recipients.

In addition to the poor who rely solely on welfare, many other Canadians—the "working poor"—are poor because their earnings from work are below the low income cut-offs. In some instances these people include welfare recipients since they are often allowed, even encouraged, to improve their economic situation by taking paid employment. This encouragement takes the form of monthly "earnings exemptions," meaning that welfare recipients are allowed to keep a portion of their earned income without it being deducted from their welfare income. These exemptions vary from province to province, by the overall employability of the individual and by the size of the family. In some provinces, they include work-related expenses such as the cost of child-care. Although the provincial and territorial governments are intent on reducing welfare rolls, and despite the low level of welfare support, some recent policy initiatives on earnings exemptions make it difficult for welfare recipients to take on paid work. For example, in 2002, British Columbia eliminated earnings exemptions for employable recipients, which means that for every dollar earned a dollar is deducted from the person's welfare cheque. The message, it would seem, is either not to work or to work illegally (National Council of Welfare, 2005: 79–86).

In short, many individuals and families are poor in Canada even though they are employed. Despite combining paid earnings with welfare or pension income, they still fall below the low income cut-offs. In addition, there are many poor Canadians, especially working-age individuals and families, who draw all their income from paid employment. According to the 2001 Census, 460 000 Canadians comprised the working poor. Because they are poorly paid—often their jobs are short term, seasonal, contract-based, and in low-wage segments of the economy such as the sales and service industries—they also live in poverty (Canada and the World Backgrounder, 2005b).

Poverty is a given for the more than half a million (547 000) Canadians who are working at or below the minimum wage set by their province (Tabi and Sussman, 2004). As poverty activists point out, to live above the approximately $20 000 a year LICO, a Canadian would have to earn $10.00 per hour and work full time, year round. Nowhere in Canada do minimum wage rates reach that standard; they vary from a low of $6.40 (January 2006) in New Brunswick to a high of $8.50 in Nunavut (March 2003). Ontario's minimum wage standards will reach $8.00 in February 2007 (Hewlett, 2005). While almost two-thirds of minimum-wage workers are under 25, a sizeable portion (31 percent) are adult workers aged from 25 to 54, and the overwhelming majority (two-thirds) of all minimum-wage workers are women (Tabi and Sussman, 2004). It is inside this pattern that we can locate the single mother who, despite her full-time employment, is living below the LICO, or the two-income teen family that earns $27 000 a year—$5 000 below the poverty line in Ontario. Whenever the worker is a single parent, when only one parent in the family is employed, when the work is minimum wage, part time, contract, short term, irregular, or unskilled, and when there are dependent children in the home, employment frequently fails to provide an escape from poverty (Kazemipur and Halli, 2000; Ross, Shillington, and Lochhead, 1994: 76–79; Gunderson and Muszynski, 1990: 68–71).

Taken as a whole, the portrait of poverty in Canada today is sobering. In 2004, 7.8 percent of Canadian families (684 000 families) were low income. An estimated 865 000 young people (12.8 percent of all Canadians under age 18) were living in poverty, down from a peak of 18.6 percent in 1996. Some 36 percent of lone-parent families headed by women were low income, down from a high of 53 percent in 1996. Almost 30 percent of unattached individuals and 5.6 percent of people above the age of 64 were living below the LICO. The low-income rate for seniors aged 65 and older has been cut dramatically since 1980 and stood at just 5.6 percent in 2004 (Statistics Canada, 2006a). This success story, along with improvements in the poverty rate for single mothers, are frequently cited as evidence that big victories can be won in the struggle against poverty.

Persistent low income tends to be concentrated among single parents, recent immigrants, people with work disabilities, unattached people between the ages of 45 and 64, and off-reserve Aboriginal people—members of these groups make up 62 percent of all people persistently below the LICO from 1996 to 2000 (Picot and Myles, 2005). The uneven geographic distribution of some of these groups—for example, recent immigrants, who tend to concentrate in Montreal, Toronto, and Vancouver—likely contributes to a distinct regional dimension in Canadian poverty. For example, according to 2003 statistics, child poverty averaged 17.6 percent in Canada but ranged from a high of 23.9 percent in British Columbia to a low of 11.3 percent on Prince Edward Island (First Call B.C. Child and Youth Advisory Council, 2005). Age is another critical determinant of poverty rates. Young families (couples with children) headed by people under the age of 25 are much more likely to be poor, as are single, widowed, and divorced women over the age of 64 (Canada and the World Backgrounder, 2005b). Families and individuals with a low level of education are more likely to be poor, as are families with only one wage-earner. Not surprisingly, participation in the paid labour force is directly related to poverty rates, with "a good job [being] the best insurance against poverty for Canadians under the age of 65" (ibid.; Lawton, 1998). Disability is a key determinant of impoverishment; 36.1 percent of people with disabilities live below the poverty line (Canada and the World

Backgrounder, 2005b). Increasingly, recent immigrant status is being recognized as an important contributor to the poverty rate. Regardless of the immigrant's age and educational background, and despite an immigration policy that has strategically selected highly skilled immigrants, there is a growing poverty and earnings gap between immigrants and Canadians who are native-born (Picot, 2004; Picot and Myles, 2005: 20). In 1980, 25 percent of recent immigrants were living below the LICO. By 2000, this figure increased to 36 percent (Statistics Canada, 2005a).

THE FEMINIZATION OF POVERTY

Canadian women are particularly at risk of being poor. The "feminization of poverty" refers to the fact that women in many industrialized Western nations, as well as in developing countries, are more likely to be poor than men (Pearce, 1978; Goldberg, 1990; Nelson 2006). Women comprise 57 percent of poor Canadian adults (National Council of Welfare, 1999: 99). Women have a higher poverty rate than men at every age level (National Council of Welfare, 1998a: 19, 36, 85). Nor is this a new problem. The ranks of the poor have long been populated by women who are deserted, widowed, or orphaned (Katz, 1975: 60).

While the reasons behind women's impoverishment are complex, they have much to do with traditional gender ideology, inequities in the labour force, flaws in family law, and the way we respond to marriage breakdown as a society. For generations, women have been expected to devote their lives to their unpaid duties in marriage and motherhood. Although many wives and mothers also worked for pay, such work was generally restricted. Lower pay rates for women, rules against the employment of married women, and the peripheralization and stigmatization of "women's work" all reinforced the notion that women's place was in the home (Duffy and Pupo, 1992: 13–40).

Throughout the twentieth century, however, these notions came under increasing attack. The women's movement, advanced education for women, and the reduction in family size, among other factors, undermined the traditional sexual division of labour. In particular, increasing numbers of Canadians have found that they cannot survive on the uncertain income of a single breadwinner. The failure of wages to keep pace with inflation, increases in taxation, high unemployment, and the loss of high-paying industrial and resource-extraction jobs have made the male-breadwinner family increasingly anachronistic. By 2003, 63 percent of women with children under age three were in the paid labour force (Statistics Canada, 2003: 7).

However, significant gender differences in work and family life persist. Many mothers continue to take time away from paid employment when their children are young and/or balance family and paid work with part-time or self-employed work (Jackson, 2005). Women who live a more traditional life—that is, marry, have children, and assume primary responsibility for domestic and child-care work—risk impoverishment. Even if they minimize their paid work interruptions or consistently maintain a presence in the part-time labour force, they run the risk of low income if their marriage ends in divorce or early widowhood. Being employed in traditionally low-paid women's occupations and taking time off to care for young children can result in economic disaster when a marriage ends in divorce, when women face long years of widowhood, or when women become single parents. These employment inequities are likely to be exacerbated if a woman is a recent immigrant or disabled or a member of a visible minority.

Single parenthood, typically the result of divorce, can have devastating effects on women's economic well-being. More than one in three single-parent mothers are poor, in contrast to a poverty rate of less than 10 percent for single-parent fathers (Statistics Canada, 2003, 2006b). Without a male breadwinner in the family and with inadequate or nonexistent support payments, many women cannot provide adequate income for their families and are likely to sink deep into poverty.

Single parenting is particularly devastating economically when combined with youthfulness or young children. Single-parent mothers under the age of 25 have a staggering poverty rate of more than 93 percent, and single-parent mothers with children under age 7 have an 80 percent rate (National Council of Welfare, 1999). However, contrary to powerful stereotypes, single mothers are not primarily teenagers having numerous babies so they can live off welfare payments. Teenage mothers comprise only 3 percent of all single parents on welfare. Forty-nine percent of single mothers have one child, and another 31 percent have two children (National Council of Welfare, 1998b: 33).

For many of these women, low income is a direct consequence of marriage breakup. The Economic Council of Canada's five-year survey of Canadian incomes found women's incomes dropped by 39 percent when they separated or divorced and rose only slightly thereafter. Three years after the marriage breakup, women's incomes were still 27 percent below their earlier level. Men's income, in contrast, increased by an average of 7 percent. Along with the labour force inequalities discussed above, inadequate support payments produce the inequity (Economic Council of Canada, 1992: 49).

Despite the neediness of single mothers, social policy initiatives have often tended to make their situation worse. For example, in Ontario, single welfare mothers of school-age children are required to sign up for workfare, and these mothers, along with other welfare recipients, have faced dramatic reductions in the dollar value of their welfare benefits. ("Workfare" is the social policy that requires able-bodied recipients of social welfare benefits to take some form of employment.) Similarly, in Alberta, new regulations restrict both eligibility for support and amount of welfare payments while also mandating that welfare recipients par-

ticipate in job training programs (Breitkreuz, 2005). Unfortunately, these efforts have tended to address inadequately the particular problems of single mothers—notably, the need for reliable, low-cost child-care and the inadequacy of women's jobs in the low-wage, low-skill sector of the market economy.

To further compound their plight, single mothers must also confront the persistent tendency to stigmatize mothers on welfare as somehow being less worthy of social support than, for example, low-income two-parent families. Popular opinion suggests that single mothers who receive social assistance are simply being encouraged to have more children.

Growing old provides no guarantee of relief for women. While policy initiatives in the 1980s and 1990s eased much of the poverty burden for the elderly, it has by no means been eliminated. Unattached women over the age of 64—typically widowed, divorced, or separated—face high rates of poverty. In 2001, 43 percent of unattached elderly women were living in poverty, and women comprised 70 percent of all poor unattached Canadians over the age of 65 (Gazso, 2005; Statistics Canada, 2006a). Unattached women aged 75 and older experience even higher rates of impoverishment. Women are particularly at risk because they are less likely to receive income from occupational pension plans, the Canada/Quebec Pension Plan, and investments. The traditional pattern—work interruptions to take care of family responsibilities, work in low-paying jobs with poor benefits, and part-time and contractual work—contribute to high rates of female impoverishment whenever women find themselves without a spouse (McDonald, 1997). These patterns also mean that women may not be able to access adequate government pension benefits to top up their income in old age and may not be able to save for their retirement through private savings plans (Gazso, 2005: 59; Statistics Canada, 2006b). In short, the traditional social structural parameters of women's lives put them at risk if they end up on their own. They are likely to confront this fate. Based on current trends in marriage, divorce, and life expectancy, an estimated 84 percent of Canadian women can expect to spend a portion of their adult lives without a male breadwinner in the home—as pregnant teens, single mothers, divorced middle-aged workers, and/or elderly widows (National Council of Welfare, 1990: 17). Yet few Canadian women live with these expectations and fewer still plan their work and marital lives to bring them financial independence and solvency (Duffy, Mandell, and Pupo, 1988). In a society that perpetuates unrealistic notions of romantic love, marital life, and parenting, and in an economy premised on the peripheralized, low-wage, ghettoized work of women, many women continue to be set up for poverty.

Predictably, certain groups of women—immigrant women, the disabled, minority women, and Native Canadians—are at greater risk. Native women, for example, have lower than average labour force participation rates, lower than average earnings, and substantially higher rates of unemployment, partly because of the remote, rural areas in which many of them live (Federal, Provincial, and Territorial Advisory Committee, 1999: 47; Abella, 1984). Visible minority and immigrant women frequently find that racial and ethnic discrimination, along with language difficulties and inadequate government policy, translate into long hours of low-wage work (Kazemipur and Halli, 2000; National Council of Welfare, 1990: 118–27). Foreign-born elderly women in all marital categories have lower average income than their Canadian-born counterparts. Elderly women who are recent immigrants or who come from less developed countries receive particularly low incomes (Boyd, 1989). Although most disabled adults live on low income, disabled women are generally worse off than their male counterparts (Ross and Shillington, 1989: 28; Barile, 1992).

THE POVERTY OF CHILDREN

Interwoven with the impoverishment of women and families is the poverty of children. Some 865 000 children—12.8 percent of Canadian children in 2004—are growing up in low-income families (Statistics Canada, 2006a). Despite a unanimous vote in the House of Commons in 1989 to eradicate child poverty by the year 2000, the Canadian child poverty rate grew from 1989 to 1996 and remains high today (National Council of Welfare, 1999). Although the number of Canadian children increased by 6 percent between 1989 and 1997, the number of poor children rose by 37 percent in the same period. Children have a consistently higher rate of poverty than adults under the age of 65 (Crane, 1999; National Council of Welfare, 1999). Placed in an international context, this is a bleak record. Canada ranked 19th out of 26 developed countries in child poverty, better than the United States and Britain, but worse than the Czech Republic, Hungary, and Poland (Canada and the World Backgrounder, 2005c).

Part of the reason for increasing child poverty is the increase in single-parent families. For example, in British Columbia, which has experienced a dramatic rise in child poverty, almost two-thirds of children living in families headed by lone-parent mothers are poor in contrast to only 15 percent of children in two-parent families (First Call B.C. Child and Youth Advisory Council, 2005). These children are poor because their parents are poor and their parents' poverty often stems from unemployment, underemployment, inadequate minimum-wage levels, and reduced social welfare supports.

Other factors intensify the problem. For example, Aboriginal children not living on reserves have a poverty rate that is almost that of non-Aboriginal children (First Call B.C. Child and Youth Advisory Council, 2005). Poverty among children from recent two-parent immigrant families has grown dramatically—from 22 percent in 1980 to 39 percent in 2001 (Canadian Council on Social Development, 2003).

THE CHANGING FACE OF POVERTY

Over time, the face of poverty has changed. In the 1960s and early 1970s, there were significant reductions in the rate and depth of poverty (Economic Council of Canada, 1992: 2). Progress slowed during the 1970s, and since 1973, the poverty rate has tended to fluctuate with the health of the economy (Ross and Shillington, 1989: 21; National Council of Welfare, 1988: 1). From the early 1980s to 1995 the poverty rate declined little and actually increased among some types of families (Zyblock and Lin, 1997). Recent evidence suggests a decline in the fortunes of people with low income. Most of the economic gains of the 1990s went to higher income families while the incomes of poor families remained the same and social transfer payments (child benefits, welfare payments) were reduced. The overall result was an increase in family income inequality. In other words, there was a widening gap between "have" and "have-not" families (Picot and Myles, 2005). Canadian families with children in the poorest 10 percent of the income spectrum experienced an 8 percent increase in income from 1993 to 2003. In contrast, families with children in the wealthiest 10 percent of income earners experienced a 35 percent increase in income. In relative terms at least, the poor are losing ground while the economic well-being of the wealthy is increasing by leaps and bounds (Canadian Council on Social Development, 2003; First Call B.C. Child and Youth Advisory Council, 2005).

Amid these troubling shifts, seniors remain the outstanding success story, demonstrating that poverty is neither inevitable nor irreversible. Policy changes, including the creation of the federal Guaranteed Income Supplement in 1967 for low-income seniors, the creation of the Canada/Quebec Pension Plan in 1966, and the implementation of provincial supplements have meant a dramatic decrease from the nearly 34 percent poverty rate among seniors in 1980

to just 5.6 percent in 2004 (Canadian Council on Social Development, 2003; National Council of Welfare, 1999: 19, 20; Statistics Canada, 2006b).

THE LOST GENERATION: THE POVERTY OF YOUNG ADULTS

One recent, alarming poverty trend, signified by the appearance of food banks on some university campuses, is the growing vulnerability of young adults (McGrath, 1998). Young people who marry and have dependents are in a particularly difficult economic position. Although in 1997 young families (those headed by someone under the age of 25) comprised only 4 percent of all Canadian families, they accounted for 11 percent of poor families; 43 percent of young families were below the LICO (Crane, 1999).

Currently, just under half of young adults in Canada have not completed a post-secondary qualification. A generation ago they might have been able to find good-paying, secure employment in the manufacturing sector but the economy has changed profoundly since then. Most employment growth has been in the service sector. As a result, young, poorly educated workers often find themselves trapped in part-time, dead-end, minimum-wage jobs (Jackson, 2005). In light of the kinds of employment available to many young people, and declining earnings among young Canadians, it is not surprising that median net worth of Canadian households where the major income recipient was between 15 and 34 years old was just $18 800, compared to $99 500 for those with an earner between 35 and 44 years old (Sauve, 2002–03). Lacking the financial resources and economic security to launch an independent adult life, many young adults must choose between prolonged dependency (as reflected in rising numbers of young adults living with their parents) and struggling to survive on a low income (Myles, 2005).

CANADIAN POVERTY IN AN INTERNATIONAL CONTEXT

Canadians often take comfort in the fact that the pattern of social inequality in Canada is better than that of the United States. In the United States, the top 1 percent of Americans own 38 percent of the nation's wealth and the bottom 40 percent own 1 percent. The bottom 20 percent of U.S. income earners not only have more debt than assets, but their incomes have barely grown in real terms since the mid-1970s (Canada and the World Backgrounder, 2004). Not surprisingly, these patterns are reflected in overall poverty rates. In 2002, when Canada's poverty rate was about 10 percent, in the United States it reached 17 percent. Furthermore, 31 percent of the U.S. poor were victims of persistent poverty (five years or more) in contrast to 24 percent of the Canadian poor (Statistics Canada, 2005a). Similarly, the U.S. child poverty rate was 7 percent higher than the Canadian rate.

However, when we compare Canadian to countries other than the United States, we find less reason for pride. In Sweden, for example, only about 6 percent of the population is poor—and less than 3 percent of all children (Jackson, 2002; Canada and the World Backgrounder, 2005c). Finland and Belgium successfully reduced poverty among lone-parent families, and Germany and the United Kingdom have substantially reduced the percentage of persistently poor people (Picot and Myles, 2005). In almost all of these success stories, the government has allocated significant resources to address poverty.

STRUGGLING WITH POVERTY: THE PERSONAL EXPERIENCE

Being poor has always meant much more than getting by at some arbitrary level of income, and understanding poverty demands more than a statistical overview. Poverty often affects people's lives, their sense of self, and their most important relationships with others. Although the toll of poverty is most apparent in the lives of children, few adults survive impoverishment unscathed (Abernathy, Webster, and Vermeulen, 2002).

For children and their families, poverty still generally translates into inadequate housing. In Calgary, Edmonton, Vancouver, and Toronto, as well as on remote reserves, poor children are likely to live with substandard heating, too little hot water, improper ventilation, generally unsafe conditions (exposed wiring and electrical outlets and so on), and too little space in which to play and study (Bragg, 1999). Even inadequate housing in large metropolitan areas may gobble up social assistance benefits, leaving little for other necessities, let alone for emergencies (Spears, 1999). Housing problems are frequently compounded by neighbourhoods plagued with high rates of crime and vandalism, inadequate play facilities, and hazardous traffic (Marsden, 1991: 8; Kitchen et al., 1991: 6).

Poor families also often lack the income to maintain a nutritious diet. High housing costs and the spectre of homelessness mean that food budgets are stretched to the limit. The end result may be ill health and frequent hospitalization, even among infants (Seguin et al., 2003). While Canada's food banks and soup kitchens provide a stop-gap solution for many families, many poor children clearly get by on too little food or food with high fat and sugar content (Kitchen et al., 1991).

Not surprisingly, the poorest of the poor, the homeless, are frequently plagued by health problems, including malnourishment, chronic respiratory and ear infections, gastrointestinal disorders, sexually transmitted diseases, and chronic infections. The psychological health of the poor also reflects the painful social and emotional environment in which they live. The pressure of poverty contributes to family breakdown and dislocation. Life often becomes unpredictable and insecure. Being poor means not knowing whether you will be able to continue living in your home, whether you will retain custody of your children, or whether your children will have to change schools and make new friends. In these and numerous other ways, the foundations of one's life may be shattered. Living with this profound uncertainty inevitably takes a toll on self-confidence and hopefulness (Neal, 2004).

Evidence also suggests that poor families are more subject to family violence, including child abuse and neglect (Statistics Canada, 2005b; MacLeod, 1987: 20–21; Gelles and Cornell, 1990: 14–15). Growing up poor often means coping with a parent or parents who are struggling with fear, anger, frustration, isolation, and despair. The emotional and psychological realities of poverty are complex, and reactions to poverty reflect the particular personal circumstances and biography of each individual. Many poor adults and children cope with courage, resourcefulness, and a sense of humour, and many poor children grow up with positive adult role models and a strong sense of family loyalty. However, the adults in most poor children's lives are also often deeply troubled by their economic straits. Poverty typically means more than doing without; it means feeling cut off from the mainstream of our consumer society. With few exceptions, the lives and experiences of the poor are not reflected sympathetically on television or in the movies; the advertisements in magazines and on subway trains underscore the insufficiencies of their lifestyle. Mothers must scramble to make sure that their children have the money to "fit in." One mother said, "Another thing that comes out [of the monthly budget] that's very important is the children's milk money for school, and their pizza and hot dog money every week, because they won't be ostracized. I won't have other children saying they're too poor to get those. . . [However, meeting these needs means that] "sometimes I can afford [heating] oil, sometimes I can't" (Power, 2005: 652).

Each day small and large events underscore the poor person's social marginality. When the school organizes a bike hike, children without bikes have to sit in the classroom and do worksheets. Frustrated parents see their children left out and

humiliated: "It visually stamps them as poor. You can hide many things, but when visually you're made poor, then something's bloody wrong" (Women for Economic Survival, 1984: 16). Day by day and incident by incident, the chasm grows between poverty and "normal life," leaving poor adults and their children feeling more isolated, stereotyped, and rejected. A 36-year-old homeless woman comments, "At one point I was sheltered in middle class society. I didn't see a lot of poverty. There is apathy in the general community. It is like they have had enough of poor people. . . . I now know there is discrimination in housing. You can't get a place if you are on welfare. They don't want welfare people. You are demoralized getting on welfare and they want to keep you that way" (Neal, 2004: 25).

When people become poor, it comes as a shock that the negative stereotype now applies to them:

> When I went down there, I felt that I just stuck right out. I thought, "Oh my God, people think I'm on welfare." Typical stereotype I guess you're led to believe. You used to think, "It's those people who are on welfare," and now you discover you're one of those people. (Burman, 1988: 86)

Being one of those people often means living with a stigma. Many poor individuals are ashamed of their identity as poor, seek to hide it whenever possible, and feel there is something "wrong" with them:

> At the beginning [of being unemployed] I was feeling so good about myself that that was a lot easier. . . . Towards the end I was feeling like such a loser. . . . You portray this, it's written all over your face. (Burman, 1988: 196)

Coping with stigmatization may mean being filled with anger at the injustices of a social system that seems to benefit only other people:

> I walked down the street one day. God, how do people buy their clothes, where are they getting their money, how come they have a job? . . . Like, I just thought SHIT! (Burman, 1988: 203)

For some, when the impoverishment seems to grind on endlessly or when their personal situation deteriorates, anger and frustration give way to despair and depression. A recent national health survey of self-reported levels of self-esteem, sense of mastery, and sense of coherence found that larger percentages of those occupying the lowest income levels report low levels of all three measures of psychological well-being (Federal, Provincial, and Territorial Advisory Committee, 1999). Poverty activists report that poor people often talk of periods of hopelessness and suicidal depression.

Many of the poor, who must rely on social assistance for all or part of their income, report that dealing with the social work apparatus compounds feelings of stigmatization and vulnerability. Even when individual welfare workers are helpful and supportive, the relationship between worker and client is structured to erode the autonomy, power, and privacy of the poor. The negativity of some welfare workers exacerbates a bad situation. One single mother comments: "Every time I come back from there I cry. They make you feel so low, they make you feel like you're worthless, and they think they're God because of what they give you. And they give you nothing." (Power, 2005: 649). Another single mother adds: "They [social services] show up at your door unannounced. They're supposed to give you 24 hours notice if they're going to come to your home. . . . They'll degrade you; they'll sit there and they'll humiliate you in a room full of 30 people and think nothing of it" (McIntyre, Officer, and Robinson, 2003: 325). Home visits by welfare workers, personal questions from workers, and the constant fear of being "reported to welfare" for not following the rules tend to undermine clients' sense of personal power and self-confidence.

Problems with the welfare apparatus are complicated by the negative reactions of the general public to welfare recipients. Commonly, landlords will not rent to people on welfare, and women on welfare may find themselves labelled as desperate and available. Degradation becomes part of everyday experience: "And then the taxi driver is looking at you, 'Oh, not another charity case'" (McIntyre et al., 2003: 324). Most commonly, the social assistance recipient has to confront the still popular belief, held by much of the general public as well as many social assistance workers, that people on welfare cheat (Blouin, 1992). Informed by the historical notions that many of the poor are not deserving or should be punished for their plight, attitudes toward the provision of adequate social assistance remain ambivalent at best.

Although a survey of welfare fraud by independent researchers indicates that fewer than 3 percent of the welfare recipients cheat, prominent members of the community continue to protest that the welfare rules on eligibility are too lax and that penalties for welfare abusers are too lenient (Armstrong, 1992: A18; Sweet, 1991a: B1). In comparison, 20 percent of Canadians admit to cheating on their income tax (McCarthy, 1992). Cheating aside, many Canadians continue to hold harsh and unsympathetic attitudes toward welfare recipients while overlooking government subsidies to corporations (Hurtig, 1999).

Despite the enormous pressure to "get back on your feet," there seem to be endless roadblocks on the path to getting off welfare. For many single mothers, adequate child-care support is a major obstacle to employment: "The day care she went to when she was a baby, every day they called. I had just started this job and every day, I swear, every day they were calling me that something was wrong with her. I'd come in, walk in at 9:00, by 10:00 she's got a rash, or pink eye or something and then I had to leave" (Mason 2003: 50). It may seem that every effort to move forward is being undermined: "There are times when I am so scared that I'm not going to find a job, I think, 'What the hell is wrong with me?' I can get scared to death. I'll have periods of insomnia. I'll get very short-tempered with my husband and with the children" (Burman, 1988: 195).

Children, lacking the life experience and coping skills of adults, are also often deeply wounded by poverty and its personal and familial consequences. Certainly, little is accomplished in terms of ensuring loyalty to social institutions and public values. When the adults in their lives are filled with confusion, frustration, anger, rage, humiliation, and fear, when their lives seem beyond their control and beyond hope, the children grow up truly impoverished.

The burdens placed on many poor children perpetuate poverty and economic vulnerability. The fallout often begins before birth with inadequate prenatal nutrition and health care. Poor children are twice as likely as other children to suffer low birth weight, death in the first year, death from accidents, poor physical health, physical disabilities, and mental disorders (Reitsma-Street et al., 1993: 7). Poor children tend not to do as well as others in school. By age 11, one in three girls from families on social assistance performs poorly in school, repeating a grade or being placed in a special class. Four of 10 children between the ages of 12 and 16 living in subsidized housing perform poorly in school (Offord, 1991: 23). Inevitably, children who do not do well in school are more likely to drop out, and dropouts are more likely to come from single-parent, minority group, or poorly educated families (Denton and Hunter, 1991: 133). Children from poor families are almost twice as likely to drop out of school as children who are not poor. While children of average and low ability from well-to-do families are likely to stay in school, even children of high ability from poor families are likely to succumb to the pressures. Without a private place to study, with parents who are preoccupied with their economic plight, and with the ever-apparent need for more family income, students from poor families often see immediate employment as their best option (Kitchen et al., 1991: 10–11). Unfortunately, in the long run their lack of education and skills may simply perpetuate their own and, later, *their* children's economic and social marginalization. To the degree a society creates the conditions for persistent poverty, it sets the stage for a polarization that may be deeply destructive on the level of the individual, the community, and the larger social order (Valetta, 2005; Reiman, 2001).

REFERENCES

Abella, R. S. 1984. *Equality in Employment: A Royal Commission Report.* Ottawa: Ministry of Supply and Services.

Abernathy, Thomas J., Greg Webster, and Marian Vermeulen. (2002). "Relationship Between Poverty and Health Among Adolescents." *Adolescence,* 37 (145): 55–68.

Armstrong, Jane. (1992). "Is Our Welfare System Being Abused?" *Toronto Star,* 7 March, A7, A18.

Barile, Maria. (1992). "Dis-Abled Women: An Exploited Genderless Under-class." *Canadian Woman Studies,* (Summer): 32–33.

Blouin, Barbara. (1992). "Welfare Workers and Clients: Problems of Sexism and Paternalism." *Canadian Woman Studies,* (Summer): 645.

Boyd, Monica. (1989). "Immigration and Income Security Policies in Canada: Implications for Elderly Immigrant Women." *Population Research and Policy Review,* 8: 5–24.

Bragg, Rebecca. (1999). "Housing Top Priority for Canada's Poor." *Toronto Star,* 26 March, E4.

Breitkreuz, Rhonda. (2005). "Engendering Citizenship? A Critical Feminist Analysis of Canadian Welfare-to-Work Policies and the Employment Experiences of Lone Mothers." *Journal of Sociology and Social Welfare,* 32 (2): 147–165.

Broadbent, Ed. 2005. "Addressing Child Poverty." *Perception* 27 (3/4): 9.

Burman, Patrick. 1988. *Killing Time, Losing Ground: Experiences of Unemployment.* Toronto: Wall & Thompson.

———. 1996. *Poverty's Bonds: Power and Agency in the Social Relations of Welfare.* Toronto: Thompson Educational Publishing.

Canada and the World Backgrounder. (2004). "Survival of the Richest." 70 (1): 17–23.

Canada and the World Backgrounder. (2005a). "Deciding Where Poverty Starts." 70 (5): 4–7.

Canada and the World Backgrounder. (2005b). "Putting a Face on Poverty." 70 (1): 8–11.

Canada and the World Backgrounder. (2005c). "Poor Families Equal Poor Children." 40 (5): 23–27.

Canadian Association of Food Banks. (2005). "Time for Action—Hungercount 2005: Canada's Only Annual Survey of Food Banks and Emergency Food Programs." On the World Wide Web at http://www.cafb-acba.ca.

Canadian Council on Social Development. (2003). "Census Shows Growing Polarization of Income in Canada," 16 May. On the World Wide Web at http://www.ccsd.ca/pr/2003/censusincome.htm.

Covenant House Toronto. (2006). "Facts and Stats About the Homeless." On the World Wide Web at http://www.covenanthouse.on.ca/web/facts_and_stats.html (1 January 2006).

Crane, David. (1999). "Children Are the 'Sound Bite' in Productivity." *Toronto Star,* 15 April, D2.

Denton, Margaret, and Alfred Hunter. (1991). "Education and the Child." In Richard Barnhorst and Laura C. Johnson, eds., *The State of the Child in Ontario* (pp. 117–38). Toronto: Oxford University Press.

Duffy, Ann, Nancy Mandell, and Norene Pupo. (1988). *Few Choices: Women, Work and Family.* Toronto: Garamond Press.

Duffy, Ann, and Norene Pupo. (1992). *Part-Time Paradox: Connecting Gender, Work, and Family.* Toronto: McClelland & Stewart.

Economic Council of Canada. (1992). *The New Face of Poverty: Income Security Needs of Canadian Families.* Ottawa: Ministry of Supply and Services.

Federal, Provincial, and Territorial Advisory Committee on Population Health for the Meeting of Ministers of Health, Charlottetown, PEI. (1999). *Toward a Healthy Future: Second Report on the Health of Canadians.* Ottawa: Minister of Public Works and Government Services.

First Call B.C. Child and Youth Advisory Council. (2005). "B.C. Campaign 2000 Fact Sheets, nos. 1–10." Available on the World Wide Web at http://www.firstcallbc.org/2005FactSheet.pdf.

Gazso, Amber. (2005). "The Poverty of Unattached Senior Women and the Canadian Retirement Income System: A Matter of Blame or Contradiction?" *Journal of Sociology and Social Welfare,* 32 (2): 41–62.

Gelles, Richard J., and Claire P. Cornell. (1990). *Intimate Violence in Families,* 2nd ed. Newbury Park, CA: Sage.

Goldberg, Gertrude Schaffner. 1990. "Canada: Bordering on the Feminization of Poverty." In Goldberg and Eleanor Kremen, eds., *The Feminization of Poverty: Only in America?* (pp. 59–89). New York: Praeger.

Gunderson, Morley, and Leon Muszynski, with Jennifer Keck. (1990). *Women and Labour Market Poverty.* Ottawa: Canadian Advisory Council on the Status of Women.

Hewlett, Dennis. (2005). "The Call for a Living Wage: Activists Fighting for Fair Wages Across the Country." *Canadian Dimension,* 39 (3): 25–28.

Hurtig, Mel. (1999). *Pay the Rent or Feed the Kids: The Tragedy and Disgrace of Poverty in Canada.* Toronto: McClelland & Stewart.

Jackson, Andrew. (2002). "Canada Beats USA—But Loses Gold to Sweden." Canadian Council on Social Development. On the World Wide Web at http://www.ccsd.ca/pubs/2002/olympic/indicators.htm.

———. (2005). *Work and Labour in Canada: Critical Issues.* Toronto: Canadian Scholars' Press.

Katz, Michael B. (1975). *The People of Hamilton, Canada West: Family and Class in a Mid-Nineteenth-Century City.* Cambridge, MA: Harvard University Press.

Kazemipur, A., and S. S. Halli. (2000). *The New Poverty in Canada: Ethnic Groups and Ghetto Neighbourhoods.* Toronto: Thompson Educational Publishing.

Kitchen, Brigitte, Andrew Mitchell, Peter Clutterbuck, and Marvyn Novick. (1991). *Unequal Futures: The Legacies of Child Poverty in Canada.* Toronto: Child Poverty Action Group and the Social Planning council in Metropolitan Toronto.

Laroche, M. (1998). "In and Out of Low Income." *Canadian Social Trends* (Autumn): 20–24.

Lawton, Valerie. (1998). "Plight of the Long-Term Jobless." *Toronto Star,* 7 November, B4.

MacLeod, Linda. (1987). *Battered But Not Beaten: Preventing Wife Battering in Canada.* Ottawa: Canadian Advisory Council on the Status of Women.

Marsden, Lorna, chair. (1991). *Children in Poverty: Toward a Better Future.* Standing Senate Committee on Social Affairs, Science and Technology. Ottawa: Ministry of Supply and Services.

Mason, Robin. (2003). "Listening to Lone Mothers: Paid Work, Family Life, and Child-care in Canada." *Journal of Children and Poverty,* 9 (1): 41–54.

McCarthy, Shawn. (1992). "Ottawa Missing $90 Billion a Year as Cheaters Use Cash to Dodge Taxes." *Toronto Star,* 30 April, A1, A32.

McDonald, Lynn. (1997). "The Invisible Poor: Canada's Retired Widows." *Canadian Journal of Aging,* 16, 3: 553–83.

McGrath, Paul. (1998). "Food Banks Part of Life on Campus," *Toronto Star,* 23 February, F1, F2.

McIntyre, Lynn, Suzanne Officer, and Lynne M. Robinson. (2003). "Feeling Poor: The Felt Experience of Low-Income Lone Mothers." *Affilia,* 18 (3): 316–31.

Myles, John. (2005). "Postponed Adulthood: Dealing with the New Economic Inequality." Canadian Council on Social Development. On the World Wide Web at http://www.ccsd.ca.

National Council of Welfare. (1988). *Poverty Profile 1988.* Ottawa: Ministry of Supply and Services.

———. (1990). *Women and Poverty Revisited.* Ottawa: Ministry of Supply and Services.

———. (1998a). *Poverty Profile 1996.* Ottawa: Minister of Public Works and Government Services Canada.

———. (1998b). *Profiles of Welfare: Myths and Realities.* Ottawa: Minister of Public Works and Government Services Canada.

———. (1999). *Poverty Profile 1997.* Ottawa: Minister of Public Works and Government Services Canada.

———. (2005). *Welfare Incomes 2004.* Ottawa: Minister of Public Works and Government Services of Canada.

Neal, Rusty. (2004). "Voices: Women, Poverty and Homelessness in Canada." Ottawa: The National Anti-Poverty Organization's Study on Homelessness.

Nelson, Adie. (2006). *Gender in Canada,* 3rd ed. Toronto: Pearson Prentice Hall.

Offord, Dan. (1991). "Growing Up Poor in Ontario." *Transition Magazine,* (June): 10–11.

Pearce, Diana. (1978). "The Feminization of Poverty: Women, Work and Welfare." *Urban and Social Change Review,* 11 (Feb.): 28–36.

Picot, Garnett. (2004). "The Deteriorating Economic Welfare of Canadian Immigrants." *The Canadian Journal of Urban Research,* 13 (1): 25–45.

Picot, Garnett, and John Myles. (2005). "Income Inequality and Low Income in Canada: An International Perspective." Statistics Canada Catalogue no. 11F0019MIE. Ottawa: Minister of Industry.

Power, Elaine M. (2005). "The Unfreedom of Being Other: Canadian Lone Mothers' Experiences of Poverty and 'Life on the Cheque.'" *Sociology,* 39 (4): 643–60.

Reiman, Jeffrey. (2001). *The Rich Get Richer and the Poor Get Prison: Ideology, Class and Criminal Justice.* Boston: Allyn and Bacon.

Reitsma-Street, Marge, Richard Carriere, Adje Van de Sande, and Carol Hein. (1993). "Three Perspectives on Child Poverty in Canada." *The Social Worker,* 61, (1): 6–13.

Ross, David. (2000). *The Canadian Fact Book on Poverty*. Ottawa: Canadian Council on Social Development.

Ross, David, and Richard Shillington. (1989). *The Canadian Fact Book on Poverty*. Ottawa: Canadian Council on Social Development.

Ross, David, Richard Shillington, and Clarence Lochhead. (1994). *The Canadian Fact Book on Poverty*. Ottawa: Canadian Council on Social Development.

Sarlo, Christopher. (1992). *Poverty in Canada*. Vancouver: Fraser Institute.

Sauve, Roger. (2002–03). "Rich Canadians, Poor Canadians and Everyone in Between." *Transition Magazine,* 32 (4). On the World Wide Web at http://www.vifamily.ca.

Seguin, Louise, Xu Qian, Louise Potvin, Maria-Victoria Zunzunegui, and Katherine L. Frohlich. (2003). "Effects of Low Income on Infant Health." *Canadian Medical Association Journal,* 168 (12): 153–58.

Spears, John. (1999). "Rent Erodes Tenants' Income, Study Shows." *Toronto Star,* 23 March, A6.

Statistics Canada. (2003). "2001 Census: Analysis Series: Income of Canadian Families." Catalogue no. 96F0030XIE2001014.

———. (2005a). "Study: Trends in Income Inequality in Canada from an International Perspective." *The Daily,* 10 February. Catalogue no. 11-001-XIE.

———. (2005b). "National Longitudinal Survey of Children and Youth: Home Environment, Income and Child Behaviour." *The Daily,* 21 February, 6–9. Catalogue no. 11-001-XIE.

———. (2006a). "Income of Canadians, 2004." *The Daily,* 30 March. On the World Wide Web at http://www.statcan.ca/Daily/English/060330/d060330a.htm (1 April 2006).

———. (2006b). "Women in Canada: A Gender-based Statistical Report." Catalogue no. 89-503-XIE.

Sweet, Lois. (1991a). "Is Welfare Cheating Running Wild?" *Toronto Star,* 2 June, B1, B7.

Tabi, Martin, and Deborah Sussman. (2004). "Minimum Wage Workers." *Perspectives on Labour and Income,* 16 (2): 5–14.

Toronto Star. 1999. "Poverty Can't Be Measured Away," 5 April, A16.

Valetta, Rob. (2005, January 31). "The Ins and Outs of Poverty in Advanced Economies: Poverty Dynamics in Canada, Germany, Great Britain and the United States." Statistics Canada Catalogue no. 75F0002MIE2005001. Income Research Paper Series.

Women for Economic Survival. (1984). *Women and Economic Hard Times: A Record.* Victoria: Women for Economic Survival and the University of Victoria.

Zyblock, Myles, and Zhengxi Lin. (1997). *Trickling Down or Fizzling Out?: Economic Performance, Transfers, Inequality and Low Income.* Ottawa: Statistics Canada.

Chapter 12

How Gender, Class, and Age Affect Self-Esteem

JULIE ANN McMULLIN AND JOHN CAIRNEY

THE PROBLEM STATED

During the early stages of writing this chapter, one of the authors (McMullin) attended a fundraiser for Brescia University College, a small women's school in London, Ontario. The aim of the event was to raise money for scholarships for disadvantaged women. Dini Petty, a famous Canadian journalist, was the guest speaker.

By all accounts, Dini Petty has had a successful career. She began her work as a traffic reporter who flew in a helicopter and reported trouble spots on Toronto's busy streets. Unlike anyone else at the time, however, Ms. Petty decided that she would prefer to both fly the helicopter and report on traffic. Soon she became one of only a few hundred women in the world to have a helicopter license. Ms. Petty subsequently held jobs as a reporter, an anchor for a 6 o'clock TV news show, the host of a Canadian talk show, and most recently, the author of a very good children's story called *The Queen, The Bear, and the Bumblebee.*

When Ms. Petty took the stage at the gala, she presented herself as a confident, self-assured, articulate, and humorous woman. Yet the focus of her talk was on her lifelong struggle to gain self-esteem. "If there were medals awarded for lack of self-esteem," said Petty, "I would have received gold." In her talk, Petty identified two key factors that contributed to her low self-esteem: (1) girls learn at an early age that they need to be nice in order to be liked; and (2) girls face a lot of pressure to be beautiful. Of course, in identifying these factors, Petty concurred with decades of feminist literature. But Petty also talked about her epiphany, the moment at which she looked in the mirror and saw a beautiful person, "both inside and out." She talked about the things she has done over the last few years to gain self-confidence and ultimately self-esteem. Not insignificantly, Petty told the audience that she would soon turn 58, a point which drew applause from some of the listeners, no doubt because she doesn't "look her age."

As Petty noted, self-esteem for young women is linked to cultural notions of beauty and femininity. Young women who perceive themselves as ugly, fat, too short, too tall, and so on, experience lower self-esteem than do those who have more positive assessments of their body (Abell and Richards, 1996). Cultural ideals of female beauty, at least in North America, are also tied to youthful appearance. Women are not considered beautiful if they are wrinkled, grey-haired, or overweight (Abu-Laban and McDaniel, 2001). Hence, one would expect that, among women, self-esteem would diminish with increasing age. Yet this hypothesis stands in contrast to Petty's experience of gaining self-esteem when she was in her fifties.

The fact that Petty's self-esteem did not decline with advancing age, but rather increased markedly, may be tied, at least in part, to her privileged structural location as a white, well-off professional. Most feminist research on self-esteem focuses on young women. Yet in light of what we know about the negative implications of age-discriminating attitudes on perceptions of body and self (Calasanti and Slevin, 2001; Hurde Clarke, 2001), the neglect of research on the relationship between aging and self-esteem is unfortunate.

PREVIOUS RESEARCH

GENDER

Self-esteem is a person's perception of his or her self-worth. The strong and consistent finding regarding gender and self-esteem is that, compared to men, women have lower self-esteem in adulthood (Josephs, Markus, and Tafarodi, 1992). Although boys and girls enjoy about the same level of self-esteem between the ages of 11 and 13, they gradually diverge during the teenage years and adulthood. Boys gain and girls lose a sense of positive self-worth (Rosenfield, 1999).

Several explanations for this relationship exist in the mental health literature. One of the most compelling is Rosenfield's view that men and women have different experiences that begin in early childhood and that are reflections of the *relative power* they enjoy. Relative power, in turn, influences self-appraisal: "Given the power, the responsibility in the public domain, receipt of support, and value placed on masculine pursuits, males generally tend toward high self-esteem" (Rosenfield, 1999: 220).

Two other compelling explanations for gender differences in self-esteem exist. First, people compare their social identities, opinions, and abilities to those of others. To the extent that they feel inferior to those with whom they interact, their self-esteem is negatively affected. This process involves the assessment of self-worth by means of *social comparison*. Second, people assess themselves through their interaction with others. People learn to see themselves as others believe them to be. If significant others do not think highly of a person, that person will come to think poorly of himself or herself. This process is known as the *reflected appraisal* of one's self-worth (Rosenberg and Pearlin, 1978).

Girls and women, more than boys and men, are socially judged on the basis of what they look like. If they diverge from socially constructed cultural ideals of beauty, others may think poorly of them and their self-esteem may suffer (through reflected appraisals). Furthermore, girls and women take part in processes of social comparison whereby they compare their beauty to that of others. If a woman feels less beautiful than the women with whom she interacts, her self-esteem is negatively affected (Abell and Richards, 1996; Furman, 1997). Men also engage in comparative beauty exercises, evaluating the appearance of their body relative to others (Oberg and Tornstam, 1999). But the fact that women place more importance than men on their physical appearance suggests that physical appearance may be more relevant to identity and self-esteem among women than among men.

SOCIAL CLASS

In the literature on the relationship between self-esteem and social class, the latter is typically measured by a person's occupational status, income, and education. In general, adults with low occupational status, income, and education have low social esteem. For instance, as Rosenberg's power theory suggests, individuals who are employed in good jobs that are characterized by high autonomy, prestige, and creativity enjoy higher self-esteem than do unemployed individuals or people who work in "bad" jobs (Gecas and Seff, 1990; Pugliesi, 1995; Rosenberg and Pearlin, 1978; Mirowsky and Ross, 1996).

Explanations of the relationship between self-esteem and social class also consider reflected appraisals and social comparisons (Rosenberg and Pearlin, 1978; Rosenberg, 1981). The reflected appraisals argument suggests that members of the working class have low self-esteem because they are judged negatively by those with whom they interact on the basis of their low-status jobs, incomes, and education. At work, for example, managers tend to see themselves as superior to non-managerial workers and treat them accordingly, while members of the working class are more likely to view themselves as inferior to members of the middle or upper classes. Thus, reflected appraisals and social comparisons negatively influence self-esteem among the working class.

In support of these arguments, Rosenberg and Pearlin (1978) argued that working-class children may not experience the negative perceptions and attitudes about their class as acutely as their parents do. They hypothesized that, as a result, the effects of social class on self-esteem should be greater in adulthood than in childhood. Their research supported their hypothesis. Although their work is now dated, the small body of research that has since been conducted on the relationship between self-esteem and social class confirms their findings (Turner and Roszell, 1994). Perhaps more importantly, the theoretical underpinnings of the argument are sound. The social class homogeneity of many school settings shelters children from social comparisons and reflected appraisals that negatively affect self-esteem.

AGING

Unfortunately, the samples that Rosenberg and Pearlin and others used to test their hypotheses were composed of people under the age of 65. It is therefore unclear how class-based reflected appraisal and social comparison arguments play out in later life. The exclusion of people 65 years old and older is in fact a characteristic of all of the work described above. Only a few studies have explored the relationship between age and self-esteem among the elderly and they have produced mixed results. Some studies show that self-esteem remains stable or increases as people age, others suggest that it decreases, and still others demonstrate that self-esteem first increases with age and then decreases after a certain age (Giarrusso, Mabry, and Bengtson, 2001).

Social scientists have proposed two explanations for the relationship between self-esteem and aging. The *maturation perspective* suggests that as people age they become more accepting of themselves. Proponents of this perspective argue that the process of social comparison is not as pronounced in later life because at that stage individuals develop "ego integrity" and a positive evaluation of their accomplishments

(Dietz, 1996). Consequently, the maturation perspective predicts stable or increasing self-esteem in later life. *Role perspectives* have also been used to explain the relationship between aging and self-esteem. According to role perspectives, the loss of social roles that is associated with old age (e.g., exit from paid work; the so-called empty nest, which involves children growing up and leaving their parents living alone at home) results in lower self-esteem.

A key problem with the maturation and role perspectives is that they do not consider how structured power relations change through the life course and how they influence development processes. Furthermore, cross-time data are required to assess accurately whether either of these perspectives adequately explains the relationship between age and self-esteem. Yet only studies that examine different categories of people at a single point in time have explored the relationship to date. Finally, we are unaware of any research that explores how gender, class, and age combine to produce different effects on self-esteem, although we do know that, in general, these variables create systems of advantage for some people and disadvantage for others in labour markets, health outcomes, and other arenas of social life (Arber and Ginn, 1995; Browne, 1998; Calasanti, 1996; Calasanti and Slevin, 2001; Hill Collins, 2000; Estes, 1999; McMullin, 2000, 2004; Palo Stoller and Campbell Gibson, 1997). Clearly, much research remains to be done on the relationships among gender, social class, aging, and self-esteem.

THE INTERSECTION OF GENDER, CLASS, AND AGE

Our literature review has identified two main types of explanations for differences in self-esteem. First, self-esteem is influenced by the relative control that individuals have over their lives—and gender, class, and age structure this control in complex ways. It is through these complexities that differences in self-esteem emerge.

We might expect, for instance, that positions of authority within families buffer the negative influence of class position on self-esteem for working-class men. We might also expect that the control that professional women have in paid work may buffer the negative effect on self-esteem that comes with their lack of control in determining who is responsible for the under-valued work of caring for children or older adults in families. For older adults, changes in self-esteem may be attributed to changes in power that come with role loss (e.g., retirement) rather than the loss of power itself. But here, class and gender structure these effects. Working-class men may feel a sense of empowerment with positive benefits to self-esteem that come with no longer having to work for anyone. Middle- and upper-class men may feel differently because they no longer have anyone under their control when they retire. The effect of class-based power for women may be similar to that of men in later life but family care and the distribution of power between men and women in the household persist. Thus, the relationship between class, age, and self-esteem cannot be separated from gender.

The second set of explanations for differences in self-esteem that we have identified focuses on the processes of social comparison and reflected appraisal. These processes are themselves influenced by the intersecting structures of gender, class, and age. For instance, research shows that self-esteem operates differently for young women and young men. Relative to young men, young women are more likely to make social comparisons and internalize reflected appraisals of themselves on the basis of socially constructed ideals of feminine beauty. For girls and women, identity is tied to their relationships with boys and men. Hence, to the extent that boys and men believe that a girl or woman is beautiful and therefore worthy of affection, the self-esteem of these girls and women will be heightened. Class is an issue here because processes of social comparison and reflected appraisal may vary if a woman's sense of identity is also linked to her paid work. Because middle-class jobs and profes-

sional employment tend to be more meaningful than working-class jobs, the connection between identity and paid work is more likely among middle- and upper-class women than it is among working-class women. Alternatively, economically well-off women, either in their own right or through their relationship with men, may have more resources to invest in maintaining their beauty, in "feeling good about themselves," and in living up to the middle-class ideal of "taking care of yourself." Of course, middle-class men also participate in the cult of self-care, emphasizing physical fitness and nutrition as means of remaining youthful in appearance. Yet the fact remains that bodily appearance is more important for women than for men (Oberg and Tornstam, 1999). As such, perceptions of attractiveness likely figure more into evaluations of self-worth for women.

How does age influence this relationship? In general, beauty is socially constructed with youth in mind (Abu-Laban and McDaniel, 2001; Calasanti and Slevin, 2001). Consumer beauty products are marketed to "combat" the effects of aging—as if we were engaged in a war (Calasanti and Slevin, 2001). For women, and to a lesser extent men, to be attractive and successful is to be young and beautiful. Social comparisons and reflected appraisals of beauty and self-worth are often made with youth as a referent. Indeed, self-appraisals are also made with a younger self as the ideal in comparison with which the older self is judged ("I'm not as young as I used to be;" "I feel younger than I look"). Of course, the connotations of these comparisons are most often negative (Hurde Clarke, 2001). Hence, through processes of self-comparison and reflected appraisal one might expect that older people would have lower self-esteem than younger people.

One of the few studies that explores the relationship between gender, age group, and body image showed that women care more about their appearance than do men, regardless of age (Oberg and Tornstam, 1999). Notably, however, 60 percent of men in the study agreed that their looks were important to them, and compared to younger men, those 75 and older were more likely to agree that their appearance was important. The study also showed that compared to men, women worry more about how their looks will change as they grow older. Except among 75- to 85-year-olds, women were less satisfied with their bodies than were men. Although body satisfaction did not vary by age group among men, older women had higher body satisfaction than did younger women. In short, appearance matters for both men and women of all ages but the relationship between gender, age, and body image is complex. Some of the complexity may be due to the relative influence of competing gender, class, and age identities in people's lives (e.g., professional versus woman, retired person versus professional, and so on).

RESEARCH QUESTIONS

The idea for this chapter was inspired by informal conversations that McMullin has had with women in varying social contexts. When discussions centred on growing old, McMullin noticed an interesting trend. Women in lower socioeconomic groups tended to reflect more negatively on the experience of growing old than did women in higher socioeconomic groups. Their assessments of aging were tied almost exclusively to their bodies. To the extent that their bodies were deteriorating relative to established norms of beauty and youth, such assessments were negative. The self-esteem of these women was threatened by the fact that they saw themselves as "looking old." On the other hand, women in higher socioeconomic groups tended to cherish the experience of growing old. They described the experience as liberating because men no longer paid attention to the way they looked. These women talked about how they loved growing old because of the self-confidence and power they had gained over the years. Like Dini Petty, these women had achieved high self-esteem and self-confidence later in life; in many ways they felt empowered with increasing age (Gibson, 1996; Browne, 1998).

McMullin's discussions with these women and our reading of the literature on self-esteem lead us to explore the following research questions:

- Is there a relationship between age, socioeconomic status, and self-esteem among Canadians? If so, what is it?
- Does gender influence the relationship between age, socioeconomic status, and self-esteem among Canadians? If so, how?

METHOD

Our sample is drawn from the National Population Health Survey (NPHS) conducted by Statistics Canada. The NPHS is a 1994 telephone survey of a representative national sample of Canadians in all ten provinces. Statistics Canada interviewers surveyed 19 600 households in which one person was selected to provide detailed personal information. People living on Native reserves, on military bases, in institutions, and in some remote areas in Ontario and Quebec were excluded.

Self-esteem is the dependent variable in the analysis and is measured by six items. The items assess how strongly one agrees or disagrees with six statements measuring self-worth:

1. You feel that you have a number of good qualities.
2. You feel that you're a person of worth at least equal to other people.
3. You are able to do things as well as most other people.
4. You take a positive attitude toward yourself.
5. One the whole, you are satisfied with yourself.
6. All in all, you're inclined to feel you're a failure.

The independent variables in our analyses include measures of age (at five-year intervals) and gender. Because gender, age, and class influence marital status and because marital status has been found to influence self-worth, we also included it in our analysis. The marital status categories used in the analysis are married (including common-law), previously married (including widowed, divorced, and separated), and single. We used years of education and household income to measure social class.

RESULTS

In support of past research, our results indicate that self-esteem falls with age. Women report lower self-esteem than do men. People who were previously married or single report lower self-esteem than married people. As education and income increase, self-esteem also increases.

To address our two research questions we needed to examine whether and how gender, age, and social class intersect in their influence on self-esteem. We graphed some of our results in Figure 12.1 (for women) and Figure 12.2 (for men). The pattern of association is similar in both graphs. Regardless of sex, the effects of income differences on self-esteem are virtually non-existent in early adolescence through to middle age. By the age of about 62, however, there is a divergence in self-esteem by income groups. Individuals in the highest income groups report higher self-esteem than those in the lowest income group. This gap widens until the age of 90, at which point income differences are most pronounced. Average self-esteem scores are somewhat higher across age groups for men than for women. Moreover, the gap in self-

esteem by income groups at the age of 90 is somewhat wider among men. Finally, the rate of decline in self-esteem and the rate of divergence in income with age appear steeper for women. Education remains significantly and positively related to self-esteem and single people have lower self-esteem than do married people.

DISCUSSION AND CONCLUSION

This chapter takes a modest step toward piecing together the complex relationships among class, gender, age, and self-esteem using Canadian data. We have shown that self-esteem is lower in older age groups, both male and female. This finding is contrary to some past research, which suggests that age has little influence on self-esteem or that self-esteem increases with age. Furthermore, in all age groups, women have lower self-esteem than do men. Corresponding with past research, we found that income tends not to influence self-esteem for young men or women but does for people in middle age. By including persons 65 years old and over in our study we see that the most pronounced income differences are for people in later life.

It is important to note that what influences self-esteem is power, social comparisons, and reflected appraisals—not an individual's gender, income, and age. Gender, class, and age relations determine the relative power of individuals in

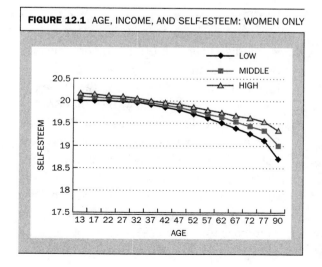

FIGURE 12.1 AGE, INCOME, AND SELF-ESTEEM: WOMEN ONLY

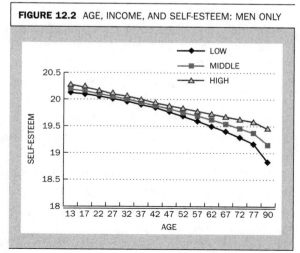

FIGURE 12.2 AGE, INCOME, AND SELF-ESTEEM: MEN ONLY

society as well as the interpersonal processes of social comparison and reflected appraisal. People with less power are poorly positioned to make favourable social comparisons and receive favourable reflected appraisals. Hence, women, members of the working class, and older adults suffer from lower self-esteem because of their structurally disadvantaged position.

This chapter provides only a glimpse into the relationship between social structure and self-esteem, so we can only speculate about how and why gender, class, and age influence self-esteem. More research is needed on this topic. Still, our research contributes to the literature on self-esteem insofar as it moves away from developmental, physiological, and role-loss approaches to aging. Our contention is that an age-based power structure is a detriment to self-esteem in later life. The fact that power decreases in later life, that old age is not highly valued, and that beauty is socially constructed with youth in mind places older people at risk of experiencing low self-esteem relative to younger people.

REFERENCES

Abell, Steven. C., and Maryse H. Richards. (1996). "The Relationship Between Body Shape Satisfaction and Self-esteem: An Investigation of Gender and Class Differences." *Journal of Youth and Adolescence,* 25: 691–703.

Abu-Laban, Sharon McIrvin, and Susan McDaniel. (2001). "Beauty, Status, and Aging." In Nancy Mandell, ed., *Feminist Issues: Race, Class, and Sexuality,* 3rd ed. (pp. 108–33). Toronto: Prentice Hall.

Arber, Sara, and Jay Ginn, eds. (1995). *Connecting Gender and Ageing: A Sociological Approach.* Buckingham: Open University Press.

Browne, Colette V. (1998). *Women, Feminism, and Aging.* New York: Springer.

Calasanti, Toni M. (1996). "Incorporating Diversity: Meaning, Levels of Research, and Implications for Theory." *The Gerontologist,* 36: 147–56.

Calasanti, Toni M., and Kate F. Slevin. (2001). *Gender, Social Inequalities, and Aging.* New York: Altamira Press.

Dietz, Bernadette E. (1996). "The Relationship of Aging to Self-Esteem: The Relative Effects of Maturation and Role Accumulation." *International Journal of Aging and Human Development,* 43: 249–66.

Estes, Carol L. (1999). "The New Political Economy of Aging: Introduction and Critique." In Merideth Minkler and Carol Estes, eds., *Critical Gerontology* (pp. 17–35). Amityville, NY: Baywood Publishing Co. Inc.

Furman, Frida Kerner. (1997). *Facing the Mirror: Older Women and Beauty Shop Culture.* New York: Routledge.

Gecas, Viktor, and Monica A. Seff. (1990). "Social Class and Self-Esteem: Psychological Centrality, Compensation and the Relative Effects of Work and Home." *Social Psychological Quarterly,* 53: 165–73.

Giarrusso, Roseann, J. Beth Mabry, and Vern L. Bengtson. (2001). "The Aging Self in Social Contexts." In Robert. H. Binstock and Linda. K. George, eds., *Handbook of Aging and the Social Sciences,* 5th ed. (pp. 295–312). San Diego: Academic Press.

Gibson, Diane. (1996). "Broken Down by Age and Gender: 'The Problem of Old Women' Redefined." *Gender and Society,* 10: 433–48.

Hill Collins, Patricia. (2000). "Moving beyond Gender: Intersectionality and Scientific Knowledge." In Myra Max Ferree, Judith Lorber, and Beth B. Hess, eds., *Revisioning Gender* (pp. 261–84). New York: Altamira Press.

Hurde Clarke, Laura. (2001). "Older Women's Bodies and the Self: The Construction of Identity in Later Life." *The Canadian Review of Sociology and Anthropology,* 38: 441–64.

Josephs, Robert A., Hazel Rose Markus, and Romin W. Tafarodi. (1992). "Gender and Self-Esteem." *Journal of Personality and Social Psychology,* 63: 391–402.

McMullin, Julie Ann. (2000). "Diversity and the State of Sociological Aging Theory." *The Gerontologist,* 40: 517–30.

———. (2004). *Understanding Inequality: Intersections of Class, Age, Gender, Ethnicity, and Race in Canada.* Toronto: Oxford University Press.

Mirowsky, John, and Catherine E. Ross. (1996). "Economic and Interpersonal Rewards: Subjective Utilities of Men's and Women's Compensation." *Social Forces,* 75: 223–45.

Oberg, Peter, and Lars Tornstam. (1999). "Body Images among Men and Women of Different Ages." *Ageing and Society,* 19: 629–44.

Palo Stoller, Eleanor, and Rose Campbell Gibson. (1997). *Worlds of Difference: Inequality in the Aging Experience.* Thousand Oaks, CA: Pine Forge Press.

Pugliesi, Karen. (1995). "Work and Well-being. Gender Differences in the Psychological Consequences of Employment." *Journal of Health and Social Behavior,* 36: 57–71.

Rosenberg, Morris. (1981). "The Self-Concept: Social Product and Social Force." In Morris Rosenberg and Ralph H. Turner, eds., *Social Psychology: Sociological Perspectives* (pp. 593–624). New York: Basic.

Rosenberg, Morris, and Leonard I. Pearlin. (1978). "Social Class and Self-Esteem Among Children and Adults." *American Journal of Sociology,* 84: 53–77.

Rosenfield, Sara. (1999). "Splitting the Difference: Gender, the Self, and Mental Health." In Carol S. Aneshensel and Jo C. Phelan, eds., *Handbook of the Sociology of Mental Health* (pp. 209–24). New York: Kluwer Academic/Plenum Publishers.

Turner, R. Jay, and Patricia Roszell. (1994). "Psychosocial Resources and the Stress Process." In William R. Avison and Ian H. Gotlib, eds., *Stress and Mental Health: Contemporary Issues and Prospects for the Future* (pp. 179–212). New York: Plenum Press.

PART 3B

ETHNIC AND RACIAL INEQUALITY

Ethnic groups are usually defined as social collectivities that are distinguished by ancestry and culture. **Races** have relatively unique ancestries and cultures too. In addition, races differ from ethnic groups and from each other in terms of visible physical characteristics, such as skin colour, that are socially defined as significant and that are significant in their social consequences.

Nearly a fifth of Canadians are members of racial minorities. The proportion is higher in large cities, reaching 25 percent in Montreal, Edmonton, Calgary, and Winnipeg; 40 percent in Vancouver; and nearly 50 percent in Toronto. Chinese, Blacks, and South Asians each account for roughly a fifth of the racial minority population. By some measures, Canada is the most ethnically and racially tolerant country in the world (see Figure 3B.1). Still, government-sponsored studies and public opinion polls find that around a third of Canadians are to some degree prejudiced against members of an ethnic or racial group. (Note that **prejudice** refers to a negative *attitude* toward members of an ethnic or racial group, while **discrimination** refers to *behaviour* that has negative consequences for such groups.)

Given the existence of ethnic and racial prejudice, most of Canada's racial minorities have fared surprisingly well economically, especially after the immigrant generation. This is a tribute to their resourcefulness and industry, and it is partly a consequence of their social background. Their economic achievements are due substantially to the country's selective immigration policy, which favours immigrants with higher education and money. Credentials and capital help to overcome the worst economic consequences of prejudice and discrimination.

FIGURE 3B.1 PERCENTAGE NOT WANTING NEIGHBOUR OF A DIFFERENT RACE, SELECTED COUNTRIES, 2000

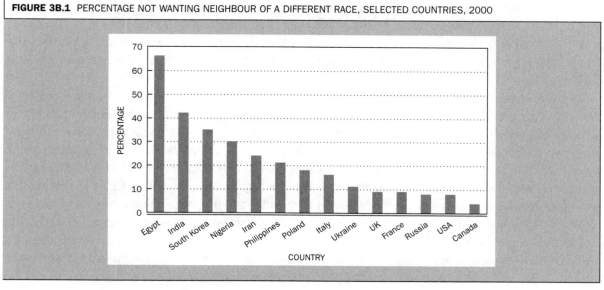

Source: *World Values Survey.* Computer dataset (2004).

Nonetheless, economic differences among racial and ethnic groups persist. They are explored in depth in Chapter 13. Hugh Lautard and Neil Guppy analyze Canadian Census data from 1931 to 2001. They conclude that occupational differences between ethnic and racial groups have decreased substantially over the period but that they are still considerable. Why do they persist? Mainly because some groups continue to be augmented by substantial numbers of immigrants, and immigrants suffer more disadvantages that native-born Canadians. For example, immigrants may lack English and French language skills and contacts in the wider community that could help them find better jobs. The Canadian-born children of immigrants are less disadvantaged in this regard, and their movement up the stratification system is therefore somewhat easier, even though discrimination persists, especially for members of some racial minority groups.

Who are the exceptions that cloud the relatively bright picture sketched above? The biggest and most glaring exception is composed of Canada's Aboriginal peoples, who have fared worse than any other ethnic or racial group in the country. Their way of life was virtually destroyed by European colonization. They were robbed of land, culture, community, and even children. As a result, they now suffer more unemployment, poverty, alcoholism, infant mortality, and day-to-day violence than any other group in the land.

Some Canadians are oblivious to the historical and social context in which Aboriginal people became victims, instead blaming them for their plight. Sociological surveys show that three out of ten Canadians believe that most of the problems of Aboriginal peoples are brought on by themselves. Most Canadians are sympathetic to Aboriginals in the abstract, but they know little about them and give Aboriginal issues a low policy priority. Aboriginal Canadians are viewed as especially problematic where they conflict with questions of ethno-national territorial control (Quebec) and least problematic in areas where they compose a small proportion of the population and make less threatening claims (Ontario).

A second exception to the generally bright picture regarding trends in ethnic and racial inequality in Canada concerns Black men. Their income is typically and substantially lower than one would expect given their level of education, years of job experience, and other factors. What is more, although the economic disadvantages of Black men fall after the immigrant generation, they remain significant. This pattern of persistent inequality is unlike that of other immigrant groups—and unlike that of Black women, whose earnings are in line with their qualifications after the immigrant generation. It is difficult to escape the conclusion that Black men are the victims of prejudice and discrimination so severe that they exert a big impact on their life chances even if they are born in this country.

The third exception to the bright picture sketched above concerns immigrants who have arrived in Canada since the 1990s. Overall, they have experienced a lower rate of upward mobility than earlier arrivals. In Chapter 14, Jeffrey Reitz explores an important reason for their relatively slow economic progress: their qualifications are insufficiently recognized in the workplace. Recent immigrants are on average better educated than Canadian-born workers, their level of fluency in the official languages is not different from that of earlier immigrants, yet they are experiencing higher levels of unemployment and lower relative earnings than immigrants did before the 1990s. Reitz argues that Canadian institutions must be changed to utilize immigrants' skills more effectively. This must be done, he writes, not just for the sake of immigrants but for the sake of Canadian society as a whole, which loses about $2 billion a year by underemploying highly qualified immigrants and suffers shortages of skilled workers in several fields, most notably medicine. The institutional changes that Reitz recommends should be studied carefully by anyone interested in keeping the "Canadian Dream" alive.

GLOSSARY

Discrimination is behaviour that has negative consequences for members of an ethnic or racial group.
Ethnic groups are social collectivities that are distinguished by relatively unique ancestries and cultures.
Prejudice refers to negative attitudes toward members of an ethnic or racial group.
Races have relatively unique ancestries and cultures but differ from ethnic groups and from each other in terms of visible physical characteristics, such as skin colour, that are socially defined as significant and that are significant in their social consequences.

CRITICAL THINKING QUESTIONS

1. Is it accurate to portray Canada as a vertical mosaic? Justify your answer with material from your readings.
2. What specific institutional changes does Jeffrey Reitz recommend to utilize the skills of immigrants more effectively? Do you think his recommendations are workable? Why or why not?

ANNOTATED BIBLIOGRAPHY

Fleras, Augie, and Jean Leonard Elliott. *Engaging Diversity: Multiculturalism in Canada.* 2nd ed. Toronto: Nelson, 2002. A comprehensive introduction to race and ethnicity in Canada.

Gould, Stephen Jay. *The Mismeasure of Man.* New York: W.W. Norton, 1981. A brilliant, award-winning study of how the measurement of human intelligence has been closely connected to racist assumptions about human behaviour.

Li, Peter S. *Destination Canada: Immigration Debates and Issues.* Toronto: Oxford University Press, 2003. A thorough treatment of immigration in Canada.

Reitz, Jeffrey, and Raymond Breton. *The Illusion of Difference: Realities of Ethnicity in Canada and the United States.* Toronto: C.D. Howe Institute, 1994. Canadians often think Canada's "ethnic mosaic" differs from the American "melting pot." This book explodes the myth.

Chapter 13

Multiculturalism or Vertical Mosaic?

OCCUPATIONAL STRATIFICATION

AMONG CANADIAN ETHNIC GROUPS

HUGH LAUTARD AND NEIL GUPPY

INTRODUCTION

Canada is primarily a land of immigrants. Most of us trace our ancestral roots to Europe, and more recently to Asia. This has meant, from the outset of our nation, a mixing of people with diverse ethnic roots. How well we have actually mixed is the focus of this chapter.

Our official government policy of multiculturalism implies a wholesome mixing of ethnic groups, an equality among peoples of distinct cultural heritages. Multiculturalism is premised upon a multiplicity of equal cultures.[1] Our diverse cultural heritages are supported through many institutions, including ethnic media outlets, ethnic churches and schools, and ethnic restaurants. The equality among these diverse cultures is most actively promoted by governments but also by, for example, the schools. Multicultural curricula now permeate the school system, in social studies courses, in recognizing different religious holidays, and in celebrating ethnic heritage days. Different cultural traditions provide separate ethnic identities within a common, egalitarian framework. Multiculturalism highlights cultural blending and ethnic equality.

A contrasting vision of Canada was proposed by sociologist John Porter (1965). Writing in the 1960s, he championed the imagery of a "vertical mosaic." "Mosaic" highlights distinct ethnic identities, but Porter saw little mixing or blending. He argued that Canada's ethnic groups were vertically arranged. According to Porter, Canada was composed of distinct social groups

defined principally by social class and ethnicity. Furthermore, these social groups were vertically ranked according to income, power, and prestige. The vertical mosaic, Porter argued, accentuates distinct cultures and ethnic inequality.

How useful are the contrasting images of the vertical mosaic and multiculturalism in understanding modern Canada? Canada's population has grown and diversified since 1965, when Porter published *The Vertical Mosaic*, and since 1971, when Canada adopted multiculturalism as official federal government policy.

Section 15.1 of the *Canadian Charter of Rights and Freedoms* (1985) proclaims: "Every individual is equal before and under the law and has the right to the equal protection and equal benefit of the law without discrimination and, in particular, without discrimination based on race, national or ethnic origin, [and] colour. . . ." However, despite the *Charter*'s grounding in multicultural language, the legacy of the vertical mosaic has required additional legislation to help enhance the *Charter*'s equality provisions. So, for example, the *Employment Equity Act* (1986) seeks to erase the subordinate positions of women, the disabled, Aboriginal peoples, and visible minorities. The Act requires employers to hire according to equity targets to overcome ethnic inequality in the labour force. While proclaiming multiculturalism as official policy, the federal government has had to enact laws simultaneously in an attempt to erode the vertical mosaic. If the key proposition of *The Vertical Mosaic* still holds—that ethnicity shapes inequality—then legislation such as the *Employment Equity Act* remains important. This implies, though, that multiculturalism remains more ideology than fact, more rhetoric than reality. Is there a causal link between your ethnicity and your socioeconomic fortunes or misfortunes? We present new data that, when compared with trends published earlier, afford the longest historical perspective yet available on the association between ethnicity and occupation, based on 70 years of census data, from 1931 to 2001. As did Porter before us, we stress both social differences (multiple ethnic groups in a mosaic) and social stratification (vertical alignment of ethnic groups).

IS THE SIGNIFICANCE OF ETHNICITY FOR INEQUALITY DECLINING?

In *The Vertical Mosaic*, Porter described Canada as a nation fractured by ethnicity. He saw the French and the British as two "charter status" groups, commanding greater power and privilege than "entrance status" groups (i.e., other immigrants). He analyzed the asymmetry of power favouring the British over the French and claimed that this asymmetry characterized non-charter immigrant groups, too. For Porter, "immigration and ethnic affiliation . . . [were] important factors in the formation of social classes" (1965: 73).

Porter focused especially on the economic elite, in which he claimed "economic power belong[ed] almost exclusively to [White Protestants] of British origin" (Porter, 1965: 286). More recent analyses of the wealthiest Canadians show less British dominance. While the Thomson family, with its strong British roots, continues to be the wealthiest Canadian family, the corridors of power are now less WASPish (Ogmundson and McLaughlin, 1990; Ogmundson and Doyle, 2001; and Nakhaie, 1997). At one time almost exclusively British, the Canadian elite, almost no matter how it is defined, now contains more people from other ethnic backgrounds.

Porter (1965) also used census data from 1931, 1951, and 1961 to make his case. By tabulating ethnic origin and occupation, he showed which ethnic groups dominated which job categories. For example, in the 1931 census he found British and Jewish groups were overrepresented in professional and financial occupations. Conversely, they were underrepresented in unskilled and primary jobs (e.g., fishing, logging). He wrote that the "French, German, and Dutch would probably rank next, followed by Scandinavian, Eastern European, Italian, Japanese, 'Other Central European', Chinese, and Native Indian" (p. 81). His 1961 census data showed that, save for the French who had slid down a little, "the rough rank order [had] persisted over time" (p. 90).

Why were different ethnic groups represented at higher and lower occupational levels? Porter proposed two complementary explanations. First, newcomers to Canada often brought with them different educational and occupational experiences. People of British heritage frequently came with professional qualifications that were officially recognized in Canada, whereas people from other ethnic backgrounds often arrived with little education and no recognized professional skills. New entrants to Canada would thus reinforce the existing link between ethnic ancestry and social class (Porter, 1965: 86, 1985: 40–51).[2]

Second, Porter argued that social mobility was correlated with ethnicity. Ethnic groups, he argued, either varied in how much they valued economic achievement and upward mobility or found that discrimination dampened their labour market success (Pineo and Porter, 1985: 360–61). Indeed, Porter felt that multiculturalism would impede ethnic assimilation and perpetuate the link between social class and ethnicity (Heath and Yu, 2005).

Much social science research has assessed the adequacy of Porter's vertical mosaic imagery. No doubt insightful in his era, is it an accurate portrayal of ethnic inequality through the last half century? Since the end of the World War II the source of Canadian immigrants has shifted dramatically away from Europe and toward other continents, especially Asia. As well, Canada has changed its immigration policy. Now greater priority is given to the skills new entrants have as opposed to their place of birth. For example, more emphasis is now placed on education and on fluency in at least one of the two official languages. Occupational experience is more valued than birthplace.

Some researchers have concluded that the vertical mosaic imagery simply needs revising to note its "colour coding." They argue that for people of visible minority background the association between ethnicity and social class has been retained. Now we have a "new ethnic mosaic . . . redrafted along lines of race and colour" (Agocs and Boyd, 1993: 333; Lian and Matthews, 1998; Ooka and Fong, 2001; Pendakur and Pendakur, 2002; Reitz, 2001).

Other research traditions have followed Porter's original lead and compared patterns of association between ethnicity and social class in successive census years. For example, Lautard and Loree (1984: 342) used detailed ethnicity and occupation data from 1931 to 1971 and concluded that "occupational inequality is still substantial enough to justify the use of the concept 'vertical mosaic' to characterize . . . ethnic relations in Canada" (Darroch, 1979; Pendakur, 2002). The census data used by Porter and Lautard and Loree combine both the foreign-born and the native-born, thus allowing researchers to examine social change by focusing on trends over time. However, the census data they used provide no test for the two explanations Porter offered about the association of ethnicity and class.

Monica Boyd's (1985) research on the influence of birthplace on occupational attainment offers a test of the immigration interpretation. For foreign-born women and men, Boyd demonstrated that ethnic ancestry was correlated with occupational attainment. Even when immigrants with the same age, education, social origin, and place of residence were compared,

the correlation existed. For women who were foreign-born, Boyd found a "double negative" that reinforced the vertical mosaic. She concluded that birthplace and sex are important factors underlying the Canadian mosaic (Boyd, 1985: 441).

The exact nature of the link between ethnicity and inequality turns, at least in part, on issues of definition and methodology. Porter used the best data available to him but his approach had weaknesses despite his best efforts. Following are the three main problems that any analyst must confront in trying to sort out whether the idea of multiculturalism or the image of a vertical mosaic best characterizes modern Canada.

ETHNICITY

Definitions matter. How broadly or finely one chooses to define ethnicity is critical in these debates. Historically, male ancestral lineage was the defining feature of ethnicity, at least as used by Statistics Canada for measurement purposes. However, this definition is problematic, not only because it privileges male descent lines. Inter-ethnic marriages occur across generations. National borders change. An increasing number of people consider themselves to be of "Canadian" ancestry since they are descendants of people who arrived in Canada generations ago.

Porter's view of the charter status groups, the French and the British, drew no distinction between the English, the Irish, the Scottish, and the Welsh. Likewise, Statistics Canada for a long time was unable to publish distinct numbers for members of different Asian ethnic groups. That is because the number of Koreans and Cambodians, for example, was too small. Typically, the following ethnic categories have been used in the census, with older census years having even fewer distinct groups: British (English, Irish, Scottish, Welsh), French, German, Italian, Jewish, Dutch, Scandinavian, Eastern European (Polish, Ukrainian), Other European, Asian, and Native Indian.

OCCUPATIONS

Porter originally used five broad occupational categories (professional and financial, clerical, personal service, primary and unskilled, and agriculture). Lautard and Loree (1984) used a more detailed occupational categorization with hundreds of separate job categories for each census.

Occupations are, in important ways, just jobs. To show that members of different ethnic groups concentrate in some jobs and not others says nothing about inequality; it is only a comment about different jobs. Only if those jobs have different rewards attached to them does inequality become an issue. But what are the most salient rewards—income, working conditions, prestige, authority? The vertical mosaic clearly implies some hierarchy, but what defines that hierarchy is not specified.

HISTORICAL COMPARABILITY

The number and kinds of occupations in Canada have changed over time. Should researchers use older census categories that tend to be broader or the full range of jobs characterizing the modern division of labour? Likewise, the detail on ethnicity has changed historically, as has the way Statistics Canada collects this information.[3] Should only broad ethnic categories that are strictly comparable over time be used?

MEASURING OCCUPATIONAL STRATIFICATION BY ETHNICITY

With the above limitations in mind you might conclude that using census data to track labour market changes for members of ethnic groups is highly problematic. Our response to this is fourfold. First, these problems must be recognized and the results interpreted cautiously in light of them. Second, even partial insight is better than ignorance. Third, if the findings of this research complement the findings of other researchers using different research methods, then the entire body of research is self-reinforcing. Fourth, if

better methods exist to answer the question we are pursuing, then we encourage others to do the research.

We use census information for 1971 and 2001 and compare our results to earlier findings, beginning either in 1931 or 1951. Depending on the availability of data, we discuss changes over a period of up to 70 years. The 2001 analysis involves examining the distribution of the members of 17 different ethnic groups, by gender, across 500 different occupations. This provides enormous detail that we need to summarize. To do so, we measure occupational differentiation by calculating an *index of dissimilarity*, and we examine occupational stratification by using an *index of net difference*.

Here first, by way of analogy, is how to understand the index of dissimilarity. In your college or university, consider the overall percentages of women and men enrolled (assume it is 55 percent and 45 percent respectively). Now think of the percentage of women and men in each of your classes. How well is the overall gender balance of 55/45 reflected in your individual courses? Extend this to all the courses offered at your institution.

To summarize this detail, begin by calculating, for each course, any difference in the percentage of women (or men) from the overall 55/45 average. This tells you how dissimilar each course is from the overall gender balance. Totalling across all courses provides a convenient summary—the higher the index number, the greater the dissimilarity. Comparing the index of dissimilarity across different faculties or different universities would tell you which has the better gender balance.

In our case, we add the percentage differences between the occupational distribution of each ethnic group and that of the rest of the labour force. A separate calculation is done for women and men. The resulting indexes are the percentages of women and men in each ethnic group who would have to be in a different occupation in order for there to be no occupational differences among ethnic groups.

For example, say the index of dissimilarity for women of British origin is 10. This means that only 10 percent of the British women in the labour force would have to be in a different occupation for there to be no difference between their occupational distribution and that of women of other ethnic origins. If the index of dissimilarity for men of Aboriginal origin is 31 percent, this indicates about three times as much difference, with nearly one in three Aboriginal men having to be in a different occupation for them to have the same occupational distribution as non-Aboriginal men. Averaging dissimilarity indexes for ethnic groups in two different census years indicates changes in occupational differentiation among ethnic groups. We present such results for 1971 and 2001, and compare them with earlier findings for 1931, 1951, and 1961, for a combined time span of 70 years.

Dissimilarity, however, does not necessarily mean disadvantage or inequality. As a method of capturing *stratification*, sociologists have adopted other methods. In this chapter, we use two separate methods to examine stratification among occupations. For 1971 we array occupations on a socioeconomic index that measures the prestige of occupations. These prestige ratings are based on the typical education and income of people in particular occupations. For 2001, where such an index is not available, we use a measure constructed by Statistics Canada to rank the variable occupational skill requirements of distinct jobs. Occupation data collected from the 2001 Census are ranked into one of four skill groups, where the groups are arrayed by estimates of educational requirements (i.e., university, college, apprenticeship training, and high school or less). To this, Statistics Canada added a "manager" category, which is unranked since the education levels of managers are diverse.

As a way of summarizing occupational inequality, we use the index of net difference. This measure (unlike the index of dissimilarity, which is always positive) may be either negative or positive. An index of net difference with a minus sign indicates the group for which it was calculated is generally lower on the occupational "ladder" relative to the rest of the labour force, while a positive index indicates higher relative position. The greater the absolute size of the index, whether positive or negative, the greater the degree of stratification, while a net difference of zero would indicate overall equality of occupational status. We use this measure to analyze occupational inequality for 1971 and 2001 and compare our results with earlier findings for 1951, 1961, and 1971.

OCCUPATIONAL INEQUALITY BY ETHNICITY, 1931 TO 2001

Table 13.1 contains indexes of occupational dissimilarity for 16 ethnic groups in 1971 and 17 groups in 2001. These scores summarize results based on just under 500 occupations in 1971 and just over 500 occupations in 2001. Generally, ethnic occupational differentiation is lower in 2001 than 1971. In 2001, average ethnic dissimilarity among men (24 percent) is 6 points lower than in 1971 (30 percent), while it is 8 points lower among women (19 percent, compared to 27 percent). Exceptions to this pattern of declining index scores occur for men and women of German, Dutch, and Scandinavian origin, for men of Ukrainian and Polish origin, and for women of Jewish origin, while the index for women of Polish origin is the same for both years.

Table 13.1 also shows that there is a generally consistent pattern of ethnic occupational differentiation. Groups of North and East European origins exhibit below-average occupational dissimilarity, while, with a few exceptions, groups of South European, Jewish, Asian, Aboriginal, and Black origins show above-average dissimilarity. The generally lower levels of ethnic differentiation in 2001 compared to 1971 are consistent with the decreases reported by Lautard and Loree (1984) for 1931 to 1971, suggesting an easing of differentiation. Nevertheless considerable occupational dissimilarity remains among ethnic groups.[4]

TABLE 13.1 OCCUPATIONAL DISSIMILARITY[a] BETWEEN SELECTED ETHNIC GROUPS AND THE REST OF THE LABOUR FORCE, BY SEX: CANADA, 1971 AND 2001

	MALE		FEMALE	
Ethnic Group	**1971**	**2001**	**1971**	**2001**
British	15	11	16	10
French	14	10	18	10
German	15	18	11	12
Dutch	16	21	15	16
Scandinavian	17	22	12	16
Ukrainian	15	16	16	12
Polish	15	17	14	14
Hungarian	21	18	20	16
Italian	35	20	38	19
Portuguese	46	29	57	24
Greek	48	31	51	23
Yugoslav	33	23	35	19
Jewish	51	45	32	33
Chinese	52	36	34	26
South Asian	46	27	31	22
Aboriginal	41[b]	31	32[b]	24
Black	NI	26	NI	24
Mean	30	24	27	19
Number of Occupations	(498)	(521)	(464)	(521)

Notes
[a]Each figure in the table indicates the percentage of the ethnic group that would have to have a different occupation in order for there to be no difference between the occupational distribution of that group and the rest of the labour force.
[b]Does not include Inuit.
NI: Not included.

Source: Special tabulations of census data.

TABLE 13.2 NET DIFFERENCE[a] IN OCCUPATIONAL STATUS (1971) AND OCCUPATIONAL SKILL GROUP (2001) BETWEEN SELECTED ETHNIC GROUPS AND THE REST OF THE LABOUR FORCE, BY SEX: CANADA

	MALE		FEMALE	
Ethnic Group	**1971**	**2001**	**1971**	**2001**
British	0.13	0.06	0.14	0.05
French	−0.06	0.04	−0.02	0.06
German	−0.08	0.04	−0.09	0.01
Dutch	−0.09	0.05	−0.10	0.04
Scandinavian	−0.08	0.07	−0.01	0.05
Ukrainian	−0.09	0.06	−0.13	0.03
Polish	−0.08	0.03	−0.12	−0.02
Hungarian	−0.06	0.07	−0.13	0.02
Italian	−0.22	0.01	−0.35	0.00
Portuguese	−0.38	−0.15	−0.62	−0.16
Greek	−0.27	0.02	−0.48	−0.04
Yugoslav	−0.12	0.03	−0.29	−0.03
Jewish	0.36	0.34	0.24	0.24
Chinese	−0.04	0.19	−0.20	0.00
South Asian	0.26	−0.05	0.19	−0.12
Aboriginal	−0.35[b]	−0.15	−0.23[b]	−0.08
Black	NI	−0.10	NI	−0.09
Mean	0.17	0.09	0.21	0.06
Number of Occupational Ranks/Skill Groups	(498)	(521)	(464)	(521)

Notes
[a]A negative figure indicates relatively lower overall occupational status/skill group, a positive figure, relatively higher status/skill group. Zero indicates overall equality of occupational status/skill group. The greater the absolute size of the index, the greater the inequality.
[b]Does not include Inuit.
NI: Not included.

Source: Special tabulations of census data.

Recall that occupational dissimilarity does not necessarily involve occupational stratification. Table 13.2 contains indexes of net difference in occupational status for 1971 and in occupational skill group for 2001 for the ethnic groups discussed previously. In 1971, with the exception of the indexes for men and women of British, Jewish, and South Asian origins, all indexes are negative, indicating the relatively low occupational status of the other groups. Note also that in 1971 both men and women of South European and Aboriginal origin have lower overall occupational status than the other groups.

In 2001, the indexes of net difference are mainly positive. In 1971, they are mainly negative. This is true for both women and men. We conclude that ethnic stratification was less pronounced in 2001 than in 1971.

Note also that the indexes for 2001 exhibit a pattern like that noted above for occupational dissimilarity among ethnic groups. Most men and women of North European origin, as well as those of Jewish origin, tend to be in higher occupational skill groups than people of South European, Aboriginal, and Black origin. Men of Chinese origin are in relatively high occupational skill groups, and women of Chinese and Italian origins are in the middle.[5]

FROM VERTICAL MOSAIC TO MULTICULTURALISM?

Has multiculturalism eclipsed the vertical mosaic? Is ethnic inequality, at least as measured by occupational stratification, only a historical fact in Canada? Our results show that between 1931 and 2001 a decline in the significance of ethnicity, for both occupational differentiation and stratification, has occurred. Yet ethnic origin continues to affect occupational inequality.

The trend in occupational dissimilarity indicates a reduction in the ethnic division of labour of about 30 percent for men and 45 percent for women in 70 years (Figure 13.1). Slowly, but surely, social differentiation based on ethnicity is eroding. With respect to occupational stratification there has been a reduction of approximately

50 percent for men and 45 percent for women, although over a shorter time span (from 1951 to 2001). From 1971 to 2001 the trend has continued. These historical comparisons have the advantage of a 70-year interval of comparison, but such a lengthy interval also makes the specific contrasts cruder than would be ideal.

Do these results imply a "collapse" of the vertical mosaic? No. Between 1971 and 2001 both occupational differentiation and occupational stratification have eroded, but for both women and men, differences persist. Furthermore, these findings are not inconsistent with recent research by Pendakur and Pendakur (2002) showing an increase in the earning gap in the 1990s for both Aboriginals and members of visible minority groups born in Canada as compared to other Canadian-born labour force participants. Also, work by Reitz (2001) shows that recent immigrants to Canada have been faring more poorly than in earlier decades in labour market integration. On the basis of this research there is no firm ground on which to conclude that multiculturalism has eliminated the vertical mosaic.

The research design that we have employed prevents us from investigating which of Porter's two dynamics best explains the continuing level of ethnic inequality: differential immigration or blocked mobility. Our reading of the research literature suggests that differential immigration continues to be the more important factor, especially in terms of visible minorities (Creese and Kambere, 2001; Sorensen, 1995; Davies and Guppy, 2006). That is, ethnicity has less of an effect on inequality for native-born Canadians than it does for immigrants. However, immigration patterns cannot be the sole explanation because our results are also consistent with research showing that some visible minorities, for example, men of Black and South Asian heritage, face earning penalties in the labour market, penalties that are consistent with the blocked mobility thesis (Geschwender and Guppy, 1995; Li, 1990; Lian and Matthews, 1998; Pendakur and Pendakur, 2002). Whatever the extent and

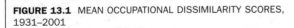

FIGURE 13.1 MEAN OCCUPATIONAL DISSIMILARITY SCORES, 1931–2001

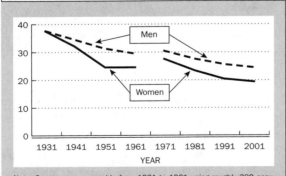

Note: Scores are comparable from 1931 to 1961 using roughly 300 occupations for women and 400 for men; between 1971 and 2001 scores increase slightly because more occupations are available for comparison (approximately 500 for both women and men).

sources of the vertical mosaic, it coexists with other aspects of ethnic and racial inequality beyond the scope of our analysis, including prejudice, hate, and violence, as well as systematic and systemic discrimination in recruitment, interviewing, hiring, promotion, training, and termination practices.

NOTES

The authors gratefully acknowledge the assistance of Jaime Caldwell and Robin Hawkshaw in preparing this paper.

1. The Canadian Heritage Web site provides the government's answer to the question: What is Multiculturalism? "Canadian multiculturalism is fundamental to our belief that all citizens are equal." On the World Wide Web at http://www.pch.gc.ca/progs/multi/what-multi_e.cfm (24 January 2006).

2. For much of Canada's history, foreign-born workers have had a higher level of education than have native-born Canadians (Légacé, 1968; Boyd, 1985). What this average hides, however, is the tendency for immigrants to be either relatively well or relatively poorly educated. Note also that earlier in Canadian history the credentials of immigrants from the United Kingdom in particular were recognized without question. Now the credentials of immigrants are frequently not accepted as legitimate professional qualifications for the Canadian labour market (Boyd and Thomas, 2001).

3. In the 1971 and earlier censuses, the census question to determine ethnic origin was: "To which ethnic or cultural group did you or your ancestor (on the male side) belong on coming to this continent?" In 1981 the question was: "To which ethnic or cultural group did you or your ancestors belong on first coming to this continent?" Notice how difficult it is for Aboriginal people especially to answer such a question accurately. Beginning in 1981, multiple ethnic origins were accepted, and the 2001 question read: "To which ethnic or cultural group(s) did this person's ancestors belong?" Our ethnic categories for 2001 are based on single responses and exclude those reporting multiple ethnic or cultural origins, except for multiple origins involving only constituent groups of certain categories. For example, "British" includes persons who report their origin(s) to be British or any one or more of English, Irish, Scottish, Welsh, and so on, but no non-British origin(s). Scandinavian includes persons who report their origin(s) as Scandinavian or any one or more of Danish, Icelandic, Norwegian, Swedish, and so forth, but no non-Scandinavian origin(s). Although the 2001 Census Guide still made it clear that ethnic origin did not refer to citizenship, "Canadian" was among the examples listed with the question itself. Our data, however, corroborate Li's (2003: 128) observation that "the growth of people reporting Canadian origin . . . did not have a measurable impact on the reporting of ethnic minorities."

4. Just as Lautard and Loree's (1984) average dissimilarity for men in 1961 (29) was about double that reported by Darroch (1979), our 1971 averages for men (30) and women (27) are roughly double Darroch's 1971 average for men and women combined. This shows why trend comparisons are so important; the dissimilarity measure is sensitive to the number of occupations used (Lautard and Lorree, 1984: 336). The level of dissimilarity reported by other authors is important as a statement about ethnic differences (i.e., how big or small they might be), but it is comparison over time, using a consistent methodology, that answers questions about how ethnic divisions are changing in Canada.

5. Data for the intervening census years, 1981 and 1991, indicate the overall decline and pattern in ethnic inequality is comparable to those reported by Lautard and Loree (1984) for the census years studied by Porter (1951 and 1961) as well as 1971 (Lautard and Guppy, 2004).

REFERENCES

Agocs, Carol, and Monica Boyd. (1993). "The Canadian Ethnic Mosaic Recast: Theory, Research and Policy Frameworks for the 1990s." In J. Curtis et al., eds., *Social Inequality in Canada: Patterns, Problems, Policies* (pp. 330–52). Toronto: Prentice-Hall.

Boyd, Monica. (1985). "Immigration and Occupational Attainment." In M. Boyd et al., eds., *Ascription and Attainment: Studies in Mobility and Status Attainment in Canada* (pp. 393–446). Ottawa: Carleton University Press.

Boyd, Monica, and Derrick Thomas. (2001). "Match or Mismatch? The Employment of Immigrant Engineers in Canada's Labor Force." *Population Research and Policy Review*, 20 (1–2): 107–33.

Creese, Gillian, and E. N. Kambere. (2001). "What Colour Is Your English?" *Canadian Review of Sociology and Anthropology*, 40 (5): 565–74.

Darroch, Gordon. (1979). "Another Look at Ethnicity, Stratification and Social Mobility in Canada." *Canadian Journal of Sociology*, 4 (1): 1–25.

Davies, Scott, and Neil Guppy. (2006). *The Schooled Society: An Introduction to the Sociology of Education.* Toronto: Oxford University Press.

Geschwender, Jim, and Neil Guppy. (1995). "Ethnicity, Educational Attainment, and Earned Income among Canadian-Born Men and Women." *Canadian Ethnic Studies*, 27 (1): 67–83.

Heath, Anthony, and S. Yu. (2005). "Explaining Ethnic Minority Disadvantage." In A.F. Heath, J. Ermish, and D. Gallie, eds., *Understanding Social Change* (pp. 187–224). Oxford: Oxford University Press.

Lautard, Hugh, and Neil Guppy. (2004). "Multiculturalism or Vertical Mosaic: Occupational Stratification among Canadian Ethnic Groups." In Robert J. Brym, ed., *Society in Question: Sociological Readings for the 21st Century*, 4th ed. (pp. 165–75). Toronto: Nelson.

Lautard, Hugh, and Donald Loree. (1984). "Ethnic Stratification in Canada, 1931–1971." *Canadian Journal of Sociology*, 9 (3): 333–44.

Légacé, Michael D. (1968). "Educational Attainment in Canada." Dominion Bureau of Statistics, Special Labour Force Survey No. 7. Ottawa: Queen's Printer.

Li, Peter. (1990). Ethnic Inequality in a Class Society. Toronto: Thompson.

———. (2003). *Destination Canada: Immigration Debates and Issues.* Don Mills: Oxford University Press.

Lian, Jason, and David Ralph Matthews. (1998). "Does the Vertical Mosaic Still Exist? Ethnicity and Income in Canada, 1991." *Canadian Review of Sociology and Anthropology*, 35 (4): 461–81.

Nakhaie, M. Reza. (1997). "Vertical Mosaic among the Elites: The New Imagery Revisited." *Canadian Review of Sociology and Anthropology*, 34 (1): 1–24.

Ogmundson, Richard, and M. Doyle. (2001). "The Rise and Decline of Canadian Labour/1960 to 2000: Elites, Power, Ethnicity and Gender." *Canadian Journal of Sociology*, 27 (3): 413–25.

Ogmundson, Richard, and J. McLaughlin. (1990). "Trends in the Ethnic Origins of Canadian Elites: The Decline of the BRITS." *Canadian Review of Sociology and Anthropology*, 29 (2): 227–42.

Ooka, Emi, and Eric Fong. (2001). "Globalization and Earnings among Native-Born and Immigrant Populations of Racial and Ethnic Groups in Canada." *Canadian Studies in Population*, 29 (1): 101–22.

Pendakur, Ravi. (2002). *Immigrants and the Labour Force: Policy, Regulation, and Impact.* Montreal: McGill-Queen's University Press.

Pendakur, Krishna, and Ravi Pendakur. (2002). "Colour My World: Have Earning Gaps for Canadian Born Ethnic Minorities Changed Over Time?" *Canadian Public Policy*, 28 (4): 489–512.

Pineo, Peter, and John Porter. (1985). "Ethnic Origin and Occupational Attainment." In M. Boyd et al., eds., *Ascription and Achieve-*

ment: *Studies and Status Attainment in Canada* (pp. 357–92). Ottawa: Carleton University Press.

Porter, John. (1965). *The Vertical Mosaic: An Analysis of Social Class and Power in Canada.* Toronto: University of Toronto Press.

———. (1985). "Canada: The Social Context of Occupational Allocation." In M. Boyd et al., eds., *Ascription and Achievement: Studies in Mobility and Status Attainment in Canada* (pp. 29–65). Ottawa: Carleton University Press.

Reitz, Jeffrey G. (2001). "Immigrant Skill Utilization in the Canadian Labour Market: Implications of Human Capital Research." *Journal of International Migration and Integration,* 2 (3): 347–78.

Sorensen, Marianne. (1995). "The Match Between Education and Occupation for Immigrant Women in Canada." *Canadian Ethnic Studies,* 27 (1): 48–66.

Chapter 14

Tapping Immigrants' Skills

JEFFREY G. REITZ

TRENDS AND ISSUES IN THE ECONOMIC STANDING OF IMMIGRANTS

Canada selects immigrants partly on the basis of their labour force skills but underutilizes those skills once newcomers settle here. A valuable opportunity is thus squandered: analysts estimate that the Canadian economy loses about $2 billion annually because immigrants' qualifications are insufficiently recognized in the workplace (Reitz, 2001a; Watt and Bloom, 2001).

The overall employment situation of immigrants is becoming worse. For more than a decade, immigrants have faced declining earnings and employment success despite rising skill and education levels (Reitz, 1997a, 1997b, 2001b; Dougherty, 1999). In 1980, the earnings of newly arrived male immigrants were about 80 percent of the earnings of Canadian-born men. By 1996, that figure fell to 60 percent. In 1980, the employment rate for newly arrived immigrant men was 86.3 percent, close to the 91 percent for Canadian-born men. By 1996, the comparable figures stood at 68.3 percent for newly arrived immigrant men and 85.4 percent for Canadian-born men. The trends for newly arrived immigrant women are similar (Reitz, 2001b: 590–95). Note too the high poverty rates among several immigrant groups, particularly in big cities such as Toronto (Kazemipur and Halli, 2000). In 1996, the poverty rate in Toronto for families of non-European origin was 34.3 percent, more than double the rate for families of European origin

(Ornstein, 2000). The poverty rate for some categories of non-European families was more than 50 percent.

Educational credentials among recent immigrants are higher on average than those of the Canadian-born work force and are rising. Recent immigrants' levels of fluency in an official language have not changed. Yet the trends in immigrants' employment and earnings are downward. This pattern suggests that the problem we are facing is not so much one of immigrants' skill levels as the extent to which those skills are accepted and utilized in the Canadian workplace.

The difficulties confronting immigrants are a problem for Canada not only in economic terms, but also because of their social and political repercussions. The fact that the great majority of immigrants to Canada today belong to racial minorities probably magnifies the impact. Overall earnings disadvantages and the extent of skill underutilization are greater for immigrants who belong to racial minorities than they are for immigrants of European ethnic origin. Thus, comparing Black immigrant men and European immigrant men *with the same level of education and other qualifications*, I found that Black men earned $6 476 less in 1996. Nearly a quarter of that difference was due to differences in access to skilled occupations (Reitz, 2001a: 367–69). In any society, the correlation between ethnic or racial status and economic success over extended periods of time is bound to become divisive and to affect intergroup relations.

Source: Adapted from Jeffrey G. Reitz, "Tapping Immigrants' Skills: New Directions for Canadian Immigration Policy in the Knowledge Economy," *IRPP Choices* (11, 1: February 2005). Reproduced with permission from IRPP (www.irpp.org).

Clearly, the emphasis in Canadian government policy on points-based immigrant selection and, in particular, on ever-higher educational standards for immigrants, is not resulting in higher employment and earnings for immigrants. One possible response would be to fine-tune the immigrant selection process. But given that sustained efforts to do so have proven ineffective, it seems inadvisable to rely entirely on that approach. There are three other alternatives to the current policy, two of which could have negative consequences.

The first option is to accept downward employment trends among current immigrants and hope for a better future for their children. The expectation of better prospects for the second generation is based in part on the importance highly educated immigrants attach to education, an attitude they tend to pass on to their children. Also, employers are more likely to accept the second generation because their education will have been acquired in Canada. Data on the offspring of immigrants generally confirm this optimism (Boyd, 1992).

The downside of this option is that even if poverty among immigrant parents does not impede their educational aspirations for their children, immigrants living in poverty could create pressures—or at least the perception of pressures—on the social welfare system. That could lead to public demands for a reduction in social programs and other support, which would affect the native-born as well as immigrants.

The second option is to cut immigration levels so as to reduce its negative social impact. For most of the period since World War II, Canada has pursued an expansionist immigration policy, and the current government is continuing that approach with a target immigration level of 1 percent of the population per year (about 300 000 immigrants annually). For much of the past decade, the actual immigration level has ranged between 200 000 and 250 000 people. On a per capita basis, these numbers are high—about three times the immigration rate of the United States, for example. Critics of

Canadian immigration suggest cutting these numbers to between 150 000 and 200 000 immigrants per year (Collacutt, 2002; Stoffman, 2002: 191).

The difficulty with doing so is that it would force Canada to forego much of the potential future economic benefits of immigration. Due to its small size and low fertility rate, Canada has relied heavily on immigration as a development strategy. Demographic projections show that, for the most part, labour force growth in Canada for the foreseeable future will stem from immigration.

Recent experience in Australia illustrates the downside of cutting immigration. Australian opposition to immigration resulted in the number of immigrants being reduced from approximately 140 000 per year in the late 1980s to between 70 000 and 90 000 in the mid-1990s. However, there was political resistance against reducing family-class immigration, so it was easier to reduce the skilled-worker-immigrant category. Consequently, out of economic necessity, Australia soon resumed accepting a larger number of immigrants. Its recent target has been in the range of 100 000 to 110 000 per year (Castles and Vasta, 2004: 146). Cutting immigration levels also had the negative consequence of reinforcing negative perceptions of immigrants, thereby exacerbating domestic race-relations problems.

By comparison, Canadians have a positive view of immigration (Simon and Lynch, 1999: 461). Surveys show that over the past 25 years most Canadians have wanted to maintain or increase immigration levels (Reitz, 2004). Arguably, popular support for immigration in Canada has helped ease the settlement process, and the absence of intense public debate over immigration levels has helped to maintain a supportive environment.

I conclude that accepting downward employment trends among immigrants and cutting immigration levels would not be advisable. The third alternative—augmenting the institutional capacity to utilize immigrants' skills more effectively—makes most sense, as I will now argue.

EFFECTS OF LABOUR MARKET CHANGE IN THE KNOWLEDGE ECONOMY

Canada's current immigration strategy rests largely on human capital theory. This theory was developed to increase our understanding of labour markets in a knowledge economy, but its weaknesses when applied to immigrants have become evident. Human capital theory suggests that workers' earnings reflect the productive value of their skills, particularly skills based on formal education and work experience. Yet immigrants' recent labour market outcomes contradict that expectation, as we have seen.

One reason for the weakness of human capital theory as applied to immigrants is that it assumes employers have effective means of assessing the productive value of prospective workers' skills. The underutilization of immigrant skills suggests that, for immigrants, they lack such means (Li, 2000; Reitz, 2001a).

Historically, immigration policy in Canada has reflected the country's stage of economic development. When agriculture was the economic priority, Canada recruited immigrants for farm work. When priorities shifted to those of an industrializing economy, Canada recruited immigrants for construction and manufacturing. Now that Canada is moving toward a postindustrial or knowledge economy, immigrants are being recruited to respond to that imperative. In the agricultural and industrial eras, it was sufficient to recruit immigrants on the basis of their capacity for physical labour and acquiring the limited skills necessary for manual work. Assessment of foreign credentials was irrelevant. In the knowledge economy, immigrants' credentials are important, and assessment of these credentials is critical to the success of the immigration program.

Any analysis of the integration of immigrants in the knowledge economy should take into account how organizational changes in the labour market and in the workplace are affecting immigrants. For example, employers place more emphasis on credentials insofar as they reflect specific skills that increase productivity (Hunter, 1988; Hunter and Leiper, 1993); organizational decision making is becoming more attentive to employee opinion; the most highly skilled employees are gaining more autonomy in their work; there is greater use of personal networks in recruitment; and there are closer links among universities, governments, and employer organizations. These changes will likely affect workers in the most highly skilled occupations, particularly in the most skill-intensive industries.

Statistics Canada defines "knowledge occupations" as those in which a high proportion of workers have a university education. They include the science and engineering professions, health and education, as well as a variety of other professional fields. "Knowledge industries" have a high proportion of knowledge workers and high levels of investment in research and development. Among them are the high-tech pharmaceutical, chemical, instrument, electronics, and machinery and equipment industries. Management is often considered a knowledge occupation too, particularly when the activities managed involve highly skilled or professional work. Between 1971 and 2001, the proportion of Canadian workers in knowledge occupations almost doubled, increasing from 14 percent to 25 percent. Education levels in these occupations also increased. At the same time, educational requirements and levels have risen in many occupations outside the knowledge category (Baldwin and Beckstead, 2003: 5; Beckstead and Vinodrai, 2003; Beckstead and Gellatly, 2004).

Because of changes in recruitment and hiring practices, qualified immigrants appear to be facing increasing difficulty gaining access to work in knowledge occupations (Reitz, 2003). As a result, they end up working in less-skilled occupations than do comparably qualified native-born Canadians. In 1996, 59 percent of native-born men with bachelors' degrees were working in knowledge occupations, compared with only 35 percent of recent immigrants with bachelors' degrees. The corresponding figures for women were 57 and 28 percent. Of men with postgraduate degrees, 79 percent of those who were born in Canada were working in knowledge occupations, compared with only 59 percent of recent immigrants. The corresponding figures for women were 78 and 49 percent. Between 1981 and 1996, as the importance of knowledge occupations increased, differences between the income levels and representation in knowledge occupations of native-born Canadians and immigrants have grown as well. Despite increases in the skill levels of new immigrants, their representation in knowledge occupations was lower in 1996 than it was in 1981. Within the knowledge occupations, immigrants have greater difficulty gaining access to managerial than to professional positions (Reitz, 2003: 485, 487; Beck, Reitz, and Weiner, 2002).

These barriers to access in professional and managerial occupations and the earnings disadvantages within these fields clearly have the effect of decreasing immigrants' earnings. Less known, but at least as important, are the earnings disadvantages of highly educated immigrants in occupations outside the knowledge sector, which are actually larger and more financially consequential than those within the knowledge sector. For example, in the knowledge occupations, the net earnings of immigrant men with bachelors' or postgraduate degrees (professions and management) are 12 to 16 percent lower than are those of native-born Canadians with similar education, but in all other occupations, they are 25 to 34 percent lower. Over time, negative earnings trends in occupations outside the knowledge sector have contributed substantially to the overall downward trend in immigrant earnings (Reitz, 2003: 493, 500).

The stereotype of immigrants with Ph.D.s driving taxis reflects the most extreme consequence of barriers to immigrant employment. Instead of working in knowledge occupations, and often experiencing greater barriers in lower level skilled work, university-educated immigrants often do unskilled work. For recent immigrants with a university degree who were employed between 1991 and 2001, "at least one in four had a job requiring no more than a high school education" (Galarneau and Morissette, 2004: 13). Most immigrants with degrees who came to Canada in the 1990s worked in just 29 occupations, including restaurant and food-service managers, taxi and

limousine drivers and chauffeurs, truck drivers, security guards and related occupations, and janitors, caretakers, and building superintendents (Statistics Canada, 2003: 13). Their earnings were substantially below those of native-born Canadians in the same occupations.

Immigrants' relative success in the professions (as opposed to management and non-knowledge jobs) implies that rigorous credential assessment processes are advantageous to them. Moreover, immigrants' difficulties outside the professions indicate that addressing the problem of credential assessment must go beyond the issue of barriers to licensing. Policy reform should also focus on sectors of the work force outside the knowledge sector, where the processes are often much less formal.

I conclude that the new knowledge economy is far from entirely immigrant-friendly. There is a well-known commitment to universality in knowledge-producing institutions such as the sciences, but the validation of knowledge-based skills in labour markets is inevitably performed by local institutions. The question is whether these local institutions can better develop the capacity for validation of skills. Employment success increasingly depends on high levels of educational attainment, but only if that education is properly assessed and utilized. The increased emphasis on education-based skills in many occupations, both inside and outside the professions, as well as the increased supply of domestically educated workers, means that immigrants now face significant competition in the labour market and cannot escape the problem of skills transferability. Creating labour market institutions that can handle a diverse work force will require institutional innovation and change.

INSTITUTIONAL CHANGE: COMPLEXITY, TIMING, AND RACIAL ATTITUDES

The success of Canada's immigration policy depends on the existence of institutions that link workers to jobs and provide for the international transferability of skills. To that end, employers need access to accurate information about the skills reflected in credentials acquired from educational institutions abroad; reliable information about people's performance in acquiring their credentials; and sound performance assessments of comparably qualified individuals who are already employed here.

While in today's labour market there should be incentive enough for employers to participate in gathering such information processes, three stumbling blocks exist. First is the complexity of the required changes. Second is the timing of the changes in relation to the decision-making processes involved and also to the different priorities of employers and immigration policymakers. Third is the effect of racial attitudes in the host society. Let us consider each of these issues in turn.

INSTITUTIONAL COMPLEXITY

In discussions of barriers to immigrant skill utilization, the role of licensing bodies has probably received the most attention. Immigrants who worked abroad as professional engineers, for example, may encounter difficulty obtaining a licence to practice in Canada. Although there has been progress in this area, more work is needed. However, important as it is, access to professional and trade licences is only a small part of the problem. Possession of a licence does not guarantee a job, and those who do get jobs in licensed occupations are not guaranteed professional advancement or promotions. As several studies have shown, the career path leading from professional to managerial responsibility, which is often successfully followed by native-born workers, is blocked for many immigrants (Reitz, 2003; Beck, Reitz, and Weiner, 2002).

Immigrants also experience difficulty in gaining a licence when there are specific gaps in their training or when specific skills are not transferable. Frequently in such cases, they are required to repeat the entire training program in Canada, which, of course, is wasteful. A more efficient way to fill specific skills gaps would be to provide some

form of bridge training, such as occupation-specific programs involving collaboration among educational institutions, governments, and regulatory bodies. The University of Toronto's Faculty of Pharmacy has developed such a program. It enables pharmacists trained outside North America to take university-based courses, thereby facilitating their preparation for professional practice in Ontario. There are a few similar programs in the health professions, and others are being developed.

Recognition of foreign educational credentials is also a problem in occupations that are not licensed or regulated. These occupations frequently require substantial educational qualifications, even though the requirements may be less specific or explicit. They include some knowledge-based occupations, such as managerial positions in knowledge-based industries. Since this labour market sector is less formally organized, institutional change may be more difficult to achieve.

One useful type of institution that is widely available in the less-regulated sector of the labour market is the credential assessment service, available in nearly all high immigration areas in Canada. For about $100, they offer immigrants an authoritative assessment of the Canadian equivalence of their foreign educational credentials. Although immigrants have so far made limited use of these services, credential assessment is making inroads and could play an important role in breaking down barriers to immigrant skill utilization. At the same time, these organizations need to gain wider acceptance among employers. For their part, the assessment services may not be providing some of the information employers need, such as information about distinctions in quality among foreign universities. Hence, it is difficult to judge the effectiveness of these services, and it would be useful if they were subjected to systematic evaluation.

The shortcomings of the institutions that certify immigrants' qualifications and promote skill utilization are epitomized by employers' notorious demand for Canadian experience. This demand has been a source of particular frustration for immigrants because of its Catch-22 character (you need Canadian experience to get Canadian experience) and also because of the suspicion that it hides prejudice against immigrants and minorities. Yet employers have a legitimate interest in knowing whether a job candidate can function effectively in the local context. In judging native-born job applicants, employers get information by means of recommendations from previous employers or well-known local educational institutions. Understandably, hiring immigrants in the absence of such information may be seen as a significant risk.

In this context, programs promoting the mentoring of new immigrant employees by more senior colleagues may well be useful. These are a kind of on-the-job training that is similar to apprenticeships or internships—a means by which the mentor can pass on knowledge about local practices in a given occupation. While employer-sponsored apprenticeship programs are not yet as common in the Canadian labour market as they are in some other countries, such as Germany, they could potentially be very useful in addressing immigrants' needs. But they must be carefully designed: programs and processes will have to be set up to match mentors with immigrants effectively. It may also be necessary to provide subsidies.

In most large and complex organizations, human resource managers are responsible for ensuring effective utilization of the skills of job applicants and employees. Increasingly, this task involves "diversity management," that is, addressing employment issues related to gender, disability, sexual orientation, ethnicity, and immigration status. Although human resource managers are likely to support and promote the institutional changes sketched above, there are limits to what they can achieve on their own. For instance, human resource managers may have the expertise to initiate immigrant mentorship, but they will need resources to do so. As well, setting up these programs may require collaboration with groups other than the employer organization.

Information is a key issue in many of these changes, and developing the means for effective communication between immigrants and employers is part of the necessary institutional response. On the immigrant side of the equation, Citizenship and Immigration Canada is creating a web site that is intended to serve as a one-stop source of information for prospective and recent immigrants. It includes information on a range of topics related to work, credential assessment, regulated professions and trades, and other labour market issues. It also features links to information about local labour markets and employers. Still in the experimental stage, neither the effectiveness of the web site in reaching its target audience nor the usefulness of the information it contains has yet been assessed. Comparable information sources for employers and other interested groups might also be useful.

Finally, institutional change requires a supportive environment. Attitudes matter. A high degree of positive commitment is necessary to bring about meaningful institutional change, inasmuch as general sympathy with the issue may or may not translate into support for concrete action in workplaces where the actual financial risks are taken. In effect, positive actions and incentives may be required to reinforce supportive work environments. Although public attitudes may provide some of these incentives, recognition of employers who develop effective best practices could be useful. *Canadian Business* magazine, in collaboration with OMNI Television, recently took a step in this direction by publishing a list of the "best employers for visible minorities" ("Minority Report," 2004).

TIMING AND DECISION-MAKING STRUCTURES

Given the complexity of the changes required, questions of timing and decision making arise. Can the institutional changes needed to avert or reverse the decline in immigrant employment outcomes be made before their negative consequences become difficult to reverse? Are the necessary decision-making processes in place? Of course, given enough time, employers might become more familiar with foreign-acquired qualifications. But working against this is the very complexity of the institutional changes needed to accommodate foreign-trained workers and the rapid increase in the supply of highly skilled native-born workers, which reduces the incentives for employers to innovate in the area. Thus, from the employer's perspective, the issue of immigrant skill utilization may be much less pressing than it is for those concerned with the broader goals of the immigration program, or for the rest of society, if there are negative economic and social consequences of declining immigrant employment outcomes.

The decline in immigrants' employment outcomes has been fairly rapid, and its negative impact could translate into a number of social problems. First, we can expect demands on the social safety net to increase. Although immigrants are known to be self-reliant and reluctant to take advantage of the social assistance for which they are eligible, high rates of poverty and social disadvantage will inevitably translate into high rates of social-service use. Second, we can expect public perceptions of immigrants as a liability or social problem to become more widespread. That perception would be heightened if social problems associated with poverty were to emerge. Third, immigrants themselves may react politically to their employment conditions. Although the time frame for these outcomes is unknown, the risks are clear. It would be prudent to ensure that the steps taken are adequate to address the problem fully.

If change is more urgent for governments than it is for employers, and if the process must be kick-started, adequate decision-making structures must be in place. Intergovernmental collaboration is crucial. In Canada, no one agency has clear responsibility for immigrant skill utilization. Responsibility resides with different levels of government and different agencies at different levels of government. At the federal level, for example, Citizenship and Immigration Canada is responsible for immigration. Yet current immigration policy is designed to minimize government involvement in matters related to the integration of immigrants in the labour force. Other federal agencies are responsible for industrial development, which includes employment issues. For example, in 2002, Human Resources and Development Canada, in cooperation with Industry Canada, committed $40 million over five years to the integration of immigrants in the labour market (Canada, 2002). More recently, further initiatives have been announced. Public statements make it clear that action on this front depends on cooperation with provincial governments because regulation of employment is formally a provincial responsibility. Unfortunately, such cooperation is far from automatic, and to date it has been minimal.

Recently, federal and provincial governments have concluded a number of agreements on immigration (in addition to the long-standing agreement involving Quebec). Much attention has been focused on two issues that are tangential to skill utilization: immigrant selection and the allocation of settlement funds. There have also been moves toward greater federal–provincial collaboration in developing a more effective immigrant employment policy. These are promising, but rapid progress is needed.

Municipalities also share the responsibility. They provide many of the services. But they are resource-poor and are fragmented among the metropolitan areas in which immigrants settle. In Toronto, for example, the need for coordination of immigration-related issues has only recently emerged as an item on the local agenda as part of a broader resurgence of attention to urban needs. While progress is being made, the question remains whether the pace of change is sufficient given the task at hand.

RACIAL ATTITUDES

Underlying all these issues are questions arising from the interrelation between immigration issues and increasing ethno-cultural and racial diversity. Because the groups affected by skills underutilization are primarily composed of racial minorities, the potential exists for inter-group tensions and prejudice to emerge. Indeed, there is already much evidence of racial prejudice and employment disparities in Canada (Boyd, 1992; Christofides and Swidinsky, 1994; Reitz and Breton, 1994; Li, 1998; Baker and Benjamin, 1994, 1997). Ethnic and racial stereotypes may affect perceptions of immigrant qualifications. Cultural differences and misunderstandings can impede efforts at cooperation. And the minority status of individual groups may have an effect on the attention they receive in the political process.

Although recognition of immigrants' foreign qualifications has not been widely viewed as a problem of racial discrimination, racial discrimination is a cause of skill underutilization. Racial discrimination occurs when negative employment decisions are based on candidates' racial origins rather than their skills. Racial discrimination is not necessarily based on racial prejudice but could arise from other individual and organizational circumstances.

The context of race relations suggests that in some circumstances resistance to better utilization of immigrant minorities' skills is not only a problem of institutional barriers in labour markets, but also one of intergroup relations. This is evident in the controversy over whether racial attitudes underlie employers' requirements for Canadian experience. Virtually any employer's judgment that a foreign-acquired qualification reflects a lower standard than its Canadian counterpart could be viewed as discriminatory.

The issues of race and employment emerged as part of the debate in Canada over employment equity. It was highly controversial, and the resulting policy initiatives have been weak, confused, and fragmented. These policy shortcomings are compounded by the fact that employment equity legislation operates differently at the federal and provincial levels. At the federal level, it was introduced in 1985 and originally included "visible minorities," among other target groups. Since then, it has been adminis-

tered, with periodic adjustments, under federal employment jurisdiction. Ontario introduced legislation in the mid-1990s similar to the federal law, but a later government scrapped it on the grounds that it amounted to the introduction of racial quotas. This disarray shows that Canadian governments have had great difficulty in directly confronting issues related to race. It illustrates how race relations complicate the process of addressing the employment circumstances of immigrant minorities.

TOWARD A NEW CANADIAN MODEL FOR IMMIGRATION

The Canadian immigration model developed as a result of the country's substantial commitment to immigration, which was dictated in part by geography and political economy. It consists essentially of two main components: immigrant selection—specifically, the points system—and the policy of multiculturalism. Today, as Canada pursues mass immigration in the context of a knowledge economy and declining employment outcomes for immigrants, the sustainability of the immigration program in the global labour market is in question.

The range of institutional innovations that will be necessary to create a global knowledge credentials network is complex. These innovations include:

- Improved Internet-based and other information sources for immigrants, both before and after they arrive in Canada.

- More support for providers of credential assessments to improve the labour market effectiveness of their services.

- Bridge-training programs to top up immigrant skills or fill gaps across a range of occupations.

- Subsidized workplace internship and mentoring programs for immigrants.

- Upgraded human resource management training programs that include training about ethnic diversity issues.

- Employer recognition of best practices.
- Improved public awareness of the problems faced by skilled immigrants in integrating into the Canadian labour market and the social and political consequences of those problems.

Broad support exists for many of the proposals just listed, but to bring about institutional change and create a new Canadian model for immigration, the various agencies and levels of governments must work together. To develop the initiatives outlined here, government leadership will be required to coordinate the institutional players that share responsibility for various aspects of the utilization of immigrants' skills: the federal government for immigration and broad economic and social policy; provincial governments for employment, education, and municipal affairs; and municipal governments for immigrant settlement and delivery of services.

To a large degree, the success of our immigration policy depends on our ability to meet the challenges outlined above. If we do not do so in a timely fashion, several consequences are likely to follow. In the short term, there may be increased pressure to reduce the size of the immigration program and its place in the nation's overall development strategy. In the longer term, there is the potential for social and political unrest. Whether Canada becomes a leader in this field remains to be seen. Several countries have been working on this issue for some time. Initiatives in Europe and the United States focus on credential assessment and recognition. The ultimate policy objective, however, is effective utilization of immigrants' skills in labour markets, which in turn depends on the broader development of labour market institutions. Fully functioning global labour markets are becoming a priority. Our heavy reliance on immigration for expansion and growth gives us a considerable incentive to focus our energies in this area.

REFERENCES

Baker, M., and D. Benjamin. (1994). "The Performance of Immigrants in the Canadian Labor Market." *Journal of Labor Economics,* 12: 369–405.

———. (1997). "Ethnicity, Foreign Birth and Earnings: A Canada/U.S. Comparison." In M.G. Abbott, C.M. Beach, and R.P. Chaykowski, eds., *Transition and Structural Change in the North American Labor Market* (pp. 281–313). Kingston: John Deutsch Institute and Industrial Relations Centre, Queen's University.

Baldwin, J. R., and D. Beckstead. (2003). *Knowledge Workers in Canada's Economy, 1971–2001.* Catalogue no. 11-624-MIE no. 004. Ottawa: Statistics Canada.

Beck, J. H., J. G. Reitz, and N. Weiner. (2002). "Addressing Systemic Racial Discrimination in Employment: The Health Canada Case and Implications of Legislative Change." *Canadian Public Policy,* 28 (3): 373–94.

Beckstead, D., and G. Gellatly. (2004). *Are Knowledge Workers Found Only in High-Technology Industries?* Catalogue no. 11-622-MIE no. 005. Ottawa: Statistics Canada.

Beckstead, D., and T. Vinodrai. (2003). *Dimensions of Occupational Changes in Canada's Knowledge Economy, 1971–1996.* Catalogue no. 11-622-MIE no. 004. Ottawa: Statistics Canada.

Boyd, M. (1992). "Gender, Visible Minority and Immigrant Earnings Inequality: Reassessing an Employment Equity Premise." In V. Satzewich, ed., *Deconstructing a Nation: Immigration, Multiculturalism and Racism in the 1990s Canada* (pp. 279–321). Toronto: Garamond Press.

Canada. Human Resources Development Canada. (2002). *Knowledge Matters: Skills and Learning for Canadians.* Ottawa: Human Resources Development Canada.

Castles, S., and E. Vasta. (2004). "Australia: New Conflicts around Old Dilemmas." In W. Cornelius, J. Hollifield, and P. Martin, eds., *Controlling Immigration: A Global Perspective,* 2nd ed. (pp. 141–73). Palo Alto, CA: Stanford University Press.

Christofides, L. N., and R. Swidinsky. (1994). "Wage Determination by Gender and Visible Minority Status: Evidence from the 1989 LMAS." *Canadian Public Policy,* 22: 34–51.

Collacutt, M. (2002). *Canadian Immigration Policy: The Need for Major Reform.* Vancouver: Fraser Institute.

Dougherty, C. (1999). "New Entrants to the Labour Market: A Comparison of the Labour Market Performance of Immigrants Landed in the 1980s and 1990s." Paper presented at the 4th International Metropolis Conference, Washington, DC, 7–11 December.

Galarneau, D., and R. Morissette. (2004). "Immigrants: Settling for Less?" *Perspectives on Labour and Income,* 5 (6): 5–16.

Hunter, A. A. (1988). "Formal Education and Initial Employment: Unravelling the Relationships between Schooling and Skills over Time." *American Sociological Review,* 53: 753–65.

Hunter, A. A., and J. M. Leiper. (1993). "On Formal Education, Skills, and Earnings: The Role of Educational Certificates in Earnings Determination." *Canadian Journal of Sociology,* 18: 21–42.

Kazemipur, A., and S. S. Halli. (2000). *The New Poverty in Canada: Ethnic Groups and Ghetto Neighbourhoods.* Toronto: Thompson Educational Publishing.

Li, P. S. (1998). "The Market Value and Social Value of Race." In V. Satzewich, ed., *Racism and Social Inequality in Canada* (pp. 115–30). Toronto: Thompson Educational Publishing.

_____. (2000). "Earnings Disparities between Immigrants and Native-born Canadians." *Canadian Review of Sociology and Anthropology,* 37 (3): 289–311.

"Minority Report: The First Canadian Business-OMNI Round up of Top Workplaces for Visible Minorities." (2004). *Canadian Business* (March).

Ornstein, Michael. (2000). Ethno-racial Inequality in Toronto: Analysis of the 1996 Census. Prepared for the Chief Administrator's Office of the City of Toronto.

Reitz, J. G. (1997a). "Priorities for Immigration in a Changing Canadian Economy: From Skill Selectivity to Skill Utilization." Workshop on "New Selection Criteria for Economic Stream Immigrants," held by the Department of Citizenship and Immigration Canada, Ottawa, 30–31 October. (Pages 189–206 in proceedings published by Citizenship and Immigration Canada.)

_____. (1997b). "Measuring Down: The Economic Performance of New Canadians Is Declining; If We Want to Change That, We Need to Rethink Immigration Policy." *Financial Post,* 8 November. Reprinted (1998) in Charles Davies, ed., *Post 2000: Business Wisdom for the Next Century* (pp. 157–63). Toronto: Key Porter Books.

_____. (2001a). "Immigrant Skill Utilization in the Canadian Labour Market: Implications of Human Capital Research." *Journal of International Migration and Integration,* 2 (3): 347–78.

_____. (2001b). "Immigrant Success in the Knowledge Economy: Institutional Change and the Immigrant Experience in Canada, 1970–1995." *Journal of Social Issues,* 57 (3): 579–613.

_____. (2003). "Occupational Dimensions of Immigrant Credential Assessment: Trends in Professional, Managerial, and Other Occupations, 1970–1996." In Charles Beach, Alan Green, and Jeffrey G. Reitz, eds., *Canadian Immigration Policy for the 21st Century* (pp. 469–596). Kingston: John Deutsch Institute for the Study of Economic Policy.

_____. (2004). "Canada: Immigration and Nation-Building in the Transition to a Knowledge Economy." In W. Cornelius, J. Hollifield, and P. Martin, eds., *Controlling Immigration: A Global Perspective,* 2nd ed. (pp. 97–133). Palo Alto, CA: Stanford University Press.

Reitz, J. G., and R. Breton. (1994). *The Illusion of Difference: Realities of Ethnicity in Canada and the United States.* Toronto: C.D. Howe.

Simon, R. J., and J. P. Lynch. (1999). "Comparative Assessment of Public Opinion Toward Immigrants and Immigration Policy." *International Migration Review,* 33 (2): 455–67.

Statistics Canada. (2003). *Earnings of Canadians: Making a Living in the New Economy.* Catalogue no. 96F0030XIE2001013. Ottawa: Minister of Industry.

Stoffman, D. (2002). *Who Gets In: What's Wrong with Canada's Immigration Program—and How to Fix It.* Toronto: Macfarlane, Walter and Ross.

Watt, D., and M. Bloom. (2001). *Exploring the Learning Recognition Gap in Canada. Phase 1 Report. Recognizing Learning: The Economic Cost of Not Recognizing Learning and Learning Credentials in Canada.* Ottawa: Conference Board of Canada.

PART 4

SOCIAL INSTITUTIONS

The social structures that comprise human societies are nested like Russian dolls or Chinese boxes. There are structures within structures within structures. The smallest are **microstructures.** Microstructures are localized sites of face-to-face interaction, such as families. Social relations in microstructures tend to be emotionally deep and enduring, which is why people value them for their own sake. **Macrostructures,** in contrast, are larger, less localized, and more impersonal. People participate in macrostructures for specific, instrumental reasons—to earn money, get an education, and so on. **Global structures** are even larger, more remote, and more impersonal. They involve relations between whole societies and between nations.

Institutions are found at both the micro- and macrostructural levels of society. Institutions are social structures that, to varying degrees, fulfill basic human needs. These needs include:

- the reproduction of the species and the nurturance and primary socialization of small children, a set of functions that is usually performed by the family (see part 4A);
- the maintenance and renewal of legitimate authority, a set of functions that is performed by the political system (see part 4B.); and
- the production and distribution of material resources, a set of functions that is performed by the economy (see part 4C).

In keeping with one of this book's major themes, the articles in this part focus on how powerful social forces, such as globalization, consumerism, and rationalization, are reshaping major social institutions. Some of the articles highlight not only the fact that social institutions fulfill basic human needs but that basic human needs are flexible and may therefore be fulfilled by a wide variety of institutional forms. The chapters also show that the adaptation of families, political systems, and economies to new conditions is often disorienting for the people who live and work in them. Some people react by organizing resistance to change and attempting to return to the old state of affairs. The very term "institution" may suggest a solid and stable establishment, but in reality social conflict is never far below the surface of any institution.

GLOSSARY

Global structures are the largest and most impersonal social relations. They include relations between societies and nations.

Institutions are micro- and macro-level social structures that address basic human needs, such as reproduction, nurturance, and primary socialization (the family), the maintenance and renewal of legitimate authority (the political system), and the production and distribution of material resources (the economy).

Macrostructures are large, non-localized, impersonal sets of social relations. People participate in them for specific, instrumental reasons.

Microstructures are small, localized, emotionally intense patterns of social relations. People value such relations for their own sake.

PART 4A

FAMILIES

Notice the italicized terms in the following sentences, taken from this part's introduction: "Institutions are social structures that, *to varying degrees,* fulfill basic human needs. These needs include the reproduction of the species and the nurturance and primary socialization of small children, a set of functions that is *usually* performed by the family." The italics signify weasel words; they allow me to squirm out of a tight spot. Here is the tight spot: the degree to which families fulfill the basic human needs of reproduction and the nurturance and primary socialization of small children has declined in recent decades.

Roughly a fifth of Canadian women between the ages of 40 and 45—women who are near the end of their reproductive years—do not have children, up from about 10 percent circa 1980. The proportion of Canadians who marry is down, the divorce rate is up, and the rate of remarriage after divorce is down. Non-family households are more common than they were a few decades ago because more single people, including the elderly, can afford to live on their own and because gay and lesbian lifestyles are more widely accepted than they used to be, especially in large urban areas. In Canada, the Netherlands, Belgium, and Spain, gays and lesbians can marry. As a result of all these factors, the **nuclear family** is no longer the overwhelmingly predominant household form. (The nuclear family consists of a husband and wife who live in the same household and have at least one child.) More than half of Canadian households are married families (many without children), a tenth are common-law families, more than a tenth are lone-parent families, and nearly three out of ten are non-family households.

The facts listed above should not lead one to conclude that the family is in a state of collapse. Sociological surveys show that more than three-quarters of Canadians regard their family as the most important thing in their lives, more important than career or religion. The great majority of adults still want to marry and have children. In one poll, more than 90 percent of respondents with children at home said that the family is becoming *more* important to them. What is happening, however, is that people are freer than they once were to establish the kinds of family arrangements that best suit them. For instance, because most adult women are now employed in the paid labour force, and because changes in divorce laws have made the division of property after divorce more equitable, women now have a measure of economic independence that gives them greater freedom to end unsatisfying marriages and seek more gratifying relationships. As this example illustrates, the facts listed in the preceding paragraph do not spell the end of the family but the possibility that family forms which better suit the *diversity* of human needs can take shape.

One alternative family form that is becoming increasingly prevalent is the gay or lesbian family. People are changing laws in some parts of the world to give partners of homosexual unions the same rights and obligations as partners in a marriage. No religious organization in Canada is compelled by the state to bless homosexual unions. But since July 20, 2005, homosexual unions can be recognized as legal marriages in this country. In Chapter 15, Adie Nelson traces the often turbulent social and legal circumstances surrounding the evolution of gay and lesbian marriage from about 1990 until 2005.

In our society, dating is usually the prelude to the formation of a long-term intimate relationship, and finding a date through the Internet is growing quickly in popularity. Chapter 16 reports results from the world's first large-scale survey of online daters, conducted in Canada in 2000. In that year, 13 percent of adult Canadian Internet users had "read personal or dating ads" online or "checked out online dating services." The percentage is undoubtedly considerably larger today. The chapter outlines the social forces that are making online dating more popular. It also discusses the similarities and differences among online daters, Internet users in general, and the Canadian population as a whole. Significantly for present purposes, 60 percent of online daters said they formed at least one long-term relationship as a result of using online dating services, 37 percent met at least one person they regarded as a "partner," and 3 percent met someone they eventually married. With a success record like that in its early years, it seems reasonable to expect that people will increasingly use online dating services to initiate long-term intimate relationships and create families.

GLOSSARY

A **nuclear family** consists of a husband and wife who live in the same household and have at least one child.

CRITICAL THINKING QUESTIONS

1. What are the major social forces (groups, ideas) for and against gay and lesbian marriage in Canada? Why did the groups (and ideas) who support gay and lesbian marriage eventually win their struggle in 2005?
2. Why has online dating grown in popularity in recent years? What are the similarities and differences among adult online daters, adult Internet users in general, and the Canadian adult population as a whole? Would you characterize online dating as less safe or safer than meeting dates in traditional ways? Why? How could you make online dating safer?

ANNOTATED BIBLIOGRAPHY

Eichler, Margrit. *Family Shifts: Families, Policies, and Gender Equality.* Toronto: Oxford University Press, 1997. A penetrating analysis of how Canadian families have changed and how public policies need to be reformed to take account of new realities.

Fox, Bonnie, ed. *Family Patterns, Gender Relations.* 2nd ed. Toronto: Oxford University Press, 2001. The definitive Canadian reader in sociology of the family.

Stack, Carol. *All Our Kin: Strategies for Survival in a Black Community.* New York: Harper and Row, 1974. This highly regarded participant-observation study shows how kinship networks adapt to conditions of extreme poverty. The author convincingly demonstrates that there are functional alternatives to the nuclear family that are required by non-middle-class social settings.

Chapter 15

What Is a Family?

NEW CHALLENGES IN DEFINING AN EVERYDAY TERM

ADIE NELSON

On the surface, answering the question "What is a family?" does not seem to pose much of a challenge. Regardless of what type of family we grew up in or what type of relationship we are currently involved in, the image of the "ideal" family comes readily to mind: the benevolent but firm father who sits at the head of the table and the household, the emotionally expressive wife/homemaker/mother and, of course, their two children. The imagery is especially potent because it is sheathed in the "charm of hominess," or a vision of Home Sweet Home in which the family is a haven in an often heartless world (Gottlieb, 1993: 270). The scene is reminiscent of a Norman Rockwell painting—the white picket fence, the gingham-clad daughter and denim-clad son playing happily with the frolicking puppy, mom's chocolate chip cookies cooling on the window sill, dad cutting the festive turkey—and creates an enticing portrait of comfort and security.

The patriarchal heterosexual nuclear family is routinely extolled by conservative political parties (Conway, 1990: xi). It is championed as universal, idyllic, and sacred. However, one of the subtle consequences of heralding this image of the family is that it constructs an evaluative framework by which all relational forms are to be judged (Abbott and Wallace, 1992: 73). Thus, a particular type of family, characterized by a gendered division of labour (that is, the male "breadwinner" and the female "housewife") is depicted "as the normal, natural and inevitable family form." Implicitly, forms of relationships that depart from or challenge this imagery are viewed as "deviant" (Gavigan, 1997)—even

though Canadian families are much more varied than this image of the family suggests. Moreover, inasmuch as "good people" enter into "good" (that is, conventional) relationships, those involved in non-traditional family forms may be regarded as suspect or inferior.

The word "family" stems from *famulus*, Latin for "servant" (Gottlieb, 1993: 7). The word *familia* was used originally in classical times to refer to the live-in staff of a household, and from there it came to mean the household itself or its members. The term *pater familias* was so commonly used to refer to a "householder" that it took on the connotation of "an ordinary citizen." *Mater familias* was also commonly used to refer to the "woman of the house" in the sense of the person who directed its domestic affairs. The gendered division of household responsibilities (man's realm was public, woman's was private) was already evident.

Our ideas of what is and is not a family are products of our society, reflecting dominant ideologies about the social roles of men and women, about their sexuality and sexual behaviour, about fertility and procreation, and about the care and socialization of children. Given that these issues intersect in discussions of the family, any attempt to answer the question "What is a family?" inevitably provokes debate.

For example, the issue of whether a long-term homosexual relationship between adults can constitute a family has considerably agitated people who categorize homosexuality as a "sexual perversion" and view homosexuals as a threat to social order (Cossman, 1996; Lancaster, 2003). Accordingly, some analysts maintain that the family must include "adults of *both* sexes, at least two of whom maintain a socially approved sexual relationship, and one or more children of their own, or adopted, of the sexually cohabiting adults" (Murdock, 1949: 1, emphasis added).

Canada's first widely publicized, unofficial gay "marriage" took place in 1977, when two gay men were married by a Unitarian-Universalist minister in Winnipeg (Jackson and Persky, 1982). Until recently, however, Canada has not been guided by a concept of "different, but equal" when it comes to same-sex relationships (Kinsman, 1996). It was only in 1969, following Prime Minister Pierre Trudeau's famous comment that the "state has no place in the bedrooms of the nation," that homosexual acts committed in private, between two consenting adults of at least 21 years of age, were decriminalized. However, it is telling that, as of 2006, the "age of consent" for engaging in the act of anal intercourse is still set higher (18) than the age at which one can legally engage in heterosexual acts (14). It is also notable that, in 1993, when Gallup Canada first attempted to gauge public attitudes toward same-sex marriage, 76 percent of Canadians expressed opposition. It was only in February 2000 that less than half (48 percent) opposed homosexual marriage. Another polling milestone was reached in June 2001, when a Leger marketing poll found majority support for gay adoption. Yet as recently as 1988 only 25 percent of Canadians agreed that gays should be allowed to adopt children (Bricker and Greenspon, 2001: 267).

Throughout the 1990s, and with growing momentum in the new millennium, many of the rights and obligations that were once exclusively associated with marriage (e.g., the right to spousal support; the right to benefit from a partner's job benefits plan) were extended to couples living in marriage-like relationships. In 1990, the Ontario government extended full coverage of supplementary health, hospital, and dental benefits to the same-sex partners of provincial government employees. In 1995, the federal government amended its policies, extending leave-related benefits (e.g., bereavement leave, leave for family-related responsibilities) to the same-sex partners of federal civil servants. In that same year, an Ontario provincial court judge ruled that, under the *Child and Family Services Act*, homosexual couples have the right to adopt a child. In the 1996 case of *M. v. H.*, the opposite-sex definition of "spouse" in Ontario's *Family Law Act* was struck down when, both at trial and on appeal, the courts ruled that M. was entitled to sue H. for support following the breakdown of their lesbian relationship. In 1998, the province of British Columbia enacted changes to its *Adoption Act* and *Family Relations Act* that gave same-sex couples who had cohabited for a period of two years the same rights and responsibilities as their opposite-sex counterparts, including pension and inheritance rights. Other changes in that year were prompted by an Ontario Court of Appeal ruling that declared the federal government's definition of "spouse" in the *Income Tax Act*, which excluded same-sex survivor benefits from employers' pension plans, was unconstitutional. A year later, the Supreme Court of Canada dismissed an appeal by Ontario's Attorney General of the 1996 *M. v. H.* Decision, upholding the right of same-sex couples to seek and obtain spousal support in the same way as opposite-sex common-law couples and informing the Ontario government that it had six months to ensure that its legislation in this area was constitutional. Although the Ontario government, in response, passed an omnibus bill in 1999 that amended 67 of its laws to include same-sex couples, it did so by creating a separate class of "same-sex partners" rather than providing same-sex couples with all of the rights of opposite-sex common-law couples. When the Quebec National Assembly unanimously passed Bill 32 in June 1999, the Quebec government became the first Canadian province to ensure that same-sex couples would receive all the benefits and responsibilities of opposite-sex couples, excluding the right to marriage. Other notable changes in that year occurred when the Alberta government joined with Ontario and British Columbia in allowing same-sex couples to jointly adopt a child and when the British Columbia government introduced the "Definition of Spouse Amendment," which expanded the definition of a spouse in that province to ensure that "persons of the same gender" would be treated the same as opposite-sex couples in relation to such matters as wills, estates, and inheritance. Although that year also witnessed the federal Parliament voting to preserve the opposite-sex definition of marriage, the tides of change were clearly moving in the opposite direction.

In 2000, for example, the federal government of Canada enacted the *Modernization of Benefits and Obligations Act*, which equalized the treatment of same-sex and opposite-sex common-law couples under 68 federal laws (EGALE, 2000). In separate legislation that year, the *Immigration Act*'s "family class" provisions were expanded to include same-sex couples. Also in that year, Nova Scotia introduced legislation that revised the definition of "spouse" in family law to include common-law and same-sex partners who had cohabited for a period of one year. The following year, Nova Scotia's same-sex couples became the first Canadians to be able to register their unions under registered domestic partnership legislation. In 2001, Quebec extended the definition of spouse to same-sex couples in a "de facto" union in 39 of its laws.

Further evidence of a shift in thinking on the question of what constitutes a family may be found in the Canadian census (EGALE, 2001). While the 1981 Census was the first to report on common-law marriages, the 2001 Census included two questions that recognized same-sex, common-law unions. It also recognized that children were being raised in same-sex households—even in jurisdictions where provincial or territorial laws did not permit same-sex couples to formally adopt or share guardianship of their children. According to Statistics Canada, a "census family" is "a now married couple (with or without never-married sons and/or daughters of either or both spouses), a couple living common-law (again, with or without never-married sons and/or daughters of either or both

partners), or a lone parent of any marital status, with at least one never-married son or daughter living in the same dwelling."

Perhaps the most noteworthy legal change has occurred in relation to the definition of marriage itself. Under the *Constitution Act*, the federal Parliament of Canada controls who may marry (i.e., the capacity of persons to marry), while the provinces regulate the technical aspects of the "solemnization of marriage" (e.g., who can perform the ceremony, how the deed is registered) (EGALE, 2004). In July 2002, three Ontario Superior Court judges made Canadian legal history when they ruled that the opposite-sex limitation in common law (which restricted marriage to the union of one man and one woman) was unconstitutional. This decision was echoed in 2003 by courts in British Columbia, Quebec, the Yukon and, in 2004, in Manitoba, Nova Scotia, Saskatchewan, Quebec, and Newfoundland and Labrador. In the fall of 2004, the federal government of Canada presented a "Reference re Same-Sex Marriage" to the Supreme Court of Canada, requesting that the Court clarify whether the opposite-sex requirement for marriage was consistent with *Charter* guarantees of equality. In response, the Supreme Court stated that the federal government had the power to change the definition of marriage to include same-sex couples and that their doing so would be constitutional. The Supreme Court of Canada likened our systems of laws to a "living tree which by way of progressive interpretation, accommodates and addresses the realities of modern life," noting that the definition of marriage in Canada's constitution "does not exclude same-sex marriage." The Court also observed that clergy could, as an expression of freedom of religion, refuse to conduct marriage ceremonies involving same-sex couples. With the passage of Bill C-38, Parliament changed the definition of marriage to comply with the *Charter* and, on July 20, 2005, the *Civil Marriage Act* received Royal Assent.

Although a November 2005 survey conducted by CBC and Environics found that two-thirds of Canadians feel that the issue of same-sex marriage has now been settled in this country and should not be revisited (EGALE, 2006), it is apparent that others hold a different opinion. For example, it is noteworthy that on the very first day of the 2006 federal election campaign, Conservative Party leader Stephen Harper declared that, if elected Prime Minister, he would reopen the equal marriage issue and ask Parliament to approve an amendment that would limit the definition of marriage to opposite-sex couples. One hundred and thirty-five law professors from across Canada issued an open letter to Harper challenging his remarks and his desire "to enact clearly unconstitutional legislation" and accused him of "playing politics with the Supreme Court and the Charter" (Choudhry et al., 2005).

For some Canadians, objections to same-sex marriage are anchored in the belief that the rights of same-sex couples to marry under the equality provisions of the *Canadian Charter of Rights and Freedoms* are secondary to the "main purpose of marriage, which is to provide a structure within which to raise children"—a view expressed in a 2001 Supreme Court of British Columbia decision (quoted in Arnold, 2001). Earlier, in 1995, the Supreme Court of Canada had expressed a similar view and identified procreation as the "ultimate purpose of marriage" in the case of *Egan v. Canada*. The flaw in this argument is that, while opposite-sex partners are uniquely able to procreate, infertile heterosexual couples or those who simply do not wish to have children are not legally prohibited from marrying. Moreover, "extending marital rights and obligations, or even marital status, to same-sex couples will not derail the state objective of encouraging procreation" (Bailey, 2000: 20).

It is also the case that gays and lesbians can and do become parents in a variety of ways. For example, new reproductive technologies allow for gay and lesbian parenting; the "lesbian baby boom" that began in the mid-1970s is largely the result of artificial insemination by donor sperm (Taylor, 1997: 75). In an attempt to genetically link the baby to both female partners, one partner in a lesbian couple may be inseminated with the sperm of a male relative of the other partner (Salholz, 1993). The new reproductive technologies have not only made possible a growing number of lesbian co-parents but (albeit less commonly) children born to gay biological fathers and surrogate mothers. Science may also hold additional breakthroughs for gay couples. For example, in September 2000, newspaper headlines reported that gay male couples may, in the near future, be able to sire "motherless" children through cell nuclear replacement, a technique originally designed to treat infertility and metabolic disorders. This procedure allows scientists to "replace the nucleus from the egg of a female donor with the nucleus from a sperm cell. The resulting 'male egg,' which would contain only male DNA, would then be fertilized in vitro by sperm from another man and implanted in the womb of a surrogate mother who would carry the child to term" (Honore, 2000).

In general, people who applaud the legalization of same-sex marriage in Canada maintain that granting gays and lesbians the right to marry is important both in practical and symbolic terms. Beyond the economic and practical advantages that marriage confers, it is believed that the right to legally marry will promote increased social acceptance of sexual minorities and function as an important source of social support for gays and lesbians as they pursue long-term relationships. As noted by Justice L'Heureux-Dubé in a dissenting opinion in *Egan v. Canada*: "Given the marginalized position of homosexuals in society, the metamessage that flows almost invariably from excluding same-sex couples from such an important social institution is essentially that society considers such relationships to be less worthy of respect, concern and consideration than relationships involving members of the opposite sex." Allowing same-sex couples the right to marry, she maintained, could go a long way toward redressing this situation and "may be of greater value and importance to those affected than any pecuniary gain flowing from that recognition" (quoted in Bailey, 2000: 46).

In marked contrast, for religious fundamentalists and other conservative groups, the case against gay marriage is unambiguous: marriage is a union of opposite-sexed persons and attempts to recognize gay families must be vigorously repelled. Consider, for example, that in June 1999, a Baptist preacher from Topeka, Kansas, announced that he and a group of his followers would be leading a demonstration on the steps of the Supreme Court of Canada to protest its decision to extend the definition of "spouse" to same-sex couples. According to the preacher, Canada had become the "sperm bank of Satan" (Anderssen, 1999). On other occasions, like-minded people have wielded posters proclaiming such sentiments as, "God made Adam and Eve, not Adam and Steve" (Smolowe, 1996). In addition, not all gay activists in Canada or elsewhere support the legalization of same-sex marriage. Some oppose same-sex marriage on the grounds that it is too derivative of heterosexual unions and mimics a traditionally repressive institution that is based on property rights and institutionalized husband–wife roles (Johnson, 1996). Such gay activists also argue that legalizing same-sex unions could further stigmatize homosexual relations that occur outside of committed, long-term relationships. Will the legalization of same-sex marriages result in further stereotypes of homosexuals and define "good gays" as those who confine themselves to sexual relations with a spouse and who parent children, and "bad gays" as those who do not? (Allen, 1997; Cossman, 1996, 1997). As one observer notes, "when same-sex couples present themselves as 'normal' in pursuit of formal recognition, the polarization of 'family' and 'not family' is effectively cemented." She rhetorically asks, "Are queers 'family?' Could queers be 'family?' Should queers be 'family?'" (Owen, 2001: 96).

Until recently, researchers studying families tended either to ignore gay families or depict them as pathological. Although in recent years there has been a knowledge explosion in this area (e.g., Arnup, 1997; Beals, Impett, and Peplau, 2002; O'Brien and Weir, 1999; Kurdek, 2003), there also exists a counter-tendency to "present fairy tale versions of our lives in which [gays and lesbians] are all happy individuals, partners and family members" (Williams, 1995: 98–99). Although research on gay and lesbian families in Canada has largely tended to draw upon small, nonrepresentative samples of white, middle-class, well-educated respondents, this body of research clearly suggests that the families of gays and lesbians may be most remarkable for their utter ordinariness (Nelson, 1993).

In 2003, the Vatican released "Considerations Regarding Proposals to Give Legal Recognition to Unions Between Homosexual Persons." The document maintained that "the absence of sexual complementarity in these [homosexual] unions creates obstacles in the normal development of children who would be placed in the care of such persons. They would be deprived of the experience of either fatherhood or motherhood. Allowing children to be adopted by such persons living in such unions would actually mean doing violence to these children, in the sense that their condition of dependency would be used to place them in an environment that is not conducive to their full human development" (Section III.7). In response, the Canadian Psychological Association (CPA) issued a press release refuting the Vatican's claim. It stated: "Psychological research into lesbian and gay parenting indicates that there is no basis in the scientific literature for [the Vatican's] perception." According to the CPA, the psychological research on lesbian and gay parenting indicates that there are "essentially no differences in the psychological development, gender identity or sexual orientation between the children of gay or lesbian parents and the children of heterosexual parents." It also emphasized that "[s]tatements that children of gay and lesbian parents have more and significant problems in the areas of psychosocial or gender development and identity than do the children of heterosexual parents have no support from the scientific literature" (Canadian Psychological Association, 2003; see also Malone and Cleary, 2002).

Similarly, despite research proclaiming lesbian couples the most egalitarian of all forms of intimate partnerships (Huston and Schwartz, 2002; Shumsky, 2001), it appears that these relationships are not immune to the violent and abusive behaviour that occurs among heterosexual and gay male couples (Ristock, 2003). Paralleling the patterns found in heterosexual relationships, violence in lesbian relationships also tends to increase in both frequency and severity over time and to be associated with the dynamics of power and dependency and the use of alcohol and other drugs (West, 2002; Fortunata and Kohn, 2003).

There can be no doubt that same-sex families challenge many of our taken-for-granted assumptions. They challenge the common-sense assumption that human beings have a heterosexual destiny and that the way in which most of us conduct our sexual affairs is both natural and morally right. They challenge classification systems surrounding the family and marriage, gender, love, and sexual experiences. Said differently, same-sex families remind us that human behaviour is not as simple as those who believe in a "natural order" suggest. The term "family" has become a very fluid concept indeed.

REFERENCES

Abbott, Pamela, and Claire Wallace. (1992). *The Family and the New Right.* London: Pluto.

Allen, Katherine R. (1997). "Lesbian and Gay Families." In Terry Arendell, ed., *Contemporary Parenting: Challenges and Issues* (pp. 196–218). Thousand Oaks, CA: Sage.

Anderssen, Erin. (1999). "Gay-Bashing Preacher Calls Off Protest." *The Globe and Mail,* 29 June. On the World Wide Web at http://www.egale.ca/archives/press/9906299gm.htm (10 January 2003).

Arnold, Tom. (2001). "B.C. Court Says No to Gay Marriage." *National Post,* 4 October, A1, A15.

Arnup, Katherine. (1997). "In the Family Way: Lesbian Mothers in Canada." In Meg Luxton, ed., *Feminism and Families: Critical Policies and Changing Practices* (pp. 80–97). Halifax: Fernwood Publishing.

Bailey, Martha. (2000). *Marriage and Marriage-Like Relationships.* On the World Wide Web at http://www.lcc.gc.ca/research_project/00_relationships-en.asp (10 January 2006).

Beals, K. P., E. A. Impett, and L. A. Peplau. (2002). "Lesbians in Love: Why Some Relationships Endure and Others End." *Journal of Lesbian Studies,* 6 (1): 53–63.

Bricker, Darrell, and Edward Greenspon. (2001). *Searching for Certainty: Inside the New Canadian Mindset.* Toronto: Doubleday Canada.

Canadian Psychological Association. (2003). "Gays and Lesbians Make Bad Parents: There Is No Basis in the Scientific Literature For This Perception." 6 August. On the World Wide Web at http://www.cpa.ca/documents/GayParenting-CPA.pdf (10 January 2006).

Choudhry, Suhjit, Jean-Francois Gaudreault-DesBiens, Wendy Adams, et al. (2005). "Open Letter to The Hon. Stephen Harper from Law Professors Regarding Same-Sex Marriage." 16 December. On the World Wide Web at http://www.law.utoronto.ca/same-sexletter.html (10 January 2006).

Conway, John F. (1990). *The Canadian Family in Crisis.* Toronto: James Lorimer and Company.

Cossman, Brenda. (1996). "Same-Sex Couples and the Politics of Family Status." In Janine Brodie, ed., *Women and Canadian Public Policy* (pp. 223–78). Toronto: Harcourt Brace and Company.

———. (1997). "Family Inside/Out." In Meg Luxton, ed., *Feminism and Families: Critical Policies and Changing Practices* (pp. 124–41). Halifax: Fernwood Publishing.

EGALE. (2000). "Omnibus Federal Law Recognizes Same-Sex Couples." On the World Wide Web at http://www.egale.ca/index.asp?lang=E&menu=21&item=400 (10 January 2003).

———. (2001). "Press Release: 2001 Census to Recognize Same-Sex Couples." 10 May. On the World Wide Web at http://www.egale.ca/pressrel/010510-e.html (10 January 2003).

———. (2004). "Quebec Becomes Third Province to Allow Same-Sex Couples to Marry." 19 March. On the World Wide Web at http://www.egale.ca/index.asp?lang=E&menu=1&item=952 (10 January 2006).

———. (2006). "Egale Asks Harper to Clarify Murky Position on the Notwithstanding Clause." 8 January. On the World Wide Web at http://www.egale.ca/index.asp?lang=E&menu=1&item=1266 (10 January 2006).

Fortunata, B., and C. S. Kohn. (2003). "Demographic, Psychosocial and Personality Characteristics of Lesbian Batterers." *Violence and Victims,* 18 (5): 557–68.

Gavigan, Shelly A. M. (1997). "Feminism, Familial Ideology and Family Law." In Meg Luxton, ed., *Feminism and Families: Critical Policies and Changing Practices* (pp. 98–123). Halifax: Fernwood Publishing.

Gottlieb, Beatrice. (1993). *The Family in the Western World from the Black Death to the Industrial Age.* New York: Oxford University Press.

Honore, Carl. (2000). "'Male Egg' Couple Enable Two Men to Conceive a Child." *National Post,* 26 September 26, A1, A12.

Huston, M., and P. Schwartz. (2002). "Gendered Dynamics in the Romantic Relationships of Lesbians and Gay Men." In A.E. Hunter and C. Forden, eds., *Readings in the Psychology of Gender: Exploring Our Differences and Commonalities* (pp. 167–278). Needham, MA: Allyn & Bacon.

Jackson, E., and S. Persky. (1982). *Flaunting It: A Decade of Gay Journalism from the Body Politic.* Toronto: Pink Triangle Press.

Johnson, Fenton. (1996). "Wedded to an Illusion: Do Gays and Lesbians Really Want the Right to Marry?" *Harper's,* November, 41–50.

Kinsman, Gary. (1996). *The Regulation of Desire: Homo and Hetero Sexualities,* 2nd ed. Montreal: Black Rose Books.

Kurdek, L. A. (2003). "Differences Between Gay and Lesbian Cohabiting Couples." *Journal of Social & Personal Relationships,* 20 (4): 411–36.

Lancaster, Roger N. (2003). *The Trouble with Nature: Sex in Science and Popular Culture.* Berkeley: University of California Press.

Malone, K., and R. Cleary. (2002). "(De)Sexing the Family: Theorizing the Social Science of Lesbian Families." *Feminist Theory,* 3 (3): 271–93.

Murdock, George. (1949). *Social Structure.* New York: Free Press.

Nelson, Fiona. (1993). *Lesbian Motherhood: An Exploration of Canadian Lesbian Families.* Toronto: University of Toronto Press.

O'Brien, Carol Anne, and Lorna Weir. (1999). "Lesbian and Gay Men Inside and Outside Families." In Nancy Mandell and Ann Duffy, eds., *Canadian Families: Diversity, Conflict and Change* (pp. 111–39). Toronto: Harcourt Brace.

Owen, Michelle K. (2001). "'Family' as a Site of Contestation: Queering the Normal or Normalizing the Queer?" In Terry Goldie, ed., *In a Queer Country: Gay & Lesbian Studies in the Canadian Context* (pp. 86–102). Vancouver: Arsenal Pulp Press.

Ristock, J. L. (2003). "Exploring Dynamics of Abusive Lesbian Relationships: Preliminary Analysis of a Multisite Qualitative Study." *American Journal of Community Psychology,* 31 (3–4): 329–41.

Salholz, Eloise. (1993). "For Better or For Worse." *Newsweek,* 24 May, 69.

Shumsky, E. (2001). "Transforming the Ties That Bind: Lesbians, Lovers and Chosen Family." In E. Gould and S. Kiersky, eds., *Sexualities Lost and Found: Lesbians, Psychoanalysis and Culture* (pp. 57–69). Madison, CT: International Universities Press.

Smolowe, Jill. (1996). "The Unmarrying Kind." *Time,* 29 April, 68–69.

Taylor, Ronald L. (1997). "Who's Parenting? Trends and Patterns." In Terry Arendell, ed., *Contemporary Parenting: Challenges and Issues* (pp. 68–91). Thousand Oaks, CA: Sage.

West, C. M. (2002). "Lesbian Intimate Partner Violence: Prevalence and Dynamics." *Journal of Lesbian Studies,* 6 (1): 121–27.

Williams, Karen. (1995). "The Good Mother." In Katherine Arnup, ed., *Lesbian Parenting: Living With Pride and Prejudice* (pp. 98–110). Charlottetown, PE: Gynergy books.

Chapter 16

Love Online[1]

ROBERT J. BRYM AND RHONDA L. LENTON

THE BIRTH OF A NEW SOCIETY

It is not often that one gets to witness the birth of a new society. Yet the birth of a new society is exactly what is happening on the Internet today.

The society is growing quickly. Numbering 40 million people in 1996, it reached 375 million in 2000. It grew to more than 700 million in 2005. In 2005, only China and India were bigger than the society of the Internet.

But is it really a society? A society is a large, enduring network of social interaction that survives by accomplishing five main tasks: (1) preserving order, (2) producing and distributing goods and services, (3) teaching new members, (4) providing its members with a sense of purpose, and (5) replacing old members (Aberle et al., 1950). Bearing this definition in mind, does the Internet form a society? We believe it does.

Internet society accomplishes many of the same tasks as other societies. For example, although control of members is much less centralized and extensive than in other societies, Internet society has established governing structures, such as those that regulate conventions in the use of HTML code, the allocation of domain names, and user behaviour on specific sites. Similarly, although e-commerce is still only a fraction of economic activity in the world of bricks and mortar, it is growing much more quickly than the economy as a whole. Meanwhile, distance education is becoming increasingly popular (some universities already offer entire degrees online), and the Internet has become an important agent of informal socialization. Thus, the first three tasks of an enduring

society—preserving order, producing and distributing goods and services, and teaching new members—are all performed by Internet society.

So is society's fourth task—providing members with a sense of purpose. More precisely, Internet society provides its members with *many* senses of purpose by enabling social interaction in a wide variety of contexts. Today, Internet users interact socially by exchanging text, images, and sound via e-mail, Internet phone, video conferencing, computer-assisted work groups, mailing lists, and chat groups. Some forms of computer-assisted interaction operate in delayed time. "A" sends a message to "B." "B" receives the message when he or she logs on, responding when convenient. Other forms of computer-assisted interaction operate in real time; people communicate by means of instant messaging.

The proliferation of computer-assisted communication in delayed and real time has resulted in the creation of "virtual communities." Virtual communities are associations of people, scattered across the country or the planet, who communicate via computer and modem about subjects of common interest. Membership in virtual communities is fluid but the communities endure. They are self-governing bodies with their own rules and norms of "netiquette" (McLaughlin, Osborne, and Smith, 1995; Sudweeks, McLaughlin, and Rafaeli, 1999). Members of virtual communities form social relationships. They exchange confidences, give advice, share resources, get emotionally involved, and talk sex. Although their true identities are usually concealed, they sometimes decide to meet and interact in real life. In the 1980s, most observers believed that social interaction by means of computer would be restricted to the exchange of information (for a review and critique of this literature, see Wellman et al., 1996). It turns out these observers were wrong. Internet society can provide its members with a sense of purpose, giving them new freedom to shape their selves as they choose (Turkle, 2001).

THE RISE OF ONLINE DATING

The fifth task of any enduring society involves replacing old members. That is, people ensure the survival of their society by dating, courting, forming long-term offline relationships, and reproducing. With respect to this task, too, Internet society is now beginning to measure up to other societies. Online dating is a growth industry, and cases of online relationships resulting in long-term relationships are increasingly common.

The first online dating services started up around 1996. Wherever the Internet extends, people now use these services. For example, China's Xinhua News Agency ran a story a few years ago about two handicapped people, one in China and the other in California, who met thanks to an online dating service and eventually married ("Internet Dating," 2000). By the middle of 2000, the seven largest online dating sites on the Internet boasted over 12 million registered members and many more "guests" or "visitors." Of these seven large sites, four are based in the U.S. The U.K., Israel, and Canada host the other three large sites. The Canadian site, Webpersonals, and its associated Womanline.com and Manline.com sites, have more than one million members, about a quarter of them Canadian residents. Advertising revenues aside, membership subscriptions generate up to $450 000 per month per million registered members. *Business Start-Ups* magazine ranked online dating as one of the top five business ideas of 2000 and beyond ("Market Overview," 2000; "Mediametrix's," 2000; "DatingClub.com," 2000; Rogers, 2000; "uDate.com," 2000).

How does an online dating site work? Typically, any Internet user may browse the ads free of charge. However, to place an ad and interact with others, one must pay to become a site member. Some sites charge a monthly fee while others operate on a fee-per-use basis. Ads include text and an optional photograph and sound recording of the member. Members may correspond by e-mail or instant messaging.

Members create a public identity—a name by which others may identify them and a user profile by which others may determine their level of interest in specific individuals. The user profile usually includes such information as the member's sex, age, locale, marital status, type of relationship preferred (e.g., romantic involvement, marriage, casual sex, online sex), sexual preferences, and so forth. The online dating service also categorizes this information and allows members to search for other members with specific characteristics. For example, one may search for heterosexual single Christian men between the ages of 35 and 44 living within a 50 km radius of one's home and wanting a romantic involvement. Some smaller sites are devoted exclusively to Christians, Blacks, Jews, gay men, and so forth (Briscoe, 2000; Crary, 2000).

Four main social forces appear to be driving the rapid growth of online dating.

A growing proportion of the population is composed of singles. Statistics Canada divides the Canadian population into four categories by marital status: married (including common-law unions), single, widowed, and divorced. Of these four categories, "married" has been growing slowest and "divorced" has been growing fastest for decades. Between 1995 and 1999, the number of married Canadians grew by 3.3 percent. The number of single, widowed, and divorced Canadians grew by 4.4 percent. With more single, widowed, and divorced people in the population, the dating and marriage markets have grown apace (Statistics Canada, 2000a).

Career and time pressures are increasing. In the 1970s, many observers predicted the advent of a "leisure society" by the end of the century. In reality, many people are working longer hours

(Schor, 1992). Among the world's rich countries, Canada ranks in the middle in terms of hours worked per week and near the bottom in terms of paid vacation days ("Mild Labor," 1999). According to a 1998 Statistics Canada survey of more than 11 000 Canadians over the age of 14, a third of Canadians identify themselves as "workaholics" and more than half worry they do not have enough time to spend with their family and friends. Nearly a fifth of Canadians reported "severe time stress" in 1998, up significantly since 1992 (Statistics Canada, 1999). Increased pressure from work makes it more difficult to find the time to engage in conventional dating methods, such as meeting eligible partners in athletic clubs and bars. People are looking for more efficient ways of meeting. Online dating has emerged as a credible alternative.

Single people are more mobile. According to the 1996 Census, more than a fifth of Canadians were not living in the same census subdivision as five years earlier. Nearly 7 percent said they had moved from another province or another country (Statistics Canada, 2000b). These numbers reflect the fact that single people, who compose nearly 80 percent of online daters, form an increasingly flexible work force, more willing to uproot and relocate in response to job market demands than in the past. (Dual careers may make it more difficult to relocate so it is questionable whether married people are more mobile.) Moreover, a growing number of jobs require frequent travel. As a result of increasing geographical mobility, single Canadians are finding it more difficult to meet other people for dating and sustained intimate relationships. Online dating is increasingly seen as a possible solution to this problem.

Workplace romance is on the decline. Due to growing sensitivity about sexual harassment in the workplace, it is more difficult to initiate workplace romances. Increasingly, people understand that sexual or romantic overtures may be interpreted as sexual harassment and result in disciplinary action or suspension. This encourages the search for alternative milieux in which to meet people for sexual and romantic involvements. Again, online dating benefits (Luck and Milich, 2000).

In short, while demand for dates is on the increase, social circumstances often make it difficult for people to find good dating partners. Thus, a 1999 Toronto Sun/COMPAS poll found that fully 52 percent of Toronto's singles were not dating, while 75 percent said they are finding it difficult or very difficult to find a good dating partner (Mandel, 1999).

A SOCIAL PROFILE OF ONLINE DATERS

To find out more about online daters in Canada, we conducted two surveys late in 2000. First, between 7 and 29 November 2000 we organized a telephone survey of 1200 randomly selected Canadians living outside the northern territories (400 in Quebec and 800 in the rest of the country). Second, we organized an online survey at the web site of Webpersonals, Canada's largest Internet dating service, between 31 November and 5 December 2000. Members and visitors to the Webpersonals sites were presented with a pop-up window when they logged on. It asked if they were willing to participate in the survey and informed them that the survey was restricted to Canadian residents. Exactly 6 581 people completed our questionnaire. From respondents who completed the questionnaire, we selected 185 men and 105 women who said online dating is "a great way to meet people" and said they were willing to be interviewed in depth by telephone. Eleven individuals were subsequently selected at random from this group of 290. They participated in 20-minute taped interviews from which we quote below.

The two surveys show that online daters differ in significant ways from the general Canadian population and from Canadian Internet users who do not use online dating services. People who use the Internet at least once a month comprise about 40 percent of the Canadian population. However, Internet users are younger, better educated, more likely to be employed in the paid labour force, and more likely to earn a higher income than Canadians in general. Using the online survey, it is also possible to compare online daters with Internet users who are not online daters. This comparison shows that the two groups are similar in some respects but different in others. Online daters are more likely to be male, single, divorced, employed, and urban. They are also more likely to enjoy higher income.

One of the enduring myths about avid computer users is that they are social isolates in the real world, locked in their basements alone for hours on end, with windows tightly sealed and shuttered. Similarly, online daters are sometimes characterized as "losers" or "lonely hearts," people who are unable to form normal social ties and enjoy normal social interaction. In this view, they pursue online dating out of desperation.

There may have been some truth to these observations when online dating was in its infancy (Klement, 1997). However, our online dating survey found little evidence to support these generalizations. It turns out that, as of the end of 2000, Canadian online daters are sociable and self-confident. Offline, they tend to be joiners of organizations. They often visit family members. They frequently engage in social and leisure activities with others. These findings are consistent with the results of other recent Canadian research on avid computer users. It turns out that the myth of the socially isolated computer enthusiast is just that—a myth (Hampton and Wellman, 1999, 2000; Wellman and Hampton, 1999).

About 30 percent of Canadians claim to belong to churches, synagogues, mosques, and temples. Membership is concentrated among people 35 years of age and older, and especially among people 55 years of age and older. Only about 15 percent of Canadians under the age of 35 say they attend church, and so forth, weekly (Bibby, 2001: 128, 132). Set beside these figures, it is surprising that almost 24 percent of online daters say they belong to churches and so forth.

That is because more than half of online daters are under the age of 35, compared to just 29 percent of the population. It seems that online daters are more likely to belong to churches and so on than non-online daters of the same age.

Additional evidence of sociability comes from a question on club membership. Respondents were asked to indicate whether they had been "a member of any clubs, such as a bridge club or athletic club, within the past year." Fully 41 percent of respondents said they belonged to such clubs. Of those who said they belonged to such clubs, 61 percent said they belonged to more than one. In striking contrast, a recent Statistics Canada study shows that only 18 percent of Canadians aged 15 and over belonged to one or more "sports and recreation organizations" (Hall et al., 1998: 43).

When respondents were asked how often they visit family or distant relatives in a typical month, only 18 percent replied that they do not visit them even once. This cannot be considered a high figure in a society with high geographical mobility. In Canada today, people often live a considerable distance from family members and cannot visit regularly. More than 82 percent of online daters visit family or relatives at least once a month and 39 percent visit them weekly or more often.

Finally, respondents were asked how often they go out with one or more people for social or leisure activities in a typical month. Only 4 percent said they typically do not go out with others at all. Roughly speaking, a quarter of respondents go out with others zero to two times per month, a quarter go out three to four times a month, a quarter go out five to eight times a month, and a quarter go out nine or more times a month. So, on average, online daters go out for social and leisure activities with others a lot. Some 53 percent typically go out with others for social or leisure activities more than once a week.

It is interesting to compare these results with comparable data from the telephone survey. About 86 percent of respondents in the telephone survey said they have never read personal or dating ads on the web or "checked out" an online dating site. These people are much more likely than online daters to belong to a religious organization (40 percent vs. 24 percent) and visit their families and relatives one or more times per week (60 percent vs. 39 percent). However, Internet users who have never read personal or dating ads on the web or checked out an online dating site are somewhat *less* likely than online daters to belong to a club (37 percent vs. 42 percent). They are also somewhat less likely to go out once a week or more for social or leisure activities (68 percent vs. 65 percent). Thus, online daters are less sociable in terms of religious and family activities but more sociable in terms of friendship and intimate activities.

Sociable people tend to be self-confident. It should therefore come as no surprise that online daters are, in general, a very self-confident group. Specifically, 70 percent of respondents said they would feel comfortable making a speech in public. Of these, 45 percent said they would feel very comfortable. Only 30 percent of respondents said they would feel uncomfortable making a speech in public. Of these, 36 percent said they would feel very uncomfortable.

Respondents were also asked about how others see them: "In terms of your personality, how do you think that people who know you well would rank your self-confidence, say, on a scale from 0 to 6, where 0 is not self-confident and 6 is very self-confident?" Only 5 percent of respondents answered in the "not self-confident" range (0–2). Another 10 percent gave a neutral response (3). Fully 86 percent of respondents answered in the "self-confident" range (4–6).

In terms of self-confidence, Internet users who have not read personal or dating ads on the web and have not checked out an online dating site are slightly more self-confident than online daters. Seventy-five percent of Internet users who have not read personal or dating ads on the web or checked out an online dating site said they would feel comfortable making a speech in public and 89 percent said that others regard them as self-confident.

In sum, the picture that emerges from these data goes a long way toward dispelling the myth of the online dater as a social isolate lacking social skills. On the whole, online daters are joiners. They often socialize with family and friends. They see themselves as self-confident. And they believe others see them that way. Although Internet users who have not read personal or dating ads on the web or checked out an online dating site differ from online daters in some ways, the two groups differ little in terms of overall sociability and self-confidence.

THE PROS AND CONS OF ONLINE DATING

People use online dating for a variety of reasons. Allowing multiple responses, the online daters we sampled often use online dating services to meet someone (78 percent), find someone for a long-term relationship (58 percent), find sexual partners (43 percent), out of curiosity or fun with no intention of making face-to-face contact (41 percent), for casual online chatting and flirting (36 percent), and to find a possible marriage partner (31 percent).

More than a million Canadians over the age of 17 have at least visited an online dating site. (21.9 million Canadians over the age of 17 × 39.1 percent Internet users × 13 percent of respondents in the telephone survey who said they had at least visited an online dating site = 1.1 million people.) What do these people see as the main advantages and disadvantages of online dating? Respondents were asked to evaluate nine possible advantages of online dating on a scale from 0 to 6. We calculated the percentage of respondents who gave each item a score between 4 and 6. For online daters, and allowing multiple responses, the three main advantages of online dating are as follows:

• It creates the opportunity to meet people one would otherwise never meet (89 percent of respondents gave this item a score of 4 to 6).

- It offers privacy and confidentiality (75 percent of respondents gave this item a score of 4 to 6).

- It's a lot more convenient than other ways of trying to meet people (74 percent of respondents gave this item a score of 4 to 6).

We conducted 11 in-depth telephone interviews of online survey respondents. When asked "What prompted you to use online dating?" they virtually unanimously stressed its convenience and the way it allows users to be selective. Typically, one woman in her twenties from Montreal said: "I feel that online I can find someone more compatible because I'm very much into the computer field and if someone has an ad up on the Internet that means that he knows how to use a computer. . . . [Also] you can get to know the person first [before dating] and sometimes see a picture, which helps." In the words of a Toronto man, also in his twenties: "You see right away if you have some compatibility. It's not like a random chance where you walk into a bar. You know right away if they're a smoker or a non-smoker, you know if they participate in some of the same activities you participate in. Some of them have photos. You can see if there's a physical attraction. Quite a long list! You can assess the person more easily." Or as a woman in her thirties from Calgary put it: "You don't have to have these lengthy, drawn-out conversations at a bar with one person. Via the Internet you can start up five or six or seven different conversations with people and kind of weed them out."

Respondents were also presented with a list of five possible disadvantages of online dating. The two biggest disadvantages:

- People online might not tell you the truth about themselves. Eighty-two percent of online daters found this a big disadvantage. Women were significantly more likely than men to find this a big disadvantage. There were no other noteworthy differences between subgroups.

- The people you meet online might be hiding something. Seventy-two percent of online daters found this a big disadvantage. Again, women were significantly more likely than men to find this a big disadvantage and there were no other noteworthy differences between subgroups.

The 11 people interviewed in depth agreed unanimously that the number one disadvantage of online dating is that some people misrepresent themselves. As one respondent put it when asked about the disadvantages of online dating: "I can't really think of any [disadvantages] other than a few people will, shall I say, exaggerate the truth."

CONTACT, MEETING, AND MISREPRESENTATION

Some people read online personal ads merely for fun, out of curiosity, or to engage in erotic verbal fantasies with no intention of meeting their correspondents. Over a third of our online survey respondents said "chatting and flirting" are important reasons why they use online dating services.

Chatters and flirters aside, other people actually meet one or more correspondents face to face. Let us now see how often people establish contact with others through online dating services and how often they meet face to face. We then discuss misrepresentation in online contacts.

Contact. Respondents in the online survey were asked how many people they had contacted by e-mail or other means as a result of an online personal ad or dating service. They were also asked how many people had contacted them. Nearly a quarter of respondents never initiated a contact. Over a third initiated one to five contacts. Nearly a fifth initiated six to ten contacts, and just over a fifth initiated more than ten contacts. Women were more likely than men to be contacted by others. Thus, nearly 16 percent of men but only about 12 percent of women had never been contacted. At the other extreme, 3 percent of men but nearly 12 percent of women had been contacted more than fifty times.

Meeting. We asked respondents how many people they had asked to meet in person as a result of online dating and how many people had asked to meet them. About a quarter of respondents said they requested no meetings with others and about half said they requested meetings with one to five other people. The remainder said they requested meetings with more than five other people. The figures are much the same for meetings requested by others. In both cases, the median number of requested meetings is two. About 2 percent more men than women asked to meet others and 8 percent more women than men were asked to meet by others.

How many people actually meet face to face as a result of using online dating services? A third of respondents reported no face-to-face meetings as a result of online dating. Nearly half reported one to five face-to-face meetings and nearly a fifth reported more than five face-to-face meetings. The median number of face-to-face meetings was two. Men reported fewer than 2 percent more face-to-face meetings than women.

About two-thirds of online daters exchanged pictures and 86 percent talked on the phone before agreeing to go out on a date. Some 55 percent of respondents spoke on the phone three or more times before first getting together with someone they met online. Only 2 percent of respondents met face to face the same day they established contact. About a third met within a week and a quarter within two weeks of first contact, with the remaining 40 percent taking more than two weeks to meet. This suggests that most respondents approach online dating cautiously, taking the time to collect information and grow comfortable before going out on a first date. On the other hand, a minority is quick—in our judgment, too quick—to date.

Misrepresentation. People do not always give accurate information when they place personal ads online. Some people misrepresent them-

selves to stimulate interest. In the online survey, people who had placed personal ads were asked if they had ever given inaccurate information about their appearance, job, education, income, age, marital status, interests and hobbies, and whether they have children. Multiple responses were allowed. Over a quarter of respondents said they had misrepresented themselves. This is a somewhat smaller percentage than we expected to find. We were also somewhat surprised not to discover big differences between men and women in their propensity to misrepresent themselves. The only sex difference worth mentioning is that slightly more men than women (11 percent vs. 8 percent) misrepresented their marital status. Age is the number one issue people misrepresent. Fourteen per cent of respondents said they had misrepresented their age. Tied for the number two spot as topics of misrepresentation are marital status and appearance (10 percent each).

SOME CONSEQUENCES OF ONLINE DATING

We asked respondents about the kinds of relationships they formed with people they met online. Multiple responses were allowed.

Of those who met other online daters face to face, 63 percent had sex with at least one person they met online. Having sex with a person first encountered online is somewhat more likely for men than women (66 percent vs. 58 percent) and for Canadians living in the East than those living in the West. Thus, 69 percent of Atlantic Canadians, 67 percent of (mainly anglophone) Quebeckers, 65 percent of Ontarians, but only 60 percent of respondents from the Prairies and British Columbia say they have had sex with someone they met online. A higher proportion of gay men (79 percent) than heterosexuals (62 percent) and lesbians (61 percent) said they have had sex with people they met online. As far as age is concerned, it is people in their forties who are most likely to have sex with someone they met online (67 percent) and people under the age of 25 who were least likely to do so (58 percent).

Sex aside, 60 percent of those who met other online daters face to face formed at least one long-term friendship. Thirty-seven percent met at least one person they regarded as a "partner." Three percent met someone they eventually married. The probability of marrying someone whom one first encounters online falls with age. The people most likely to marry a person first encountered online are in their twenties. The people least likely to do so are more than 39 years old. The probability of marrying an online date is not associated with one's income or education. However, the people most likely to marry someone they meet online tend to live in small towns near major cities or in the suburbs of major cities. Such people compose 25 percent of all online daters but 56 percent of online daters who married someone they met through an online dating service.

What pre-dating practices are associated with the establishment of long-term relationships among online daters? We asked respondents: "How many, if any, of the people that you have met as a result of online dating have become a long-term friend, a partner, or a spouse?" Our data show that people who formed long-term relationships were more likely to have taken a long time to get to know other people online. They were also more likely to engage in a protracted exchange of information and emotion before the first date. Specifically, people who found long-term friends, partners, and spouses online were more likely than others to have sent photos to people they eventually dated, seen photos of those people, talked to them on the phone ten or more times, and waited more than a month before first meeting them. It may be that daters looking for long-term relationships are generally more selective than daters looking for casual relationships. It may also be that people who spend more time getting to know others before meeting them face to face inadvertently increase the chance of finding a good match and therefore forming a long-term rela-

tionship. In either case, the duration and intensity of pre-dating "courtships" is likely to be greater for people who eventually form long-term relationships.

Despite the apparently high "success rate" of online daters, 42 percent of people who went out on a date with someone they met online reported at least one bad experience on a date. For 38 percent of people who went out on a date, the bad experience involved "disappointment" at least once. Another 33 percent "felt uncomfortable" at least once. More seriously, 10 percent said they felt "frightened" at least once and 26 percent said they were "pestered" at least once after a date. (Multiple responses were allowed.)

It is important to note that the 10 percent of daters who said they were frightened at least once on a date were not frightened enough to change their positive opinion about online dating in general. There was no difference in attitude toward online dating between people who were frightened and those who were never frightened. The same finding—no difference in attitude toward online dating—held for the 26 percent of daters who reported being pestered at least once after a date. It also held for men and women considered separately. We conclude that, in the great majority of cases, the more serious negative experiences reported by our respondents were not all that serious.

They were almost certainly less common than the kinds of negative experiences people have during conventional dates. For example, one nationwide survey of dating in Canadian universities found that, in the year preceding the survey, more than half the men and women who dated were insulted or sworn at by a date and more than half experienced a date throwing, smashing, or kicking something. Nearly 12 percent of men and 20 percent of women were pushed, grabbed, or shoved by a date in the year preceding the survey (DeKeseredy and Schwartz, 1998: 60). Seen in this context, it is quite possible that online dating is safer than conventional dating. That was certainly the strong consensus of the 11 online daters we interviewed in depth. "It just seems safer doing it this way. . . . Online dating gives you more control," said one woman in her forties from Northern Ontario. When asked whether she would recommend online dating to others, a woman in her thirties from Calgary replied: "Oh, definitely, yes. Because it's safe. . . . It's risk free. You can get to know somebody anonymously before you meet them." These responses must be taken with a grain of salt because the 11 individuals interviewed in depth were selected on the grounds that they thought Internet dating is "a great way to meet people." Still, if seen in the context of other data presented above, it seems reasonable to conclude that Internet dating is rarely the risky activity sometimes portrayed by the mass media.

NOTE

1. This article summarizes a report published in 2001. For the full report, see Robert J. Brym and Rhonda L. Lenton, *Love Online: Digital Dating in Canada* (Toronto: MSN.CA, 2001), on the World Wide Web at http://www.nelson.com/nelson/harcourt/sociology/newsociety3e/loveonline.pdf. This summary is published with permission of Donna Hindson and MSN.CA.

REFERENCES

Aberle, D. F., A. K. Cohen, A. K. Davis, M. J. Levy, Jr., and F. X. Sutton (1950). "The Functional Prerequisites of a Society." *Ethics*, 60: 100–11.

Bibby, Reginald. (2001). "Religion." In Robert J. Brym, ed., *New Society: Sociology for the 21st Century*, 3rd ed. (pp. 117–43). Toronto: Harcourt Canada.

Briscoe, Connie. (2000). "Mr.right.com." *Essence*, 31, 4: 112–14.

Crary, David. (2000). "Weary Christian Singles Also Find Love on Internet." *Florida Times Union*, 1 September, B4.

"DatingClub.com Reaches One Million Members on Eve of Third Anniversary On Internet." (2000). *Business Wire*, 24 July.

DeKeseredy, Walter S., and Martin D. Schwartz. (1998). *Woman Abuse on Campus: Results from the Canadian National Survey.* Thousand Oaks, CA: Sage.

Hall, Michael, Tamara Knighton, Paul Reed, Patrick Bussière, Don McRae, and Paddy Bowen. (1998). *Caring Canadians: Highlights from the 1997 National Survey of Giving, Volunteering and Participating.* Ottawa: Statistics Canada.

Hampton, Keith N., and Barry Wellman. (1999). "Netville On-Line and Off-Line: Observing and Surveying a Wired Suburb." *American Behavioral Scientist*, 43: 475–92.

———. (2000). "Examining Community in the Digital Neighbourhood: Early Results from Canada's Wired Suburb." In Toru Ishida and Katherine Isbister, eds., *Digital Cities: Technologies, Experiences, and Future Perspectives* (pp. 475–92). Heidelberg, Germany: Springer-Verlag.

"Internet Dating Leads to Marriage of Handicapped Couple." (2000). *Xinhua News Agency*, 14 July.

Klement, Jo Anne. (1997). "Love at First Byte: Internet Romance is Cheaper, Less Stressful Than a Blind Date." *The Salt Lake Tribune*, 8 September, B1.

Luck, Adam, and Emily Milich. (2000). "Lonely Heart Britain Floods Dating Firms." *Sunday Times*, 2GN edition, 13 August, 9.

Mandel, Michele. (1999). "The Dating Game: Your Place or Mine?" *Toronto Sun*, 24 September. On the World Wide Web at http://www.canoe.ca/CNEWSLifeSexSurvey/six.html (22 December 2000).

"Market Overview." (2000). On the World Wide Web at http://corporate.udate.com/udatecorp.asp?MenuItem=3,0 (23 December 2000).

McLaughlin, Margaret L., Kerry K. Osborne, and Christine B. Smith. (1995). "Standards of Conduct on Usenet." In Steven G. Jones, ed., *CyberSociety* (pp. 90–112). Thousand Oaks, CA: Sage.

"MediaMetrix's July 2000 Statistics Confirm uDate.com as the Fastest Growing Online Matchmaking Site." (2000). *PR Newswire*, 23 August.

"Mild Labor: The World at Work and Play." (1999). *Wired,* 7 (12): 144.

Rogers, Scott. (2000). Team Director, Webpersonals. com. Personal communication, 15 September.

Schor, Juliet B. (1992). *The Overworked American: The Unexpected Decline of Leisure.* New York: Basic Books.

Statistics Canada. (1999). "General Social Survey: Time Use." *The Daily,* 9 November. On the World Wide Web at http://www.statcan. ca/Daily/English/991109/d991109a.htm (23 December 2000).

———. (2000a). "Population by Marital Status and Sex." On the World Wide Web at http://www.statcan.ca/english/Pgdb/ People/Families/famil01.htm (23 December 2000).

———. (2000b). "Population 5 Years and Over by Mobility Status, 1991 and 1996 Censuses." On the World Wide Web at http://www.statcan.ca/english/Pgdb/People/ Population/demo42a.htm (18 December 2000).

Sudweeks, Fay, Margaret McLaughlin, and Sheizaf Rafaeli, eds. (1999). *Network and Netplay: Virtual Groups on the Internet.* Menlo Park, CA: AAAI Press.

Turkle, Sherry. (2001). "Identity in the Age of the Internet." In Robert J. Brym, ed., *Society in Question: Sociological Readings for the 21st Century,* 3rd ed. (pp. 49–55). Toronto: Harcourt Canada.

"u.Date.com Reports Record 309% Growth in Third Quarter Revenues." (2000). On the World Wide Web at http://www.stockgenie. com/udatrel.htm (23 December 2000).

Wellman, Barry, and Keith N. Hampton. (1999). "Living Networked in a Wired World." *Contemporary Sociology,* 28: 648–54.

Wellman, Barry, Janet Salaff, Dimitrina Dimitrova, Laura Garton, Milena Gulia, Caroline Haythornthwaite. (1996). "Computer Networks as Social Networks: Collaborative Work, Telework, and Virtual Community." *Annual Review of Sociology,* 22: 213–38.

PART 4B

POLITICS AND SOCIAL MOVEMENTS

Voters are unhappy in Canada, no less than in other democratic countries. Surveys repeatedly show that Canadians are growing increasingly cynical about politics and distrustful of politicians. As a result, fewer Canadians are voting; while more than 80 percent of eligible voters cast ballots in the 1958 federal election, fewer than 65 percent did so in 2006. In addition, political loyalty is antique. Voters are more willing than ever to switch their allegiance from one party to the next in succeeding elections. They are swayed less by ideologies, principles, and programs than by personalities and fleeting issues. Consequently, Canada's political landscape gyrates wildly from one election to the next. The fortunes of some parties rise as quickly as the fortunes of other parties decline.

According to some commentators, widespread discontent with politics resulted in a fundamental shift in the Canadian party system in 1993. For three decades before the federal election of that year, Canada was a "two-and-a-half party system." Strong Liberal and Progressive Conservative parties vied for power while a weak NDP usually captured about a seventh of the popular vote. These parties failed to represent strong regional voices, however, so in 1993 two new parties emerged—the Bloc Québécois and the Reform Party. They placed second and third, respectively, as half the electorate switched parties from 1988, and they had strong regional bases of support, the Bloc in Quebec and Reform in the West.

In Chapter 17, Lawrence Leduc, writing from the perspective of the 2006 federal election, disputes the view that 1993 saw the emergence of a new Canadian party system. Instead, he argues, the Canadian party system today is little different from what it has been since the end of World War II: a system of "brokerage politics" and "dealigned voters."

Brokerage politics involves party leaders organizing focus groups, public opinion polls, and informal canvasses of voters to determine the hot issues of the day. With this information in hand, they delineate the varied interests of the electorate. They then work out a strategy for organizing a coalition of diverse interests that, they hope, will support their party. They use advertising firms, public relations experts, and "spin doctors" to help them project an image of the party and its leaders that will appeal to the diverse interests in their desired coalition. In this way, party leaders "broker" a coalition of supporters.

The components of the brokered coalition change over time. That is because new political exigencies emerge, and they often require that parties strengthen their ties to some interest groups and weaken their ties to others. As a result, party policies are also in flux. The goal of parties in a system of brokerage politics is not to adhere to relatively fixed sets of principles but to manipulate the electorate in order to gain and maintain power. (That is why, for example, the Liberals did a quick flip-flop on the free trade issue in the early 1990s; they felt they had to switch from an anti-free trade to a pro-free trade position in order to win office.) The system of brokerage politics seems highly democratic because parties listen intently to the opinions of groups of voters. But the system is in fact unresponsive to voters' group interests, which are likely to be watered down or sacrificed entirely as parties seek to broker coalitions between diverse groups. Brokerage politics is a major source of voters' cynicism. It produces a **dealigned electorate,** voters whose allegiances are easily swayed from one election to the next in response to the issues of the day and the appeal (or lack of appeal) of party leaders. Leduc's review of recent voter surveys convincingly demonstrates that the Canadian electorate remains dealigned. As a result, we can expect dramatic swings in voter support in upcoming federal elections.

Brokerage politics notwithstanding, the Bloc Québécois remains a powerful voice in Ottawa. It is not just the federal voice of Quebec. It is the *separatist* voice of Quebec at the federal level, a party for the large number of Quebeckers who want to opt out of Confederation. Quebec separatism is, of course, Canada's perennial and, according to many analysts, biggest political problem. Separatism is not, however, either the first or the most recent vision of the ideal future (or "utopia") that has animated Quebec politics since, say, 1950. In Chapter 18, Jean-Philippe Warren recaps the utopian visions that have animated Quebec politics over the past half-century. These utopias include the desire for (1) the creation of a true democracy, (2) the creation of a culture of openness, (3) the renewal of nationalism (in both federalist and separatist variants), and (4) the establishment of a social democracy in which social justice prevails. Warren boldly evaluates the extent to which it is worthwhile for Quebeckers to continue fighting the battles of their predecessors. He also assesses the extent to which old ideas could usefully give way to a new understanding of Quebec's present condition and ideal future.

Politics has been likened to a machine that determines "who gets what, when, and how." From this point of view, politics involves more than just elections and the passage of laws by legislatures. It also involves riots, petitions, sit-ins, occupations, boycotts, strikes, and other forms of collective action against people in positions of authority. This is politics "beyond the rules," as it were. Canadians are more likely than past generations to express their political interest and sophistication by participating in non-conventional forms of politics. In a 2000 survey, more than a quarter of Canadians said they had joined in a boycott, attended an unlawful demonstration, joined an unofficial strike or occupied a building or a factory at least once. Participation in non-conventional politics was most common among young, highly educated people.

In Chapter 19, I examine one such form of collective action: the strike. I show how changing government and corporate policies have influenced patterns of strike activity in Canada. From the end of World War II until the mid-1980s, the frequency of strike activity in Canada was sensitive to the phase of the business cycle. During boom periods, unemployment was low and strikes were relatively numerous. That is because in boom times workers were in a good bargaining position. Union strike coffers were full, alternative jobs were available, and employers wanted to settle strikes quickly so they could continue earning high profits. In contrast, during economic slumps workers were in a poor bargaining position. Strike coffers were strapped for cash, alternative jobs were few, and employers had little interest in meeting workers' demands because business was slow. As a result, strikes were infrequent.

Beginning in 1973, however, governments and corporations began to take actions and pass laws that undermined union power and the effectiveness of strikes as a weapon in the struggle to improve workers' standard of living. They felt compelled to limit workers' demands due to rising competitiveness in the global economy. The full economic recovery of Germany and Japan from World War II, the rise of South Korea, Taiwan, and other "Asian Tigers" as major players in international commerce, and Canada's agreement to establish a free trade zone with the United States and Mexico all pushed Canadian governments and corporations to keep wages and benefits down, even if that meant undermining unions and their ability to mount effective strikes. After 1986, sensing that they could achieve little by striking, workers tended not to strike even in boom periods. The association between the phase of the business cycle and the strike rate thus disappeared. In this manner, heightened international competition among businesses changed the nature of Canadian politics in general and the effectiveness and frequency of strike action in particular.

GLOSSARY

Brokerage politics involves parties that lack clear ideological and issue differentiation and stable bases of voter support. They cobble together new coalitions of support in every election, basing their platforms on the results of public opinion polls, focus groups, and informal canvasses of voters, and swaying public opinion by using advertising firms, public relations experts, and "spin doctors."

A **dealigned electorate** is comprised of voters whose allegiances are easily swayed from one election to the next in response to the issues of the day and the appeal (or lack of appeal) of party leaders.

CRITICAL THINKING QUESTIONS

1. What is more democratic—a system of brokerage politics or a system in which various group interests are firmly aligned with specific parties?
2. Outline the utopian visions that have animated Quebec politics over the past half-century. According to Jean-Philippe Warren, how worthwhile is it for Quebeckers today to fight the battles of their predecessors? What alternative does he propose?
3. In Canada, how did strike frequency vary with the phase of the business cycle between 1945 and 1986? Between 1987 and 2000? What changes in government and corporate policy altered the association between the phase of the business cycle and the frequency of strikes in Canada after the mid-1980s?

ANNOTATED BIBLIOGRAPHY

Baer, Doug, ed. *Political Sociology: Canadian Perspectives.* Toronto: Oxford University Press, 2002. Covers the major issues in the study of Canadian politics from a sociological perspective.

Carroll, William K., ed. *Organizing Dissent: Contemporary Social Movements in Theory and Practice.* 2nd ed. Toronto: Garamond, 1997. A useful collection of articles on non-conventional politics in Canada.

McRoberts, Kenneth. *Quebec: Social Change and Political Crisis.* 3rd ed., with a postscript. Toronto: Oxford University Press, 1999 [1976]. The definitive account in English of the political, economic, and social dimensions of the Quebec question.

Chapter 17

Political Volatility in Canada:

BROKERAGE PARTIES AND A DEALIGNED ELECTORATE

LAWRENCE LeDUC

THE 1993 "EARTHQUAKE"

From the early 1960s until 1993, the Canadian party system comprised two strong parties—Liberal and Progressive Conservative—and a weak New Democratic Party. In the 1993 Canadian federal election, however, two new parties appeared to shatter the old system. The Bloc Québécois and the Reform Party emerged as major players on the Canadian political scene and made it more difficult to weave together a national majority. Reassembling the much-weakened Progressive Conservative Party was found to be a more difficult task than anyone imagined. Three successive leaders sought to construct a new party that could compete against the Liberals—first as the Reform Party, then the Canadian Alliance, and finally the new Conservative Party of Canada. A foreign visitor familiar with the old "two-and-a-half" party system might easily be convinced that Canadian federal politics had changed beyond all recognition.

But how different, in reality, is the new political world from the one that it replaced? In this chapter, I examine several competing interpretations of the federal party system in the light of recent political events, including the 2006 federal election, which saw the defeat of the Liberal Party after 12 consecutive years in power. I argue that, despite the political turbulence of recent years and the dramatic victory of the Harper Conservatives in 2006, older interpretations of Canadian party politics hold up well when tested against these events. While powerful changes have taken place in federal party politics, the source of those changes remains deeply embedded in the very nature of Canadian political parties. Set alongside other dramatic periods of change in modern Canadian history—the Diefenbaker victories in 1957–58, the ups and downs of the Trudeau years, or the Mulroney landslide of 1984, for example—the political events of 1993 and 2006 are more readily understood.

THREE INTERPRETATIONS OF CANADIAN POLITICAL PARTIES

A NEW PARTY SYSTEM

Some scholars interpret the 1993 election as the start of a major political realignment in which the foundations of an entirely new party system were formed. One group of researchers refers to the new configuration as Canada's "fourth party system."[1] In this view, each party system has had distinctive characteristics that produced attachments to political parties spanning several elections. Other observers argue that the new party system, with its entrenched bases of regional support, "looks like Canada." One would expect a party system that so clearly reflects the political realities of the country to have considerable staying power.

Superficial evidence supports the view that the 1993 election signalled the advent of a new party system. Thus, after four federal elections (1993, 1997, 2000, and 2004) producing broadly similar electoral patterns, it became increasingly difficult to argue that 1993 was a temporary aberration similar to those of 1962 or 1979. Right through the 2006 federal election, the Bloc Québécois has retained its appeal among Quebec voters, and the new Conservative Party of Canada has captured most of the electoral support won by its predecessors, Reform and the Canadian Alliance. The Liberal share of the vote has fluctuated only between a high of 41 percent in the 1993 and 2000 elections and a low of 30 percent in 2006 despite the Liberals' fall from power in the most recent election. The new, highly regionalized alignment makes it increasingly difficult for *any* party to win a majority of votes, or even of seats, across the country. Accordingly, minority governments of the kind elected in 2004 and 2006 may become the new norm, heralding more frequent elections and weaker and more unstable federal governments. But partisan attachment in such a system could well be stronger, because voters would be less likely in any given election to move outside the prevailing regional alignments.

LIBERAL HEGEMONY

The second interpretation of Canadian political parties is the theory of Liberal hegemony. Liberal Party has been in power federally through much of Canada's modern history and has been extraordinarily successful at bridging the regional, ethnic, and linguistic divisions of Canadian society and adapting to new political and economic circumstances. One might argue that, despite the Liberal minority government that emerged from the 2004 election and the loss of the Liberals in the 2006 election, the recent period still resembles other long periods of Liberal hegemony, punctuated by occasional setbacks. Parties that are primarily "power seeking," as the Liberals historically have tended to be, are often particularly good at adapting to changed political circumstances.[2]

Contemporary analysts of the 1958 or 1984 landslide elections, or even of Joe Clark's defeat of Trudeau in 1979, might easily have misread those events as signalling the demise of the Liberals. But in each instance, the Liberals were back in power within a few years. Surveys of the electorate consistently show that more Canadians

identify with the Liberal party than with any of its competitors. Some analysts thus argue that the Liberal support base continues to be wide and deep.[3] In their view, Liberal continuity has been evident despite the 1993 shattering of the old party system. Despite his victory in 2006, Stephen Harper may find his tenure in office cut short by a reinvigorated Liberal Party under an appealing new leader. The race within the Liberal Party to bring about precisely that outcome was under way within weeks of the 2006 election. Those who have seen the Liberal Party rise time and again from electoral defeat expect to see yet another rebirth of what many analysts regard as "Canada's natural governing party."

BROKERAGE POLITICS

The third and final interpretation of Canadian political parties is the theory of brokerage politics. Canadian political parties of the past have traditionally been brokerage parties. Lacking stable support groups in the electorate, and avoiding clear ideological and even issue differentiation from their competitors, the parties and their leaders approach each election anew, hoping to cobble together a winning coalition of support across the electorate.[4] In election campaigns, brokerage parties do not seek to appeal to voters on the basis of long-standing principles or ideological commitment. They are not bound by positions or actions they have taken in the past, and they sometimes appear inconsistent as they search for electorally successful formulations or respond to new versions of old problems. They organize around leaders rather than around principles or ideologies, and expect the leader to work out the many compromises required for electoral success. A variety of conflicting and contradictory policy stances may sometimes coexist inside a brokerage party.

Some analysts have suggested that the Canadian preoccupation with issues of national unity, ethnic and/or linguistic relations, and federal–provincial divisions of responsibility has prevented the emergence of an electoral politics of social class or ideology.[5] In the past, the major parties have generally attempted to accommodate interests on the opposing sides of important social, linguistic, or regional cleavages. Under this interpretation, the success of the Liberals throughout Canadian history has come, not from the natural dominance of the party, but from its success at fashioning new coalitions of support. However, brokerage politics, by its very nature, leads to weak parties, limited commitments from voters, and considerable volatility, or at least the potential for volatility, in elections.[6]

Arguably, recent events suggest that brokerage politics is returning to the federal political arena. The 2003 merger of the Canadian Alliance with the remnants of the old Progressive Conservative Party provided the framework for the construction of a new brokerage party with a potentially broader range of appeal than its immediate predecessors. As the 2006 campaign waged by the new party demonstrated, the key to its victory lay in refashioning old political coalitions and mobilizing short-term discontent. Any long-time observer of Canadian federal politics might well say, "Plus ça change, plus c'est la même chose."

THE 2006 ELECTION: TESTING THE HYPOTHESES

At first, the post-1993 world seemed very different from the traditional world of brokerage politics to which Canadians had long been accustomed. With the Canadian Alliance promoting an agenda of a "united right" and the Bloc Québécois committed to its long-term project of achieving Quebec sovereignty, Canadian federal politics appeared to have become segmented into parties and groups representing narrower and more specific ideological, interest, or issue positions than had been the case in the past. Even the Liberals, with weaker representation from Quebec and the West, appeared increasingly to speak largely for the interests of Ontario or the major urban centres. In this political world, it seemed that the Liberals could win

national elections by default as long as they could portray themselves as the only credible alternative to smaller parties with narrow appeal.

The 2006 election, however, saw a return to the practice of brokerage politics and yielded a result that is likely to revive and reaffirm the predominance of brokerage parties in Canada. Stephen Harper fashioned his victory not by uniting the right but by deliberately positioning his party closer to the centre of the ideological spectrum and appealing directly to interests outside of his secure western base. The Bloc, although running candidates only in Quebec, sought to broaden its appeal to federalists and other voters, emphasizing in its campaign not sovereignty but rather the sponsorship scandal. And both the NDP and the Liberals pitched large parts of their 2006 campaign to each other's voters, de-emphasizing issue and ideological positions and appealing instead for "strategic" votes.

Given that the "new party system" of the post-1993 period had seemingly become solidified, many of these developments came as something of a surprise. At the beginning of the 2004 election campaign, the new Conservative Party of Canada surged ahead of the Liberals in the polls, only to fall back in the final weeks of the campaign.[7] The weakness of the Liberals in that campaign, and the minority outcome, should have provided clues as to what lay ahead. In 2006, the Harper-led Conservatives moved from an initial deficit of about eight percentage points at the time of the government's defeat in Parliament to a lead of as much as twelve percentage points at the start of the final week of the campaign (Figure 17.1). Unexpectedly, the Conservatives suddenly became a force in Quebec, ultimately winning ten seats and a stunning 25 percent of the popular vote in a province where they had all but been written off and where support for the Bloc seemed unshakable. Volatility and uncertainty had made a dramatic return to the Canadian federal political arena.

But the surface evidence available from the events of the 2004 and 2006 federal elections is of course not in itself a definitive test of the var-

FIGURE 17.1 PUBLIC OPINION POLLS IN THE 2006 FEDERAL ELECTION CAMPAIGN

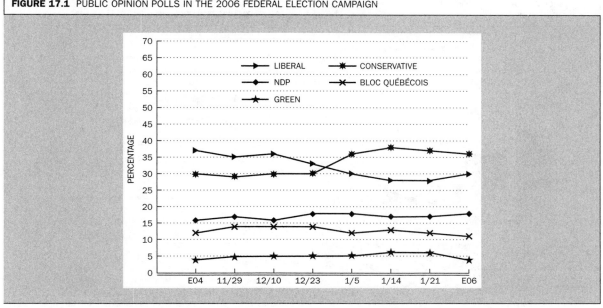

Sources: Strategic Counsel/*Globe and Mail*; Ekos Research/*Toronto Star*; Ipsos Reid/*National Post*; SES Research/*CPAC* (29 November 2005–21 January 2006). E04, E06 denote actual vote percentages in the 2004 and 2006 elections (Ottawa: Elections Canada).

ious theoretical interpretations of the Canadian party system discussed earlier. It is entirely possible that the 2006 election represented something of an aberration, given the role played by the sponsorship scandal and other events of a purely short-term nature. There is however other evidence available that speaks more directly to these issues, and which is not affected by the specific issues and events of 2004 and 2006. Further evidence can be found in data from some of the recent Canadian National Election Studies, which shows that the Canadian electorate since 1993 continues to be largely dealigned, and thus highly susceptible to brokerage appeals.[8] Neither the "liberal hegemony" hypothesis nor the "new party system" line of argument stands up well when examined in the light of available survey data revealing the attitudes and attachments of Canadian voters. Given the right electoral circumstances, significant numbers of Canadian voters can still be moved by short-term appeals emanating from an election campaign or other sources.

A DEALIGNED ELECTORATE

As Figure 17.2 shows, about a third of Canadian voters identify in some way with the Liberal Party. But just over 6 percent of respondents consider themselves "very strong" Liberals. In fact, in 2004 fewer than 15 percent of Canadians saw themselves as "very strong" supporters of *any* party, and another fifth of the electorate held no partisan attachment at all.[9] Added together, there are more weak partisans or non-partisans in the Canadian electorate than there are Liberals, and the percentage of Canadians who do not identify with any of the federal political parties has risen substantially, from about 12 percent of the total in surveys conducted during the 1980s to more than 20 percent in 2004 (Figure 17.3).

In short, if we are searching for a solid base of party support in the Canadian electorate, it is increasingly difficult to find one. While the Liberals enjoy an advantage over all competitors, they find it increasingly difficult to win an election through appeals to partisans alone, includ-

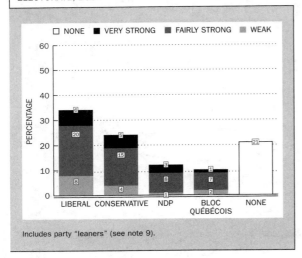

FIGURE 17.2 PARTY IDENTIFICATION IN THE CANADIAN ELECTORATE, 2004

Includes party "leaners" (see note 9).

Source: Canadian National Election Study (2004), post-election wave. N = 3052.

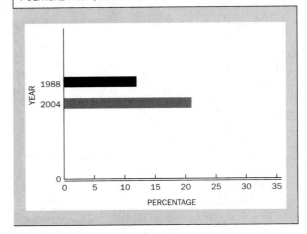

FIGURE 17.3 RESPONDENTS NOT IDENTIFYING WITH *ANY* POLITICAL PARTY, 1988 AND 2004

Source: Canadian National Election Studies (1988, 2004).

ing weak partisans. This distribution of partisan attachment does not suggest a return to the days of Liberal hegemony. The Liberal Party is considerably weaker today in terms of core support than it was in the 1960s and 1970s.

While the Liberals since 1993 seem to have settled at a lower level of support than they previously enjoyed, the Conservatives nevertheless remained well short of overtaking them, at least in the proportion of Canadians identifying themselves as supporters of the new party. But as the 2006 result demonstrates, this does not necessarily preclude a successful electoral appeal across party lines, and/or the migration of partisan attachment from one party to another.[10]

The ideological underpinnings of the Canadian party system are extraordinarily weak compared to party systems in many other Western democracies. While the terms "left" and "right" are widely used by political commentators and other elites in Canada, they do not resonate with much of the electorate. Figure 17.4 displays the ideological self-identification of Canadians surveyed in 2000. By far the largest component of the electorate is found in the political centre (39 percent), and 29 percent of respondents reject the concept of ideological placement entirely or

are unable to locate themselves on a left–right continuum. Just 31 percent of respondents describe themselves in ideological terms. Of these, 18 percent placed themselves on the right and 13 percent on the left. The observation that Canadian voters are not particularly ideological in their orientation to politics is not exactly new; we have known as much since the 1980s.[11] This relative lack of ideological fervour does not appear to favour the prospects of those who believe that the future of the Canadian party system lies in uniting the right or in presenting voters with more ideologically polarized choices. Neither a united right nor a more radical left would appear to be well placed to win the allegiance of a very large cross-section of Canadian voters on a continuing basis.

My conclusion is reinforced by the relatively weak linkage between ideological self-placement and party alignment (Figure 17.5). Even supporters of the Conservatives, the most ideologically coherent of the parties that contested the 2004 and 2006 federal elections, did not uniformly place themselves on the political right. Similarly, only about half of NDP supporters identify with the left. The ideological portrait of identifiers with the other parties was even more fragmented. Among the large and growing segment of the Canadian electorate that does not

FIGURE 17.4 IDEOLOGICAL SELF-PLACEMENT IN THE CANADIAN ELECTORATE

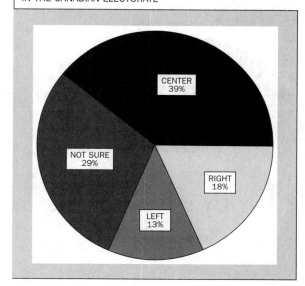

CENTER 39%

NOT SURE 29%

RIGHT 18%

LEFT 13%

Source: Canadian National Election Study (2000), campaign wave.
N = 2691.

identify with *any* of the four main political parties, there are few adherents of either the left or the right.

Harper's success in the 2006 election came from his party's strategic decision to mount an appeal to the political centre, de-emphasize polarizing issues, and base the campaign on popular short-term fixes such as "accountability" and tax relief. This was essentially the key to the success of the Mulroney Conservatives in 1984 and 1988 and, to some extent, of the Diefenbaker Tories in the 1950s. It has also been the preferred strategy of the Liberals throughout much of their modern history. It was, after all, Mackenzie King whose formula for political success was to "campaign from the left, but govern from the right." The mention of particular leaders in this context is important. Given the weakness of ideology in the Canadian party system, along with the relative fluidity of issue and policy agendas, individual political leaders have assumed great importance in explanations of voting behaviour in Canada throughout much of its modern political history.[12] Parties have been most electorally successful when they have found a leader who

was able to capture the public imagination and reflect the mood of a particular time. Diefenbaker did this in breaking the Liberal hold on national politics in 1957–58 and Pierre Trudeau represents perhaps the clearest example of a leadership-driven politics in recent years. During the Trudeau years, the image of the leader came to define the party, rather than the other way around. It is thus not surprising that there are fewer Liberal partisans in the electorate now than during the Trudeau era. In the present political environment in Canada, there has not been any single political leader who has been able to capture the public imagination like Trudeau did. To some extent, this may be part of the reason why Canadian party politics appeared to stall around the weak 1993 alignment. Harper was more successful in the 2006 election in neutralizing some of the negative qualities of his image as a leader, although it would be stretching the evidence to argue that the two most recent elections turned as heavily on leader images as did some of those of the 1970s and 1980s. Nevertheless, it is clear that Harper's greater acceptability as a potential prime minister played a role in the minority outcome of 2006.[13]

In this political setting, voters do not make choices easily. It is not simply a matter of reaffirming support for a party or voting one's ideological identity. Surveys of the electorate consistently show that only half or fewer voters are able to decide how they are going to vote before the campaign actually begins (Figure 17.6). As the campaign progresses, more voters are able to reach a decision based on their assessment of the leaders, issues, and the context of a particular election. Increasingly, high-profile events such as the televised leaders' debates play a crucial role in this process. In a typical election, a significant number of voters remain "undecided," sometimes until the final days leading up to the election. This makes the actual campaign period vital to the election outcome, as the sharp turnaround in public opinion polls during the 2006 campaign clearly demonstrated.

FIGURE 17.5 IDEOLOGICAL SELF-PLACEMENT BY PARTY IDENTIFICATION, 2004

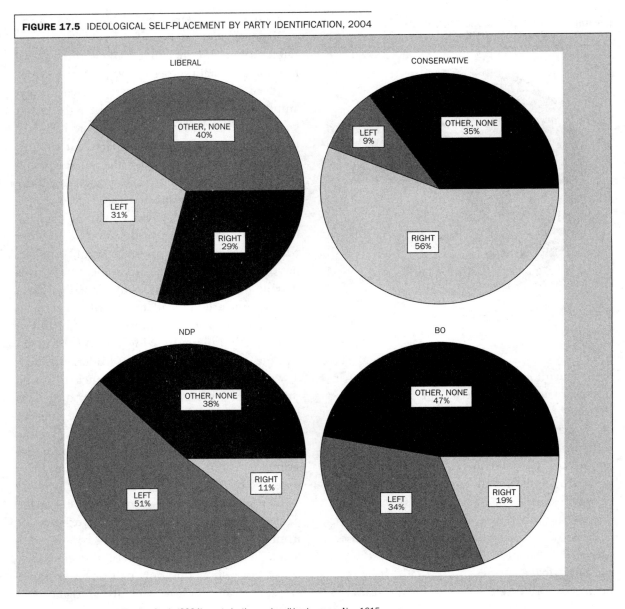

Source: Canadian National Election Study (2004), post-election and mail-back waves. N = 1615.

THE CONSEQUENCES OF BROKERAGE POLITICS

A certain style of politics has persisted throughout much of modern Canadian history and does not appear to have been significantly altered by events since 1993. The style makes for exciting election campaigns but not necessarily for a healthy democracy. Parties and their leaders become cynical and manipulative, and voters turn distrustful as they come to believe that the electoral choices presented to them are not meaningful. As one group of researchers wrote:

> Voters are profoundly and almost universally dissatisfied with brokerage politics. [Many] believe that the parties do not offer real choices and think that the parties fail to tell the voters about the really important problems facing the country. Moreover, there is virtual consensus

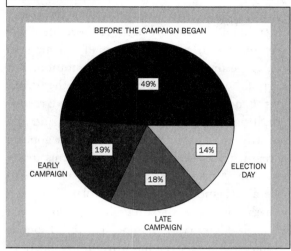

FIGURE 17.6 REPORTED TIME OF VOTE DECISION, 2004 FEDERAL ELECTION

Source: Canadian National Election Study (2004), post-election wave. N = 2360.

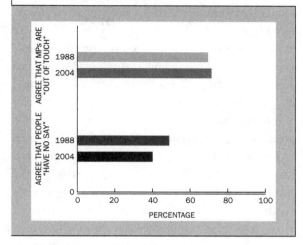

FIGURE 17.7 ATTITUDES TOWARD POLITICS AND GOVERNMENT, 1988 AND 2004

Source: Canadian National Election Studies (1988, 2004).

that political parties pay too much attention to winning elections and not enough to governing afterwards, and to gaining partisan advantage rather than to solving important problems. . . . 91% of respondents agreed that there was a big difference between what a party says it will do and what it actually does if it wins an election.[14]

As Figure 17.7 suggests, data from both recent and older surveys confirm the impression of voter cynicism. In 1988 and 2004, nearly half of all Canadians surveyed agreed that "the people have little or no say in what the government does." Nearly three-quarters of respondents in both surveys also agreed that "Members of Parliament lose touch with the people soon after they are elected." Survey findings of this type do not vary substantially from election to election and appear to have changed little over the past three decades.

The events that immediately followed the 2006 election seemed almost designed to reinforce such cynicism. When a previous Liberal Minister crossed the floor to join the new Conservative Cabinet within days of the election, there was widespread condemnation of his decision. At the same time, the appointment of a Conservative

Party campaign co-chairman to the Senate and his assignment to the Public Works portfolio, which had been a lightning rod of scandal in the previous government, brought further criticism. "Different party, same old tricks," wrote *Globe and Mail* columnist Jeffrey Simpson. "Is this how Harper ushers in a new era?" asked *The Globe and Mail* on its editorial page following the Cabinet appointments.[15] The new Prime Minister's Cabinet appointments might not have provoked such a reaction had they not appeared so much at variance with the Conservatives' resounding criticism over the course of the campaign of similar Liberal actions in the past. Voters who were hopeful that the change of government might strike a new tone of political accountability were quickly disillusioned.

Malaise in contemporary Canadian federal politics is also reflected in the declining turnout of voters in federal elections over the past two decades (Figure 17.8). While part of this decline can be explained by patterns of generational change and other demographic factors, there is little doubt that voter cynicism and the characteristics of the current party system have also contributed to the withdrawal of voters from the electoral process.[16] Dealigned voters with weak partisan attachments are more difficult to mobilize in elections. The strong regional patterns that have been evident in recent years have also contributed to the withdrawal of many Canadians from electoral participation because it has made elections less competitive in many areas of the country, and the choices presented less meaningful.[17] Turnout in 2006 rose slightly, in part because of the greater uncertainty regarding the outcome of that election. But it is unlikely that the pattern of decline has been broken because most of the factors underlying it remain in place. Voters in many parts of the country could easily believe that their vote would have little influence on the outcome of the election, either nationally or in their own constituencies. If they also believe that there is little real difference between the parties or that politicians cannot be trusted to keep their promises, the motivation to participate is further diminished.

The Canadian electorate has been distrustful of political parties and politicians for some time, creating the possibility that the political future in Canada could be much like the past. In the present political environment, all three of the interpretations advanced at the beginning of this chapter continue to have some degree of plausibility. Canada could be in the early stages of an

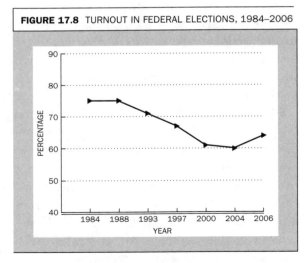

FIGURE 17.8 TURNOUT IN FEDERAL ELECTIONS, 1984–2006

Source: Elections Canada. On the World Wide Web at http://www.elections.ca.

ongoing process of realignment, in which some version of the present party system might yet solidify. Under this interpretation, the party system could eventually become more ideologically polarized, perhaps eventually leading to some type of new two-party configuration. But most of the present evidence indicates that this is not the most likely direction of any future reconfiguration of Canadian party politics, and the minority outcome of the 2006 election appears to reaffirm our skepticism regarding this interpretation. The second hypothesis—a return to Liberal hegemony—seems more plausible, even with the defeat of the Liberals in 2006. Given the thin Conservative minority, the Liberals could certainly recover and win a future election. But even if the Liberals recover, this interpretation is not the most compelling. The Liberal base is weaker than ever, and it was weak even before the sponsorship scandal took its toll. The Conservatives could just as readily convert their minority victory of 2006 into a majority in a subsequent election, particularly if the party's 2006 breakthrough in Quebec continues to undermine the hold of the Bloc on Quebec voters. But either of these possible outcomes would tell us little about the future of Canadian parties beyond one or two elections. In the past, Conservative governments, even some with large majorities, have had little staying power, and seeming Liberal hegemony did not insulate the party from sometimes crushing electoral defeats.

The interpretation that I have advanced here is that the Canadian electorate continues to be highly dealigned, in part because of the nature of brokerage politics. In this setting, elections are unpredictable and tend to be dominated by short-term issues, personalities, and events. With a dealigned electorate, the potential for sudden and unpredictable change is always high. Parties will continue to search for electorally successful formulae and to position themselves for short-term political advantage, even if that involves repudiation of past issues and ideological commitments. In a polity dominated by brokerage parties, an attractive new leader or a compelling issue easily ignites a process of sudden change. It happened in the elections of 1958, 1968, 1984, and 1993. Given what we know about the nature of the Canadian electorate, there is no reason to believe that it could not happen again, perhaps soon.

NOTES

1. R. Kenneth Carty, William Cross, and Lisa Young, *Rebuilding Canadian Party Politics* (Vancouver: University of British Columbia Press, 2000); R. Kenneth Carty, "Three Canadian Party Systems," in *Canadian Political Party Systems: A Reader,* ed. R. K. Carty (Peterborough: Broadview Press, 1992), 563–86.

2. Kaare Strøm, "A Behavioral Theory of Competitive Political Parties," *American Journal of Political Science,* 34 (1990): 565–98; Peter Mair, "Myths of Electoral Change and the Survival of Traditional Parties," *European Journal of Political Research,* 24 (1993): 121–33; Stephen Clarkson, *The Big Red Machine* (Vancouver: University of British Columbia Press, 2005), 3–27.

3. Neil Nevitte, André Blais, Elisabeth Gidengil, and Richard Nadeau, *Unsteady State: The 1997 Canadian Federal Election* (Toronto: Oxford University Press, 2000), 67–69, 127–135; André Blais, Elisabeth Gidengil, Richard Nadeau, and Neil Nevitte, *Anatomy of a Liberal Victory* (Peterborough: Broadview Press, 2002), 115–25.

4. Harold D. Clarke, Jane Jenson, Lawrence LeDuc, and Jon H. Pammett, *Absent Mandate: Canadian Electoral Politics in an Era of Restructuring* (Toronto: Gage, 1996), 15–21; Janine Brodie and Jane Jenson, *Crisis, Challenge and Change: Party and Class in Canada Revisited* (Ottawa, Carleton University Press, 1988).

5. Robert Alford, *Party and Society* (Chicago: Rand McNally, 1963), 250–86; John Porter, *The Vertical Mosaic* (Toronto: University of Toronto Press, 1965); Jon H. Pammett, "Class Voting and Class Consciousness in Canada," *Canadian Review of Sociology and Anthropology,* 24 (1987): 269–90.

6. Clarke et al., *Absent Mandate.*

7. Stephen Clarkson, "Disaster and Recovery," in *The Canadian General Election of 2004,* ed. Jon H. Pammett and Christopher Dornan (Toronto: Dundurn Press, 2004), 28–65.

8. The 2004 Canadian National Election Study (CNES) was conducted by André Blais, Elisabeth Gidengil, Neil Nevitte, Patrick Fournier, and Joanna Everitt. The 1993, 1997, and 2000 Canadian National Election Studies were conducted by André Blais, Neil Nevitte, Elisabeth Gidengil, and Richard Nadeau. The 1988 CNES, which is used as a basis for comparison in Figure 17.3 and subsequent figures, was conducted by Richard Johnston, André Blais, Henry Brady, and Jean Crête. The field work for all of these studies was carried out by the York University Institute for Social Research, and the studies were funded by the Social Sciences and Humanities Research Council of Canada. Neither the funding agencies nor the principal investigators are responsible for the analyses or interpretations presented here. Some of the findings of the 1997–2000 studies are reported in Nevitte et al., *Unsteady State,* and in Blais et al., *Anatomy of a Liberal Victory.* On the 1988 study, see Richard Johnston, André Blais, Henry Brady, and Jean Crête, *Letting the People Decide* (Montreal and Kingston: McGill-Queen's University Press, 1992).

9. There are different methods of measuring party identification in surveys. In the findings reported here, we use data from the post-election wave of the Canadian National Election Studies to maximize comparability with the older surveys. Respondents reporting any party "leanings" are counted as identifiers even though they may have rejected identification with a party in their first response.

This produces a somewhat more conservative estimate of non-identification than might be obtained by other methods of classification. The standard sequence of questions employed in the CNES surveys is: "Generally speaking, do you think of yourself as a Liberal, Conservative, NDP, etc.?" [IF PARTY] "How strongly do you feel—very strong, fairly strong, or not very strong?" [IF NO PARTY] "Do you feel a bit closer to any of the federal parties?" [IF YES] "Which party is that?" On some of the issues involved in employing different measures and methods of classification, see Richard Johnston, "Party Identification Measures in the Anglo American Democracies: a National Survey Experiment," *American Journal of Political Science,* 36 (1992): 542–59.

10. Lawrence LeDuc, Harold D. Clarke, Jane Jenson, and Jon H. Pammett, "Partisan Instability in Canada: Evidence from a New Panel Study," *American Political Science Review,* 78 (1984): 470–84; Clarke et al., *Absent Mandate,* 50–69.

11. Ronald D. Lambert, James Curtis, Steven Brown, and Barry Kay, "In Search of Left/Right Beliefs in the Canadian Electorate," *Canadian Journal of Political Science,* 19 (1986): 542–63.

12. Clarke et al., *Absent Mandate.*

13. Public opinion polls show that, at about the mid-point of the 2006 campaign, Stephen Harper overtook Paul Martin as "the leader who would make the best prime minister." His rating as a leader who made a "favourable impression" also rose sharply during the second half of the campaign. Strategic Counsel/*Globe and Mail,* Ekos Research/*Toronto Star* surveys (29 November 2005–21 January 2006).

14. Clarke et al., *Absent Mandate,* 180–81; André Blais and Elisabeth Gidengil, *Making Representative Democracy Work,* vol. 17 of the Research Studies of the Royal Commission on Electoral Reform and Party Financing (Toronto: Dundurn Press, 1991).

15. Jeffrey Simpson, "Different party, same old tricks," *The Globe and Mail,* 7 February 2006, A1; Editorial, *The Globe and Mail,* 8 February 2006, A8.

16. Blais et al., *Anatomy of a Liberal Victory.* See also Jon H. Pammett and Lawrence LeDuc, *Explaining the Turnout Decline in Canadian Federal Elections: A New Survey of Non-Voters* (Ottawa: Elections Canada, 2002).

17. Jon H. Pammett and Lawrence LeDuc, "Four Vicious Circles of Turnout: Competitiveness, Regionalism, Culture and Participation in Canada," paper presented to the Joint Sessions Workshops of the European Consortium for Political Research, Uppsala, Sweden, April 2004; Jon H. Pammett and Lawrence LeDuc, "Behind the Turnout Decline," in *The Canadian General Election of 2004,* ed. Jon H. Pammett and Christopher Dornan (Toronto: Dundurn Press, 2004), 338–60.

Chapter 18

French Quebec, the Quiet Revolution, and After:

GLORIES AND MISERIES OF FOUR UTOPIAS[1]

JEAN-PHILIPPE WARREN

This essay focuses on four visions of the ideal society ("utopias") formulated by the French population in Quebec in the past four decades. My starting point is the Quiet Revolution (1960–70). During the 1960s, Quebec undertook massive reforms aimed at getting rid of what many observers judged to be its backward character. Blaming mostly the Catholic Church's domination of the province, French Canadian intellectuals and militants dreamed of establishing a society in which democracy, tolerance, justice, and openness would prevail. This is how, in the space of just a decade, a largely traditionalist and closed society was transformed by the dreams of a new generation of *Québécois*.[2] This essay relates the story of these dreams and their fate.

The four utopias of the 1960s and the 1970s were as follows:

1. the realization of a thoroughly democratic political system;
2. the achievement of Quebec independence or the construction of a completely bilingual Canada;
3. the establishment of a socialist society ("social democracy"); and
4. the translation of the old language of values into a new humanism adapted to the technological age in the making.

Analysis of these utopias can help us better understand the ideologies and commitments of Quebec social movements during the past four decades, reveal the main political and social tendencies of this period, and, consequently, underline the challenges facing Quebec society today. You will see that, following two decades of struggle and great expectations (the 1960s and 1970s), a period of disillusionment set in. In this respect, Quebec was no different from other countries in the Western world, where the radical 1960s and 1970s eventually gave way to a more conservative era. Reassessing the utopias of the 1960s and 1970s will also serve to emphasize the importance of not forgetting them, even if they must now be understood in a new light.

1. DEMOCRACY

It is easy to forget today, but one of the chief debates that helped Jean Lesage and his Liberal Party get elected in 1960 turned on the question of political morality. The Union Nationale Party, led by Maurice Duplessis, dominated Quebec politics since the 1930s. Duplessis was premier from 1936 to 1939 and from 1944 to 1959. He turned patronage (e.g., hiring and giving government contracts to political friends) and corruption (e.g., accepting bribes) into a political system. Characteristically, Duplessis once started a speech by addressing his audience as "Électeurs, électrices, électricité" ("Male Electors, Female Electors, Electricity"), reminding voters in the small village he was speaking in

Source: © Jean-Philippe Warren (2006).

that they had better vote for his party if they wanted to get connected to the province's electrical grid.

Duplessis organized politics into an efficient machine for reinforcing his personal domination. Companies had to pay a "commission" for every government contract they obtained, and the regime's friends had to contribute to Union Nationale coffers if they expected personal favours. Duplessis was also careful to discredit the provincial Liberal Party. He accused it of being a refuge for French Canada's enemies. Did the Liberal Party not support compulsory military service in 1942, forcing the *Québécois* to fight "England's" war against Germany, as if Quebec were still an English colony, he persistently asked the electorate? Was the Liberal Party not a nest of dangerous socialists, as evidenced by its support for more state intervention in economic life? Duplessis's propaganda tarnished the reputation of everybody who stood in his way. Nor did he stop at words. He took action—often brutal action—to rid himself of opponents. He crushed the prolonged and bitter Asbestos strike (1948) by sending in the police to beat up the strikers. He imposed restrictive new regulations at Laval University that compelled Father Georges-Henri Lévesque to resign as dean of the *Faculté des sciences sociales*. And so forth.

One of the most famous articles published in Quebec in the 1950s was Gérard Dion and Louis O'Neill's "L'Immoralité politique dans la province de Québec" (1956). The authors denounced the "flood of stupidity" that Quebec was witnessing and the complete "perversion of conscience." Their words were harsh for they feared the destruction of democracy in Quebec. This is why, for both of them, an urgent reform of political morals by means of general civic education seemed necessary. "The work has to speed up before demagogues and would-be fascists render the masses so stupid that any effort to right the situation becomes impossible."[3] This was also what the intellectuals grouped around the *Rassemblement* (formed in 1956) and the *Unions des forces démocratiques* (formed in 1958) believed.

These two political organizations did not seek to become political parties. Rather, they sought to purify Quebec's politics by educating ordinary *Québécois*. "In 1958, French Canadians must begin to learn democracy from scratch," wrote the young Pierre Elliott Trudeau.[4] If the masses were not ready to exercise their political rights, the solution was not to abolish democracy altogether but to elevate political consciousness.

The generation that came of age after World War II was dedicated to establishing liberal democracy in Quebec like no generation before. At last, for instance, Aboriginal peoples gained the right to vote at the federal and provincial level in the 1960s. To be sure, there were violent elements in provincial politics, including people who thought traditional liberal democracy was a sham and were willing to plant bombs in mailboxes to prove their point. In 1970 the Front de Libération du Quebec (FLQ) proclaimed: "We wash our hands of the British parliamentary system; the Front de Libération du Québec will never let itself be distracted by the electoral crumbs that the Anglo-Saxon capitalists toss into the Quebec barnyard every four years."[5]

Believing Quebec was on the eve of a popular uprising, the FLQ kidnapped and murdered Pierre Laporte, Quebec Vice-Premier and Minister of Labour, plunging the country into the 1970 "October crisis," during which martial law was declared, federal troops marched into the province, and arbitrary mass arrests were made. Yet this outburst of violence cannot make us forget the peaceful and democratic way in which most of Quebec's political disputes were dealt with. Many democratic struggles elsewhere— notably the civil rights movement in the United States, which sought to heal much deeper and more painful wounds—witnessed bitter violence. Most of the members of the postwar generation believed that the people were the sole repository of power and that transparency was the cardinal quality of a democratic regime. This meant an insistence on participatory democracy (universal, mass participation in politics) and the eradication of corruption from public affairs.

Notwithstanding the absurdity of most of their claims, the radical groups of the 1970s (the FLQ, the Marxist-Leninists, the Maoists, extremists in labour unions, etc.) attacked liberal democracy for not being democratic enough and extended the critique of the parliamentary system as a system of corruption and favouritism.

In 1978 the ruling party, the *Parti Québécois*, adopted laws restraining companies and trade unions from contributing to the electoral funding of political parties and forcing the latter to state their incomes and expenses. Recently, the *Bloc Québécois* has been trying to adhere to these funding rules in Ottawa despite the fact that other federal parties do not follow similar principles and have no intention of doing so. Numerous other provincial laws confirm the commitment of *Québécois* to the health of their democracy.

In Canada, the Trudeau government did not have similar success in its attempt to change the electoral process and political organization in general. Of course, less needed to be done because most of Canada outside Quebec was already a vigorous, albeit imperfect, democracy in the 1970s. It is nevertheless obvious that Bay Street did not lose control over Parliament, that thousands of jobs for political friends were created in the 1970s, and that networks of political patronage remained strong. Characteristically, of the 25 cabinet ministers appointed to Trudeau's first government, 15 were given prestigious federal offices after they left politics.[6] Trudeau's commitment to establishing participatory democracy during his 1968 leadership campaign soon vanished, leaving Canadian politics in pretty much the same state as when he came to power.

This is not to say that Canada is not a democracy and should not, as such, be regarded with envy by the world community. It is to say that democracy, here and abroad, is a work in progress, and that *Québécois*, having made considerable headway in their province, must continue to fight for greater openness of public institutions at the federal and provincial levels. Major changes await us if we want to live up to the dreams of our predecessors. At the provincial level, one of these might involve reassessing the constituency-based, simple majority ballot. In the 1998 Quebec election, fully one-third of the deputies were elected with less than 50 percent of the popular vote in their ridings because so many people voted for losing candidates. Many analysts are now talking about partly adopting a system of proportional representation, as in Western Europe. In addition to the traditional vote for local candidates, this would involve people voting for a province-wide list of candidates established by each political party. It might take, say, 40 000 votes from anywhere in the province to elect each person on a party's list. In that case, few votes would be wasted and representation in the Quebec legislature would much more closely reflect the political will of the people. The fact that the percentage of people exercising their right to vote is slowly but inexorably dropping election after election is one indication among others that democracy in Quebec (and Canada as a whole) is amenable to improvement. The concentration of ownership of the Canadian press in the hands of a few giant conglomerates is another big problem area for Quebec and Canadian democracy.

2. A NATION IN THE MAKING

Louis Tardivel, the religious owner of the newspaper *La Vérité*, and Henri Bourassa, the founder of the newspaper *Le Devoir*, knew each other well and respected each other's commitments. But while Louis Tardivel wrote a novel (*Pour la Patrie*, 1895) in which he predicted an independent Quebec by 1945, Henri Bourassa wrote and spoke to convince English Canadians to help him build a bilingual and bicultural Canada respectful of the two founding nations. When Bourassa died in 1952, neither dream had become reality. The national question remained unresolved. The Quiet Revolutionaries split on this issue, most of the older half joining the federalist camp and most of the younger half joining the nationalist camp.

The historical context nurtured the dreams of both federalists and nationalists. On the one hand, nationalism had been discredited by the horrible atrocities of the fascist regimes during World War II. Furthermore, the Western European countries were trying to unite into a single political body, paving the way, according to optimists, to a world government. On the other hand, colonies around the globe (including, ironically, Canada, which adopted its flag in 1965, its national anthem in 1980, and repatriated its Constitution from London in 1982) were striving for independence from their metropolises while invoking the principle of self-determination recognized by the United Nations.

For French-Canadian federalists, Canada belonged to both francophones and anglophones even if the two founding peoples did not always act like equal partners. With this view in mind they helped to enact the Official Languages Bill (1969) in spite of strong resistance from conservative factions in English Canada, who feared so-called "French power." French-Canadian federalists believed that nearly every Canadian would eventually speak English and French fluently. Moreover, they felt that once Canada was a bilingual country, Quebec would not have the right to speak for all French Canadians.

In contrast, separatists did not believe Canada could ever be a true home for Francophones. English Canadians, they said, had never respected them. They argued, for example, that during World War II the federal government asked the provinces to temporarily hand over their control of income tax but never gave it back. Historically, the federal government even refused things as trivial as bilingual postage stamps, insisting instead on stamps extolling Canada's attachment to the British Empire. French Quebec, said the separatists, shared nothing with the rest of Canada. Moreover, lost in what appeared to be a North American ocean, many *Québécois* felt in danger of being assimilated to the English majority. Securing the *Québécois* nation could only be achieved through the political autonomy of the province, they concluded.

Quebec's last 40 years of history has been summarized by some analysts as a political struggle between sovereigntists and federalists. But these analysts fail to underline how much both camps came to share as they evolved:

1. *Culture as a state policy.* Despite their continuous quarrelling, Quebec federalists and Quebec separatists were both convinced nationalists, proud of being a citizen either of Quebec or Canada. Jacques Parizeau, leader of the *Parti Québécois* during the 1995 referendum, once said that he and Trudeau agreed on everything except where to put the national capital. And in fact, while the Quebec government was adopting programs to promote local culture, the federal government, under the guidance of those who exercised "French power," was mounting a campaign to protect Canadian culture from American influence. Artists, magazines, television and radio broadcasting, as well as thousands of institutions, associations, groups, and organizations received government funding conditional on promoting "Canadian content." The federal government gave itself the mandate of building a Canadian nation out of British, French, Aboriginal, and other elements, while the Quebec government imagined having a mandate to forge a Quebec nation out of (for the most part) the *Québécois*. Yet despite heading in different directions, the principles at the crux of Canada's and Quebec's actions were similar. Opposed when they were addressing Canadian cultural issues, they stood shoulder to shoulder at international consultation tables for the protection of local particularities. They tried to save Quebec and Canadian culture from the invasion of "McWorld" by creating state cultural institutions (Radio Canada, *Télé Québec*), distributing grants to artists and intellectuals (Canada Council for the Arts, Ministère de la culture), establishing quotas on "Canadian" and "Quebec" content, and controlling

investment in cultural institutions (some companies engaged in cultural production must be two-thirds Canadian-owned by law).

2. *Language as the only legitimate criterion for defining a nation.* A second area of commonality between sovereigntists and federalists involves the criterion they employ for defining a nation. They did not always agree on this matter. In the 1960s, the federal Commission on Bilingualism and Biculturalism had legitimized the "two equal founding nations" idea. In 1972, however, the federal government passed a bill on multiculturalism. Many Quebec nationalists accused Trudeau of betrayal, of watering down the idea of two equal founding nations. To the sovereigntists it seemed that other immigrant groups were now being awarded almost the same status as the *Québécois.* Partly in reaction, the Quebec government passed Bill 101 in 1977. Its aim was to protect not just the French language, but also the values and traditions of the *Québécois.* Yet in the 1980s and 1990s more and more Quebec nationalists came to acknowledge that a state can promote only language and that cultural diversity is not a dilution but an enrichment of national traditions. The Quebec nation many *Québécois* have come to believe in is a "nation of cultures"—very much like Canada with its multiculturalist policies—and not a homogeneous nation composed exclusively of people of French descent. For example, historian Gérard Bouchard, a leading separatist thinker, asserts that the *Québécois* should be defined "strictly by a linguistic criterion."[7] As a result of the widespread acceptance of this idea, promoting *Québécois* culture now involves little more than subsidizing the creation of cultural products in Quebec, regardless of their cultural content. This is similar to the situation in the rest of Canada, where cultural products created in Canada are equated with Canadian culture.

3. *Quebec as a people.* A third area of commonality between sovereigntists and separatists concerns the idea that French-Canadian Quebeckers form a *Québécois* people. The *Québécois* have come a long way since the nineteenth century, when they called themselves *Canadiens* to distinguish themselves from the British, and since the turn of the twentieth century, when they called themselves French Canadians to distinguish themselves from Canadians who spoke English. Today, the *Québécois* feel little or no attachment to their linguistic "brothers" and "sisters" in other provinces. For their part, the leaders of the provincial and federal Liberal parties speak of *Québécois* interests without even trying to convince the *Québécois* that they are members of the same family as Francophones outside Quebec. The same recognition was embodied in the ill-fated Meech Lake Accord, which was designed to entice Quebec to recognize Canada's constitution. The Accord recognized Quebec—not French Canada—as a "distinct society," that is, a society enjoying special status in Confederation.

Today the national question remains unresolved. The 1980 and 1995 Quebec referenda on sovereignty ended in bitter defeat for the sovereigntists. Trudeau's dream of a bilingual Canada is an almost complete failure, except in the Acadian part of New Brunswick and despite episodic vitality in other French-Canadian communities outside Quebec. Not only is French as a first language not progressing outside Quebec, its only chance of maintaining itself as a first language is to stay within Quebec's borders. The numbers are there to remind anyone of the fragility of the French fact in Canada. In 1971, the percentage of people speaking French at home outside Quebec was a mere 4.4 percent. In 1981, it was down to 3.8 percent. Ten years later, it fell to 3.2 percent. In 1996, it dropped to 2.9 percent. This picture is discouraging for anyone hoping to achieve

Henri Bourassa's and Pierre Trudeau's dream of a Canada which would be not just officially bilingual but where French as a first language would flower from coast to coast.

3. SOCIAL JUSTICE

The generation that came of age after World War II committed itself to erecting a welfare state in Canada and Quebec. (A "welfare state" guards citizens from the ravages of the market by providing some level of protection against ill health, unemployment, poverty, etc.) The federal and Quebec bureaucracies were in their infancy in 1940. Twenty years later, things had changed dramatically. Governments were playing a large and growing role in public affairs. In 1950, Quebec was, according to some observers, a "priest-ridden province." In 1980, it was a state-controlled province.

Trudeau made speeches in the 1950s on behalf of establishing socialism in Canada and flirted with the New Democratic Party. He was not alone. In Quebec, many people advocated state intervention in domains previously reserved for the Roman Catholic Church. Soon, education, previously controlled by the Church, came under state jurisdiction and state social programs replaced private charities.

An interventionist state was thought to be necessary for many reasons. The state was a rational institution in an age when efficiency and functionality became watchwords. In an age of universalism, it was viewed as a neutral and inclusive institution in which people of different national origins and religions could be treated equally. The state was regarded, moreover, as a means of "domesticating capital," that is, avoiding recurrent financial and industrial crises. Finally, an interventionist state was widely construed as a means of leading Canadians to the creation of a "just society" in which equality would prevail. Labour unions in particular were fighting for a more equitable distribution of wealth and power.

Many of Trudeau's articles in the 1950s constituted a defence of Keynesian economic theory. (John Maynard Keynes was the leading British economist who first advocated massive state intervention to end the Great Depression of 1929–39.) Thus, it is not surprising that under Trudeau's government state intervention reached new heights. The federal debt grew nine-fold under his administration. He fostered a national energy policy, restricted foreign investment in Canada, created regional development, programs, and so forth. Quebec did not trail behind for long. In the U.S. State Department, Quebec came to be known as "Cuba North." In a little less than a decade, Quebec created thousands of municipal councils and regional boards, hundreds of health institutions, innumerable social services, programs for the protection of agricultural lands, giant Crown Corporations such as Hydro-Quebec, and so on. The state intervention movement even radicalized itself in the 1970s. Concluding that socialism could never be implemented in Canada, some revolutionaries turned their hopes towards an independent Quebec. Pierre Vallières, for example, the author of the famous *White Niggers of America*,[8] intertwined nationalist sentiments with socialist beliefs.

The deep and prolonged recession of 1981–82, by far Canada's worst economic crisis since World War II, rattled the foundations of the welfare state ideologically and practically. Practically, it meant that the Trudeau spending years were over. In Quebec, the return of Liberal Robert Bourassa to power (1985) brought an end to the liberal spending policies of the *Parti Québécois* years (1976–85). However, privatization of government-owned enterprises and cuts in social programs did not reduce the size of the state as much as is sometimes thought. In fact, in absolute numbers, the state apparatus continued to grow along with Quebec's population. Government transfers (welfare payments, unemployment insurance, etc.) as a percentage of personal income even increased, from 10 percent in 1970 to 17 percent in 1990 to approximately 20 percent in 2000. In comparison with the United States, Quebec and Canada maintained their social-democratic proclivity. The continuation of a national health-care system is testimony to the country's disputed but still strong commitment to social democracy.

Ideologically the change was more drastic. The state changed its role from arbiter and organizer of the economy to a merchandiser of labour and a servant of the market. The new ideology (known as neo-conservatism in the United States but more accurately called neo-liberalism), does not oppose the state as such. It only wants the state to eliminate all values from its vocabulary save the value of cost-efficiency and let nothing other than the market determine social priorities. The neo-liberal state defines people more as paying clients than citizens with rights. This ideology accompanied the signing of the Free Trade Agreement between Canada and the United States in 1989 (largely supported by *Québécois*, in contrast with the rest of Canada), its broadening to include Mexico in 1993, and subsequent discussions to eventually create a free trade zone encompassing all of North and South America. This process can only contribute to a further subordination of politics to financial and industrial priorities and interests.

4. A NEW HUMANISM

The first publishing success in Quebec in the second half of the twentieth century was Jean-Paul Desbiens's *Les Insolences du frère Untel*,[9] a book in which the author, a young friar, declared war on Quebec's traditional culture. That 50 000 copies were sold in less than three months reveals how popular and long-awaited Desbiens's criticisms were. Desbiens criticized French-Canadian culture in three ways. First, he said, it was an outmoded island in the midst of a progressive American continent. The French Canadians might use "an American clock" but they lived in "the Middle Ages." The inventions of science, new literary currents, new conceptions in the arts—all this was censored by a clerical

authority that associated modernity with evil and erected ideological walls to "protect" French Canadians from the "perverse" influence of an English and Protestant continent. Second, according to Desbiens, French-Canadian culture imposed a cult of mediocrity on French Canada. "Joual" (the French dialect of the *Québécois*) was for him the self-evident syndrome of this cult. For Desbiens, Joual represented a defeat of the spirit and a laziness of the mind. It was evidence of the abysmal lack of education in the province. Not only did people speak Joual, he complained, they thought Joual. The language crisis was terrible and patent proof of the crisis of French-Canadian civilization, wrote Desbiens. Finally, he argued, French-Canadian culture advocated fear and obedience: "What we are practicing here is purity by sterilization, orthodoxy by silence, security by material repetition. We imagine there is only one way to walk straight, to go nowhere, only one way to never be mistaken, never search for anything, only one way to never get lost: sleep. We have invented a radical means of fighting the caterpillars: cut down the trees."[10] The Catholic Church's doctrine was one reason this situation came to prevail in Quebec, according to Desbiens. By insisting continuously on one's duties and not on one's freedom, by exercising its omnipresence and overwhelming authority over almost every field of activity, the clergy served as a sentinel against rebellious, dissident, and deviant attitudes and beliefs, ending up obliterating the very meaning of free will.

Contrary to what has often been stated, however, the Church was not inactive in the secularization of Quebec society. After all, Desbiens himself was a friar in the Mariste order. He was the expression of a new religious ethic that catalyzed the will for social reform and promoted the individual's triumph over authoritarian institutions. It is no coincidence that the Quiet Revolution took place during the Vatican II Council. Abbot Louis O'Neill, Father Lévesque, and committed Catholics like Fernand Dumont and Robert Lalonde drew from this new religious ethic the moral energy to confront the Catholic Church itself.

The search for a new culture took two directions, both closely connected to reform of the educational system. For a century, French-Canadian intellectuals had considered education the core of all reform. "Without school," said early-twentieth-century Quebec nationalist intellectual Lionel Groulx, "nothing is possible. With school, everything is possible." This is close to what many intellectuals of the 1960s believed.

Firstly, some intellectuals tried to adapt the classical colleges' humanism to the new conditions of a technological and modern society. Humanism, they argued, had to incorporate the developments of the human sciences, to be more open to other cultures and beliefs, and to be founded on the rights of the individual. A 1963 government report ratified this perspective: culture was not a catechism of questions and listed answers but a toolkit that enabled every citizen to prepare for the modern industrial world. The creation of the CEGEPS (two-year college) system in 1969 grew out of this report. Spending two years in CEGEPS between high school and university, each student would now have an opportunity to learn the basics of philosophy, humanities, and the social sciences, thus assimilating the lessons of a general but ever-changing humanism.

Secondly, some intellectuals, going further, insisted on a culture that would not only help individuals adapt to the new era, but would encourage them to question society as it was and strive for a better world. Sociologist Marcel Rioux, fearing a world in which all creativity would disappear under the steamrollers of machinery, technology, and computerization, associated education with the imaginative search for new possibilities: "To speak of culture in our modern society is to speak . . . of surpassing oneself through values, imagination, and creativity."[11] Rioux insisted among other subjects on the teaching of art in schools so as to introduce students to a world where they could be their own creation.

In the 1960s and 1970s, Quebec's culture flourished like never before, at least quantitatively. The Quiet Revolution brought about the creation of the *Ministère des Affaires culturelles du Québec*, the founding of many publishing houses (the number of titles published annually rose from 260 to 4 000 between 1962 and 1977), the establishment of the National Film Board, the popularity of *chansonniers* like Gilles Vigneault and Georges D'or, who were not just singers but cultural icons, and so on. Between 1960 and 1970, the number of university students doubled. The number of artists and art teachers grew from 683 to 3 805 between 1951 and 1971.[12] Television transformed itself from a medium of information to an agent of socialization.

More generally, the decline of the traditional nuclear family, the erosion of religious practice, the liberalization of sexual behaviour, and the emancipation of women deeply affected Quebec society. Looking back at the 1950s through the films of the era can be a big shock to anyone who is unaware of the rapid and radical cultural transformations that originated in the 1960s and created a vastly more open and progressive culture in place of the earlier conservatism. Unique to Quebec was the almost complete secularization of social life that was brought about by restricting the Catholic Church to a very narrow role in private affairs. In the 1960s, the "priest-ridden province" rid itself of the widespread influence of the priesthood.

The quest for a new culture—specifically, for a new humanism—ended with the rise of a consumer society. The great celebration of "we-ness" in the 1960s raised hopes of a more fraternal and convivial society. But the 1970s and 1980s opened the way to an increasingly individualistic society in which people were increasingly concerned with their own destiny. The 1960s also raised hopes for an authentic human culture that would enable every person to discover his or her real self. But disillusionment swiftly replaced this optimism. The pervasive influence of American culture—Hollywood cinema, Walt Disney philosophy, a fast-food mentality—jeopardized the formulation of a new humanism. As Rioux put it: "The Americanization of Quebec is, to my eyes, a most important and anguishing question. . . . Humanity, which was once condemned to a thermonuclear death . . . is now more and more threatened by a cultural death. . . ."[13]

Notwithstanding Rioux's condemnation, the consumer society made more and more inroads into Quebec culture. In 2000, 50 percent of Quebec households had two colour television sets, 46 percent owned a gas barbecue, and two-thirds were connected to cable TV. In 1990, 300 000 movie performances were shown on theater screens; in 2000, the number rose to about 650 000—and 85 percent of all movies were American productions. Instead of turning their liberty into an existential or spiritual search, the *Québécois* soon preferred inquiring about the latest car models. Instead of taking advantage of the cultural opportunities offered to them, they became couch potatoes enslaved to their television sets. At least, this is what the generation that came of age in the aftermath of World War II tended to believe. What was missing among the younger generation and in Quebec society as a whole, they said, was what Fernand Dumont called "transcendence." He wrote: "A society is not an aggregate of people pursuing their individual roads according to their interests; nor is it a closed field where factions struggle for their privileges independently of any rules other than the power of numbers or money."[14] A society, continued Dumont, must be capable of judging its inner value by resorting to some abstract transcendence. Failing to achieve such a judgment, a society condemns itself, according to Dumont, to disappearance as a distinct entity.

This cultural revolution had perhaps a deeper impact in Quebec than elsewhere in Canada, for the will to escape a closed and homogeneous religious universe resulted in calling into question all institutionalized authorities. But, in opposition to Rioux's and Dumont's harsh judgments, the general Americanization of French

Canadian culture did not only mean the progressive establishment of an atomized and materialist society. It also meant the rise of pluralism, a greater tolerance toward different ways of living, and an attachment to simple and fundamental human values. "Beyond political rhetoric," concluded two sociologists on the basis of a national survey, "Quebec's uniqueness can readily be seen in the province's young people of the 1990s."[15] Among other unique features, Quebec's teenagers, they declared, are more open than teenagers elsewhere in Canada to premarital sex, homosexuality, and abortion, and they enjoy their family life more. Overall, their main characteristic seems to be a "lifestyle flexibility" that regards culture as a series of options and opportunities rather than a set of widely accepted values.

CONCLUSION

The reader has certainly noticed that the four great utopias of the Quiet Revolution did not materialize in contemporary Quebec, at least not completely. This observation allows me to reach three conclusions.

Conclusion 1: If one were obliged to summarize in a single sentence the development of Quebec after 1960, one would have to underline two radical social changes that are unique to Quebec history when compared to the rest of North America. First, with the Quiet Revolution, "French Canadians" began to call themselves "*Québécois*." Second, clerical French Canada gave way to a state-controlled Quebec. But besides these two changes, the challenges Quebec faces today resemble pretty much those of every other Western society. For example, the fact that Quebec is a minority nation struggling for the recognition of its rights is not unique. In Canada, Aboriginal peoples are also trying to achieve national recognition. Corsicans in France, Basques in Spain, and the Scottish in the United Kingdom are only some of the other small nations searching for a way to preserve their language and to promote local autonomy through new political arrangements. It is one of the great lessons of the twentieth century that modern states have to find a way to accommodate basic human rights with the collective ambition of nations. Canada has not yet found all the answers to the dilemma nor the secret to equilibrium. But it represents one of the greatest social laboratories of what that equilibrium could be like and leads the way for other countries that today confront the same problems.[16]

Conclusion 2: The Quiet Revolution failed to achieve some of its goals. Bare statistics show the failure of the attempt to create a bilingual Canada. A sovereign Quebec now seems a remote dream. Canadian and Quebec social democracy are on the decline. Democracy is experiencing a crisis. There seems to be little desire to renew humanism. On the other hand, the Quiet Revolution accomplished a complete and largely beneficial transformation of morals and attitudes. For example, in spite of persistent sexism in many quarters, women have gained a status they lacked in the 1950s. Lately, *Québécois* have been found in national surveys to be very tolerant toward immigrants and visible minorities—in spite of a certain level of persistent racism (anti-Semitism, for example, has a long history in Canada, particularly in Quebec). Multiculturalism has brought about a recognition of Canada as a nation of nations. The Charter of Rights and Freedoms is accepted by the vast majority of the provincial population, the only question being whether it should have precedence over the National Assembly in Quebec City. It is worth noting that Quebec passed a *Chartre des droits et libertés de la personne* in 1975 (the provisions of which were extended in 1981) that has quasi-constitutional status and covers not only public law, like its Canadian counterpart, but also private law. The Quebec government was also the first provincial government to sign treaties with First Nations' representatives and has encouraged a new policy of negotiation instead of sterile confrontation.

Conclusion 3: I am not one to believe that a utopia is something that can be fully realized here and now. A utopia is first and foremost a source of inspiration. Obviously, democracy, nationalism, social democracy, and humanism have made inroads in Quebec over the years. But much more must be done if we want Canada to be a place where justice, tolerance, openness, and transparency prevail. If this lesson in humility is remembered, the utopias of the 1960s and 1970s, with all their excesses and their self-evident weaknesses, will not have been dreamt in vain. In this sense, they constitute a useful reminder that if the Canada of 2007 cannot be changed, the Canada of 2057 is yet to be built. That Canada, inescapably, we will have to build together.

NOTES

1. I thank Robert Brym and Valérie de Courville Nicole for their useful comments on a draft of this essay.

2. In this chapter, *"Québécois"* refers to French Quebeckers and "Quebeckers" refers to the entire population of Quebec.

3. Gérard Dion and Louis O'Neill, "L'Immoralité politique dans la province de Québec," *Le Devoir* (14 August 1956).

4. Pierre Elliott Trudeau, "Some obstacles to democracy in Quebec," *Canadian Journal of Economics and Political Science* XXIV: 3 August 1958: 303.

5. "FLQ Manifesto," on the World Wide Web at http://www.ola.bc.ca/online/cf/documents/1970FLQManifesto.html#top (23 November 2002).

6. Stéphane Kelly, "Pierre Elliott Trudeau et son maître. Une éducation politique," *Argument* (I, 1: Fall 1998) 29–40.

7. Gérard Bouchard, *La Nation québécoise au futur et au passé* (Montreal: VLB, 1999) 69.

8. Pierre Vallières, *White Niggers of America: The Precocious Autobiography of a Quebec "Terrorist,"* Joan Pinkham, trans. (Toronto: McClelland and Stewart, 1971). [First French edition, 1969.]

9. Jean-Paul Desbiens, *Les Insolences du frère Untel* (Montreal: Les Éditions de l'homme, 1960).

10. Ibid., 55–56.

11. Marcel Rioux, *Rapport de la Commission d'enquête sur l'enseignement des arts au Québec* (Quebec: l'Éditeur officiel du Québec, 1968) quoted in Pierre W. Bélanger et Guy Rocher, dir., *École et société au Québec: Éléments d'une sociologie de l'éducation* (Montreal: HMH, 1970) 462.

12. Marcel Fournier, *Les Génération d'artistes* (Quebec: IQRC, 1986) 97.

13. Marcel Rioux, "Remarques sur les industries de l'âme," *Question de culture*, 7, "*La culture: une industrie?*" (Quebec: IQRC, 1984) 50 and 49.

14. Fernand Dumont, *Raisons communes* (Montreal: Boréal, 1995) 218.

15. Reginald W. Bibby and Donald C. Posterski, *Teen Trends. A Nation in Motion* (Toronto: Stoddart, 2000), 115–36. [First non-abridged edition, 1991].

16. Michael Ignatieff, *The Rights Revolution* (Toronto: Anansi, 2000).

Chapter 19

Affluence, Power, and Strikes in Canada, 1973–2000

ROBERT J. BRYM

Common sense suggests affluence breeds contentment. On this assumption, people with secure jobs, good working conditions, and high wages are happier than people who face the prospect of unemployment, poor working conditions, and low wages. Moreover, according to the common-sense view, happier workers are less likely to strike. After all, compared to unhappy workers, their needs and demands seem closer to having been met. They appear to lack the deprivations that would motivate them to strike.

It follows from the common-sense view that there ought to be an observable association between measures of strike activity and measures of economic well-being. Figure 19.1, covering the 1973–2000 period, seems to suggest there is such an association.[1] The graph's horizontal axis shows *GDPpc* (Gross Domestic Product per capita), or the total value of goods and services produced in Canada in a year divided by the number of people living in the country at year end. GDPpc is an indicator of the economic well-being of the average Canadian. It is measured in constant (1992) dollars to eliminate the influence of inflation. In effect, this indicator of economic well-being shows the purchasing power of the average Canadian in a given year. Meanwhile, the graph's vertical axis shows *weighted strike frequency*, or the number of strikes that took place in Canada each year divided by the number of non-agricultural workers in the

country. The curve formed by annual scores on these two variables slopes downward. This suggests that when well-being is low, propensity to strike is high; and when well-being is high, propensity to strike is low. Affluence, it seems at first glance, does breed contentment.

Case closed? Hardly. GDPpc is an average, and averages can mask more than they reveal. For instance, GDPpc could conceivably rise when the purchasing power of high-income earners (a minority of the population) rises a lot and the purchasing power of middle- and low-income earners (a majority of the population) falls a little. In that case, rising GDPpc would mask the fact that most people are worse off.

Because workers who strike are unlikely to be rich, we need a better measure of workers' well-being than GDPpc. One candidate is the *unemployment rate*. Unemployment is more likely to affect ordinary workers than the well-to-do. Doctors rarely lose their jobs, and business executives, even if they are fired, can live relatively comfortably off savings in the typically short period before they find work again. On the other hand, unemployment is likely to result in a sharp decline in living standards for ordinary workers, and sometimes the period before they find a new job is protracted.

How then does strike activity vary with the unemployment rate? Figures 19.2 and 19.3 provide the surprising answer. During the first half

Source: Copyright © Robert J. Brym (2006). Originally published in James Curtis, Edward Grabb, and Neil Guppy, ed., *Social Inequality in Canada: Patterns, Problems, Policies 4th ed.*, (Scarborough: Prentice-Hall Canada, 2003). I thank Jonah Butovsky, John Fox, Morley Gunderson, Alan Harrison, Reza Nakhaie, Gregg Olson, and Michael Shalev for helpful comments on a draft of this chapter.

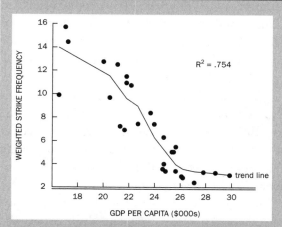

FIGURE 19.1 WEIGHTED STRIKE FREQUENCY BY GDP PER CAPITA (1992$), 1973–2000

Notes: (1) R^2 measures the degree to which the independent variable is associated with (or "explains") variation in the dependent variable. If the independent variable accounts for none of the variation in the dependent variable, the value of R^2 is 0. If it accounts for all of the variation, its value is 1. The R^2 given here is adjusted for the number of cases. (2) The "trend line" is a LOWESS curve. LOWESS stands for "locally weighted scatterplot smoothing." After dividing the values of the independent variable into a number of equal parts, the LOWESS curve computes least squares regression lines for each part and then smoothes the lines. This reveals patterns in the data that may be obscured by a single linear regression line computed over all values of the independent variable.

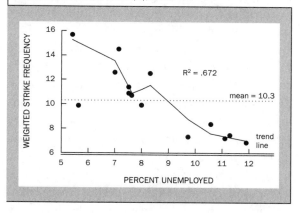

FIGURE 19.2 WEIGHTED STRIKE FREQUENCY BY UNEMPLOYMENT RATE (%), 1973–86

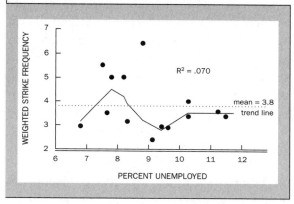

FIGURE 19.3 WEIGHTED STRIKE FREQUENCY BY UNEMPLOYMENT RATE (%), 1987–2000

of the 1973–2000 period, weighted strike frequency fell when the unemployment rate rose, and rose when the unemployment rate fell (see Figure 19.2). In other words, when workers were most economically deprived, they were *least* inclined to strike, and when they were most secure in their jobs, they were *most* inclined to strike. This is just the opposite of the common-sense view, outlined above. Equally unexpected are the results for the second half of the 1973–2000 period (see Figure 19.3). After 1986, the relationship between the unemployment rate and weighted strike frequency virtually disappeared. Thus, the trend line summarizing the association between weighted strike frequency and the unemployment rate shows little trend. What accounts for the inverse association between the unemployment rate and weighted strike frequency in the 1973–86 period? What accounts for the near disappearance of this inverse association after 1986? These are the intriguing questions I address in the remainder of this chapter.

STRIKE RESEARCH ON THE EFFECT OF THE BUSINESS CYCLE

The existing body of strike research goes a long way toward explaining the trend for the 1973–86 period, although not, as you will see, for the 1987–2000 period. Many strike researchers begin with the observation that capitalist economies undergo recurrent "boom and bust" cycles. During bad times, unemployment is high and business profitability low. During good times, unemployment is low and business profitability high. They then go on to note the existence of an association between the business cycle and strike frequency (Rees, 1952). They argue that, as unemployment falls, strike incidence rises.

That is because workers are in a better bargaining position during good economic times. Accordingly, at the peaks of business cycles workers are more likely to enjoy higher savings and alternative job opportunities. At the same time, workers know employers are eager to settle strikes quickly since business is so profitable. Strikes are therefore relatively low-risk. In contrast, during economic downturns, workers are less well off and have fewer job alternatives. They understand employers have little incentive to meet their demands because profitability is low and inventories high. Workers avoid strikes during troughs in the business cycle since they are riskier than in economic good times. From this point of view, workers' contentment, levels of felt deprivation, and other states of mind are unimportant as causes of strike activity. What matters is how *powerful* workers are. Their bargaining position or their ability to get their own way despite the resistance of employers is what counts. Said differently, strike research suggests we can arrive at superior explanations for variations in strike activity by thinking like sociologists, not psychologists.

The association between strike incidence and the business cycle (or its proxy, the unemployment rate) was first demonstrated empirically for the United States (Ashenfelter and Johnson, 1969) and shortly thereafter for Canada (Smith, 1972). Since then, researchers have shown that the association between strike incidence and the business cycle was a feature of most advanced capitalist countries in the twentieth century (Hibbs, 1976). However, later research also introduced three important qualifications to the argument.

First, before World War II, the North American system of collective bargaining between workers and employers was not well institutionalized. In Canada, for example, the legal right to organize unions, bargain collectively, and strike with relatively little constraint dates only from 1944. Before then, strikes were often fights for union recognition. They were therefore less responsive to economic conditions (Cruikshank and Kealey, 1987; Jamieson, 1973 [1957]: 102; Palmer, 1987; Snyder, 1977). As a result, in Canada and the United States, the effect of the business cycle on strike incidence is stronger for the post–World War II period than for the pre–World War II period.

The second important qualification concerns the fact that, in much of Western Europe, the institutional environment mitigates the effect of economic conditions on strike frequency. One important aspect of the institutional environment is the degree of centralization of bargaining units. Strikes are negotiating tools. They are therefore more frequent during periodic contract renewals than between contracts. In much of Western Europe, however, centralized, nationwide bargaining among workers, employers, and governments means that entire sectors of the work force come up for contract renewal and negotiation at the same time. Thus, aggregate measures of strike frequency are affected not just by the phase of the business cycle but by the periodicity of contract renewal schedules. In contrast, the absence of a centralized bargaining structure in Canada and the United States makes aggregate measures of strike frequency more sensitive to the business cycle in North America (Harrison and Stewart, 1994; Snyder, 1977; Franzosi, 1989).

Union density, or the proportion of the non-agricultural labour force that is unionized, is another aspect of the institutional environment that influences strike activity. Unions educate workers and enable them to speak with one voice. Their organizational assets allow unions to mobilize workers. It follows that union density will influence strike action, although strike frequency is often less affected than are strike duration and the average size of strikes (Shorter and Tilly, 1971).

Finally, the third condition limiting the impact of the business cycle on strike frequency is political. In many Western European countries, left-wing or social democratic parties have formed governments or at least achieved representation in Cabinets. This has the effect of moving negotiations over the division of rewards in society from the labour market, where strikes are important bargaining tools, to the political sphere. Where labour is powerful enough to negotiate favourable income redistribution and welfare policies at the political level, industrial conflict tends to recede.[2] Agreeing to limit strike action has even been used as a bargaining chip in exchange for income redistribution and welfare concessions in Sweden, Germany, and other Western European countries. Thus, in the 1970s and 1980s, strike frequency in Sweden, for example, was relatively insensitive to the business cycle (Franzosi, 1989; Hibbs, 1978).

In sum, a substantial body of research demonstrates an association between the business cycle and strike frequency. Moreover, it shows that the association is strongest in North America in the post–World War II era because that is the setting least influenced by mitigating institutional and political variables (Paldam and Pedersen, 1982).

In the context of this research, Figure 19.2 is as ordinary as Figure 19.3 is puzzling. The strong inverse relationship between the unemployment rate and strike frequency for the 1973–86 period is wholly in line with expectations derived from the research literature. However, contrary to what we are led to expect by the research literature, there is little discernible trend for the 1987–2000 period. The unemployment rate is very *weakly* associated with strike frequency in the latter period. Said differently, cyclicality appears to have been largely wrung out of Canada's labour relations system in the last 14 years of the twentieth century, at least in terms of its influence on the incidence of industrial disputes. With respect to its impact on strike incidence, the business cycle was somehow repressed—and this in precisely the setting (post–World War II North America) where its impact was previously the greatest.

Why? What accounts for the repression of the business cycle as a determinant of the incidence of Canadian industrial disputes? That is the question on which the remainder of this chapter turns. An intimation of my answer lies embedded in my decision to divide the recent history of Canadian industrial disputes into two 14-year periods, as in Figures 19.2 and 19.3. Inspection of scatterplots suggested that a shift in the direction of the relationship between the unemployment rate and weighted strike frequency took place after 1986. Since data were available for 14 years following 1986, I chose to examine the relationship for a period of equal duration before 1987. That period ends in 1973.

Using 1973 as the cut-off is also justifiable on historical grounds, for 1973 was the year of the first oil shock. In that year, due to war in the Middle East, the price of oil on world markets tripled, intensifying already high inflation and galloping wage demands. As a result, a strike wave that had been growing since the mid-1950s gained force and crested in 1974–75. In the entire history of Canadian labour, the only strike action that matched that crest was the Winnipeg General strike of 1919 and the ensuing sympathy strikes that stretched all the way from Amherst, Nova Scotia to Victoria, British Columbia (see Figure 19.4). Understandably, therefore, the strikes of 1974–75 caused a strong reaction among government and corporate leaders. They soon took measures to make it substantially more costly for workers to strike. Thus, 1973 marks the beginning of an historical era, one aspect of which is the substantive focus of this chapter.

In the balance of this chapter, I outline how, from the mid-1970s to the 1990s, government and corporate leaders weakened unions and made it more difficult for workers to achieve their goals. These actions had the effect of making strikes less frequent and repressing the effect of the business cycle on the propensity to strike. As you will see, they explain the near-trendless trend line in Figure 19.3.

FIGURE 19.4 WEIGHTED STRIKE FREQUENCY, 1901–2000

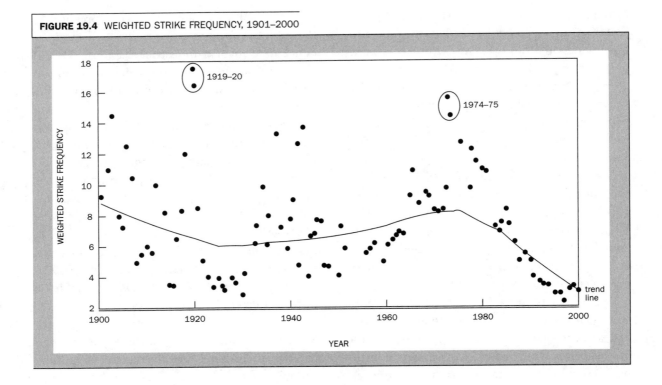

A NEW ECONOMIC AND POLITICAL CONTEXT

Government and business leaders reacted to the 1919–20 strike wave by sending in troops to restore order, throwing union leaders in jail, legislating strikers back to work, and changing laws to allow the deportation of British-born immigrants, who were thought to dominate the strike leadership (Bercuson, 1990 [1974]). Faced with a strike wave of similar proportions in 1974–75, government and business leaders again felt drastic action was necessary. However, the political, institutional, and cultural environment had changed between these two extraordinary episodes of labour unrest. As a result, strategies for controlling labour were different. In 1944, Canadian workers had won the right to organize, bargain collectively, and strike with relatively little constraint. In the context of three decades of post-war prosperity, their new rights allowed them to win substantial gains in real earnings and a massive expansion of state supports and services. In the mid-1970s, business leaders and

governments sympathetic to business felt they had to control labour unrest while fighting wage gains and the growth of the welfare state. To accomplish these tasks, they organized a neo-conservative "counter-revolution" that continues to this day.

The neo-conservative counter-revolution was, however, motivated by more than just the strike wave that crested in the mid-1970s. Rising government debt and global competition also contributed to the decision to go on the political offensive (Johnston, 2001).

Government borrowing rose quickly in the 1970s and 1980s. By the end of that period, interest payments were consuming a quarter of the federal government's annual budget. With indebtedness threatening to cripple government programs, the neo-conservative claim that debt reduction is sound public policy made sense to more and more people.

At the same time, global competition was becoming fiercer. By the early 1970s, Japanese and West German industry had fully recovered from the destruction of World War II. Manufacturers in these countries were exporting massive quantities of finished goods to North America and other markets. In the 1980s, South Korea, China, and other countries followed suit. With growing global competition threatening the welfare of Canadian industry, big business had to develop new strategies to survive and prosper. One such strategy involved restructuring: introducing computers and robots, eliminating middle management positions, outsourcing parts manufacturing, and so forth. Another strategy aimed at increasing business opportunities and ensuring job growth by creating a free trade zone encompassing Canada and the United States (MacDonald, 2000).

Controlling labour while cutting debt, restructuring, and promoting free trade required deep ideological change. Business leaders therefore set about the task of redefining in the public mind the desirable features of the market, the state, and the relationship between the two. From roughly the end of World War II until the mid-1970s, labour demands focused on improving wages and state benefits. Now, an imposing ideological machine sought to convince the public that high wages and generous state benefits decrease the ability of Canadians to compete against workers in other countries. Massive job losses will result (the neo-conservative argument continued) unless wages are held in check and state benefits slashed. That was the main message of Canada's two neo-conservative, corporate-funded think tanks and pressure groups, the Fraser Institute, founded in 1974, and the Business Council on National Issues (BCNI), founded in 1976. The creation of these bodies in the mid-1970s signalled that, like its counterpart in the United States, the Canadian business elite was becoming more ideologically and politically organized and unified (Akard, 1992; Langille, 1987).

One important sign of neo-conservative success was the outcome of the 1988 "free trade" federal election (Richardson, 1996). Just four days before the election, a Gallup poll showed the pro–free trade Progressive Conservatives with the support of only 31 percent of Canadians intending to vote. The anti–free trade Liberals enjoyed a commanding 43 percent of the popular vote while the anti–free trade New Democratic Party stood at 22 percent. At about the same time, an Angus Reid poll disclosed that most Canadians opposed free trade by a margin of 54 percent to 35 percent. A majority of Canadians apparently sensed that free trade might open the country to harmful competition with giant American companies, thus leading to job losses and deteriorating living standards.

Then, a mere 100 hours before the first votes were cast, a little-known organization, the Canadian Alliance for Trade and Job Opportunities (CATJO), swung into high gear. CATJO was funded exclusively by the BCNI. With a campaign budget larger than that of the two opposition parties combined, CATJO bankrolled a media blitz promoting the PCs and their free trade policies. A barrage of brochures, newspaper ads, and radio and television commercials supported the idea that Canadian prosperity depends on the removal of all taxes and impediments to trade between Canadian and the United States. CATJO argued that if goods and services could be bought and sold across the border without hindrance, and capital invested without restraint, good jobs would proliferate and Canada's economic future would be assured. The CATJO onslaught succeeded in overcoming some of the public's fears and drawing attention away from the opposition. On election day, the PCs won with 43 percent of the popular vote. The free trade agreement with the United States was signed just six weeks later.

The free trade agreement, later broadened to include Mexico, sharply increased competition for investment between jurisdictions, leading to a "downward harmonization" of labour policies (Gunderson, 1998). Just as water seeks its lowest level, capital that is allowed to flow freely between jurisdictions will seek the jurisdiction with the lowest costs and therefore the highest profit potential, all else the same. Increasingly, jurisdictions will compete for investment by offering outright tax concessions to investors and ensuring competitive labour costs in the form of lower state benefits, wages, and rates of labour disruption due to strikes. As Canadian workers learned, persistent demands for higher wages—indeed, failure to make wage and other concessions—increase the prospect of plant closings. Where capital mobility is unrestricted, it is only a short hop from southern Ontario to "right to work" states like Georgia or the Maquiladora free trade zone of northern Mexico. In this context, unions lose bargaining power and strikes become riskier actions with a lower probability of achieving their aims.[3]

The slew of government budget cutbacks that took place in the 1990s also had a negative influence on strike incidence. Since workers who go on strike sometimes quit or lose their jobs, declining income-replacing state benefits make strikes riskier for them. In other words, many of the cutbacks of the 1990s increased the potential cost of job loss to workers and therefore ensured that strike incidence would drop. Restricting eligibility for employment insurance and welfare were two of the most important policy measures affecting the readiness of workers to strike.

High government debt, intense global competition, and neo-conservative publicity and lobbying continued to push the Canadian electorate to the right in the 1990s. The Reform Party became the official opposition, its popularity aided by the defection of members of the working class, most of them non-unionized, from the Liberals and the NDP (Butovsky, 2001). The ruling Liberals, meanwhile, adopted much of the neo-conservative agenda. To varying degrees, all major parties supported the new industrial relations regime that had begun to crystallize in the mid-1970s.

A NEW INDUSTRIAL RELATIONS REGIME

Beginning in the mid-1970s, governments adopted a series of measures aimed at better controlling labour (Panitch and Swartz, 1993 [1988]).

Among them was the establishment of wage and price controls that limited only wages in practice yet claimed to require equal sacrifices from labour and business. That strategy was followed in 1975 by the Trudeau government establishing the Anti-Inflation Board for a three-year period. Blessed by business and condemned by the labour movement, the anti-inflation program suspended collective bargaining for all workers in Canada. By undermining the ability of strikes to achieve wage gains, it also dampened labour militancy. A similar approach was taken in 1982, when the federal government passed the Public Sector Compensation Restraint Act. The act imposed a two-year wage limit on federal employees, eliminating their right to bargain and strike. The provinces soon passed similar laws. In some cases, provincial cutbacks were even more draconian than those implemented at the federal level. Public employees in Quebec, for example, took a 20 percent pay cut. In 1991, the federal government announced a one-year wage freeze for federal employees, followed by a 3 percent limit on wage increases for the next two years. By 1993, even the Ontario NDP was backing wage restraint. In that year, the government of Bob Rae introduced a "Social Contract" that overruled the provisions of existing collective agreements and effectively reduced the wages of all 900 000 provincial employees for a three-year period.

A second method of labour control involved amending a variety of laws and regulations. For example, governments persistently broadened the definitions of "management" and "essential service," thereby denying many public sector workers the right to strike. Thus, in 1984 nearly 76 percent of public service workers negotiating contracts were designated as providing managerial or essential services. In the preceding set of negotiations, fewer than 47 percent of those workers were so designated. In addition, and to varying degrees, governments imposed restrictions on political strikes and secondary picketing (picketing beyond the plant or department affected by a strike). They increased employers' rights to fight organizing drives and employees' rights to attempt decertification. They banned strikes in designated work sites, weakened the ability of unions to discipline members who carried out anti-union activities, permitted unions to be sued, and, in most jurisdictions, allowed the use of replacement workers. One result of these actions was that, beginning in 1984, union density began to decline (see Figure 19.5).

Finally, throughout the 1980s, and particularly after Brian Mulroney's Progressive Conservative government was elected in 1984, federal and provincial governments increasingly adopted *ad hoc* back-to-work legislation to weaken workers' bargaining position and thereby limit strike action. Used on average only 0.2 times per year in the 1950–54 period, back-to-work laws were passed on average 5.0 times per year in the 1975–79 period and 5.4 times per year in the 1985–89 period.

At first, limiting the right to strike was widely viewed as a temporary measure necessitated by fear of a resurgence of the strike wave of 1974–75, the highest inflation rates Canada had ever seen, and the deep recessions of 1981–82 and 1991–92. However, limiting the right to strike became a matter of enduring if unstated public policy, largely because economic and political conditions required a less expensive and less militant work force. By the mid-1980s, a new labour relations regime had crystallized. One of

its main purposes was to render labour's ultimate bargaining tool—the strike—increasingly superfluous as a means of bargaining for improved terms of employment.

CONCLUSION: THE WITHERING AWAY OF THE STRIKE?

About 1960, some influential social scientists predicted that the strike was "withering away." The working class, they wrote, had become "embourgeoisified" due to growing affluence. Class conflict was supposedly becoming "institutionalized" in stable systems of collective bargaining. These developments were viewed as a sort of natural evolutionary process, part of the peaceful unfolding of the "inner logic of industrialization" (Ross and Hartman, 1960; Dahrendorf, 1959).

In the 1960s and 1970s, an international strike wave caught these social scientists by surprise. It cast doubt on the validity of their generalizations. Now, however, amid an international "resurgence of labour quiescence" (Shalev, 1992) that has lasted more than two decades, some observers may be tempted to argue that affluence has at last caused the strike to wither away. For them, the generalizations of 1960 may appear valid after all.

My analysis suggests we should avoid this conclusion. I have shown that a measure of average affluence (GDPpc) is inversely associated with weighted strike frequency but is a poor measure of the economic conditions that shape the lives of Canadian workers. The unemployment rate is a much better indicator of workers' economic conditions; and for the 1973–86 period, the unemployment rate varied inversely with weighted strike frequency. This suggests that the relative power or bargaining position of workers—not their level of affluence—determined their propensity to strike. Complicating the story, however, is a fact most researchers have overlooked. In the 1987–2000 period, the inverse relationship between the unemployment rate and weighted strike frequency nearly disappeared.[4] The business cycle had little effect on workers'

FIGURE 19.5 UNION DENSITY, 1973–2000

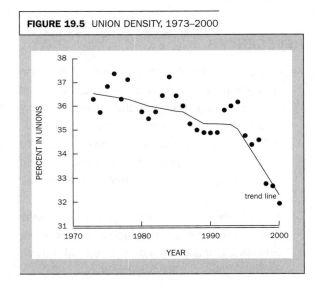

propensity to strike. The reason? Actions taken by employers and governments from the mid-1970s to the late 1990s—introducing free trade, cutting budgets for a wide range of government assistance programs, passing laws and regulations that undermined unions—disempowered workers and rendered the strike a less effective weapon.

In sum, the history of Canadian industrial relations since the mid-1970s suggests that the "inner logic" of industrial capitalism is driven by power, not alleged evolutionary imperatives such as the rising average level of affluence. Industrial relations systems *are* institutionalized forms of class conflict, that is, enduring legal resolutions of historically specific struggles between workers and employers. But "enduring" does not mean "permanent." Trends lasting a few decades should not be confused with the end of history. Industrial relations systems change when power is massively redistributed between classes. In Canada, for example, a massive redistribution of power in favour of workers took place from the mid-1940s onward, when workers won the legal right to unionize and strike and were in a position to extract increased disposable income and benefits from employers and governments. Another massive redistribution of power, this time in favour of employers, took place after the mid-1970s. The Canadian industrial relations regime was transformed on both occasions. The transition from the first regime to the second was marked by a change in the relationship between strike frequency and the business cycle. It follows that, however difficult it might be to imagine in the current industrial relations climate, another massive shift in the distribution of power in society could once again help the strike regain its former popularity.

NOTES

1. Data sources for this chapter are as follows:
   - *Population:* CANSIM (2002b).
   - *Gross Domestic Product per capita:* CANSIM (2002a).
   - *Strikes:* "Series E190-197 . . ." (2001); "Chronological Perspective . . ." (2001).
   - *Union membership:* "Series E175-177 . . ." (2001); Human Resources Development Canada (2001); "Union membership. . ." (2000).
   - *Non-agricultural workers* (1902–10 and 1912–20 interpolated): *Fifth Census . . .* (1915), Table 1, p. 13; *Labour Organizations . . .* (1973) pp. xxii–xxiii; *1994– 1995 Directory . . .* (1995) p. xiii; "Union membership . . ." (2000).
   - *Unemployment:* CANSIM (2001).

2. That is why the influence of union density on strike action peaks at intermediate levels of union density and then tapers off. In countries with the highest proportion of unionized workers, unions tend to exert considerable political influence.

3. As Morley Gunderson commented on a draft of this chapter, the argument developed here is also an argument about wage concessions. Moreover, for strike incidence to fall, the *joint* cost of strikes to both workers *and employers* must increase. In the present case, the cost of strikes to employers has increased, partly because strikes threaten the loss of global market share.

4. See, however, Cramton and Tracy (1994), who reach similar conclusions about the United States in the 1980s.

REFERENCES

Akard, Patrick J. (1992). "Corporate Mobilization and Political Power: The Transformation of U.S. Economic Policy in the 1970s." *American Sociological Review, 57*: 587–615.

Ashenfelter, Orley and George Johnson. (1969). "Bargaining Theory, Trade Unions, and Industrial Strike Activity." *American Economic Review, 59*: 35–49.

Bercuson, David Jay. (1990 [1974]). *Confrontation at Winnipeg: Labour, Industrial Relations, and the General Strike*, rev. ed. Montreal: McGill-Queen's University Press.

Butovsky, Jonah. (2001). *The Decline of the New Democrats: The Politics of Postmaterialism or Neoliberalism?* Ph.D. dissertation, Department of Sociology, University of Toronto.

CANSIM. (2001). "Unemployment Rate Age 15+ SA CDA." On the World Wide Web at http://chass.utoronto.ca/cansim/ (4 April).

———. (2002a). "G.D.P., Expenditure-Based, 1992$/Gross Domestic Pr at Market Prices." On the World Wide Web at http://chass.utoronto.ca/cansim/ (7 January).

———. (2002b). "Population of Canada, by Province/Canada." On the World Wide Web at http://chass.utoronto.ca/cansim/ (7 January).

"Chronological Perspective on Work Stoppages in Canada (Work Stoppages Involving One or More Workers), 1976–2000." (2001). On the World Wide Web at http://labour-travail. hrdc-drhc.gc.ca/doc/wid-dimt/eng/wsat/ table.cfm (27 March).

Cramton, Peter C. and Joseph S. Tracy. 1994. "The Determinants of U.S. Labour Disputes." *Journal of Labor Economics, 12*: 180–209.

Cruikshank, Douglas and Gregory S. Kealey. (1987). "Strikes in Canada, 1891–1950." *Labour/Le Travail, 20*: 85–145.

Dahrendorf, Ralf. (1959). *Class and Class Conflict in Industrial Society*. London: Routledge & Kegan Paul.

Fifth Census of Canada, 1911, Vol. VI. (1915). Ottawa: Census and Statistics Office, Department of Trade and Commerce.

Franzosi, Roberto. (1989). "One Hundred Years of Strike Statistics: Methodological and Theoretical Issues in Quantitative Strike Research." *Industrial and Labor Relations Review, 42*: 348–62.

Gunderson, Morley. (1998). "Harmonization of Labour Policies under Trade Liberalization." *Industrial Relations* 53. On the World Wide Web at http://www.erudit.org/erudit/ri/ v53no1/gunder/gunder.html (9 April 2001).

Harrison, Alan and Mark Stewart. 1994. "Is Strike Behavior Cyclical?" *Journal of Labor Economics* 12: 524–53.

Hibbs, Douglas. (1976). "Industrial Conflict in Advanced Industrial Societies." *American Political Science Review, 70*: 1033–58.

———. (1978). "On the Political Economy of Long-Run Trends in Strike Activity." *British Journal of Political Science, 8*: 153–75.

Human Resources Development Canada. (2001). Special tabulation on union membership, 1960–2000.

Jamieson, Stuart. (1973 [1957]). *Industrial Relations in Canada*, 2nd ed. Toronto: Macmillan.

Johnston, William A. (2001). "Class and Politics in the Era of the Global Economy." In Doug Baer, ed., *Political Sociology: Canadian Perspectives* (pp. 288–306). Don Mills ON: Oxford University Press.

Labour Organizations in Canada 1972. (1973). Ottawa: Economics and Research Branch, Canada Department of Labour.

Langille, David. (1987). "The Business Council on National Issues and the Canadian State." *Studies in Political Economy, 24*: 41–85.

MacDonald, L. Ian, ed. (2000). *Free Trade: Risks and Rewards*. Montreal and Kingston: McGill-Queen's University Press.

1994–1995 Directory of Labour Organizations in Canada. (1995). Ottawa: Minister of Supply and Services Canada.

Paldam, Martin, and Peder Pedersen. (1982). "The Macroeconomic Strike Model: A Study of Seventeen Countries, 1948–1975." *Industrial and Labor Relations Review*, 35: 504–21.

Palmer, Bryan D. (1987). "Labour Protest and Organization in Nineteenth Century Canada, 1820–1890." *Labour/Le Travail, 20*: 61–83.

Panitch, Leo, and Donald Swartz. (1993 [1988]). *The Assault on Trade Union Freedoms: From Wage Controls to Social Contract*, 2nd ed. Toronto: Garamond Press.

Rees, Albert. (1952). "Industrial Conflict and Business Fluctuations." *Journal of Political Economy, 60*: 371–82.

Richardson, R. Jack. 1996. "Canada and Free Trade: Why Did It Happen?" In Robert J. Brym, ed. *Society in Question* (pp. 200–09). Toronto: Harcourt Brace Canada.

Ross, Arthur M. and Paul T. Hartman. (1960). *Changing Patterns of Industrial Conflict*. New York: Wiley.

"Series E175-177: Union Membership in Canada, in Total, as a Percentage of Non-agricultural Paid Workers, and Union Members with International Affiliation, 1911 to 1975 (thousands)." (2001). On the World Wide Web at http://www.statcan.ca/english/freepub/11-516-XIE/sectione/sectione.htm#Unions (29 March).

"Series E190-197: Number of Strikes and Lockouts, Employers and Workers Involved and Time Loss, Canada, 1901 to 1975." (2001). On the World Wide Web at http://www.statcan.ca/english/freepub/11-516-XIE/sectione/sectione.htm#Unions (29 March).

Shalev, Michael. (1992). "The Resurgence of Labour Quiescence." In Marino Regini, ed., *The Future of Labour Movements* (pp. 102–32). London: Sage.

Shorter, Edward, and Charles Tilly. (1971). "The Shape of Strikes in France, 1830–1960." *Comparative Studies in Society and History*, *13*: 60–86.

Smith, Douglas A. (1972). "The Determinants of Strike Activity in Canada." *Industrial Relations*, *27*: 663–77.

Snyder, David. (1977). "Early North American Strikes: A Reinterpretation." *Industrial and Labor Relations Review*, 30: 325–41.

"Union Membership in Canada—2000." (2000). *Workplace Gazette: An Industrial Relations Quarterly*, 3 (3): 68–75.

PART 4C THE ECONOMY AND WORK

When the twentieth century was young, the celebrated German sociologist Max Weber wrote admiringly of the "technical superiority" of **bureaucracies** over any other form of organization. Bureaucracies, wrote Weber, are more precise, faster, less ambiguous, more discrete, and cheaper than all other ways of organizing business, education, law, the military, and so forth. They achieve their efficiency because they employ a specialized division of labour, a strict hierarchy of authority, clear regulations, impersonality, and a staff that is technically qualified to do its job.

Weber also recognized the dark underside of bureaucracy. Bureaucracies, he wrote, create cadres of powerful non-elected officials, thus making the world less democratic. Bureaucracies also lead people to focus on the means of achieving goals that have been specified by their superiors, not on questioning and helping to decide those goals. For these reasons, Weber likened the modern era to an "iron cage." In Chapter 20, George Ritzer carries Weber's analysis a step further. He agrees that the rationalization of the world is occurring in much the way Weber predicted. However, argues Ritzer, the model for this process is not bureaucracy so much as the fast-food restaurant. "McDonaldization," as Ritzer calls it, combines the principles of bureaucracy with those of the assembly line and "scientific management." Ritzer shows that, since the mid-1950s, McDonaldization has spread to larger and larger areas of life, and is now taking over pre-birth and post-death as well. He discusses several countervailing forces, but concludes that they are not sufficiently powerful to overwhelm the continued McDonaldization of the world.

Bureaucratization is one master trend governing the social organization of work. A second such trend is *job polarization.* Job polarization refers to the rapid growth of "bad jobs," the slower growth of "good jobs," and the still slower growth of medium-quality jobs. Bad jobs don't pay much and require the performance of routine tasks under close supervision. Working conditions are unpleasant and sometimes dangerous. Bad jobs require little formal education. In contrast, good jobs often require higher education. They pay well. They are not closely supervised and they encourage the worker to be creative in pleasant surroundings. Good jobs offer secure employment, opportunities for promotion, and fringe benefits. In a bad job, you can easily be fired, you receive few if any fringe benefits, and the prospects for promotion are few. If, over a decade or more, the number of bad jobs grows quickly, the number of medium-quality jobs grows slowly, and the number of good jobs grows at an intermediate rate, the occupational structure will start to assume the shape of an hourglass. Increasingly, jobs will be polarized or concentrated at the high and low ends of the occupational structure. This sort of polarization appears to have taken place in Canada in recent years.

In Chapter 21, Wallace Clement analyzes one of the main forces that has led to the creation of many bad jobs in Canada since the 1990s: the free trade agreements that Canada signed with the U.S. and Mexico. Before free trade, Canadian workers enjoyed higher wages and more state benefits than workers in the other North American countries. However, by making cross-border trade and investment easier, the free trade agreements put downward pressure on both wages and benefits. If employers in Canada continued paying high wages under free trade, and if Canadian governments continued taxing citizens at high rates to pay for generous state benefits, employers could simply shift their investment to more hospitable regimes. That is just what some employers have done. Consequently, unemployment remained high throughout the decade. As Clement shows, to prevent further deterioration of the

Canadian job market, wage levels were forced down and governments slashed their budgets. Bad jobs proliferated. The first years of the new century altered the picture somewhat. For example, particularly after the terrorist attacks of 11 September 2001, job growth continued in Canada but stalled in the United States. According to Clement, it is still too early to tell whether this is a long-term change in the economic environment or a temporary aberration from the longer trend. However, the Canadian Imperial Bank of Commerce (CIBC) regularly publishes a job quality index that sheds light on this question. It measures the quality of a job in terms of its average pay and whether it is part time and involves self-employment. The CIBC found that, overall, the quality of jobs in Canada declined by 8 percent between 1988 and 2006.

The globalization of production extends beyond North America. It encompasses most of the world. In the last few decades, for example, transnational corporations involved in apparel and sports shoe production have moved their factories to low-wage countries such as Malaysia, Indonesia, and Vietnam. There, workers are paid extremely low wages and toil very long hours in often dangerous conditions. In the West, a movement has emerged among university students, labour unions, human rights organizations, religious groups, and other activists to protest the existence of these Third World sweatshops—and the athletes such as Michael Jordan and Tiger Woods who have lent their support to Nike and make large sums of money by appearing in Nike ads.

Activists are especially adept at using the Internet to embarrass Nike into changing its labour practices. For example, in 2001, Jonah Peretti, a graduate student at MIT, discovered that for US$50 Nike lets consumers personalize their shoes by submitting a word or phrase that can be stitched onto the shoes under the swoosh. Peretti filled out the form and sent them $50, asking them to stitch "SWEATSHOP" onto his shoes. Following is the e-mail correspondence that ensued.

From: "Personalize, NIKE iD" <nikeid_personalize@nike.com
To: "'Jonah H. Peretti'" <peretti@media.mit.edu
Subject: RE: Your NIKE iD order o16468000

Your NIKE iD order was cancelled for one or more of the following reasons: 1) Your Personal iD contains another party's trademark or other intellectual property 2) Your Personal iD contains the name of an athlete or team we do not have the legal right to use 3) Your Personal iD was left blank. Did you not want any personalization? 4) Your Personal iD contains profanity or inappropriate slang, and besides, your mother would slap us. If you wish to reorder your NIKE iD product with a new personalization please visit us again at www.nike.com

Thank you, NIKE iD

From: "Jonah H. Peretti" <peretti@media.mit.edu
To: "Personalize, NIKE iD" <nikeid_personalize@nike.com
Subject: RE: Your NIKE iD order o16468000

Greetings,
My order was canceled but my personal NIKE iD does not violate any of the criteria outlined in your message. The Personal iD on my custom ZOOM XC USA running shoes was the word "sweatshop." Sweatshop is not: 1) another party's trademark, 2) the name of an athlete, 3) blank, or 4) profanity. I choose the iD because I wanted to remember the toil and labor of the children that made my shoes. Could you please ship them to me immediately?

Thanks and Happy New Year,
Jonah Peretti

From: "Personalize, NIKE iD" <nikeid_personalize@nike.com
To: "'Jonah H. Peretti'" <peretti@media.mit.edu
Subject: RE: Your NIKE iD order o16468000

Dear NIKE iD Customer,

Your NIKE iD order was cancelled because the iD you have chosen contains, as stated in the previous e-mail correspondence, "inappropriate slang". If you wish to reorder your NIKE iD product with a new personalization please visit us again at nike.com

Thank you, NIKE iD

From: "Jonah H. Peretti" <peretti@media.mit.edu
To: "Personalize, NIKE iD" <nikeid_personalize@nike.com
Subject: RE: Your NIKE iD order o16468000

Dear NIKE iD,

Thank you for your quick response to my inquiry about my custom ZOOM XC USA running shoes. Although I commend you for your prompt customer service, I disagree with the claim that my personal iD was inappropriate slang. After consulting Webster's Dictionary, I discovered that "sweatshop" is in fact part of standard English, and not slang. The word means: "a shop or factory in which workers are employed for long hours at low wages and under unhealthy conditions" and its origin dates from 1892. So my personal iD does meet the criteria detailed in your first email. Your web site advertises that the NIKE iD program is "about freedom to choose and freedom to express who you are." I share Nike's love of freedom and personal expression. The site also says that "If you want it done right . . . build it yourself." I was thrilled to be able to build my own shoes, and my personal iD was offered as a small token of appreciation for the sweatshop workers poised to help me realize my vision. I hope that you will value my freedom of expression and reconsider your decision to reject my order.

Thank you, Jonah Peretti

From: "Personalize, NIKE iD" <nikeid_personalize@nike.com
To: "Jonah H. Peretti'" <peretti@media.mit.edu
Subject: RE: Your NIKE iD order o16468000

Dear NIKE iD Customer,

Regarding the rules for personalization it also states on the NIKE iD web site that "Nike reserves the right to cancel any personal iD up to 24 hours after it has been submitted". In addition, it further explains: "While we honor most personal iDs, we cannot honor every one. Some may be (or contain) other's trademarks, or the names of certain professional sports teams, athletes or celebrities that Nike does not have the right to use. Others may contain material that we consider inappropriate or simply do not want to place on our products. Unfortunately, at times this obliges us to decline personal iDs that may otherwise seem unobjectionable. In any event, we will let you know if we decline your personal iD, and we will offer you the chance to submit another." With these rules in mind, we cannot accept your order as submitted. If you wish to reorder your NIKE iD product with a new personalization please visit us again at www.nike.com

Thank you, NIKE iD

From: "Jonah H. Peretti" <peretti@media.mit.edu
To: "Personalize, NIKE iD" <nikeid_personalize@nike.com
Subject: RE: Your NIKE iD order o16468000

Dear NIKE iD,

Thank you for the time and energy you have spent on my request. I have decided to order the shoes with a different iD, but I would like to make one small request. Could you please send me a color snapshot of the ten-year-old Vietnamese girl who makes my shoes?

Thanks,
Jonah Peretti

Nike did not respond to Peretti's final e-mail but the correspondence was published on the Web and in *The Village Voice,* causing a public relations fiasco for Nike.

The campaign against Nike forms the subject of Chapter 22, by Graham Knight and Josh Greenberg. Knight and Greenberg explain why Nike is the focus of persistent anti-sweatshop protests even though its production practices are no different from those of some other large transnational corporations. They show that it is precisely Nike's success economically and symbolically that makes it the main target of anti-sweatshop protest. They also argue that the kind of social activism typified by the anti-sweatshop campaign will pose an ongoing problem for some transnational corporations. That is because the movement is decentralized, ethically based, and uses tactics that are able to turn a corporation's pro-motional power against its interests and image.

GLOSSARY

Bureaucracies are associations that operate more precisely, faster, less ambiguously, more discretely, and cheaper than other forms of organization. They achieve their efficiency because they embody a specialized division of labour, a strict hierarchy of authority, clear regulations, impersonality, and a staff that is technically qualified to do its job.

Job polarization refers to the rapid growth of "bad jobs," the slower growth of "good jobs," and the still slower growth of medium-quality jobs.

CRITICAL THINKING QUESTIONS

1. What does George Ritzer mean by the statement, "McDonaldization is expanding both in time and space"? Give examples to support your answer.
2. "McDonaldization is a global phenomenon even though it is at odds with many of the basic tenets of globalization theory." Explain what Ritzer means by this statement.
3. The American unemployment rate fell in the 1990s while the Canadian unemployment rate remained high. Why?
4. To what extent do you think global forces compelled the Canadian government and corporations to enter into a free trade agreement with the United States and Mexico? To what extent do you think Canada has political leeway in this regard?

ANNOTATED BIBLIOGRAPHY

Ehrenreich, Barbara. *Nickel and Dimed: On (Not) Getting By in America.* New York: Henry Holt, 2001. An eye-opening first-person account by a leading sociologist of what it's like to try to get by working a minimum-wage job. In brief: nearly impossible.

Krahn, Harvey J., and Graham S. Lowe. *Work, Industry and Canadian Society.* 4th ed. Toronto: Nelson, 2002. A highly regarded Canadian overview of the sociology of work.

Laxer, Gordon. *Open for Business: The Roots of Foreign Ownership in Canada.* Toronto: Oxford University Press, 1989. An award-winning study of the social and historical roots of Canada's peculiar and prob-lematic economic structure.

Chapter 20

The McDonaldization Thesis:

IS EXPANSION INEVITABLE?

GEORGE RITZER

The "McDonaldization thesis" (Ritzer, 1983, 1993, 1996) is derived, most directly, from Max Weber's (1968 [1921]) theory of the rationalization of the Occident and ultimately the rest of the world (Kalberg, 1980). Weber tended to see this process as inexorable, leading, in the end, to the iron cage of rationalization from which there was less and less possibility of escape. Furthermore, with the corresponding decline in the possibility of individual or revolutionary charisma, Weber believed that there was a decreasing possibility of the emergence of a revolutionary counterforce.

Time has been kind to the Weberian thesis, if not to the social world. Rationalization has progressed dramatically in the century or so since Weber developed his ideas. The social world does seem to be more of an iron cage and, as a result, there does seem to be less possibility of escape. And it does appear less likely that any counterrevolution can upset the march toward increasing rationalization.

It is this theory and empirical reality that forms the background for the development of what has been termed the "McDonaldization thesis." This thesis accepts the basic premises of rationalization as well as Weber's basic theses about the inexorable character of the process. Its major point of departure from the Weberian theory of rationalization is to argue that the paradigm of the process is no longer, as Weber argued, the bureaucracy, but it is rather the fast-food restaurant. The fast-food restaurant has combined the principles of the bureaucracy with those of other rationalized precursors (for example, the assembly line, scientific management) to create a particularly powerful model of the rationalization process. It is a relatively new paradigm, traceable to the opening of the first restaurant in the McDonald's chain in 1955. While there were a number of predecessors to the first McDonald's outlet in the fast-food industry, it is McDonald's that was the truly revolutionary development in not only that industry, but in the history of the rationalization process.

Embodying perfectly the principles of rationalization, McDonald's became the model to be emulated first by other fast-food chains and later by other types of chain stores. It was not long before the success of McDonald's caught the eye of those in other types of businesses, and ultimately in virtually every other sector of society. Today, not only is McDonald's a worldwide success, but it offers an alluring model to those in a wide variety of leadership positions. It is in this role that McDonald's is playing the key role in the still-further expansion of the process of rationalization. Indeed its participation is so central that the contemporary manifestations of this process can be aptly labelled "McDonaldization."

Like Weber, I have tended to view this process as inexorable in a variety of senses. First, it is seen as migrating from its roots in the fast-food industry in America to other types of businesses and other social institutions. Second,

Source: Adapted from "The McDonaldization Thesis: Is Expansion Inevitable?" *International Sociology* 11, 3 (September 1996): 291–307. Reprinted by permission of the author.

McDonaldization is spreading from the United States to more and more societies around the world. Third, McDonaldization is viewed as having first concentrated on the rationalization of processes central to life itself, but more recently it has moved to encompass the birth process (and before) as well as the process of death (and beyond).

To put this expansionism in contemporary theoretical terms, McDonaldization is expanding in both space and time (Giddens, 1984; Harvey, 1989). Spatially, McDonaldization is encompassing more and more chains, industries, social institutions, and geographic areas of the world. Temporally, McDonaldization has moved from the core of life itself both backward to the birth process as well as the steps leading up to it and forward to the process of dying and its aftermath.

The evidence on the spatial and temporal advance of McDonaldization is overwhelming. However, in this essay I want to do more than review this evidence. I want to reexamine the issue of inexorability. Do its past and present successes mean that McDonaldization is truly inexorable? Is there no hope that the process can be slowed down or even stopped? Is it possible to avoid an iron cage of rationalization that encompasses time (from birth and before to death and beyond) and space (geographic areas within the United States and throughout the world)? Before getting to these issues, I need to review the basic parameters of the McDonaldization thesis.

McDONALDIZATION

I begin with a foundational definition: *McDonaldization is the process by which the principles of the fast-food restaurant are coming to dominate more and more sectors of American society, as well as of the rest of the world.* The nature of the McDonaldization process may be delineated by outlining its five basic dimensions: efficiency, calculability, predictability, control through the substitution of technology for people, and, paradoxically, the irrationality of rationality.

First, a McDonaldizing society emphasizes *efficiency*, or the effort to discover the best possible means to whatever end is desired. Workers in fast-food restaurants clearly must work efficiently; for example, burgers are assembled, and sometimes even cooked, in an assembly-line fashion. Customers want, and are expected, to acquire and consume their meals efficiently. The drive-through window is a highly efficient means for customers to obtain, and employees to dole out, meals. Overall, a variety of norms, rules, regulations, procedures, and structures have been put in place in the fast-food restaurant in order to ensure that *both* employees and customers act in an efficient manner. Furthermore, the efficiency of one party helps to ensure that the other will behave in a similar manner.

Second, there is great importance given to *calculability*, to an emphasis on quantity, often to the detriment of quality. Various aspects of the work of employees at fast-food restaurants are timed, and this emphasis on speed often serves to adversely affect the quality of the work, from the point of view of the employee, resulting in dissatisfaction, alienation, and high turnover rates. Only slightly over half the predominantly part-time, teenage, non-unionized, generally minimum-wage work force remains on the job for one year or more (Van Giezen, 1994). Similarly, customers are expected to spend as little time as possible in the fast-food restaurant. In fact, the drive-through window reduces this time to zero, but if the customers desire to eat in the restaurant, the chairs are designed to impel them to leave after about twenty minutes. All of this emphasis on speed clearly has a negative effect on the quality of the "dining experience" at a fast-food restaurant. Furthermore, the emphasis on how fast the work is to be done means that customers cannot be served high-quality food, which, almost by definition, requires a good deal of time to prepare.

Third, McDonaldization involves an emphasis on *predictability*. Employees are expected to perform their work in a predictable manner, and customers are expected to respond with similarly predictable behaviour. Thus, when customers enter, employees will ask, following scripts (Leidner, 1993), what they wish to order. For their part, customers are expected to know what they want, or where to look to find what they want, and they are expected to order, pay, and leave quickly. Employees (following another script) are expected to thank them when they do leave. A highly predictable ritual is played out in the fast-food restaurant, and it is one that involves highly predictable foods that vary little from one time or place to another.

Fourth, there is great *control* in a McDonaldizing society, and a good deal of that control comes from technologies. While these technologies currently dominate employees, increasingly they will be replacing humans. Employees are clearly controlled by such technologies as French-fry machines that ring when the fries are done and even automatically lift the fries out of the hot oil. For their part, customers are controlled both by the employees, who are constrained by such technologies, as well as more directly by the technologies themselves. Thus, the automatic fry machine makes it impossible for a customer to request well-done, well-browned fries.

Finally, both employees and customers suffer from the various *irrationalities of rationality* that seem inevitably to accompany McDonaldization. Many of these irrationalities involve the opposite of the basic principles of McDonaldization. For example, the efficiency of the fast-food restaurant is often replaced by the inefficiencies associated with long lines of people at the counters or long lines of cars at the drive-through window. While there are many others, the ultimate irrationality of rationality is dehumanization. Employees are forced to work in dehumanizing jobs and customers are forced to eat in dehumanizing settings and circumstances. In Harry Braverman's terms, the fast-food restaurant is a source of degradation for employees and customers alike (Braverman, 1974).

EXPANSIONISM

McDonald's has continually extended its reach, within American society and beyond. As McDonald's chairman put the company's objective, "Our goal: to totally dominate the quick service restaurant industry worldwide. . . . I want McDonald's to be more than a leader. I want McDonald's to dominate" (Papiernik, 1994).

McDonald's began as a suburban and medium-sized-town phenomenon, but in recent years it has moved into big cities and smaller towns (Kleinfeld, 1985; L. Shapiro, 1990) that supposedly could not support such a restaurant, not only in the United States but also in many other parts of the world. A huge growth area is in small satellite, express, or remote outlets opened in areas that are not able to support full-scale fast-food restaurants. These are beginning to appear in small store fronts in large cities, as well as in non-traditional settings like department stores and even schools. These satellites typically offer only limited menus and may rely on larger outlets for food storage and preparation (Rigg, 1994). McDonald's is considering opening express outlets in such locations as museums, office buildings, and corporate cafeterias.

Another significant expansion has occurred as fast-food restaurants have moved onto college campuses (the first such facility opened at the University of Cincinnati in 1973), instead of being content merely to dominate the strips that surround many campuses. In conjunction with a variety of "branded partners" (for example, Pizza Hut and Subway), Marriott now supplies food to almost 500 colleges and universities (Sugarman, 1995).

Another, even more recent, incursion has occurred: we no longer need to leave the highway to dine in our favourite fast-food restaurant. We can obtain fast food quickly and easily at convenient rest stops along the highway and then proceed with our trip. Fast food is also increasingly available *in* service stations (Chan, 1994). Also in the travel realm, fast-food restaurants are more and more apt to be found in hotels (E. McDowell, 1992), railway stations, and airports, and their products are appearing even on the trays of in-flight meals. The following newspaper advertisement appeared a few years ago: "Where else at 35 000 feet can you get a McDonald's meal like this for your kids? Only on United's Orlando flights." Now, McDonald's so-called Friendly Skies Meals are generally available to children on Delta flights. In addition, in December 1994, Delta began offering Blimpie sandwiches on its North American flights (*Phoenix Gazette*, 1994). (Subway sandwiches are also now offered on Continental flights.) How much longer before McDonaldized meals will be available on all flights everywhere by every carrier? In fact, on an increasing number of flights, prepackaged "snacks" have already replaced hot main courses.

In other sectors of society, the influence of fast-food restaurants has been more subtle, but no less profound. While we are now beginning to see the appearance of McDonald's and other fast-food restaurants in high schools and trade schools (Albright, 1995), few lower-grade schools as yet have in-house fast-food restaurants, but many have had to alter school cafeteria menus and procedures so that fast food is readily and continually available to children and teenagers (Berry, 1995). We are even beginning to see efforts by fast-food chains to market their products in these school cafeterias (Farhi, 1990).

The military has been pressed into offering fast-food menus on its bases and ships. Despite the criticisms by physicians and nutritionists, fast-food outlets are increasingly turning up *inside* hospitals. No homes have a McDonald's of their own, but dining within the home has been influenced by the fast-food restaurant. Home-cooked meals often resemble those available in fast-food restaurants. Frozen, microwavable, and pre-prepared foods, also bearing a striking resemblance to McDonald's meals and increasingly modelled after them, often find their way to the dinner table. Then there is the home delivery of fast foods, especially pizza, as revolutionized by Domino's.

As powerful as it is, McDonald's has not been alone in pressing the fast-food model on American society and the rest of the world. Other fast-food giants, such as Burger King, Wendy's, Hardee's, Arby's, Big-Boy, Dairy Queen, TCBY, Denny's, Sizzler, Kentucky Fried Chicken, Popeye's, Subway, Taco Bell, Chi Chi's, Pizza Hut, Domino's, Long John Silver, Baskin-Robbins, and Dunkin' Donuts, have played a key role, as have the innumerable other businesses built on the principles of the fast-food restaurant.

Even the derivatives of McDonald's and the fast-food industry more generally are, in turn, having their own influence. For example, the success of *USA Today* has led to changes in many newspapers across the nation, with shorter stories and colour weather maps, for example. As one *USA Today* editor put it: "The same newspaper editors who call us McPaper have been stealing our McNuggets" (Prichard, 1987: 232–33).

Sex, like virtually every other sector of society, has undergone a process of McDonaldization. In the movie *Sleeper*, Woody Allen not only created a futuristic world in which McDonald's was an important and highly visible element, but he also envisioned a society in which even sex underwent the process of McDonaldization. The denizens of his future world were able to enter a machine called an "orgasmatron" that allowed them to experience an orgasm without going through the muss and fuss of sexual intercourse. In fact, we already have things like highly specialized pornographic movies (heterosexual, homosexual, sex with children, sex with animals) that can be seen at urban multiplexes and are available at local video stores for viewing in the comfort of our living rooms. In New York City, an official called a three-story pornographic centre "the McDonald's of sex" because of its "cookie-cutter cleanliness and compliance with the law" (*The New York Times*, 1986: 6). The McDonaldization of sex suggests that no aspect of our lives is immune to its influence.

IS McDONALDIZATION TRULY INEXORABLE?

I want to discuss this issue both spatially and temporally. First, there is the spatial issue of whether McDonaldization is destined to spread from its

American roots and become a global phenomenon. Second, there is the temporal issue of whether McDonaldization will inevitably spread from its control over the core of life to colonize birth and before as well as death and beyond.

GLOBALIZATION

We can discuss the first issue under the heading of globalization, or the spread of McDonald's, and more importantly the principles of McDonaldization, around the world. However, in using the term globalization here, it should be pointed out that, as we will see below, there are some differences between its usage here and the way it has been used in the currently voguish globalization theory.

While there are significant differences among globalization theorists, most if not all would accept Robertson's advocacy of the idea that social scientists adopt "a specifically global point of view," and "treat the global condition as such" (Robertson, 1992: 61, 64). Elsewhere, Robertson (1990: 18) talks of the "study of the world as a whole." More specifically, Robertson argues that we need to concern ourselves with global processes that operate in relative independence of societal sociocultural processes. Thus, Robertson (1992: 60) argues, "there is a general autonomy and 'logic' to the globalization process, which operates in *relative* independence of strictly societal and other conventionally studied sociocultural processes." Similarly, Featherstone (1990: 1) discusses the interest in processes that "gain some autonomy on a global level."

While the reach of McDonaldization is global, it does not quite fit the model proposed by globalization theorists. The differences between them are clear when we outline those things rejected by globalization theorists:

1. A focus on any single nation-state.
2. A focus on the West in general, or the United States in particular.
3. A concern with the impact of the West (westernization) or the United States (Americanization) on the rest of the world.
4. A concern with homogenization (rather than heterogenization).
5. A concern with modernity (as contrasted with postmodernity).
6. An interest in what used to be called modernization theory (Tiryakian, 1991).

The fact is that while McDonaldization *is* a global process, it has all of the characteristics *rejected* by globalization theorists: it does have its source in a single nation-state; it does focus on the West in general and the United States in particular; it is concerned with the impact of westernization and Americanization on the rest of the world; it is attentive to the homogenization of the world's products and services; it is better thought of as a modern than a postmodern phenomenon (because of its rationality, which is a central characteristic of modernity); and it does have some affinity with modernization theory (although it is not presented in the positive light modernization theory tended to cast on all western phenomena). Thus, McDonaldization is a global phenomenon even though it is at odds with many of the basic tenets of globalization theory.

The global character of this American institution is clear in the fact that it is making increasing inroads around the world (B. McDowell, 1994). For example, in 1991, for the first time, McDonald's opened more restaurants abroad than in the United States (Shapiro, 1992). This trend continues and, as we move toward the next century, McDonald's expects to build twice as many restaurants each year overseas as it does in the United States. Already by the end of 1993 over a third of McDonald's restaurants were overseas. As of the beginning of 1995, about half of McDonald's profits came from its overseas operations. As of this writing, one of McDonald's latest advances was the opening of a restaurant in Mecca, Saudi Arabia (*Tampa Tribune*, 1995).

Other nations have developed their own variants of this American institution, as is best exemplified by the now large number of fast-food croissanteries in Paris, a city whose love of fine cuisine might have led one to think that it would prove immune to the fast-food restaurant. India has a chain of fast-food restaurants, Nirula's, which sells mutton burgers (about 80 percent of Indians are Hindus who eat no beef) as well as local Indian cuisine (Reitman, 1993). Perhaps the most unlikely spot for an indigenous fast-food restaurant was then war-ravaged Beirut, Lebanon; but in 1984, Juicy Burger opened there (with a rainbow instead of golden arches and J.B. the clown replacing Ronald McDonald), with its owners hoping that it would become the "McDonald's of the Arab world" (Cowan, 1984).

Other countries not only now have their own McDonaldized institutions, but they have also begun to export them to the United States. For example, the Body Shop is an ecologically sensitive British cosmetics chain with, as of early 1993, 893 shops in many countries; 120 of those shops were in the United States, with 40 more scheduled to open that year (Elmer-Dewitt, 1993; E. Shapiro, 1991). Furthermore, American firms are now opening copies of this British chain, such as the Limited, Inc.'s, and Bath and Body Works.

This kind of obvious spread of McDonaldization is only a small part of that process's broader impact around the world. Far more subtle and important are the ways in which McDonaldization and its various dimensions have affected the way in which many institutions and systems throughout the world operate. That is, they have come to adopt, and adapt to their needs: efficiency, predictability, calculability, and control through the replacement of human by non-human technology (and they have experienced the irrationalities of rationality).

How do we account for the global spread of McDonaldization? The first and most obvious answer is that material interests are impelling the process. That is, there is a great deal of money to be made by McDonaldizing systems, and those who stand to profit are the major motor force behind it.

Culture is a second factor in the spread of McDonaldization. There appears to be a growing passion around the world for things American, and few things reflect American culture better than McDonald's and its various clones. Thus, when Pizza Hut opened in Moscow in 1990, a Russian student said: "It's a piece of America" (*Washington Post*, 1990: B10). Reflecting on the growth of Pizza Hut and other fast-food restaurants in Brazil, the president of Pepsico (of which Pizza Hut is part) said of Brazil that this nation "is experiencing a passion for things American" (Blount, 1994: F1). Many people around the world identify strongly with McDonald's; in fact to some it has become a sacred institution (Kottak, 1983). On the opening of the McDonald's in Moscow, one journalist described it as the "ultimate icon of Americans," while a worker spoke of it "as if it were the Cathedral in Chartres . . . a place to experience 'celestial joy'" (Keller, 1990: 12).

A third explanation of the rush toward McDonaldization is that it meshes well with other changes occurring in American society as well as around the world. Among other things, it fits in well with the increase in dual-career families, mobility, and affluence and with a society in which the mass media play an increasingly important role.

A fourth factor in the spread of McDonaldization and other aspects of American culture (the credit card [Ritzer, 1995], for example), is the absence of any viable alternative on the world stage. The path to worldwide McDonaldization has been laid bare, at least in part, because of the death of communism. With the demise of communism the only organized resistance can come from local cultures and communities. While the latter can mobilize significant opposition, it is not likely to be nearly as powerful as one embedded in an alternate worldwide movement.

Given the spread of McDonaldization and the powerful reasons behind it, what can serve to impede this global development? First, there is the fact that many areas of the world offer little in the way of profits to those who push McDonaldization. Many economies are so poor that there is little to be gained by pushing McDonaldized systems on them. Other institutions within such societies may want to McDonaldize their operations, but they are likely to be so overwhelmed by day-to-day concerns that they will have little time and energy to overhaul their systems. Furthermore, they are apt to lack the funds needed for such an overhaul. Thus their very economic weakness serves to protect many areas of the world from McDonaldization.

Second, we cannot overlook the importance and resilience of local culture. Globalization theorists, in particular, have emphasized the strength of such cultures. While it is true that McDonaldization has the power to sweep away much of local culture, it is not omnipotent. For example, while the eating habits of some will change dramatically, many others will continue to eat much as they always have. Then, even if the eating habits of an entire culture change (a highly unlikely occurrence), other aspects of life may be partly or even wholly unaffected by McDonaldization. It is also likely that too high a degree of McDonaldization will lead to a counterreaction and a reassertion of local culture. Also worth mentioning are the many ways in which local cultures affect McDonaldizing systems, forcing them to adapt in various ways to local demands and customs (for example, as discussed above, the mutton burgers in India).

The combination of a comparative lack of economic incentive to the forces behind McDonaldization and the opposition of local cultures will serve to impede the global spread of McDonaldization. However, when a given local culture advances economically, those who profit from McDonaldization will begin to move into that domain. In such cases, only local resistance will remain as a barrier to McDonaldization. It seems clear that while some local cultures will successfully resist, most will fail. In the end, and in the main, the only areas of the world that will be free of McDonaldization are those that lack the economic base to make it profitable.

The only hope on the horizon might be international groups like those interested in health and environmental issues. McDonaldized systems do tend to pose health risks for people and do tend to threaten the environment in various ways. There has, in fact, been some organized opposition to McDonaldized systems on health and environmental grounds. One could envision more such opposition, organized on a worldwide basis, in the future. However, it is worth noting that McDonaldized systems have proven to be quite adaptable when faced with opposition on these grounds. That is, they have modified their systems to eliminate the greatest threats to their customers' health and the greatest environmental dangers. Such adaptations have thus far served to keep health and environmental groups at bay.

THE COLONIZATION OF LIFE AND DEATH

While spatial expansion is covered in the previous section under the heading of globalization, in this section I deal with temporal expansion. McDonaldization first focused on a variety of things associated with *life*. That is, it is the day-to-day aspects of living—food, drink, clothing, shelter, and so on—that were initially McDonaldized. Firmly ensconced in the centre of the process of living, McDonaldization has pressed outward in both directions until it has come to encompass as many aspects as possible of both the beginning (birth) and the end of life (death). Indeed, as we will see, the process has not stopped there, but has moved beyond what would, at first glance, appear to be its absolute limits to encompass (again, to the degree that such a thing is possible) "prebirth" and "postdeath." Thus, this section is devoted to what might be termed the "colonization" (Habermas, 1987) of birth (and its antecedents) and death (and its aftermath) by the forces of McDonaldization.

In recent years a variety of steps have been taken to rationalize the process leading up to birth: burgeoning impotence clinics, including chains (Jackson, 1995), or soon-to-be-chains; artificial or, better, "donor" (Baran and Pannor, 1989) insemination; in vitro fertilization (DeWitt, 1993); surrogate mothers (Pretorius, 1994); "granny pregnancies" (*Daily Mail*, 1994); home pregnancy and ovulation-predictor tests (Cain,

1995); sex-selection clinics (Bennett, 1983); sex-determination tests like amniocentesis (Rapp, 1994); and tests including chorionic villus sampling, maternal serum alpha-fetoprotein, and ultrasound to determine whether the fetus is carrying such genetic defects as Down's syndrome, hemophilia, Tay-Sachs, and sickle-cell disease. All of these techniques are collectively leading to "high-tech baby making" (Baran and Pannor, 1989), which can be used to produce what have been called "designer pregnancies" (Kolker and Burke, 1994) and "designer babies" (Daley, 1994).

The rationalization process is also manifest in the process of giving birth. One measure of this is the decline in the very human and personal practice of midwifery. In 1900 about half of American births were attended by midwives, but by 1986 that had declined to only 4 percent (Mitford, 1993). Then there is the bureaucratization of childbirth. In 1900, less than 5 percent of births in the United States took place in hospitals, by 1940 it was 55 percent, and by 1960 the process was all but complete with nearly 100 percent of births taking place in hospitals (Leavitt, 1986: 190).

Hospitals and the medical profession developed standard, routinized (McDonaldized) procedures for handling childbirth. One of the best-known viewed childbirth as a disease (a "pathologic process") and its procedures were to be followed even in the case of low-risk births (Treichler, 1990). First, the patient was to be placed in the lithotomy position, "lying supine with legs in air, bent and wide apart, supported by stirrups" (Mitford, 1993: 59). Second, the mother-to-be was to be sedated from the first stage of labour on. Third, an episiotomy[1] was to be performed to enlarge the area through which the baby must pass. Finally, forceps were to be used to make the delivery more efficient. Describing this type of procedure, one woman wrote "Women are herded like sheep through an obstetrical assembly line [needless to say, one of the precursors of McDonaldization], are drugged and strapped on tables where their babies are forceps delivered" (Mitford, 1993: 61). This procedure had most of the elements of McDonaldization, but it lacked calculability, but that was added in the form of the "Friedman Curve" created in 1978. This curve envisioned three rigid stages of labour with, for example, the first stage allocated exactly 8.6 hours during which cervical dilation went from 2 to 4 cm (Mitford, 1993: 143).

A variety of non-human technologies (e.g., forceps) have been employed in the delivery of babies. One of the most widespread is the scalpel. Many doctors routinely perform episiotomies during delivery so that the walls of the vagina are not stretched unduly during pregnancy.

The scalpel is also a key tool in caesareans. A perfectly human process has come, in a large number of cases, to be controlled by this technology and those who wield it (Guillemin, 1989). The first modern caesarean took place in 1882, but as late as 1970 only 5 percent of all births involved caesareans. The use skyrocketed in the 1970s and 1980s, reaching 25 percent of all births in 1987 in what has been described as a "national epidemic" (Silver and Wolfe, 1989). (By 1989 there had been a slight decline to just under 24 percent.)

Once the baby comes into the world, there is a calculable scoring system, Apgar, used on newborns. The babies are given scores of 1 to 2 on five factors (for example, heart rate, colour), with 10 being the top (healthiest) total score. Most babies have scores between 7 and 9 a minute after birth, and 8 to 10 after five minutes. Babies with scores of 0 to 3 are in distress.

We move now to the other frontier: from the process of being born to that of dying. The McDonaldization of death begins long before a person dies; it commences in the efforts by the medical system to keep the person alive as long as possible: the increasing array of technologies designed to keep people alive; the focus of medicine on maximizing the *quantity* of days, weeks, or years a patient remains alive, and the lack of emphasis on the *quality* of life during that extra time; computer systems that assess a patient's chances of survival; and the *rationing* in the treatment of the dying person.

Turning to death itself, it has followed much the same path as birth. That is, it has been moved out of the home and beyond the control of the dying and their family members and into the hands of medical personnel and hospitals. Physicians have played a key role here by gaining a large measure of control of death just as they won control over birth. And death, like birth, is increasingly likely to take place in the hospital. In 1900, only 20 percent of deaths took place in hospitals, in 1949 it was up to 50 percent, by 1958 it was at 61 percent, and by 1977 it had reached 70 percent. By 1993 the number of hospital deaths was down slightly (65 percent), but to that must be added the increasing number of people who die in nursing homes (11 percent) and residences such as hospices (22 percent) (National Center for Health Statistics, 1995). Thus, death has been bureaucratized, which means it has been rationalized, even McDonaldized. The latter is quite explicit in the growth of hospital chains and even chains of hospices, using principles derived from the fast-food restaurant, which are increasingly controlling death. One result of all of this is the dehumanization of the very human process of death, as we are increasingly likely to die (as we are likely to be born) impersonally, in the presence of total strangers.

However, even the best efforts of modern, rationalized medicine inevitably fail and patients die. But we are not free of McDonaldization even after we die. For example, we are beginning to witness the development of the changeover from largely family-owned to chains of funeral homes (Corcoran, 1992; Finn, 1991). The chains are leaping into this lucrative and growing market, often offering not only funeral services, but cemetery property and merchandise such as caskets and markers.

Perhaps the best example of the rationalization of death is the cremation. It is the parallel to caesareans in the realm of birth. Cremations are clearly more efficient than conventional funerals and burials. Ritual is minimized, and cremations have a kind of assembly-line quality; they lead to "conveyor belt funerals." Cremations also lend themselves to greater calculability than traditional funerals and burials. For example, instead of allowing lying in state for a day, or more, the city of London crematorium has the following sign: "Please restrict service to 15 minutes" (Grice, 1992: 10). Then there is the irrationality of the highly rational cremation, which tends to eliminate much of the human ceremony associated with a traditional funeral-burial.

The period after one dies has been rationalized in other ways, at least to some degree. There are, for example, the pre-arranged funerals that allow people to manage their affairs even after they are dead. Another example is the harvesting of the organs of the deceased so that others might live. Then there is cryogenics, where people are having themselves, or perhaps just their heads, frozen so that they might be brought back to life when anticipated advances in the rationalization of life make such a thing possible.

Given the rationalization of birth and before as well as death and beyond, are there any limits to this expansion? Several are worth mentioning:

- The uniqueness of every death (and birth): "Every life is different from any that has gone before it, and so is every death. The uniqueness of each of us extends even to the way we die" (Nuland, 1994: 3).

- The often highly nonrational character of the things that cause death (and cause problems at birth):

    Cancer, far from being a clandestine foe, is in fact berserk with the malicious exuberance of killing. The disease pursues a continuous, uninhibited, circumferential, barn-burning expedition of destructiveness, in which it heeds no rules, follows no commands and explodes all resistance in a homicidal riot of devastation. Its cells behave like members of a barbarian horde run amok—leaderless and undirected, but with a single-minded purpose: to plunder everything within reach. (Nuland, 1994: 207)

If ever there was a daunting nonrational enemy of rationalization, cancer (and the death it often causes) is it.

- Midwifery has enjoyed a slight renaissance *because* of the dehumanization and rationalization of modern childbirth practices. When asked why they have sought out midwives, women complain about things like the "callous and neglectful treatment by the hospital staff," "labour unnecessarily induced for the convenience of the doctor," and "unnecessary caesareans for the same reason" (Mitford, 1993: 13).

- The slight decline in caesareans is reflective of the growing concern over the epidemic of caesareans as well as the fact that the American College of Obstetricians came out for abandoning the time-honoured idea, "once a caesarean, always a caesarean."

- Advance directives and living wills tell hospitals and medical personnel what they may or may not do during the dying process.

- The growth of suicide societies and books like Derek Humphrey's *Final Exit* give people instructions on how to kill themselves; on how to control their own deaths.

- The growing interest in euthanasia, most notably the work of "Dr. Death," Jack Kevorkian, shows that more people wish to exercise control over their own deaths.

CONCLUSION

I have discussed the spatial and temporal expansion of McDonaldization under the headings of globalization and the colonization of birth and death. It is abundantly clear that McDonaldization is expanding dramatically over time and space. However, there remains the issue of whether or not this growth is inexorable. A number of the barriers to, and limits on, the expansion of McDonaldization have been discussed in this chapter. There clearly are such limits and, perhaps more importantly, McDonaldization seems to lead to various counterreac-

tions that serve to limit this spread. The issue, of course, is whether or not these counterreactions can themselves avoid being McDonaldized.

While there is some hope in all of this, there is not enough to allow us to abandon the Weberian hypothesis about the inexorable march toward the iron cage of, in this case, McDonaldization. In spite of this likely scenario, I think there are several reasons why it is important for people to continue to try to contain this process. First, it will serve to mitigate the worst excesses of McDonaldized systems. Second, it will lead to the discovery, creation, and use of niches where people who are so inclined can escape McDonaldization for at least a part of their day or even a larger portion of their lives. Finally, and perhaps most important, the struggle itself is ennobling. As a general rule, such struggles are nonrationalized, individual, and collective activities. It is in such struggles that people can express genuinely human reason in a world that in virtually all other ways has set up rationalized systems to deny people the ability to behave in human ways; to paraphrase Dylan Thomas, instead of going gently into that next McDonaldized system, rage, rage against the way it's destroying that which makes life worth living.

NOTE

1. An episiotomy is an incision between the vagina and the anus to enlarge the opening needed for a baby to pass.

REFERENCES

Albright, M. (1995). "Inside Job: Fast-food Chains Serve a Captive Audience," *St Petersburg Times* 15 January: 1H.

Baran, A. and Pannor, R. (1989). *Lethal Secrets: The Shocking Consequences and Unresolved Problems of Artificial Insemination*. New York: Warner Books.

Bennett, N., ed. (1983). *Sex Selection of Children.* New York: Academic Press.

Berry, M. (1995). "Redoing School Cafeterias to Favor Fast-Food Eateries," *The Orlando Sentinel* 12 January: 11.

Blount, J. (1994). "Frying Down to Rio," *Washington Post-Business* 18 May: F1, F5.

Braverman, H. (1974). *Labor and Monopoly Capital: The Degradation of Work in the Twentieth Century.* New York: Monthly Review Press.

Cain, A. (1995). "Home-Test Kits Fill an Expanding Health Niche," *The Times Union-Life and Leisure* (Albany, NY) 12 February: 11.

Chan, G. (1994). "Fast-Food Chains Pump Profits at Gas Stations," *The Fresno Bee* 10 October: F4.

Corcoran, J. (1992). "Chain Buys Funeral Home in Mt Holly," *Burlington County Times* 26 January.

Cowan, A. (1984). "Unlikely Spot for Fast Food," *The New York Times* 29 April: 3: 5.

Daily Mail (1994). "A New Mama, Aged 62," 19 July: 12.

Daley, J. (1994). "Is Birth Ever Natural?" *The Times* (London) 16 March.

DeWitt, P. (1993). "In Pursuit of Pregnancy," *American Demographics* May: 48ff.

Elmer-Dewitt, P. (1993). "Anita the Agitator," *Time* 25 January: 52ff.

Farhi, P. (1990). "Domino's Is Going to School," *Washington Post* 21 September: F3.

Featherstone, M. (1990). "Global Culture: An Introduction," in M. Featherstone (ed.) *Global Culture: Nationalism, Globalization and Modernity,* pp. 1–14. London: Sage.

Finn, K. (1991). "Funeral Trends Favor Stewart IPO," *New Orleans City Business* 9 September.

Giddens, A. (1984). *The Constitution of Society: Outline of the Theory of Structuration.* Berkeley: University of California Press.

Grice, E. (1992). "The Last Show on Earth," *The Times* (London) 11 January: 10.

Guillemin, J. (1989). "Babies by Caesarean: Who Chooses, Who Controls?" in P. Brown (ed.) *Perspectives in Medical Sociology,* pp. 549–58. Prospect Heights, IL: Waveland Press.

Habermas, J. (1987). *The Theory of Communicative Action. Vol. 2., Lifeworld and System: A Critique of Functionalist Reason.* Boston, MA: Beacon Press.

Harvey, D. (1989). *The Condition of Post-modernity: An Inquiry into the Origins of Cultural Change.* Oxford: Blackwell.

Jackson, C. (1995). "Impotence Clinic Grows into Chain," *The Tampa Tribune–Business and Finance* 18 February: 1.

Kalberg, S. (1980). "Max Weber's Types of Rationality: Cornerstones for the Analysis of Rationalization Processes in History," *American Journal of Sociology* 85: 1145–79.

Keller, B. (1990). "Of Famous Arches, Beeg Meks and Rubles," *The New York Times* 28 January: 1: 1, 12.

Kleinfeld, N. (1985). "Fast Food's Changing Landscape," *The New York Times* 14 April: 3: 1, 6.

Kolker, A. and Burke, B. (1994). *Prenatal Testing: A Sociological Perspective.* Westport, CT: Bergin and Garvey.

Kottak, C. (1983). "Rituals at McDonald's," in M. Fishwick (ed.) *Ronald Revisited: The World of Ronald McDonald,* pp. 52–58. Bowling Green, OH: Bowling Green University Press.

Leavitt, J. (1986). *Brought to Bed: Childbearing in America, 1750–1950.* New York: Oxford University Press.

Leidner, R. (1993). *Fast Food, Fast Talk: Service Work and the Routinization of Everyday Life.* Berkeley: University of California Press.

McDowell, B. (1994). "The Global Market Challenge," *Restaurants & Institutions* 104, 26: 52ff.

McDowell, E. (1992). "Fast Food Fills Menu for Many Hotel Chains," *The New York Times* 9 January: D1, D6.

Mitford, J. (1993). *The American Way of Birth.* New York: Plume.

National Center for Health Statistics. (1995). *Vital Statistics of the United States,*

1992–1993, Volume II—Mortality, Part A. Hyattsville, MD: Public Health Service.

The New York Times. (1986). 5 October: 3: 6.

Nuland, S. (1994). *How We Die: Reflections on Life's Final Chapter.* New York: Knopf.

Papiernik, R. (1994). "Mac Attack?" *Financial World* 12 April.

Phoenix Gazette. (1994). "Fast-Food Flights," 25 November: D1.

Pretorius, D. (1994). *Surrogate Motherhood: A Worldwide View of the Issues.* Springfield, IL: Charles C. Thomas.

Prichard, P. (1987). *The Making of McPaper: The Inside Story of USA Today.* Kansas City, MO: Andrews, McMeel and Parker.

Rapp, R. (1994). "The Power of 'Positive' Diagnosis: Medical and Maternal Discourses on Amniocentesis," in D. Bassin, M. Honey and M. Kaplan (eds.) *Representations of Motherhood,* pp. 204–19. New Haven, CT: Yale University Press.

Reitman, V. (1993). "India Anticipates the Arrival of the Beefless Big Mac," *Wall Street Journal* 20 October: B1, B3.

Rigg, C. (1994). "McDonald's Lean Units Beef Up NY Presence," *Crain's New York Business* 31 October: 1.

Ritzer, G. (1983). "The McDonaldization of Society," *Journal of American Culture* 6: 100–7.

———. (1993). *The McDonaldization of Society.* Thousand Oaks, CA: Pine Forge Press.

———. (1995). *Expressing America: A Critique of the Global Credit Card Society.* Thousand Oaks, CA: Pine Forge Press.

———. (1996). *The McDonaldization of Society,* rev. ed. Thousand Oaks, CA: Pine Forge Press.

Robertson, R. (1990). "Mapping the Global Condition: Globalization as the Central Concept," in M. Featherstone (ed.) *Global Culture: Nationalism, Globalization and Modernity,* pp. 15–30. London: Sage.

———. (1992). *Globalization: Social Theory and Global Culture.* London: Sage.

Shapiro, E. (1991). "The Sincerest Form of Rivalry," *The New York Times* 19 October: 35, 46.

———. (1992). "Overseas Sizzle for McDonald's," *The New York Times* April 17: D1, D4.

Shapiro, L. (1990). "Ready for McCatfish?" *Newsweek* 15 October: 76–7.

Silver, L. and Wolfe, S. (1989). *Unnecessary Cesarian Sections: How to Cure a National Epidemic.* Washington, DC: Public Citizen Health Research Group.

Sugarman, C. (1995). "Dining Out on Campus," *Washington Post/Health* 14 February: 20.

Tampa Tribune. (1995). "Investors with Taste for Growth Looking to Golden Arches," *Business and Finance* 11 January: 7.

Tiryakian, E. (1991). "Modernisation: Exhumetur in Pace (Rethinking Macrosociology in the 1990s)," *International Sociology* 6: 165–80.

Treichler, P. (1990). "Feminism, Medicine, and the Meaning of Childbirth," in M. Jacobus, E. Keller and S. Shuttleworth (eds.) *Body Politics: Women and the Discourses of Science,* pp. 113–38. New York: Routledge.

Van Giezen, R. (1994). "Occupational Wages in the Fast-Food Industry," *Monthly Labor Review* August: 24–30.

Washington Post. (1990). "Wedge of Americana: In Moscow, Pizza Hut Opens 2 Restaurants," 12 September: B10.

Weber, M. (1968 [1921]). *Economy and Society.* Totowa, NJ: Bedminster Press.

Chapter 21

Work and Society:

CANADA IN CONTINENTAL CONTEXT

WALLACE CLEMENT

THE WORST OF BOTH WORLDS

In the late 1980s and 1990s, Canada became increasingly integrated into the U.S. economy through several free trade agreements. The agreements facilitated cross-border trade and investment. Closer integration of the two countries had some paradoxical effects. On the one hand, Canadians witnessed an erosion of their hard-won rights to various welfare-state benefits—state-funded medical services, subsidized higher education, and the like. In this sense, Canada became more like the U.S., where citizens have historically enjoyed fewer welfare-state entitlements than Canadians. On the other hand, Canada failed to participate fully in the "boom" economy of the U.S., at least until the altered circumstances at the turn of the century. For example, while the proportion of working-age Americans in the labour force remained exceptionally high throughout the 1990s, the corresponding proportion in Canada fell. After the turn of the century, this trend reversed. Thus, the Canadian labour market failed to emulate the American model while the system of Canadian citizenship entitlements began to do so. In terms of labour market and state benefits, then, Canada experienced the worst of both worlds. The question before us now is "What does the post-September 11th, 2001, era hold in store for us?"

COMPARING LABOUR MARKETS

Before 1981, Canada and the United States had nearly identical unemployment rates. During the 1980s, however, a 2 percent gap in unem-ployment rates opened between the two countries. The gap grew to 5 percent in the early 1990s, reached nearly 8 percent in 1999, and then began to decline.[1] In 2004, the Canadian unemployment rate was 7.2 percent while the U.S. rate was 5.5 percent, a difference of just 1.7 percent (see Table 21.1).[2]

The gap between Canadian and U.S. unemployment rates is due in part to Canada lagging behind the United States in its capacity to create new jobs, but other factors are at work too. For one thing, the United States imprisons more of its citizens per 100 000 population than any other country. Incarceration became particularly popular in the U.S. in the 1980s and 1990s. Today, more than two million Americans are behind bars and the rate of incarceration is more than six times higher than in Canada. The high incarceration rate keeps many hard-to-employ Americans out of the labour force while providing many jobs for police and prison guards.[3] Also helping to

TABLE 21.1 UNEMPLOYMENT IN CANADA AND THE UNITED STATES (IN PERCENT)

	1992–2002	2001	2002	2003	2004
Canada	9.0	7.2	7.7	7.6	7.2
United States	5.4	4.7	5.8	6.0	5.5

Source: Based on Table 0.3. Unemployment in OECD countries (source: *OECD Economic Outlook*, No. 77, May 2005) and Table A. Standardised unemployment rates in 27 OECD countries (source: *OECD Main Economic Indicators*, 2005), OECD Employment Outlook - 2005 Edition, © OECD 2005.

Source: Adapted from Wallace Clement, "Work and Society: Canada in a Continental and Comparative Context," presented in the Department of Sociology, Bishop's University, Lennoxville, 9 November 1999. Revised 2005. Reprinted by permission of the author.

keep the U.S. unemployment rate low is the growing population of "illegal immigrants." There are about twelve million illegal immigrants in the United States, most from Mexico.[4] That is proportionately far more than in Canada. Illegal immigrants are likely to experience higher unemployment rates than legal immigrants and non-immigrants, yet they are not calculated among the officially unemployed because they are in the country as "undocumented workers." Finally, the American armed forces comprise 0.5 percent of the American population but only 0.2 percent of the Canadian population. The higher level of militarization of the United States also keeps the American unemployment rate lower.[5]

Compared to the U.S., Canada was more deeply affected by the recession of the early 1990s and its population grew more quickly. These factors also contributed to the growing gap in unemployment rates between the two countries up to 1999. True, by the middle of 2000, Canada's unemployment rate fell to its lowest level in ten years (6.8 percent) compared to 4.0 percent in the U.S. But it is important to note that much of this decline was due to the growth of part-time, not full-time, jobs. Part-time jobs are less secure, pay less, and offer fewer benefits than full-time jobs. Not until 1998 did the number of full-time jobs regain their 1989 level, with most new jobs in this nine-year period coming from more precarious sources such as part-time work and self-employment.[6] Moreover, some of the decline was due to people dropping out of the labour force. Declining unemployment rates due to people dropping out of the labour force and taking part-time work are less impressive and less beneficial than declining unemployment rates due to the growth of full-time jobs.

One of the strongest patterns of change in Canada's labour force during the free trade era is the rise in self-employment. Self-employment accounted for three-quarters of all new jobs created between 1989 and 1997. The self-employed in 2004 comprised 18 percent of Canada's labour force. Ninety percent of these new jobs are in the service sector, led by business, health, and social services. Significantly, earnings of self-employed

workers are more polarized than earnings of employees, resulting in a bigger earnings divide in the entire labour force. Thus, 45 percent of self-employed workers, compared to 26 percent of employees, earn less than $20 000 annually. At the other extreme, only 1 percent of employees, compared to 4 percent of self-employed workers, earn more than $100 000 annually.[7]

A Statistics Canada study contrasting labour market developments in Canada and the United States between 1989 and 1997 found that self-employment grew by 39 percent in Canada while the number of employees rose by only 1.6 percent. In the United States over the same period, both self-employment and employment in general grew by about 10 percent[8] (see Table 21.2). The difference in self-employment in the two labour markets is striking when one considers that self-employment accounted for four-fifths of total job growth in Canada and only one-tenth in the United States between 1989 and 1997. Equally stunning is the difference in the share of growth from part-time employment in the two countries. Canada's full-time employees took a major hit over the period. Thus, not only was Canada's job growth much slower than in the United States, it was characterized by the more rapid growth of so-called marginal or "contin-

TABLE 21.2 COMPONENTS OF EMPLOYMENT GROWTH, CANADA AND THE UNITED STATES, 1989–1997 (IN PERCENT)

GROWTH	CANADA	UNITED STATES
Total employment	6.5	10.4
Percent of total growth from:		
Self-employment	79.4	9.5
Part-time	47.8	6.2
Full-time	31.6	3.3
Employees	20.6	90.5
Part-time	47.3	20.4
Full-time	−26.7	70.1

Source: Adapted from the Statistics Canada publication "Labour Force Update," Catalogue 71-005, Autumn 1998, Vol. 2, No. 04, November 24, 1998, Table 4, page 17.

gent" jobs that offer less job security, lower wages, more seasonal work, and fewer benefits.

The growth of contingent jobs affects different segments of the labour force to varying degrees. Compare women and men, for example. A recent Canadian study reports that nearly two-thirds of women who have been employed in the paid labour force have had their work interrupted for six or more months. This compares to just over a quarter of men. Moreover, while 88 percent of women's labour force interruptions were due to family responsibilities in the 1950s, this figure fell to 47 percent in the 1990s. Meanwhile, economic reasons such as layoffs accounted for nearly a quarter of female labour force interruptions in the 1990s.[9] Another gender difference is evident in the proportion of women and men who work part time. In all countries, women are more likely than men to work for pay fewer than 30 hours a week. In the U.S. in 2004, about 8 percent of men and 19 percent of women worked for pay fewer than 30 hours a week. In Canada, the respective figures were substantially higher: about 11 percent of men and 29 percent of women.

Part-time work may be voluntary or involuntary. In Canada, an increasingly large share of the part-time labour force is involuntary, which is to say it consists of people who want to work full time but cannot find full-time jobs. Thus, between 1975 and 1994, part-time employment rose from 11 to 17 percent of the labour force, while those seeking full-time employment but having to settle for part-time work rose from 11 to 35 percent. In 40 percent of cases, the involuntary part-time worker was the primary earner in their family.[10] Finally, shift work is becoming more common, and the health and family implications of this development are unclear. For 2000–01, in the core labour force age group (18–54 years old) 30 percent of men and 26 percent of women had nonstandard work schedules (evening, rotating, or irregular shifts).[11]

We now seem to be on the edge of a new era with unclear outcomes. This period began with the attacks on the United States on September 11, 2001, and soon involved much economic dislocation and military mobilization. The U.S.

seems to have been especially hurt in employment terms, and has experienced modest employment growth since the attacks. In Canada, the picture is mixed: job growth has taken place in the state sector (mainly health and education) but has slowed in the private sector.[12] Whether the federal Liberals were forced to expand the state sector after they formed a minority government in 2004 we cannot say with any certainty. We do know that the labour market is in a state of flux, with the number of Canadian self-employed people still rising and the share of the labour force in part-time employment still higher than in the United States. Women continue to make up about 70 percent of part-time workers in both Canada and the United States. The part-time share of the labour force in Canada remains higher than in the United States (see Table 21.3). In 2004, part-timers represented 13.2 percent of the U.S. labour force and 18.5 percent in Canada.

It is important to stress the difference between the expansion of the "own-account" self-employed category in Canada and its contraction in the United States. (Own-account self-employed workers have no employees.) In Canada, the own-account self-employed category grew by 65 percent between 1987 and 1998, accounting for 80 percent of all self-employed people by 1998. Individuals in the own-account category earned only 53 to 68 per-

TABLE 21.3 PART-TIME EMPLOYMENT BY SEX IN CANADA AND UNITED STATES (as percent of total labour force)

Canada	1990	2001	2002	2003	2004
Men	9.2	10.5	11.0	11.1	10.9
Women	26.8	27.0	27.7	27.9	27.2
United States					
Men	8.6	8.0	8.0	8.0	8.0
Women	20.2	18.0	18.5	18.8	18.8

Note: Part time is less than 30 hours per week in main job. U.S. data for wage and salary workers only; Canada includes entire labour market, including self-employed.

Source: OECD, *Employment Outlook 2005* (Paris: OECD, 2005), Table E, p. 252.

cent of the average income of other workers in this period.[13] While Canada experienced a dramatic increase in the number of own-account self-employed workers and the number of hours they worked, both declined in the United States between 1987 and 1998. These findings show fundamental differences between the self-employed sectors in the two countries.[14] Self-employed Americans are much more likely than self-employed Canadians to hire employees and earn more. Should Canadians be concerned? Yes, primarily because these new jobs are of low quality compared with other forms of employment. We are not headed in the right direction.

CITIZENSHIP AND THE WELFARE STATE

On the basis of the foregoing discussion it seems safe to conclude that, since the advent of free trade in the late 1980s, Canada has not participated in many aspects of the boom economy enjoyed by its southern neighbour until it faced the attack of September 11th, 2001. Whether we examine labour force participation rates, unemployment rates, change in GDPpc, or growth in full-time non-contingent jobs, Canada has lagged behind the United States. That, however, is only half the story I want to tell. The other half has to do with the decline of welfare-state benefits or entitlements. Here Canada *has* begun to resemble the United States. That is largely because of free trade. If Canada kept welfare-state benefits much higher than U.S. levels, investment capital would tend to flow out of the country because total labour costs would be higher here. Free trade thus puts downward pressure on Canadian welfare-state benefits.

The main differences between Canadian and U.S. entitlements are in the realm of health care and postsecondary education. In the mid-1990s, just under 45 percent of American health-care costs were covered by government. In Canada, the comparable figure was just over 70 percent. Similarly, the Canadian government heavily subsidizes postsecondary education, while American postsecondary education is largely private.

However, these and other differences between the Canadian and American welfare states are weakening in the free trade era. Canadian government spending on health care and postsecondary education was cut throughout the 1990s. Tuition fees have gone up and private health care is making inroads, especially in Alberta.

Here I must distinguish entitlements based on employment from those based on citizenship. To the extent that access to health care is based on private insurance plans or plans paid by employers rather than awarded as a right of citizenship, health-care insurance is turned into a commodity. In Canada, basic health care, including doctor's fees and hospitalization, are covered by a nationally financed health insurance scheme. Other features of health care—dentistry, drugs, eyewear, types of hospital rooms, and so on—are covered either privately or through employment benefits. In Canada, employers face modest demands in wage negotiations for health-care coverage, whereas in the U.S., health-care insurance demands are high because state funding partially covers only the elderly and the poor.

For education, Canada's primary and secondary levels are fully state-funded with near-universal utilization of the system. Preschool child-care is a private responsibility, and a once-promised national daycare program still remains a dream, although some progress has been made in recent years. Postsecondary education is fee-based but tuition has traditionally been modest and all universities are public institutions. In the United States, a large proportion of primary and secondary students are in private schools because of the low quality of many state-funded schools. Postsecondary education is sharply divided between (1) state-sponsored institutions with high tuition fees and (2) private colleges with very high tuition fees.

In Canada, the contributory "employment insurance" scheme became more restrictive in the 1990s as eligibility criteria were tightened and a shrinking proportion of unemployed people were deemed entitled to benefits. People excluded from employment insurance are pushed into the means-tested welfare system. While

83 percent of unemployed Canadians qualified for employment insurance benefits in 1989, only 43 percent were eligible in 1997. This declining coverage resulted from 1996 reforms disqualifying "voluntary" job leavers and seasonal and part-time workers. Benefits were cut from 67 percent of previous salary to 55 percent. The result was a cash cow for the government; $19.5 billion in employment insurance contributions was collected in 1997 but only $12.5 billion was paid in benefits and administration.[15]

In terms of public expenditures on labour markets, Canada and the United States are not in the same league. Active labour market measures facilitate people's ability to find work. Passive measures compensate them for not working. While active labour market support diminished in Germany and Sweden in the 1990s, these countries remained active in their labour market support throughout the decade. Canada and Australia were high on passive support but low on active support and moderate overall. Japan and the United States were inactive and provided little even in the way of passive labour market support (see Table 21.4).

Compared to the United States, Canada spends more on employment services and labour market training. However, Canada follows the meagre U.S. pattern for youth measures, subsidized employment, and disability measures. During the 1990s, countries such as Australia, Germany, and Sweden dedicated more resources to actively combating unemployment. Canada is in the same league as the United States and Japan in this respect. Still, it is exceptional because, compared to these two countries, Canada suffers from high unemployment.

Canada's dramatic reduction in passive payments was achieved by cutting coverage, not by reducing unemployment, as in the United States. Indeed, Canada's unemployment increased as its expenditures decreased. In terms of its welfare-state expenditures, it is acting like the United States but it is doing so on a labour market foundation dramatically different from its neighbour's.

CONCLUSION

What, in the final analysis, can be said about the relationship between work and society during the free trade era in Canada? Work in Canada has become more marginal or contingent in many respects. There are more self-employed workers, more part-time workers, and more unemployed people (although by 2001 the unemployment gap between the two countries declined to the low level of the 1980s). Instead of becoming more like the American labour market, where people tend to work longer hours

TABLE 21.4 PUBLIC EXPENDITURES IN LABOUR MARKET PROGRAMS AS PERCENTAGE OF GDP, SELECTED COUNTRIES, 2003–2004

EMPLOYMENT	CANADA	USA	AUSTRALIA	JAPAN	GERMANY	SWEDEN
Services	0.17	0.04	0.19	0.26	0.28	0.24
Training	0.12	0.05	0.03	0.04	0.40	0.37
Incentives	0.02	0.01	0.01	0.02	0.11	0.15
Subsidized	0.03	0.01	0.10	0.00	0.20	0.04
Disabled	0.02	0.03	0.05	0.01	0.15	0.48
Compensation	0.77	0.37	0.74	0.46	2.27	1.22
Active	0.37	0.16	0.39	0.32	1.14	1.29
Passive	0.77	0.37	0.74	0.46	2.31	1.22
Total	1.14	0.53	1.13	0.79	3.46	2.51

Source: Based on Table H. Public expenditure and participant inflows in labour market programmes in OECD countries, OECD Employment Outlook - 2005 Edition, © OECD 2005.

during longer work lives, Canada has become a place where people work less because less work is available, especially good work in the public sector and large corporations. Postindustrialism has not been kind to the Canadian labour force.

In areas like unemployment insurance, the Canadian government is putting more stress on employment-based benefits that are typically unavailable for self-employed and part-time workers. The Canadian state has not yet declined to American levels because its citizens continue to insist on a higher level of social support. Canada stands between the American job machine with its abundance of cheap labour and the more supportive labour markets of Sweden and Germany.

Are Canadians, as citizens and workers, better off under free trade? We cannot answer this question fully because we will never know the outcome of alternative policy choices. Nonetheless, it seems that many Canadians have paid dearly for the path Canada's political leaders chose and its economic leaders demanded. The labour market and social service effects of September 11th, 2001, remain unclear, but indications are that the United States experienced more negative effects than Canada. By 2004, the United States appeared to be recovering from the effects of September 11, 2001, but new challenges loomed, including the effects of disastrous hurricanes on the Gulf Coast, the ongoing war in Iraq, and the rising price of oil. Canada has attached its employment wagon to an unstable and inequitable society to its south with disquieting consequences.

NOTES

1. See *Labour Force Update* (Ottawa: Statistics Canada, Autumn 1998), p. 3.
2. See Organisation for Economic Co-operation and Development, *Employment Outlook 2005* (Paris: OECD, 2005), Table 1.3, p. 20.
3. Bruce Western and Katherine Beckett, "How Unregulated is the US Labor Market?: The Penal System as a Labor Market Institution," *American Journal of Sociology,* 104 (4) (January 1999): 1030–60; H. L. Ginsburg, J. Zaccone, G. S. Goldberg, S. D. Collins, and S. M. Rosen, "Special Issue on the Challenge of Full Employment in the Global Economy, Editorial Introduction," *Economic and Industrial Democracy,* 18 (1997): 24; "U.S. surpasses Russia as world leader in rate of incarceration," *The Sentencing Project* (2001). On the World Wide Web at http://www.sentencingproject.org/brief/usvsrus.pdf (18 October 2002).
4. See Min Zhou, "Growing Up American: The Challenge Confronting Immigrant Children and the Children of Immigrants," *Annual Review of Sociology,* 23 (1997): 63–95; *New York Times,* 31 August 1997.
5. "Defence expenditure and size of armed forces of NATO and partner countries," *NATO Review: 2001.* On the World Wide Web at http://www.nato.int/docu/review/2001/defence0103-en.pdf (18 October 2002).
6. See Ekuwa Smith and Andrew Jackson, "Does a Rising Tide Lift All Boats? The Labour Market Experience and Incomes of Recent Immigrants, 1995–1998" (Ottawa: Canadian Council on Social Development, February 2002).
7. See *Canadian Social Trends* (Ottawa: Statistics Canada, Spring 1998), p. 28.
8. See *Labour Force Update* (Autumn 1998), p. 13.
9. See Janet Fast and Moreno Da Pont, "Changes in Women's Work Continuity," *Canadian Social Trends* (Ottawa: Statistics Canada, Autumn 1997), pp. 3–5.
10. Grant Schellenberg, "'Involuntary,' Part-Time Workers," *Perception,* 18 (1996): 3–4.
11. See Statistics Canada, *The Daily,* 25 July 2002.
12. See Statistics Canada, *The Daily,* 9 August 2002.
13. See John Baldwin and James Chowham, "The Impact of Self-Employment on Labour-Productivity Growth: A Canada and United States Comparison" (Ottawa: Statistics Canada, August 2003), pp. 10–11.
14. Ibid., p. 29.
15. See *Globe and Mail,* 13 February 1998, A3.

Chapter 22

Promotionalism and Subpolitics:

NIKE AND ITS LABOUR CRITICS

GRAHAM KNIGHT AND JOSH GREENBERG

INTRODUCTION

On May 12, 1998, Phil Knight, CEO of the sportswear giant Nike, appeared at the National Press Club in Washington to announce "new initiatives to further improve factory working conditions worldwide and provide increased opportunities for people who manufacture Nike products" (Nike, 1999). Knight admitted that Nike's products—and by implication its corporate identity—had become "synonymous with slave wages, forced overtime and arbitrary abuse" (Dionne, 1998). The context for Knight's speech was political as well as economic. Nike had recently suffered a significant drop in its share price in connection with the Asian financial crisis and projections about sales and profits had been revised downwards. But the speech also came on the heels of a series of public relations problems in regard to the campaign being waged by non-governmental organizations (NGOs), labour unions, student groups, and other activists in the U.S. and elsewhere against sweatshop labour practices in developing countries. These practices included below-subsistence wages, hazardous and stressful working conditions, forced overtime, long working hours, abusive management, and denial of worker rights to organize independent unions. While several western transnational corporations (TNCs) have been targets of anti-sweatshop criticism, Nike in particular has become the principal object of anti-sweatshop activism and the growing media publicity of the issue (Greenberg and Knight, 2001), especially since the mid-1990s. In its coverage of Knight's speech *The New York Times* noted that Nike had recently been "pummelled in the public relations arena" over its handling of sweatshop allegations (Cushman, 1998).

In this chapter, we address two questions: firstly, why Nike has become the most prominent target of anti-sweatshop criticism, given that its production practices do not vary significantly from those of its major competitors, and secondly, why Nike has faced persistent public relations problems over the issue. We make two arguments. The first is that Nike is the principal target of anti-sweatshop activism because of its symbolic as well as economic prominence. Nike has become a celebrity corporation as a result of its high-profile advertising and promotional practices, which have made it into not only a commercial success but also a magnet for activist criticism. Secondly, we argue that social activism poses a challenge for corporate public relations because it is ethically motivated, has a decentred network form of organization, and relies on the use of "reflexive" tactics that turn the kind of promotional power corporations rely on against corporate interests and image.

PROMOTIONALISM: COMMUNICATING CORPORATE IDENTITY

Nike has become a principal target of anti-sweatshop activism not only because it is the largest company in the global sports shoe and apparel industry, but also because it has achieved public prominence as a celebrity corporation. Nike has successfully integrated the way it has constructed and communicated different aspects of its corporate identity into an effective promotional strategy that associates its brand name and image with positive social values ranging from athleticism and fitness to social and environmental responsibility to patriotism (Cole, 1996; Cole and Hribar, 1995). Nike has been adept at using promotionalism to craft a flexible, multi-faceted identity that enables the company to represent itself simultaneously as serious and "cool," socially conscious and fashionable, earnest and ironic, image-conscious and technologically sophisticated (Goldman and Papson, 1998). Following Wernick's (1991) definition, promotionalism can be seen as a mode of corporate image-making that extends beyond conventional advertising and integrates different types of communication to the point where functional differences between them become blurred. So, for example, when Tiger Woods, Mia Hamm, and Lance Armstrong promote Nike, Nike also promotes Woods, Hamm, and Armstrong, and there is no clear or fixed distinction between who or what is doing the promoting and who or what is being promoted.

Promotionalism entails the management of a corporation's public presence with a view to translating it into an asset that serves the corporation's economic success. The construction and circulation of a corporate identity is the mechanism by which public presence is managed (Cheney and Christensen, 2001). Corporate identity, which is signified above all by the brand name, logo, and slogan, serves several functions. Externally, corporate identity aims to distinguish the corporation from market rivals. This operates economically, in terms of the range, appeal, and price of the company's products, but also socially, in terms of determining the corporation's place and reputation in the wider community. Corporate identity is used strategically to motivate consumer and investor identification with the organization and its products, and as a way to legitimate the corporation and its activities. Internally, corporate identity is designed to secure organizational unity as well as identification, loyalty, and motivation on the part of staff. In all respects, identity concerns the generation of trust.

Although it is widely recognized that corporate identity is becoming increasingly significant, that significance varies structurally. Identity and promotionalism play an especially critical role for brand name, consumer goods companies that operate in buyer-driven commodity chains. Buyer-driven commodity chains are typical of the apparel and athletic footwear industries where high rates of product turnover are the norm. In buyer-driven chains, economic success depends on control over and heavy investment in the initial and final stages of the production process—over product conception, design, and styling on the one hand, and marketing, advertising, product display, and consumer relations on the other—where symbolic values are paramount (Gereffi, 1994; Korzeniewicz, 1994). The intervening stages of production are contracted out to factories in developing countries where low skilled, cheap labour—especially young migrant women who are also considered to be more compliant and reliable—is relatively plentiful (Carty, 1997). These are also countries where local political elites often seek to attract investment from Western transnational corporations (TNCs) by ensuring environmental and labour standards are poorly enforced or non-existent, and where social stability often depends on authoritarian (and even violent) methods of social control.

Buyer-driven commodity chains entail a dissociation of production and consumption that is economic as well as geographical. Manufacturing labour costs are only a small fraction of the final price consumers will pay for the product. The total costs of promotion, including product styling and design, outweigh those of actual production as new styles, models, and lines are constantly required to ensure the growth of consumer demand. Constant product innovation and turnover mean that the brand name and logo become the principal means to stabilize corporate identity and public recognition.

NIKE'S PROMOTIONAL STRATEGY

Nike's promotional strategy has comprised two major aspects. The first is the use of endorsements and sponsorships to promote not only its products but also social causes, such as protection of the environment or support for the rights and aspirations of the socially disadvantaged or excluded (e.g., African Americans, women, and the disabled), by emphasizing self-empowerment and personal affirmation through sport, fitness, and physical activity (Cole, 1996; Cole and Hribar, 1995; Stabile, 2000). The use of endorsements and sponsorships as a way to promote social causes blurs the line that normally separates commercial and noncommercial activity. Nike's products and brand name, its corporate identity, its social activism on behalf of others (especially the disadvantaged or those at risk), the identity of celebrity endorsers, and the identity of the sports these endorsers play, all feed into the promotional mix. The integration of endorsements and sponsorships enables Nike to represent itself as a socially responsible corporate citizen promoting sport as a solution to social problems. However, the problems these causes address, such as environmental degradation or poverty, tend to be defined in a way that strips them of their material determinants. They are defined chiefly as problems of attitude and disposition for which Nike and the corporate economy should not be held responsible. Material inequalities and social divisions are at once acknowledged and effaced through the fusion of ethical and commercial interests and the promotion of affirmative values (Cole and Hribar, 1995; Cole, 1996).

Nike's "If you let me play" advertising campaign vaunting the personal and social benefits of female participation in sport and its Participate in the Lives of American Youth (P.L.A.Y.) program, launched in 1994, are the most prominent examples of the integration of commercial and ethical promotionalism. Both were framed as the response to a problem of social exclusion and disadvantage. This was articulated more explicitly in the case of the P.L.A.Y. program. According to Phil Knight, P.L.A.Y. was the company's reaction to a "crisis in America," as children were denied access to sport and play due to cutbacks in school sport programs and the lack of safety in community playgrounds (Business Wire cited in Goldman and Papson, 1998: 109). The publicity campaign promoting the P.L.A.Y. program on television made use of Nike endorsers such as Michael Jordan and Olympic track star Jackie Joyner-Kersee to narrate visual images of the "social alienation of poverty and their transcendence via sports" (Goldman and Papson, 1998: 109; see also Cole, 1996). If the responsibility for providing youth access to sport and recreation was no longer being met by the state, Nike represented itself as willing to step in and fill the void.

The second aspect of Nike's promotional strategy has been the extensive use of information subsidies. In Gandy's formulation, "information is characterized as a subsidy because the source of that information causes it to be made available at something less than the cost a user would face" otherwise (1992: 61). Gandy distinguishes "direct" from "indirect" information subsidies. Nike provides direct information subsidies to the media inasmuch as it acts as a source of information about its business activities, sponsorships, community programs, and so forth. The reciprocal effect is that the media also provide indirect information subsidies to Nike inasmuch as media coverage, at least good news coverage, enhances the presence and value of Nike's identity in the public sphere, where consumers and investors acquire the information that determines how they act.

Nike's ability to make use of information subsidies has been expanded by the development of the Internet as a communications tool. As part of its "nikebiz" web site, Nike republishes selected press coverage in edited and unedited form. While much of this consists of favourable coverage, Nike has also included some coverage of its critics, by including its own FAQ page on labour issues, letters responding to activist groups such as the Clean Clothes Campaign, and, recently, a 12-minute virtual video tour of Nike factories in Asia. The web site plays a role similar to that of the department store window. Several items are put on display, and the browser is positioned as a consumer who is free to pick and choose which elements strike his or her interest: products to buy, share price trends to contemplate, or ethical concerns to allay. In this way, the web site enables Nike to unify its communication with different audiences and audience segments in a single virtual space. Answering its critics is a way to display openness and to reassure consumers concerned about the ethics of its products. It is also a way to speak to investors whose decisions are calculated in terms of prospective sales and revenue.

PROMOTIONALISM AS ITS OWN PROBLEM

The extent to which promotional culture has become dominant in the public sphere speaks not only to the importance of corporate identity in the marketplace, but also to the blurring of boundaries between the marketplace and the wider social, political, and cultural environment. Promotionalism is directed ultimately at increasing consumption. For example, when Nike lost market share and leadership to Reebok in the mid-1980s, its response was to refocus its promotionalism on female consumers by incorporating an appeal to and celebration of women's aspirations for autonomy and self-empowerment (Cole and Hribar, 1995). Similarly, Nike's use of African-American celebrity endorsers like Michael Jordan to promote both social causes and commodities makes use of racial imagery in a way that goes beyond and effaces specifically racial meanings (Cole, 1996). Jordan is represented in Nike's promotionalism as the personification of universal values rather than the values of a particular community whose interests have been shaped by social exclusion.

In addition to these strategies, which have been aimed primarily at expanding market share, Nike has also used a promotional logic to address problems that have arisen outside the marketplace. As Cole (1996) and Stabile (2000) note, Nike's integration of marketing and social responsibility has generally been a response to controversy and crisis originating in civil society. The P.L.A.Y. program, for example, came in the wake of bad publicity Nike suffered in the late 1980s and early 1990s from its association with a wave of "sneaker crimes" when media reports of youths being mugged and even killed for their sport shoes began to circulate. The finger was pointed at Nike precisely because of the powerful effect its promotionalism was thought to have on creating an obsession to own Nike products on the part of those unable to pay. The racialized coding of the sneaker crime wave put Nike in particular in the spotlight because of the company's association with African-American sports celebrities like Michael Jordan.

What the sneaker crime crisis represents is an example of promotionalism's *reflexive* character. Reflexivity denotes both reflection (or representation) and reflex (or reaction). In the former sense, promotionalism reflects the identity that corporations such as Nike try to convey (e.g., rebellious, progressive, cool, ironic) through their advertising, marketing, sponsorships, and so on. At the same time, promotionalism is also reflexive to the extent that it reacts back upon itself in ways that undermine its intended aims. In this sense, promotionalism is not only a solution to corporate communication and identity, it is also a source of new problems that result precisely from the side effects of success (Beck, 1997). By making Nike into a celebrity corporation with a prominent public profile and presence, promotional success has also made Nike into a prominent public target of social criticism levelled in terms of the alleged breach between what the company claims to represent and what the effects of its practices are. In the case of the sneaker crime crisis, the reflexive effect of promotionalism was confined to the negative side effects of consumption. In the case of anti-sweatshop criticism, on the other hand, the effect of reflexivity has shifted to the sphere of production. Activists have criticized and protested the working conditions in Nike's factories in terms of a failure to respect and implement the values that Nike invokes in its claims of social responsibility and individual empowerment. Because corporate identity has to circulate in the public sphere where its meaning cannot be totally controlled, activists have been able to open up a space between Nike's preferred identity and its actual image, and counter-brand the company as a sweatshop employer.

COUNTER-BRANDING NIKE: ACTIVISM AND SUBPOLITICS

The counter-branding of Nike as a sweatshop employer should be understood in the context of social activism as a form of "subpolitics" (Beck, 1997). Subpolitics is the politics of interest groups, social movements, activism, and advocacy groups whose interests radiate out beyond the sphere of institutional politics, and whose targets include power centres other than the state. If politics represents the intervention of the state and market economy in the everyday life-world of social and cultural experience, then subpolitics represents the life-world's reciprocal feedback effect on the system (Habermas, 1987).

Subpolitics confronts the state and the market with their attempts to appropriate and exploit the norms and expectations of everyday life. Central to the motivation of the anti-sweatshop movement is a belief that Nike is hypocritical in the way it lays claim to social responsibility yet continues to exploit young female workers in the developing world. The logic of the anti-sweatshop critique is thus one of "communicative action" geared to mutual understanding and consensus rather than "strategic action," which is aimed at competitive success (Habermas, 1987). This is a general feature of new social movements (NSMs), which are oriented not towards the immediate, material self-interest of participants but to questions of shared meaning, social justice, and social solidarity (Carroll, 1997; Jasper, 1997). Many NSMs share an altruistic dimension as their actions entail an interest in the welfare of others (Melucci, 1996). In much the same way, the subpolitics represented by the anti-sweatshop movement is less about achieving material gains for the movement than it is about creating social understanding and support for others. Anti-sweatshop activism involves a desire to empathize with and care about the situation, interests, and aspirations of those at a distance (workers in developing countries) while assuming a critical stance towards something that is culturally and geographically more proximate (the corporation).

Subpolitics also differs from formal politics in that it is oriented more to questions of short-term tactics rather than long-term strategy. NSMs such as the anti-sweatshop movement assume a looser, more mobile and flexible form than more bureaucratically structured organizations. Whereas state and corporate organizations constitute definite centres of power where binding decision-making occurs, NSMs are typically organized in terms of network arrangements (Castells, 1996). This makes NSMs transient and reliant on a more pluralistic range of tactics that may also lack a strong sense of overall strategy. The anti-sweatshop movement consists of a network of different groups (unionists, students, religious groups, etc.) engaged in diverse activities such as culture jamming (mass media sabotage), conventional public protests, participation in shareholders' meetings, and regulatory initiatives such as the Worker Rights Consortium (Klein, 2000; Sage, 1999; Shaw, 1999). The communicational success of NSM groups such as the anti-sweatshop movement can also be attributed to the growing use of the Internet as a tool for information sharing. The Internet is seen by many to have levelled the playing field of corporate-activist relations by diminishing the corporation's gatekeeper role in the communication of critical information (Coombs, 1998; Heath, 1998). For example, according to Medea Benjamin of the international NGO, *Global Exchange*, "every time we do an action, we send an e-mail and a hundred people show up. It's like magic. We couldn't do it without e-mail" (Bullert, 1999: 4).

As we argued previously, the anti-sweatshop movement differs from conventional social movements in that its organizational structure is decentred, mobile, and transient. In part, this is a result of the way in which new communication technologies such as the Internet bind the participants together in a virtual, rather than actual, geographical space. But at the same time, it is also because the movement consists of a coalition of groups that, under other circumstances, might find themselves on different sides of the political and ideological fence (e.g., environmental activists and labour unionists). What makes NSMs such as the anti-sweatshop movement so powerful is that traditional activist groups such as the labour movement, whose interests tend to be more particularistic (e.g., preserving jobs), can work cooperatively with other groups such as religious organizations and students, whose interests are based on considerations that are more ethical and normative than material. Indeed, it was not until the anti-sweatshop movement spread onto university campuses in the mid- to late 1990s that the issue demanded intense and ongoing attention in the mainstream media (Greenberg and Knight, 2001).

The anti-sweatshop campus campaigns began in earnest in 1997, when a small but well-organized group of students at Duke University successfully pressured the administration there to adopt a "Code of Conduct" that would require the university to purchase and authorize the sale of clothing bearing the university's logo only from dealers that abided by standards pertaining to health and safety, wage, child-labour provisions, and factory location disclosures. In July 1998, a national coalition of student anti-sweatshop groups was formed under the umbrella name United Students Against Sweatshops (USAS). In a short time, thanks to the use of the Internet, close to 200 campus organizations had sprung up across North America (though less extensively in Canada, where university logo-wear is less pop-

ular and intercollegiate sports less commercially minded and funded). Newspaper reporting on the sweatshop problem increasingly referred to campus sit-ins and other student protests. At Georgetown University, students occupied the university president's office for four days to demand a meeting with the administration in order to establish a Code of Conduct there. Similarly, at the University of Wisconsin, student activists staged a 97-hour sit-in at the main administrative buildings before finally being granted a meeting with the administration. The UW protest was hugely successful, as nearly all of the students' demands were met (Hausman, 1999). In a more spectacular case, the University of North Carolina anti-sweatshop group, Students for Economic Justice, held a nude-optional party titled "I'd Rather Go Naked Than Wear Sweatshop Clothes." Shortly afterwards, in a show of solidarity, 12 student activists at Syracuse University in upstate New York cycled nude across their campus in late March to demonstrate their commitment to abolishing the sale of sweatshop garments there. Between February and April 2000, anti-sweatshop sit-ins had been held at universities in Pennsylvania, Michigan, Wisconsin, Oregon, Iowa, and Kentucky, as well as SUNY-Albany, Tulane, Purdue, and Macalester (Featherstone, 2000). In Canada, anti-sweatshop campaigns were organized at Concordia University, George Brown College, the University of Guelph, McMaster University, Queen's University, Ryerson University, the University of Toronto, the University of Waterloo, the University of Western Ontario, and York University. An organization linking Canadian college and university groups—Students Against Sweatshops-Canada—was formed in February 1999 (Students Against Sweatshops-Canada, 2000). For the first time in nearly three decades, university students had become politically engaged and the power elite had taken notice.

By raising controversy over Nike's labour practices, the anti-sweatshop movement has not only questioned the reality of production conditions and workers' rights in developing countries. It has also thrown Nike's sincerity and credibility into question (Habermas, 1987). Nike has been presented with a problem whose resolution is not only practical, but also communicational. Its communication problem is particularly acute inasmuch as issues of sincerity and credibility penetrate to the heart of corporate identity. Nike's public relations response to the anti-sweatshop movement, however, has compounded this communication problem. Despite the view that corporate public relations have become increasingly proactive, Nike's response to its anti-sweatshop critics has been largely reactive and marked by a reluctance to take seriously its critics' arguments and claims. Nike has relied on a strategy of issues management aimed at deflecting and dispersing blame, making rhetorical commitments to social responsibility, and subduing controversy.

NIKE'S RESPONSE TO ITS CRITICS

Boje (1999; see also Harvard Business School, 2000) has identified four stages through which Nike's response to sweatshop criticisms has developed. The first stage, up to the early 1990s, was one of avoidance: Nike disclaimed responsibility by displacing blame onto its contractors. In stage two, from 1993 to 1996, Nike's response switched to one of denial that the problem existed in a systematic and widespread way, and pointed to its own corporate code of conduct, first formulated in 1992, as evidence of this. This was followed in 1996 and 1997 (stage three) by a period of intensified media publicity after the 1995 discovery of the El Monte sweatshop in California and the 1996 exposé of the Kathy Lee Gifford line of Wal-Mart clothing being made under sweatshop conditions. Though not directly implicated in these events, Nike claimed its monitoring system was independent and commissioned a report by the global auditing firm GoodWorks International to testify to this. The GoodWorks report, which gave Nike a largely favourable review, was subsequently crit-

icized by the media and academics as well as activists for its shoddy methodology and failure to acknowledge the key issue of wages (Boje, 1998). Knight's National Press Club appearance in May 1998 marked the beginning of the fourth stage and the prospect of some material improvement in working conditions.

Nike's reactive posture, its reluctance to address criticisms on major issues like wage levels, and its continued hostility towards some critics point to the limitations of promotionalism and the difficulty that promotionally oriented issues management has in coming to terms with anti-sweatshop subpolitics. The heart of issues management is a concern on the part of the corporation to manage the public policy process in a way that minimizes interference by outside actors, such as the state (Heath, 1988). In this respect, Nike's reluctance to address the issue of manufacturing wage levels, despite the relatively small proportion of total costs they comprise, represents a desire to preserve autonomy in the marketplace. When Nike translates social responsibility into philanthropic initiatives such as environmental projects, micro loans for local entrepreneurs, or education and fitness programs in developing countries, it also demonstrates a concern to maximize promotional returns. These are initiatives to which Nike can attach its name and corporate identity in a more visible and lasting way than wage increases.

The rise of issues management in the 1970s coincided with the neo-liberal turn in economic thinking, as governments began to redefine their role from one of legislative and regulatory intervention to one of facilitation and mediation in circumstances where corporate conduct became socially problematic. This was the model adopted by the American government in response to the growing controversy about sweatshops. In 1996 the Clinton administration brokered an agreement—the Apparel Industry Partnership (AIP)—between several apparel industry companies and other interested parties, including labour and human rights NGOs. The AIP, which gave rise to the Fair Labor

Association (FLA), included Nike as a charter member. The formation of the AIP/FLA marked the institutionalization of sweatshops as a multilateral issue whose resolution was seen to lie in long-term consensus building around voluntary corporate codes of labour conduct, monitoring, and public accountability, rather than legislative or regulatory intervention.

The construction of an issue by means of this kind of multilateral process has two consequences for how the issue is framed and communicated publicly. Firstly, responsibility is generalized and dispersed among several parties so that no single organization bears the burden of accountability. Membership in the AIP/FLA enabled Nike to share its responsibility for the sweatshop issue with other corporate members and demonstrate publicly its willingness to resolve the problem in a voluntary and cooperative way. This means that Nike and other TNCs that are caught in the spotlight of bad publicity are able to point to one another as evidence that the problem is systemic rather than specific. Secondly, the generalization and dispersion of the issue implicates all the parties to institutional arrangements like the AIP/FLA in the responsibility for resolution. Resolution for the problem then becomes a matter of organizational politics, of negotiation and compromise. Because there are so many different actors to coordinate efforts with, Nike is unable to act on its own without disrupting the broader environment in which other participants must also act.

What has emerged from the interaction between Nike and anti-sweatshop activists is a dialectic of issues and crisis management. Nike's attempts to construct the issue in a systematic and institutionally manageable way are constantly punctured by activist claims about local crisis situations such as the recent controversy over the Kukdong factory in Atlixco, Mexico (Maquilla Solidarity Network, 2001; Nike, 2001; Verité, 2001). The effect of this is to reframe the issue of sweatshops as a problem of both Nike's factory conditions and its public credibility and sincerity. Nike's vulnerability to the publicity of sweatshop criticism stems from the fact that activists do not fit the mould of typical corporate stakeholders such as investors, consumers, or even employees. Stakeholders are assumed to have a direct, objective stake in the corporation's performance; they are assumed to have a vested interest of some kind that defines this stake and the issues or concerns that arise from it. Each stakeholder puts something at risk in his or her relationship with the corporation, and also stands to benefit directly from that relationship. It is the balance of benefits and risks that induces stakeholders to limit their claims and that allows for compromise solutions when stakeholder interests conflict. The interests of most anti-sweatshop activists, however, do not involve direct personal benefit and cost (with the possible exception of the labour movement). Their stake is really a mediated and mediating one, namely the interests of other stakeholders, Nike's workers in developing countries, who are already disregarded or marginalized. This means that activists' actions and claims are less likely to be constrained by considerations of material self-interest than those of other stakeholders.

CONCLUSION

Nike is faced with two problems. It must address in a substantive way criticisms of the conditions of production in its contract factories. It must also convince its critics that it is sincere in its claims and efforts to make acceptable improvements, while taking account of the way expectations and standards can be constantly revised. Because Nike has attempted so extensively to turn its claim to social responsibility into promotional capital, its sincerity problem in particular can be addressed successfully only in ways that reduce the appearance of direct promotional benefit. Regardless of the practical steps it can take to improve working conditions, wages, and worker rights, activist criticism, public suspicion, and the uncertainty these imply will doubtless persist as long as Nike continues to treat social responsibility as simply part of a promotional strategy.

For the anti-sweatshop movement the challenge of communicating its views is one of both access and content. Although the Internet has something of a democratizing effect on the capacity to communicate, it functions primarily as a tool to inform and motivate those who are already aware of and sympathetic to the anti-sweatshop campaign. Initial awareness still relies on "old" media such as face-to-face communication, public spectacles like demonstrations, and coverage in mainstream news outlets. The effectiveness of these depends on the cyclical character of protest activism, and the fact that social problems and causes vie for popular attention and support (Tarrow, 1994). Social movements can compensate for this by building on and renewing the way they frame social problems and their resolution (Snow and Benford, 1992). The sweatshop issue is a complex one, to be sure. The anti-sweatshop movement has been most effective in drawing attention to aspects such as wage levels that can be framed and communicated in a simplified but effective way, such as comparing the average Nike worker's wages to the sums paid to top Nike executives or celebrity athletes. The movement will have to continue to develop the framing of key issues like wages in an accessible yet innovative way. This is especially so if it is to attract the attention of the elite mainstream media whose influence is essential in legitimating the issue, but whose own search for new story topics and angles creates its own cyclical effects.

As economic globalization creates the conditions under which new forms of subpolitics cut across social, cultural, political, and geographical distances, TNCs will see their symbolic power challenged in the public sphere. Despite the dominance of promotionalism, the public sphere has not lost altogether its function as an arena where critical views can be expressed and support mobilized to challenge dominant institutions. As economic globalization extends and intensifies the logic of market relations, TNCs such as Nike, which are the principal agent of this process, will be confronted increasingly with the side effects of commercial success in the form of mobile, diffuse, and decentred subpolitics. This subpolitics, whose authority rests essentially on its ethical resonance, will continue to turn the power of publicity back onto the marketplace and reclaim the values of civil society as an affirmation of identification, mutual understanding, and social solidarity, rather than competitive success.

REFERENCES

Beck, U. (1997). *The Reinvention of Politics: Rethinking Modernity in the Global Social Order.* Trans. By M. Ritter. Cambridge: Polity Press.

Boje, D. M. (1998). "The Swoosh Goddess Is a Vampire: Nike's Environmental Accounting Storytelling." In G. A. Rossile, ed., *International Business and Ecology Research Yearbook* (pp. 23–32). Slippery Rock, PA: International Association of Business Disciplines Publication.

———. (1999). "Is Nike Roadrunner or Wile E. Coyote? A Postmodern Organization Analysis of Double Logic." *Journal of Business and Entrepreneurship,* 2:77–109.

Bullert, B. J. (1999). "Strategic Public Relations, Sweatshops, and the Making of a Global Movement." The Joan Shorenstein Center on the Press, Politics and Public Policy, Working Paper #2000-14. Cambridge, MA: Harvard University.

Carroll, W. (1997). "Social Movements and Counterhegemony: Canadian Contexts and Social Theory." In W. Carroll, ed., *Organizing Dissent: Contemporary Social Movements in Theory and Practice,* 2nd edition. Toronto: Garamond.

Carty, V. (1997). "Ideologies and Forms of Domination in the Organization of the Global Production and Consumption of Goods in the Emerging Postmodern Era: A Case Study of Nike Corporation and the Implications for Gender." *Gender, Work and Organization,* 4: 189–201.

Castells, M. (1996). *The Information Age: Economy, Society and Culture. Vol. I: The Rise of the Network Society*. Oxford: Blackwell.

Cheney, G., and Christensen, L. T. (2001). "Organizational Identity: Linkages between Internal and External Communication." In F. M. Jablin and L. L. Putnam, eds., *New Handbook of Organizational Communication*. London: SAGE.

Cole, C. (1996). "American Jordan: P.L.A.Y., Consensus and Punishment." *Sociology of Sport Journal*, 13:366–397.

Cole, C. and Hribar, A. (1995). "Celebrity Feminism: Nike Style Post-feminism, Transcendence, and Consumer Power." *Sociology of Sport Journal*, 12:347–369.

Coombs, W. T. (1998). "The Internet as Potential Equalizer: New Leverage for Confronting Social Irresponsibility." *Public Relations Review*, 24:289–303.

Cushman Jr., J. H. (1998, May 13). "Nike Pledges to End Child Labor and Apply U.S. Rules Abroad." *The New York Times*, D1.

Dionne, E. J. (1998, May 15). "Bad for Business." *The Washington Post*, A27.

Featherstone, L. (2000, May 15). "The New Student Movement." *The Nation*, pp. 11–18.

Gandy, O. (1992). "Public Relations and Public Policy: The Structuration of Dominance in the Information Age." In E. Toth & R. L. Heath, eds., *Rhetorical and Critical Approaches to Public Relations* (pp. 111–130). Hillsdale, NJ: Erlbaum.

Gereffi, G. (1994). "The Organization of Buyer-Driven Commodity Chains." In G. Gereffi and M. Korzeniewicz, eds., *Commodity Chains and Global Capitalism* (pp. 95–122). Westport: Praeger.

Goldman, R., and Papson, S. (1998). *Nike Culture: The Sign of the Swoosh*. London: SAGE.

Greenberg, J., and Knight, G. (2001). "Framing Nike: Globalized Production, Sweatshop Labor and the American Media." Paper presented at the Global Village/Global Image Conference, London: British Film Institute.

Habermas, J. (1987). *The Theory of Communicative Action Vol. 2. Lifeworld and System: A Critique of Functionalist Reason*. Trans. by T. McCarthy. Boston: Beacon Press.

Harvard Business School. (2000, January 19). Hitting the Wall: Nike and International Labor Practices. HBS Case N1-700-047. Prepared by J. L. Burns under the supervision of D. L. Spar.

Hausman, T. (1999, February 26). "Students Leading the Sweatshop Battle." Retrieved from http://www.alternet.org.

Heath, R. L. (1988). "Conclusion: Balancing the interests of competing stakeholders: The new role for issues management." In R. L. Heath and Associates, eds., *Strategic Issues Management: How Organizations Influence and Respond to Public Interests and Policies* (pp. 386–394). San Francisco & London: Jossey-Bass Publishers.

———. (1998). New Communication Technologies: An Issues Management Approach. *Public Relations Review*, 24:273–288.

Jasper, J. (1997). *The Art of Moral Protest: Culture, Biography and Creativity in Social Movements*. Chicago: University of Chicago Press.

Klein, N. (2000). *No Logo: Taking Aim at the Brand Bullies*. Toronto: Knopf Canada.

Korzeniewicz, M. (1994). "Commodity Chains and Marketing Strategies: Nike and the Global Athletic Footwear Industry." In G. Gereffi and M. Korzeniewicz, eds., *Commodity Chains and Global Capitalism* (pp. 247–265). Westport: Praeger.

Maquilla Solidarity Network. (2001, January 26). "Two Independent Reports Confirm that Mexican Nike Workers' Rights Violated." Memo: Codes Update Number 4. Toronto: Maquilla Solidarity Network.

Melucci, A. (1996). *Challenging Codes: Collective Action in the Information Age*. Cambridge: Cambridge University Press.

Nike. (1999). "Nike Chairman and CEO Phil Knight New Labor Initiatives." On the World Wide Web at http://www.nikebiz.com/labor/speech_trans.shtml.

———. (2001). "Nike Develops Remediation Plan for Kukdong Based on Recently Completed Independent Audit." On the World Wide Web at http://www.nikebiz.com/media/n_kukdong6.shtml.

Sage, G. (1999). "Justice Do It! The Nike Transnational Advocacy Network: Organization, Collective Actions, and Outcomes." *Sociology of Sport Journal*, 16:206–235.

Shaw, R. (1999). *Reclaiming America: Nike, Clean Air and the New National Activism*. Berkeley: University of California Press.

Snow, D. A. and Benford, R. D. (1992). "Master Frames and Cycles of Protest." In A. D. Morris and C. McClurg Mueller, eds., *Frontiers in Social Movement Theory* (pp. 133–155). New Haven and London: Yale University Press.

Stabile, C. (2000). "Nike, Social Responsibility and the Hidden Abode of Production." *Critical Studies in Media Communication*, 17: 186–204.

Students Against Sweatshops-Canada (2000). On the World Wide Web at http://www.campuslife.utoronto.ca/groups/opirg/groups/sweatshops/sas-c.html (30 October 2002).

Tarrow, S. (1994). *Power in Movement: Social Movements, Collective Action and Politics*. Cambridge: Cambridge University Press.

Verité. (2001). Comprehensive Factory Evaluation Report on Kukdong International Mexico, S. A. de C. V. On the World Wide Web at http://www.nikebiz.com/media/nike_verite_report.pdf.

Wernick, A. (1991). *Promotional Culture: Advertising, Ideology and Symbolic Expression*. London: SAGE.

PART 5

DEVIANCE AND CRIME

Deviance is behaviour that departs from a norm. It ranges from harmless fads to the most violent crimes. In a sense, all deviance is anti-institutional since it seeks to achieve acceptable goals, such as getting rich or happy, by generally disapproved, and often illegal, means. But deviance is also institutionalized behaviour because it is socially learned, organized, and persistent. Accordingly, an individual is more likely to become a deviant if he or she is exposed to more deviant than non-deviant role models. Moreover, the deviant role is learned by means of socialization; just as medical students are socialized into the role of doctor, so professional robbers must learn the moral code of thieves. And deviants, including criminals, establish counter-institutions—cliques, gangs, mafias, and so forth—with their own rules of behaviour and their own subcultural norms.

Criminal behaviour worries the Canadian public more today than it used to. There is much talk about crime waves and mounting random violence, particularly among youth. The roughly 20 percent spike in the number of Toronto homicides in 2005 fuelled the fear. Many people are afraid to walk alone outside at night. In large cities, many people equip their homes with burglar alarms and install steel bars on their basement windows.

There is no doubt that crime rates have risen since the early 1960s, but are current fears exaggerated? A dispassionate analysis of crime statistics suggests as much. In 2003, Canada's homicide rate (the number of homicides per 100 000 people) reached its lowest point since 1967. Violent crime in general was down by 10 percent since 1992. In 2004, Canada's rate of youth crime had been stable for a decade. Ontario had the lowest crime rate of any province in 2003 and 2004. Toronto's homicide rate was just below the national average in 2004 and was average among Canada's major cities. The American homicide rate is 3 times higher than Canada's; Chicago's homicide rate is 13 times higher than Toronto's.

Clearly, there is a disconnection between most people's perception of crime and actual crime rates. Why is this so? Most people rely on the mass media for information about crime trends. The police rely on information they collect in the course of doing their work. Reported criminal incidents, apprehensions, convictions, and incarcerations are all recorded to determine, among other things, whether crimes of various types are on the rise. Both public and police sources of information are, however, subject to bias. The mass media often exaggerate the extent of criminal behaviour because doing so increases audience size and therefore the amount of money that businesses are willing to pay for advertisements. The police may record more crime not just because there is more, but also because more officers are looking harder for certain types of criminals and because the public is more willing to report certain types of crimes.

Due to these biases, sociologists prefer to supplement official police statistics with "victimization surveys," polls of representative samples of citizens that seek to determine whether and under what circumstances people are victims of crime. Recent Canadian victimization surveys find that under a quarter of Canadians are victims of at least one crime in the year preceding the surveys. Overall, victimization rates are remaining steady or *decreasing,* depending on the type of crime examined. Victimization surveys also show that while Canadians think that crime rates are rising, they believe the rise is taking place some place other than their own neighbourhood. Thus it is not personal experience that accounts for recent perceptions of rising crime rates. Rather, such perceptions result partly from mass media "hype" and partly from the fact that robberies and assaults more frequently take place in public settings than they used to. Discrepancies between police statistics and victimization surveys are partly due to the fact that victims of some crimes, such as spousal assault and school violence, are more willing to report events to the authorities than they used to be. Increased reporting does not, however, necessarily mean increased crime.

In Chapter 23, Reginald Bibby analyzes patterns of violence, sexual behaviour, and drug use among Canadian teenagers. Bibby finds strong evidence that violence among teens is not all media hype. For example, some 40 percent of males and 25 percent of females claim they have a close friend who has been physically attacked at school. That said, teen violence has been declining in recent years, contrary to what many people believe. Moreover, it is perhaps this contrary belief itself that helps explain why punishment for violence is often harsher for young offenders than for adults.

The picture of teen sexual behaviour and attitudes that emerges from Bibby's sketch is rather more conservative than many people would predict. For example, while 75 percent of Canadian teenagers think that homosexuals are entitled to the same rights as other Canadians (higher than the corresponding figure for adults), only 55 percent think that it should be possible to obtain a legal abortion for any reason (lower than the corresponding percentage for Canadian adults). Religiosity is a major determinant of how liberal or conservative teenagers are with respect to sexual behaviour and attitudes. Finally, the data on drug use show that 28 percent of teenagers smoke cigarettes monthly or more often, 20 percent drink alcohol at least once a week, 15 percent smoke marijuana or hashish weekly or more, and 3 percent use other illegal drugs on a weekly basis.

Patricia Erickson's analysis of Canadian drug law in Chapter 24 complements Bibby's statistics on teenage drug use. Erickson goes beyond the numbers to show that the way in which drugs have been controlled in Canada has been strongly influenced by social and cultural forces. One might assume that stricter control and harsher punishment are associated with more dangerous drugs. The plain fact is, however, that alcohol, tobacco, opium, heroin, cocaine, and marijuana have been controlled more or less stringently by the state at different times. As Erickson shows, which drugs are singled out for how much control depends on the ability of particular groups of "moral crusaders" to sway public opinion and government policy in particular directions. This was evident as early as 1908, when the government first imposed harsh penalties for the use of opium. The law was directed at Chinese labourers at a time when anti-Chinese race riots first broke out in Canada (in Vancouver in 1907). This was also a time when growing unemployment led white racists inside and outside government to restrict Chinese immigration and force Chinese workers to return to China by imposing a special, exorbitant tax on them (the so-called "head tax"). Similarly, in 1986, Canada mounted a harsh campaign against cocaine when Ronald Reagan announced his "war against drugs" and the American media made much of the American drug problem. Yet in the 1980s the Canadian rate of cocaine use was only about a fifth as high as the American rate. Fewer than 1 percent of Canadian adults had used cocaine, and the rate of cocaine use among students was declining. In this context, the Canadian "drug crisis" had to be largely manufactured by the Canadian government and police officials. What links 1908 with 1986 is that on both occasions drug taking was criminalized in response to moral crusades by influential groups.

Some Canadians believe that crime is in part a racial phenomenon. Canadian Blacks in particular rank high in the public's perception of criminal villains. In October 2002, a series of articles in the *Toronto Star* demonstrating that Black people in Toronto are more likely to be charged with crime than others may have reinforced this perception. Some people—including a handful of academics, such as

University of Western Ontario psychology professor Philippe Rushton—go so far as to claim that there is a *genetic* link between race and crime. Rushton contends that "Negroids" (Blacks) are genetically predisposed to commit more criminal acts than "Caucasoids" (whites), while whites are genetically predisposed to commit more criminal acts than "Mongoloids" (Orientals). He cites crime statistics from the U.S., the U.K., and other countries showing that crime rates do indeed vary along racial lines, as he predicts.

In Chapter 25, Julian Roberts and Thomas Gabor criticize Rushton's views. They show, among other things, that crime rates vary *within* racial groups, depending on historical period and society. Homicide rates are very low among Blacks in Africa and Chinese in Hong Kong, but very high among Blacks in the Bahamas and even higher among Filipinos in the Philippines. Yet if Rushton's genetic theory were correct, Blacks would have universally higher crime rates than Orientals. Roberts and Gabor also show that race-specific crime rates vary by type of crime. For instance, in the United States, whites have much higher rates of white-collar crime (fraud, embezzlement, etc.) than do Blacks. These and other facts analyzed by Roberts and Gabor demonstrate that genetic factors peculiar to each race do not cause crime. Roberts and Gabor instead attribute high rates of "street crime" among Blacks in the U.S. and the U.K. exclusively to social factors: where they face high levels of discrimination, widespread poverty, and differential treatment by the criminal justice system, Blacks are convicted of more street crime.

Crime statistics by race are not widely available in Canada, but those that are available often contradict Rushton's argument. For example, the homicide rate among Aboriginal Canadians is more than ten times higher than among whites, but Rushton's theory predicts the opposite since Aboriginal Canadians are of Mongoloid descent. Canadian Aboriginals do, however, resemble American Blacks in terms of the social conditions in which they live, a fact consistent with Roberts's and Gabor's theory.

And the *Toronto Star* statistics? They show that while Blacks form 8.1 percent of Toronto's population, they compose 23.3 percent of all arrests in the city. However, in interpreting these figures one must remember three things. First, there is racism in the criminal justice system. For example, the *Toronto Star* statistics show that Blacks charged with simple drug possession are taken to the police station 13 percent more often than whites faced with the same charge. They are held at the station overnight for a bail hearing at twice the rate of whites. In other words, whites are more likely than Blacks to be released at the scene of the crime and less likely to be held overnight. Other research shows that Black men in Toronto are nearly four times more likely than white men to be stopped by the police while driving. These figures suggest that the criminal justice system is biased against Black people, men in particular, searching them out and treating them more harshly than whites. Second, crime is associated with age; young men commit most crimes. This is important because the Black community in Toronto is younger than the white community. On purely demographic grounds one would therefore expect to find a higher crime rate among Blacks. And finally, Black men form one of the very few ethnic or racial categories that appears to experience persistently high levels of discrimination in the paid labour force, even after the immigrant generation. Relatively low per capita income and high unemployment contribute to crime *directly* insofar as people with a low standard of living are more likely than others to explore illegal means of improving their lot in life. Poor economic conditions contribute to crime *indirectly* because they make it more difficult to keep families intact. As a result, young people growing up in poor families are more likely to be brought up by a single parent, usually their mother. Accordingly, they tend to be subject to less adult supervision and discipline in the family. They are less likely to benefit from the kind of early social control that can lead to lower crime rates.

GLOSSARY

Deviance is behaviour that departs from a norm.

CRITICAL THINKING QUESTIONS

1. Describe patterns of violence, sexual behaviour, and drug use among Canadian teenagers.
2. In what sense is illegal drug use "socially constructed" rather than determined by the "nature" of drug use itself?
3. What social factors contribute to the crime rate? Does society make criminals, or is criminality based on biology?

ANNOTATED BIBLIOGRAPHY

Goode, Erich, and Nachman Ben-Yehudah. *Moral Panics: The Social Construction of Deviance.* Cambridge, UK: Cambridge University Press, 1995. Drug panics and witch crazes illustrate the ways in which deviance and crime are not "given" but created by social reactions.

Miller, Jerome G. *Search and Destroy: African-American Males in the Criminal Justice System.* Cambridge, UK: Cambridge University Press, 1996. This infuriating book shows how the American justice system has been turned into a system of racial segregation and control. It can be read as a warning to Canadians about some of the potential effects of neoconservative, anti-welfare policies.

Silverman, Robert A., James J. Teevan, and Vincent F. Sacco, eds. *Crime in Canadian Society.* 6th ed. Toronto: Nelson, 2000. A standard, comprehensive overview of Canadian criminology.

Chapter 23

Violence, Sex, and Drugs Among Canadian Teenagers

REGINALD W. BIBBY

VIOLENCE

During the past few years, adults have been increasingly concerned about teenage violence, stimulated in large part by a series of violent acts in Canada and the United States. On April 20, 1999, 12 students and a teacher were killed at Columbine High in Littleton, Colorado, followed on April 28 by the shooting of two students, one fatally, in Taber, Alberta. Ever since, threats of violence in schools across Canada have been seen as abounding.[1] A knife attack on the one-year anniversary of Columbine in April 2000 resulted in the wounding of four students and one staff member at Cairine Wilson High School in the Ottawa suburb of Orléans. In November 2000 a Toronto teen admitted he had shown classmates a list of fourteen students he planned to kill and had attempted to buy an assault rifle over the Internet to carry out his plan.[2] The same month a student was stabbed to death at Calgary's Lester B. Pearson High School.[3]

Parents are among those feeling new pressures. *National Post* columnist Jane Christmas described the ambivalence she felt when her 14-year-old wanted to stay away from his Hamilton school on the day of the Columbine anniversary. In the end, she decided to let him. But it required the confirmation of her mother, her doctor, and word of what happened in Ottawa—what she describes as three votes of confidence. "Did I overreact?" she asks, and then answers her own question: "I don't believe anything you do in the interest of protecting your child is an over-reaction."[4] The headline of her article referred to the times as "the age of Columbine."

Violence among young people has not been limited to schools. On November 14, 1997, Victoria teenager Reena Virk was beaten by a group of girls she'd sought to befriend, then drowned by one of the girls and a teenage male companion.[5] Eight young people, seven of them girls between the ages of 14 and 16, were charged, and one of the girls was subsequently convicted of second-degree murder and sentenced to five years in prison before she can apply for parole. Virk's mother told the presiding judge, "My dream to raise and love my child is shattered like a vase."[6] In November of 1999, 15-year-old Dmitri Baranovski was punched and kicked to death in a Toronto park by eight to ten males wearing balaclavas and blue bandanas who demanded cigarettes, drugs, and money from the victim and his friends.[7] Just two days later, a 14-year-old Toronto girl was found bruised and bleeding with cigarette burns on her back; she'd been tortured for two hours by four older teenage girls.[8] In November of 2000, a 14-year-old Edmonton boy was taken off life support two weeks after being brutally beaten beyond recognition by two older teens behind a junior high school.[9] And youth violence was further highlighted when an eight-year-old boy in Lytton, Quebec, used his father's high-powered rifle to shoot and critically wound a 64-year-old man, claiming he was shooting at a tree to scare the man.[10]

In light of these and other forms of violent acts—including child abuse, sexual assault, and suicide—it's important to hear what young people have to say.

Violence in schools is seen as a "very serious" problem by significant numbers of teenagers. But the difference by gender is fairly dramatic. Some 65% of females see the issue as extremely serious, compared to just 40% of males. Nonetheless, out of 18 issues posed, violence in schools is among those most widely cited by males as being particularly serious (see Table 23.1).

One 17-year-old male from a small northern Alberta city expresses his concern this way: "We have had threats and it makes me scared to come here and learn. I mean, just the other day there was a fight in our hallways." A 15-year-old who lives in a small community in northern Ontario says she doesn't feel safe at school, adding, "I could at any time be shot." But another female, 16, from Regina warns against stereotyping teens: "In reaction to the recent school shootings, I would like to say it isn't all kids in black who listen to Marilyn Manson, have black trench coats, and get beat up at school who do these kinds of things. I would never do anything that stupid and I am a goth, black trench–owning, Marilyn Manson–loving freak who gets picked on."

In addition to violence in schools, some 50% to 65% of females and 30% to 45% of males view *child abuse, teenage suicide, violence against women,* and *crime* as "very serious" problems. In each instance, the concern levels for females are significantly higher than those of males. About 35% of females and 30% of males see youth gangs as "very serious."

Beyond perception of the seriousness of these various issues, teens were asked if they have a *close friend* who personally has encountered violence or has had depression or suicide-related experiences (see Table 23.2).

- Some five in ten, led by females, say they have had a close friend who has been *severely depressed*, while four in ten indicate that they have a close friend who has *attempted suicide*. In both cases the levels for females exceed those for males.

- Almost 40% of males and 25% of females report that they have had a close friend who has been *physically attacked at school*; conversely, around 40% of females and 25% of males say a close friend has been *physically abused at home*.

- Three in ten females and just under two in ten males confide that they have a close friend who has been *sexually abused*.

- About 30% of males and 20% of females say a close friend has been a victim of *gang violence*.

TABLE 23.1 PERCEPTIONS OF SERIOUSNESS OF VIOLENCE, CRIME, AND SUICIDE

	% Viewing as "Very Serious"		
	NATIONALLY	FEMALES	MALES
Child abuse	56%	66	44
Violence in schools	50	59	40
Teenage suicide	49	60	36
Violence against women	42	51	33
Crime	40	49	29
Youth gangs	31	34	28

TABLE 23.2 EXTENT TO WHICH PROBLEMS HAVE BEEN EXPERIENCED BY A CLOSE FRIEND

	NATIONALLY	FEMALES	MALES
Has been severely depressed	48%	57	39
Has attempted suicide	41	50	31
Physically attacked at school	32	25	39
Physically abused at home	31	37	25
Has been sexually abused	26	32	18
A victim of gang violence	24	21	28

Some caution needs to be used in interpreting such findings; one's close friend may also be the close friend of others. To find that three in ten females has a close friend who has been sexually abused, for example, does not mean that three in ten females have been sexually abused; obviously the figure, based on such an item, is somewhat lower.

Still these findings suggest that the incidence of depression and suicide attempts, physical attacks and abuse is startlingly high. What is disconcerting is that the violence is frequently found not only at school but also at home.

A final note on bullying. Alan King's 1998 national health survey found that just under 30% of males and females in grade 10 reported that they had been bullied during the school term. Such physical, verbal, or psychological intimidation has few clear-cut correlates, other than being disproportionately directed at males who feel isolated. Bullying tends to be cyclical: those who are bullied bully, and in turn receive similar treatment.[11]

DIFFERENCES ACROSS THE COUNTRY

Overall there are few distinct differences in the perception and incidence of school and home violence among regions and communities, regardless of size (see Table 23.3). Simply put, perception and behaviour are distributed fairly evenly across Canada.

Concern about violence in schools is somewhat less in Quebec than elsewhere, despite the fact that students there are marginally more likely than others to say they do not feel safe at school; presumably such concern has been normalized. Contrary to what I suspect is widely believed, teens in cities of over 400 000 are slightly *less* inclined than young people living elsewhere to view school violence as "very serious," and no more likely than others to say they do *not* feel safe at school. Teens living on farms are the least likely to report that they have close friends who either have been attacked at school or physically abused at home.

TABLE 23.3 CONCERN ABOUT VIOLENCE BY REGION, COMMUNITY SIZE, AND BIRTHPLACE

	SCHOOL VIOLENCE A VERY SERIOUS PROBLEM	CLOSE FRIEND ATTACKED AT SCHOOL	NOT SAFE AT SCHOOL	NOT SAFE AT HOME	CLOSE FRIEND PHYSICALLY ABUSED AT HOME
Nationally	50%	32	22	7	31
B.C.	51	30	19	7	30
Prairies	49	32	17	5	30
Ontario	53	32	22	7	32
Quebec	43	33	27	7	33
Atlantic	54	30	21	8	27
North	53	34	19	2	31
>400 000	44	35	21	5	32
399 999–100 000	51	32	21	7	34
99 999–30 000	56	36	28	7	31
Cities/towns <30 000	53	29	21	8	33
Rural non-farm	52	32	18	7	27
Farm	50	24	19	6	25
Born in Canada	50	31	21	7	32
Born outside Canada	47	35	26	6	28

There is little difference in concern about violence at school and at home between young people born in Canada and those born outside the country. There is, however, a slightly greater tendency for teens who have come to Canada to say both that (1) they have a close friend who has been attacked at school and (2) they themselves don't feel safe at school. As might be expected, as teens from outside Canada share in Canadian life, their inclination to engage in offences comes to resemble those of teens born here—a pattern noted, for example, by Brandon sociologist Siu Kwong Wong in a recent study of Winnipeg teens of Chinese descent.[12]

Concern about youth violence has led to proactive measures in cities such as Toronto. In June 2000, a Youth Violence Task Force comprising Toronto police, Catholic and public school boards, and the transit commission recommended that:

- police officers be assigned to schools, recreational centres, and subway stations during lunchtime and after-school hours;
- police disclose conditions of release for young offenders to schools as permissible under the *Young Offenders Act*; and
- a young offender program be implemented to target high-risk, repeat offenders.

A member of the task force, 17-year-old Krista Lopes, noted the need to work together "to combat the ever-increasing problem of youth violent crimes," while Toronto Police Chief Julian Fantino noted that "the ol' thing is no longer adequate," adding, "We need to do things that are more strategic and we need to count on parents, politicians, educators, and certainly the police community and all others, but especially the youth, to turn things around."[13]

In order to understand current youth violence in relation to the past, it is important to first ask, what constitutes violence? By way of illustration, a 1999 survey of 2 000 grade 7 to 12 students in Alberta by the Canadian Research Institute for Law and the Family found violence to be highest among grades 8 and 9 students. Some 40% of grade 9 students, for example, admitted to slapping, punching, or kicking someone in the past year, compared to 32% of grade 12 students. About 16% of students acknowledged they had brought weapons to school, with the most common being illegal knives, replica weapons—mostly plastic guns, clubs, and bats. The least common were pellet guns and handguns. In addition, more than half the students surveyed said they had been victimized at least once during the past year at school; perhaps significantly, almost the same percentage said they had been victimized while they were *not* at school. The most frequent forms of victimization—similar in all Alberta communities—included being slapped, punched, or kicked, having something stolen, being threatened with bodily harm, and having property damaged. The least frequent included being attacked by a group or gang and being threatened by a weapon. Such survey findings prompted the Calgary police chief at the time, Christine Silverberg, to call for an expansion of school resource programs in junior high schools.[14]

It is clear from such research that "violence" is being applied to an extremely wide range of activities beyond beatings, stabbings, and shootings. Such a broad application of "violence" undoubtedly is associated with a "zero tolerance" response to any physically aggressive act toward another person. *Hear me clearly*: this is in no way to minimize the gravity of such acts today. But it is to say the bar that defines violence has been raised considerably over where it has been in the past. Adults also may be placing the bar at a higher level than where many teens—especially males, but also some females—are placing it. Among them is a 16-year-old female from a small town near Calgary who comments, "School violence has been around since schools came about. Let kids be kids," she says, "Don't punish them for wrestling. Punish them for guns and severe fighting."

A REALITY CHECK

It is worthwhile to compare our survey perceptions and reports with additional information on young people. A victimization analysis released in December 1995 by Statistics Canada using data from police departments indicated that teenagers are certainly vulnerable when it comes to violent crime. In fact, they are at greater risk of violent crime than either adults or children. Young people between the ages of 12 and 19 made up 20% of the victims of violent crime in the mid-'90s, even though they represented just 11% of the population. About 80% of violent incidents against teenagers were assaults, some 15% being of a sexual nature; most of the others involved robbery. Victims of violent crime were equally likely to be males and females; however, a large majority of victimized females were victims of sexual offenses, whereas males were more likely to be victims of assault and robbery. Police statistics also revealed that about five in ten violent incidents against teenagers involved acquaintances, and three in ten strangers, while two in ten were committed by family members, with parents implicated in half of those incidents.[15] Further, Statistics Canada survey data for 1999 show that young people 15 to 24 are reporting the highest rate of personal victimization, more than twice the national average. Seniors 65 and over, by the way, are reporting the lowest rates of victimization.[16]

In July 2000, Statistics Canada released a new report, also based on police records, revealing that the national crime rate in 1999 fell to its lowest level in two decades. Young people under the age of 20 were more likely than people in other age groups to commit both violent and property crimes. Youth crime, however, was down more than 7% from 1998 and was 21% lower than in 1989. The rate of youths charged with violent crime fell 5%, the largest year-to-year drop since the *Young Offenders Act* was introduced in 1984. While the 1990s saw an increase in violent crimes among females, the female rate as of 1999 was still only one-third of the male rate. The report reminded readers that many non-violent young offenders are diverted from the formal justice system, but also said that available statistics indicate the number of youths being diverted has also been decreasing in recent years.[17] Coincidentally, the same day the report was released, Britain released crime statistics for England and Wales, which showed a large jump in violent crime in those two countries over the past year.[18]

A third Statistics Canada report, made available in August 2000, is also worth acknowledging. An analysis of sentences given to young offenders (12 to 17) who were convicted in youth court during 1998–99 reveals that one-third were put in some form of custody. Males were more likely to be sentenced to custody than females. A comparison of the sentencing of adults and youths for the most common offences for nine of the most frequent offences—such as common assault, breaking and entering, and possession of stolen property—showed that young people were less likely to be placed in custody. But when they were jailed, they were more likely to receive longer sentences than the adults. For example, in the case of common assault, the report found that 65% of young offenders were sentenced to more than one month in jail, compared to 43% of adults.[19] Commenting on the report, Robert Gordon, the director of the Department of Criminology at Simon Fraser University, suggested the sentencing differences reflect public calls for stiffer penalties for offences involving young people.[20]

Taken together, these three reports indicate that (1) a disproportionate number of teens are victims of violent crime, (2) the rate of violent crime committed by young people has been decreasing in recent years, and (3) young offenders who are placed in custody tend to be punished to a greater degree than adult offenders. These findings document that teen violence is a serious problem. But contrary to widely held perception, teen violence has actually been declining. In addition, reaction to young offenders in recent years, in some instances at least, has been harsher than that shown adults.

Even in the face of the Calgary school homicide in November 2000, Dennis Eastcott, the founder of the Alberta Association of School Resource Officers and the officer in charge of Edmonton's youth and crime prevention services, maintained that statistics do not support the notion that kids are becoming more violent or are getting "out of whack." As for school violence, Staff Sgt. Eastcott commented, "Studies based on where kids are victimized show one of the safest places for them is at school."[21] Obviously not everyone agrees.

It therefore is not surprising that it's difficult to obtain a consensus on how to respond to so-called youth crime. At a conference of victims'-rights advocates held in Hamilton in October of 1999, Justice Minister Anne McLellan said that Ottawa would do what it thinks is right to deal with young offenders, regardless of pressure from the provinces. "Quebec is telling me: 'Your legislation is too tough.' Ontario is telling me: 'It's not tough enough.' Well, you know what that tells me? Canadians are generally right in the middle and I think our legislation reflects that balanced approach."[22]

SAFETY AT SCHOOL AND AT HOME

Although teens are aware of friends who have been attacked and abused, 19 in 20 say they feel safe at home, 16 in 20 feel safe at school.

	% INDICATING FEEL SAFE	
	AT HOME	**AT SCHOOL**
Nationally	93%	78
Males	94	79
Females	94	78

A national survey of 400 American teenagers, 14 to 17, conducted in April 2000 for *Time* magazine found 86% felt either "very safe" or "somewhat safe" from violence at school.[23]

SEXUALITY

Our sexually liberated society is characterized by considerable openness about sex, led by the media. If Pierre Trudeau took the government out of the bedrooms of the nation, the media takes us into the bedrooms of the nation on a daily if not hourly basis. TV programs such as *Sex and the City*, the *Sunday Night Sex Show*, and *The Sex Files* lead the way explicitly. But sex is to be found everywhere, spanning sitcoms, movies, stand-up comedy, and, for reasons well known to all of us, even nightly newscasts in the U.S. and Canada on a regular basis during 1999.

Craig Colby, the Toronto producer of *The Sex Files* that airs on the Discovery Channel, recently commented, "There's definitely a lot more permissiveness in society." Colby says that two events have been new groundbreakers—the Monica Lewinsky affair, which made oral sex and phone-sex discussion topics, and the memorable "Master of His Domain" episode on *Seinfeld*, that "completely destigmatized" masturbation.[24] Yes, these are days of sexual freedom and openness. And with the morning-after pill becoming more accessible to women, making it possible to prevent pregnancy within three days of intercourse,[25] some would argue that the incidence and enjoyment of sexual activity, marital and otherwise, will only increase.

In the midst of all this, adults worry a great deal about teenagers and sex for any number of reasons. And they should, if the words of this 17-year-old female from Hamilton are accurate: "Sex is like an everyday thing for teens now."

The survey shows that Canada's youth are divided almost evenly when it comes to sexual attitudes and behaviour, although males typically hold more liberal attitudes than females and are more sexually active (see Table 23.4).

- Approximately six in ten teens, led by males, maintain that *consenting adults* should be able to do whatever they want sexually. Moreover, the same proportion of males and a smaller proportion of females feel that *con-*

TABLE 23.4 SEXUAL ATTITUDES

	% "Strongly Approve" or "Approve"		
	NATIONALLY	**FEMALES**	**MALES**
Sexual Tolerance Limits			
Consenting adults doing whatever they want sexually	61%	67	56
Consenting teens 15 to 17 doing whatever they want sexually	56	66	46
Sexual Behaviour and Rights			
Sex before marriage when people LOVE each other	82	85	80
Sex before marriage when people LIKE each other	58	68	48
Sexual relations between two people of the same sex	54	41	66
Homosexuals are entitled to the same rights as other Canadians	75	62	87
A married person having sex with someone other than marriage partner	9	13	4
Cohabitation			
A couple who are not married living together	86	89	83
A couple having children without being married	63	61	64
Abortion			
It being possible to obtain a legal abortion when a female has been raped	84	85	83
It being possible to obtain a legal abortion for any reason	55	58	52

senting teens between the ages of 15 and 17 also should be able to do whatever they want sexually. One 17-year-old from the B.C. Interior sums things up this way: "I believe in people's rights to do whatever they want sexually, as long as it doesn't hurt any other living thing. In the case of teenagers, however, more thought has to go into it because they are less able to deal with accidental pregnancy than adults."

• Some 80% of young people approve of sex before marriage *when people love each other*, with little disagreement between males and females. In addition, close to 60% think that sex before marriage is all right *when people like each other*. Here there is a significant difference in opinion between males (68%) and females (48%). A Burnaby, B.C., 16-year-old says, "I'm worried about diseases in Canada; more people are having unprotected sex." The issues of birth control and pregnancy are expressed starkly by a 17-year-old from

Alberta: "Teens should have more information about protection if they are going to have sex. People should be told how to take birth control properly, along with the fact methods aren't 100% effective against pregnancy." She signed her comments, "A pregnant teen who was on birth control." Few young people would disagree: 92% maintain that "birth control information should be available to teens who want it." More possibilities, incidentally, are on the way. As you might be aware, a new monthly injectable contraceptive known as Lunelle, the first new birth control method since 1992, was introduced in the U.S. in late 2000. It is an alternative to Depo-Provera, an injectable drug that is given every three months. Both are administered by a physician.[26]

• About one in two teenagers (54%) approve of *homosexual* relations, with females (66%) considerably more likely than males (41%) to express approval. But 75%, led by females, maintain that homosexuals are entitled to the same rights as other Canadians. Among males expressing consternation is this 15-year-old male from Regina who says, "Gays should not have a special week or the right to adopt children." A grade 11 male from a small Alberta town comments, "One thing I would like to stress is that homosexuality is wrong. If they really want to be gay, they should do it in secret and not adopt kids." (See Figure 23.1.)

- Merely 9% of young people condone *extra-marital* sexual relations. It seems quite obvious that such behaviour has not been adding much to lives, however heralded it might have been by some at the time of the sexual revolution.

- *Cohabitation* receives the approval of almost nine in ten teenagers, while having *children without being married* is regarded as all right by about six in ten. Stigma in the latter case seemingly is higher for teenage single parents than couples. A 16-year-old in the Atlantic region says that, despite the fact that her boyfriend has stood with her in raising her child, "I get a lot of discrimination against my parenting skills."

- The availability of *legal abortion* when a female has been *raped* is approved of by some 80%, abortion *on demand* by just over 50%. One twelfth grader from Vancouver says he "applauds the availability of birth control in British Columbia" and adds that "abortion should never be withheld under any circumstances." The introduction of the RU-486 pill as an alternative to surgical abortion may or may not alter such attitudes. The pill, which can terminate a pregnancy up to about seven weeks after conception, was approved and made available to some U.S. doctors in late 2000[27] and is being tested in Canada. It has been met with strong opposition from pro-life groups. RU-486 has been made available in France since 1989 and is also sold in Britain, Sweden, and China.[28]

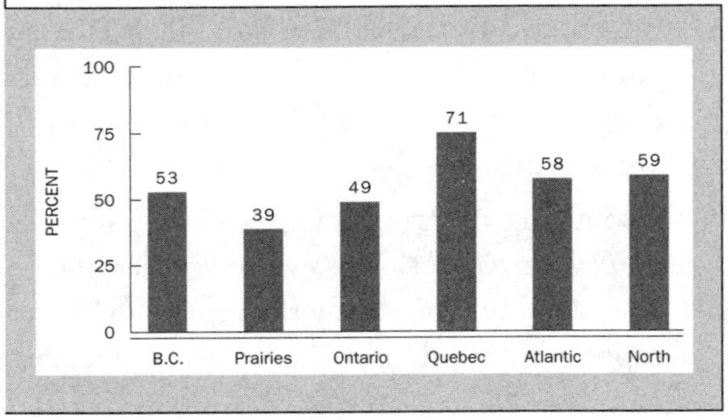

In short, while one in two Canadian teenagers indicate that, in theory, consenting individuals technically and legally have "the right" to do what they want, teens nonetheless have some strong personal feelings as to what is sexually appropriate and what is not.

We asked teens pointedly how often they engage in sex. About 25%, including 27% of males and 22% of females, claim they have sex at least once a week (see Table 23.5). Around another 10% indicate they have sex two to three times a month, a further 15% say less often. Approximately 50% of teenagers say they never engage in sex, with this category including some 45% of males and 55% of females. Among them is a 16-year-old male from southern Alberta who comments, "None of my friends or anyone I know have had sex. My friends and I feel that you should not have sex unless you are married." As for the one in two who do engage in sex, a *Globe and Mail* editorial has put it this way: "There is a principal reason why people engage in consensual sex: They enjoy it. Liking sex has little to do with age. Thinking about sex in terms of preventing unwanted consequences rather than preventing the sex act itself simply recognizes the fact that teenage sex is, well, common."[29] In responding to the question of how often she engages in sex, a 16-year-old female from suburban Montreal may speak for much of the nation in admitting, "When the chance comes up." In her case, she says, it's "hardly ever."

FIGURE 23.1 APPROVAL OF HOMOSEXUALITY BY REGION

SEXUAL ATTITUDES AND SERVICE ATTENDANCE

Differences in sexual attitudes are readily apparent between teens who attend religious services weekly versus those who attend less often.

	WEEKLY	% APPROVING LESS THAN WEEKLY
Consenting adults doing what they want sexually	38%	68
Consenting teens 15 to 17 doing what they want sexually	28	63
Sex before marriage when people LOVE each other	49	91
Sexual relations between two people of the same sex	25	62
Sex with someone other than one's marriage partner	4	10
Homosexuals entitled to same rights as other Canadians	59	79
A couple who are not married living together	57	94
A couple having children without being married	29	72
It being possible to obtain a legal abortion for any reason	24	64

A cautionary note: "engage" in sex undoubtedly means "sexual intercourse" for most teens, but not all. One 15-year-old female from Williams Lake, British Columbia, reminds us that "some people engage in sexual activity which does not include actual sex," and that "there is a lot more sexual activity between 'neck and pet' and 'sex.'"

In sum, around 50% of teens are currently sexually involved, and 50% are not. A national survey of teenagers carried out in the mid-1990s by Statistics Canada reports similar levels of activity and adds some further details. First, 44% of males and 43% of females had had at least one sex partner in the year that the survey covered. Second, 21% of teen males had sex with at least two partners, compared to 13% of females. Third, close to three in four males (71%) but only one in two females (49%) claimed that condoms were used.[30]

Yet our current survey findings on sexual activity underestimate the lifetime sexual experiences of teenagers, because the item is asking specifically about *current* sexual behaviour. Fifty percent of teens are not virgins. An additional survey item reveals that 15%–16% of males, 14% of females—are not sexually involved *currently*, but just 41% of teens (33% of males, 48%

TABLE 23.5 TEENAGE SEXUAL ACTIVITY

"About how often do you engage in sex?"			
	NATIONALLY	**FEMALES**	**MALES**
Daily	6%	9	3
Several times a week	10	10	10
About once a week	8	8	9
2 to 3 times a month	7	8	6
About once a month	5	7	3
Hardly ever	13	14	12
Never	51	44	57
Totals	100	100	100

of females) say they have *never* been sexually involved. The "currently involved" and "previously involved" total consequently appears to be closer to 60%.

As for appropriate behaviour on dates, nine in ten teens think it is all right for two people to *hold hands* on the first date if they like each other and more than seven in ten approve of kissing on the first date (see Table 23.6 on page 250). *Necking and petting*, however, is seen by six in ten

TABLE 23.6 APPROPRIATE BEHAVIOUR ON DATES

"If two people on a date like each other, do you think it is all right for them to . . ."			
	YES, ON THE FIRST DATE	YES, AFTER A FEW DATES	NO
Hold Hands	89%	10	1
Males	92	8	<1
Females	87	12	1
Kiss	73	26	1
Males	78	21	1
Females	68	30	2
Neck and Pet	32	57	11
Males	43	50	7
Females	22	63	15
Have Sex	11	40	49
Males	18	50	32
Females	4	32	64

THE LIMITED IMPACT OF AIDS

"Has the existence of AIDS influenced your own personal sexual habits?"

	YES	NO
Males	58%	44
Females	62	38

teenagers as something that should not take place until after a few dates. Here, males and females differ significantly. Young women are much more inclined to indicate a few dates should have taken place, and about 15% don't think necking and petting should occur at all. In case you are wondering, no, we weren't all that excited about using the terms "necking and petting," but we wanted to use terms consistent with our previous surveys and, frankly, "making out" is too general. A 17-year-old from Nunavut was among those who wanted to make a distinction. Drawing an arrow to "necking," she said, "Yes, we did that after two months of going out. Me and my boyfriend neck, but I don't know what you mean by pet. If you mean 'feel up,' then no, never!" That's what we meant, and I think that's what most teens thought we meant.

Males and females differ sharply in their sense of when and if *sexual relations* are appropriate. Almost seven in ten males say sex is all right within a few dates, but fewer than four in ten females share their opinion.

Two common assertions of people observing the teenage sex scene is that the threat of AIDS has been (1) contributing to a reduction in sexual activity and/or (2) resulting in more protected sex. While the first assertion is seriously in doubt, about 60% of teens who say they are sexually involved acknowledge that AIDS has influenced their sexual habits. The remaining 40% apparently have been relatively unfazed by the existence of the fatal disease. One 16-year-old, who lives in a small city in northeastern Quebec, seems to express the sentiments of many teens in this latter category when she says, "Since I have been sexually active, AIDS has existed. For me, nothing has changed."

DRUGS

Since at least the 1960s, considerable publicity has been given to the problem of drug use among young people. It remains an area of major concern for adults. For example, we saw earlier that some 25% of males and 15% of females note that they frequently have conflict with their parents over the issue of drugs. Parents' and adults' fears are not neutralized by what they sense is the ready availability of drugs. If anything, those fears may be heightened when they learn of the current survey's finding that no less than 44% of teenage males and 49% of females acknowledge they have a close friend with "a severe alcohol or drug problem."

There is little doubt that Canadian teens have ample access to illegal drugs. No less than 77% say that if they wanted to use drugs, it is "not very difficult" (26%) or "not difficult at all" (51%) to obtain them; 6% think it is "difficult" and the remaining 17% say they "don't know" (see Table 23.7). What's particularly striking is that access is not limited by whether or not

TABLE 23.7 ACCESS TO DRUGS

	% "NOT VERY DIFFICULT" OR "NOT DIFFICULT AT ALL"
Nationally	77%
Males	80
Females	74
B.C.	81
Prairies	76
Ontario	75
Quebec	78
Atlantic	80
North	81
<400 000	77
399 999–100 000	79
99 999–30 000	76
Cities/towns <30 000	80
Rural non-farm	75
Farm	76

someone is female or male, lives in one region of the country or another, or resides in a large city, small city, or a rural area. Illegal drugs appear to be just about everywhere. A 16-year-old in one Western Canadian city decries the availability of drugs where he lives:

I think the drug problem is very bad here. I mean, I try to stop doing drugs, but they are so readily available that it is very hard. There are so many drug traffickers in my school and I go to the best Catholic high school in the city. Kids need to be stopped from turning to drugs, but not by another one of the government's corny programs. Also, more stores should call for identification when people buy alcohol because I can buy it easily and I don't look a day over 16.

A grade 12 student from New Westminister says "drugs are available on today's streets" and that "it is easier to buy drugs than alcohol." A 17-year-old in Hamilton notes, "Drugs are everywhere. I can get marijuana any time I want, day or night." A 16-year-old in a small city north of Edmonton concurs: "Pot is so easy to get, and

cheap." Another Albertan, a 16-year-old male from a small town south of Calgary, takes the position that drugs are so readily available that laws should be relaxed: "I believe it shouldn't matter how old you are to buy liquor or cigarettes or pot because they are very easy to get if you are underage."

Availability, of course, doesn't equal use. A 15-year-old from Moose Jaw, Saskatchewan, observes, "There are a lot of drugs around here, but not all people use them." Yet the concern about drug abuse is shared by significant numbers of teenagers. As we saw earlier, almost one in two teens say that drug use is a "very serious" problem in Canada. One male, 16, who lives just outside Ottawa comments, "I really do feel that the use of drugs among teenagers is a big problem. I have many friends who engage in drugs weekly, daily, or monthly. I see this becoming more of a problem because I don't have a friend who hasn't at least tried drugs once or twice." A Grande Prairie, Alberta, teen expresses his alarm this way: "I strongly feel that heroin and crack cocaine are being strongly abused by teens and parents. This is breaking up families and lives. I am very worried about it and scared for the future of our society." A 16-year-old female from a small Ontario town acknowledges that the problem exists and offers an explanation as to why: "I think that in our town a lot of our drug and alcohol problems are because we have nothing to do—no movie theatre, no bowling alley, no mall, nothing."

Given the prevalent consternation and access, what actually is happening?

Some 28% of teenagers say they smoke *cigarettes* monthly or more often, 9% rarely, and 63% never. Female smoking levels are marginally above those of males (see Table 23.8 on page 252). These figures are consistent with Statistics Canada data for early 1999 that found 28% of teens, 15 to 19, to be smokers.[31]

Around 20% of teens say they drink *beer, wine, or other forms of alcohol* at least once a week, with the level for those under 18 only slightly lower than that of 15- to 19-year-olds as a whole. The

TABLE 23.8 DRUG USE AMONG TEENAGERS

	"How often do you yourself . . ."			
	WEEKLY OR MORE	ONCE OR TWICE A MONTH	LESS THAN ONCE A MONTH	NEVER
Smoke Cigarettes	23%	5	9	63
Males	22	5	9	64
Females	24	6	9	61
Drink Beer, Wine, Other Alcohol	22	30	26	22
Males	29	29	22	20
Females	16	31	28	25
Under 18 total	18	29	26	27
Males	26	31	22	21
Females	14	31	29	26
Smoke Marijuana or Hashish	14	10	13	63
Males	19	11	13	57
Females	9	8	14	69
Use Other Illegal Drugs	3	4	7	86
Males	4	4	8	84
Females	2	4	7	87

weekly level for males is almost twice that of females; yet 75% of females drink at least on occasion, compared to 80% of males. One 15-year-old female from Edmonton helps to clarify the nature of alcohol use for some young people: "My parents often let me have wine or a cooler but I feel because of this I have grown a respect for alcohol. Because it's always available at home, I don't go out and get drunk with friends."

Approximately 15% of teenagers say they *smoke marijuana or hashish* weekly or more, with male use about twice that of females. However, about four in ten males and three in ten females admit to being occasional marijuana users.

Just 3% of young people acknowledge that they are using *other illegal drugs* on a regular weekly basis, including 4% of males and 2% of females. But again, occasional use is not insignificant—another 15% for males and 11% for females.

A 17-year-old from Montreal sums up the place of drugs in her life in a fairly matter-of-fact manner: "Every weekend I consume alcohol when I go to a pub or go out to eat at a restaurant. When I go to a rave I take illegal drugs, but I only go about once a month." A grade 11 student who lives in a small community in New Brunswick explains her use of marijuana:

> When you asked the question, "Do you smoke pot," I replied yes. This doesn't make me a drug addict. I'm getting an 80% average in school and doing well at work. I enjoy having a toke but I am very responsible. I never come to school or work high. I hope this shows that every teen who smokes pot is not a delinquent.

It's important not to lose sight of the fact that sizable numbers of young people maintain that they are *not* using drugs of any kind, including—in close to one in four cases—alcohol. Among them is another Montrealer, a 16-year-old female, who says, "Drugs do not interest me at all. I find cigarettes distasteful and I don't want to know anything about illegal drugs."

TOP FIVE MOST POPULAR DRUGS

1.	Marijuana	87%
2.	Ecstasy	3
3.	Hashish	2
4.	Mushrooms	<1
5.	Cocaine	<1

TWO AREAS OF CONTROVERSY

One drug that has become increasingly controversial is marijuana. Use is extensive and the public seemingly divided as to whether or not it should continue to be treated as illegal. Interest groups have been arguing that its effects, short-term and long-term, pale compared to legal drugs such as alcohol and nicotine. Those opposed argue that its affects are highly detrimental, contributing to short-term dysfunctions and long-term disabilities.

In late July of 2000, the Ontario Court of Appeal ruled that Canada's marijuana law prohibiting the possession of marijuana is unconstitutional and gave Ottawa a year to amend it. People who require marijuana for medicinal purposes can apply for an exemption; the Ontario court asked that the exemption be written into law. At the same time, the court upheld a lower-court decision prohibiting the possession of marijuana for recreational purposes.[32] On the heels of the decision, Ontario NDP leader Howard Hampton called for the decriminalization of marijuana, saying that too many people are being turned into criminals for "smoking a little pot," and that such a move would free up police to fight real crime.[33] Indications that marijuana use may be on the increase means the debate can be expected to intensify.

Young people are not lost for views on the topic. One in two favour the legalization of the use of marijuana, with males (58%) more likely to be in favour than females (42%). A 15-year-old male from Hamilton protests, "No matter what anyone says, marijuana is addictive," while a 16-year-old Calgary-area female offers these thoughts:

> I feel that the use of marijuana should not be illegal because it helps people relax; also, everyone does it nowadays so there is no way the law can keep it under control. If marijuana is illegal, then alcohol should be illegal, because it does the same things to your body and is just as dangerous or even more dangerous.

We saw earlier that 18% of teens say they attend raves monthly or more, with the figure for males (21%) higher than that for females (15%). The media have given extensive attention to raves; *Maclean's*, for example, carried a cover story entitled "Rave Fever" in its April 24, 2000, issue. Writer Susan Oh noted that many see Toronto as the rave capital of North America, and that ravers can "dance until dawn most weekends" in other cities such as Vancouver, Calgary, Edmonton, Montreal, and Halifax, as well as some other smaller locales.[34] Critics say that these all-night parties are replete with drugs, notably ecstasy, which was given emphasis in the *Maclean's* story. In Ontario, a 13-day inquest was held in May 2000 following the death of Allan Ho, 21, who died at a Toronto rave after taking ecstasy. The inquest resulted in 27 recommendations to ensure the all-night parties are safe.[35] Concern about ecstasy was heightened in late August 2000 with news that Canada Customs officials in Montreal had seized a record-breaking shipment of ecstasy that was on its way to Toronto.[36]

Raves, according to Toronto police chief Julian Fantino, are "threatening the very fabric of Canadian life." Others, however, say they represent a new cultural party expression and are no more problematic than party gatherings in the past—and typically less turbulent than gatherings in bars. Edward Adlaf, a research scientist at Toronto's Centre for Addiction and Mental Health, has said, "In many ways, the concerns raised over the rave scene are not that much different than for rock concerts in the 1970s." He points out that, in Ontario, about 60% of students who attended raves in the past year used cannabis but no other illegal substance. Just over 4% of all students surveyed had taken ecstasy in the past year.[37] A June 2000 article in *Time* magazine argued, "First we had the Beat Generation; now we have the Beats-per-Minute Generation. And it's not just about ecstasy." Rave culture, said writer Christopher John Farley, has started to exert a potent influence on pop music, advertising, films, and even computer games. According to some observers, rave culture has become youth culture. Drugs may or may not be part of "the rave scene."[38]

One of our survey participants, a 17-year-old male from Kelowna, B.C., has the following to say:

> I know lots of kids who go to them and I went to them extensively myself. The thing is drugs! So many hard drugs are taken by kids ages 14 to 25 it's amazing. I've done ecstasy about 10 times and it was really fun, although I won't do it again, and I was able to stop unassisted. I know of kids who go to every rave that's put on (about 1 to 2 times a week) and do ecstasy, crystal, mushrooms, smoke dope, use acid, drink, huff nitric acid, snort coke. People don't really know about this underground rave culture and parents would freak if they found out their 15-year-old daughter went to raves, got f . . . d out of her mind, and hooked up with some older guy. I can see how kids get addicted to raves but the drugs are the scary thing and it makes me laugh that parents have no clue!

Despite such alarming reports, journalists such as Kevin Grace maintain that a consensus is forming in some cities, including Toronto: attempts to ban raves only drive them underground. He cites one suburban-Vancouver municipal councillor who says, "They're not something I would ever go to, but my parents' generation had the same opinion of the dances we went to when I was young."[39] *Calgary Sun* columnist Bill Kaufmann writes, "The hysteria that swept city hall in the wake of an isolated stabbing incident following a rave was amusing to behold. It's as if raves have just arrived in Calgary in the past few weeks. In fact, they've been filling halls, party rooms and underground venues for years with little fallout." Predicts Kaufmann, "This current manifestation of youth culture—like so many others before it—will play itself out."[40]

So what do the data actually say?

To begin with, 6% of teens tell us that they go to raves once a week or more, 5% say they go two to three times a month, and another 7% about once a month. A further 18% say they "hardly ever" attend raves, and 64% say they never do. Almost 50% of monthly-plus ravers come from cities of 100 000 or more, but these consist of only about 15% of the teens in those same cities. Surprisingly, 40% of those who say they attend raves at least once a month come from communities of fewer than 10 000, suggesting that the term "rave" has come to have a fairly broad interpretation. Keeping things in perspective, approximately 20% of the young people living in those smaller communities go to raves that often.

An examination of general drug use among young people who attend raves and those who don't shows that rave-attendees are more inclined than non-attendees to use marijuana and other illegal drugs (see Figure 23.2). It is not clear where exactly such use is taking place. However, what is clear is that about 40% of teens who attend raves at least once a week say that they *never* use marijuana, and almost 70% claim they *never* use any other illegal drugs, including ecstasy. In short, lots of teens who attend raves claim they are partying without drugs.

Tracy Ford, a social worker with the Ministry of the Attorney General in Toronto and described as "a former enthusiast of the rave scene," is a member of the Party People's Project (PPP), a community-based group formed to protect the rights of ravers. Writing in a publication of the Alberta Alcohol and Drug Abuse Commission in late 2000, she maintains that false stereotypes of violence and rampant drug use have been used to discredit raves. What is required, she suggests, is not the outlawing of raves, but rather a combina-

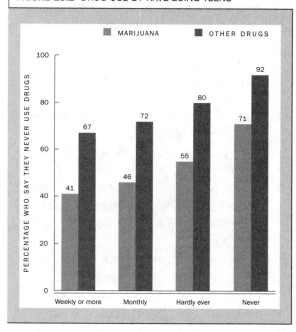

FIGURE 23.2 DRUG USE BY RAVE-GOING TEENS

tion of support, trained supervision, and education that can reduce rave-related harms. "The harm reduction model," she says, "accepts the choices of young people, and supports them, rather than criminalizing them." Ford writes:

> The rave community is a place where young people can find a creative and open network of individuals that love to dance and love music. Young people have basic civil rights to associate, express themselves and enjoy the same freedoms accorded all Canadians in their leisure time. Whatever our concerns about the safety of young people, we must find options that will foster their development, and support their ability to make informed choices.[41]

There is little reason to disagree.

NOTES

1. See, for example, the *National Post* story of April 21, 2000, "Threats of violence abound in schools since Taber, Columbine," by Ian MacLeod.

2. "Teen pleads guilty to making hit list of students," Canadian Press, Toronto, November 28, 2000.

3. Robert Remington and Chris Wattie, "$30 debt seen as motive in killing," *National Post,* November 21, 2000.

4. Jane Christmas, "A parent's dilemma in the age of Columbine," *National Post,* April 21, 2000.

5. For a summary article on the sentencing of one of Virk's assailants, see Rod Mickleburgh, "Virk's killer gets minimum sentence," *Globe and Mail,* April 21, 2000.

6. "Virk's killer off to prison," Canadian Press, Vancouver, April 20, 2000.

7. Details are provided by Jim Rankin and Michelle Shephard in their article, "Teen beaten to death didn't defend himself," in *Toronto Star,* November 17, 1999.

8. See Michelle Shephard, "Four teens charged with torturing girl, 14," *Toronto Star,* November 18, 1999.

9. Ian Williams, "Teens charged with murder after boy's death," *Edmonton Journal,* November 17, 2000.

10. "Kid says he used dad's gun to 'scare' man he shot," Canadian Press, Lytton, Quebec, November 27, 2000.

11. Alan J. C. King, William F. Boyce, and Matthew A. King, *Trends in the Health of Canadian Youth,* Ottawa: Health Canada, 1999:23.

12. Siu Kwong Wong, "Acculturation, peer relations, and delinquent behaviour of Chinese-Canadian youth," *Adolescence* 34, 1999: 107–19.

13. "Advisory group recommended to reduce youth crime," Canadian Press, Toronto, June 22, 2000.

14. "Junior high violence shocks officials," Canadian Press, Calgary, May 8, 2000. For a summary of a parallel earlier study in Calgary, see Joanne J. Paetsch and Lorne D. Bertrand, "Victimization and delinquency among Canadian youth," *Adolescence* 34, 1999:351–67.

15. *The Daily,* Statistics Canada, December 19, 1995.

16. *The Daily,* Statistics Canada, November 2, 2000.

17. "Crime rate drops to 20-year low," Canadian Press, Ottawa, July 18, 2000.

18. "British statistics show jump in violent crime," Reuters, London, July 18, 2000.

19. "Sentencing of young offenders," *The Daily,* August 1, 2000.

20. "Teens given more jail time than adults for same crime," Canadian Press, Vancouver, August 1, 2000.

21. Janine Ecklund, "Schools safe, say police," *Lethbridge Herald,* December 1, 2000.

22. "Ottawa, provinces disagree on youth crime," Canadian Press, Hamilton, ON, October 4, 1999.

23. "The Perception Gap," *Time,* April 24, 2000: 40–41.

24. "The Sex Files on Discovery pushing the envelope," Canadian Press, Toronto, October 4, 2000.

25. See, for example, Vanessa Lu and Richard Brennan, "No-prescription test for morning-after pill," *Toronto Star,* September 8, 2000.

26. "Injectable birth control approved in U.S.," Associated Press, New York, October 6, 2000.

27. Tanya Talaga, "American women get approval to use abortion pill RU-486," *Toronto Star,* September 29, 2000.

28. Graeme Smith, "Doctors to test French abortion pill here," *Toronto Star,* July 7, 2000.

29. Editorial, "The consequences of sex," *Globe and Mail,* December 1, 1999.

30. "Multiple-risk behaviour in teenagers and young adults," *The Daily,* Statistics Canada, October 29, 1998.

31. "Tobacco use," *The Daily,* Statistics Canada, January 20, 2000.

32. "Pot possession law ruled unconstitutional," Canadian Press, Toronto, July 31, 2000.

33. "Ontario NDP wants marijuana decriminalized," Canadian Press, Toronto, August 2, 2000.

34. Susan Oh, "Rave fever," *Maclean's,* April 24, 2000:39–43.

35. "Inquest urges steps for safer raves," Canadian Press, Toronto, June 1, 2000.

36. "Ecstasy seized in major drug bust," *Globe and Mail,* August 22, 2000.

37. Cited in Susan Oh, "Rave fever," *Maclean's,* April 24, 2000:41.

38. Christopher John Farley, "Rave new world," *Time,* June 5, 2000:42–44.

39. Kevin Michael Grace, "Spontaneous congestion," *The Report,* July 24, 2000:47.

40. Bill Kaufmann, "Rave hysteria amusing," *Calgary Sun,* Jun 5, 2000.

41. Tracy Ford, "Regulating the rave: Keeping ravers safe in Toronto," *Developments,* AADAC, Oct/Nov 2000.

Chapter 24

The Selective Control of Drugs

PATRICIA ERICKSON

INTRODUCTION

As the twentieth century commenced, the public could choose from a broad array of legally available psychoactive substances. The growing temperance movement focused on alcohol as the root cause of most of society's problems. Opium, heroin, and cocaine were readily obtainable from the local pharmacy, and were, along with alcohol, major components of many popular and widely used patent medicines (Murray, 1988). The modern tobacco cigarette, competing with pipes, cigars, and snuff, was just beginning to be marketed in quantity. Marijuana was grown primarily for the production of hemp cloth and birdseed. None of the users of the substances was regarded as sick, criminal, or seriously deviant, and extreme cases of addiction were viewed as a matter of individual misfortune or personal vice.

Soon all this changed. Forces routed drugs down various paths of social control, with varying degrees of severity of societal response. Today, the crack users are as feared and despised as the heroin "junkie" of an earlier era. The seller of illegal "narcotics"—that is, cannabis, opium, cocaine, or PCP (or phencyclidine)—faces a maximum sentence of life imprisonment under current Canadian law. Alcohol, which was banned briefly during the First World War, was soon re-established as society's drug of choice; now messages promoting its use compete with those for moderation. The cigarette smoker

pursued his (and increasingly her) glamorous, Hollywood-endorsed habit for several decades, unimpeded except by pocketbook and hours in the day. However, current smokers confront higher prices and a barrage of no-smoking signs. Mood-modifying prescription drugs like Valium are dispensed by medical professionals as a legitimate source of relief for modern-day stresses and anxiety. For those whose tension-relieving or recreational drugs of choice are prohibited, heavy fines or jail sentences are a possible side effect of indulgence.

This chapter will address four major topics in the social construction of deviance in Canada as reflected in the varying social response to psychoactive substances: (1) the historical development of social meanings attached to different drugs, (2) the perceived harm of drugs and the actual extent of their use and related problems, (3) the institutional response to drug users, and (4) the various ways the drug users themselves concede or resist the imputation of the deviant identity.

HISTORY: A DIVERGENCE OF SOCIAL MEANINGS

The first major fork in the path of social control occurred in 1908 with the creation of the Opium Act, which was directed at Chinese labourers. Subsequent debates, concerned also with morphine and cocaine, led to the Opium and Drug

---

Act of 1911 and the Opium and Narcotic Drug Act of 1920. Each modification of a previous statute provided harsher penalties and fewer legal protections for illicit drug users and sellers. Possession, importation, manufacture, and trafficking were not differentiated in terms of sentences available. A series of amendments in the 1920s stipulated progressively more severe penalties for all these offences and greatly extended the police's powers of search and seizure.

By 1929, mandatory minimum penalties and a maximum of seven years' imprisonment, plus whipping and hard labour, were in effect. In 1922, police officers received the right to search, without a warrant, any place except a dwelling in which they suspected illicit drugs were concealed. Police powers to search dwellings were expanded further in 1929 through a measure called the writ of assistance. The writ was issued to a particular officer, rather than in relation to a specific search in limited circumstances, as would be the case in the normal, judicially approved, search warrant procedure. Until 1985, the designated officer could:

> aided and assisted by such person or persons as he may require, at any time enter and search any dwelling house within Canada in which he reasonably believes there is a narcotic and search any person found in such a place and as he deems necessary, break open any door, window lock, fastener, floor, wall, ceiling, compartment, plumbing fixture, box container or anything (Narcotic Control Act, RSC 1970, s. 10[4]).

These penalties and unusually broad police powers set the stage for defining as criminals all those involved with illegal narcotics, including the physicians who supplied them.

This pattern, with some modification, has persisted up to the present. The dominance of the criminalization approach to "narcotics" (including cannabis, so defined without debate in 1923) is attributable to two principal factors (Giffen, Endicott, and Lambert, 1991). The first is that opium use was associated with Asians, a negatively stereotyped racial group, as well as unconventional, low-status whites. The creation of the "dope fiend" mythology encouraged a moral crusade against narcotic addiction, one that demanded harshly punitive measures. Any pharmacological distinction between different drugs, as long as they originated from exotic, faraway places, was irrelevant to the mythology. Soon-to-be Prime Minister MacKenzie King was skillful in mobilizing this cultural antagonism on behalf of political interest groups who wanted to prevent further Asian immigration. During this early period, Canadian representatives played a prominent role in the international movement among Western nations to criminalize the use and distribution of narcotics through various conferences and treaties.

The second factor in the persistence and expansion of criminalization is the power base established by the centralized drug bureaucracy during the formative period of Canadian narcotic law. The Division of Narcotic Control in the national Department of Health, in conjunction with the federal enforcers and the federal prosecutors, gained a virtual monopoly over drug policies during the crucial early years. The Canadian medical profession, only weakly organized at the time, was easily intimidated and provided little advocacy for a medical approach to addiction; indeed ninety-one physicians were prosecuted in the 1920s for prescribing opiates (Giffen, Endicott, and Lambert, 1991:324). The formidable early chiefs of the Division of Narcotic Control, Cowan and Sharman, coordinated reports from police and prosecutors concerning their expressed need for greater powers, met regularly with politicians and top civil servants, and saw to it that legislative support was forthcoming (Giffen, Endicott, and Lambert, 1991). The bureaucratic partnership of social control agents remained virtually unchallenged until the 1950s when the treatment issued gained prominence and was further assailed by the marijuana controversy that erupted in the late 1960s.

For alcohol consumers, the first serious control efforts took a different path. Early temperance efforts focused on local jurisdictions, with some success in rural areas in Ontario and the Maritimes (Smart and Ogborne, 1986). A national referendum on prohibition in 1898, held under the authority of the Canada Temperance Act of 1879, received approval in all provinces except Quebec, but with only 44 percent turnout of voters. With an eye for trouble, Prime Minister Wilfrid Laurier refused to implement the ban, and temperance organizations had to wait until the First World War. Then national prohibition was imposed in all provinces, only to be defeated by 1929 in postwar votes everywhere except Prince Edward Island, which held out until 1948.

Alcohol prohibition in Canada never amounted to a total ban on buying and drinking alcohol. Rather, alcoholic beverages containing no more than 2.5 percent of ethanol were allowed, alcohol was available by prescription, and production for export was permitted (Smart and Ogborne, 1986). Canadians made fortunes supplying the "dryer" American market. Manufacturers and distributors, not consumers, were the targets of enforcement within Canada. Thus users of alcohol never had a criminal identification like that already associated with illicit drug users in this era. At the same time, the medical or "disease" model of alcoholism was beginning to gain some currency (Blackwell, 1988). This set the stage for the expansion of the treatment approach in the 1950s and 1960s, and the definition of the alcoholic as "sick" rather than bad, contagious, and morally suspect.

Cigarettes became the object of a short-lived prohibitionist campaign in 1908. Despite debates in the House of Commons describing nicotine as the "narcotic poison of tobacco" with the capability of "impairing health, arresting development [and] weakening intellectual power," members of Parliament nevertheless failed to pass any legislation other than that forbidding sale to those under sixteen years of age, but also approved a bill protecting domestic tobacco producers and manufacturers from foreign competition (Giffen, Endicott, and Lambert, 1991:50). For the ensuing decades, the tobacco industry freely marketed and promoted its product, offi-

cially *not* a drug, and by 1960 Canada had one of the highest levels of per capita consumption of cigarettes in the world.

Also in contrast to the Chinese opium situation in these early years was the growing influence of vested interests in the fledgling pharmaceutical industry (Murray, 1988). The Proprietary and Patent Medicine Act of 1908, intended explicitly "to safeguard the public interest without committing injustice to the business interests" contained weak restrictions and penalties. The act required only that the ingredients of any medicine had to be listed on the bottle. Cocaine and "excessive" amounts of alcohol were forbidden, but opium and morphine were not, and even heroin could be included in the miracle cures in "safe" amounts. The maximum penalty for infractions was $100, compared to $1 000 and/or three years' imprisonment under the Opium Act of the same year (Giffen, Endicott, and Lambert, 1991:50). Although stricter requirements were later imposed, the principle that the production of "medicine" was in the control of legitimate manufacturers was established.

It is evident that the first decades of the 20th century were extremely important in establishing historical dividing lines between licit and illicit drugs. This led to very different social definitions of their acceptability and appropriate controls. The system of complete prohibition that was established for "narcotics" suppressed all legitimate availability and provided severe criminal penalties for a variety of offences involving importation, cultivation, trafficking, and possession. In contrast, regulatory schemes permitted controlled access to many other substances. Licit drugs were subject to varying limits on conditions of sale, to certain standards for the quality of the product, and to professional guidelines for medical prescription. Violations of regulatory statutes were subject to milder penalties such as fines or loss of licences.

Alcohol, after Canada's brief fling with partial "prohibition," was clearly differentiated from medicines and re-established as a socially approved, recreational beverage. Physicians eventually gained more control of prescribing an ever-increasing array of pharmaceuticals produced by a global industry. Almost no controls over tobacco products existed. The label "drug user" was a highly negative one, synonymous with *illicit* use of "narcotics," when the 1960s ushered in a new era of psychoactive drug use.

DANGERS REAL AND IMAGINARY: USE AND ABUSE IN CULTURAL CONTEXT

Nearly all human societies (the traditional Inuit were an exception) have indulged in some form of mind-altering substance use with indigenous plants (McKenna, 1992). It is also accurate to state that in no society where drug use was subject to cultural rituals and restrictions has destructive use been the norm (Heath, 1992). Individuals and societies find ways of avoiding serious harm by using informal social controls (Maloff et al., 1979). These include rules for appropriate use generated in social interaction between friends, family, and peers. The modern, rapid diffusion of new, more potent drugs into societies lacking a traditional cultural context for their appropriate use has led to some harmful patterns of use. When identified as a threat, these help to spawn an overreliance on more repressive, external, formal controls (Peyrot, 1984).

Official and popular assessments of the harm caused by alcohol and other drugs differ from culture to culture and also shift within a particular culture over even relatively short time periods. This establishes an important principle about understanding drug problems: they are not simply inherent in the pharmacology of the substance but rather emerge in the interaction between the drug, the user, and the social and physical environment (Heath, 1992). In other words, there are no "bad" (or "good") drugs, but rather more or less harmful consequences, depending on how the drug is used and who is using it. The designation of a pejorative label is

largely arbitrary. Drug "abuse" is in the eye of the beholder, reflecting a socially constructed reality. A new prohibition or "war on drugs" is imposed on those who conform to the stereotype of the evil, dangerous, often foreign, users and pushers (Duster, 1970; Musto, 1973). Such approaches may have little to do with an objective reality that recognizes a continuum of drug use/misuse, regardless of the drug's legal status (Goode, 1990; Jensen and Gerber, 1993).

Reviews of the pharmacological properties of drugs, including their short- and long-term effects and addictive capacity, are available in a number of sources (Alexander, 1990; Jacobs and Fehr, 1987). For sociological analysis, the concern is the perception of drug effects—their imputed properties—as a basis for social stigma and punitive social control. These perceptions are important because many of the intensely moralistic judgements about narcotics are based on conceptions of the physiological consequences of the drugs (Duster, 1970:29).

Cannabis was portrayed in the 1930s as leading to "reefer madness" then, in an about-face in the 1970s, to the "amotivational syndrome." Beginning to be valued as a relaxant and euphoriant by some in the "counterculture," its scientific reputation was also briefly rehabilitated by various national commissions that concluded that the adverse consequences of cannabis had been exaggerated. Then a counter-reaction in the 1980s attributed anew both physical and mental damage to marijuana (Erickson, 1985). Such a reaction was hardly surprising, given the enormous resources that were invested in animal studies to establish any possible harms of cannabis, rather than any assessment of benefits of safer dosages for human users (Fehr and Kalant, 1983). The research effort petered out quickly once the wave of decriminalization ended (Negrete, 1988). This has meant that we have very little knowledge about the long-term effects of cannabis use in relation to varying amounts and frequency of intake. The image of cannabis as a dangerous narcotic has persisted despite scientific opinion that like alcohol, tobacco, or any other psycho-pharmacologically active agent, cannabis can produce detrimental effects if enough is taken, and can be used in sufficiently low amounts so that no detriment results (Kalant, 1982).

The drugs subject to the most persistent demonizing mythology have been the opiates, particularly heroin. An unrivalled analgesic (pain-killer), the most deleterious effects of chronic opiate use are severe constipation and reduced libido (Jacobs and Fehr, 1987). Throughout most of the 20th century, medical and scientific commentators have agreed that opiates are not otherwise significantly damaging to the minds and bodies of regular users (Brecher et al., 1972:21–7). A quote from Nobel prizewinner, Solomon Snyder, expresses this perspective: "opiate addiction in and of itself is not physically dangerous. Ingesting opiate extracts by mouth is safer than injecting morphine, but if dosage is reasonably well controlled, even opiates by injection are not inherently dangerous" (Snyder, 1989:38).

The undeniable poor health and degraded lives of "street" opiate addicts are rather attributable to the damaging, deprived, and marginal lifestyle generated by the prohibition itself (Alexander, 1990; Lindesmith, 1965). The major risks of opiate injection are related to the unknown potency and impurity of the drug, the possible contamination of needles with hepatitis and HIV, and unsafe injecting practices. In addition, involvement in the criminal black market with its inherent violence in order to obtain opiates at inflated prices generates further individual and social costs (Faupel, 1991). The image of the opiate user as a hopelessly passive misfit has nevertheless been challenged by evidence that many lead very demanding lives in their job of "hustling," many fluctuate in their usage patterns according to availability, and many stabilize in relatively productive lives (Blackwell, 1983; Preble and Casey, 1969).

Cocaine and, more recently, crack have been the latest "headliners" in the drug crisis industry (Reinarman and Levine, 1989). Cocaine, like amphetamine, is a powerful stimulant that acts on the central nervous system to create short-term feelings of euphoria, energy, and well-being. Since the lethal dose is unknown, its potentially deadly effects are unpredictable (Smart and Anglin, 1987). Repeated heavy use can lead to a well-documented phenomenon known as cocaine psychosis, marked by paranoia and "formication" (i.e., the sensation of insects crawling under the skin) (Jacobs and Fehr, 1987). Clearly, cocaine use is not without risks.

Cocaine has gone through extreme cycles of popularity in which it has been portrayed as a benign, non-addictive tonic and as the most powerfully addictive drug on earth (Erickson et al., 1987; Murray, 1987). The confusion about cocaine's addictive potential is attributable in part to the absence of a clear-cut physical withdrawal syndrome after the cessation of regular use. This confusion is also attributable to a behavioural pattern of compulsive, socially destructive use by a small proportion of those who try cocaine. The contrast between cocaine and heroin, which can produce an extremely unpleasant though not life-threatening withdrawal syndrome, is captured by William S. Burroughs in *Naked Lunch*:

> You can smell it going in, clean and cold in your nose and throat then a rush of pure pleasure right through the brain lighting up those C[ocaine] connections. Ten minutes later you want another shot, you will walk across town for another shot. But if you can't score for C, you eat, sleep and forget about it (Burroughs, 1959:19).

The currently dominant notion of cocaine's powerful addictive quality is a considerable overstatement: between 5 percent and 10 percent of those who ever try cocaine will use it weekly or more often; most users will not continue, and the majority of those who do will use it infrequently. Of the more frequent users (weekly or more often), about one-tenth to one-quarter will develop uncontrolled use patterns at some time (Erickson et al., 1987). Even crack use, when studied outside of treatment settings, is not necessarily compulsive (Cheung, Erickson, and Landau, 1991). The natural history of the recent crack epidemic in the United States has been described as differing little from that of previous (drug) epidemics (Fagin and Chin, 1989: 606). Cocaine use patterns, then, span a continuum. Although persistent uncontrolled use is the outcome for a small minority, many more users stop for periods of time, maintain moderate use, stop completely, or regain control over their cocaine use (Erickson, 1993).

Since all psychoactive drugs have the potential for harm, the selection of particular drugs for harsh repression is a social process that has little relationship to objective evidence. During the alternating waves of panic and indifference (Giffen, Endicott, and Lambert, 1991) that have marked the 20th century's response to illicit drugs, Canada's most deadly drugs were quietly gaining ground. Tobacco and alcohol are used, respectively, by about 32 percent and 78 percent of the population aged fifteen years and older, according to a national survey conducted in 1989 (Health and Welfare Canada, 1992). For tobacco, this represents a decline from peak levels of consumption in 1966 when 82 percent of Canadians smoked. While the proportion of alcohol drinkers has remained quite stable, per capita consumption of alcohol has declined slightly in the 1980s to about 11 L of absolute alcohol by 1989. Of course, these more widely used legal drugs generate substantial government revenue. Nevertheless, an estimated 15 000 people now die annually in Canada from alcohol-related causes and 35 000 from tobacco-related causes. Nor are medically prescribed drugs immune from excessive or inappropriate use. In contrast, the deaths attributable each year to all the illicit drugs combined number in the hundreds; these occur among the approximately 7 percent to 10 percent of Canadians who are cannabis users, 1.4 percent who are cocaine users, and the much less than 1 percent who regularly inject opiates (Health and Welfare Canada, 1992). Such figures are the basis for the conclusion that the drugs carrying the greatest health and safety risks are not, in fact, illegal (Addiction Research Foundation, 1987–8: 10).

INSTITUTIONAL RESPONSE: THE PERSISTENCE OF CRIMINALIZATION

A reliance on strict enforcement and punishment has traditionally been Canada's primary strategy for the control of illicit drugs. The upsurge in drug use, especially marijuana and hashish, by otherwise normal, middle-class youth in the 1960s precipitated the questioning and some selective penalty modification of the dominant policy (Erickson, 1980). Before 1969, limited sentencing options in the Narcotic Control Act meant that half of all cannabis possession offenders were imprisoned. The courts were overloaded with several thousand of this new breed of "cannabis criminals." The federal government's initial response to the public controversy was to provide a "fine only" sentencing option in the Narcotic Control Act in 1969, and to appoint the Royal Commission of Inquiry into the Non-medical Use of Drugs, the Le Dain Commission (Erickson and Smart, 1988).

During the 1970s, cannabis was at centre-stage in an unprecedented public debate over illicit drug policy. Although the government did not act on the findings of the Le Dain majority report recommending the decriminalization of cannabis possession, it did provide the new sentencing alternative of a discharge (which still imposes a criminal record) in a Criminal Code amendment in 1972. Judges were quick to utilize the fine and discharge options; a lower proportion of possession offenders were imprisoned. The rapid increase in the number of convictions, however, resulted in greater *numbers* of these cannabis offenders actually being incarcerated than in the 1960s (Erickson, 1980:22). During this decade, annual arrests and convictions for cannabis climbed dramatically, numbering about

41 000 convictions in 1980, over 90 percent of them for possession. In contrast, convictions for each of heroin, cocaine, LSD, and other drugs did not exceed 1 000 in any given year (Erickson and Cheung, 1992).

Despite ongoing controversy over the appropriate social response to cannabis and Prime Minister Trudeau's remark to students in 1977 that "if you have a joint and you're smoking it for your private pleasure, you shouldn't be hassled," no other significant legal changes occurred. A proposal to move cannabis into the less restrictive but still criminal statute, the Food and Drugs Act, surfaced several times, but never progressed through Parliament. Despite increasing numbers of young people subjected to criminalization, a combination of the decline in sentence severity for cannabis possession, the low-visibility of police enforcement activity, and the greater efficiency of the courts in processing these offenders helped to defuse the earlier pressure for meaningful law reform (Erickson, 1982; Erickson and Murray, 1986). By the beginning of the 1980s, cannabis users and society had, it appeared, learned to live with prohibition (Erickson, 1989).

As the 1980s advanced, most forms of illicit drug use declined, arrests for cannabis decreased while those for cocaine gradually increased, and heroin convictions remained low. Cannabis use had become normalized to some extent. It is difficult to continue regarding as seriously deviant a behaviour that has been engaged in by over 4.5 million Canadians, or about one-quarter of the adult population (Health and Welfare Canada, 1991). The passage of the Charter of Rights and Freedoms in 1982 resulted in the removal of some of the procedural disadvantages accruing to suspected drug users and sellers. It seemed possible that illicit drug use would gradually wane in importance and like other previously criminalized acts (e.g., abortion and homosexuality) would follow the cycle of diminished social concern, less enforcement, minimal intervention, and greater tolerance (Glaser, 1985).

This trend was reversed, like those before it, with the emergence of a new drug of concern, cocaine. Panic again dominated the cycle of response. Despite evidence that use levels in Canada were one-fifth or one-quarter of those in the United States, Canadian perceptions of their cocaine "problem" tended to be shaped by the extreme views presented in the American media (Erickson et al., 1994). Within two days of President Reagan's declaration in 1986 that "Drugs are menacing our society, there is no moral middle ground," Prime Minister Mulroney departed from a prepared speech to warn that "Drug abuse has become an epidemic that undermines our economic as well as our social fabric" (Erickson, 1992:248). Levels of cocaine use in the 1985 national survey indicated that less than 1 percent of adults had used cocaine in the previous year (Erickson et al., 1987). The only trend data available in the 1980s from the Ontario surveys showed that cocaine use was declining among students and was stable among adults (Adlaf and Smart, 1991; Adlaf, Smart, and Canale, 1991). As a senior health official commented about this rediscovery of Canada's drug crisis, "When [the Prime Minister] made that statement, then we had to make it a problem" (Erickson, 1992:248).

The result was the resurgence of criminalization, fuelled both by the concerns about cocaine and crack emanating from the United States, and by the direction of additional resources into enforcement as part of Canada's new "drug strategy" launched in 1987 (Erickson, 1992). Cocaine charges went up by a factor of ten in the 1980s, seizures of cocaine increased markedly, and cocaine products became the avowed target of antidrug activity (Erickson and Cheung, 1992). The proportion of cocaine possession offenders who were jailed rose from 19 percent in 1980 to 29 percent in 1989. The proportion of inmates incarcerated federally from all narcotic offences went up from 9 percent to 14 percent between 1986 and 1989.

During this same period, the Royal Canadian Mounted Police's investigation of suspected traffickers in cocaine or cannabis increasingly focused on small-scale dealers (Royal Canadian Mounted Police, 1990). For example, the proportion of traffickers investigated for the smallest amount of drug tripled for both cocaine and cannabis, while those pursued for the largest amounts actually declined (Erickson, 1992). Cannabis possession offenders were also caught up in this slipstream of antidrug activity, and the decline in charges halted in 1986 and stabilized at about 28 000 yearly for the rest of the decade. Thus during a period of declining illicit drug use, the overall drug crime rate (i.e., recorded drug law offences per 100 000 population) actually climbed from 221.9 in 1986 to 258.9 in 1989 (Erickson, 1992). The United States might have been waging a drug war, but Canada, it appeared, was waging a drug strategy.

How has the perception of an emerging crack problem in Canada been portrayed as a basis for an intensification of criminalization? There were no seizures of crack before 1986, but once it began to appear, the Canadian media and police reports alerted the public to the arrival of a "crack epidemic." The *Toronto Star* informed its readers that this drug was a "one-way ticket to hell for the user" (1989a) and that crack posed "the greatest threat to society over the past fifteen years" (1989b). Crack use quickly reached "crisis proportions," according to the *Globe and Mail*, and was being used by a "very, very paranoid, psychotic group" (1989). A deadly plague of drugs was described by *Maclean's* to be infesting Toronto and other Canadian cities. In 1987, the Royal Canadian Mounted Police reported that crack comprised a very modest proportion of all cocaine seizures in Canada, and in 1989 it reported that the "use of crack is not widespread in Canada at the point" (Royal Canadian Mounted Police, 1989:42). The same report, however, also referred to the greatly increased number of seizures, especially in Toronto, and referred to crack as "almost instantly addictive." In combination with local news stories and police reports of a growing crime problem linked to crack, it is not surprising that the public perceived a growing "crack menace" (Cheung and Erickson, 1997).

While there was considerable evidence that cocaine and crack misuse were responsible for a substantial increase in drug-related problems in the United States in the middle to late 1980s (Goode, 1990), this situation was not reflected to nearly the same extent in Canada (Erickson et al., 1994). As noted earlier, Canadian surveys showed stable or declining use at fairly low levels in adult and student populations during this period. It was therefore possible to answer no to the question of a major crack epidemic (Smart, 1988). A study of crack users in Toronto dispelled some of the myths about crack's "instantly addictive" property and the lack of control purportedly displayed by all those exposed to this form of cocaine (Cheung, Erickson, and Landau, 1991). Some indicators of cocaine problems, such as treatment admissions and drug-related deaths, did show some increase during the latter part of the 1980s, but levelled off by the end of the decade (Single et al., 1992). Such trends in problem indicators also likely reflect the greater purity and lower price of cocaine that was available on the street, where the price had dropped from $100 000 in 1981 to $34 000 per kilogram in 1989 (Erickson and Cheung, 1992). Despite the relatively minor nature of the problem in Canada, sufficient public concern was generated to revive a call for tougher action against drug users and sellers.

The intensified criminal justice response to illicit drugs in the 1980s continued a well-established tradition, aided and abetted by the influx of additional resources to enforcement in Canada's Drug Strategy. Since recorded offences for activities like drug use and sale depend on proactive police discovery, a growing drug crime rate in part reflects this deployment rather than any real increase in actual deviant behaviour (Hagan, 1991). Thus the police have been able to demonstrate and maintain a high level of productivity in overall investigations, seizures, arrests, and charges during a period of decreased illicit drug use. This occurred despite the avowed purpose of the new strategy, which was to balance enforcement with prevention and treatment and take Canada's drug policy in a new, less punitive direction (Erickson, 1992).

In sum, after a wave of repression that accompanied the upsurge in illicit drug use in the 1960s, Canada appeared to be less wedded to its traditional responses for a brief period in the early 1980s. This shift of emphasis was marked by decreases in drug use, reductions in cannabis arrests and convictions, less severe sentences, various proposals for law reform, increased protection of the rights of drug offenders, and greater social tolerance of drug use. Then, fuelled by the latest American antidrug crusade and Canada's local version of the cocaine scare, the pendulum swung back from about 1987 onwards. The resurgence of criminalization was characterized by an increase in drug charges, especially for cocaine, more investigations of small-scale traffickers, severe sentences, and several other measures that have not been presented due to space limitations. These include new state powers of seizure and forfeiture of assets of those arrested on drug charges, the military's involvement in interdiction efforts, banning of drug paraphernalia, expansion of workplace drug testing, and proposals to limit the parole eligibility of convicted drug traffickers (Erickson, 1992). Canada's institutions of social control of illicit drugs, i.e., repressive laws, broad police powers, highly discretionary criminal justice procedures, and substantial community support for punitive measures, have remained ascendant and impeded fundamental change in drug policy.

In 2006, despite a new drug law passed in 1997, the Controlled Drugs and Substances Act, and further proposals to remove criminal records for cannabis possession, the penalties on the books for cannabis remain fundamentally the same as a decade earlier (Erickson, 2005). Over 50 000 cannabis possession charges were laid in 2002—more than double the figures for 1992 (Erickson, Hathaway, and Urquhart, 2004). The most recent national survey data from 2004 showed that 45 percent of Canadians have used cannabis at least once (Adlaf, Begin, and Sawka, 2005).

RESISTANCE OR CAPITULATION: THE DEVIANT STRIKES BACK?

Norwegian criminologist Nils Christie has called illicit drug users the "easy enemy": poor, often sick, and powerless. Some Canadian research is relevant to this question: to what extent have drug users been the helpless targets of narcotic laws, and to what extent have they resisted and reshaped the current policies? The evidence suggests that drug users have not been a viable political force in Canada, but have often personally resisted the stigmatization of a deviant identity and supported others in doing so. In the wake of the AIDS epidemic, injection drug users have become better organized around public health issues in Europe and Australia, and this may influence future directions in Canada.

Historically, it is clear that Chinese opium smokers had little power to resist increasingly harsh penalties, including deportation, once prohibition was in place (Giffen, Endicott, and Lambert, 1991). Before that, Chinese merchants had sought recompense from Mackenzie King for the destruction of their opium stocks in the anti-Asiatic riot of 1907 in Vancouver. This marked the last legitimacy of the narcotic drug dealer in this century. Canadian heroin addicts, few in number and marginalized, have expressed an almost fatalistic view of the hardships of their lives on the street (Stoddart, 1988, 1991). The revolving cycle of arrest and imprisonment, the search for a "fix," has changed little since Stephenson and colleagues first reported in 1956. Recently, however, a small group of opiate users called a press conference in Toronto to protest the shortage of methadone maintenance places in the province. Users were also represented at an international harm reduction conference in Toronto in 1994 (and will be again in Vancouver in 2006).

The cannabis controversy of the early 1970s led to a far more open political debate than had occurred previously (e.g., in the punishment versus treatment controversy of the 1950s). Drug users themselves testified before the Le Dain Commission (Erickson and Smart, 1988). Many different interest groups were involved—the medical and legal professions, social service workers, and treatment representatives—to challenge the bureaucratic hegemony of the social control agents. At several points, change in the drug laws seemed imminent. In the end, however, no significant alteration to the dominant social policy occurred.

A Toronto sample of ninety-five first-time offenders for cannabis possession were interviewed in depth at the time of their sentencing and again one year later (Erickson, 1980). Their responses indicated a wide variety of reactions to the experience of being caught and officially labelled a "cannabis criminal." Some reported humiliating or frightening experiences at the hands of the police; for others, the processing was routine, even good-natured. For many, the arrest and the waiting period before going to court provoked anxiety that their employer, family, or others might learn about the charge. Others arrived at court with several friends or parents in attendance to show support. Nearly all (about 95 percent) did not consider themselves as criminals after their court appearance, and thought that peers shared that perception. Most were fairly long-term, regular cannabis users who had no intention of changing their behaviour, and indeed had not one year later. A replication study several years later found little change in offenders' attitudes and experiences of criminalization, but these criminalized users were more confident that employers would be unlikely to learn of their record (Erickson and Murray, 1986). The stigma attached to becoming a criminal for cannabis use seemed to decrease progressively for these deviants, resembling a state of *de facto* decriminalization despite the lack of legal change.

Interviews with experienced drug users who are in the community rather than in prison or treatment institutions consistently reveal the "normalcy" of their behaviour to themselves and their friends (Erickson, 1980; Erickson et al., 1994). Drug use is rarely the focal point of their lives, but is an important part of their recreational activities. Considerable effort and planning are devoted to acquiring drugs for special occasions such as birthdays or parties. Concern about health risks, rather than fear of apprehension, is more likely to influence users to cut down their intake or cease use (Cheung, Erickson, and Landau, 1991; Erickson, 1989; Erickson and Murray, 1989).

A sample of long-term cannabis users (average duration was thirteen years) had no trouble maintaining a regular source of supply and were far from unanimous in their support for more liberal legal availability (Erickson, 1989). The support by a minority for continued penalties for trafficking to those who would sell cannabis to a new generation of youthful users helps to explain the lack of coherent political lobbying for drug law reform. As Mugford (1990) has noted with regard to similar findings in Australia, it also illustrates the persistence of the antidrug ideology.

Thus Canadian drug users have had little success in actively resisting the operation of public policy that declares them to be criminals. The policy objective has been to suppress all use rather than to reduce the harmful consequences of use. Those who are officially criminalized are only the tip of the iceberg of several million current or former illicit drug users. Shared knowledge and experience of both the risks and benefits of drug use in informed social control networks can reduce harmful effects (Erickson, 1993). Fears about the transmission of the AIDS virus among injection drug users has helped to orient a more public health approach towards the consequences of drug use. Perhaps the "shadow line" (Gomme, 1993)—that vague boundary between the official, highly deviant, criminalized world of illicit drug users and the reality of casual, widespread use of illicit substances by the younger mainstream of the population—will continue to be blurred until a more rational public policy emerges. The Le Dain Commission envisioned a gradual withdrawal of criminal sanctions as they were replaced by more effective, less costly forms of social control (Commission of Inquiry into the Non-Medical Use of Drugs, 1972, 1973). While this strategy is far from being fully implemented, high-risk street drug users have benefited from harm reduction initiatives such as needle and syringe exchange, greater availability of methadone, and safe injection sites. These initiatives have been put in place in major cities, with Vancouver leading the way (Vancouver, 2001) and Toronto recently endorsing similar ideas (Toronto, 2005).

CONCLUSION

The future of the social construction of drug problems in Canadian society may reflect more stigmatization of the currently legal drugs, alcohol and tobacco. Canada has some of the strictest antismoking laws in the world. It has also instituted a number of checks on the availability of alcohol and mounted antidrinking/ driving and moderate drinking campaigns. The neo-temperance ideology, which has strong roots in English Canada (Levine, 1992), relies on external controls to reinforce the internal controls. These are seen as essential to check drug-induced intoxication. In cultures where loss of self-control is not so negatively valued, temperance ideology has never had widespread support. Thus, for example, Quebec has always expressed a different alcohol culture, and also has a much lower rate of cannabis criminalization than other provinces (Moreau, 1988). Even if punitive responses to illicit drugs are relaxed again in the future, and convergence develops in policy approaches to all psychoactive substances, it is difficult to envision a major change without a concomitant shift in the social evaluation of the acceptability of losing self-control. In Canada, such behaviour is the basis for being viewed as deviant.

NOTES

The views expressed in this chapter are mine and do not necessarily reflect those of the Addiction Research Foundation or the Centre for Addiction & Mental Health.

I thank Benedikt Fischer, Gordon Walsh, Russell Callaghan, and Andrew Hathaway for their helpful comments.

POSTSCRIPT ON METHAMPHETAMINE (A.K.A. CRYSTAL METH, ICE, SPEED)

The latest drug to make Canadian headlines is "crystal meth." A recent *Toronto Star* article proclaimed a new drug menace in rural southern Ontario "hooking hundreds and it's on the rise. It's in the schools, on the streets and addiction has soared" (*Toronto Star*, 2005). But how new is crystal meth? Methamphetamine, a psychostimulant known for its euphoric, energizing, and sexually arousing effects lasting several hours, has been around since the 1930s in Canada and many other countries (Jacobs and Fehr, 1987). It was often taken, even prescribed, in pill form to combat weight gain and promote alertness. The drug gained notoriety in the 1960s and early 1970s when patterns of intense injection use were associated with violence, suicide, and paranoid reactions, leading to the motto, "speed kills." Greater control over legal production, culminating in a complete ban on possession and sale, in tandem with the market developing an equally attractive stimulant (cocaine), led to a decline in use and its disappearance from the public eye, though never completely from the street drug scene.

Then, in the 1980s, first note was made of the practice of smoking the crystalline form of methamphetamine, referred to as "ice," in Hawaii (Miller and Kozel, 1991). Although apparently peaking there in 1988, evidence began to indicate a gradual spread to the west coast of the U.S. in the 1990s. Reports of Canadian use soon followed (Toronto Public Health, 2005) and by 2006, the United Nations' drug control agency was warning of a global pandemic (*The Guardian*, 2006). The president of the International Narcotics Control Board described crystal meth as "a dance and sex drug which is more addictive than crack cocaine" and the "number 1 problem drug in North America."

While all this might remind one of the crack scare of the late 1980s, it is important to ask what evidence is available about the crystal meth problem in Canada in the early years of the twenty-first century. Certainly many adverse effects of methamphetamine use, similar to those of cocaine, have been documented over the years (Jacobs and Fehr, 1987). Concern was expressed recently by Canadian public health and enforcement officials about trends of growing availability and use of crystal meth. A meeting of experts in 2005 convened by the Chief Medical Officer of British Columbia found some evidence of increases in several standard drug problem indicators: arrests, border seizures, concentrations of the drug in street samples, coroner's reports, and treatment admissions (Kendall, 2005). Based on drug user surveys, methamphetamine was described as "taking significant market share from other illicit drugs," but trends varied according to the age and other characteristics of the people examined.

In general, surveys of different populations of drug users can provide important information about new and emerging trends. However, such surveys may be limited by the time lag in asking about a drug that has recently come onto the scene. Also, people can only report what they think they are taking, not necessarily what the drug actually is. Since the 2004 Canadian Addiction Survey did not include specific questions on methamphetamine use, but rather on stimulants more generally, no national data are available. Localized student surveys such as those in British Columbia and Ontario indicate very low levels of crystal meth or ice use among high school students—about 2 percent in the past year—with some indication of a recent decline (Kendall, 2005; CAMH, 2005). High risk youthful (<25 years) populations such as injection drug users, young offenders, and street youth report much higher levels of use of methamphetamine. In contrast, older illicit drug users are more likely to stay with heroin, cocaine, or crack.

One of the more worrisome aspects of the recent infusion of methamphetamine into Canadian society is its apparent appeal to youth. Even more mainstream younger members of society are increasingly exposed to crystal meth as a "party" or "club" drug. Ongoing analysis of drugs confiscated from various rave, concert, and club events by police have indicated increased concentrations of methamphetamine combined with Ecstasy and other substances.

Methamphetamine was found in 22 percent of samples of drugs confiscated from various rave, concert, and club events in Vancouver by security or police personnel in 2001 but increased every subsequent year to 69 percent in 2005 (Rintoul, 2005). Thus it has the potential to permeate society more widely than traditional "hard" drugs such as opiates, cocaine, and crack.

There have been different responses to the apparent spread of crystal meth use in Canada. One response has been the traditional criminal justice get-tough approach. In 2005, politicians moved all amphetamine substances from Schedule 3 to Schedule 1 of the Controlled Drugs & Substances Act, thus increasing the maximum penalty to life imprisonment for production, import, export, or sale. Local police forces have reportedly stepped up efforts to locate production laboratories (*Toronto Star*, 2005; Rintoul, 2005). Since crystal meth is a manufactured drug, efforts at source are not plant-directed as are eradication efforts for coca and opium, but rather focus on the chemicals that are used in the production process. Since many of the chemicals are readily available and used for other legitimate purposes (e.g., ephedrine in cold medications) it is impossible to eliminate them. The UN narcotics chief called for more border controls and monitoring (*The Guardian*, 2006). These enforcement and interdiction efforts are unlikely to meet with much success, as is always the case with illicit markets where large profits are involved.

Another strategy is prevention. It is not known whether drug education in Canadian schools has been expanded to include crystal meth, but enterprising crusaders have produced educational material for purchase. For example, a video series entitled, "Meth: Big Time Drug in Small Town America," provides profiles of the casualties of this drug "in a small rural community. On the surface it looks peaceful and wholesome. But meth has found a home here . . ." (*You Have the Power*, 2005). In Canada, a new drug testing technology called Drugwipe was introduced at a crystal meth conference in Saskatoon. It was promoted to parents as an "early warning system" able to detect drugs on surfaces of their children's rooms, since "in the case of crystal meth, addiction can happen very quickly" (EVIDENT Corporate Investigations, 2005).

Thus, another drug has recycled to produce a moral panic, taking crack's place and gaining popularity among users, the media, and enforcement officials. Crack use never became widespread in the population (Erickson, Hathaway, and Urquhart, 1994) and, in all likelihood, neither will crystal meth. Nevertheless, its risks are considerable and its harms will add to those already affecting the most vulnerable members of drug using groups. The challenge will be to address these consequences without impairing the harm reduction gains that have been made since the mid-1990s. The movement to reform cannabis laws, even in a modest way, has been stalled with no resolution in sight, and may be further hampered by the extreme portrayals of more dangerous drugs such as crystal meth.

REFERENCES

Addiction Research Foundation. 1987–8. *Annual Report*. Toronto: Addiction Research Foundation.

Adlaf, E. M., and R. G. Smart. 1991. "Drug Use Among Adolescent Students in Canada and Ontario: The Past, Present and Future." *Journal of Drug Issues* 21:59–72.

———, R. G. Smart, and M. D. Canale. 1991. *Drug Use Among Ontario Adults 1977–1991*. Toronto: Addiction Research Foundation.

———, P. Begin, and E. Sawka (Eds.) 2005. *Canadian Addiction Survey (CAS): A national survey of Canadian's use of alcohol and other drugs*. Ottawa: Canadian Centre on Substance Abuse.

Alexander, B. 1990. *Peaceful Measures: Canada's Way Out of the War on Drugs*. Toronto: University of Toronto Press.

Blackwell, J. C. 1983. "Drifting, Controlling, and Overcoming: Opiate Users Who Avoid Becoming Chronically Independent." *Journal of Drug Issues* 13:219–35.

———. 1988. "Sin, Sickness, or Social Problem? The Concept of Drug Dependence." In *Illicit Drugs in Canada: A Risky Business*, edited by J. C. Blackwell and P. G. Erickson, 158–74. Toronto: Nelson Canada.

Brecher, E. M., et al. 1972. *Licit and Illicit Drugs*. Mount Vernon: Consumers Union.

Burroughs, W. A. 1959. *Naked Lunch*. New York: Grove Weidenfeld.

CAMH [Centre for Addiction & Mental Health]. 2005. CAMH Population Studies eBulletin, Nov/Dec. *Drug Use Highlights from the 2005 Ontario Student Drug Use Survey*.

Cheung, Y. W., and P. G. Erickson. (1997). "Crack Use in Canada: A Distant American Cousin." In *Crack in America: Demon Drugs and Social Justice*, edited by C. Reinarman and H. G. Levine, 175–93, Berkeley: University of California Press.

———, P. G. Erickson, and T. C. Landau. 1991. "Experience of Crack Use: Findings from a Community-Based Sample in Toronto." *Journal of Drug Issues* 21:121–40.

Commission of Inquiry into the Non-Medical Use of Drugs. 1972. *Cannabis.* Ottawa: Information Canada.

———. 1973. *Final Report.* Ottawa: Information Canada.

Duster, T. 1970. *The Legislation of Morality.* New York: Free Press.

Erickson, P. G. 1980. *Cannabis Criminals: The Social Effects of Punishment on Drug Users.* Toronto: ARF Books.

———. 1985. "Cannabis Law Reform: An Unfinished Era." *Psychotropes* 2:96–8.

———. 1989. "Living with Prohibition: Regular Cannabis Users, Legal Sanctions, and Informal Controls." *The International Journal of Addictions* 24: 175–88.

———. 1992. "Recent Trends in Canadian Drug Policy: The Decline and Resurgence of Prohibitionism." *Daedalus* 121:239–67.

———. 1993. "The Prospects of Harm Reduction for Psychostimulants." In *Psychoactive Drugs and Harm Reduction: From Faith to Science,* edited by N. Heather et al., 184–210. London: Whurr.

———. 2005. "Alternative sanctions for cannabis use and possession." In *Substance Abuse in Canada: Current Challenges and Choices,* edited by P. Begin and J. Weekes, 39–43. Ottawa: Canadian Centre on Substance Abuse.

———, and Y. W. Cheung. 1992. "Drug Crime and Legal Control: Lessons from the Canadian Experience." *Contemporary Drug Problems* 19:247–77.

———, A. D. Hathaway, and C. D. Urquhart. 2004. "Backing into cannabis reform: The CDSA and Toronto's diversion experiment." *Windsor Review of Legal and Social Issues* XVII (March):9–27.

———, and G. F. Murray. 1986. "Cannabis Criminals Revisited." *British Journal of Addiction* 81:81–5.

———, and R. G. Smart. 1988. "The Le Dain Commission Recommendations." In *Illicit Drugs in Canada: A Risky Business,* edited by J. C. Blackwell and P. G. Erickson, 336–44. Toronto: Nelson Canada.

———, et al. 1987. *The Steel Drug: Cocaine in Perspective.* Lexington: D.C. Heath and Company.

———, et al. 1994. *The Steel Drug: Cocaine and Crack in Perspective,* 2nd ed. New York: Macmillan.

EVIDENT Corporate Investigations. 2005. Drugwipe. Presented at the Crystal Meth Conference, Saskatoon, Sask. Nov. 28, 2005. Global Detections & Reporting, Inc. www.evident.ca

Fagin, J., and K. L. Chin. 1989. "Initiation into Crack and Cocaine: A Tale of Two Epidemics." *Contemporary Drug Problems* 16:579–618.

Faupel, C. E. 1991. *Shooting Dope: Career Patterns of Hard Core Heroin Users.* Gainesville: University of Florida Press.

Fehr, K. and H. Kalant. 1983. *Cannabis and Health Hazards: Proceedings of an ARF/WHO Scientific Meeting on Adverse Health and Behavioural Consequences of Cannabis.* Toronto: Addiction Research Foundation.

Giffen, P. J., S. Endicott, and S. Lambert. 1991. *Panic and Indifference: The Politics of Canada's Drug Laws.* Ottawa: Canadian Centre on Substance Abuse.

Glaser, D. 1985. "The Criminal Law's Nemesis: Drug Control." *American Bar Foundation Research Journal,* 619–26.

Globe and Mail (Toronto). 1989. "Crack Use Near Epidemic Toronto Police Warn" (11 February).

Gomme, I. M. 1993. *The Shadow Line: Deviance and Crime in Canada.* Toronto: Harcourt Brace Jovanovich.

Goode, E. 1990. "The American Drug Panic of the 1980s: Social Construction or Objective Threat?" *The International Journal of the Addictions* 25:1083–98.

The Guardian (UK). 2006. "UN warns of crystal meth pandemic" (01 March). Special Report. Drugs in Britain.

Hagan, J. 1991. *The Disreputable Pleasures: Crime and Deviance in Canada,* 3rd ed. Toronto: McGraw-Hill Ryerson.

Health and Welfare Canada. 1992. *Alcohol and Other Drug Use by Canadians: A National*

Alcohol and Other Drug Survey (1989): Technical Report. Prepared by E. Eliany et al. Ottawa: Minister of Supply and Services Canada.

Heath, D. B. 1992. "U.S. Drug Control Policy: A Cultural Perspective." *Daedalus* 121:269–91.

Jacobs, M. R., and K. Fehr. 1987. *Drugs and Drug Abuse: A Reference Text,* 2nd ed. Toronto: Addiction Research Foundation.

Jensen, E. L., and J. Gerber. 1993. "State Efforts to Construct a Social Problem: the 1986 War on Drugs in Canada." *Canadian Journal of Sociology* 18, no. 4:453–62.

Kalant, H. 1982. "Commentary on the Home Office Report on the Effects of Cannabis Use." *British Journal of Addiction* 77:341–5.

Kendall, P. 2005. *Trends in BC regarding Methamphetamine use.* Unpublished draft statement, Centre for Addictions Research BC and the Centre for Social Responsibility. Vancouver.

Levine, H. G. 1992. "Temperance Cultures: Concerns About Alcohol Problems in Nordic and English-Speaking Cultures." In *The Nature of Alcohol and Drug-Related Problems,* edited by G. Edwards and M. Lader, 15–36. London: Oxford University Press.

Lindesmith, A. 1965. *The Addict and the Law.* Bloomington: Indiana University Press.

Maloff, D., et al. 1979. "Informal Social Controls and Their Influence on Substance Use." *Journal of Drug Issues* 9:161–84.

McKenna, T. 1992. *Food of the Gods.* New York: Bantam Books.

Miller, M. A., and N. J. Kozel. 1991. *Methamphetamine Abuse: Epidemiologic Issues and Implications.* NIDA Research Monograph 115. Rockville MD: National Institute on Drug Abuse.

Moreau, J. A. E. 1988. "Appendix A: Selected Statistics on Convictions for Illicit Drug Use in Canada." In *Illicit Drugs in Canada: A Risky Business,* edited by J. C. Blackwell and P. G. Erickson, 449–55. Toronto: Nelson Canada.

Mugford, S. K. 1990. "Drug Policy and Criminal Consequences: The Australian Experience." Paper presented at the annual meeting of the American Society of Criminology, Baltimore, Maryland.

Murray, G. F. 1987. "Cocaine Use in an Era of Social Reform: The Natural History of a Social Problem in Canada." *Canadian Journal of Law and Society* 29–43.

———. 1988. "The Road to Regulation: Patent Medicines in Canada in Historical Perspective." In *Illicit Drugs in Canada: A Risky Business,* edited by J. C. Blackwell and P. G. Erickson, 721–87. Toronto: Nelson Canada.

Musto, D. F. 1973. *The American Disease: Origins of Narcotic Control.* New Haven: Yale University Press.

Narcotic Control Act, RSC 1970, s. 10[4].

Negrete, J. C. 1988. "What Happened to the Cannabis Debate?" *British Journal of Addiction* 83:354–72.

Peyrot, M. 1984. "Cycles of Social Problem Development: The Case of Drug Abuse." *The Sociological Quarterly* 25:83–95.

Prebel, E., and J. J. Casey. 1969. "Taking Care of Business: The Heroin User's Life on the Streets." *The International Journal of Addictions* 4:1–24.

Reinarman, C., and H. G. Levine. 1989. "The Crack Attack: Media and Politics in America's Latest Drug Scare." In *Images of Issues: Current Perspectives on Social Problems,* edited by J. Best, 115–37. New York: Aldine DeGruyter.

Rintoul, S. 2005. "Ecstasy, methamphetamine or chemical cocktails." Paper presented at the Issues of Substance Abuse Conference, Markham, ON, Nov. 14.

Royal Canadian Mounted Police. 1987. *National Drug Intelligence Estimates 1986/1987.* Ottawa: Minister of Supply and Services Canada.

———. 1989. *National Drug Intelligence Estimates 1988/1989.* Ottawa: Minister of Supply and Services Canada.

———. 1990. *National Drug Intelligence Estimates 1989/1990.* Ottawa: Minister of Supply and Services Canada.

Single, E., et al. 1992. "Policy Developments in Canada." In *Drug Problems in Society: Dimensions and Perspectives,* edited by J. White, 63–72. Parkside: Drug and Alcohol Services Council.

Smart, R. G. 1988. "Crack Cocaine Use in Canada: A New Epidemic?" *American Journal of Epidemiology* 127:135–17.

———, and L. Anglin. 1987. "Do We Know the Lethal Dose of Cocaine?" *Journal of Forensic Sciences* 32:303–12.

———, and A. C. Ogborne. 1986. *Northern Spirits: Drinking in Canada Then and Now.* Toronto: ARF Books.

Snyder, S. 1989. *Brainstorming: The Science and Politics of Opiate Research.* Cambridge: Harvard University Press.

Stoddart, K. 1988. "The Enforcement of Narcotics Violations in a Canadian City: Heroin Users' Perspectives on the Production of Official Statistics." In *Illicit Drugs in Canada: A Risky Business,* edited by J. C. Blackwell and P. G. Erickson, 244–62. Toronto: Nelson Canada.

———. 1991. "It's Easier for the Bulls Now: Official Statistics and Social Change in a Canadian Heroin-Using Community." *Journal of Drug Issues* 21:83–103.

Toronto. 2005. City Council. *"A Drug Strategy for the City of Toronto."*

Toronto Public Health. 2005. *Drug Use in Toronto: Facts on Methamphetamine.* www.toronto.ca/drugcentre.

Toronto Star. 1989a. "Aroused Public Needed to Fight Drugs Mayor Says" (16 June).

———. 1989b. "New Group Joins Fight to Curb Cocaine Trade" (24 February).

———. 2005. "Crystal Meth in the Country" (18 June), A1.

Vancouver. 2001. City Council. *"A Framework for Action: A Four Pillar Approach to Drug Problems in Vancouver."*

You Have the Power. 2005. Video series: *Meth: Big Time Drug in Small Town America.* Nashville Tennessee. www.yhtp.org.

Chapter 25

Race and Crime:

A CRITIQUE

JULIAN V. ROBERTS AND THOMAS GABOR

Canadian criminologists have been challenged recently by the work of a professor of psychology, Philippe Rushton, who claims to have uncovered evidence of significant interracial differences in many areas of human behaviour, including criminality (Rushton, 1987, 1988, 1989). In January 1987, Professor Rushton delivered a paper at the American Association for the Advancement of Science conference in San Francisco (Rushton, 1987). He proposed a genetically based hierarchy in which Blacks (who supposedly evolved earlier than whites or orientals) were, *inter alia*, less intelligent and law-abiding than whites and orientals. Rushton asserts that there are substantial interracial differences in crime rates, and that these are accounted for by genetic factors. We shall examine later the credibility of genetic explanations of variations in crime rates. First, it is important to address the context of these assertions, and their likely impact upon society.

Rushton's speculations about race and crime have achieved national coverage exceeding that accorded any research project undertaken by criminologists (*The Globe and Mail*, 1989). Part of the reason for this is the aggressive posture adopted by Rushton: he has been interviewed in several newspapers and has appeared on several television programs with national audiences. In contrast, the reaction from criminologists, but not other professional groups (*The Globe and Mail*, 1989), has been muted. His monopolization of media coverage may, we believe, have had a detrimental impact upon public opinion. It is important, therefore, that criminologists

in Canada respond to his statements. While Rushton's claims about racial influences upon intelligence have been challenged, his assertions about crime have not.

THE EFFECT OF RUSHTON'S VIEWS ON PUBLIC THEORIES OF CRIME CAUSATION

The race/crime controversy has important consequences for public opinion in the area of criminal justice. Many of the important questions in the field of criminology—such as the relative deterrent effect of capital punishment—cannot be addressed by experiments. Accordingly, criminologists have used sophisticated correlational procedures to untangle the relative effects on crime of correlated variables such as genetic and environmental factors. The existence of a simple statistic, then, such as the overrepresentation in some crime statistics of certain racial minorities, will by itself convince few scholars. Criminologists have become sensitized to the possibility of alternative explanations for apparently straightforward relationships. Members of the public, however, are not so sophisticated in drawing inferences from statistical information. In fact, a great deal of recent research in social psychology has documented numerous ways in which the layperson is led into making unjustified inferences from material such as that which appears in newspapers (Fiske and Taylor, 1984; Nisbett and Ross, 1980).

Source: Excerpted from "Lombrosian Wine in a New Bottle: Research on Crime and Race," *Canadian Journal of Criminology* 32, 2 (April 1990): 291–313. Reprinted by permission of the Canadian Journal of Criminology.

Rushton's theories may affect public opinion in this area for several reasons. First, as already noted, the average layperson may not readily seek alternative (i.e., nongenetic) explanations for the overrepresentation of Blacks in certain types of crime. Second, laypersons are less likely to realize that studies on race and crime are essentially correlational, rather than causal, in nature. Third, the race/crime hypothesis comes from a highly credible source, namely a well-published and tenured university professor. Fourth, it is vital to remember that, to the average member of the public, crime is a relatively unidimensional phenomenon: it usually involves violence, loss of property, and is a consequence of a "criminal disposition." Members of the public tend to regard offenders as a relatively homogeneous group (Roberts and White, 1986) varying somewhat in their actions but not their motivations. Criminologists have long been aware of the deficiencies of this perception of crime; the multidimensional nature of crime and the complexity of motivation render sweeping statements about the etiology of crime invalid. Finally, but not last in importance, some people may be particularly receptive to racial explanations of crime. Thus, views such as those expressed by Professor Rushton may have the unintended effect of inflaming racism in Canada.

Furthermore, Rushton's views received what many laypersons might interpret as substantial support within days of the news media's coverage of his San Francisco address. On February 16, a representative of the Toronto Police Force released statistics showing that Blacks were overrepresented in the crime statistics in the Jane–Finch area of Toronto (*The Toronto Star*, 1989). These data are likely to be misinterpreted by members of the public to constitute evidence supporting a genetic explanation of crime.

For the vast majority of the public, the mass media constitute their primary source of information about crime and criminal justice. Public conceptions of deviance are a consequence of what people read, hear, and see in the media. An abundance of research has demonstrated a direct correspondence between public misperceptions of crime and distorted media coverage of criminal justice issues (Doob and Roberts, 1982). Since criminologists have failed to refute Rushton in the news media, we have also relinquished access to the one means of influencing public opinion on this issue. Criminologists may be highly skeptical of Rushton's opinions in the area of crime, but the only way that this skepticism can affect the public is through coverage in the news media. Once again, we note that while Rushton has been criticized by various behavioural geneticists (such as David Suzuki), his assertions regarding race and crime have remained uncontested.

We believe, therefore, that it is important to address the hypothesis that inherited racial traits affect crime rates. We shall examine some methodological issues relating criminality to race. A comprehensive survey of the literature on this topic would occupy a whole issue of a journal; we can only highlight the research findings and point out what we perceive to be the principal flaws in Rushton's argument. We shall draw upon data from Canada, the United States, and the United Kingdom. Finally, it should be made clear from the outset that we are addressing Rushton's theory as it pertains to the phenomenon of crime. We are not behavioural geneticists, to whom we cede the question of whether the general theory of racial differences withstands scientific scrutiny.

THE SCIENTIFIC ARGUMENT: EMPIRICAL RESEARCH ON RACE AND CRIME

PROBLEMS WITH THE DEFINITION OF RACE

Rushton relates an independent variable (race) to a dependent variable (crime). The interracial comparisons cited by Rushton are predicated on the assumption that people are racially pure. Each racial "category" is held to be homogeneous, but this is now accepted by contemporary anthropologists and biologists to be an antiquated and dangerous myth. Centuries of interbreeding reduce Rushton's rather crude tripartite classification (Black, white, oriental) to the level of caricature. For example, Radzinowicz and King (1977) note that in the United States, close to 50 percent of those classified as Black are over half white by lineage (see also Herskovits, 1930; and, for a study of offenders, Hooton, 1939). Many American whites, as well, have some Black ancestry; Haskell and Yablonsky (1983: 95) note that:

> Estimates of the number of Blacks who have "passed" into the white society run as high as 7 million. In addition to those millions who have introduced an African mixture into the "white" population of the United States in the relatively recent past, there must have been millions of Africans who were assimilated into the population of Spain, Portugal, Italy, Greece, and other Mediterranean countries. Descendants of those people are now part of the "white" population of the United States.

Wolfgang and Cohen (1970) cite data showing that no more than 22 percent of all persons designated as Black, in the United States, were of unmixed ancestry. Fully 15 percent of persons classified as Black were more white than Black (Wolfgang and Cohen, 1970: 7). The pervasiveness of such racial overlap calls genetically based racial theories of crime into question. (For the rest of this article, for convenience only, we shall continue to refer to interracial differences. This does not mean we endorse the racial trichotomy of Blacks, orientals, and whites advanced by Professor Rushton.) Finally, it is important to bear in mind that crime statistics deal with race as a sociological and not a biological category. In short, the independent variable, as it were, is highly problematic. Now we turn to the dependent measure, official and unofficial measures of crime.

THE ISSUE OF OVERREPRESENTATION IN OFFICIAL CRIME STATISTICS

Rushton's evidence for a genetic influence consists of the overrepresentation of Blacks in official statistics of crime in the United States, the United Kingdom, and elsewhere. Specifically he asserts that:

> African descended people, for example, while constituting less than one-eighth of the population of the United States or of London, England, currently account for over 50% of the crimes in both places. Since about the same proportion of victims say their assailant was Black, the arrest statistics cannot really be blamed on police prejudice. (Rushton, 1987: 3)

There are at least two factually incorrect elements here, but first we offer a general comment regarding the issue of overrepresentation.

A simple correlation between two variables does not constitute evidence of a *causal* relationship. A multitude of other confounding factors must be ruled out before one can contemplate a causal relationship. Even if the relationship between race and crime holds up after careful secondary analyses, this is hardly convincing evidence of genetic influences. The fact that parental alcoholism is correlated with alcoholism in the offspring does not prove a genetic component to alcoholism. Alcohol abuse can be a learned behaviour as well. The same argument applies to the race/crime relationship.

Another point is relevant to the issue of a disproportionate involvement in crime. Virtually every society contains racial and ethnic groups, usually minorities, who are more criminally active in certain crimes than the rest of the population. According to Rushton's theory of criminal behaviour, Native Canadians should display lower, not higher, crime rates than the non-Native population. Unfortunately for the theory, this is not true. The overrepresentation of Native offenders in the criminal justice statistics has been apparent for some time (Griffiths and Verdun-Jones, 1989; LaPrairie, 1989). Explanations in terms of the social strata in our society occupied by indigenous peoples can easily explain these findings; Rushton's racial theory cannot. According to Rushton's typology this group, being oriental or mongoloid, should display lower, not higher, rates of criminality.

According to Rushton's genetic explanation of crime, the crime rates for Blacks should be higher than the white crime rates, *and* the rates for Native Canadians should be *lower* than the non-Native population. The two categories (Blacks and Native people) are genetically dissimilar; their rates of criminality should reflect this difference (relative to the white population). The fact is that both Black Americans and Native Canadians share an elevated risk of certain kinds of criminality (relative to the comparable white populations in their respective countries). Such an outcome is, of course, perfectly consistent with a sociological explanation: both minority groups share a protracted history of constrained social opportunity, as well as overt discrimination.

Also in Canada, French Canadians are the most active in the crime of robbery (Gabor et al., 1987). In England, Irish immigrants have been overrepresented in crimes of assault for years (Radzinowicz and King, 1977). In Israel, the Arab population and non-European Jews are more criminally active in conventional crimes than the European Jews (Fishman, Rattner, and Weimann, 1987). Such overrepresentation, then, is the rule rather than the exception across different societies.

To return to Rushton's suggestion, two errors can be identified. First, he cites data published in the *Daily Telegraph* (a British newspaper) showing that Blacks account for over 50 percent of the crimes in the United States and the United Kingdom (Rushton, 1988). By any measure, this is a considerable exaggeration. If he refers to all reported crimes and not merely index crimes, Blacks account for about 29 percent of all persons charged in the United States (United States Department of Justice, 1989). Index crimes are those included in official crime indices; they exclude many white-collar crimes, for example.

As well, aggregate statistics based on index crimes alone misrepresent the true picture. Crime is not, as suggested by Rushton's publications, a homogeneous category of behaviours. While Blacks in the United States account for over 60 percent of arrests for robbery and almost 50 percent of arrests for murder, they account for about 30 percent of arrests for burglary and theft, less than 24 percent of those arrested for arson and about 20 percent of those arrested for vandalism (United States Department of Justice, 1987). Using Rushton's own data, Blacks are underrepresented in crimes like tax fraud and securities violations. In fact, arrest statistics for white-collar crimes such as fraud and embezzlement are significantly higher for whites. Treating crime as a unitary phenomenon obscures this diversity. These variations reflect differential opportunities for offending, and not, we submit, offence-specific genetic programming.

Differential Treatment of Blacks by the Criminal Justice System

Finally, arrest statistics reflect, to a degree, the more rigorous surveillance by police to which minorities are subject. Data on this point are hard to obtain; the magnitude of the problem is hard to quantify. Nevertheless, the recent release of the "Guildford Four" in England, after fifteen years of imprisonment following a wrongful conviction based upon fabricated police evidence, reveals the dangers posed to minorities by an overzealous police force.

Research in the United States sustains the view that the police are more likely to arrest and charge Blacks (Black and Reiss, 1967; Lundman, Sykes, and Clark, 1978). Wolfgang and Cohen (1970: 71) summarize some of this research:

> In comparing arrest statistics for Blacks and whites, it is important to remember, then, that one reason for the high arrest rates among Blacks is that they are more likely to be stopped, picked up on suspicion and subsequently arrested.

Furthermore, the bias does not remain at the police station: British data (Landau, 1981; Landau and Nathan, 1983) show that prosecution is more likely for persons of Afro-Caribbean origin. Bias persists at most critical stages of the criminal justice process. As Paul Gordon (1988: 309) noted, summarizing data on the issue:

> Black people's experience of the British criminal justice system shows clearly that the rhetoric of the law does not accord with the reality of its practice. The law is not colour-blind, but a means by which Black people have been subject to a process of criminalization.

Most recently, Albonetti and her colleagues (1989) have demonstrated that while the influence of race upon pretrial decisions is complicated, white suspects have the edge over Black suspects.

To summarize the data on contact with the criminal justice process, American Blacks are clearly overrepresented in violent crime statistics, slightly overrepresented in property crimes, and underrepresented in white-collar crimes. In order to explain this diverse pattern, one has to strain the genetic explanation beyond the breaking point. Are Blacks genetically predisposed toward street crimes while whites are programmed to commit white-collar crimes? A far more plausible explanation exists: social groups commit crimes as a consequence of their social situations and in response to prevailing criminal opportunities. This environmental perspective explains more findings and requires fewer assumptions. The law of parsimony, then, clearly favours environmental over genetic theories of crime. In short, Rushton's explanation of crime by reference to genetic influences requires acceptance of the position that specific antisocial behaviours are directly related to genetic structure. Modern behavioural geneticists would undoubtedly reject this view.

OVERREPRESENTATION AND ALTERNATIVE SOURCES OF CRIME STATISTICS: VICTIMIZATION SURVEYS AND SELF-REPORTED CRIMINALITY

There is convincing evidence that arrest data exaggerate the true incidence of Black criminality. Two alternative sources of information on crime make this clear. Overall, FBI data indicate that 46.5 percent of all violent crimes reported to the police are committed by Blacks. However, the victimization survey conducted by the U.S. Department of Justice found that Blacks account for only about 24 percent of violent crimes (United States Department of Justice, 1986). Which source presents a more accurate picture of crimes actually committed? With regard to crimes of violence, data derived from victims would appear to be more accurate than arrest data. But it is not just victimization surveys that cast doubt upon the official statistics. A third source of information on crime patterns also shows discrepancies. Rojek (1983) compared police reports with self-reports of delinquency. In the police database, race was a significant factor in several offence categories, but this was not true for the self-reports. Other studies using the self-report approach (Williams and Gold, 1972) have found a similar pattern: no difference between Black and white respondents (Pope, 1979) or only slight differences (Hirschi, 1969).

Unreported versus Reported Crime

Another explanation for the elevated incidence of Black offenders in official crime statistics concerns the issue of unreported crimes. As we have noted, official crime data indicate that Blacks are more likely than whites to commit certain crimes (personal injury offences) and less likely than whites to commit other types of crimes. The problem with crime statistics is that the reporting rate is highly variable, depending upon the offence. The types of offences committed by Blacks are more likely to be reported than the offences committed by whites. Any examination of aggregate crime statistics is going to overestimate the true incidence of crime committed by Blacks relative to the amount of crime committed by whites.

To conclude, the extent of overrepresentation of Blacks, even in those offences where it occurs, has been exaggerated. In perhaps the most comprehensive study to date which relates crime to race, Michael Hindelang (1982) tested various theories that attempted to explain interracial differences. He concluded that the theories of delinquency that best explain the patterns of data were sociological rather than biological. These included Merton's reformulation of anomie theory (Merton, 1968), Cloward and Ohlin's opportunity theory (Cloward and Ohlin, 1960), and Wolfgang's subculture of violence theory (Wolfgang and Ferracuti, 1982).

A final word on the crime statistics utilized by Rushton consists of a caveat: recorded crime is exactly that: it is only a small fraction of all reported and unreported crime. A recent article by Tony Jefferson (1988: 535) makes the point succinctly:

> We do not *know* what the real rate of Black crime is, nor whether it is on the increase. Take robbery for instance. The British Crime Survey reveals that only 8% of robberies were recorded. If those figures applied to London this would mean that there is a suspect for only 1 in 100 robberies. The comparable figure for burglaries would be 5 in 100. This means that *whatever* the arrest figures, and whatever the victim identifications, the "unknown" element is so great, especially for those crimes where Black "over-representation" is seen as greatest, as to make all estimates of Black offending strictly conjectural.

When there is sound reason to suppose that the police are more vigilant with regard to Black suspects and offenders, it is clear that if we were able to replace reported with unreported crime rates, the interracial differences would diminish still further.

Self-report studies provide insight in another area as well. While Professor Rushton associates "lawlessness" with being Black, there is overwhelming evidence indicating that most people, at one point or another, commit acts for which they could be prosecuted. As an example, in a now classic study, Wallerstein and Wyle (1947) surveyed 1700 New York City residents without a criminal record. Fully 99 percent admitted to involvement in at least one of 49 offences. This evidence suggests that rule breaking is normal activity on the part of most citizens in Western societies. The selection of norm violators to be prosecuted therefore is critical to an understanding of who becomes officially classified as a criminal. Many observers of the criminal justice system believe that race may be a key factor affecting that selection process. Another classic study, Hartshorne and May's (1928) investigation of children, also showed that dishonesty was both pervasive and situation-specific. There was little cross-situational consistency: children that were dishonest in one situation were honest in others. This emphasis on the social situation as the determinant of behaviour is consistent with an environmental view of crime, and inconsistent with Rushton's genetic theory. (A large body of evidence, drawn from longitudinal, self-report, experimental, and observational research, suggests that law breaking is widespread in North American society.)

WITHIN RACE COMPARISONS

Comparisons over Time

In the next two sections, we examine variation in crime rates within race, but across time and cultures. If genetic factors have an important impact upon crime, rates should be relatively stable within race, across both time and cultures. This, however, is not the case. Further undermining Rushton's thesis are the temporal and cross-cultural variations in crime patterns for the Black population. Street crime by Blacks in the United Kingdom has only recently increased significantly. Just over a decade ago, Radzinowicz and King (1977) were able to write that, with the exception of prostitution and other victimless crimes, the Black community was as law abiding as other Britons. Any increase in crime rates within a generation obviously cannot be attributed to genetic factors. This point was made recently by Anthony Mawson (1989) in the context of explanations of homicide in terms of Darwinian selection (Daly and Wilson, 1988). Mawson (1989: 239) notes the inability of biological explanations of homicide to account for fluctuations in homicide rates over a short period of time:

> Thus, it seems doubtful whether a selectionist explanation can be applied to changing homicide rates, even those occurring over a thousand years.

The same argument applies in the context of Rushton's work: increases in offending by Blacks over a period of ten to fifteen years cannot possibly be explained by reference to genetic influence.

In the United States as well, the proportional involvement of Blacks in crime has risen over the past few decades. One major factor in this rise has been the proliferation of illicit drug usage. Heroin use became pervasive in the 1950s, and "crack" cocaine is creating an explosion of violent crime in this decade. As well, the erosion of taboos relating to interracial crimes has been associated with increased victimization of whites by Blacks (Silberman, 1978). A third major development has been the greater accessibility of firearms. These are three potent environmental factors affecting Black criminality. One would be hard-pressed to find a genetic explanation for the changing criminal activity pattern of a race over such a short period of time.

Comparisons across Jurisdictions

The variations in Black, white, and oriental crime from one society to another also demonstrate the potency of environmental factors in the etiology of crime. Levels of violent crime in the American South are greater for both Blacks *and* whites than they are in other parts of the country. As well, there is substantial variation in the homicide rates for Blacks in different American states. For example, in Delaware the homicide rate for Blacks is 16.7 per 100 000. This is considerably lower than the homicide rate for Black residents of other states; in Missouri, for example, the rate is 65 per 100 000 (Carroll and Mercy, 1989).

Cross-national, within-race comparisons make the same point. Black Americans have a higher homicide rate than their more racially pure counterparts in Africa: this fact directly contradicts Rushton's thesis. The author (Bohannan, 1960: 123) of a study of African homicide concludes:

> if it needed stressing, here is overwhelming evidence that it is a cultural and not biological factor which makes for a high homicide rate among American negroes.

More recent data (International Criminal Police Organization, 1988) demonstrate the same variations: the homicide rate per 100 000 inhabitants varies from .01 (Mali) to 29 (Bahamas) and 22.05 (Jamaica). It is noteworthy also that the Caribbean homicide rates are far in excess of even the African countries with the highest rates (e.g., Rwanda, 11 per 100 000; Tanzania, 8 per 100 000). This despite the fact that residents of the Caribbean are more racially mixed than Blacks from Africa. According to Rushton's theory, homicide rates should be higher not lower in the more racially pure African states.

Furthermore, orientals do not constitute a monolith of law-abiding citizens. The homicide rates in the Far East also vary considerably, from 39 per 100 000 residents in the Philippines to 1.3 per 100 000 in Hong Kong. In Thailand, the homicide rate exceeds the rate of homicide in Japan by a factor of twelve (International Criminal Police Organization, 1988). In all these comparisons, the genetic explanation falls short.

The magnitude of these intraracial differences suggests that the potency of environmental factors to explain crime rates far exceeds that of genetic factors. In statistical terms, these data imply that the percentage of variation in crime rates explained by genetic factors is negligible, if it exists at all.

VICTIMIZATION PATTERNS

There is another form of overrepresentation of which Professor Rushton appears unaware: Blacks are at much higher risk of becoming the victims of violent crime. In the United States, Black males are 20 times more likely than whites to be shot, cut, or stabbed, and Black females are 18 times more likely to be raped than white women (Wolfgang and Cohen, 1981). Black Americans are also more likely than whites to be victims of burglary, motor vehicle theft, assault, robbery, and many other offences (United States Department of Justice, 1983). Although Blacks constitute only 12 percent of the general United States population, over 40 percent of homicide victims are Black. See Barnett and Schwartz (1989) for recent data showing Black victimization rates to be approximately four times higher than white rates. The same trends are apparent in other countries, such as England. The overrepresentation of Blacks as victims is substantial, yet no one has posited that such overrepresentation is due to a genetically based susceptibility to criminal victimization. While this finding is not inconsistent with an explanation based upon genetic factors, it does underscore the importance of environmental factors such as propinquity and accessibility. Violent crimes are a result of an interaction between offender and victim. To posit an overriding genetic basis of crime is to ignore the role of the victim and situational factors (Boyd, 1988; Wolfgang, 1958). When we examine the dynamics of the violent crime most commonly associated with Blacks—armed robbery—we readily see the importance of situational determinants. Actually, recourse to physical violence occurs only in a small minority

of robberies. Usually the violence that does occur arises in response to victims who resist the robbers' demands (Gabor et al., 1987). The violence, therefore, is often instrumental and situation-specific.

If Blacks are more likely to be both offenders and victims in relation to certain types of crime, then a plausible explanation for their overrepresentation on both counts is that they tend to live in areas in which violence is a normal consequence of stress, threat, and frustration. This essentially is Wolfgang and Ferracuti's (1982) subculture of violence thesis. Aside from living in environments where violence is normative behaviour, Blacks tend disproportionately to live in poverty. Furthermore, they are overrepresented among urban dwellers. Economic status and urban residence are linked to a number of crime indices. A fair examination of Black and white criminality would therefore necessitate comparison between persons situated similarly in society.

But even the presence of a correlation between race and certain indices of crime, after other plausible environmental factors have been pointed out, does not demonstrate a genetically based race/crime link. As Charles Silberman (1978) has pointed out, the experience of Black Americans has been very different from the experience of any other disadvantaged group. The generations of violence, deprivation, disenfranchisement, and exclusion from educational and vocational opportunities to which they have been subjected has not been shared by any other ethnic or racial group. Moreover, much of this racial discrimination persists, to this day, and in this country, as recent research has documented (Henry and Ginzberg, 1985). Discrimination of this kind can engender social patterns and attitudes toward authority that lead to law breaking.

Careful epidemiological research can result in samples of Black and white citizens that are "matched" on many important background variables such as social class, income, education, age, and family size and composition. Comparison between such groups is preferable to comparison based upon unmatched samples, but the effects of long-term discrimination, brutality, and oppression over generations cannot be captured by the most rigorous multiple regression analysis. As John Conklin (1989: 140) notes:

> to argue that Blacks and whites of similar backgrounds will have the same crime rate is to argue that centuries of discrimination have had no long-term effects on Blacks that are conducive to criminal behavior.

Our opposition to Rushton's views should not be interpreted to mean that we deny the existence of any genetic influences upon human behaviour. Rather, we take issue with the attribution of racial differences in criminality to genetic factors. In our view, there is little scientific basis for his rather sweeping assertions about the relative "law-abidingness" of different racial groups. The few statistics he provides are susceptible to a multitude of highly probable alternative explanations derived from an environmental perspective. Given the incendiary nature of the theory and its policy implications, we feel that the burden of proof is upon Professor Rushton to provide more convincing data than the few ambiguous statistics he has to date brought forth. We leave it to others (Lynn, 1989; Zuckerman and Brody, 1989) to evaluate the scientific credibility of Professor Rushton's genetic explanation of other phenomena such as: intelligence, sexual restraint, personality, political preferences, and the efficacy of the German army in the Second World War (*The Globe and Mail*, 1989). In the area of criminality, his evidence, in our view, falls short of discharging a scientific burden of proof.

NOTE

The authors would like to acknowledge that this manuscript has benefited from the comments of Michael Petrunik (University of Ottawa), the editorial committee of the *Canadian Journal of Criminology,* and two anonymous reviewers.

REFERENCES

Albonetti, Celesta, Robert Hauser, John Hagan, and Ilene Nagel. 1989. "Criminal justice decision making as a stratification process: The role of race and stratification resources in pre-trial release." *Journal of Quantitative Criminology* 5: 57–82.

Barnett, Arnold and Elliot Schwartz. 1989. "Urban homicide: Still the same." *Journal of Quantitative Criminology* 5: 83–100.

Black, D. and Albert Reiss. 1967. *Studies of Crime and Law Enforcement in Major Metropolitan Areas.* Washington, DC: Government Printing Office.

Bohannan, Paul. 1960. *African Homicide and Suicide.* Princeton, NJ: Princeton University Press.

Boyd, Neil. 1988. *The Last Dance: Murder in Canada.* Toronto: Prentice-Hall.

Carroll, Patrick and James Mercy. 1989. "Regional variation in homicide rates: Why is the west violent?" *Violence and Victims* 4: 17–25.

Cloward, Richard A. and Lloyd Ohlin. 1960. *Delinquency and Opportunity: A Theory of Delinquent Gangs.* New York: Free Press.

Conklin, John. 1989. *Criminology.* (Third edition.) New York: Macmillan.

Curie, Elliot. 1985. *Confronting Crime.* New York: Pantheon.

Daly, Martin and Margo Wilson. 1988. *Homicide.* New York: Aldine.

Doob, Anthony N. and Julian V. Roberts. 1982. *Crime: Some Views of the Canadian Public.* Ottawa: Department of Justice.

Fishman, G., Arye Rattner, and Gabriel Weimann. 1987. "The effect of ethnicity on crime attribution." *Criminology* 25: 507–24.

Fiske, Susan T. and Shelley E. Taylor. 1984. *Social Cognition.* Reading, MA: Addison-Wesley.

Gabor, Thomas, Micheline Baril, M. Cusson, D. Elie, Marc LeBlanc, and André Normandeau. 1987. *Armed Robbery: Cops, Robbers, and Victims.* Springfield, Ill.: Charles C. Thomas.

The Globe and Mail. 1989. February 11: 14.

Gordon, Paul. 1988. "Black people and the criminal law: Rhetoric and reality." *International Journal of the Sociology of Law* 16: 295–313.

Griffiths, Curt and Simon Verdun-Jones. 1989. *Canadian Criminal Justice.* Toronto: Butterworths.

Hartshorne, M. and M. A. May. 1928. *Studies in Deceit.* New York: Macmillan.

Haskell, M. R. and L. Yablonsky. 1983. *Criminology: Crime and Criminality.* Boston: Houghton Mifflin.

Henry, F. and E. Ginzberg. 1985. *Who Gets the Work: A Test of Racial Discrimination in Employment.* Toronto: Urban Alliance on Race Relations and the Social Planning Council.

Herskovits, Melville J. 1930. *The Anthropometry of the American Negro.* New York: Columbia University Press.

Hindelang, Michael. 1982. "Race and Crime." In Leonard D. Savitz and N. Johnston, eds., *Contemporary Criminology.* Toronto: John Wiley.

Hirschi, Travis. 1969. *Causes of Delinquency.* Berkeley: University of California Press.

Hooton, Ernest A. 1939. *Crime and the Man.* Cambridge: Harvard University Press.

International Criminal Police Organization. 1988. *International Crime Statistics* 1985–86.

Jefferson, Tony. 1988. "Race, crime and policing: Empirical, theoretical and methodological issues." *International Journal of the Sociology of Law* 16: 521–39.

Landau, Simha. 1981. "Juveniles and the police." *British Journal of Criminology* 21: 27–46.

——— and G. Nathan. 1983. "Selecting delinquents for cautioning in the London metropolitan area." *British Journal of Criminology* 28: 128–49.

LaPrairie, Carol. 1989. *The Role of Sentencing in the Over-Representation of Aboriginal People in Correctional Institutions.* Ottawa: Department of Justice.

Lundman, R., R. Sykes and J. Clark. 1978. "Police control of juveniles: A replication." *Journal of Research in Crime and Delinquency* 15: 74–91.

Lynn, Michael. 1989. "Race difference in sexual behaviour: A critique of Rushton and Bogaert's evolutionary hypothesis." *Journal of Research in Personality* 23: 1–6.

Mawson, Anthony. 1989. "Review of *Homicide*" (Daly and Wilson, 1988). *Contemporary Sociology* March: 238–40.

Merton, Robert K. 1968. *Social Theory and Social Structure.* Glencoe: Free Press.

Nisbett, Richard and Lee Ross. 1980. *Human Inference: Strategies and Shortcomings of Social Judgement.* Englewood Cliffs, NJ: Prentice-Hall.

Pope, Carl E. 1979. "Race and crime revisited." *Crime and Delinquency* 25: 345–57.

Radzinowicz, Leon and Joan King. 1977. *The Growth of Crime: The International Experience.* London: Penguin.

Roberts, Julian V. and Nicholas R. White. 1986. "Public estimates of recidivism rates: Consequences of a criminal stereotype." *Canadian Journal of Criminology* 28: 229–41.

Rojek, Dean G. 1983. "Social status and delinquency: Do self-reports and official reports match?" In Gordon P. Waldo, ed., *Measurement Issues in Criminal Justice.* Beverly Hills: Sage.

Rushton, J. Philippe. 1987. "Population differences in rule-following behaviour: Race, evolution and crime." Paper presented to the 39th Annual Meeting of the American Society of Criminology, Montreal, November 11–14.

———. 1988. "Race differences in behaviour: A review and evolutionary analysis." *Personality and Individual Differences* 9: 1009–24.

———. 1989. "Race differences in sexuality and their correlates: Another look at physiological models." *Journal of Research in Personality* 23: 35–54.

Silberman, Charles. 1978. *Criminal Violence, Criminal Justice.* New York: Vintage.

The Toronto Star. 1989. February 17: 20.

United States Department of Justice. 1983. *Sourcebook of Criminal Justice Statistics.* Washington, DC: Bureau of Justice Statistics.

———. 1986. *Criminal Victimization in the United States.* Washington, DC: Bureau of Justice Statistics.

———. 1987. *Sourcebook of Criminal Justice Statistics.* Washington, DC: Bureau of Justice Statistics.

———. 1989. *Sourcebook of Criminal Justice Statistics.* Washington, DC: Bureau of Justice Statistics.

Wallerstein, James S. and Clement J. Wyle. 1947. "Our law-abiding lawbreakers." *Probation* 25: 107–12.

Williams, Jay and Martin Gold. 1972. "From delinquent behaviour to official delinquency." *Social Problems* 20: 209–29.

Wolfgang, Marvin. 1958. *Patterns in Criminal Homicide.* Philadelphia: University of Pennsylvania Press.

——— and Bernard Cohen. 1970. *Crime and Race: Conceptions and Misconceptions.* New York: Institute of Human Relations Press.

———. 1981. "Crime and race: The victims of crime." In Burt Galaway and Joe Hudson, eds., *Perspectives on Crime Victims.* St. Louis: C.V. Mosby.

——— and Franco Ferracuti. 1982. *The Subculture of Violence.* Beverly Hills: Sage.

Zuckerman, Marvin and Nathan Brody. 1989. "Oysters, rabbits and people: A critique of 'race differences in behaviour' by J. P. Rushton." *Personality and Individual Differences* 9: 1025–33.

PART 6

GLOBAL DEVELOPMENT AND THE ENVIRONMENT

The industrial revolution began in Britain about 230 years ago. Nature seemed exploitable without limit, a thing to be subdued and dominated in the name of economic progress and human development. In the last few decades, however, circumstances have forced a growing number of people to recognize that industrial-era attitudes toward nature are not just naive, but arrogant and foolhardy. For example:

- Since the industrial revolution, humans have been using increasing quantities of fossil fuels (coal, oil, gasoline, etc.). When burned, they release carbon dioxide into the atmosphere. The accumulation of carbon dioxide allows more solar radiation to enter the atmosphere and less solar radiation to escape. The result of this "greenhouse effect" is global warming and potentially catastrophic climactic change, including the partial melting of the polar ice caps and the flooding of heavily populated coastal regions.
- Various gaseous compounds widely used in industry and by consumers are burning a hole in the atmosphere's ozone layer. Ozone is a form of oxygen that blocks ultraviolet radiation from the sun. Let more ultraviolet radiation reach ground level and, as we are now witnessing, rates of skin cancer increase.
- The world's forests help to clean the air since photosynthesis uses up carbon dioxide and produces oxygen. The tropical rain forests contain a large and variegated plant life that is an important source of new drugs. The rain forests also produce moisture, which is carried by wind currents to other parts of the globe and falls as rain. Despite the enormously important role the forests play, however, they are being rapidly depleted as a result of strip mining, the construction of pulp and paper mills and hydro-electric projects, and the deforestation of land by farmers and cattle grazers.
- Fleets of trawlers belonging to the highly industrialized countries have been equipped with sonar to help locate large concentrations of fish. Some of these ships use fine mesh nets to increase their catch. As a result, fish stocks in some areas of the world, such as cod off the coast of Newfoundland, have been greatly depleted, devastating fishing communities and endangering one of the world's most important sources of protein.
- A wide range of toxic gases and liquids enters the environment as a result of industrial production, often with devastating consequences. For example, sulphur dioxide and other gases emitted by coal-burning power plants, pulp and paper mills, and motor vehicle exhaust help to form an acid in the atmosphere which rains down on the earth, destroying forests and lakes.

Canada is one of the world's big polluters. While the United States, Australia, Norway, and Iceland produce more carbon dioxide per capita than anyone else, Canada is in the second tier of greenhouse gas emitters along with Russia, Japan, and the Eastern European countries. Of the 60 states and provinces in the United States and Canada, Ontario ranks fourth (behind Ohio, Texas, and Pennsylvania) in its total release of industrial chemicals into the environment.

Exposure to environmental risk is not evenly distributed across the Canadian population. As Maude Barlow and Elizabeth May show in Chapter 26, for example, there is a disturbing pattern of **environmental racism** in the distribution of toxic waste in Canada. Toxic waste sites are more likely to be found near communities with a high proportion of Aboriginal and poor people. (In the United

States, Black and Hispanic people are more likely to live near toxic waste sites.) Barlow and May also show that the Canadian government has been slow to clean up toxic waste sites, partly because of political pressure from industry, partly because the free trade agreement with the United States has eroded some of Canada's capacity to act in this regard.

Environmental degradation is one of the major problems confronting humanity. A related problem of equal magnitude is rapid population growth, which puts enormous strains on the earth's resources. From a demographic point of view, the less industrialized countries are now in the position that Europe and North America were in 200 years ago. Their populations are growing rapidly because people are living longer yet women's birth rates remain high. As a result, by 2100 the less developed countries are expected to increase their share of world population to 86 percent of the total.

The U.S. Census Bureau expects the 6.6 billion inhabitants of the planet in 2007 to multiply to 9.2 billion by 2050. Yet demographers are pretty confident that world population will level off sometime between 2070 and 2100, reaching its peak at no more than 10.2 billion people. Two main factors are causing the rate of world population growth to fall: economic development and the emancipation of women. Agricultural societies need many children to help with farming but industrial societies require fewer children. Since many countries are industrializing, the rate of world population growth is falling apace. The second main factor responsible for this decline is the improving economic status and education of women. Once women enter the non-agricultural paid labour force, they quickly recognize the advantages of having few children. The birth rate plummets. In many less developed countries, that is just what is taking place.

In other less developed countries the position of women is not as satisfactory. This can be seen most clearly by examining the ratio of women to men (the **sex ratio**). In Canada in 2000, the sex ratio was about 1.02. That is, there were 102 women for every 100 men. This is a little on the low side for a highly developed country but still in the same ballpark. (The sex ratio for the United States was 1.03 and for Germany and Japan, 1.04). The "surplus" of women reflects the fact that men are more likely than women to be employed in health-threatening occupations, consume more cigarettes and alcohol, and engage in riskier and more violent behaviour, while women are the hardier sex biologically speaking.

In the world as a whole, the picture is reversed. There were just 98 women for every 100 men in 2000, while in India and China there were only 94 women for every 100 men. What accounts for this variation? According to Amartya Sen in Chapter 27, the sex ratio is low where women have less access to health services, medicine, and adequate nutrition than do men. In highly developed countries, women and men have approximately equal access to health services, medicine, and adequate nutrition, so there are about 103 women for every 100 men. By this standard, the world as a whole is "missing" about 5 women for every 100 men (since 103 − 98 = 5). This works out to about 100 million women missing in 2000 due to unequal access to resources of the most basic sort. Although there are big variations within regions, which Sen discusses, Asia and North Africa are the regions that suffer most from a deficit of women due to high levels of gender inequality.[1]

Sen has argued elsewhere that human development is really about increasing our freedom—freedom from want and oppression, freedom of expression and assembly, freedom to work and to elect governments, and so on. From this point of view, gender inequality is a measure of lack of freedom insofar as it restricts the access of women to resources that would make them as free as men are. In *Human Development Report 2002,* a section of which is reprinted here as Chapter 28, United Nations researchers adopt Sen's argument. They document trends around the world in democratization, the protection of human rights, freedom of the press, women's education, poverty, environmental protection, and other indicators of human development. While they find progress in many areas, they find grotesque disparities in others. They then outline a set of achievable development targets for the year 2015.

Many of the UN's development targets require sacrifice and cooperation on the part of the world's rich countries. Substantially increasing foreign aid to less developed countries, monitoring aid to ensure it is used effectively, cancelling the debt of the poorest countries, removing tariffs to increase the import of agricultural goods from less developed countries, reducing the emission of greenhouse gases and other toxic substances, allowing developing countries to override patents and manufacture generic drugs for the fight against HIV/AIDS—these and other actions outlined by the UN could do much to promote human development worldwide. They would also cost taxpayers in Canada and other rich countries a lot of money.

It is unclear whether we are willing to pay. One thing is, however, crystal clear. If people continue to think of themselves only as members of a particular nation, class, or race, and not as part of humanity as a whole, the UN recommendations are likely to fall on deaf ears. In that event, many citizens of the privileged countries will believe that it is in their self-interest to cut aid to the less industrialized countries, to use just as many scarce resources as they wish to and can afford, and to object to the imposition of high environmental taxes on fossil fuels. They will be blind to the fact that such a narrow definition of self-interest may devastate humanity.

Much now seems to depend on whether we will be able to think and act as members of a single human group whose members share a common interest in survival. If we fail to take such a global view, if we insist instead on fighting to protect our narrow group privileges rather than humanity's general interest, we may not go the way of the dinosaurs, but future generations will likely suffer an existence that is nastier, more brutish, and shorter than that which we now enjoy.

GLOSSARY

Environmental racism is the unequal distribution of environmental risk by race.
The **sex ratio** is the ratio of women to men in a society.

CRITICAL THINKING QUESTIONS

1. On what grounds do Barlow and May contend that Canada practices environmental racism?
2. Explain what Sen means when he writes that 100 million women are missing.
3. Sen argues that purely cultural and purely economic arguments fail to explain variations in the sex ratio worldwide. Explain his reasoning.
4. How does the UN define human development? Do you think the UN development targets for 2015 are politically achievable? Why or why not?

ANNOTATED BIBLIOGRAPHY

Barber, Benjamin R. *Jihad vs. McWorld: How Globalism and Tribalism Are Reshaping the World.* New York: Ballantine, 1996. The central conflict of our times is incisively analyzed in this heralded work.

Halweil, Brian, and Lisa Mastny. *State of the World 2006.* New York. W.W. Norton, 2006. In this definitive and widely acclaimed annual, the authors give up-to-the-minute details on the world's environmental crisis and its political, economic, and social ramifications.

Hobsbawm, Eric. *Age of Extremes: The Short Twentieth Century, 1914–1991.* London: Abacus, 1994. It's long, it's opinionated, and it's a masterpiece by one of the world's greatest historians. Magnificently expands one's understanding of global twentieth-century development.

NOTE

1. My sex ratios differ from Sen's because his data are from the mid-1980s. Note, however, that the number of "missing women" remained constant at about 100 million between 1985 and 2000 despite a nearly 25 percent increase in world population. The number of missing women did not increase because the sex ratio in the highly developed countries fell while the sex ratio in the less developed countries rose. The latter trend reflects an improvement in women's relative position in society while the former trend results from a disproportionately large number of men ceasing health-threatening practices, such as working in dangerous industries and smoking tobacco.

Chapter 26

Industrial Pollution in Canada

MAUDE BARLOW AND ELIZABETH MAY

We have the arsenic, we have the naphthalene, we have the lead.
The ground is poison, the air turns your lungs raw, now there is
orange goo oozing across the cellar.
Welcome to Sydney.
— Debbie Ouellette, Frederick Street resident

Spring 1998 was unusually warm. Juanita McKenzie had driven home from work one balmy evening and remembers how pleasant it was after a harsh winter to shed her heavy winter wools for a light spring coat. She pulled up in front of her Frederick Street home in Sydney, Nova Scotia, and stepped out of the car. Across the street, she saw a scene out of a grade B science fiction movie. Behind her neighbour Debbie Ouellette's house, two men, dressed in sealed white E.T.-type environmental hazard suits, complete with breathing apparatus, were posting a sign that read Human Health Hazard. Juanita McKenzie looked down at her cotton shirt and pants and asked herself, "Am I underdressed?"

For months, Juanita, Debbie, and their families had been sick with every kind of ailment they could imagine and some they couldn't. Kidney infections, nosebleeds, nausea, diarrhea, headaches, tingling joints, ear infections, bloody stools, bloody urine, and severe coughs were sweeping through the families that lived in the 17 homes of Frederick Street. All the dogs had died, one after it had literally glowed in the dark. Deformed mice, with batlike heads and kangaroo-like feet, had appeared. Lilacs and roses had bloomed pitch black and then disintegrated. One day in early May, when Debbie Ouellette was cleaning up her backyard, she noticed a bright yellow goo seeping out of the embankment directly behind her house and fluorescent orange chemicals lighting up the creek that runs through her property. Juanita and Debbie were terrified.

Perhaps, they now think, they shouldn't have been surprised. Residents of Frederick and nearby Tupper streets, and Lingan Road as well, had been dying of cancer in disproportionate numbers for years. Cancer was their uninvited, dreaded and constant companion.

For their homes border the worst toxic site in Canada and arguably the worst in North America. Behind Debbie Ouellette's house is a 3-metre-high chain-link fence surrounding the 50-hectare heavily contaminated coke ovens site that drains to the infamous Sydney tar ponds, the toxic legacy of 100 years of steel-making. The coke ovens site, polluted to depths of 24 metres, contains uncalculated amounts of deadly PAHs (polycyclic aromatic hydrocarbons, the largest group of cancer-causing chemicals in the world) and heavy toxic metals. The estuary contains 700 000 tons of toxic sludge, a witch's brew of carcinogenic chemicals 35 times worse than New York's infamous Love Canal, Hooker Chemical's abandoned toxic site upon which a housing subdivision was built. For years, the residents of Frederick Street lived with their fears and the unconfirmed risks to their health.

But suddenly everything seemed immeasurably worse. When Environment Canada officials confirmed that the backyard soil and brook running behind the homes contained arsenic and other deadly chemicals in concentrations many times over the allowable limit, the women knew that they and their children were in mortal danger. "My heart hit the floor," says Juanita.

ENVIRONMENTAL RACISM

When we look more closely at pollution of neighbourhoods in Canada and the United States a common theme emerges. Deadly toxic waste sites are more likely to be found near First Nations communities, or near non–First Nations communities of poorer people, people of colour, and politically marginalized people. This phenomenon has been given a name: "environmental racism."

In the United States, the Environmental Protection Agency has created a large environmental justice program to address the problem. The statistics are overwhelming: more poor people, aboriginals, and people of colour have their health compromised by pollution than wealthier, white communities. Sydney residents are right in believing that the conditions in which they live would not be tolerated in Toronto or Vancouver. There is no mystery about this reality—communities like Rosedale in Toronto, Rockcliffe Park in Ottawa, Westmount in Montreal, or Shaughnessy in Vancouver are simply not threatened with dump sites.

First Nations communities are more exposed to environmental risk than other Canadians. The Lubicon First Nation in Alberta experienced dramatic increases in illness since their reserves were surrounded with sour gas wells. Within a two-year period in the early 1980s, over 400 oil wells were drilled within a 24-kilometre radius of the Lubicon village of Little Buffalo. UNOCAL, a California-based oil and gas company, built a

sour gas battery plant within 5 kilometres of the same community. Sour gas is exactly what it smells like, and the rotten-egg smell of hydrogen sulphide emissions is posing health problems for the Lubicon.

Their health is also compromised by logging. As traditional sources of food in the bush are no longer available, the Lubicon are forced to rely on store-bought food. The rates of diabetes have soared, as have suicides and other social problems. What was once a healthy, self-sustaining community has been devastated. Currently, 95 percent of the population is on welfare, while 35 percent have health problems, ranging from tuberculosis to respiratory problems to cancer—at rates that exceed the national average.[1] Oil and gas development was rushed through approval processes before air emissions regulations could catch up.

In the 1940s, when the Inuit men of Deline in the Northwest Territories were recruited to mine uranium, they were never told that it was destined for nuclear weapons. When the bomb was dropped on Hiroshima, they never dreamt that they had unknowingly played a part. They were also never warned of any danger in carrying uranium out of the mine in sacks on their backs. As early as 1931, the government knew the dangers of the ore that the Inuit called "money rock." The men of Deline were carelessly, even criminally, exposed to excessive radiation from the uranium ore. The environment around them was also heavily contaminated. Nearly 2 million tons of radioactive tailings were dumped into Great Bear Lake.

As the men died, survivors began to ask questions. The town of Deline, now known as the "Village of the Widows," is finally closer to answers—if no closer to justice. A federal Crown corporation knowingly allowed unprotected workers to be massively exposed to radioactive materials. The lake is still full of the 1.7 million tons of uranium waste dumped there. Survivors are demanding a health study, cleanup and compensation. An apology would also be in order, but so far it is the Inuit who have apologized. A delegation from Deline travelled to Hiroshima for commemorative ceremonies at the fiftieth anniversary of the bombing, August 6, 1995. They offered their heartfelt apologies for the part they unwittingly played in the annihilation of the city. Japanese citizens learned for the first time that the men who mined the uranium that killed hundreds of thousands had themselves paid with their lives.

Throughout the North, toxic chemicals have also affected the Inuit. Levels of exposure and accumulation of persistent toxic chemicals are at their worst in Inuit communities. The patterns of atmospheric cycling have made the North a dumping ground for industrial chemicals that were never used there. The Inuit diet is primarily from the wildlife of the North. The chemicals bio-accumulate, delivering a higher level of toxic concentration to each level up the food chain. As a result, the breastmilk of Inuit mothers is ten times as contaminated as that of southern Canadian women.

MAPPING THE HOT SPOTS

"The legacy of 100 years of steelmaking" is the common phrase to describe the toxic mess known as the tar ponds and coke ovens in Sydney. With that description comes a subtle and misleading message that such disasters are historical—a thing of the past.

Sydney residents are still living with the ongoing health threat of the contamination, and the surrounding environment is still more polluted by government failure to clean up the tar ponds. Worse, the nature of government decision-making suggests that such disasters are not merely products of a time when we did not realize the consequences of industrialization. Instead, they reveal today's negligence and indifference. Despite a generation raised since the birth of the environmental movement and the creation of governmental departments charged with protecting the biosphere, Canada still lacks basic tools to protect human health and the environment and is allowing trade deals to undermine the tools we do have.

At the provincial and federal level, every environment department, whether federal or provincial, has seen its budget slashed by at least one-third in the last decade. Meanwhile, more responsibilities, including those for toxic waste sites, are being downloaded from federal to provincial responsibility.

Many communities across Canada have toxic waste sites, yet Environment Canada does not even attempt to maintain a list of such sites. From 1989 to 1995, a preliminary list was assembled but, before it could be organized into a proper inventory, budget cuts shut down the program. Why bother collecting the information when, unlike the United States, Canada has no national program for cleanup? The federal government has not even cleaned up those sites that were created by government itself, much less by its myriad of Crown corporations, such as those in the nuclear industry.

At best, there are estimates. The federal public accounts for 1999, tabled in the House of Commons in the fall of 1999, estimated the extent of liability of both government and corporations for contaminated sites at $30 billion.[2] There are an estimated 10 000 toxic sites across Canada—half of them on federal land.[3] The worst federal polluter has been the Department of National Defence, as well as former U.S. bases under DND responsibility. The Distant Early Warning System (DEW) line in Canada's North is dotted with toxic sites. DND sites are contaminated with fuel tanks, lead bullets, heavy metals and PCBs. In October 1999, Environment Minister David Anderson announced intentions to develop a plan to deal with contaminated sites, but only on federal lands.[4]

When there is a plan, much progress occurs. While it is a long way from being fully implemented, the 1987 Great Lakes Water Quality Agreement did result in significant cleanup efforts. The goals of the agreement were ambitious and stated in clear, unequivocal language. The agreement affirmed the commitment of the governments of Canada and the United

States, as well as the governments of Ontario and certain U.S. states, to swimmable beaches, edible fish, and drinkable water. Sadly, the sludge on the floor of our largest freshwater lakes will remain contaminated with PCBs and other persistent bio-accumulative toxic substances for a long time. Scientists fear that disturbing them in a cleanup could worsen the problem.

Another steel town, Hamilton, Ontario, has seen millions of dollars in Canada and U.S. funding spent on cleanup. Hamilton Harbour was extensively contaminated but it was made a priority under the Great Lakes Water Quality Agreement. Collins Bay within the harbour has been sufficiently remediated to be removed from the list of areas of concern. But, even though substantial progress has been made, the area still has many toxic hot spots. Randle Reef in Hamilton Harbour was badly polluted by Stelco, and the sediment is highly contaminated, primarily with PAHs. The cleanup of Randle Reef has yet to begin.

WHO PROTECTS PUBLIC HEALTH AND THE ENVIRONMENT?

The Canadian Environmental Protection Act (CEPA) is the most important piece of legislation in Canada for the regulation of toxic chemicals. It is administered jointly by the ministries of environment and health and operates on a chemical-by-chemical basis.

Between the spring and fall of 1999, the Prime Minister's Office forced the passage of amendments that weakened and redrafted CEPA to satisfy the industry lobby. Originally passed in 1988, the act cobbled together various bits, such as the Ocean Dumping Act, pre-existing regulations to control nutrients in water and, its primary basis, the Commercial Chemicals Act. From the very beginning it failed to live up to its name—excluding large classes of toxic substances of concern to Canadians. If a chemical is so toxic that its primary purpose is to kill things, then CEPA only operated if the chemicals were left lying around. As long as the chemicals were being widely dispersed over the environment, they fell under the Pest Control Products Act. If the toxic material also happened to be radioactive, CEPA would not apply.

Still, CEPA did promise comprehensive management of regulated substances—from "cradle to grave" as the press release at the time of passage touted. The problem is that studying and listing toxic chemicals, one substance at a time, is a long and difficult process. The deficiencies in Canada's toxic chemical management were set out in the 1999 report of the Commissioner for Environment and Sustainable Development, Brian Emmett. In his view, the system was so flawed that the health of Canadians was at risk. Of the 23 000 toxic substances in Canada, only 31 have been subjected to a conclusive review process. The Priority Substances List, which was intended to fast-track the operation of CEPA, has been an exercise in slow motion.

Commissioner Emmett's report also highlighted the lack of information-sharing between departments as was evident in the [Sydney] tar ponds disaster. The shared role of environment and health ministers should have worked to integrate our life support systems—the air we breathe, the water we drink, the food we eat—with our state of health. It did not. Instead, unsafe chemicals have remained in use while health and environment bureaucrats engage in turf warfare.

The only good news in the last ten years has come from the Supreme Court of Canada. It reconfirmed the importance of the federal role in protecting public health and the environment from poisonous substances.

After heroic efforts by the House of Commons environment committee to improve the act through its mandatory five-year review, the industry lobby went to war against the committee. It was the worst, most protracted and unpleasant parliamentary process of any bill in memory.

When the all-party committee presented its report, the chemical and aluminum industries used every weapon in their arsenal to gut the bill. The CEO of Alcan Aluminium Ltd., Jacques Bougie, wrote to Prime Minister Chrétien, warning him that if the bill was enacted into law as written, "it could force the closure of all aluminum smelters in Canada."[5] It was not necessary for Mr. Bougie to remind Mr. Chrétien that one of the threatened smelters was in the prime minister's Shawinigan riding. The source of Bougie's concern was that the bill might be used to regulate PAHs. Already listed on the toxic substances list, PAHs have been under a special review within CEPA for the last five years to determine the appropriate approach to regulation. The multi-stakeholder advisory committee includes industry, of course, and consensus has not been possible.

Some of the very same poisons that poured out of the coke ovens are also emitted from aluminum smelters. Benzopyrene turns up in the St. Lawrence downstream from smelters, and according to Alcan's vice-president, "There is no smelting technology that does not emit a detectable, almost negligible, level of PAHs."[6] Thus, when beluga whales wash up dead in the St. Lawrence River, their flesh must be treated as hazardous waste.

The industry focused on CEPA's new goal of the "virtual elimination" of certain inherently toxic and bio-accumulative chemicals, deciding that the concept had to be rejected. Such lobbying was not new. In response to industry pressure a year before, Environment Canada staff had prepared an analysis of wording changes demanded by the aluminum industry. The memo noted that the language demanded by industry would "create an internal contradiction that would make virtual elimination impossible." Yet the bill that was brought before the House for passage had nearly identical language to that rejected a year before as unworkable.

The result was predictable. Key sections of CEPA were made unintelligible. The drafting was incomprehensible. It moved tentatively towards the possibility of virtual elimination, but failed to adopt a goal to achieve it. The industry also demanded that the precautionary principle, which requires that actions to protect public health and the environment not await 100 percent proof when caution would require action, also be gutted. The bill sent to the House was amended to require that actions of a precautionary nature only be allowed when "cost-effective." Nothing in the new "improved" CEPA creates an imperative to clean up toxic waste sites—or even to catalogue them.

CEPA was so badly damaged by the prime ministerial cave-in to industry that a most extraordinary parliamentary rebellion took place. The three members of parliament within the governing Liberal Party, those most knowledgeable about the bill, voted against it. Charles Caccia, a former minister of the environment under Pierre Trudeau, was chair of the House of Commons committee that had dedicated years to the review and amendment process for CEPA. Joining him in rejecting the bill were Karen Kraft-Sloan, an Ontario MP and former parliamentary secretary to the environment minister who had also worked on the House Committee process, and Quebec's former environment minister, who was now a federal politician, Clifford Lincoln.

All three MPs believed the government had so emasculated the bill that it was now worse than the version of the bill passed in 1988. Efforts focused on the Senate to improve the bill, with progressive positions adopted by Tory senator Mira Spivak and committee chair Ron Ghitter. But the Prime Minister's Office and the Senate Liberal leader pushed all Liberal senators hard to approve the bill without changes. The lack of enthusiasm for the task was evidenced in a report that accompanied the bill to the Senate floor. The Liberal majority of the Senate committee urged that upon passage, the bill should be subjected to an immediate review to deal with its failings.

TOXIC DUMPING

While corporate lobbyists successfully gut our legislative tools, the potential profits from toxic waste are eroding our standards. The economic benefits of becoming a toxic dumping ground are beginning to change Canada's reputation. We will accept PCBs for disposal and incineration in Canada. The United States will not. We are pushing hard for the right to be the long-term repository for highly radioactive plutonium, removed from the warheads of U.S. and U.S.S.R. missiles. The campaign originates not with the former Soviet Union or the United States, but within Canada from the massively subsidized Crown corporation, Atomic Energy of Canada, Limited (AECL), supported by this country's biggest booster of nuclear energy, Prime Minister Jean Chrétien. Expert analysis of the disposal methods for plutonium favours leaving the plutonium where it is, and then encasing it in glass—a process called vitrification. Vitrification wins on every point as the least expensive, and safest, from an environmental and security viewpoint. But Chrétien and AECL are desperate to establish a global trade in plutonium waste so that AECL will have a long-term contract for disposal.

The open door policy to hazardous waste is not restricted to federal agencies. Ontario's Harris government has drastically increased the importation of toxic waste to the province. From 1997 to 1999, the province had asked the federal environment department to accept all hazardous waste applications from U.S. companies wishing to dump materials in Ontario. The blanket approvals letter was recently revoked by the province's new environment minister, Tony Clement. Meanwhile, in the first six months of 1998, nearly 11 million tones of hazardous materials were shipped into Ontario from the United States.[7]

Industry analysts know why companies are prepared to ship materials hundreds of kilometres from the source to ultimate disposal in Canada—our regulations are lax, our costs are lower, and there is less chance of being sued or prosecuted.

TRADING AWAY ENVIRONMENTAL PROTECTION

The federal government continues to sign international trade agreements that prohibit all levels of Canadian government from passing legislation to protect the environment. The sad story of MMT shows just how much control the federal government has given away through such agreements.

In 1997, the federal government took the unusual step of banning a persistent neurotoxic substance used as an anti-knock agent in gasoline. The move was unusual because the government rarely bans a toxic chemical in Canada, tending instead to treat toxic chemicals as though they had constitutional rights—innocent until proven guilty. In fact, the banning of MMT was an appropriate use of the "precautionary principle." The science on the key ingredient in MMT, manganese, is well established. Manganese in occupational exposure can lead to a disease called "manganism" which closely resembles the tremors and nervous system breakdown in Parkinson's disease. Manganese exposure can cause a progressive deterioration of the brain. This condition is particularly dangerous for older people, leading to premature and accelerated aging of the brain.

MMT was introduced in the early 1970s as a gasoline additive by the same company that had manufactured and sold leaded gas, Ethyl Corporation of Richmond, Virginia. After decades of defending leaded gas as a safe product, Ethyl Corp. knew the jig was up. Leaded gas was on the way out, and the company wanted to protect its prime business as a manufacturer of gasoline additives. Ethyl Corp. began flogging MMT as a replacement for lead in gas.

The U.S. Government soon rejected registration of MMT. Canada, relying on the same data, decided it could be registered for use. Health Canada did note, however, that there were significant data gaps about how MMT might affect vulnerable groups, such as children, pregnant women, and the elderly.

By the 1990s, the automakers were complaining to the government about MMT. They said that it was gumming up the onboard diagnostic systems of cars, compromising the air pollution control devices. The Big Three car manufacturers became very concerned about the financial repercussions of violated warranties if MMT reduced the effectiveness of catalytic converters. Pressure to ban it was exerted on Environment Minister Sheila Copps. Environmental and health groups supported the ban, arguing that MMT not only increased air pollution, but could poison the brains of Canadians. Twenty years after registration, Health Canada had done nothing to deal with the "data gaps" around its health impacts.

Laboratory studies suggested that MMT could provoke increased aggression in animals, as well as create symptoms that could be described as attention deficit disorder if they occurred in humans. The experience with leaded gas had proven that if you wanted to introduce a toxic heavy metal into the blood and brains of children, then adding it to gasoline was a good delivery mechanism.

In the spring of 1997, MMT was finally banned in Canada. A decade earlier that would have been the end of the matter. But Ethyl Corp. did not accept the regulatory decision. Now it has recourse through the North American Free Trade Agreement (NAFTA) to challenge Canada's decision. In fact, under provisions of Chapter II of NAFTA, companies from one of the three NAFTA countries who lose profits based on a regulatory decision in one of the other countries can sue the government for damages. Thus, Ethyl Corp, as a U.S.-based company, was able to sue the government of Canada for banning its neurotoxic gasoline additive, claiming damages in the amount of $350 million (Canadian) for lost profits and damage to its reputation. The hearings would be completely private. A three-person arbitration panel would hear the arguments of the Canadian government and Ethyl Corp. No independent scientific briefings would be allowed by environmental or health groups.

Under NAFTA Chapter II it didn't really matter if the government had been right to ban MMT or not. The real issue was whether Ethyl Corp. had rights to profits "expropriated." As Ethyl Corp.'s Canadian lawyer Barry Appleton has said, it wouldn't matter if a substance was liquid plutonium destined for a child's breakfast cereal. If the government bans a product and a U.S.-based company loses profits, the company can claim damages under NAFTA.

In the summer of 1998, the government caved in. It withdrew the regulation removing MMT from use, paid Ethyl Corp. $19 million as compensation for its "trouble," and issued a public apology in which Christine Stewart, then minister of the environment, explained that the government had never had adequate grounds to ban MMT. A spokesperson for Ethyl said at the time, "It's a very happy day, a significant step for Ethyl Corp. and its business worldwide."

Within days of the MMT settlement, Barry Appleton filed a claim for another U.S.-based corporation, S.D. Myers of Ohio, a company in the business of hazardous waste. It wanted PCBs from Canada for disposal in its Ohio plant. Myers claimed damages from a nine-month-long ban against the export of PCBs to the U.S. from Canada, initiated by Sheila Copps, and upholding the principles of the Basel Convention on hazardous wastes. The ban was removed quickly under a NAFTA threat. Even though Sierra Club in the U.S. had successfully sued to prevent Canadian PCBs from entering the U.S., it was still possible for S.D. Myers to sue for damages on a moot point.

Other cases are piling up: from a company wanting to export water from B.C., from a wood product company claiming that Canada's forest export rules deprive it of access to forest products, and even from a Canadian company, Methanex, challenging a California ban on a carcinogenic gas additive, MTBE.

LESSONS UNLEARNED

Here, then, is the greatest tragedy of the Sydney tar ponds story. It would appear that the residents of Sydney, and especially the residents of Whitney Pier and Frederick Street, have suffered and fought in isolation and perhaps in vain. We appear not to have learned one thing from their ordeal. We continue to talk about the "trade-off" between jobs and the environment; jobs and health. The tar ponds saga should have taught us that such trade-offs are wrong economically, environmentally, and morally.

There are now several decades of documented proof of the deep harm done to humans, other species, and the earth by the noxious and toxic chemicals so cavalierly dumped into open waterways around the Sydney steel plant and at other poisoned sites right across Canada. Yet governments and many corporations continue to turn a blind eye to the clear and present danger these chemicals pose to the very future of humankind. In the end, our collective failure to learn from their suffering may be a greater offence to the courageous people of Sydney than the toxic site itself.

It is never too late to change our behaviour, our values, and our laws. But it is late in the day. The sun is setting on a chemical-safe world; Sydney, Nova Scotia, has sounded the alarm. Will we hear it in time?

NOTES

1. John Goddard, *Last Stand of the Lubicon Cree* (Vancouver: Douglas and McIntyre, 1992).
2. Jim Bronskill and James Baxter, "Government on the hook for billions," *Ottawa Citizen,* 27 October 1999.
3. Andrew Duffy, "Toxic waste cleanup list in the works: federal environment minister preparing national strategy," *Ottawa Citizen,* 12 October 1999.
4. Ibid.
5. Donna Jacobs, "How industry beat the Environmental Protection Act," *Ottawa Citizen,* 7 September 1999.
6. Ibid.
7. Martin Mittelstaedt, "Ontario to receive hazardous waste—Ottawa approved transfer of 473 000 tonnes of toxins from Michigan, papers show," *Globe and Mail,* 27 September 1999.

Chapter 27

More than 100 Million Women Are Missing

AMARTYA SEN

It is often said that women make up a majority of the world's population. They do not. This mistaken belief is based on generalizing from the contemporary situation in Europe and North America, where the ratio of women to men is typically around 1.05 or 1.06, or higher. In South Asia, West Asia, and China, the ratio of women to men can be as low as 0.94, or even lower, and it varies widely elsewhere in Asia, in Africa, and in Latin America. How can we understand and explain these differences, and react to them?

1.

At birth, boys outnumber girls everywhere in the world, by much the same proportion—there are around 105 or 106 male children for every 100 female children. Just why the biology of reproduction leads to this result remains a subject of debate. But after conception, biology seems on the whole to favor women. Considerable research has shown that if men and women receive similar nutritional and medical attention and general health care, women tend to live noticeably longer than men. Women seem to be, on the whole, more resistant to disease and in general hardier than men, an advantage they enjoy not only after they are forty years old but also at the beginning of life, especially during the months immediately following birth, and even in the womb. When given the same care as males, females tend to have better survival rates than males.[1]

Women outnumber men substantially in Europe, the U.S., and Japan, where, despite the persistence of various types of bias against women (men having distinct advantages in higher education, job specialization, and promotion to senior executive positions, for example), women suffer little discrimination in basic nutrition and health care. The greater number of women in these countries is partly the result of social and environmental differences that increase mortality among men, such as a higher likelihood that men will die from violence, for example, and from diseases related to smoking. But even after these are taken into account, the longer lifetimes enjoyed by women given similar care appear to relate to the biological advantages that women have over men in resisting disease. Whether the higher frequency of male births over female births has evolutionary links to this potentially greater survival rate of women is a question of some interest in itself. Women seem to have lower death rates than men at most ages whenever they get roughly similar treatment in matters of life and death.

The fate of women is quite different in most of Asia and North Africa. In these places the failure to give women medical care similar to what men get and to provide them with comparable food and social services results in fewer women surviving than would be the case if they had equal care. In India, for example, except in the period immediately following birth, the death rate is higher for women than for men fairly consistently in all age groups until the late thirties. This relates to higher rates of disease

Source: Sen, Amartya. "More than 100 Million Women Are Missing." *The New York Review*, December 20, 1990. pp. 61–66. Reprinted with permission from The New York Review of Books. Copyright © 1990 NYREV, Inc.

from which women suffer, and ultimately to the relative neglect of females, especially in health care and medical attention.[2] Similar neglect of women vis-à-vis men can be seen also in many other parts of the world. The result is a lower proportion of women than would be the case if they had equal care—in most of Asia and North Africa, and to a lesser extent Latin America.

This pattern is not uniform in all parts of the world, however. Sub-Saharan Africa, for example, ravaged as it is by extreme poverty, hunger, and famine, has a substantial excess rather than deficit of women, the ratio of women to men being around 1.02. The "third-world" in this matter is not a useful category, because it is so diverse. Even within Asia, which has the lowest proportion of women in the world, Southeast Asia and East Asia (apart from China) have a ratio of women to men that is slightly higher than one to one (around 1.01). Indeed, sharp diversities also exist within particular regions—sometimes even within a particular country. For example, the ratio of women to men in the Indian states of Punjab and Haryana, which happen to be among the country's richest, is a remarkably low 0.86, while the state of Kerala in southwestern India has a ratio higher than 1.03, similar to that in Europe, North America, and Japan.

To get an idea of the numbers of people involved in the different ratios of women to men, we can estimate the number of "missing women" in a country, say, China or India, by calculating the number of extra women who would have been in China or India if these countries had the same ratio of women to men as obtained in areas of the world in which they receive similar care. If we could expect equal populations of the two sexes, the low ratio of 0.94 women to men in South Asia, West Asia, and China would indicate a 6 percent deficit of women; but since, in countries where men and women receive similar care, the ratio is about 1.05, the real shortfall is about 11 percent. In China alone this amounts to 50 million "missing women," taking 1.05 as the benchmark ratio. When that number is added to those in South Asia, West Asia, and North

Africa, a great many more than 100 million women are "missing." These numbers tell us, quietly, a terrible story of inequality and neglect leading to the excess mortality of women.

2.

To account for the neglect of women, two simplistic explanations have often been presented or, more often, implicitly assumed. One view emphasizes the cultural contrasts between East and West (or between the Occident and the Orient), claiming that Western civilization is less sexist than Eastern. That women outnumber men in Western countries may appear to lend support to this Kipling-like generalization. (Kipling himself was not, of course, much bothered by concerns about sexism, and even made "the twain" meet in romantically masculine circumstances: "But there is neither East nor West, Border, nor Breed, nor Birth, / When two strong men stand face to face, tho' they come from the ends of the earth!") The other simple argument looks instead at stages of economic development, seeing the unequal nutrition and health care provided for women as a feature of underdevelopment, a characteristic of poor economies awaiting economic advancement.

There may be elements of truth in each of these explanations, but neither is very convincing as a general thesis. To some extent, the two simple explanations, in terms of "economic development" and "East-West" divisions, also tend to undermine each other. A combined cultural and economic analysis would seem to be necessary, and, I will argue, it would have to take note of many other social conditions in addition to the features identified in the simple aggregative theses.

To take the cultural view first, the East-West explanation is obviously flawed because experiences within the East and West diverge so sharply. Japan, for example, unlike most of Asia, has a ratio of women to men that is not very different from that in Europe or North America.

This might suggest, at least superficially, that real income and economic development do more to explain the bias against providing women with the conditions for survival than whether the society is Western or Oriental. In the censuses of 1899 and 1908, Japan had a clear and substantial deficit of women, but by 1940 the numbers of men and women were nearly equal, and in the postwar decades, as Japan became a rich and highly industrialized country, it moved firmly in the direction of a large surplus, rather than a deficit, of women. Some countries in East Asia and Southeast Asia also provide exceptions to the deficit of women: in Thailand and Indonesia, for example, women substantially outnumber men.

In its rudimentary, undiscriminating form, the East-West explanation also fails to take into account other characteristics of these societies. For example, the ratios of women to men in South Asia are among the lowest in the world (around 0.94 in India and Bangladesh, and 0.90 in Pakistan—the lowest ratio for any large country), but that region has been among the pioneers in electing women as top political leaders. Indeed, each of the four large South Asian countries—India, Pakistan, Bangladesh, and Sri Lanka—either has had a woman as the elected head of government (Sri Lanka, India, and Pakistan), or has had women leading the main opposition parties (as in Bangladesh).

It is, of course, true that these successes in South Asia have been achieved only by upper-class women, and that having a woman head of government has not, by itself, done much for women in general in these countries. However, the point here is only to question the tendency to see the contrast between East and West as simply based on more sexism or less. The large electoral successes of women in achieving high positions in government in South Asia indicate that the analysis has to be more complex.

It is, of course, also true that these women leaders reached their powerful positions with the help of dynastic connections—Indira Gandhi was the daughter of Jawaharlal Nehru, Benázir Bhutto the daughter of Zulfikar Bhutto, and so on. But it would be absurd to overlook—just on that ground—the significance of their rise to power through popular mandate. Dynastic connections are not new in politics and are pervasive features of political succession in many countries. That Indira Gandhi derived her political strength partly from her father's position is not in itself more significant than the fact that Rajiv Gandhi's political credibility derived largely from his mother's political eminence, or the fact (perhaps less well known) that Indira Gandhi's father—the great Jawaharlal Nehru—initially rose to prominence as the son of Motilal Nehru, who had been president of the Congress party. The dynastic aspects of South Asian politics have certainly helped women to come to power through electoral support, but it is still true that so far as winning elections is concerned, South Asia would seem to be some distance ahead of the United States and most European countries when it comes to discrimination according to gender.

In this context it is useful also to compare the ratios of women in American and Indian legislatures. In the U.S. House of Representatives the proportion of women is 6.4 percent, while in the present and last lower houses of the Indian Parliament, women's proportions have been respectively 5.3 and 7.9 percent. Only two of the 100 U.S. Senators are women, and this 2 percent ratio contrasts with more than 9 and 10 percent women respectively in the last and present "upper house," Rajya Sabha, in India. (In a different, but not altogether unrelated, sphere, I had a much higher proportion of tenured women colleagues when I was teaching at Delhi University than I now have at Harvard.) The cultural climate in different societies must have a clear relevance to differences between men and women—both in survival and in other ways as well—but it would be hopeless to see the divergences simply as a contrast between the sexist East and the unbiased West.

How good is the other (i.e., the purely economic) explanation for women's inequality? Certainly all the countries with large deficits of women are more or less poor, if we measure poverty by real incomes, and no sizable country with a high gross national product per head has such a deficit. There are reasons to expect a reduction of differential female mortality with economic progress. For example, the rate of maternal mortality at childbirth can be expected to decrease both with better hospital facilities and the reduction in birth rate that usually accompanies economic development.

However, in this simple form, an economic analysis does not explain very much, since many poor countries do not, in fact, have deficits of women. As was noted earlier, sub-Saharan Africa, poor and underdeveloped as it is, has a substantial excess of women. Southeast and East Asia (but not China) also differ from many other relatively poor countries in this respect, although to a lesser degree. Within India, as was noted earlier, Punjab and Haryana—among the richest and most economically advanced Indian states—have very low ratios of women to men (around 0.86), in contrast to the much poorer state of Kerala, where the ratio is greater than 1.03.

Indeed, economic development is quite often accompanied by a relative worsening in the rate of survival of women (even as life expectancy improves in absolute terms for both men and women). For example, in India the gap between the life expectancy of men and women has narrowed recently, but only after many decades when women's relative position deteriorated. There has been a steady decline in the ratio of women to men in the population, from more than 97 women to 100 men at the turn of the century (in 1901), to 93 women in 1971, and the ratio is only a little higher now. The deterioration in women's position results largely from their unequal sharing in the advantages of medical and social progress. Economic development does not invariably reduce women's disadvantages in mortality.

A significant proportional decline in the population of women occurred in China after the economic and social reforms introduced there in 1979. The Chinese Statistical Yearbooks show a steady decline in the already very low ratio of women to men in the population, from 94.32 in 1979 to 93.42 in 1985 and 1986. (It has risen since then, to 93.98 in 1989—still lower than what it was in 1979.) Life expectancy was significantly higher for females than for males until the economic reforms, but seems to have fallen behind since then.[3] Of course, the years following the reforms were also years of great economic growth and, in many ways, of social progress, yet women's relative prospects for survival deteriorated. These and other cases show that rapid economic development may go hand in hand with worsening relative mortality of women.

3.

Despite their superficial plausibility, neither the alleged contrast between "East" and "West," nor the simple hypothesis of female deprivation as a characteristic of economic "underdevelopment" gives us anything like an adequate understanding of the geography of female deprivation in social well-being and survival. We have to examine the complex ways in which economic, social, and cultural factors can influence the regional differences.

It is certainly true that, for example, the status and power of women in the family differ greatly from one region to another, and there are good reasons to expect that these social features would be related to the economic role and independence of women. For example, employment outside the home and owning assets can both be important for women's economic independence and power; and these factors may have far-reaching effects on the divisions of benefits and chores within the family and can greatly influence what are implicitly accepted as women's "entitlements."

Indeed, men and women have both interests in common and conflicting interests that affect family decisions; and it is possible to see decision making in the family taking the form of the pursuit of cooperation in which solutions for the conflicting aspects of family life are implicitly agreed on. Such "cooperative conflicts" are a general feature of many group relations, and an analysis of cooperative conflicts can provide a useful way of understanding the influences that affect the "deal" that women get in the division of benefits within the family. There are gains to be made by men and women through following implicitly agreed-on patterns of behavior; but there are many possible agreements—some more favorable to one party than others. The choice of one such cooperative arrangement from among the range of possibilities leads to a particular distribution of joint benefits. (Elsewhere, I have tried to analyze the general nature of "cooperative conflicts" and the application of the analysis of such conflicts to family economics.[4])

Conflicts in family life are typically resolved through implicitly agreed-on patterns of behavior that may or may not be particularly egalitarian. The very nature of family living—sharing a home and experiences—requires that the elements of conflict must not be explicitly emphasized (giving persistent attention to conflicts will usually be seen as aberrant behavior); and sometimes the deprived woman would not even have a clear idea of the extent of her relative deprivation. Similarly, the perception of who is doing "productive" work, who is "contributing" how much to the family's prosperity, can be very influential, even though the underlying principles regarding how "contributions" or "productivity" are to be assessed may be rarely discussed explicitly. These issues of social perception are, I believe, of pervasive importance in gender inequality, even in the richer countries, but they can have a particularly powerful influence in sustaining female deprivation in many of the poorer countries.[5]

The division of a family's joint benefits is likely to be less unfavorable to women if (1) they can earn an outside income; (2) their work is recognized as productive (this is easier to achieve with work done outside the home); (3) they own some economic resources and have some rights to fall back on; and (4) there is a clear-headed understanding of the ways in which women are deprived and a recognition of the possibilities of changing this situation. This last category can be much influenced by education for women and by participatory political action.

Considerable empirical evidence, mostly studies of particular localities, suggests that what is usually defined as "gainful" employment (i.e., working outside the home for a wage, or in such "productive" occupations as farming), as opposed to unpaid and unhonored housework—no matter how demanding—can substantially enhance the deal that women get.[6] Indeed, "gainful" employment of women can make the solution of "cooperative conflicts" less unfavorable to women in many ways. First, outside employment for wages can provide women with an income to which they have easier access, and it can also serve as a means of making a living on which women can rely, making them less vulnerable. Second, the social respect that is associated with being a "bread winner" (and a "productive" contributor to the family's joint prosperity) can improve women's status and standing in the family, and may influence the prevailing cultural traditions regarding who gets what in the division of joint benefits. Third, when outside employment takes the form of jobs with some security and legal protection, the corresponding rights that women get can make their economic position much less vulnerable and precarious. Fourth, working outside the home also provides experience of the outside world, and this can be socially important in improving women's position within the family. In this respect outside work may be "educational" as well.

These factors may not only improve the "deal" women get in the family, they can also counter the relative neglect of girls as they grow up. Boys are preferred in many countries because they are expected to provide more economic security for their parents in old age; but the force of this bias can be weakened if women as well as men can regularly work at paid jobs. Moreover, if the status of women does in general rise and women's contributions become more recognized, female children may receive more attention. Similarly, the exposure of women to the world through work outside the home can weaken, through its educational effect, the hold of traditional beliefs and behavior.

In comparing different regions of Asia and Africa, if we try to relate the relative survival prospects of women to the "gainful employment" of both sexes—i.e., work outside the home, possibly for a wage—we do find a strong association. If the different regions of Asia and Africa (with the exception of China) are ranked according to the proportion of women in so-called gainful employment relative to the proportion of men in such employment, we get the following ranking, in descending order.[7]

1. Sub-Saharan Africa
2. Southeast and Eastern Asia
3. Western Asia
4. Southern Asia
5. Northern Africa

Ranking the ratios of life expectancy of females to those of males produces a remarkably similar ordering:

1. Sub-Saharan Africa
2. Southeast and Eastern Asia
3. Western Asia
4. Northern Africa
5. Southern Asia

That the two rankings are much the same, except for a switch between the two lowest-ranking regions (lowest in terms of both indicators), suggests a link between employment and survival prospects. In addition to the overall correspondence between the two rankings, the particular contrasts between sub-Saharan Africa and North Africa, and that between Southern (and Western) Asia and Southeast (and Eastern) Asia are suggestive distinctions *within* Africa and Asia respectively, linking women's gainful employment and survival prospects.

It is, of course, possible that what we are seeing here is not a demonstration that gainful employment causes better survival prospects but the influence of some other factor correlated with each. In fact, on the basis of such broad relations, it is very hard to draw any firm conclusion; but evidence of similar relations can be found also in other comparisons.[8] For example, Punjab, the richest Indian state, has the lowest ratio of women to men (0.86) in India; it also has the lowest ratio of women in "gainful" employment compared to men. The influence of outside employment on women's well-being has also been documented in a number of studies of specific communities in different parts of the world.[9]

4.

The case of China deserves particular attention. It is a country with a traditional bias against women, but after the revolution the Chinese leaders did pay considerable attention to reducing inequality between men and women.[10] This was helped both by a general expansion of basic health and medical services accessible to all and by the increase in women's gainful employment, along with greater social recognition of the importance of women in the economy and the society.

There has been a remarkable general expansion of longevity, and despite the temporary setback during the terrible famines of 1958–1961 (following the disastrous failure of the so-called Great Leap Forward), the Chinese life expectancy at birth increased from the low forties around 1950 to the high sixties by the time the economic reforms were introduced in 1979. The sharp reduction in general mortality (including female mortality) is all the more remarkable in view of the fact that it took place despite deep economic problems in the form of widespread industrial inefficiency, a rather stagnant agriculture, and relatively little increase in output per head. Female death rates declined sharply—both as a part of a general mortality reduction and also relatively, vis-à-vis male mortality. Women's life expectancy at birth overtook that of men— itself much enhanced—and was significantly ahead at the time the economic and social reforms were introduced in 1979.

Those reforms immediately increased the rate of economic growth and broke the agricultural stagnation. The official figures suggest a doubling of agricultural output between 1979 and 1986—a remarkable achievement even if some elements of exaggeration are eliminated from these figures. But at the same time, the official figures also record an *increase* in the general mortality rates after the reforms, with a consistently higher death rate than what China had achieved by 1979. There seems to be also a worsening of the relative survival of women, including a decline, discussed earlier, of the ratio of women to men in the population, which went down from 94.3 in 1979 to 93.4 in 1985 and 1986. There are problems in interpreting the available data and difficulties in arriving at firm conclusions, but the view that women's life expectancy has again become lower than that of men has gained support. For example, the World Bank's most recent *World Development Report* suggests a life expectancy of sixty-nine years for men and sixty-six years for women (even though the confounded nature of the subject is well reflected by the fact that the same *Report* also suggests an average life expectancy of seventy years for men and women put together).[11]

Why have women's survival prospects in China deteriorated, especially in relative terms, since 1979? Several experts have noted that recently Chinese leaders have tended, on the whole, to reduce the emphasis on equality for women; it is no longer much discussed, and indeed, as the sociologist Margery Wolf puts it, it is a case of a "revolution postponed."[12] But this fact, while important, does not explain why the relative survival prospects of women would have so deteriorated during the early years of the reforms, just at the time when there was a rapid expansion of overall economic prosperity.

The compulsory measures to control the size of families which were introduced in 1979 may have been an important factor. In some parts of the country the authorities insisted on the "one-child family." This restriction, given the strong preference for boys in China, led to a neglect of girls that was often severe. Some evidence exists of female infanticide. In the early years after the reforms, infant mortality for girls appeared to increase considerably. Some estimates had suggested that the rate of female infant mortality rose from 37.7 per thousand in 1978 to 67.2 per thousand in 1984.[13] Even if this seems exaggerated in the light of later data, the survival prospects of female children clearly have been unfavorably affected by restrictions on the size of the family. Later legal concessions (including the permission to have a second child if the first one is a girl) reflect some official recognition of these problems.

A second factor relevant to the survival problems of Chinese women is the general crisis in health services since the economic reforms. As the agricultural production brigades and collectives, which had traditionally provided much of the funding for China's extensive rural health programs, were dismantled, they were replaced by the so-called "responsibility system," in which agriculture was centered in the family. Agricultural production improved, but cutbacks in communal facilities placed severe financial restrictions on China's extensive rural medical services. Communal agriculture may not have done much for agricultural production as such, but it had been a main source of support for China's innovative and extensive rural medical services. So far as gender is concerned, the effects of the reduced scope of these services are officially neutral, but in view of the pro-male bias in Chinese rural society, the cutback in medical services would have had a particularly severe impact on women and female children. (It is also the pro-male bias in the general culture that made the one-child policy, which too is neutral in form, unfavorable to female children in terms of its actual impact.)

Third, the "responsibility system" arguably has reduced women's involvement in recognized gainful employment in agriculture. In the new system's more traditional arrangement of work responsibilities, women's work in the household economy may again suffer from the lack of recognition that typically affects household work throughout the world.[14] The impact of this change on the status of women within the household may be negative, for the reasons previously described. Expanded employment opportunities for women outside agriculture in some regions may at least partially balance this effect. But the weakening of social security arrangements since the reforms would also have made old age more precarious, and since such insecurity is one of the persistent motives for families' preferring boys over girls, this change too can be contributing to the worsening of care for female children.[15]

5.

Analyses based on simple conflicts between East and West or on "underdevelopment" clearly do not take us very far. The variables that appear important—for example, female employment or female literacy—combine both economic and cultural effects. To ascribe importance to the influence of gainful employment on women's prospects for survival may superficially look like another attempt at a simple economic explanation, but it would be a mistake to see it this way. The deeper question is why such outside employment is more prevalent in, say, sub-Saharan Africa than in North Africa, or in Southeast and Eastern Asia than in Western and Southern Asia. Here the cultural, including religious, backgrounds of the respective regions are surely important. Economic causes for women's deprivation have to be integrated with other—social and cultural—factors to give depth to the explanation.

Of course, gainful employment is not the only factor affecting women's chances of survival. Women's education and their economic rights—including property rights—may be crucial variables as well.[16] Consider the state of Kerala in India, which I mentioned earlier. It does not have a deficit of women—its ratio of women to men of more than 1.03 is closer to that of Europe (1.05) than those of China, West Asia, and India as a whole (0.94). The life expectancy of women at birth in Kerala, which had already reached sixty-eight years by the time of the last census in 1981 (and is estimated to be seventy-two years now), is considerably higher than men's sixty-four years at that time (and sixty-seven now). While women are generally able to find "gainful employment" in Kerala—certainly much more so than in Punjab—the state is not exceptional in this regard. What is exceptional is Kerala's remarkably high literacy rate; not only is it much higher than elsewhere in India, it is also substantially higher than in China, especially for women.

Kerala's experience of state-funded expansion of basic education, which has been consolidated by left-wing state governments in recent decades, began, in fact, nearly two centuries ago, led by the rulers of the kingdoms of Travancore and Cochin. (These two native states were not part of British India; they were joined together with a small part of the old Madras presidency to form the new state of Kerala after independence.) Indeed, as early as 1817, Rani Gouri Parvathi Bai, the young queen of Travancore, issued clear instructions for public support of education:

> The state should defray the entire cost of education of its people in order that there might be no backwardness in the spread of enlightenment among them. That by diffusion of education they might be better subjects and public servants and that the reputation of the State might be advanced thereby.[17]

Moreover, in parts of Kerala, property is usually inherited through the family's female line. These factors, as well as the generally high level of communal medicine, help to explain why women in Kerala do not suffer disadvantages in obtaining the means for survival. While it would be difficult to "split up" the respective contributions made by each of these different influences, it would be a mistake not to include all these factors among the potentially interesting variables that deserve examination.

In view of the enormity of the problems of women's survival in large parts of Asia and Africa, it is surprising that these disadvantages have received such inadequate attention. The numbers of "missing women" in relation to the numbers that could be expected if men and women received similar care in health, medicine, and nutrition, are remarkably large. A great many more than a hundred million women are simply not there because women are neglected compared with men. If this situation is to be corrected by political action and public policy, the reasons why there are so many "missing" women must first be better understood. We confront here what is clearly one of the more momentous, and neglected, problems facing the world today.

NOTES

1. An assessment of the available evidence can be found in Ingrid Waldron's "The Role of Genetic and Biological Factors in Sex Differences in Mortality," in A. D. Lopez and L. T. Ruzicka, eds., *Sex Differences in Mortality* (Canberra: Department of Demography, Australian National University, 1983). On the pervasive cultural influences on mortality and the difficulties in forming a biological view of survival advantages, see Sheila Ryan Johansson, "Mortality, Welfare and Gender: Continuity and Change in Explanations for Male/Female Mortality Differences over Three Centuries," in *Continuity and Change,* forthcoming.

2. These and related data are presented and assessed in my joint paper with Jocelyn Kynch, "Indian Women: Well-being and Survival," *Cambridge Journal of Economics,* Vol. 7 (1983), and in my *Commodities and Capa-*

bilities (Amsterdam: North-Holland, 1985), Appendix B. See also Lincoln Chen et al., "Sex Bias in the Family Allocation of Food and Health Care in Rural Bangladesh," in *Population and Development Review,* Vol. 7 (1981); Barbara Miller, *The Endangered Sex: Neglect of Female Children in Rural North India* (Cornell University Press, 1981); Pranab Bardhan, *Land, Labor, and Rural Poverty* (Columbia University Press, 1984); Devaki Jain and Nirmala Banerji, eds., *Tyranny of the Household* (New Delhi: Vikas, 1985); Barbara Harriss and Elizabeth Watson, "The Sex Ratio in South Asia," in J. H. Momsen and J. G. Townsend, eds., *Geography of Gender in the Third World* (State University of New York Press, 1987); Monica Das Gupta, "Selective Discrimination against Female Children in Rural Punjab, India," in *Population and Development Review,* Vol. 13 (1987).

3. See the World Bank's World Development Report 1990 (Oxford University Press, 1990), Table 32. See also Judith Banister, *China's Changing Population* (Stanford University Press, 1987), Chapter 4, though the change in life expectancy may not have been as large as these early estimates had suggested, as Banister herself has later noted.

4. "Gender and Cooperative Conflicts," Working paper of the World Institute of Development Economics Research (1986), in Irene Tinker, ed., *Persistent Inequalities: Women and World Development* (Oxford University Press, 1990). In the same volume see also the papers of Ester Boserup, Hanna Papanek, and Irene Tinker on closely related subjects.

5. The recent literature on the modeling of family relations as "bargaining problems," despite being usefully suggestive and insightful, has suffered a little from giving an inadequate role to the importance of perceptions (as opposed to objectively identified interests) of the parties involved. On the relevance of perception, including perceptual distortions (a variant of what Marx had called

"false perception"), in family relations, see my "Gender and Cooperative Conflicts." See also my *Resources, Values and Development* (Harvard University Press, 1984), Chapters 15 and 16; Gail Wilson, *Money in the Family* (Avebury/Gower, 1987).

6. See the case studies and the literature cited in my "Gender and Cooperative Conflicts." A pioneering study of some of these issues was provided by Ester Boserup, *Women's Role in Economic Development* (St. Martin's, 1970). See also Bina Agarwal, "Social Security and the Family," in E. Ahmad, et al., *Social Security in Developing Countries,* to be published by Oxford University Press in 1991.

7. Details can be found in my "Gender and Cooperative Conflicts."

8. For example, see Pranab Bardhan, *Land, Labor, and Rural Poverty* on different states in India and the literature cited there.

9. See the literature cited in my "Gender and Cooperative Conflicts."

10. See Elisabeth Croll, *Chinese Women Since Mao* (M. E. Sharpe, 1984).

11. See *World Development Report 1990,* Tables 1 and 32. See also Banister, *China's Changing Population,* Chapter 4, and Athar Hussain and Nicholas Stern. *On the recent increase in death rate in China,* China Paper #8 (London: STICERD/London School of Economics, 1990).

12. See Margery Wolf, *Revolution Postponed: Women in Contemporary China* (Stanford University Press, 1984).

13. See Banister, *China's Changing Population,* Table 4.12.

14. On this and related matters, see Nahid Aslanbeigui and Gale Summerfield, "The Impact of the Responsibility System on Women in Rural China: A Theoretical Application of Sen's Theory of Entitlement," in *World Development,* Vol. 17 (1989).

15. These and other aspects of the problem are discussed more extensively in my joint book with Jean Drèze, *Hunger and Public Action* (Oxford University Press, 1989).

16. For interesting investigations of the role of education, broadly defined, in influencing women's well-being in Bangladesh and India, see Martha Chen, *A Quiet Revolution: Women in Transition in Rural Bangladesh* (Schenkman Books, 1983); and Alaka Basu, *Culture, the Status of Women and Demographic Behavior* (New Delhi: National Council of Applied Economic Research, 1988).

17. Kerala has also had considerable missionary activity in schooling (a fifth of the population is, in fact, Christian), has had international trading and political contacts (both with east and west Asia) for a very long time, and it was from Kerala that the great Hindu philosopher and educator Sankaracarya, who lived during AD 788–820, had launched his big movement of setting up centers of study and worship across India.

Chapter 28

The State and Progress of Human Development

UNITED NATIONS

Human development is about people, about expanding their choices to lead lives they value. Economic growth, increased international trade and investment, technological advance—all are very important. But they are means, not ends. Whether they contribute to human development in the 21st century will depend on whether they expand people's choices, whether they help create an environment for people to develop their full potential and lead productive, creative lives.

Fundamental to enlarging human choices is building human capabilities: the range of things that people can do or be. The most basic capabilities for human development are leading a long and healthy life, being educated, having access to the resources needed for a decent standard of living and being able to participate in the life of one's community. As this Report emphasizes, assuring people's dignity also requires that they be free—and able—to participate in the formation and stewardship of the rules and institutions that govern them. A poor man who cannot afford to send his children to school, but must send them to work in the fields, is lacking in human development. So is a wealthy educated woman whose gender excludes her from voting in elections.

In today's new era of global integration, is human development moving forward? There has been clear progress in some areas. The share of the world's people living in extreme poverty is slowly but steadily declining, from 29 percent in 1990 to 23 percent in 1999.[1] Primary school enrollments have risen worldwide, from 80 percent in 1990 to 84 percent in 1998.[2] Since 1990, 800 million people have gained access to improved water supplies, and 750 million to improved sanitation.[3] There also have been great improvements in political and civil rights: since 1980, 81 countries have taken significant steps in democratization,[4] with 33 military regimes replaced by civilian governments.[5]

But in a globalizing world the increasing interconnectedness of nations and peoples has made the differences between them more glaring. A girl born in Japan today may have a 50 percent chance of seeing the 22nd century[6]—while a newborn in Afghanistan has a 1 in 4 chance of dying before age 5. And the richest 5 percent of the world's people have incomes 114 times those of the poorest 5 percent.[7] Every day more than 30 000 children around the world die of preventable diseases,[8] and nearly 14 000 people are infected with HIV/AIDS.[9] In Botswana, more than a third of adults have the disease, in Swaziland and Zimbabwe more than a quarter. If tuberculosis control does not improve, 1 billion people will contract it by 2020—and 35 million will die from it.[10]

In Sub-Saharan Africa, human development has actually regressed in recent years, and the lives of its very poor people are getting worse. The share of people living on $1 a day was about the same at the end of the 1990s—47 percent—as at the start.[11] Thus, because of population growth, the number of poor people in the region has increased. And while most of the world has increased the share of children who are immunized against the leading diseases, since 1990 immunization rates in Sub-Saharan Africa have fallen below 50 percent.[12]

Global progress on political freedoms has also been uneven. The spread of democratization appears to have stalled, with many countries failing to consolidate and deepen the first steps towards democracy and several slipping back into authoritarianism. Some 73 countries—with 42 percent of the world's people—still do not hold free and fair elections,[13] and 106 governments still restrict many civil and political freedoms.[14] In addition, conflict continues to blight the lives of millions: since 1990, 3.6 million people have died in civil wars and ethnic violence, more than 16 times the number killed in wars between states.[15]

There is growing recognition that all countries pay a price for these global injustices. And there is greater acceptance of the need for action to narrow the gap between global potential and reality—and to advance global human development in its deepest sense.

In surveying the progress of countries towards human development in its many dimensions, this chapter highlights the directions for change in the years ahead—and how far it will need to go. The chapter begins by looking at global trends in political participation and democracy, the subjects of this Report. It then considers the Millennium Development Goals, set by the global community to monitor development along a number of dimensions. It assesses progress towards the goals, showing that many countries are on track but that many others are lagging and unlikely to achieve the goals.

TRENDS IN POLITICAL PARTICIPATION AND DEMOCRACY AROUND THE WORLD

Political participation and freedom are fundamental parts of human development. The world has more democratic countries and more political participation than ever, with 140 countries holding multiparty elections (Table 28.1). Of 147 countries with data, 121—with 68 percent of the world's people—have some or all of the

---

TABLE 28.1 MOST PEOPLE CAN NOW VOTE IN MULTIPARTY ELECTIONS, 1999

REGION OR COUNTRY GROUP			
	Number of Countries with Multiparty Electoral Systems (countries with data)	Population of Countries with Multiparty Electoral Systems (millions)	Share of Regional Population Living in Countries with Multiparty Electoral Systems (percent)
Sub-Saharan Africa	29 (42)	464	77.2
Arab States	4 (7)	115	48.5
East Asia and the Pacific	9 (16)	401	22.0
South Asia	4 (8)	1 170	85.5
Latin America and the Caribbean	25 (26)	468	94.9
Central and Eastern Europe and CIS	21 (25)	350	88.0
OECD	30 (30)	1 120	100.0
Low human development	23 (36)	527	64.4
World	140 (189)	3 923	65.8

NOTE: Low human development countries are also included in their respective regional groups. Regional data do not sum to the world total because some countries included in the world total are not included in a regional group.

Source: Human Development Report Office calculations based on Alvarez and others 2002.

elements of formal democracy in 2000 (Figure 28.1).[16] This compares with only 54 countries, with 46 percent of the world's people, in 1980. Since then 81 countries have taken significant steps in democratization, while 6 have regressed.[17] Scores of authoritarian regimes have been replaced by governments more accountable to the people—a real achievement for human development. But true democratization means more than elections. It requires the consolidation of democratic institutions and the strengthening of democratic practices, with democratic values and norms embedded in all parts of society.

The last two decades of the 20th century have been dubbed the "third wave" of democratization, as dictatorial regimes fell in scores of countries.[18] Like history's other movements for liberation, these democratic revolutions were propelled by people. In the 1980s, growing pressures against the excesses of military dictatorships in Latin America caused them to topple one after another, starting with Ecuador and Peru. In Central and Eastern Europe and what is now the Commonwealth of Independent States (CIS), the fall of the Berlin Wall in 1989 was the turning point. In Africa, rising opposition through the 1980s and 1990s tossed out many long-standing dictators, including Mali's Moussa Traoré in 1991 and Malawi's Kamuzu Banda in 1994. People's power in the Philippines removed Ferdinand Marcos in 1986.

For some countries the transition has been less dramatic, as with the move to civilian rule in the Republic of Korea and Thailand and the introduction of elections in Nepal. Perhaps most striking was the advent of full democracy in South Africa in 1994—the result of long negotiations. Democratic reforms have been relatively modest in the Arab States, with a few cases of democratic ferment. But monarchies such as Jordan and Morocco have increased space for people's participation in the political life of the community, and Tunisia has taken steps to expand political participation. Still, the region has been slower to democratize than other parts of the world, and only 4 of 7 countries have multiparty electoral systems.[19]

The global shift from authoritarian to democratic regimes shows up in various indications of governance. The number of authoritarian countries fell from almost 70 in 1980 to fewer than 30 in 2000.[20] Over the same period the number of democratic regimes doubled, from 41 to 82. The breakup of the Soviet Union contributed to the

FIGURE 28.1 THE WORLD BECOMING MORE DEMOCRATIC

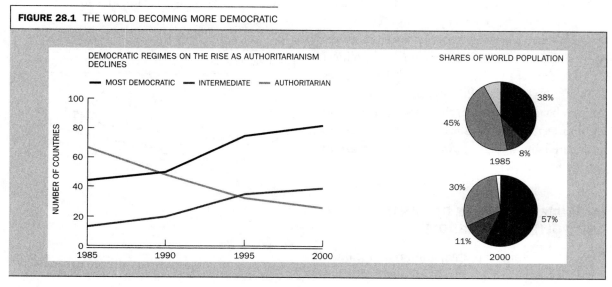

Source: Polity IV 2002.

jump in country coverage. Overall, the former Soviet Union and the rest of Eastern Europe have become more democratic.

General indicators do not capture the complexity of political transitions. Most attempts at democratization are fragmented, involving small steps and large, forward and back. Take Peru. In 1980, after 12 years of military rule, it shifted to a democratic regime. But the situation slowly deteriorated, with president Alberto Fujimori's regime becoming increasingly authoritarian. Despite irregularities that led international observers to withdraw, Fujimori was proclaimed the winner of the 2000 elections. But public outrage over political scandals ultimately forced him to flee the country. Alejandro Toledo was elected president after elections in 2001.

While the long-term and recent trends have been impressive, the slight drop in measured democracy in Sub-Saharan Africa and South Asia in the second half of the 1990s reflects the fact that the "third wave" of democratization seems to have stalled. Of the 81 countries that have taken steps in democratization, only 47 are considered full democracies.[21] Many others do not seem to be in transition to anything or have lapsed back into authoritarianism—or conflict, as in the Democratic Republic of Congo, Sierra Leone, and others. This has been especially common in Sub-Saharan Africa and Central Asia. In Belarus, Cameroon, Togo, Uzbekistan, and elsewhere, one-party states have allowed elections but ended up permitting only limited opening for political competition. Most of these "limited" democracies suffer from shallow political participation, where citizens have little trust in their governments and are disaffected from politics, or the countries are dominated by a single powerful party or group despite formal elections.[22]

BROADER MEASURES OF PARTICIPATION AND POLITICAL FREEDOM

Democratic political participation requires more than elections for governments—truly democratic politics requires civil and political rights to provide the space for effective participation. Illustrating the greater importance attached to human rights worldwide, the number of countries ratifying the six main human rights conventions and covenants has increased dramatically since 1990 (Figure 28.2). Upholding human rights is crucial for guaranteeing people's well-being and securing a humane and non-discriminatory society—and for enabling an active and engaged citizenry. Freedoms of association and assembly, of expression and conscience, as laid out in the International Covenant on Civil and Political Rights, are fundamental to political participation.

A free and active press is particularly important for the creation and consolidation of democracy. Freedom House's Freedom of the Press Index indicates levels and trends worldwide, showing that press freedom has also been increasing (Figure 28.3).

In addition to civil and political rights, equitable opportunities for participation are crucial to democratic politics. But around the world, women are seriously underrepresented in domestic politics, accounting for only 14 percent of national parliamentarians. There is little difference between industrial and developing countries. In most industrial countries—including France, Japan and the United States—women account for 10–20 percent of parliamentarians.[23] Positive exceptions worldwide include both

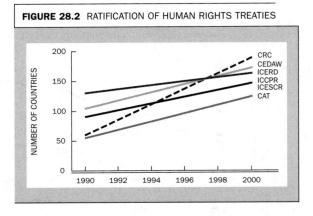

FIGURE 28.2 RATIFICATION OF HUMAN RIGHTS TREATIES

Source: Human Development Report Office calculations based on UNOHCHR 2002.

FIGURE 28.3 THE PRESS BECOMES FREER

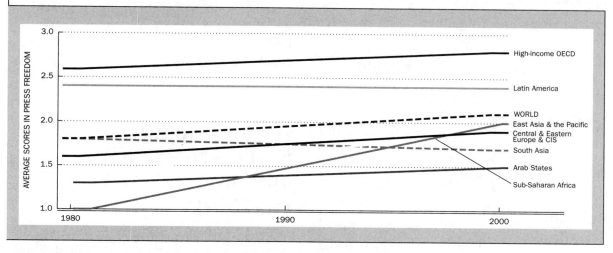

Source: Human Development Report Office calculations based on Freedom House 2000.

developing and industrial countries (Figure 28.4). Nordic countries do particularly well, but in Argentina, Mozambique, and South Africa about 30 percent of parliamentarians are women. Meanwhile, a number of Arab states have no female representation.

THE PROLIFERATION OF CIVIL CONFLICT

The stalling of democratic transitions highlights the fragility of democracies. The proliferation of conflicts, particularly internal conflicts, highlights the fragility of states (Figure 28.5 on page 312). Internal conflicts today vastly out-number wars between states. Since 1990 an estimated 220 000 people have died in wars between states—compared with nearly 3.6 million in wars within states.[24]

Particularly tragic is the fact that civilians, not soldiers, are increasingly the victims of con-flicts. Civilians have accounted for more than 90 percent of the casualties—either injured or killed—in post-cold war conflicts.[25] Moreover, internal conflicts are usually fought with small

FIGURE 28.4 WOMEN'S PARTICIPATION LAGS EVERYWHERE

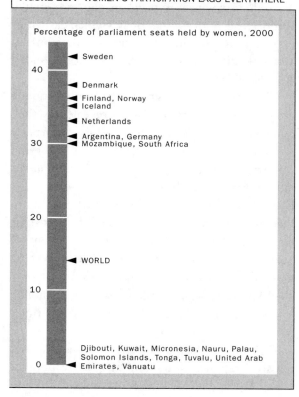

Source: IPU 2000c and indicator table 23.

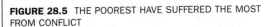

FIGURE 28.5 THE POOREST HAVE SUFFERED THE MOST FROM CONFLICT

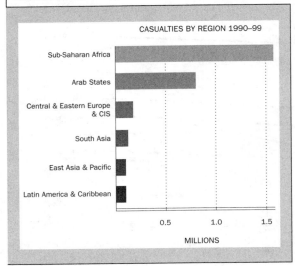

Source: Human Development Report Office calculations based on Marshall 2000.

weapons, and combatants use strategies that have the strongest impact on the vulnerable. Children account for half of all civilian casualties in wars,[26] and worldwide there are an estimated 300 000 child soldiers—in Sierra Leone, Sudan and elsewhere.[27]

Civil wars also have grave effects on economic growth and food production, as revealed by such human development indicators as infant mortality rates and school enrollments.[28] Seven of the ten countries with the lowest human development indices have recently suffered major civil wars. During Mozambique's 16-year civil war more than 40 percent of schools were destroyed or forced to close, and more than 40 percent of health centres were destroyed. Industries were so damaged that postwar production was only 20–40 percent of prewar capacity, with economic losses estimated at $15 billion—several times Mozambique's prewar GDP.[29]

Fighting between and within states also causes massive refugee flows and displaced populations. At the end of 2000, more than 12 million people were refugees, 6 million were internally displaced and nearly 4 million were returning refugees, asylum-seekers or people otherwise of concern to the UN High Commissioner for Refugees[30]—in all, 50 percent more than in 1990.[31] The increase in refugees and displaced populations indicates that today's armed conflicts are more intense.

THE MILLENNIUM DEVELOPMENT GOALS: COMMITMENTS AND PROSPECTS

At the UN General Assembly in 2000, heads of state and government took stock of the gross inequalities in human development worldwide and recognized "their collective responsibility to uphold the principles of human dignity, equality, and equity at the global level."[32] In addition to declaring their support for freedom, democracy and human rights, they set eight goals for development and poverty eradication, to be achieved by 2015:

- Eradicate extreme poverty and hunger.
- Achieve universal primary education.
- Achieve gender equality and empower women.
- Reduce child mortality.
- Improve maternal health.
- Combat HIV/AIDS, malaria, and other diseases.
- Ensure environmental sustainability.
- Develop a global partnership for development.[33]

Most of the Millennium Development Goals have quantifiable, monitorable targets to measure progress against standards set by the international community. This Report assesses how likely countries are to achieve goals by 2015 if recent trends continue, classifying them as achieved, on track, lagging, far behind, or slipping back. The analysis assumes that trends over the next decade will be the same as over the past decade. Whether countries fall behind or surpass this expectation will depend on their actions and those of the global community between now and 2015.

Many countries have made progress. But much of the world, generally the poorest countries, seems unlikely to achieve the goals. Although 55 countries, with 23 percent of the world's people, are on track to achieve at least three-quarters of the goals, 33 countries with 26 percent of the world's people are failing on more than half (Figure 28.6A). Especially extraordinary efforts will be needed in Sub-Saharan Africa, where 23 countries are failing and 11 others do not have enough data to be assessed—a possible indication that they are even further behind. That leaves just 10 Sub-Saharan countries on track to meet at least half of the goals (Figure 28.6B).

Lack of data makes it difficult to assess progress on the goal of halving income poverty.

But slow growth in average incomes indicates that many countries will have to struggle to achieve the goal. Optimistic estimates suggest that 3.7 percent annual growth in per capita GDP will be needed, yet in the 1990s only 24 countries achieved such growth (Figure 28.7 on page 314).[34] China and India, the most populous countries, are in this group. But incomes in nearly 130 countries, with 40 percent of the world's people, are not growing fast enough—including 52 countries that actually had negative growth in the 1990s. Again, progress is most elusive in the poorest countries: 40 of 44 Sub-Saharan countries, with 93 percent of the region's people, grew too slowly. Half of those 40 countries, with more than half of the region's people, are poorer now than in 1990. These include 11 of the world's 20 poorest countries.

Countries have come closer to some goals than others. Many developing countries have already achieved or are on track to achieve

FIGURE 28.6A COUNTRIES ON TRACK TO MEET THE MILLENNIUM DEVELOPMENT GOALS

All UN member countries excluding high-income OECD

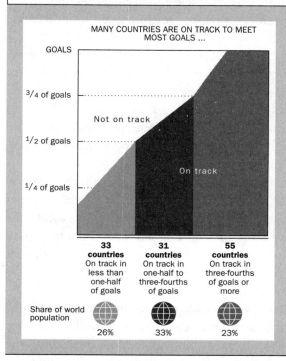

Source: Human Development Report Office calculations based on appendix table A1.3.

FIGURE 28.6B COUNTRIES ON TRACK TO MEET THE MILLENNIUM DEVELOPMENT GOALS

Sub-Saharan Africa

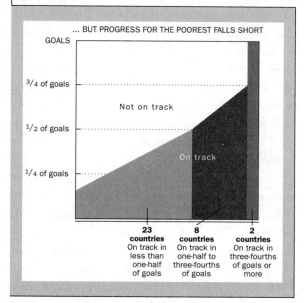

Source: Human Development Report Office calculations based on appendix table A1.3.

FIGURE 28.7 FAILING TO GROW OUT OF POVERTY

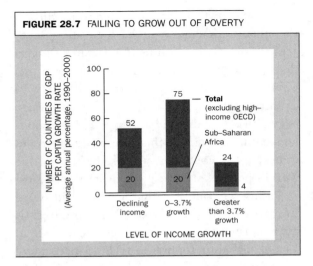

Source: Human Development Report Office calculations based on indicator table 12.

GOAL 1—ERADICATING EXTREME POVERTY AND HUNGER

Target 1a: Halve the Proportion of People Living on Less than $1 a Day

In 1999, 2.8 billion people lived on less than $2 a day, with 1.2 billion of them barely surviving at the margins of subsistence on less than $1 a day (Table 28.2). During the 1990s the number of extremely poor people dropped only slightly. But because of population growth, the share of the world's people living in extreme poverty fell from 29 percent in 1990 to 23 percent in 1999.

The declining share of people in extreme poverty is hopeful, but the level remains disturbingly high. And the failure to reduce poverty in Sub-Saharan Africa, the world's poorest region, is a grave concern.

Per Capita Income. A country's income poverty rate is determined by its per capita income and by the distribution of that income. Though there is no guarantee that poor people will benefit from an increase in their country's average per capita income, aggregate growth typically does increase their incomes.[35]

Since the mid-1970s, growth in per capita income has varied dramatically across regions. East Asia and the Pacific's impressive poverty reduction is primarily due to a quadrupling in its per capita GDP between 1975 and 2000. But Sub-Saharan Africa ended the millennium 5 percent poorer than in 1990.

Central and Eastern Europe and the CIS was the only other region to suffer a decline in per capita income during the 1990s. Growth in the region is picking up, and a few countries have done quite well. But in many countries incomes remain far lower than in the past.

Income Inequality within Countries. The amount of growth required to reduce poverty depends on a country's level of inequality—the more unequal is the distribution of income, the fewer are the benefits of growth to poor people. Studies of inequality trends within countries

universal primary education and gender equity in education. Given the importance of education to so many other areas of development, this bodes well for accelerating progress towards the other goals. Most developing countries have also achieved or are on track to achieve the targets for eradicating hunger and improving water supplies (part of the environmental goal). But more than 40 countries, with 28 percent of the world's people, are not on track to halve hunger by 2015. And 25 countries, with 32 percent of the world's people, may not halve the share of people lacking access to an improved water source. Most pressing, however, is child mortality: 85 countries with more than 60 percent of the world's people are not on track to achieve the goal.

A goal that cannot be monitored cannot be met or missed—and one of the most startling conclusions is the lack of data. The targets for poverty, HIV/AIDS and maternal mortality cannot be monitored directly with current international data. Even targets that can be monitored have many gaps in the data. Complicating matters, countries lacking data may have the worst performance, giving an inflated impression of the proportion of countries that are progressing.

TABLE 28.2 WORLDWIDE, THE NUMBER OF PEOPLE LIVING ON LESS THAN $1 A DAY BARELY CHANGED IN THE 1990S

REGION	SHARE (PERCENT)		NUMBER (MILLIONS)	
	1990	1999	1990	1999
Sub-Saharan Africa	47.7	46.7	242	300
East Asia and the Pacific Excluding China	18.5	7.9	92	46
South Asia	44.0	36.9	495	490
Latin America and the Caribbean	16.8	15.1	74	77
Eastern Europe and Central Asia	1.6	3.6	7	17
Middle East and North Africa	2.4	2.3	6	7
Total	**29.0**	**22.7**	**1 276**	**1 151**
Excluding China	**28.1**	**24.5**	**916**	**936**

NOTE: $1 a day is $1.08 in 1993 purchasing power parity (PPP) prices.

Source: World Bank 2002c.

suffer from a lack of reliable, comparable data. The limited available evidence indicates that worldwide, within-country income inequality has been increasing for the past 30 years.[36] Among the 73 countries with data (and 80 percent of the world's people), 48 have seen inequality increase since the 1950s, 16 have experienced no change and only 9—with just 4 percent of the world's people—have seen inequality fall.[37] The increase in inequality has impeded poverty reduction. Given current inequality levels, most countries are not growing fast enough to meet the poverty target. Thus efforts must focus on making growth more pro-poor.[38]

Target 1b: Halve the Proportion of People Suffering from Hunger

Children suffer doubly from hunger: it affects their daily lives and has devastating consequences for their future mental and physical health. In 50 countries with almost 40 percent of the world's people, more than one-fifth of children under the age of five are underweight.[39] That 17 of those countries are in the medium human development category underscores hunger's pervasiveness. Still, the problem is worst among the world's poorest countries. In Sub-Saharan Africa only South Africa has less than a 10 percent incidence of child malnourishment. In six Sub-Saharan countries that figure is more than 40 percent.

A rough indication of how countries are moving towards halving hunger by 2015 comes from changes in the number of malnourished people—a less precise indicator of hunger than child malnutrition rates, based on national food availability and estimated distribution. In 1997–99 an estimated 815 million people were undernourished: 777 million in developing countries, 27 million in transition economies, and 11 million in industrial countries.[40]

There are some reasons for optimism. Fifty-seven countries, with half of the world's people, have halved hunger or are on track to do so by 2015. But progress is far from universal. Twenty-four countries are far behind in achieving the target. And in 15 more—6 from Sub-Saharan Africa—the situation worsened in the 1990s.

While the proportion of hungry people has been declining, the world's booming population means that the number of malnourished people has not been falling fast enough. During the 1990s it declined by just 6 million people a year.[41] At this rate it would take more than 130 years to rid the world of hunger.

GOAL 2—ACHIEVING UNIVERSAL PRIMARY EDUCATION

Target 2a: Ensure That Children Everywhere—Boys and Girls Alike— Complete a Full Course of Primary Education

Education is important in its own right and has strong spillover benefits to mortality rates, income and even social cohesion. Worldwide, primary enrollments have been improving, rising from 80 percent in 1990 to 84 percent in 1998. But that still means that of the 680 million children of primary school age, 113 million are not in school—97 percent of them in developing countries.[42]

Many countries have good prospects for achieving universal primary education. But there is little middle ground: most of those not on track to achieve the goal are far behind or have worsening primary enrollments. Sub-Saharan Africa fares worst—of the 21 countries with data, 14 are far behind the target or have deteriorating enrollments. Furthermore, 93 countries with 39 percent of the world's people do not have sufficient data to make a judgement.

Enrolling children in primary school is only half the battle, because it is meaningful only if they complete it—which requires that they and their families be able to resist the pressures of forgone income and work in the home. Of the few countries with data on primary school completion, most seem to be on track. But again the news is worse for Sub-Saharan Africa, where 6 countries are on track and 5 are far behind or slipping back—and the 33 countries without data are likely to be among the poor performers.

Literacy. One of the most important outcomes of primary education is literacy. And literacy rates are slow to change, reflecting the education of previous generations of children and the history of school enrollment. Since 1975, literacy rates have increased substantially in all developing regions. East Asia and the Pacific and Latin America and the Caribbean seem to be converging, with close to 90 percent adult literacy. But Sub-Saharan Africa, South Asia and Arab States, despite significant progress, are much further behind, with adult literacy rates of about 60 percent. In the past 25 years, literacy rates in low human development countries have doubled—though only to 50 percent.

Functional Literacy. Among OECD countries, literacy rates are often assumed to be close to 100 percent. But the truth is very different. The concept of functional illiteracy describes the inability to understand and use common channels of communication and information in an everyday context, from newspapers and books to pamphlets and instructions on medicine bottles. Based on this measure, in most OECD countries an incredible 10–20 percent of people are functionally illiterate, with Sweden and Norway doing relatively well at 8 percent and 9 percent while Ireland, the United Kingdom and the United States have levels over 20 percent.

GOAL 3—ACHIEVING GENDER EQUALITY AND EMPOWERING WOMEN

Target 3a: Eliminate Gender Disparities in Primary and Secondary Education, Preferably by 2005, and In All Levels of Education by 2015

The Millennium Development Goal for gender equality in education responds to dramatic gender disparities in many parts of the world, particularly South Asia and West, Central, and North Africa. In India, the enrollment ratio of boys aged 6–14 is 17 percentage points higher than that of girls the same age; in Benin, 21 percentage points. Yet in many developing countries, mostly in Latin America, girls have no disadvantage or even a small advantage.[43] Still, of the world's estimated 854 million illiterate adults, 544 million are women—and of the 113 million children not in primary school, 60 percent are girls.[44] The world is still a long way from achieving equal rights and opportunities between females and males.

The gaps are closing in primary and, to a lesser extent, secondary enrollments: 90 countries, with more than 60 percent of the world's people, have achieved or are on track to achieving gender equality in primary education by 2015—and more than 80 in secondary education.

Perhaps most surprising is the performance of Arab States—countries generally associated with high gender inequality. All but one of those with data are on track to meet the target for primary enrollments. Again, Sub-Saharan Africa is making the least progress, but even there most countries have achieved or are on track to achieve gender equality in primary enrollment.

Education is just one aspect of human development in which there is discrimination between the sexes. Around the world, women still earn only around 75 percent as much as men. Domestic violence against women is common in many societies. And around the world there are an estimated 100 million "missing" women—50 million in India alone—who would be alive but for infanticide, neglect, or sex-selective abortions. A recent survey in India found 10 000 cases of female infanticide a year, and a study of a clinic in Bombay found that 7 999 of 8 000 aborted foetuses were female.[45]

Worse outcomes for women in many aspects of human development result from the fact that their voices have less impact than men's in the decisions that shape their lives. This inequality in empowerment is partly captured by the gender empowerment measure (GEM), introduced in *Human Development Report 1995* to help assess gender inequality in economic and political opportunities. This year the GEM has been estimated for 66 countries. Some observations:

- GEM values range from less than 0.300 to more than 0.800—indicating enormous variation around the world in empowering women.

- Only 5 of the 66 countries—Denmark, Finland, Iceland, Norway and Sweden—have a GEM above 0.800, while 22 have a GEM below 0.500.

- Some developing countries outperform much richer industrial countries. The Bahamas and Trinidad and Tobago are ahead of Italy and Japan. Barbados's GEM is 25 percent higher than Greece's. The message: high income is not a prerequisite to creating opportunities for women.

Inequalities beyond Gender. The Millennium Development goals consider gender inequality in education—but this is only one aspect of unfair access to schooling. While gender gaps in education are large in some countries and nonexistent in others, wealth gaps exist the world over. Extreme examples include Senegal, where the enrollment ratio for 6–14-year-olds from the poorest households is 52 percentage points lower than for those from the richest households, and Zambia, with a 36 point difference. Such wealth gaps perpetuate the cycle of poverty: those born poor are likely to die poor. Furthermore, in some countries (Egypt, India, Morocco, Niger, Pakistan) the gender gap in education is much larger for poor households. In India the gender gap in enrollment is only 3 percentage points in the richest households, but 34 points in the poorest.[46]

One cause of such gaps is that in many countries, public spending on education is skewed towards the rich. In Ecuador the poorest 20 percent of households receive only 11 percent of public education spending, while the richest 20 percent receive 26 percent—more than twice as much.[47] Even when public spending is distributed more equitably, rich parents can buy a far better education for their children at private schools. In Chile, Peru, the Philippines and Thailand private spending accounts for more than 40 percent of education spending.[48]

Education inequality is also a serious problem in some industrial countries. In the United States, race is a significant factor: minorities have lower schooling levels and less access to high-quality schooling. Controlling for parental education and immigrant status, young African Americans perform worse in functional literacy tests than do young white Americans—on average, by the equivalent of four to five years of schooling. The gap for Hispanic Americans is one and a half to two years.[49]

GOAL 4—REDUCING CHILD MORTALITY

Target 4a: Reduce Infant and Under-Five Mortality Rates by Two-Thirds

Every year about 11 million children die of preventable causes,[50] often for want of simple and easily provided improvements in nutrition, sanitation, and maternal health and education. Some developing regions have made rapid improvements in this area—especially Arab

States, where 6 percent of children die before age five, down from 20 percent in 1970.

Although Latin America and the Caribbean are doing well as a whole, eight countries are far from achieving the infant mortality target. In East Asia and the Pacific, 13 countries are on track but 3, including China, are far behind—and in Cambodia, under-five mortality rates are increasing. Central and Eastern Europe and the CIS, doing badly as a whole, combine good performance from the European countries and worse performance from the more populous CIS countries. In Sub-Saharan Africa, 34 of 44 counties are far behind or slipping back.

Immunizations against leading diseases are a vital element in improving child survival. After soaring in the 1980s, immunizations in developing countries levelled off at about 75 percent in the 1990s. And in recent years the proportion of children immunized in Sub-Saharan Africa has fallen below 50 percent.

Child mortality has a dramatic effect on a country's life expectancy, which is part of the HDI and is an excellent indicator of a country's overall health. Between 1975 and 2000, East Asia and the Pacific increased life expectancy by about 8 years, to almost 70 (Figure 28.8). South Asia, Latin America and the Caribbean, and Arab States also achieved consistent increases. But high-income OECD countries are still head and shoulders above the rest, with a life expectancy of 77 years—7 years more than the next-highest region.

Sub-Saharan Africa, ravaged by HIV/AIDS and conflict, saw life expectancy reverse in the 1990s from already tragically low levels. Eastern Europe and the CIS also suffered a decline, and is the only other region where life expectancy is lower now than in 1990.

GOAL 5—IMPROVING MATERNAL HEALTH

Target 5a: Reduce Maternal Mortality Ratios by Three-Quarters

Every year more than 500 000 women die as a result of pregnancy and childbirth,[51] with huge regional disparities (Table 28.3). The situation

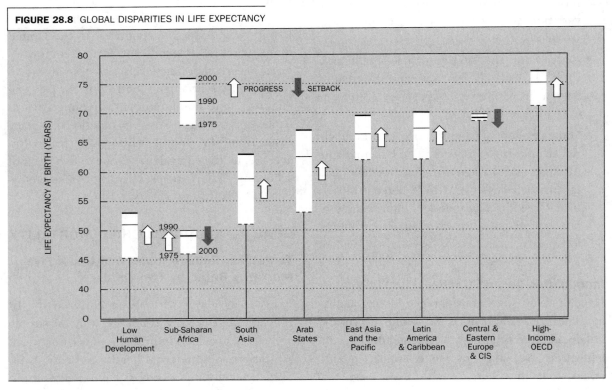

FIGURE 28.8 GLOBAL DISPARITIES IN LIFE EXPECTANCY

Source: Human Development Report Office calculations based on UN 2001d.

TABLE 28.3 MATERNAL MORTALITY IS MUCH HIGHER IN SOME REGIONS

REGION	LIFETIME CHANCE OF DYING IN PREGNANCY OR CHILDBIRTH
Sub-Saharan Africa	1 in 13
South Asia	1 in 54
Middle East and North Africa	1 in 55
Latin America and the Caribbean	1 in 157
East Asia and the Pacific	1 in 283
Central and Eastern Europe and CIS	1 in 797
OECD	1 in 4 085

NOTE: Data refer to most recent year available.

Source: UNICEF 2002.

FIGURE 28.9 DEVASTATION FROM HIV/AIDS—LIFE EXPECTANCY IN SUB-SAHARAN AFRICA PLUMMETS

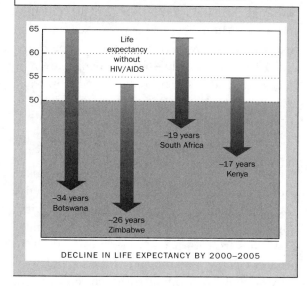

DECLINE IN LIFE EXPECTANCY BY 2000–2005

Source: UVDESA 2001.

is worst in Sub-Saharan Africa, where a woman has a 1 in 13 chance of dying in pregnancy or childbirth.

Increasing the number of births attended by skilled health personnel is key to reducing maternal mortality ratios, and again there is wide variation—with as few as 29 percent of births attended by skilled personnel in South Asia and 37 percent in Sub-Saharan Africa.[52]

There are not enough data on maternal mortality or births attended by skilled health personnel to assess how countries are progressing towards this important goal, indicating an urgent need for more complete, comparable data on this vital issue.

GOAL 6—COMBATING HIV/AIDS, MALARIA, AND OTHER DISEASES

Target 6a: Halt and Begin to Reverse the Spread of HIV/AIDS

By the end of 2000, almost 22 million people had died from AIDS, 13 million children had lost their mother or both parents to the disease, and more than 40 million people were living with the HIV virus—90 percent of them in developing countries, 75 percent in Sub-Saharan Africa.[53]

In Botswana, the most affected country, more than a third of adults have HIV/AIDS and a child born today can expect to live only 36 years—about half as long as if the disease did not exist (Figure 28.9). In Burkina Faso, the 20th most affected country, 330 000 adults are living with HIV/AIDS, and life expectancy has fallen by 8 years.[54]

The toll on life expectancy is only the beginning. In Thailand, one-third of AIDS-affected rural families saw their incomes fall by half because the time of farmers, and those caring for them, was taken from the fields.[55] At the same time, medical expenses shoot up. In Côte d'Ivoire, caring for a male AIDS patient costs an average of $300 a year, a quarter to half of the net annual income of most small farms.[56] The effect on poor households, with little or no savings to cope with such shocks, is devastating. In urban Côte d'Ivoire, food consumption dropped 41 percent per capita, and school outlays halved.[57]

HIV/AIDS is also a concern in the Caribbean, the region with the second highest infection rate. In Latin America, 1.3 million people have HIV/AIDS. Central and Eastern Europe and the CIS have fast-rising infection rates—240 000 people are now infected in Ukraine.[58] And there are warnings that Asia is on the verge of an epidemic. In Ho Chi Minh City, Vietnam, one sex worker in five is HIV positive, up from almost none in the mid-1990s. And nearly 4 million people are now infected in India, second only to South Africa.[59] Without strong preventative measures, as in Thailand, the epidemic could rage out of control.

There are no comparable trend data for assessing how well countries are fighting the disease. But it is clear that policies can make a difference and that contraceptive prevalence and reproductive rights for women are vital. Through preventive measures, Uganda reduced HIV rates from 14 percent in the early 1990s to around 8 percent by the end of the 1990s.[60]

Also vital is providing treatment and care to those already affected. But at a cost of $300 per year per patient—well over half the GDP per capita of Sub-Saharan Africa—antiretroviral drugs that can prolong life expectancy are out of reach for the average African HIV patient. As homes to the leading pharmaceutical companies, some industrial countries have pressured developing countries not to manufacture generic alternatives of these patented drugs. But in November 2001 the World Trade Organization ministerial conference in Doha, Qatar, adopted the Declaration on Trade-Related Intellectual Property Rights and Public Health, affirming the sovereign right of governments to protect public health. The legal status of this declaration is not yet clear, but it indicates that rulings on disputes may now favour public health. One issue that remains uncertain is whether countries can override patents and produce generic drugs for export to other developing countries—a crucial question for all developing countries with no pharmaceutical industry of their own. Goal 8, developing a global partnership for development, includes the aspiration of resolving this problem with the help of pharmaceutical companies. Whether this proves to be possible, in the wake of the Doha declaration, it is clear that international law must put global public health first.

Target 6b: Halt and Begin to Reverse the Incidence of Malaria and Other Major Diseases

Every year there are more than 300 million cases of malaria, 90 percent of them in Sub-Saharan Africa.[61] And every year 60 million people are infected with tuberculosis.[62] Current medical technologies can prevent these diseases from being fatal, but lack of access means that tuberculosis kills 2 million people a year[63] and malaria 1 million.[64] The poorest people typically suffer most.

Without much more effective control, by 2020 nearly 1 billion people will be infected and 35 million will die from tuberculosis.[65] In addition to its human costs, disease takes a heavy economic toll: for instance, high malaria prevalence can lower economic growth by 1 percent or more a year.[66] Work is underway to strengthen national health systems and increase international support, and there are some encouraging signs: the World Health Organization, for example, has struck a deal with the Swiss firm Novartis on the drug Coartem, an extremely effective malaria treatment. The price of this drug, which can reduce infection and fatality rates by 75 percent, has fallen to less than $2.50 a treatment.[67] But this is still far more than many people can afford—and only the beginning of efforts to overcome these diseases.

GOAL 7—ENDURING ENVIRONMENTAL SUSTAINABILITY

The diversity of environmental issues across countries and regions makes it extremely difficult to set global targets, so this goal sets out general principles for achieving sustainability and reducing the human costs of environmental degradation.

Target 7a: Integrate the Principles of Sustainable Development into Country Policies and Programmes and Reverse the Loss of Environmental Resources

Global warming is a universal concern—and carbon dioxide emissions are one of its main causes. Such emissions have increased dramatically, to more than 6.6 billion tons in 1998, up from 5.3 billion in 1980.[68] High-income countries generate a far higher proportion than their share of the world's population (Figure 28.10).

Around the world, goods production has generally become more energy-efficient in the past few decades. But the increased volume of global production means that such improvements are far from sufficient to reduce world carbon dioxide emissions. So the Kyoto Protocol to the Framework Convention on Climate Change aims to reduce emissions, mainly through controls on industrial pollution. The protocol could be a big step towards controlling emissions. But 165 countries, responsible for 89 percent of global carbon dioxide emissions, have yet to ratify it. The key missing player is the United States, responsible for almost one-quarter of the world's carbon dioxide emissions.

The ratification of international treaties can be a useful means of measuring a country's formal commitment to key environmental issues that are not globally monitorable. Deforestation, risks to endangered species and the state of the world's fisheries are broadly covered by the 1992 Convention on Biological Diversity, ratified by 168 countries. But such treaties are no guarantee of action. What is needed is detailed understanding of the situation in each country, with plans to ensure that people's enjoyment of the Earth is not at the expense of others—today or in the future.

To that end, Agenda 21, adopted in 1992 by governments at the United Nations Conference on Environment and Development (UNCED) in Rio de Janeiro, establishes principles for achieving sustainable development based on the need to manage the economy, the environment and social issues in a coherent, coordinated fashion. By March 2002, 73 countries had signed Agenda 21 and 33 countries had ratified it.[69]

One major topic addressed by Agenda 21 is desertification. Dryland ecosystems—covering more than a third of the world's land area—are extremely vulnerable to overexploitation and inappropriate land use. Poverty, political instability, deforestation, overgrazing, and bad irrigation practices can all undermine the land's productivity.

The human cost is enormous. More than 250 million people living off the land are directly affected by desertification. In addition, the livelihoods of 1 billion people in more than a hundred countries are at risk. These include many of the world's poorest, most marginalized and politically powerless people.

The United Nations Convention to Combat Desertification—ratified by 115 countries—aims to combat desertification and mitigate the effects of drought, particularly in Africa. This requires long-term integrated strategies that focus on increasing the productivity of land and on rehabilitating, conserving, and sustainably managing land and water resources.[70]

Target 7b: Halve the Proportion of People without Sustainable Safe Drinking Water

Target 7c: Achieve, by 2020, a Significant Improvement in the Lives of at Least 100 Million Slum Dwellers

Environmental conditions particularly affect the health of poor people. Traditional hazards such as lack of safe drinking water, sanitation, and

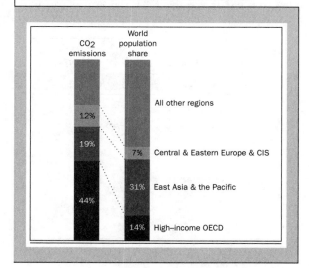

FIGURE 28.10 CARBON DIOXIDE EMISSIONS ORIGINATE DISPROPORTIONATELY IN HIGH-INCOME COUNTRIES

Source: Indicator table 19 and Human Development Report Office calculations basd on indicator table 5.

waste disposal lead to major outbreaks of diarrhoea, malaria, and cholera. Modern hazards such as urban and indoor air pollution can lead to respiratory infections, while exposure to agroindustrial chemicals and waste also causes harm.

The Millennium Declaration separates the goals for safe water and sanitation, using sanitation as an indicator of improving the lives of slum dwellers. In 2000, 1.1 billion people lacked access to safe water, and 2.4 billion did not have access to any form of improved sanitation services.[71]

The health consequences are significant. About 4 billion cases of diarrhoea occur each year, leading to 2.2 million deaths, predominantly among children—representing 15 percent of child deaths in developing countries. Other concerns include intestinal worms, which infect about 10 percent of people in the developing world, and trachoma, which has left 6 million people blind and another 500 million at risk.[72]

Human dignity is also at stake. A survey in the Philippines found that among the reasons given for wanting latrines, rural households cited the desire for privacy, cleaner surroundings, lack of flies, and lack of embarrassment ahead of health benefits.[73]

There was progress in the 1990s: 800 million more people now have access to improved water than in 1990, and 750 million more to improved sanitation.[74] Most countries with data are on track to halving the proportion of people without access to improved water sources. But the challenge remains enormous, with 27 percent of the world's people living in countries that are far behind the target.

GOAL 8—DEVELOPING A GLOBAL PARTNERSHIP FOR DEVELOPMENT

The implications of goal 8 are clear: global action must create an environment in which all people and countries have the chance to realize their potential.

International Aid for the Millennium Development Goals

A key to responsibility is finance. Aid from official and new sources is essential to kickstart the performance of countries failing to achieve the goals—as well as to keep on track those doing well. But how much aid is needed? Accurately estimating the costs of achieving the millennium goals is almost impossible—but it is important for understanding the size of the responsibility of richer nations. Detailed country assessments should be the basis of global estimates. These would allow thorough investigations of how countries are progressing towards the goals, better understanding of the areas for policies to focus on, and a much more accurate estimate of the costs of these policies and possible sources of finance. Currently, there are too few country studies of this type to paint a global picture.

Calculating an overall estimate of the cost of achieving all the goals using less direct means is tricky because it must take into account the positive side effects of achieving success in different areas. Some consensus is being reached on a figure that takes these synergies into account—giving a rough total of $40–60 billion a year in addition to the current $56 billion (Figure 28.11).

While approximate, these numbers give an idea of what is required. When compared with

FIGURE 28.11 OFFICIAL DEVELOPMENT ASSISTANCE MUST DOUBLE TO MEET THE MILLENNIUM DEVELOPMENT GOALS

Total ODA required to meet all goals $96 to $116 billion

Current ODA $56 billion

ODA

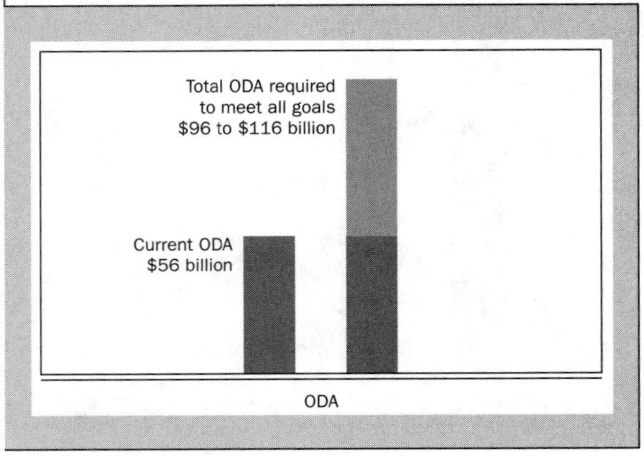

Source: World Bank and IMF 2001.

current official development assistance from industrial countries, around $56 billion a year, it is clear that aid needs to double. That would amount to about 0.5 percent of GNP of the countries on the Development Assistance Committee (DAC) of the Organisation for Economic Cooperation and Development— substantially less than the 0.7 percent agreed at the UN General Assembly in 1970.

The Millennium Declaration set no specific targets for aid, but if it had, most OECD countries would be performing badly. Of the 22 countries on the DAC, 17 give less than 0.5 percent of their GNP in foreign aid, and 11 give less than 0.3 percent—and most gave less in 2 000 than in 1990 (Figure 28.12).[75] Countries with big economies give the most in absolute terms but not as a percentage of GNP. At $13.5 billion, Japan gives the most aid of all countries, though as a share of its GNP it is in the middle of the range. The United States gives the second highest amount but the lowest proportion.

Aid has fallen substantially in recent years, but announcements in March 2002—at the UN's International Conference on Financing for Development—suggest that this trend may be reversing. The Bush administration proposed increasing aid over the next three fiscal years so that from the third year onwards the United States would give an additional $5 billion a year over the current level—representing a 50 percent increase, to about 0.15 percent of GNP.[76] EU heads of state and government announced a new target of 0.39 percent of GNP, to be achieved by 2006, representing an additional $7 billion a year.[77] Though short of doubling aid, and the 0.5 percent of GNP needed, the proposed increases are a step in the right direction.

Some countries, generally smaller, have bucked the recent trend of diminishing aid. During the 1990s, Ireland doubled its aid from 0.16 percent of GNP to 0.30 percent, and Luxembourg tripled its aid from 0.21 percent to 0.71 percent.

Alternative forms of financing have become more important but fall far short of substituting for increased official aid. Though small relative to official development assistance, resources generated by non-governmental organizations (NGOs) are substantial (Table 28.4). The same is true of contributions by philanthropists. The George Soros Foundation Network gives about $500 million a year, most of it in developing and transition countries, with a focus on human rights, culture and economic and social development.[78] And the Bill and Melinda Gates Foundation has given more than $4 billion since the beginning of 2000, with half of it spent on global health initiatives.[79]

FIGURE 28.12 AID HAS DECREASED FROM MOST DAC MEMBER COUNTRIES, 1990–2000

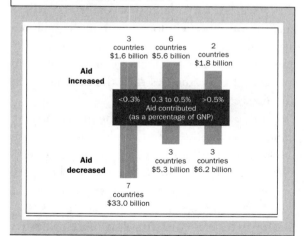

Source: Human Development Report Office calculations based on indicator table 15.

TABLE 28.4 EXPORTS AND DEBT SERVICE DOMINATE RESOURCE FLOWS TO AND FROM DEVELOPING COUNTRIES

TYPE OF FLOWS	PERCENTAGE OF DEVELOPING COUNTRIES' GDP, 2000
Exports	26.0
Debt service	6.3
Net foreign direct investment	2.5
Aid	0.5
Net grants from NGOs	0.1

Source: Human Development Report Office calculations based on indicator tables 14, 15, and 16.

Many developing countries still pay enormous sums in debt. Not all debt is bad: borrowing today to provide returns tomorrow is often prudent. But in many countries debt strangles the public purse—and is often for money spent unproductively long ago, by authoritarian regimes.

The most recent move to reduce debt is the Heavily Indebted Poor Countries (HIPC) initiative, launched by the World Bank and the International Monetary Fund (IMF) in 1996 to provide comprehensive debt relief to the world's poorest, most heavily indebted countries.[80] For low human development countries, 28 of them part of the initiative, debt service fell from 5.1 percent of GDP in 1990 to 3.6 percent in 2000. But there have been calls, led by Jubilee 2000, that the relief is not enough—and that too many countries desperately in need are not included. Recent new commitments by the World Bank and the IMF to deepen and broaden debt relief are positive developments.[81]

Better Aid

More aid may be needed to achieve the goals, but there is no guarantee it will have the right impact in the right places. For transfers to hit the targets laid out in the Millennium Declaration, there needs to be not only more aid, but better aid.

Who should receive it? Donors are concentrating aid in countries with a demonstrated ability to monitor and use it effectively.[82] While understandable, this approach also bears great risks. It means that the countries falling behind in achieving the goals, and in greatest need of resources, are least likely to receive aid.

Not only does aid need to be directed to the countries that need it most, it must also go to the right sectors. Only $2 billion of the annual aid from DAC countries is directed towards education.[83] To achieve the goals for education, this will have to increase by $9–12 billion, from about 3.5 percent of aid to well over 10 percent. Similarly, a larger proportion of aid will need to

go to other basic social services to achieve the goals. But that raises tough issues of setting priorities and reaching an understanding of how best to distribute aid among competing areas.

Trade and Foreign Direct Investment

One-way financial transfers will not be enough to build a global partnership, nor should they be. Developing countries need to compete and prosper in the world economy to drive their own development. The financial flows that developing countries receive from exports dwarf those from other sources, indicating how integrated many of these countries already are (see Table 28.4). And during the 1990s, foreign direct investment grew faster than other financial flows to developing countries, from 0.9 percent of their GDP to 2.5 percent. Developing countries—especially the poorest countries—still receive only a tiny fraction of total foreign direct investment, but that inflow is now greater than official development assistance.

In principle, participating in the global market offers the same benefits as a flourishing market economy within a country. But global trade is highly regulated, with the powerful holding sway and the playing field far from level. The average poor person in a developing country selling into global markets confronts barriers twice as high as the typical worker in industrial countries,[84] where agricultural subsidies alone are about $1 billion a day—more than six times total aid. These barriers and subsidies cost developing countries more in lost export opportunities than the $56 billion in aid they receive each year.[85]

If there were a levelling of the global playing field, many of the gains would come in low-income, low-skill areas such as agriculture, textiles, and clothing. So in many cases both the poorest countries and the poorest people would benefit.[86] Eliminating trade barriers and subsidies in industrial countries that inhibit imports from developing countries is therefore an urgent priority, and potentially a route to greatly accelerated development.

The Millennium Declaration's call for a non-discriminatory trading system places a clear responsibility on the world's richer countries, but it is a small step towards changing the system. And while liberalizing trade will bring substantial gains overall, it is not universally a win-win situation—some sectors in some countries will lose out, and they are likely to voice opposition.

But the losers must be seen as more than lobbying groups to overcome. They are individuals, families, and communities whose lives change immediately and for the worse because of globalization and foreign competition. People across the globe share this despair, and as trade continues to liberalize, their numbers will grow.

Although the question remains a subject of vigorous debate, a number of recent studies have suggested that increased international trade was a factor in the sharp increase in inequality in industrial countries in the 1980s and 1990s.[87] But holding trade back is most likely to hurt those who are even poorer in developing countries.

Since trade increases overall income, the answer to this moral dilemma—which appears to pit poor workers in industrial countries against even poorer workers in developing countries—is to redistribute some of the overall gain to those who directly lose out. That means providing greater social security and more help in finding alternative employment for people who lose their jobs. Canada and Denmark have successfully used fiscal transfers and social security to counter rising inequality in before-tax market wages, showing that the inevitable sectoral losses from increased trade can be distributed fairly within each economy.

To ensure that the gains from globalization are more widely distributed, industrial countries need to eliminate trade barriers against developing countries. The 2001 World Trade Organization meeting in Doha produced a framework for lowering trade barriers worldwide, but there is concern that reductions in the most important areas—barriers against textiles and subsidies for agriculture—may stall when the formal rules are developed. Industrial countries must also ensure that domestic workers in sectors hit by global competition do not shoulder the full burden of the adjustments that global innovation and integration can bring.

The new era of global integration offers enormous potential benefits. But they will not be realized unless more of the world's people are included. This has important implications for national and international policies in industrial as well as developing countries. Perhaps the most important is the need to include more people in the decisions that shape their lives in the modern world—and to include more people in the economic and social gains.

NOTES

1. World Bank 2002b.
2. UNESCO 2000, p. 9.
3. WHO, UNICEF and WSSCC 2000, p. v.
4. Human Development Report Office calculations based on Polity IV 2002. Following Marshall and Jaggers 2000, p. 12, a change of 3 or more in the polity score is considered significant. Countries that were members of the Soviet Union in 1980 are given its score.
5. Human Development Report Office calculations based on Alvarez and others 2002.
6. Oeppen and Vaupel 2002
7. Milanovic 2001a.
8. WHO 1997.
9. Human Development Report Office calculations based on WHO 2001.
10. WHO 2002a.
11. World Bank 2002b.
12. UNICEF 2002, p. 10.
13. Freedom House 2002.
14. Freedom House 2002. Figure refers to number of countries described as "not free" or "partly free."
15. Human Development Report Office calculations based on Marshall 2000.
16. Human Development Report Office calculations based on Polity IV 2002.

17. Human Development Report Office calculations based on Polity IV 2002. Following Marshall and Jaggers 2000, p. 12, a change of 3 or more in the polity score is considered significant. Countries that were members of the Soviet Union in 1980 are given its score.
18. Huntington 1991.
19. Human Development Report Office calculations based on Alvarez and others 2002.
20. Human Development Report Office calculations based on Polity IV 2002.
21. Human Development Report Office calculations based on Polity IV 2002, where a polity score of 6 or higher denotes full democracy.
22. Carothers 2002.
23. Indicator table 23.
24. Human Development Report Office calculations based on Marshall 2000.
25. UNHCR 2000.
26. UNICEF 1996.
27. UNHCR 2001a, p. 12.
28. Stewart and Fitzgerald 2000.
29. Carnegie Commission on Preventing Deadly Conflict 1997, p. 20.
30. Human Development Report Office calculations based on UNHCR 2002. Besides returning refugees and asylum-seekers, people otherwise of concern to the UN High Commissioner for Refugees include forced migrants, stateless persons and others.
31. Human Development Report Office calculations based on indicator table 20 and UNHCR 2001, p. 4.
32. UN 2000, paragraph 2.
33. UN 2000, pp. 56–58.
34. Hanmer and Naschold 2000.
35. Dollar and Kraay 2001.
36. Dikhanov and Ward 2001. The authors find that the worldwide within-country Theil index of inequality increased steadily from 0.211 in 1970 to 0.267 in 1999.
37. Cornia and Kiiski 2001.
38. Cornia and Court 2001.
39. Human Development Report Office calculations based on indicator table 3.
40. FAO 2001.
41. FAO 2001.
42. UNESCO 2000, pp. 8–9.
43. Filmer 1999.
44. UNESCO 2000.
45. Hunger Project 2002.
46. Filmer 1999.
47. World Bank 2001, p. 80.
48. OECD and UNESCO Institute for Statistics 2001.
49. Willms 1999.
50. WHO 1997.
51. UNICEF 2002, p. 11.
52. UNICEF 2002, p. 12.
53. UNAIDS 2001.
54. UNDESA 2001.
55. UNAIDS 2000b.
56. UNAIDS 2000b, p. 32.
57. UNAIDS 2000b, p. 27.
58. UNAIDS 2000b.
59. UNAIDS 2001.
60. UNAIDS 2000a.
61. WHO 2000.
62. WHO 2000.
63. WHO 2000.
64. WHO 2001.
65. WHO 2000.
66. Sachs 2001, p. 25.
67. WHO 2001.
68. CDIAC 2001.
69. UNCCD 2002.
70. UNCCD 2002.
71. WHO, UNICEF and WSSCC 2000, p. v.
72. WHO, UNICEF and WSSCC 2000.
73. WHO, UNICEF and WSSCC 2000, p. 34.
74. WHO, UNICEF and WSSCC 2000, p. v.
75. Greece lacks 1990 data and so is not included in Figure 28.12.
76. Larson 2002.
77. EU 2002.
78. Open Society Institute 2001, p. 9.
79. Bill and Melinda Gates Foundation 2002.
80. World Bank 2002c.
81. World Bank 2002c.
82. Morrisey 2002.
83. Naschold 2002.
84. World Bank 2002b.

85. Mehrotra 2001.
86. World Bank 2002b.
87. See discussion in Atkinson 1999, pp. 6–7.

REFERENCES

Alvarez, Michael, José Antonio Cheibub, Jennifer Gandhi, Fernando Limongi, Adam Przeworski and Sebastian Saiegh. 2002. "D&D2000." Dataset provided in correspondence. March.

Atkinson, Anthony B. 1999. "Is Rising Income Inequality Inevitable? A Critique of the Transatlantic Consensus." Annual Lecture 3. United Nations University and World Institute for Development Economics Research, Helsinki, Finland. [http://www.wider.unu.edu/events/annuel1999a.pdf].

Bill and Melinda Gates Foundation. 2002. "Grant Highlights." [http://www.gatesfoundation.org/grants/default.htm]. April 2002.

Carnegie Commission on Preventing Deadly Conflict. 1997. *Preventing Deadly Conflict: Final Report.* New York: Carnegie Corporation of New York. [http://www.ccpdc.org/pubs/rept97/finfr.htm]. April 2002.

Carothers, Thomas. 1999. Aiding Democracy Abroad: The Learning Curve. Washington, D.C.: Carnegie Endowment for International Peace.

Carter, Lynn, Zeric Smith and Joseph Siegal. 2002. "Memorandum on Measuring Voice and Accountability."

CDIAC (Carbon Dioxide Information Analysis Center). 2001. "Trends: A Compendium of Data on Global Change." [http://cdiac.ornl.gov/trends.html]. April 2002.

Cornia, Andrea, and Julius Court. 2001. "Inequality, Growth and Poverty in the Era of Liberalization and Globalization." Policy Brief 4. United Nations University and World Institute for Development Economics Research, Helsinki, Finland. [http://www.wider.unu.edu/publications/publications.htm]. April 2002.

Cornia, Andrea, and Sampsa Kiiski. 2001. "Trends in Income Distribution in the Post–World War II Period: Evidence and Interpretation." Discussion Paper 2001/89. United Nations University and World Institute for Development Economics Research, Helsinki, Finland. [http://www.wider.unu.edu/publications/dps/dp2001-89.pdf]. April 2002.

Court, Julius. 2002. "Input for Trends in Political Participation and Democracy around the World."

Court, Julius, and Goran Hyden. 2000. "A World Governance Survey: Pilot Phase." United Nations University, Tokyo. [http://www.unu.edu/p%26g/wgs/index.htm]. April 2002.

Dikhanov, Yuri, and Michael Ward. 2001 "Evolution of the Global Distribution of Income 1970–99." Paper prepared for the 53rd session of the International Statistical Institute, Seoul, Republic of Korea, 22–29 August.

Dollar, David, and Art Kraay. 2001. "Growth Is Good for the Poor." Policy Research Working Paper 2587. World Bank, Washington, D.C. [http://www-wds.worldbank.org/servlet/WDSContentServer/WDSP/IB/2001/05/11/000094946_01042806383524/Rendered/PDF/multi0page.pdf]. April 2002.

EU (European Union). 2002. "EU Commitments: Going Beyond the Monterrey Consensus." Announcement distributed to delegates, nongovernmental organizations and the media at the UN Conference on Financing for Development, Monterrey, Mexico, 20 March.

FAO (Food and Agriculture Organization). 2001. *The State of Food Insecurity in the World.* Rome. [http://www.fao.org/DOCREP/003/Y1500E/Y1500E00.HTM]. April 2002.

Filmer, Deon. 1999. "The Structure of Social Disparities in Education: Gender and Wealth." Working paper 5. World Bank, Development Research Group and Poverty Reduction and Economic Management Network. [http://www.worldbank.org/gender/prr/wp5.pdf]. April 2002.

Freedom House. 2000. *Press Freedom Survey 2000.* [http://www.freedomhouse.org/pfs2000]. April 2002.

———. 2002. *Freedom in the World 2001/2002: The Democracy Gap.* New York. [http://www.freedomhouse.org/research/survey2002.htm]. April 2002.

Hanmer, Lucia, and Felix Naschold. 2000. "Attaining the International Development Targets: Will Growth Be Enough?" *Development Policy Review* 18(1): 11–36.

Hunger Project. 2002. "The Condition of Women in South Asia." [http://www.thp.org/sac/unit4/index.html]. April 2002.

Huntington, Samuel P. 1991. *The Third Wave: Democratization in the Late Twentieth Century.* Norman: University of Oklahoma Press.

ILO (International Labour Organization). 2002. "Women in National Parliaments." [http://www.ipu.org/wmn-e/world.htm]. April 2002.

Larson, Alan P. 2002. Press conference transcript, UN Conference on Financing for Development, 19 March, Monterrey, Mexico.

Marshall, Monty G. 2000. "Major Episodes of Political Violence, 1946–1999." University of Maryland, Center for Systematic Peace, College Park. [http://members.aol.com/CSPmgm/warlist.htm]. April 2002.

Marshall, Monty G., and Keith Jaggers. 2000. "Polity IV Project: Dataset Users Manual." [http://www.bsos.umd.edu/cidcm/inscr/polity/]. April 2002.

Mehrotra, Santosh. 2001. "The Rhetoric of International Development Targets and the Reality of Official Development Assistance." Working Paper 85. United Nations Children's Fund, Innocenti Research Centre, Florence, Italy.

Milanovic, Branko. 2001. "True World Income Distribution, 1988 and 1993: First Calculation Based on Household Surveys Alone." Policy Research Working Paper 2244. World Bank, Washington, D.C. [http://www-wds.worldbank.org/servlet/WDSContentServer/WDSP/IB/1999/12/30/000094946_99121105392984/Rendered/PDF/multi_page.pdf]. April 2002.

Morrisey, Oliver. 2002. "ODI Opinions on Effective Expansion of Aid." Opinion 1. Overseas Development Institute, London. [http://www.odi.org.uk/opinions/1_intro_opinions.html]. April 2002.

Naschold, Felix. 2002. "Aid and the Millennium Development Goals." Opinion 4. Overseas Development Institute, London. [http://www.odi.org.uk/opinions/4_MDGs.html]. April 2002.

OECD (Organisation for Economic Co-operation and Development) and UNESCO (United Nations Educational, Scientific and Cultural Organization) Institute for Statistics. 2001. *Teachers for Tomorrow's Schools: Analysis of World Education Indicators 2001 Edition.* Paris. [http://www.uis.unesco.org/en/pub/doc/WEI/wei_execsum_EN.pdf]. April 2002.

Oeppen, Jim, and James W. Vaupel. 2002. "Enhanced: Broken Limits to Life Expectancy." *Science* 296: 1029–31.

Open Society Institute. 2001. *Building Open Societies: Soros Foundation Network Annual Report 2000.* New York. [http://www.soros.org/annual/2000/]. May 2002.

Polity IV. 2002. "Political Regime Characteristics and Transitions, 1800–2000." [http://www.bsos.umd.edu/cidcm/inscr/polity/index.htm. April 2002.

Sachs, Jeffrey D. 2001. *Macroeconomics and Health: Investing in Health for Economic Development.* Geneva: World Health Organization.

Stewart, Frances, and Valpy Fitzgerald. 2000. *The Economic and Social Consequences of Conflict.* Oxford: Oxford University Press.

UN (United Nations). 2000. "Report of the Open-ended Working Group on the Question of Equitable Representation on and Increase in the Membership of the Security Council and Other Matters Related to the Security Council." Document A/54/57. General Assembly Official Records, Fifty-fourth Session, New York.

———. 2001. World Population Prospects 1950–2050: The 2000 Revision. Database. Department of Economic and Social Affairs, Population Division, New York.

UNAIDS (Joint United Nations Programme on HIV/AIDS). 2000a. "Country Successes."

Factsheet.Geneva.[http://www.unaids.org/ fact_sheets/files/Successes_Eng.html]. April 2002.

———. 2000b. "Report on the Global HIV/AIDS Epidemic." Geneva. [http://www.unaids.org/ epidemic_update/report/index.html]. April 2002.

———. 2001. "AIDS Epidemic Update—December 2001." [http://www.unaids.org/epidemic_ update/report_dec01/index.html]. April 2002.

UNCCD (United Nations Convention to Combat Desertification). 2002. "The United Nations Convention to Combat Desertification: An Explanatory Leaflet." [http://www.unccd.int/ convention/text/leaflet.php]. April 2002.

UNDESA (United Nations Department of Economic and Social Affairs). 2001. "HIV/AIDS: Population Impact and Policies 2001." [http:// www.un.org/esa/population/publications/ aidswallchart/MainPage.htm]. May 2002.

UNESCO (United Nations Educational, Scientific and Cultural Organization). 2000. "Education For All: 2000 Assessment, Statistical Document." [http://unesdoc.unesco.org/images/ 0012/001204/120472e.pdf]. April 2002.

UNHCR (United Nations High Commissioner for Refugees). 2000. *The State of the World's Refugees: Fifty Years of Humanitarian Action.* Oxford: Oxford University Press. [http://www. unhcr.ch/pubs/sowr2000/sowr2000toc. htm]. April 2002.

———. 2001a. "Children." [http://www.unhcr.ch/ children/index.html]. April 2002.

———. 2001b. "Refugees by Numbers 2001 Edition." [http://www.unhcr.ch/cgi-bin/texis/ vtx/home?page=basics]. April 2002.

———. 2002. Correspondence on refugees and internally displaced persons. February. Geneva.

UNICEF (United Nations Children's Fund). 1996. "Wars against Children." [http://www.unicef. org/graca/]. April 2002.

———. 2002. *The State of the World's Children 2002.* New York: Oxford University Press.

[http://www.unicef.org/pubsgen/sowc02/ sowc2002-eng-full.pdf]. April 2002.

WHO (World Health Organization). 1997. *Health and Environment in Sustainable Development: Five Years after the Earth Summit.* Geneva.

———. 2000. "Tuberculosis." Factsheet 104. Geneva. [http://www.who.int/inf-fs/en/fact104. html]. April 2000.

———. 2001. "WHO and Norvartis Join Forces to Combat Drug Resistant Malaria." Press release. [http://www.who.int/infpr-2001/en/ pr2001-26.html]. April 2002.

WHO (World Health Organization), UNICEF (United Nations Children's Fund) and WSSCC (Water Supply and Satiation Collaborative Council). 2000. "Global Water Supply and Sanitation Assessment 2000 Report." [http://www.who. int/water_sanitation_health/Globassessment/ GlobalTOC.htm]. April 2002.

Willms, Douglas J. 1999. *Inequalities in Literacy Skills among Youth in Canada and the United States.* Statistics Canada International Adult Literacy Survey Monograph 89-552-MIE99006. National Literacy Secretariat/Human Resources Development, Canada.

World Bank. 2001. *World Development Report 2000/2001.* New York: Oxford University Press.

———. 2002a. "Countries and Regions." [http://www.world-bank.org/html/extdr/ regions.htm]. April 2002.

———. 2002b. Global Economic Prospects and the Developing Countries 2002: Making Trade Work for the World's Poor. Washington, D.C.

———. 2002c. "The HIPC Initiative: Background and Progress through December 2001." [http://www.worldbank.org/hipc/progress-to- date/may99v3/may99v3.htm]. April 2002.

World Bank and IMF (International Monetary Fund). 2001. "Financing for Development." [http://www.imf.org/external/np/pdr/2001/ ffd.pdf]. February 2001.

Index